AUTHENTICATING THE WORDS OF JESUS

NEW TESTAMENT TOOLS
AND STUDIES

EDITED BY

BRUCE M. METZGER, Ph.D., D.D., L.H.D., D. Theol., D. Litt.

Professor of New Testament Language and Literature, Emeritus
Princeton Theological Seminary
and
Corresponding Fellow of the British Academy

AND

BART D. EHRMAN, Ph.D.

Associate Professor, Department of Religious Studies
University of North Carolina at Chapel Hill

VOLUME XXVIII,1

AUTHENTICATING THE WORDS OF JESUS

EDITED BY

BRUCE CHILTON AND CRAIG A. EVANS

BRILL

LEIDEN · BOSTON · KÖLN

1999

This book is printed on acid-free paper.

Die Deutsche Bibliothek – CIP-Einheitsaufnahme

Authenticating the words of Jesus / ed. by Bruce D. Chilton and
Craig A. Evans. - Leiden ; Boston ; Köln : Brill, 1998
(New Testament tools and studies ; Vol. 28.1)
ISBN 90–04–11301–0
ISBN 90–04–11141–7 (Bd. 1 und 2)

Library of Congress Cataloging-in-Publication Data

Library of Congress Cataloging-in-Publication Data is also available

ISSN 0077-8842
ISBN 90 04 11141 7

PRINTED IN THE NETHERLANDS

IN MEMORY OF BEN F. MEYER

CONTENTS

Preface ix
Abbreviations xi
Contributors xv

PART ONE
METHODS AND ASSUMPTIONS

CRAIG A. EVANS
Authenticating the Words of Jesus 3

BRUCE D. CHILTON
Assessing Progress in the Third Quest 15

BRUCE J. MALINA
Criteria for Assessing the Authentic Words of Jesus:
Some Specifications 27

TOM HOLMÉN
Doubts about Double Dissimilarity: Restructuring
the Main Criterion of Jesus-of-History Research 47

BEN F. MEYER
How Jesus Charged Language with Meaning:
A Study in Rhetoric 81

STANLEY E. PORTER and MATTHEW BROOK O'DONNELL
The Implications of Textual Variants for Authenticating
the Words of Jesus 97

PART TWO
AUTHENTICATING THE WORDS OF JESUS

DOUGLAS E. OAKMAN
The Lord's Prayer in Social Perspective 137

NORMAN METZLER
The Lord's Prayer: Second Thoughts on the First Petition 187

ECKHARD J. SCHNABEL
The Silence of Jesus: The Galilean Rabbi Who was More
than a Prophet 203

BRUCE CHILTON
(The) Son of (the) Man, and Jesus 259

DALE C. ALLISON, JR.
Q 12:51-53 and Mark 9:11-13 and the Messianic Woes 289

HOWARD CLARK KEE
Jesus: A Glutton and Drunkard 311

J. IAN H. MCDONALD
Questioning and Discernment in Gospel Discourse:
Communicative Strategy in Matthew 11:2-9 333

SCOT MCKNIGHT
Public Declaration or Final Judgment? Matthew 10:26-27 =
Luke 12:2-3 as a Case of Creative Redaction 363

WILLIAM KLASSEN
The Authenticity of the Command: "Love Your Enemies" 385

CHARLES L. QUARLES
The Authenticity of the Parable of the Warring King:
A Response to the Jesus Seminar 409

WESLEY HIRAM WACHOB and LUKE TIMOTHY JOHNSON
The Sayings of Jesus in the Letter of James 431

Index of Biblical Literature 451

Index of Modern Authors 471

PREFACE

It was the suggestion of David Orton, one of E. J. Brill's academic editors, that led to the production of *Authenticating the Words of Jesus* and *Authenticating the Activities of Jesus*. He proposed that we continue the collaborative work begun in the collection of critical studies entitled *Studying the Historical Jesus: Evaluations of the State of Current Research* (NTTS 19; Leiden: E. J. Brill, 1994). Because critical response to the latter book has been positive, we were pleased to take this work a step further. We hope that it will further refine and clarify at many points our own studies that appeared recently in the jointly-authored *Jesus in Context: Temple, Purity, and Restoration* (AGJU 39; Leiden: E. J. Brill, 1997).

The present volume is intended to review the appropriate criteria and necessary steps in assessing the Jesus tradition, particularly the words of Jesus. The title *Authenticating the Words of Jesus* should not be taken to mean that the contributors have as their aim some sort of apologetical goal, whose purpose is to prove that Jesus said everything attributed to him in the Gospels. Rather, the purpose is to clarify what procedures should be undertaken to distinguish tradition and meaning that stem from Jesus from that which stems from later tradents and evangelists, and to inquire into the various forces and situations that led to the emergence of the tradition as we have it.

The editors are grateful to Dr. Orton for his suggestion and to Dr. Theo Joppe for guiding the completed manuscripts through the press. The editors also wish to thank the series editors, Professors Bruce Metzger and Bart Ehrman, as well as the many contributors, whose labors have made the volumes possible, and Mr. Chris Young for his assistance in the preparation of the indexes.

Bruce Chilton   September, 1998
Bard College
Annandale-on-Hudson, New York

Craig A. Evans
Trinity Western University
Langley, British Columbia

ABBREVIATIONS

AB	Anchor Bible (Commentary)
ABD	D. N. Freedman (ed.), *The Anchor Bible Dictionary* (6 vols., New York: Doubleday, 1992)
ABRL	Anchor Bible Reference Library
AGJU	Arbeiten zur Geschichte des antiken Judentums und des Urchristentums
ANF	A. Roberts and J. Donaldson (eds.), *The Ante-Nicene Fathers* (10 vols., Edinburgh: T. & T. Clark, 1898; repr. Grand Rapids: Eerdmans, 1989)
ANRW	W. Haase and E. Temporini (eds.), *Aufstieg und Niedergang der römischen Welt*
ANTJ	Arbeiten zum Neuen Testament und Judentum
ArBib	The Aramaic Bible
ATANT	Abhandlungen zur Theologie des Alten und Neuen Testaments
ATR	*Anglican Theological Review*
BAGD	W. Bauer, *A Greek-English Lexicon of the New Testament and Other Early Christian Literature* (2nd ed., revised by W. F. Arndt, F. W. Gingrich, and F. W. Danker; Chicago: University of Chicago Press, 1979)
BARev	*Biblical Archaeology Review*
BBB	Bonner biblische Beiträge
BBR	*Bulletin for Biblical Research*
BDB	F. Brown, S. R. Driver, and C. A. Briggs (eds.), *A Hebrew and English Lexicon of the Old Testament* (Oxford: Clarendon, 1907).
BDF	B. Blass, A. Debrunner, and R. W. Funk, *A Greek Grammar of the New Testament and Other Early Christian Literature* (Chicago: University of Chicago Press, 1961)
BECNT	Baker Exegetical Commentary on the New Testament
BETL	Bibliotheca ephemeridum theologicarum lovaniensium
BFCT	Beiträge zur Förderung christlicher Theologie
BGBE	Beiträge zur Geschichte der biblischen Exegese
BibSem	The Biblical Seminar
BJS	Brown Judaic Studies
BKAT	Biblischer Kommentar: Altes Testament
BLG	Biblical Languages: Greek
BTB	*Biblical Theology Bulletin*
BTZ	*Berliner theologische Zeitschrift*
BWANT	Beiträge zur Wissenschaft vom Alten und Neuen Testament
BZ	*Biblische Zeitschrift*
BZNW	Beihefte zur *Zeitschrift für die neutestamentliche Wissenschaft*

CBQ Catholic Biblical Quarterly
CBQMS Catholic Biblical Quarterly Monograph Series
CGTC Cambridge Greek Testament Commentaries
CNT Commentaire du Nouveau Testament
ConBNT Coniectanea biblica, New Testament
DJD Discoveries in the Judaean Desert
DJG J. B. Green, S. McKnight, and I. H. Marshall (eds.), *Dictionary of Jesus and the Gospels* (Downers Grove: InterVarsity, 1992)
DSD *Dead Sea Discoveries*
EBC F. E. Gaebelein (ed.), *Expositor's Bible Commentary*
EDNT H. R. Balz and G. Schneider (eds.), *Exegetical Dictionary of the New Testament* (Grand Rapids: Eerdmans, 1990-93)
EKK Evangelisch-katholischer Kommentar (Vorarbeiten)
EKKNT Evangelisch-katholischer Kommentar zum Neuen Testament
ETL *Ephemerides theologicae lovanienses*
EUS European University Studies
ExpTim *Expository Times*
FAT Forschungen zum Alten Testament
FB Forschung zur Bibel
FFRS Facets and Foundations—Reference Series
FRLANT Forschungen zur Religion und Literatur des Alten und Neuen Testaments
HervTS *Hervormde Teologiese Studies*
HNTC Harper's New Testament Commentaries
HTKNT Herders theologischer Kommentar zum Neuen Testament
HTR *Harvard Theological Review*
HUCA *Hebrew Union College Annual*
ICC International Critical Commentary
IDB G. A Buttrick (ed.), *The Interpreter's Dictionary of the Bible* (1962)
IRT Issues in Religion and Theology
JAAR *Journal of the American Academy of Religion*
JAC Jahrbuch für Antike und Christentum
JBL *Journal of Biblical Literature*
JJS *Journal of Jewish Studies*
JNSL *Journal of Northwest Semitic Languages*
JR *Journal of Religion*
JRS *Journal of Roman Studies*
JSNT *Journal for the Study of the New Testament*
JSNTSup *Journal for the Study of the New Testament*, Supplement Series
JSP *Journal for the Study of the Pseudepigrapha*
JSPSup *Journal for the Study of the Pseudepigrapha*, Supplement Series
JTS *Journal of Theological Studies*
LCL Loeb Classical Library
MeyerK H. A. W. Meyer (ed.), Kritisch-exegetischer Kommentar über das Neue Testament
MM J. H. Moulton and G. Milligan (eds.), *The Vocabulary of the Greek New Testament* (London: Hodder & Stoughton, 1930; repr. Grand Rapids: Eerdmans, 1974)

MPER	Mitteilungen aus der Papyrussammlung der Österreichischen Nationalbibliothek (Papyrus Erzherzog Rainer) New Series
NA	E. Nestle and K. Aland (eds.), *Novum Testamentum Graece*
NCB(C)	New Century Bible (Commentary)
Neot	*Neotestamentica*
NIC	New International Commentary
NICNT	New International Commentary—New Testament
NIDOTTE	W. vanGemeren (ed.), *New International Dictionary of Old Testament Theology and Exegesis* (5 vols., Grand Rapids: Zondervan, 1997)
NIGTC	New International Greek Testament Commentary
NovT	*Novum Testamentum*
NovTSup	Novum Tetamentum, Supplements
NPNF 1	P. Schaff (ed.), *A Selection of the Nicene and Post-Nicene Fathers: First Series* (14 vols., Edinburgh: T. & T. Clark, 1886; repr. Grand Rapids: Eerdmans, 1954-71)
NTAbh	Neutestamentliche Abhandlungen
NTD	Das Neue Testament Deutsch
NTL	New Testamnt Library
NTOA	Novum Testamentum et Orbis Antiquus
NTS	*New Testament Studies*
NTTS	New Testament Tools and Studies
OBO	Orbis biblicus et orientalis
OBT	Overtures to Biblical Theology
OTP	J. H. Charlesworth (ed.), *The Old Testament Pseudepigrapha* (2 vols., ABRL 13-14; New York: Doubleday, 1983-85)
OTS	Oudtestamentische Studiën
PRS	*Perspectives in Religious Studies*
QD	Quaestiones disputatae
RevQ	*Revue de Qumran*
RHPR	*Revue d'histoire et de philosophie religieuses*
RILP	Roehampton Institute London Papers
RNT	Regensburger Neues Testament
RSR	*Recherches de science religieuse*
SBB	Stuttgarter biblische Beiträge
SBEC	Studies in the Bible and Early Christianity
SBLMS	Society of Biblical Literature Monograph Series
SBLSP	Society of Biblical Literature Seminar Papers
SBT	Studies in Biblical Theology
SecCent	*Second Century*
SFEG	Schriften der Finnischen Exegetischen Gesellschaft
SJLA	Studies in Judaism in Late Antiquity
SJT	*Scottish Journal of Theology*
SNTSMS	Society for New Testament Studies Monograph Series
SNTU	Studien zum Neuen Testament und seiner Umwelt
SR	*Studies in Religion/Sciences religieuses*
STDJ	Studies on the Texts of the Desert of Judah
STK	*Svensk teologisk kvartalskrift*

SUNT   Studien zur Umwelt des Neuen Testaments
TBei   *Theologische Beiträge*
TDNT   G. Kittel and G. Friedrich (eds.), *Theological Dictionary of the New Testament* (1964-74)
Th   *Theology*
TNTC   Tyndale New Testament Commentaries
TRu   *Theologische Rundschau*
TSK   *Theologische Studien und Kritiken*
TU   Texte und Untersuchungen
TWNT   G. Kittel and G. Friedrich (eds.), *Theologisches Wörterbuch zum Neuen Testament*
TZ   *Theologische Zeitschrift*
UBSGNT   United Bible Societies *The Greek New Testament*
VT   *Vetus Testamentum*
WBC   Word Biblical Commentary
WMANT   Wissenschaftliche Monographien zum Alten und Neuen Testament
WPC   Westminster Pelican Commentaries
WUNT   Wissenschaftliche Untersuchungen zum Neuen Testament
ZNW   *Zeitschrift für die neutestamentliche Wissenschaft*
ZTK   *Zeitschrift für Theologie und Kirche*

CONTRIBUTORS

Dale C. Allison, Jr.
Pittsburgh Theological Seminary
Pittsburgh, Pennsylvania
USA

Bruce Chilton
Bard College
Annandale-on-Hudson, New York
USA

Craig A. Evans
Trinity Western University
Langley, British Columbia
Canada
Roehampton Institute London
London, England
UK

Tom Holmén
Åbo Academy University
Institute of Exegetics
Turku
Finland

Luke Timothy Johnson
Emory University and
Candler School of Theology .
Atlanta, Georgia
USA

Howard Clark Kee
University of Pennsylvania
Haverford, Pennsylvania
USA

William Klassen
École Biblique et Archéologique
Française
Jerusalem
Israel

Bruce J. Malina
Creighton University
Omaha, Nebraska
USA

J. Ian H. McDonald
The University of Edinburgh
Edinburgh, Scotland
UK

Scot McKnight
North Park College
Chicago, Illinois
USA

Norman Metzler
Concordia University
Portland, Oregon
USA

Ben F. Meyer
McMaster University
Hamilton, Ontario
Canada

Douglas E. Oakman
Pacific Lutheran University
Tacoma, Washington
USA

Matthew Brook O'Donnell
Roehampton Institute London
London, England
UK

Stanley E. Porter
Roehampton Institute London
London, England
UK

Charles L. Quarles
Clear Creek Baptist College
Pineville, Kentucky
USA

Eckhard J. Schnabel
Trinity International University
Deerfield, Illinois
USA

Wesley Hiram Wachob
Emory University and
Candler School of Theology
Atlanta, Georgia
USA

PART ONE

METHODS AND ASSUMPTIONS

AUTHENTICATING THE WORDS OF JESUS*

Craig Evans

Jesus research is no easy task.[1] This is so, among other things, because of the number and complexities of the primary source materials. These complexities involve problems that arise from imperfect preservation of sources, uncertain literary relationships among the documents themselves, and even less certain knowledge of their respective provenances. In short, we know little about the individuals and communities (the latter often no more than an assumption) which generated and transmitted them.

Jesus research is not difficult because we lack sufficient quantity of source material. On the contrary, we have a fair amount of material. Within the Christian canon of Scripture we have four Gospels. The first three, the Synoptic Gospels, are clearly interdependent, but the Fourth Gospel, which has been traditionally known as the Gospel of John, is probably independent of the Synoptics.[2] From the Synoptics we are able to infer Q, the source common to Matthew and Luke. We have, therefore, as many as three independent sources. Outside of the Christian canon we have several other Gospels, fragments, and sayings attributed to Jesus. Among these are the *Gospel of Peter*, the *Gospel of Thomas*, the Egerton Papyrus 2, and the *Secret Gospel of*

---

* Portions of this introduction have appeared in C. A. Evans, "Images of Christ in the Canonical and Apocryphal Gospels," in S. E. Porter et al. (eds.), *Images of Christ: Ancient and Modern* (RILP 2; Sheffield: Sheffield Academic Press, 1997) 34-72.

[1] Some of the problems are reviewed in C. A. Evans, "Recent Developments in Jesus Research: Presupposition, Criteria, and Sources," in Evans, *Jesus and His Contemporaries: Comparative Studies* (AGJU 25; Leiden: Brill, 1995) 1-49; idem, "The Life of Jesus," in S. E. Porter (ed.), *Handbook to Exegesis of the New Testament* (NTTS 25; Leiden: Brill, 1997) 427-75.

[2] See C. H. Dodd, *Historical Tradition in the Fourth Gospel* (Cambridge: Cambridge University Press, 1963). Since Dodd's influential study most Gospel scholars have assumed or argued for Johannine independence of the Synoptic Gospels. However, a goodly number have argued that the fourth evangelist knew of and perhaps had even read one or more of the Synoptics, but did not use them as sources.

Mark. To these many other Gospels, largely preserved in patristic quotations, could be added (e.g. the *Gospel of the Ebionites*, the *Gospel of the Hebrews*, and the *Gospel of the Nazarenes*).

The extra-canonical Gospels have been discussed in other contexts.[3] Suffice it to say here that other than a few sayings in *Thomas*, we do not think that these sources offer the historian any reliable data that can supplement, or supplant, that provided by the New Testament Gospels.[4] But how should we assess the canonical Gospels?

ASSESSING THE SOURCES: PRELIMINARY CONSIDERATIONS

When we think of the "canonical" Gospels, we usually have in mind Matthew, Mark, Luke, and John. But, depending upon one's solution to the synoptic problem and the question of the development of the Johannine tradition, we may have six, not four canonical sources. The synoptic problem attempts to explain the literary relationship among the first three Gospels. The majority of Gospel scholars believe that Mark and the sayings source called Q were the literary sources upon which the Matthean and Lukan evangelists later drew in composing their respective Gospels. If this solution is correct, and I believe that it is,[5] then in reality we have four synoptic sources: Q, Mark, Matthew, and Luke (in the probable order of their composition).[6] With regard to the fourth Gospel, many scholars

---

3   See J. H. Charlesworth and C. A. Evans, "Jesus in the Agrapha and Apocryphal Gospels," in B. D. Chilton and C. A. Evans (eds.), *Studying the Historical Jesus: Evaluations of the State of Current Research* (NTTS 19; Leiden: Brill, 1994) 479-533; Evans, "Recent Developments in Jesus Research," 26-45. For a cautious statement of the limited value of *Thomas*, see B. D. Chilton, "The Gospel According to Thomas as a Source of Jesus' Teaching," in D. Wenham (ed.), *The Jesus Tradition Outside the Gospels* (Gospel Perspectives 5; Sheffield: JSOT Press, 1984) 155-75.

4   *Pace* J. D. Crossan, "Materials and Methods in Historical Jesus Research," *Forum* 4.4 (1988) 3-24; idem, *The Historical Jesus: The Life of a Jewish Mediterranean Jewish Peasant* (San Francisco: HarperCollins, 1991) 427-34.

5   I summarize what I regard to be the primary arguments in favor of the Two Source hypothesis in C. A. Evans, "Source, Form and Redaction Criticism: The 'Traditional' Methods of Synoptic Interpretation," in S. E. Porter and D. Tombs (eds.), *Approaches to New Testament Study* (JSNTSup 120; Sheffield: Sheffield Academic Press, 1995) 17-45, esp. 20-26. But see Bruce Chilton's qualifications offered in the essay that follows, "Assessing Progress in the Third Quest."

6   Some scholars add two more sources: "M" (a source utilized by the Matthean evangelist) and "L" (a source utilized by the Lucan evangelist). As one might

believe that a document consisting largely of Jesus' miracles, referred to as "signs," was incorporated. If this view is correct, and again I think it is,[7] then we have two Johannine sources: the signs source and the Johannine Gospel itself. Thus, all together we may very well have six sources preserved in the four New Testament Gospels; and, conceivably, we could have six distinct images of Jesus.

Once we step outside of the New Testament, we are confronted with several Gospels, preserved for the most part as fragments and excerpts in later sources. The portraits of Jesus preserved in these writings display a great deal of variety. As we shall see, our knowledge of their provenance is limited. Our conclusions must remain tentative, though again, as we shall see, there are some who believe that they can infer many things from these writings.

The same problems and caveats apply in the case of the hypothetical sources extracted from the New Testament Gospels: Q and the Johannine signs source. Q presents a special problem, in light of its popularity in Jesus research. It is popular with scholars because of widespread assumptions regarding its antiquity and its alleged more primitive portrait of Jesus.[8] Q may indeed be quite old and its

---

expect, these hypothetical sources are much debated. Along with many others, I am not convinced that there ever were such sources, at least as distinct, coherent literary works.

7   On this question, see the discussion and bibliography below.

8   For a representative sampling of Q studies, in which these views in various forms are recommended, see A. von Harnack, *The Sayings of Jesus: The Second Source of St. Matthew and St. Luke* (New Testament Studies 3; London: Williams and Norgate; New York: Putnam's Sons, 1908); J. M. Robinson, "ΛΟΓΟΙ ΣΟΦΩΝ: Zur Gattung der Spruchquelle Q," in E. Dinkler (ed.), *Zeit und Geschichte: Dankesgabe an Rudolf Bultmann zum 80. Geburtstag* (Tübingen: Mohr [Siebeck], 1964) 77-96; ET: "LOGOI SOPHON: On the Gattung of Q," in J. M. Robinson and H. Koester, *Trajectories through Early Christianity* (Philadelphia: Fortress, 1971) 71-113; S. Schulz, *Q—Die Spruchquelle der Evangelisten* (Zurich: Theologischer Verlag, 1971); R. A. Edwards, *A Theology of Q: Eschatology, Prophecy, and Wisdom* (Philadephia: Fortress, 1976); A. Polag, *Die Christologie der Logienquelle* (WMANT 45; Neukirchen-Vluyn: Neukirchener Verlag, 1977); J. S. Kloppenborg, *The Formation of Q: Trajectories in Ancient Wisdom Collections* (Studies in Antiquity and Christianity; Philadelphia: Fortress, 1987); A. D. Jacobson, *The First Gospel: An Introduction to Q* (Sonoma: Polebridge, 1992); D. R. Catchpole, *The Quest for Q* (Edinburgh: T. & T. Clark, 1993); B. L. Mack, *The Lost Gospel: The Book of Q and Christian Origins* (San Francisco: HarperCollins, 1993); C. M. Tuckett, *Q and the History of Early Christianity* (Edinburgh: T. & T. Clark, 1996).

tradition may well be primitive, but in my view scholars say far too much about this hypothetical source. We hear confident assertions about the "christology of Q" and the "community of Q." We are even told, on the basis of silence, what the Q community did not regard as important, e.g. Jesus' miracles, death, and resurrection. From these observations we now know, we are assured, that the portrait of Jesus in Q was substantially different from those preserved in the synoptic Gospels themselves.[9]

There is no Q document extant, but that has not stopped James Robinson and company from attempting to reconstruct it on the basis of what is found in Matthew and Luke.[10] But how do we know that a sufficient amount of Q has been preserved to make such reconstruction possible,[11] and the inferences that inevitably derive from it?

The problem may be illustrated by imagining that our only access to Mark comes via Matthew and Luke. Let us suppose that we possess Matthew, Luke, and Q—but not Mark. It becomes readily apparent that Matthew and Luke had access to a common narrative Gospel, one that began with Isa 40:3 and the preaching of John the Baptist, and ended with Jesus' crucifixion and the discovery of the empty tomb. How much of Mark could we, with confidence, reconstruct from Matthew and Luke?

Together Matthew and Luke contain approximately 96% of Mark. But we know this only because we have Mark and so know what Matthew and Luke actually borrowed from it. Because Luke only contains approximately 60% of Mark, we would not know for certain that that part of Mark preserved *only in Matthew* was in fact

---

[9]   For a more cautious assessment of what can be known about the date and provenance of Q, see Tuckett, *Q and the History of Early Christianity*, 83-106.

[10]   J. M. Robinson, "The Sayings of Jesus: Q," *Drew Gateway* 54 (1983-84) 26-38; idem, "A Critical Text of the Sayings Gospel Q," *RHPR* 72 (1992) 15-22; idem, "The Sayings Gospel Q," in F. Van Segbroeck et al. (eds.), *The Four Gospels 1992* (F. Neirynck Festschrift; 3 vols., BETL 100; Leuven: Peeters and Leuven University Press, 1992) 1.361-88.

[11]   According to A. T. Honoré ("A Statistical Study of the Synoptic Problem," *NovT* 10 [1968] 95-147, esp. 135-36) Matthew and Luke preserve only 10–14% of the original wording of Q. In contrast to this conservative assessment, we have the much more inclusive proposal of H. Schürmann ("Zum Komposition der Redenquelle: Beobachtungen an den lukanischen Q-Vorlage," in C. Bussmann and W. Radl [eds.], *Der Treue Gottes trauen* [G. Schneider Festschrift; Freiburg: Herder, 1991] 325-42, and other studies) who includes a great deal of Luke's *Sondergut*.

from Mark. All that we would know for certain that came from Mark was what we found *in both Matthew and Luke*, that is, less than two-thirds of Mark. For example, only Matthew preserves both of Mark's feeding stories. Would scholars assume that two stories had been present in Mark, or would they assume that Matthew, who is fond of doublets (e.g. two demoniacs, 8:28-33; two sets of two blind men, 9:27-31 + 20:29-34; two donkeys, 21:1-9), made a doublet out of what would probably be assumed to have been only one feeding story in Mark?

What would Mark look like, reconstructed in this manner? The following table of contents gives us an overview:

1:2-8	The ministry of John the Baptist
1:9-11	The baptism of Jesus
1:12-13	The temptation of Jesus
1:16-20	The calling of the disciples
1:29-34	The healing of many
1:40-45	The cleansing of the leper
2:1-12	The healing of the paralytic
2:13-17	The calling of Levi
2:18-22	The question of fasting
2:23-28	Plucking grain on the sabbath
3:1-6	Healing on the sabbath
3:7, 12	Withdrawal and silencing of demons
3:13-19	Appointment and empowerment of the Twelve
3:22-27	Accusation of being in league with Beelzebul
3:28-29	On blasphemy
3:31-32, 34-35	On Jesus' true family
4:1-9	Parable of the Sower
4:10-12	On teaching in parables
4:13-20	The meaning of the Parable of the Sower
4:21-23	On what will be revealed
4:24-25	Measure for measure
4:30-32	The Parable of the Mustard Seed
4:35-41	Stilling the storm
5:1-20	The Gerasene demoniac
5:21-43	The raising of a daughter, and the healing of a woman
6:4	"A prophet is not without honor"
6:7-13	The mission of the Twelve
6:14-16	Is John raised from the dead?
6:35-44	The feeding of the 5,000
8:12	No sign for this generation
8:15	"Beware of the leaven of the Pharisees"

8:27-30	Peter's confession
8:31	First prediction of the passion
8:34–9:1	The way of the cross
9:2-8	The transfiguration
9:14-27	Healing of boy
9:30-32	Second prediction of the passion
9:33-37	Teaching about greatness
9:38-40	Another casts out demons
9:42	The millstone saying
9:50	The salt saying
10:11-12	Teaching on divorce
10:13-15	Receiving the kingdom like a child
10:17-22	The rich man
10:23-31	The danger of wealth
10:32-34	Third prediction of the passion
10:42-44	A different style of leadership
10:46-52	The healing of the blind man (or men)
11:1-10	Entry into Jerusalem
11:15-18	Action in the Temple
11:27-33	The question of authority
12:1-10, 12	The Parable of the Wicked Vineyard Tenants
12:13-17	On paying taxes to Caesar
12:18-27	On the resurrection
12:35b-37	Whose son is the Christ?
12:39	Places of honor and the best seats
13:1-2	Prediction of the Temple's destruction
13:3-13	Signs of the end
13:14-23	Tribulation before the end
13:24-31	The coming of the son of man
13:33, 36	The warning to watch
14:1-2	The plot to kill Jesus
14:10-11	Judas' agreement to betray Jesus
14:12-25	The last supper
14:30	The prediction of Peter's denials
14:36-38	"Remove this cup from me"
14:43-49	The arrest
14:54-55, 61-65	The hearing before the Jewish council
14:66-72	Peter's denials
15:1-15	The trial before Pilate
15:21	Simon of Cyrene
15:22-31	The crucifixion
15:33-41	The death of Jesus
15:42-47	The burial of Jesus
16:1-8	The discovery of the empty tomb

16:15   Commission to go and preach
16:19   Ascension into heaven

Not only are there several pericopes missing, but many of the pericopes listed above would be considerably reduced in size or greatly altered from the way they are preserved in Mark, if they were reconstructed strictly on the basis of the parallel materials found in Matthew and Luke. (The apparent lengths of the respective passages in the list above are misleading, in that they create the impression of far more recoverable material than would actually be the case.) From this reconstructed Mark would we be able to discern Mark's christology? Could we infer from reconstructed Mark the situation and the interests of the Markan community?

Mark's opening verse, considered by most commentators and interpreters of Mark as vital to the understanding of the Gospel, would not be part of this reconstruction. Would we know that Mark's key christological formulation is that Jesus is "the son of God"? Not only is Mark 1:1 missing, but Jesus' bold affirmation in response to the High Priest's question, "Are you the Christ, the son of the Blessed?" (Mark 14:61-62), would be blunted in a reconstruction based on the Matthean and Lukan parallels. Whereas Matthew follows Mark fairly closely, Luke does not. Luke splits up the High Priest's question into two parts, "Are you the Christ?" (Luke 22:67a) and "Are you the son of God?" (22:70a), and has Jesus answer evasively: "If I tell you, you will not believe" (22:67b); "You say that I am" (22:70b). Moreover, Mark's confession through the Roman centurion would also be lost: "Truly this man was the son of God!" (Mark 15:39). Whereas Matthew again follows Mark closely, Luke reads: "Certainly this man was innocent!" (Luke 23:47). Given these deviations from Mark, would scholars really be in a position to discern with precision the christology of a Mark reconstructed from Matthew and Luke?

Controversial aspects of Jesus' ministry are also largely missing in a reconstructed Mark. The unbelief and opposition of Jesus' family are absent. Much of the material that casts the disciples in a negative light is also absent. One immediately thinks of the hypersensitive redaction-critical interpretations of Mark produced in the 1960s and 1970s. Would Theodore Weeden have found in Mark an implicit criticism of the triumphalist christology that had come to be associated with the apostles, had his access to Mark been limited to a reconstruction based on the Matthean-Lukan overlaps?[12] It seems rather unlikely. In my opinion, many of the interpretations of Mark in the last quarter of a century would never have suggested themselves.[13]

Finally, a Mark reconstructed from Matthean and Lukan parallels might actually include a small amount of Easter appearance tradition, which would in all probability be completely misleading, given the almost certainty that Mark 16:9-20 is a later, spurious ending, which drew upon Matthew, Luke, John, and Acts. In other words, a reconstruction based on Matthew and Luke in this instance might actually give us too much Mark!

The point of all of this, with regard to attempts to interpret Q, should be quite clear. If a reconstruction of Mark based solely on what can be extracted from Matthew and Luke is missing so many important elements, then why should we assume that in the case of Q, which must be reconstructed from Matthew and Luke, the situation is different in any significant sense? Inferences regarding the theology and community (if we can even speak of a "community") of hypothetical sources like Q, or the signs source many think was incorporated into the fourth Gospel, must be articulated with the appropriate degree of tentativeness.

Let us review the materials usually assigned to Q and some of the discussion about Q's value for recovering the historical Jesus and the

---

12   T. J. Weeden, Jr., *Mark—Traditions in Conflict* (Philadelphia: Fortress, 1971). Weeden believes that the Markan evangelist has attacked a divine man christology that placed great emphasis on miracles but had little stomach for persecution and suffering. Because the advocates of this christology appealed to the example of the apostles, the evangelist found it necessary to debunk them. This he has done by taking over much of his opponents' material (consisting mostly of miracle stories, now found in Mark 1–8) and then countering it with a lengthy passion story (Mark 11–15), complete with several passion predictions (Mark 8–10) and a portrayal of the disciples as increasingly uncomprehending and faithless as the Passion nears. Weeden's interpretation and many like it were for a time quite popular. In recent years, however, these interpretations appear to exert little influence. For a recent and devastating critique of them, see R. H. Gundry, *Mark: A Commentary on His Apology for the Cross* (Grand Rapids: Eerdmans, 1993).

13   As, for example, in W. H. Kelber (ed.), *The Passion in Mark: Studies on Mark 14–16* (Philadelphia: Fortress, 1976). Even with the full text of Mark before them, the speculative hypotheses of many scholars are dubious. See the appropriate criticisms expressed in M. Hengel, *Studies in the Gospel of Mark* (Philadelphia: Fortress, 1985) 31-45.

earliest christology. The following materials, which according to convention are placed in the Lukan order, are thought by most scholars to belong to Q (L = Luke; M = Matthew):[14]

L 3:7-9, 16-17	Preaching of John	M 3:7-12
L 4:1-13	Temptations	M 4:1-11
L 6:20-26	Beatitudes	M 5:1-12
L 6:27-36	Love of enemies	M 5:39-42, 44-48; 7:12
L 6:37-42	Admonitions	M 7:1-5; 10:24-25; 15:14
L 6:43-45	A tree and its fruit	M 7:16-20; 12:33-35
L 6:46-49	Two foundations	M 7:21, 24-27
L 7:1-10	Healing of the centurion's slave	M 7:28a; 8:5-10, 13
L 7:18-23	John's question	M 11:2-6
L 7:24-28	Jesus praises John	M 11:7-11
L 7:31-35	Fickle children	M 11:16-19
L 9:57-62	Would-be followers	M 8:19-22
L 10:2-12	The mission speech	M 9:37-38; 10:7-16
L 10:13-15	Woe on unbelieving cities	M 11:21-23
L 10:16	Hearing and rejecting	M 10:40
L 10:21-24	Praise of the Father	M 11:25-27; 13:16-17
L 11:2-4	Lord's Prayer	M 6:9-13
L 11:9-13	Ask, seek, knock	M 7:7-11
L 11:14-20, 23	Beelzebul accusation	M 12:22-30; 9:32-34
L 11:24-26	Return of unclean spirit	M 12:43-45
L 11:16, 29-32	Request for a sign	M 12:38-42
L 11:33	Lamp and bushel basket	M 5:15
L 11:34-35	Eye and light	M 6:22-23
L 11:39-52	Religious hypocrisy	M 23:4, 6-7, 13, 23, 25-27, 29-32, 34-36
L 12:2-12	Revelation and faith	M 10:26-33; 12:32; 10:19-20
L 12:22-31	On anxieties	M 6:25-33
L 12:33-34	On possessions	M 6:19-21
L 12:39-46	On preparedness	M 24:43-51
L 12:49-53	Sword, not peace	M 10:34-36
L 12:54-56	Knowing the times	M 16:2-3
L 12:57-59	Before the judge	M 5:25-26
L 13:18-21	Mustard seed and leaven	M 13:31-33
L 13:23-30	Two ways	M 7:13-14; 25:10-12;

---

14   See F. Neirynck, "Recent Developments in the Study of Q," in Neirynck, *Evangelica II* (BETL 99; Leuven: Peeters and Leuven University Press, 1991) 409-64, esp. 416.

		7:22-23; 8:11-12; 20:16
L 13:34-35	Jerusalem indicted	M 23:37-39
L 14:11; 18:14	Exaltation and debasement	M 23:12
L 14:16-24	Parable of the Great Banquet	M 22:2-10
L 14:26-27	Hating one's family	M 10:37-38
L 14:34-35	Tasteless salt	M 5:13
L 15:4-7	Parable of Lost Sheep	M 18:12-14
L 16:13	Two masters	M 6:24
L 16:16	Law and prophets	M 11:12-13
L 16:17	Importance of the Law	M 5:18
L 16:18	On divorce	M 5:32
L 17:1	Millstone	M 18:7
L 17:3-4	On forgiveness	M 18:15, 21-22
L 17:6	On faith	M 17:20
L 17:23-24, 26-30, 33-35, 37	The coming of the Son of Man	M 24:26-28, 37-41; 10:39
L 19:12-27	Parable of the Noble Man	M 25:14-20
L 22:28-30	On twelve thrones	M 19:28

An image of Jesus can be tentatively extracted from this material. A first impression is that Jesus is a sage, a teacher of a way of life. Much of the material found in the Sermon on the Mount/Plain falls into this category. Many of the teachings found in Q reflect themes found in Jewish wisdom tradition, as found, for example, in Proverbs, Sirach, and Wisdom of Solomon. Only one miracle story is told (Luke 7:1-10 = Matt 8:5-10, 13) and the point mostly has to do with faith ("Not even in Israel have I found such faith!"). There is no story of the passion; nor is the resurrection mentioned. But we cannot infer from these omissions that the "Q community," if there was one, had no interest in the death and resurrection of Jesus. To make such a claim would be an inappropriate use of the argument from silence. This is so for two reasons: (1) The purpose of the Q collection may have been primarily didactic and admonitory. Therefore, miracle stories and the passion story were unnecessary. (2) Because we have no way of knowing how much of Q is missing, we cannot be certain that it originally did not contain references to the passion and resurrection.

Q does contain some important elements of christology. John's question ("Are you the Coming One?") and Jesus' positive reply, in which he alludes to passages from Isa 35:5-6 and 61:1-2 (Luke 7:18-23 = Matt 11:2-6), should probably be understood as a messianic affirmation. This is probable because of the discovery of 4Q521 in which a similar allusion to the Isaian passages is found in the context of a description of the deeds of the Messiah. That is, John has asked Jesus if he is the Messiah, and Jesus has replied indirectly (as modesty and messianic tradition apparently required) that he was, as seen by his messianic deeds.[15] Elsewhere Jesus warns his generation of the danger of judgment for their lack of faith. They have no excuse, for a preacher greater than Jonah is present, and a sage wiser than Solomon is present (Luke 11:29-32 = Matt 12:40-42). Indeed, he who acknowledges Jesus before people will be acknowledged before the angels of God (Luke 12:8-9 = Matt 10:32-33). On account of Jesus, families will be divided (Luke 12:51-53 = Matt 10:34-36). The allusion to Mic 7:6 is significant here, for it appears in the Mishnah's only significant mention of the Messiah (cf. *m. Soṭa* 9:15). It is probable that in predicting family divisions on account of himself, Jesus implies that he is Israel's Messiah. Finally, the saying about the disciples sitting on thrones judging the twelve tribes of Israel (Luke 22:28-30 = Matt 19:28), at the time when the son of man is seated on his throne of glory (so Matthew), or when his disciples will sit at table with Jesus "in [his] kingdom" (so Luke), clearly implies a messianic self-understanding on the part of Jesus.

Thus, although we may not be certain what views the author(s) of the Q material held with respect to the death and resurrection of Jesus (and silence gives us little to go on!), we cannot say that there is no christology in Q or that Q's christology is a low christology. What christology is present coheres, as we shall see, with the christology present in the other New Testament Gospel sources.

Jesus research inevitably involves reaching behind the extant sources, inferring from what lies before us the nature of the material upon which the evangelists drew. But this activity of reaching behind the sources must be done with caution and with a generous dose of common sense.

The essays that follow elaborate on this theme. Bruce Chilton's chapter—which will further introduce the present volume—speaks

---

[15] See the discussion in J. D. Tabor and M. O. Wise, "4Q521 'On Resurrection' and the Synoptic Gospel Tradition: A Preliminary Study," *JSP* 10 (1994) 149-62; J. J. Collins, *The Scepter and the Star: The Messiahs of the Dead Sea Scrolls and Other Ancient Literature* (ABRL; New York: Doubleday, 1995) 117-22. Wise and Tabor ("The Messiah at Qumran," *BARev* 18.6 [1992] 60-65) were the first to recognize the significance of the parallel between 4Q521 and Jesus' reply to John the Baptist.

very much to the need for greater nuance in source-critical work and exegetical contextualization, while Bruce Malina attempts to refine certain aspects of the criteria for assessing authentic words of Jesus. Tom Holmén's essay offers trenchant and much deserved criticism of the criterion of double dissimilarity. The essay by the late Ben Meyer probes an aspect of Jesus' style of teaching that has been largely neglected. Stan Porter's and Matthew Brook O'Donnell's study of the textual variants found in the Greek Jesus tradition represents the first systematic treatment of this important, though overlooked aspect of research. The remaining essays treat specific passages, themes, and self-designations, all of which probe significant elements of the teaching and words of Jesus.

ASSESSING PROGRESS IN THE THIRD QUEST

Bruce Chilton

A LITERARILY HISTORICAL JESUS

The purpose of the Gospels is such that Jesus can only be known by means of literary inference, owing to the indirect relationship between the sources and what we call historical information. There is a reasonable degree of consensus that Mark was the first of the Gospels to be written, after 70 CE in the environs of Rome. As convention has it, Matthew was subsequently composed, near 80 CE, perhaps in Damascus (or elsewhere in Syria), while Luke came later, say in 90 CE, perhaps in Antioch. John is generally assigned to Ephesus, circa 100 CE, and the *Gospel according to Thomas* to Edessa sometime during the middle of the second century.

The close relationship among the first three Gospels, in their wording, order, and content, has led to their designation as "Synoptic," and to various hypotheses of their literary relationship. The hypothesis which once enjoyed a commanding position in the discipline has it that Mark was the written source of Matthew and Luke, all three of whom are often personified as authors on the hypothesis, and that Matthew and Luke used a source of Jesus' sayings, known as "Q[uelle, 'source']," as well as other written sources.

The popularity of the hypothesis of a genetic, literary relationship among the Synoptic Gospels has encouraged certain misleading assumptions. Chief among the them is the notion that the verbal similarity among the Gospels actually proves their literary connection: the fact is that the rate of verbal correspondence in comparable passages is as great or greater in Rabbinic literature, where the influence of oral transmission is known to have been substantial. The notion of "the Evangelists" as authors is another distortion. The Gospels simply were not produced within the sort of literary circles which gave us the Josephan corpus, and any critical reading reveals that there are layers of interpretative reflection within each of the Gospels, no single one of which can claim the authority of "the Evangelist" as a personal author in the modern sense.

Once "the Evangelist" is assumed to be an authorial scribe, his work is easily misconstrued as a mechanical compilation of documents. Moreover, the social function of the Gospels within the development of early Christianity tends to be ignored, because a model of professional, literary production is simply taken for granted. But the "hypothesis" (which among some scholars approaches to being an axiom) of Markan priority and the genetic relationship of the Synoptic Gospels has also left us with the most misleading apprehension of all: the supposition that there is a "real" Jesus "behind" the Gospels, who is to be identified by excavating and paring away "late" material and getting down to what is "primitive."

The persistence of the fallacious analogy between a critical reading of the Gospels and textual archaeology, or stratigraphy (the more fashionable designation today) requires that its inadequacy be identified. The point is evident, but apparently it has not been taken to heart, that the analogy of texts to archaeological tells presupposes that inert matter overlays the "original" object beneath, which only requires to be uncovered to be discovered in its pristine primitivity. But a text is not a tell, and meaning is not conveyed from generation to generation of tradents by permitting the erection of whatever seems convenient upon what has gone before. A text by definition conveys some set of meanings, and—in the case of the Gospels—the complexity is that earlier meanings may be conveyed within later meanings, and that we have access to earlier meanings only through later meanings. We know Jesus in a critical sense only insofar as the texts which claim to convey him in fact do so. There is no "primitive," "historical," "authentic," or otherwise real Jesus apart from what texts promulgate. In the first instance, therefore, Jesus is only knowable as a literarily historical phenomenon: what the Gospels point to as their source.

The understanding that Jesus is an inference of literary history distinguishes our approach from "the quest of the historical Jesus" and from "the new quest."[1] The positivistic first quest (from 1778), still represented in much discussion today, assumed that Jesus was

---

[1]   See W. R. Telford, "Major Trends and Interpretive Issues in the Study of Jesus," in B. D. Chilton and C. A. Evans (eds.), *Studying the Historical Jesus. Evaluations of the State of Current Research* (NTTS 19; Leiden: Brill, 1994) 33-74. Telford is justifiably skeptical about the contention that a "third quest" is in progress. On my reading of the present volumes (i.e. *Authenticating the Words of Jesus* and *Authenticating the Activities of Jesus*), the contours of the third quest for the historical Jesus are now discernible.

knowable apart from or behind the sources; the hermeneutical second quest (from 1953) permitted unduly of the influence of interpreters' theological agendas in their constructions of Jesus. We have set ourselves the task of what has been called generative exegesis.[2] Jesus for us, at the beginning of critical inquiry, is neither a unchanging datum covered over by the sources nor a function of how certain readers encounter certain texts in the light of their faith or their ideological commitment. Rather, our orientation allows that the literary reference of the Gospels must be the point of departure for critical reflection. There is no Archimedian fulcrum, which permits history to be lifted away from text (as in the first quest) or text to be lifted away from history (as in the second quest).

THE PLURALISM OF LITERARY HISTORY

In the instance of Jesus' occupation of the Temple, widely agreed to be a well-attested incident, the Gospels in fact present us with distinct portraits of Jesus. In Mark, we are informed that Jesus "did not permit anyone to carry a vessel through the Temple" while he occupied it (11:16). The uniquely Markan assertion implies that Jesus effectively brought sacrificial activity to a halt. In much the same way, a uniquely Markan explanation earlier in the Gospel (chap. 7) has it that "the Pharisees and all the Jews" (v. 3) keep many practices "of washings of cups and pots and bronze things and beds" (7:4): Mark's Jesus represents the end of all that.

By contrast, the Matthean Jesus, precisely in his occupation of the Temple, represents the fulfillment of Davidic hopes. He heals the blind and the lame, and is hailed as David's son (21:14-15). Within Matthew particularly, the designation "son of David" alludes to Solomon's power to heal, which Jesus also is understood to exert. The high priests and scribes become angry precisely because Jesus is so recognized in the Temple, and his response is to affirm that the praise itself fulfills God's intent (21:15-16).

Luke presents the most condensed version of the occupation within

---

2   An approach I first used in *Profiles of a Rabbi: Synoptic Opportunities in Reading about Jesus* (BJS 177; Atlanta: Scholars Press, 1989) and *The Temple of Jesus: His Sacrificial Program Within a Cultural History of Sacrifice* (University Park: The Pennsylvania State University Press, 1992) 113-21, and then developed in *A Feast of Meanings: Eucharistic Theologies from Jesus through Johannine Circles* (NovTSup 72; Leiden: Brill, 1994).

the canonical Gospels, and yet here too there is unique matter. The notice is appended that Jesus taught every day in the Temple, and that the high priest and scribes were unable to act against him, owing to the support of "the people" (Luke 19:47-48). The Temple is therefore established as a place where, as in the book of Acts, Christian teaching is a proper activity.

The simple, literary fact that the Synoptic Gospels are each substantially unique in their presentation of Jesus' action in the Temple, one of the most stable elements in the Synoptic tradition, ought long ago to have warned the discipline against a reductionistic, purely documentary solution of the "Synoptic Problem." A more adequate approach would recognize that the similarity of the first three Gospels is a function of their shared origin in the catechesis of the early Church, and that their uniqueness is a measure of the differences among the catechetical programs current in Antioch, Damascus, and Rome.

Indeed, the "Synoptic Problem" is an artifact of the assumption that the relationship among the Gospels is a documentary cipher which can be solved as a puzzle, whereas in fact, it is a matter of both the consensus and the distinctiveness of apostolic Christianity. Similarly, the dichotomy between oral and written transmission within the process of Synoptic formation, frequently assumed in recent discussion, is all to easily exaggerated: catechesis is essentially a matter of preparing baptisands, and whether one does so from written notes or from memory, the point of the exercise is to transmit what is held to be vital.

The "solution" of "the Synoptic Problem," of course, is not our purpose here. In aggregate, however, the contributors in fact represent a range of models in their work, from support of a qualified version of the priority of Mark and the existence of "Q," through some defense of the priority of Matthew, and on to a more thoroughly oral paradigm of how the Gospels as we know them emerged. Our work reflects a deep ferment which characterizes the study of the origins of the Gospels, and at the same time attests that we are engaged in a generative exegesis which allows for the limits of our certainty and therefore permits scholars who deploy different models to continue to speak to one another. The discipline of the study of the New Testament has for too long been hobbled by fashions so strong they approach to being dogma: "uncritical" is the adjective dogmatists use to protect their preferred fashions from any questioning. By showing here that we disagree at the same time that we all grow toward more comprehensive models of analysis, we hope that we do our part to put the conventionalism of the discipline behind us. In much of what is presented here, there is sharp and sometimes trenchant criticism (much of it directed toward "The Jesus Seminar"). When a statement is inaccurate, we try to correct it; when theory is deployed without reflection, we insist upon a critical appraisal of how that solecism might instruct work in the future. But the global rejection of critical viewpoints, simply because they do not accord with our own, is an indulgence which does not serve the interests of scholarship. These volumes develop an approach and its cognate methods; they do so with a variety of emphases and intellectual strategies, but without recourse to a single fashion of constructing Jesus.

The principal point of consensus among the Synoptic Gospels in their portrayal of the occupation of the Temple, which—in turn—makes them unique in comparison with John and *Thomas*, is the attribution to Jesus of some form of the biblical citation, a hybrid of passages in Isaiah and Jeremiah, "My house will be a house of prayer, but you have made it a den of thieves" (Luke 19:46; cf. Matt 21:13; Mark 11:17). The Synoptic placement of the occupation within the presentation of the passion of Jesus, preceding an extensive prediction of the destruction of the Temple, associates his action with divine judgment against the cult, a judgment which is assumed to have been executed in 70 CE. By means of a variety of narrative devices, the Synoptics bring out and vivify the connection between Jesus' occupation and subsequent death with the end of the Temple, but their stability in making that connection tends to suggest it was a prominent part of early catechesis.

The connection between Jesus' death and the destruction of the Temple is attenuated in John, and is transformed into the theme of the general irreconcilability of Jesus and "the Jews." Jesus' statement, "Destroy this Temple, and in three days I will raise it," is misunderstood by "the Jews" to refer to the Temple building; Jesus is alleged thereby to have referred to his own resurrection (John 2:18-22). The scriptural citation of the Synoptics, and its apparent denunciation of commercialism, does not appear; instead, Jesus' disciples think of Ps 69:10, "Zeal for your house will consume me" (John 2:17). The plane of the Johannine presentation, in other words, is the thematic axiom, "he came into his own, and his own received him not" (1:11), and the placement of the occupation near the beginning of the Gospel demonstrates that the dominant concern of the Gospel is discursive. Reflection upon central themes of belief is here more important than catechesis, and the impact is even less "historical" (in the modern sense of that term) than in the case of the Synoptics.

If John's logic is discursive, that of *Thomas* is aphoristic: sayings of Jesus are presented as if they provided their own contextual meaning, although in fact the questions which generally lead into a given section provide an interlocutory, and obviously artificial context. *Thomas* is no mere hodgepodge of traditional materials, although association by catchword and topic is a feature of organization. Evidently, the sayings were handed on orally within the community of *Thomas*, but the peculiar shape of the Thomaean tradition as we know it, in a documentary form, was achieved when an interlocutory structure was imposed upon the whole. The structure of interlocutions usually has disciples ask questions or make statements, to which Jesus is alleged to respond in the sayings which follow. A governing context is thereby generated for each saying, shorn of any narrative context (such as in the canonical Gospels, to which the Thomaean logia are usually comparable).

The interlocutions of disciples target our attention on the particular issues raised by contextual definition throughout *Thomas*. Didymos Judas Thomas, that is, Judas "the Twin" is introduced as the guardian of Jesus' words, and the first saying immediately makes the correct interpretation of those words the guiding concern of the entire work (cf. §1, with the superscription). In that strings of sayings are made to reply to the disciples' remarks, those remarks are the primary determinants of the context—and therefore the meaning—of Jesus' aphorisms. Prayer, fasting, and alms-giving (§6, §104), radically challenged by Jesus here, are made key issues, as are right leadership within the community (§12), the purpose of discipleship (§18), entering the kingdom and finding Jesus (§20, §21, §22, §24, §113, §114), the identity of Jesus (§43, §61.2), the world to come (§51, §52, §53), human (especially physical) relationships (§79, §99), and human government (§100). The interlocutory structure of the document makes it apparent that a community centered upon Jesus as an enduring, interpretative reality is the fundamental presupposition and aim of the whole. Full separation from Judaism is intimated not only by that exclusive perspective, but by the absence of reference to the Hebrew scriptures, the dismissal of prophetic testimony as the speech of "the dead" (§52), and the rejection of literal circumcision (§53). It is no accident that, when the disciples ask who Jesus is, he responds sarcastically that, in even posing the question, they have become like "the Jews" who cannot understand the whole of revelation (§43).

In §64.12, the laconic statement is made, "Tradesmen and merchants shall never enter the places of my father"; it follows the statement of Salome in §61.2, "Who are you, Lord? For in one you have climbed on my couch and eaten from my table." The inter-locutory context establishes that the thematic interest is in the identity of Jesus, and the key to that identity is that he is a single "one," inte-grated with his heavenly counterpart, knowledge of which Salome's very question betrays an awareness. But §64 itself is immediately followed by the parable of the vineyard in §65, which is closely associated with the Temple within the Synoptic tradition; §66 is the key text concerning, "The stone that the builders rejected," the climax of the parable in the Synoptics. The association of §64.12 with the Temple in the tradition before *Thomas* is therefore evident, and that association makes sense of the term "places" within the saying. The architectural complexity of the Temple appears to be reflected in the plural; the form of the saying is an instance of an independent tradition in *Thomas* closely associated with the catechesis which produced the Synoptics.

A review of the contents of the earliest Gospels (including *Thomas*) as they concern Jesus' occupation of the Temple makes it evident that none of them (as it stands) is what could be called historical. A given Gospel might be catechetical, as in the case of the Synoptics (but even then, the tenor of the catechesis involved varies greatly), theologically discursive (as in John), or aphoristically interpretative (as in *Thomas*). There is no stemma of the relationship among the five, so that the "most primitive" is identifiable from the outset, and even if there were such a stemma, our experience of the texts to hand would make us suspicious of any claim that what was most primitive happened also to be the most historical. All of the texts are programmatic, and in that sense tendentious; none of them is historical in its governing intention, even to the extent that, say, Josephus is.

Yet the Gospels are "historical" in effect, even though not by intention. In the process of the Synoptic catechesis, the Johannine homily of traditions, and the Thomaean interpretation of them, those traditions, some deriving from Jesus and his first followers, are permitted to come to speech. Moreover, the Gospels refer back to. Jesus as their source: *the literarily historical Jesus is a fact of which any reading of the Gospels must take account*, even if the question of "the historical Jesus" itself remains unsettled. That is to say, we cannot understand the documents at all, unless we can identify what they believe they are referring to (whether or not we accept that they in fact do so). That reference constitutes the literarily historical Jesus for a particular document, and the community of tradents which produced it.

With or without wishing to, those tradents were in the best possible position to know things about Jesus, and their documents are sometimes informative because or in spite of their particular programs. *Thomas* §64.12 does not wish to tell us that the principal issue in the occupation of the Temple was tradesmen and merchants; its concern is the lifestyle of disciples generally. But the logion nonetheless tells us something historical. Similarly, John 2:15 has Jesus make a whip of cords to drive animals away, and thereby confirms what an approach on the basis of the concern for purity in the Temple would suggest, that it was trade in the outer court which upset Jesus. And the Synoptic citation of Isaiah and Jeremiah (Matt 21:13; Mark 11:17; Luke 19:46) quite clearly indicates an enduring interest in the Temple, not an explanation for its imminent destruction. Because the ancient sources often speak historically despite themselves, no method can be commended which attempts to remove any Gospel from consideration on the grounds it is more secondary than another on literary grounds.

Our methods must reject the misleading analogy of archaeological strata, and attend to the historical unfolding of meaning by exegetical means. Our first and principal concern is for what we must presuppose of Jesus to explain the shape of a given text. Sometimes, of course, nothing must be presupposed: on occasions, the Gospels may simply speak the language of folk piety (as is the case, if much scholarly opinion is any guide, in the instance of the narratives of Jesus' birth). But it is difficult to understand how the Gospels came to speak of the kingdom of God as they do, for example, had Jesus not been concerned with the topic. Jesus' position can not be known directly, but by means of the sources to hand, we can infer his theology from the five sources that make a tenable claim to represent him: that is, in a process akin to triangulation in mapping, we may infer from our reading of texts what his position must have been to produce what we read. We are engaged in what we might call pentagulation. That course is unquestionably demanding, but it is the only course available for the critical apprehension of Jesus.

If we press the model of pentagulation further, another consideration presents itself. No cartographer can map a territory simply on the basis of the data of a survey. It is true that the measurement of angles from various perspectives will permit one to place objects, but only on the assumption of a certain geometry. Triangulation is as dependent upon Euclid for the conception of space which it assumes as for the method of measurement which is its more obvious feature. So in the case of the Gospels, we must appreciate from the outset that, if we wish to speak of Jesus in critical terms, he must be located in the space of early Judaism. Any language which alleges Jesus' rejection or transcendence of Judaism is to be rejected at the outset as an instance of apologetic.

There are, then, precisely two indices of Jesus as he may be known historically:

1. What may be said of him in aggregate as the presupposition of the canonical Gospels and *Thomas*,
2. within a critical understanding of Judaism prior to the destruction of the Temple.

Other alleged measures (all represented in the much-worked "criteria for authenticity"), such as his distinction or dissimilarity from Judaism, or the alleged primitivity of a given source, or the multiple attestation of a saying or action, are only helpful to the extent they help to explain the emergence of the texts to hand through the communities of their tradents. As the Gospels are read, it is crucial that they be assumed at no point (and at no hypothetical level) to convey a historical perspective directly. Rather, we may infer the literarily historical Jesus to which a given source refers on exegetical grounds, and then further conceive by abstract reasoning of the historical Jesus who presumably gave rise within early Judaism to that source, and others. Throughout, an attempt is being made to identify, insofar as that is possible, the historical performance of meaning which is called Jesus, and which gave rise to the transformation of that meaning into a catechetical program (the earliest version of the tradition which became Synoptic) and a collection of sayings (the proverbial or mishnaic source known as "Q"), which by a further set of permutations, combinations, and fresh developments became—in chronological order—the Synoptic Gospels, John and *Thomas.*

COHERENCE IN THE STUDY OF MEANING

Readers of these volumes will quickly see that our generative concern typically targets one of three issues: the connection between Jesus and a given source, or the shape and program of a particular source, or the framing conception of Jesus which one might use to apprehend him within a source or within the process which led up to the production of that source. Jesus, the sources that refer to him, and the conceptions of Jesus we deploy to understand the whole unfolding of meaning attested in the Gospels: these are focal issues within the generative approach we have found productive. The association among all three issues is fundamental within the attempt at insight into the critical matter of Jesus; although each of the articles which follow attend principally to one or another of them, they all attest the connections among the three.

The Jesus referred to by a source, the purpose of a source, our capacity to make sense of the source, have all emerged as interesting and irreducibly important programs of study within the third quest of the historical Jesus as it has emerged here. As one looks back to the contributions which have enabled the current approach to emerge, perhaps none is as evocative as Ben F. Meyer's book, *The Aims of Jesus.*[3] The logic and method Meyer deployed are not always spelled out there, and his article in the present volumes help one to appreciate the total intellectual project to which he was committed during his productive career. But the generative attempt to grapple with Jesus, the sources that refer to him, and the conceptual frame we use to outline both Jesus and the sources, owes more to Meyer than to any other single scholar.

The basic logic of "reasoning from consequent to antecedent" in the formation of a hypothesis was called Retroduction or Abduction by Charles S. Peirce (to distinguish that inference from deduction and induction).[4] Peirce's refinement of an Aristotelian understanding of syllogism has been taken up within a socially scientific reading of

---

3   B. F. Meyer, *The Aims of Jesus* (London: SCM Press, 1979). See B. D. Chilton, "Jesus within Judaism," in J. Neusner (ed.), *Judaism in Late Antiquity II. Historical Syntheses* (Handbuch der Orientalistik 70; Leiden: Brill, 1995) 262-84.

4   See P. P. Wiener, *Charles S. Peirce: Selected Writings (Values in a Universe of Chance)* (New York: Dover, 1958) 366-71.

the New Testament by Bruce Malina,[5] who rightly notes the affiliation with generative exegesis. Analyzing a text in a generative
manner implies a willingness to infer how Jesus, source, and Gospel
might relate to one another in a given case and in related instances.
The movement is dialectical, between text and explanation, under the
clear understanding that the hypothesis which best accounts for the
meaning of the text to hand is to be preferred.

Because composite texts are at issue in the traditions concerning
Jesus, no facile equation which collapses the creation of a document
into a single moment during its emergence can commend itself to us
on methodological grounds. Whether in the guise of postulating a
one-to-one correspondence between the Jesus of history and the text
of a Gospel, or in the guise of postulating that the anonymous
"author" was "responsible for the final form of the text," such exercises in reductionism, by their very failure to account for variegation
within the Gospels, only underline the necessity for more complex
and flexible thinking. What is "generative" in the exegesis proposed
is its capacity to move among the categories of "Jesus," "source," and
"Gospel" in a way which permits us to relate them—through the
inferences and hypotheses we form as we read—to one another. The
lucidity of the text in its received form under our analysis becomes
our measure of success or failure. That exegetical movement
involves discovering—and tracing the relations among—new and
perhaps unexpected meanings, revealing constructions of Jesus which
have long been marginalized in Christian thinking, and adjudicating
among the different and sometimes competing claims about Jesus
which the documents attest. That is to be expected, because a
generative exegesis must account for Jesus and the emergence of the
various sources concerning him, first within Judaism, and then
within the movement which became Christianity. The itinerary of the
third quest leads neither around the issue of faith in Jesus (as in the
first quest), nor through particular constructions of faith (as in the
second quest), but by means of critical assessments which involve
Jesus in the explanation of how faith in him emerged.

---

[5] In addition to "Criteria for Assessing the Authentic Words of Jesus: Some
Specifications" in this volume, see his review of *A Feast of Meanings*, in *Biblical
Interpretation* 5 (1997) 220.

CRITERIA FOR ASSESSING THE AUTHENTIC WORDS OF JESUS: SOME SPECIFICATIONS

Bruce J. Malina

The quest for the discovery of the authentic words of Jesus has been pursued along several tracks. The range of criteria that has become classic among researchers all presuppose that the investigator has a rather accurate grasp of the story of Jesus in terms of the social system in which that story took place. While no one can fault the criteria and the degree of probability they might yield, there is much to be desired in the scenarios that professional New Testament readers bring to their reading of the extant documents. Given the circular process involved in postulating criteria, applying them to some preconceived story, and then verifying the application of the criteria, the process is a typical example of reasoning called "abduction," by the U.S. philosopher, Charles S. Peirce (see Malina 1991). Bruce Chilton has successfully employed this dimension of human reasoning, calling it "generative history" (Chilton 1994; 1996). The purpose of this essay is to take the abduction process seriously in the area of assessing the authenticity of the words of Jesus. I will begin with a brief overview of the rather abstract, general criteria of judging the authentic words of Jesus, then apply these criteria to the whole story of Jesus presented in the gospels in order to disclose some less abstract, general perspectives at work in the life of Jesus as told in the whole story. Finally I take these less abstract, general perspectives and assess statements attributed to Jesus in terms of them. I believe this is the sort of reasoning in a circle that characterizes abduction, and that can assist in the task of assessing the authenticity of statements attributed to Jesus.

GENERAL PRINCIPLES

The rather abstract, general principles used to evaluate the authenticity of statements attributed to Jesus include the following: criteria of discontinuity, embarrassment, incongruity, multiple attestation, explanation and coherence (Barr 1995: 467-73; Duling 1994:

520-23). There is general consensus that statements ascribed to Jesus that express ideas militating against Second-Temple Israelite behavior as well as against behavior espoused by later Jesus Messiah groups (discontinuity) trace back to Jesus with high probability. Similarly, Jesus' statements that express sentiments and values awkward for Jesus Messiah groups (embarrassment) have a very high probability of tracing back to Jesus himself. Further, there is likewise general consensus that a statement attributed to Jesus in tension with other ideas in the same work (incongruity) as well as the statement found in a number of early sources (multiple attestation) has a high probability of tracing back to Jesus himself. Statements attributed to Jesus that account for his rejection and crucifixion (explanation) along with those that add up to produce a cogent portrait of a "believable" person (coherence) are generally viewed as possible to probable in value.

APPLYING THE GENERAL PRINCIPLES

First of all, these criteria will be applied to aspects of the general story of Jesus told in the New Testament, rather than to individual statements (excluding John, see Malina and Rohrbaugh 1998). The result will provide some less abstract general orientations with which to evaluate what Jesus is supposed to have said. Consider the following assertions and the reasons for judging them to trace back to Jesus with high probability. Thus:

1. Jesus proclaimed a forthcoming kingdom of God (or of Heaven or of the Sky) (Matt 4:17; Mark 1:15; Luke 4:42): criteria involved would be embarrassment (no such theocracy emerged); incongruity (behavior urged in Matt and Luke is for fictive kin groups, not theocracy); multiple attestation (all Synoptics, notably lacking in Paul); coherence (Jesus was crucified for causing political unrest).

2. The harbinger of this kingdom, Jesus said, would be a celestial or astral entity called "the Son of Man" (Matt 24:30; Mark 13:26; Luke 21:27; see also Matt 16:27; Mark 8:38; Luke 9:26): criteria involved would be embarrassment (no such celestial entity appeared); incongruity (Jesus is identified with this celestial entity); multiple attestation (all Synoptics mention this, notably lacking in Paul), coherence (Jesus often spoke of celestial or astral phenomena; final discourse is in astrological forecast terms).

3. Jesus recruited a group of persons to assist him in the task of

proclaiming the forthcoming theocracy (Matt 4:18-22; Mark 1:16-20; Luke 5:1-11): criteria involved include embarrassment (the proclamation proved vacuous); incongruity (in the Synoptics these recruits act like a fictive kinship group rather than a political religion group); multiple attestation (all Synoptics mention this recruitment and an initial attempt at proclamation); coherence (all Synoptics report that group members accompany Jesus on his final trip to Jerusalem; they flee).

4. The theocracy proclaimed by Jesus and his group was an exclusively Israelite theocracy (Matt 10:5, explicitly; Mark 6:7; Luke 9:2, contextually): criteria include embarrassment (in Matthew, no Samaritans, while Luke includes them; in Acts and Paul problems with admitting non-Israelites to Jesus Messianist groups); incongruity (none in Matthew, Mark or John which are solidly against non-Israelites; for John Samaritans are Israelites but not Judeans; the incongruity surfaces in Acts and Paul's Galatians); multiple attestation (all Synoptics report Jesus having no theocratic outreach to non-Israelites; at most there are healings which are not distinctive to Jesus); coherence (all Synoptics report that Jesus' career is oriented to Israel, to Jerusalem, to obeying the God of Israel).

5. The "God" to whom Jesus refers and relates is always "the God of Israel" (Matt 15:31; Mark 12:29; Luke 1:68; ancestral God Matt 22:32; Mark 12:26; Luke 20:37; Acts 3:13; 7:32; Matt 8:11 and compare Luke 13:29): criteria involved again include embarrassment (in Paul and Revelation, there is but one God, no specific "God of Israel"); incongruity (none in the Synoptics, hints of incongruity in Acts, e.g. in Peter's vision of one God of all people; Paul and Revelation); multiple attestation (all Synoptics report Jesus relating to the traditional God of Israel, referring to the Shema which refers explicitly to Israel's God); coherence (all Synoptics report that the theocracy Jesus proclaimed refers to the rule of Israel's God over Israel).

HYPOTHESIS FOR ASSESSING THE AUTHENTICITY
OF THE WORDS OF JESUS

The foregoing assertions describe Jesus' project. They derive from a set of data that set the limits for a general scenario for the story of Jesus' career. If any key to assessing the authenticity of the words of Jesus is to be found, it must somehow relate this general scenario, and thus adequately and sufficiently fit Jesus' project and historical context. This is the general scenario deriving from the social system operative at the time and place, and realized in the language of the sources at various chronological levels. Information about Jesus' career, of course, is prismed through the Jesus tradition espoused by Jesus groups situated at least at three chronological levels: the period of Jesus' activity, the period of initial compilations and formulations of what Jesus said, and the period of those groups for whom the final form of the gospel documents were composed (Luke 1:1-4). From the perspective of social scientific analysis, these three chronological levels point to three different institutional arrangements set within a general Mediterranean social matrix and a more focused Hellenistic society norming life in first-century Galilee and Judea.

If the general scenario based on the foregoing assertions are prismed through the general social system of the first-century Eastern Mediterranean, and the specific cultural configurations in vogue at the time in the house of Israel, it produces a set of perspectives within which to place the inquiry into the authenticity of Jesus' statements. These perspectives include the following:

1. It is historically certain (that is highly probable) that Jesus proclaimed a political religion, not kinship religion. The proclamation of the kingdom of God (or of Heaven or of the Sky) is the proclamation of theocracy. As a social institution, theocracy is political. As a first-century Mediterranean institution it features religion and economics embedded in politics (see Malina 1986; 1994; 1996a). Like economics, so too the religious institution was embedded both in politics and the household. There was political religion and domestic religion, but no religion pure and simple. Similarly, there was political economy and domestic economy, but no economy pure and simple. The separation of bank/market and state and the separation of church and state take place in the eighteenth century A.D.

Political religion used the roles, values, and goals of politics in the articulation and expression of religion: religious functionaries were political personages, focus was on the deity(ies) as source of power and might, expected to provide order, well-being and prosperity for the body politic and its power wielders (nobles) to the benefit of subjects. Temples were political buildings, temple sacrifices were for the public good; the deity of the temple had a staff similar to the one a monarch had in the palace. Democratic cities altered monarchic temples into democratic ones, owned and run by city councils or noble council members, etc.

Domestic religion used the roles, values, and goals of the household in the articulation and expression of religion: religious functionaries were domestic personages (notably fathers and inside the household, mothers as well, oldest sons, ancestors), focus was on the deity(ies) as source of solidarity, commitment, belonging mediated through ancestors, expected to provide well-being, health, and prosperity for the kin group and its patriarchs to the benefit of family members. The house had its altars and sacred rites (focused on the hearth=life) with father (patriarch) and mother (first in charge at home) officiating. Deities were tribal/household ones (e.g. God of Abraham, Isaac, Jacob etc.) as well as ancestors who saw to the well-being, prosperity and fertility of the family members.

As we know from our detached religious institution, religion looks specifically to meaningfulness, the meaning of it all and how one (individualistic or collectivistic) fits into it all, ultimate meaningfulness. Thus when embedded, political religion seeks meaning through power: an ultimately meaningful existence derives from power access and/or power wielding. When societal values are readily attainable, it is power exercised on behalf of society by those above, due to the deity(ies). But when societal values are simply desiderata, it is power deriving from and experienced within the group, notably through central patrons or brokers (see Malina 1986).

Domestic religion, in turn, seeks meaning through belonging: an ultimately meaningful existence derives from belonging. Again, when societal values are readily realizable, it is belonging to the proper ranking in one's hierarchical society; but when societal values are dimly attainable, it is belonging to a proper kin and/or fictive kin group.

In Roman Hellenism, with the demise of *polis* life and the rise of *imperium*, various associations come to institutionalize fictive kinship, i.e. organization "brothers," "sisters," or "friends" (see, e.g. Barton and Horsley 1981; Kloppenborg and Wilson 1996). The result is fictive domestic religion, with family roles, values and goals emerging, notably for those types of persons who found such associations attractive over and above their own domestic religion (if they had a household to belong to).

However in Second-Temple Israel during the same period, a

number of political factions espousing a range of political-religious programs were salient: Pharisees, Sadducees, Essenes, Herodians and the like. With his proclamation of the "kingdom of the God," Jesus was proclaiming a forthcoming theocracy. Hence any statement attributed to Jesus that deals with political religion has highest probability of authenticity.

As we shall later note, the political religion faction inaugurated by Jesus did, indeed, adjourn, only to emerge for a time as a renewed political religion association looking to the advent of Jesus as Israel's Messiah. With the destruction of the focal apparatus of Israel's political religion and concern with "men of Israel" (Acts 2:2; 3:12; 5:35; 13:16), it seems this Jesus Messiah group developed into a domestic religion association of "brothers." The point is that Jesus' concerns were with theocracy, an Israelite political religion. Hence, statements dealing with kinship/fictive kinship religion reflect social settings postdating Jesus' activity. The problem here, of course, is that some political religious statements have been re-employed in the new domestic religious social situation. For example, the directive on reconciliation in Matt 5:23-24 directly relates to family life in political Israel as Jesus knew it (level 1), but in its present context it reflects fictive kinship relations in Matthew's Jesus Messiah group (level 3).

2. It is equally historically certain that Jesus sought help to have Israel learn about the forthcoming theocracy. To this end he recruited a faction to assist him. A faction is a type of coalition, that is a group recruited for a given purpose for a limited time. Factions differ from other coalitions in that a faction results from a single person's enlisting help to realize his own program (see Malina 1996b). The Jesus faction, according to the Synoptics, lasted for only a single dry season (March to October) interrupted by the rainy season (October to March), and concluded with a trip to Jerusalem at the onset of the next dry season.

Jesus' faction was a small group. As a small group, it developed and adjourned like other small groups, following a pattern that has been cross-culturally verified. Small groups unfold, if they come to term, through the following five stages: forming, storming, norming, performing and adjourning. We shall shortly consider these five stages. During forming, storming and adjourning, all group members are in the same phase of group socialization, while such is not the case for the norming and performing stages.

(Tuckman 1965: 384-99, synthesized by Moreland and Levine 1988: 151-81). Groups form at all as solutions to social problems (see Malina 1995). Further, small groups are formed for one of two purposes: task fulfillment or social and emotional support. Some groups exist for pragmatic, action oriented purposes. Their orientation is outward, to have effect on some outgroup. Other groups are formed for social and emotional support. Their orientation is inward, to have effect on the ingroup, whether singly or as a whole. Jesus' political religion faction was of the pragmatic type. The various Jesus Messiah groups and their domestic religious focus were of the social/emotive type. Of course pragmatic groups can develop social/emotive features, but they are not structured to fulfill social and emotive functions as are non-pragmatic groups.

Now consider the five stages of group development:

(1) *Forming*: The forming stage is the period when the group is put together. Jesus put his faction together to help him in the pragmatic task of announcing the forthcoming, if undefined, Israelite theocracy. This activity is articulated in the Synoptic tradition in the so-called "mission" charge: to proclaim God's taking over the country soon, to urge Israelites to get their affairs in order to this end, and to heal those in need of healing (Matt 10:1-16; Mark 6:7-11; Luke 9:2-5). Mark intimates that group recruits were chosen with healing ability in tow (Mark 3:14-15), while Q states that Jesus bestowed this ability on his recruits (Matt 10:1; Luke 9:1-2). During the forming stage, group members discuss the nature of their task and how it might be performed.

Jesus Messiah associations that followed Jesus' public career were not task oriented like the Jesus faction. Rather Jesus Messiah groups were social activity groups. During the forming stage, individuals were invited to join the group or sought it out themselves by means of networking procedures. The forming stage develops group dependence.

At the forming stage, members of both types of groups are anxious and uncertain about belonging to the group. They exhibit typically cautious behavior. Each member carefully tries to ascertain whether the group will meet his (or her) aspirations. The behavior of group members toward each other is tentative; commitment to the group is low.

(2) *Storming*: At the storming stage, group recruits jockey for position and ease into interpersonal stances. Members of task activity

groups such as the Jesus faction resist the need to work closely with one another. Conflict among members emerges, with emotions getting free expression (e.g. question of precedence: Matt 20:21; Mark 10:37; about reward: Matt 19:27-28; Mark 10:28; Luke 22:30).

Jesus Messiah social activity groups likewise break out in conflict, with group members arguing with each other and heaping criticism on the leader.

In both types of groups, group members become more assertive and each tries to change the group to satisfy personal needs (thus Peter as moral entrepreneur Matt 16:16; Mark 8:29; Luke 9:20). Resentment and hostilities erupt among group members with differing aspirations (again Peter in Matt 16:22; Mark 8:32). Each members attempts to persuade the others to adopt group goals that will fulfill his (or her) expectations. The behavior of group members toward one another is assertive, and their commitment to the group is higher than it was before.

(3) *Norming*: The norming stage is marked by interpersonal conflict resolution in favor of mutually agreed upon patterns of behavior. This phase is one of exchange in task activity groups such as the Jesus faction (upon returning from a trip: Mark 6:30; Luke 9:10; 22:35). Everyone in the group shares ideas about how to improve the group's level of performance (Jesus must show how it is done: Matt 17:16; Mark 9:18; Luke 9:40).

In social activity groups such as Jesus Messiah fictive kin groups, on the other hand, it is a phase of cohesion. Group members begin to feel more positive about their membership in their particular group.

In both cases, norming involves group members in the attempt to resolve earlier conflicts, often by negotiating clearer guidelines for group behavior.

(4) *Performing*: With the performing stage, group participants carry out the program for which the group was assembled. Performing marks the problem-solving stage of task activity groups. Members solve their performance problems and work together productively.

Social activity groups, on the other hand, move into the performing stage by role-taking. Members take social roles that make the group more rewarding to all. They work together cooperatively to achieve mutual goals.

From the evidence provided in the New Testament documents, it is clear that the Jesus faction moved into a performing stage. The sending of the seventy (-two; Luke 10:1-20) points to enlarged activity. This implies further recruitment or forming, with subsequent storming and norming to lead to greater performing.

On the other hand, there is little, if any, evidence for a performing stage in Pauline groups. The problems addressed in the Pauline corpus reveal storming and norming. The desiderata listed in the Pastorals concerning group leadership still look like items desired and not yet realized.

(5) *Adjourning*: With adjourning, group members gradually disengage from both task activities as well as from social activities, in a way that reflects their efforts to cope with the approaching end of the group.

In the gospel story, the adjourning phase is rather abrupt, distinguished by the crucifixion of Jesus. As regards the core Jesus faction, the post-crucifixion stories liberally attest to this phase. But with the experience of the appearance of the Risen Jesus, a feedback loop revives the process with new forming and storming, norming and initial performing, as described telescopically in the final sections of Matthew and Luke, but at length in opening of Acts. The new norms point initially to heightened political religion concerns in Israel. But outreach to emigre Israelite communities indicates the beginning of fictive kinship concerns. The ritual of baptism commanded in Matthew for Israelites of all nations (Matt 28:19) and described in Acts points to such fictive kinship focus. The quality of these groups as fictive kin groups is further indicated by the main group ceremony, the common meal (see Esler 1987: 71-109). Thus in the development of Jesus movement organizations, the adjournment of the initial Jesus faction signaled by the crucifixion of Jesus loops back to renewed forming and storming for former Jesus faction members, around whom another political religious group emerges, awaiting the coming of Jesus as Israel's Messiah. (Outside Roman Palestine and at a later stage in Palestine, after 70 CE, these groups emerge as fictive kin groups.). The trigger event for this loopback was their experience of Jesus after his death, an experience understood as the work of God, now perceived as "He who raised Jesus from the dead" (Acts 3:15; Rom 8:11).

I should like to note in conclusion, with Moreland and Levine (1988: 164) that "most theories of group socialization implicitly assume that the group is in the performing stage of development."

This of course is the situation in studies of early Jesus Messiah groups, whether of "wandering charismatics" or Pauline communities! Our New Testament documents come from storming and norming situations for the most part and are studied by scholars in performing (or adjourning) phases. Furthermore, the documents are used in churches that are into performing. Obviously inattention to this state of affairs can lead to some distortion due to a sort of Doppler effect caused by scholars reading volatile storming and norming traditions while they stand fixed in performing situations.

3. The pivotal inaugurating sign of the emergence of the theocracy was the coming of the Son of Man from the Sky (see Malina 1997). Jesus' forecast about the destruction of Jerusalem and the coming of the celestial Son of Man indicate that Jesus had astral prophetic abilities. The astral entity known as the Son of Man (*1 Enoch* 37–71; Revelation 12) has a central role in the forthcoming Israelite theocracy. Hence the astral prophecies of Jesus, no matter how edited by various final authors, have a high probability of being authentic.

4. The theocracy Jesus proclaimed was an exclusively Israelite theocracy. Jesus either ignored non-Israelites or was insulting toward them. Statements like the one in Matthew, "Go nowhere except to the lost sheep of the house of Israel" (Matt 10:4), are quite authentic. So are Matthew's "many" statements, which should be read as "many in Israel" (for example, Matt 7:13.22; 8:11; 13:17; 19:30; 20:28; 22:14; 24:5, 10-11; 26:28, 60; 27:52-53, 55). Similarly, the repartees to non-Israelites are equally authentic (e.g. the Syro-Phoenician woman Matt 15:21-28; Mark 7:24-30; the proverb about dogs and swine Matt 7:6). Jesus' answer to the centurion, "I tell you not even in Israel have I found such faith" (Luke 7:1-10; Matt 8:5-13), is fully embedded in an Israelite context so that it fits Israel well (it forms a put down of Israel by highlighting Gentiles).

5. The "God" to whom Jesus refers is always "the God of Israel." The theology underpinning this reference must be understood in the matrix of the henotheistic value systems of the time espoused by Israelite elites of the time. Hence any statement that makes full sense with reference to the God of Israel alone has high probability of authenticity. On the other hand, if statements can be understood as referring to some universal or monotheistic God of all people, then it surely postdates Jesus' activity. Monotheism emerges in the Resurrected Jesus Group, when the Roman emperor was used as analogy for understanding God as a universal divine monarch, "like

an emperor of the world, of infinite power and majesty" (Tertullian, *Apol.* 24).

6. Given the fact that Jesus set up a political religious faction, the sayings of Jesus relative to his political movement group may fit one (or more) of the following group development stages:

Forming (invitation to join a faction for Jesus' project: to proclaim theocracy in Israel)

Storming (about what's in it for us if we join)

Norming (rules for ingroup and outgroup relations of those who proclaim the theocracy)

Performing (behavior among the people of Israel, proclaiming the theocracy)

Adjourning (with the collapse of Jesus' project)

7. Jesus does not present himself as Israel's Messiah. There is no indication of this in what is reported concerning Jesus' political religious program. Jesus proclaimed a forthcoming theocracy, but said nothing about any role he might have in that theocracy. In terms of the model of small group development, with the adjourning of Jesus' own political religious faction, the faction's core members followed a feedback loop to a new forming rooted in the experience of Jesus raised by the God of Israel and the meaning of this event. This experience was interpreted variously.

8. As for the group re-formed after Jesus' death and appearance, we learn from Acts that initially, the experience of Jesus raised from the dead by the God of Israel was interpreted to mean that Jesus was Israel's Messiah who would soon come to inaugurate the theocracy Jesus spoke about. This ideology served as a cue for the (re)-forming of another task oriented group, now charged with making known to all Israel that Jesus is Israel's Messiah to come and this would be soon. Jesus's former recruits now continue their healing and exorcizing as they take the word to Israel in Judea, Galilee, Perea (and even Samaria, according to Acts). In the Israelite heartland, the message was perceived as one of political religion. Acts tells of conflict with political authorities because of the message.

However those who embraced the ideology of Jesus as Messiah to come had to wait it out. They did so by forming fictive kinship religion groups, "brothers and sisters" who met and prayed and shared while awaiting the coming of the Messiah in power.

Some members of the fictive kinship religion group felt urged to take the message of Jesus as Israel's Messiah to Israelite emigres or colonists in other parts of the Mediterranean and the Middle East. (see Matt 28:16-20), While such a task oriented group in Judea would appear as a political religion group (until 70 CE), outside Judea it seemed more a fictive kinship religion association, whose adherents met as the Jerusalem group with a view to waiting for the coming of Israel's Messiah in Jerusalem.

On the other hand, one segment of the Jesus Messiah fictive kinship group saw in Jesus more than Israel's Messiah to come. Due to their experience of non-Israelites wishing to join their ranks, members of this group came to view Jesus as a new revelation of the God of Israel. What the burning bush was to Moses, the resurrected Jesus was to members of this segment. The result was that two major forms of Jesus Messiah fictive kinship groups emerged: the Israel-only Jesus Messianist fictive kinship group and the Outsiders-too Resurrected Jesus fictive kinship groups. The Israel-only group required outsiders to become Israelites (by circumcision and keeping all the Torah) or to live by the Torah requirements of residents aliens in Israel (as listed in Acts 15). The God whose Messiah Jesus is, is the God of Israel.

The Outsiders-too group took another tack. In forming its ideology, its concerns were something like the following. Since the role of Messiah is Israel specific, the resurrection of Jesus indicated that Jesus was more than Israel's Messiah. Rather by that event, the God of Israel reveals that there is no other God at all; there is but one and only one God, the one who raised Jesus from the dead. Hence it would make no sense for non-Israelites who sought to join Jesus Messiah groups to bother with Israel specific ideology, values and behavior. With the resurrection of Jesus, God is revealed as a monotheistic being for all human beings.

Furthermore, all initial instances of non-Israelites joining Jesus Messiah groups occur because God Himself did it: the vision to Cornelius in Acts 10:1-8; the repeated confirmatory vision to Peter in Acts 10:9-16; "God opens the door of faith to Gentiles" Acts 14:27; 15:24; Paul's own call Gal 1:12. These are so many instance of God at work "founding" the Outsiders-too Resurrected Jesus group.

Thus, Luke and Paul explain in their own way that it was God's raising Jesus from the dead along with God's own initiative that eventually allowed for Israelite outgroups to join the Jesus Messiah fictive kinship groups. Their coming resulted in a refashioning of those groups, with a new focus on Jesus as raised by a universal God, rather than on Jesus as God's Messiah for Israel. The Israel-only Jesus Messianist fictive kinship groups are witnessed to by Matthew; John; James, Hebrews; the Outsiders-too Resurrected Jesus fictive kinship groups are witnessed to by Luke; Paul; Revelation.

9. All statements about "following" Jesus and "discipleship" must be interpreted in terms of the quality of the small group involved. Small groups are formed for one of two purposes. Some groups exist for pragmatic, action oriented purposes. Their orientation is outward, to have effect on the outgroup. Other groups are formed for social and emotional support. Their orientation is inward, to have effect on the ingroup, whether singly or as a whole. Jesus' political religion faction was of the pragmatic type. The various Jesus Messianist groups and their domestic religious focus were of the social/emotive type.

In the stories about Jesus, there are two types of following of Jesus: there are followers who join to assist Jesus in his political task, there are followers who join Jesus as though he were a teacher/founder of a philosophical school, to learn a way of life. Statements relating to the task oriented following trace back to Jesus; statements relating to following as disciple trace back to Jesus Messianist movement groups.

Pragmatic following deals with helping the faction founder with his self chosen task: announcing the forthcoming theocracy and healing people to this end. This is political religious factionalism. Way of life following, following a teacher, is social and emotional; here following connotes following a way of living, a life style, undertaken for one's own well being. This is fictive kinship religious group formation (much like contemporary philosophical schools).

The first type of following is typical of the Jesus movement and Jesus movement group adherents. This is what the historical Jesus was concerned about—and it failed. The appropriation of this story for fictive kinship religion resonates quite explicitly in Matthew (and implicitly in Mark, and "historically" in Luke). These Jesus Messianist groups believed Jesus will come soon as Messiah of Israel so his program ought be continued in the hope that when he comes soon the theocracy would begin. In the meantime, Jesus Messianists form and live in their fictional kinship groups, open only to Israel, according to the directives of Q.

10. As a social-emotional support group with a way of living project, Jesus Messianist fictive kinship movement groups preserve sayings of Jesus that fit one (or more) of the following group development stages:

> Forming (a group to follow a way of living based on what the God of Israel did to Jesus, designating him as Israel's forthcoming Messiah)
>
> Storming (about roles and benefits for a way of living based on what God did to Jesus when he comes as Messiah with power)
>
> Norming (about rules for a way of living based on what the God of Israel did to Jesus as Israel's forthcoming Messiah)
>
> Performing (rather conflict free way of living typical of Jesus Messianist movement groups—this does not emerge in the New Testament period)
>
> Adjourning (expected adjourning when "all things are submitted to Christ and Christ to the God of Israel")

11. But there was a third type of following that is really no following at all. This orientation was typical of those branches of the Jesus Messianist movement groups that dismissed the centrality of Israel, such as the Pauline and Lukan types. The ideology of these groups held that even though Jesus was wrong in his political expectations and aspirations, God raised him anyway, thus (and in order to) revealing himself (God) as "he who raised Jesus from the dead." As fictive kinship religion groups, the focal concern of these groups was not Jesus' return as Israel's Messiah, but on pleasing and obeying God revealed by the presence of the resurrected Jesus (through the Spirit) in their midst. These fictional kinship groups learned about the story of Jesus and behavioral directives such as Q only as historical information about Jesus and his program "according to the flesh." The Lukan and Pauline groups were not concerned about following the "teachings of Jesus," but instead took their cues from emerging social interaction of the groups "in Christ" and their relationship with outgroups (as in Paul; I believe Luke does "antiquarian" history to explain to groups such as Pauline groups who Jesus was and what God has revealed through the resurrection of Jesus).

Thus any statement relevant to the Israel-only Jesus Messianist movement groups (e.g. fasting) that stands opposed to Jesus's behavior (e.g. he did not fast) underscores the authenticity of statement. The reason for this is that it is hard to conceive of early Jesus Messianists contradicting Jesus's behavior since they sought to "follow" Jesus in his way of life. If their following meant contradicting Jesus, their witness must be accepted since their behavior contradicted Jesus; of course rationales for contradictory behavior are inauthentic (e.g. when the bridegroom is taken away Matt 9:15; Mark 2:20; Luke 5:35).

On the other hand, the Outsiders-too Resurrected Jesus movement groups were not concerned about what Jesus said and did as basis for a way of life (Luke in Acts) or not at all (Paul). It was the God revealed in the Resurrection of Jesus who counted. For the Outsiders-too Resurrected Jesus movement groups, the universal God was the founder of their group (i.e. of Jesus Messiah Groups).

POPULAR CONTEMPORARY APPROACHES

Among contemporary reconstructions of the life of Jesus, obviously the pragmatic, task oriented, groups recruited by Jesus to proclaim theocracy fall closer to images of Jesus as leader of a peasant rebellion (exit the Cynic Jesus). Although Jesus did indeed live in a society with an advanced peasant economy, there is little in the documents (or the history of the period) to warrant identifying the Jesus movement group with contemporary peasant societies (Horsley 1987 is too anachronistic, if very relevant for the twentieth century).

On the other hand, the fictive kinship religion groups of Jesus Messianism are social and emotional in their orientation. By imagining Jesus himself to have founded such groups, the image of Jesus comes closer to a settled, non-political portrait. The political dimensions tend to disappear. Among contemporary story tellers, Crossan's attempt to wed the pragmatic and the social/emotional types of groups (Jesus the peasant for peasants and the wandering Cynic) is like the wedding of oil and water (Crossan 1991). It is a mismatch that is socially impossible. Similarly Mack's picture of Jesus as Cynic is quite on target if Jesus did in fact found fictive kinship religious groups (Mack 1988). But this seems highly unlikely, if not impossible given the duration of Jesus' activity (in the Synoptics, two dry seasons and one rainy season).

Yet there are quite clear reminiscences of conflict with kinship groups whose sons were recruited by Jesus for his political religion faction. It was Jesus' conflict with Israelite families, including his own, it seems, that provoked those memorable words of Jesus that

seem to resonate with the experience of later fictive kinship religion
groups. One must hate one's family to assist in proclaiming the.
forthcoming theocracy since families as a rule will have nothing of it.
After all theocracy is political and is the concern of those in charge
of the political institutions (one can discern the political institutions
by following the trail of the political economy: who gets the taxes—>
monarchs, aristocrats, priests). There are also statements fitting such
family conflicts that seem to have wandered far from their original
setting in the process of appropriation, e.g. the basic four beatitudes
of Luke, originally asserting the honor of the "disobedient son" (see
the perceptive study of Neyrey 1995). While one might imagine
Jesus himself having been ejected from his own kin group and
village, thus left to seek out a new family, there seems to have been
little need for such a nurturing group if in fact God's kingdom were
coming soon.

In sum, Jesus was not a peasant rebel, but a peasant prophet
(perhaps like Amos, the man from Tekoa), emerging as a holy man
(the Israelite equivalent of a shaman) with a prophetic proclamation.
He recruited a faction to help with the task—to be completed soon
since the theocracy he proclaimed was forthcoming. Cynics (and all
Hellenistic philosophers) are concerned with a way of living, "good"
living. There is no evidence that Jesus cared about this at all, except
mediately and indirectly to make points in challenge riposte with
opponents (e.g. kin groups which opposed his recruiting of their
sons; Pharisees and Sadducees who were directly concerned with the
existing theocracy and their way of living Torah; early Jesus Messiah
groups, after their political phase, surely were concerned with
"good" living).

Thus in the story of Jesus and the emergence of early Jesus
Messianism, political religion and fictive kinship religion were
sequential.

1. Jesus was interested solely in political religion.

2. With the death-resurrection of Jesus, the meaning of Jesus'
appearance and God's intentions bifurcates in the emerging ideology
developed among Jesus' recruited following:

2.1. The Israel-only group (Matthew, Mark) see Jesus as Messiah
to come soon for Israel to inaugurate theocracy; in the meanwhile
true Israel forms fictive kin groups with developing directives while
awaiting the coming of Jesus with power.

2.1.1. Some fictive kin directives are applications of Jesus's theocratic message to the temporary fictive kin group, e.g. four beatitudes deriving from family conflict are refashioned into moral beatitudes.

2.1.2. Most fictive kin directives are developed by Jesus Messianist seers and prophets for their ingroup as words of the risen Jesus to new Israel.

2.1.3. The collections labeled *GThom*, Q^1 and Q^2 are early collections of fictive kin directives for the Israel-only group, to be practiced by such groups. There are no statements in the story of Jesus indicating openness to non-Israelites. For example, it is only when non-Israelites begin to read these documents as directed to themselves that they find Matthew's conclusion ("Make disciples of all nations") and even Q as open to non-Israelites. When read from an Israel-only perspective, Matthew's conclusion ("Make disciples of Israelites of all nations), and all Q statements make very good Israel-only sense. Thus Q 3:7-10 is a wonderful insult in a region full of stones that outnumber the local population. After calling people "snake bastards" (i.e. "brood of vipers"), to put them down by saying their achieved honor is of as much value as the stones of the land is quite strong, as one might expect.

2.2. The Gentiles-too group (Luke, Paul) see Jesus as revelation of the God of Israel to all peoples. Theirs is a new theology. Their role for Jesus is as Lord in power. Their fictive kinship norms do not trace back to Jesus, but develop from their ingroup experiences and interaction with the outgroup. The Gentiles-too group, such as Luke, wish to tell the authentic story of Jesus for antiquarian reasons, as prolegomenon to the Gentiles-too experience of God. Thus any parallels to *GThom*, Q^1 and Q^2 in Luke are not there to supply norms, but to tell about what Jesus thought while he "went in and out among us." Now that Jesus is cosmic Lord, such are of antiquarian interest, mirroring life "in Israel," rather than life "in Christ."

CONCLUSIONS

Given the foregoing hypothetical postulates and clarifying observations, I submit the following criteria as initial social scientific principles for assessing the authenticity of statements of Jesus in the sources:

If a statement attributed to Jesus makes direct and immediate political sense, then it is authentic.

If a statement attributed to Jesus makes fictive-kinship sense, then it is not authentic.

Corollaries:

If a statement of Jesus is pragmatic, task-oriented with a view to a forthcoming theocracy (i.e. political religion), then it is authentic.

If a statement of Jesus is concerned with small group formation for the sake of ingroup support (social and emotional) or living a way of life for the good of the follower, then it is inauthentic.

BIBLIOGRAPHY

Barr, David L. *New Testament Story: An Introduction* (2nd ed., Belmont: Wordsworth, 1995).

Barton, S.C., and G.H.R. Horsley. "A Hellenistic Cult Group and the New Testament Churches." *JAC* 24 (1981) 7-41.

Chilton, Bruce. *A Feast of Meanings: Eucharistic Theologies from Jesus through Johannine Circles*. NovTSup 72. Leiden: Brill, 1994.

—. "A Generative Exegesis of Mark 7:1-23." *Journal of Higher Criticism* 3 (1996) 18-37. Revised and reprinted in B. Chilton and C. A. Evans, *Jesus in Context: Temple, Purity, and Restoration* (AGJU 39; Leiden: Brill, 1997) 297-317.

Crossan, John Dominic. *The Historical Jesus: The Life of a Mediterranean Peasant* (San Francisco: HarperCollins, 1991).

Duling, Dennis C. *The New Testament: Proclamation and Parenesis, Myth and History*. 3rd ed. Fort Worth: Harcourt, Brace, 1994.

Esler, Philip F. *Community and the Gospel in Luke-Acts: The Social and Political Motivations of Lucan Theology*. SNTSMS 57. Cambridge: Cambridge University Press, 1987.

Horsley, Richard A. *Jesus and the Spiral of Violence: Popular Jewish Resistance in Roman Palestine*. San Francisco: Harper & Row, 1987.

Kloppenborg, John S., and Stephen G. Wilson, eds. *Voluntary Associations in the Graeco-Roman World*. London and New York: Routledge, 1996.

Mack, Burton L. *A Myth of Innocence : Mark and Christian Origins*. Minneapolis: Fortress, 1988.

Malina, Bruce J. "Religion in the World of Paul: A Preliminary Sketch." *BTB* 16 (1986) 92-101.

—. "Religion in the Imagined New Testament World: More Social Science Lenses." *Scriptura* 51 (1994) 1-26.

—. "Interpretation: Reading, Abduction, Metaphor." Pp. in 253-66 David Jobling, Peggy L. Day and Gerald T. Sheppard, eds. *The Bible and the Politics of Exegesis: Essays in Honor of Norman K. Gottwald on His Sixty-Fifth Birthday*. Cleveland: Pilgrim Press, 1991.

—. *Christian Origins and Cultural Anthropology.* Atlanta: John Knox, 1986.

—. "Early Christian Groups: Using Small Group Formation Theory to Explain Christian Organizations." Pp. 96-113 in P. F. Esler, ed. *Modelling Early Christianity: Social-Scientific Studies of the New Testament in its Context.* London and New York: Routledge, 1995.

—. "Mediterranean Sacrifice: Dimensions of Domestic and Political Religion." *BTB* 26 (1996a) 26-44.

—. "Patron and Client: The Analogy Behind Synoptic Theology." Pp. 143-75 in *The Social World of Jesus and the Gospels.* London and New York: Routledge, 1996.

—. "Jesus as Astral Prophet." *BTB* 27 (1997) 83-98.

— and Richard L. Rohrbaugh. *Social Science Commentary on the Gospel of John.* Minneapolis: Fortress, 1998.

Moreland, Richard L., and John M. Levine. "Group Dynamics Over Time: Development and Socialization in Small Groups." Pp. 151-81 in J. E. McGrath, ed. *The Social Psychology of Time: New Perspectives.* Newbury Park: Sage Publications, 1988.

Neyrey, Jerome H. "Loss of Wealth, Loss of Family and Loss of Honour: The Cultural Context of the Original Makarisms in Q." Pp. 139-58 in P. F. Esler, ed. *Modelling Early Christianity: Social-scientific Studies of the New Testament in Its Context.* London and New York: Routledge, 1995.

Tuckman, B. W. "Developmental Sequence in Small Groups." *Psychological Bulletin* 63 (1965) 384-99.

DOUBTS ABOUT DOUBLE DISSIMILARITY
Restructuring the main criterion of Jesus-of-history research

Tom Holmén

The present article seeks to reevaluate the theoretical groundwork of *the criterion of dissimilarity*, especially the contention that both dissimilarity to Judaism and dissimilarity to Christianity need to be established before the criterion can be appealed to. Further, the article delves into the question of what exactly is the role of dissimilarity to Judaism in determining authenticity. As a result of the observations made, the logical structure of the criterion is considered anew.

WHAT IS THE CRITERION OF DISSIMILARITY?

The criterion of dissimilarity (or "the criterion of discontinuity"[1]; also "the dissimilarity test"[2]) is one of *the criteria of authenticity* employed in distinguishing authentic Jesus traditions.[3] The criterion

---

[1] J. P. Meier, *A Marginal Jew: Rethinking the Historical Jesus.* Volume one: *The Roots of the Problem and the Person* (ABRL 3; New York: Doubleday, 1991) 171.

[2] D. L. Mealand, "The Dissimilarity Test," *SJT* 31 (1978) 41-50.

[3] When dealing with the Gospel texts, we have to reckon with the fact that they are a result of development and that the traditions about Jesus they relate may not be conserved in their original forms and contents. The conventional procedure has been at first to use traditio-criticism to reconstruct the earliest recoverable forms of the traditions. Now, these reconstructions cannot offhandedly be considered to embody the genuine teaching of Jesus; the traditions may simply have originated from the early Church itself. For identification of the actual Jesuanic material, then, the so-called criteria of authenticity have been employed. For general treatments of these criteria, see, for example, F. C. Grant, "The Authenticity of Jesus' Sayings," in W. Eltester (ed.), *Neutestamentliche Studien für Rudolf Bultmann* (BZNW 21; Berlin: Töpelmann, 1954) 137-43; W. O. Walker, "The Quest for the Historical Jesus: A Discussion of Methodology," *ATR* 51 (1969) 38-56; M. Lehmann, *Synoptische Quellenanalyse und die Frage nach dem historischen Jesus* (BZNW 38; Berlin: Töpelmann, 1970) 163-205; F. Lentzen-Deis, "Kriterien für die historische Beurteilung der Jesusüberlieferung in den Evangelien," in F. Hahn (ed.), *Rückfrage nach Jesus: Zur Methodik und Bedeutung der Frage nach dem*

has, relatively speaking, lived a long life.[4] Despite the fact that it has
been shown that much caution is required in its application, it is still
counted among the most reliable criteria. For a definition of the
criterion the formulation of Ernst Käsemann is usually recalled:

> Einigermaßen sicheren Boden haben wir nur in einem einzigen Fall unter
> den Füßen, wenn nämlich Tradition aus irgendwelchen Gründen weder aus
> dem Judentum abgeleitet noch der Urchristenheit zugeschrieben werden
> kann.[5]

Hence, if a tradition is dissimilar to both Judaism and Christianity
and therefore most likely not derivative from either one,[6] it can only
have originated from Jesus.[7] It is this basic idea scholars today still

---

historischen Jesus (Freiburg: Herder, 1974) 78-117; R. T. France, "The Authen-
ticity of the Sayings of Jesus," in C. Brown (ed.), *History, Criticism & Faith.
Four exploratory studies* (Leicester: Inter-Varsity, 1976) 101-43; R. H. Stein, "The
'Criteria' for Authenticity," in R. T. France and D. Wenham (eds.), *Studies of
History and Tradition in the Four Gospels* (Gospel Perspectives 1; Sheffield: JSOT
Press, 1983) 225-63; D. Polkow, "Method and Criteria for Historical Jesus
Research," in K. H. Richards (ed.), *Society of Biblical Literature 1987 Seminar
Papers* (SBLSP 26; Atlanta: Scholars Press, 1987) 336-56; C. A. Evans, "Authen-
ticity Criteria in Life of Jesus Research," *Christian Scholar's Review* 19 (1989) 6-
31; Meier, *A Marginal Jew*, 167-95. The phrase "Jesus traditions" in the text is
used in order to include all kinds of information about Jesus, not only what he is
reported to have said but also accounts of his deeds.

4   A comprehensive review of the use of the criterion in Jesus-of-history
research is now available in G. Theissen and D. Winter, *Die Kriterienfrage in der
Jesusforschung: Vom Differenzkriterium zum Plausibilitätskriterium* (NTOA 34;
Göttingen: Vandenhoeck & Ruprecht; Freiburg: Universitätsverlag, 1997) 28-174.

5   E. Käsemann, *Exegetische Versuche und Besinnungen I* (Göttingen: Vandenhoeck & Ruprecht, 1960) 205. However, the principle is of earlier origin; see,
for instance, R. Bultmann, *Die Geschichte der synoptischen Tradition* (2nd ed.,
Göttingen: Vandenhoeck & Ruprecht, 1931) 222.

6   As usual, here we exploit the generalizing terms "Judaism" and "Christianity." For the problems arising from being compelled to reflect two such
heterogeneous and incompletely definable entities, see, for example, the discussion
in M. D. Hooker, "On Using the Wrong Tool," *Th* 75 (1972) 570-81, esp. 575;
and Polkow, "Method," 348-49. See also n. 21 below.

7   We should, of course, not assume that we can ever *prove* that certain
particular words were actually uttered by Jesus. We can only determine grounds—
or rationale—by means of which we isolate the material that *relatively* has the best
options to be Jesuanic (cf. F. M. Fling, *Outline of Historical Method* [repr. New
York: Franklin, 1971] 78). The criteria of authenticity should constitute such
grounds. Scholarship has thereby endeavored to set terms for considering some

evoke when they appeal to the criterion of dissimilarity.[8]

Since Käsemann, however, many qualifications concerning the correct application of the criterion have been put forward. For instance, it has been acknowledged—correctly, I think—that the criterion must not be used negatively, to single out what is inauthentic.[9] There is no "criterion of similarity" suggesting that when a piece of information parallels the teachings of the early Church (or contemporary Judaism) it should be regarded as inauthentic. While it

---

particular piece of information *more likely* to be trustworthy. All claims made about Jesus should then rely on material distinguishable by these terms, or criteria, *rather than* on material which does not allow appeal thereto. This relativity may be recognized by speaking of a "claim for authenticity" (cf. for instance, N. Perrin, *Rediscovering the Teaching of Jesus* [New York: Harper & Row, 1967] 32), which a Jesus tradition can be considered to possess if supported by one or more criteria. For the appropriateness of the word "criterion" for this kind of usage, see n. 44 below.

[8]   Virtually all who methodically pursue the quest for the historical Jesus reason in this way. In more recent contributions to the theme, for instance, M. J. Borg, *Conflict, Holiness and Politics in the Teachings of Jesus* (New York and Toronto: Edwin Mellen, 1984) 20; R. Riesner, *Jesus als Lehrer* (2nd ed., Tübingen: Mohr [Siebeck], 1984) 89-91; E. P. Sanders, *Jesus and Judaism* (London: SCM Press, 1985) 16-17; M. E. Boring, "The Historical-Critical Method's 'Criteria of Authenticity': The Beatitudes in Q and Thomas as a test case," *Semeia* 44 (1988) 9-44, esp. 17-21; D. Kosch, *Die eschatologische Tora des Menschensohnes: Untersuchungen zur Rezeption der Stellung Jesu zur Tora in Q* (Göttingen: Vandenhoeck & Ruprecht, 1989) 20; J. Gnilka, *Jesus von Nazaret: Botschaft und Geschichte* (Freiburg: Herder, 1990) 29-30; B. Witherington, *The Christology of Jesus* (Minneapolis: Fortress, 1990) 28; Meier, *A Marginal Jew*, 171; H. Merkel, "Die Gottesherrschaft in der Verkündigung Jesu," in M. Hengel and A. M. Schwemer (eds.), *Königsherrschaft Gottes und himmlischer Kult im Judentum, Urchristentum und in der hellenistischen Welt* (Tübingen: Mohr [Siebeck], 1991) 119-61, esp. 131-32; C. A. Evans, *Jesus and His Contemporaries: Comparative studies* (AGJU 25; Leiden: Brill, 1995) 19-21; J. Becker, *Jesus von Nazaret* (Berlin and New York: de Gruyter, 1996) 17-19. A profound modification of the criterion is offered by Theissen and Winter, *Die Kriterienfrage*, 175-217; see my critical comments in n. 106 below.

[9]   See, for example, M. D. Hooker, "Christology and Methodology," *NTS* 17 (1970-71) 480-87, esp. 486; D. G. A. Calvert, "An Examination of the Criteria for Distinguishing the Authentic Words of Jesus," *NTS* 18 (1971-72) 209-18, esp. 211-13; France, "The Authenticity," 110-14; Mealand, "Test," 47; Riesner, *Lehrer*, 90; B. F. Meyer, "Objectivity and subjectivity in Historical Criticism of the Gospels," in D. L. Dungan (ed.), *The Interrelations of the Gospels* (BETL 95; Leuven: Peeters and Leuven University Press, 1990) 546-65, esp. 548; Evans, *Jesus*, 21.

is reasonable to think that the early Christians would not invent teachings of Jesus they themselves disagreed with, we cannot conversely presume that they just could not willingly agree with anything he taught. Therefore, if a tradition does not pass the dissimilarity test, it does not mean that the tradition would be inauthentic, but merely that on the point of this particular tradition—and others like it—the criterion itself is inapplicable. The criterion of dissimilarity is not suited for cases where there is no dissimilarity. In such cases it is simply "incompetent to deliver an opinion."[10]

Further, it has been recognized that because the criterion of dissimilarity thus is able to identify as authentic such material only where Jesus appears to differ from the views and theology of the early Church (and Judaism), it cumulatively results in a biased picture of Jesus. The functionality of the criterion is restricted to a very particular kind of material and consequently, what it inevitably produces is a particular selection of authentic traditions.[11] This does not mean that the criterion would err in its judgments of the authenticity of the individual traditions, but the overall picture of Jesus that the selected material taken as a whole imparts will be one-sided and biased towards detaching Jesus from his surroundings.[12] For this reason, when seeking to gather together authentic sayings and deeds of Jesus, the criterion of dissimilarity should not be the only tool of authenticity applied. Criteria capable of probing the authenticity of such traditions, too, where Jesus' teaching appears to accord with the views of the early Church (and Judaism), ought to accompany it.[13] Only then a too one-sided picture of Jesus is avoided,

---

[10]   In effect this means disqualification of the word "nur" in Käsemann's definition of the criterion quoted above.

[11]   Hooker, "Christology," 482: "The method dictates its own conclusions." See also Stein, "The 'Criteria'," 242-43.

[12]   For, "if authentic materials contrary to church tendencies were conserved in the gospel tradition, authentic materials in accord with church tendencies were *a fortiori* conserved" (Meyer, "Objectivity," 548). And it is that latter type of authentic material the criterion of dissimilarity will totally miss.

[13]   Cf. Meier, *A Marginal Jew*, 173: "Especially with this criterion, complementary and balancing insights from other criteria are vital." However, the case is not easily balanced. There are actually only two generally accepted main criteria which are not restricted the way the criterion of dissimilarity is: *The criterion of multiple attestation* (of forms and sources) and *the criterion of coherence*. Now, the criterion of coherence focuses on sayings or deeds of Jesus which are coherent with those whose authenticity has already been verified by some other criteria. When

a picture which leaves no possibility for continuity between Jesus and Judaism on the one hand and between Jesus and Christianity on the other.[14]

In addition to these, a number of further cautions and refinements have been advanced, and careful scholars usually try to comply with them.[15] However, a major observation concerned with the basic thought of the criterion has not acquired the attention it deserves. In 1979 B. F. Meyer in his book *The Aims of Jesus* discussed the criterion and opposed the requisite of a *double* test of dissimilarity, namely the allegation—inherent in the dual form of the criterion's definition—that the authenticity of a piece of information can be sustained on grounds of this criterion, only if it is found to be dissimilar *both* to Christianity *and* to Judaism. According to Meyer, dissimilarity to the views of the primitive Church alone suffices as an indication of authenticity.[16]

Though masterly argued and substantial in meaning, Meyer's observation has so far largely escaped the notice of biblical scholarship. In what follows I shall first recollect Meyer's argument, then develop it further, evaluating how it actually affects the way the

---

relying on material identified as authentic with the criterion of dissimilarity, then, the criterion of coherence is likely only to magnify the tendencies of the dissimilarity test (Hooker, "Christology," 483; nevertheless, this is not always the case; cf. the example in Mealand, "Test," 44). For the *criterion of embarrassment*, see Conclusions below.

[14] Recognition of the need for "balancing" criteria naturally ensues from aiming at a method which will not import to the texts any ideas of what genuinely Jesuanic material ought to look like. It is the traditions, of course, we turn to in order to learn about Jesus. Therefore, when developing tools for identifying authentic teaching of Jesus scholarship tries to refrain from knowing *a priori* what kind of material comes from him. Quite different is the methodological approach of the "Jesus Seminar" which precisely sets out from a particular and articulated knowledge of "Jesus' wit and wisdom, his mode of teaching, his style"; see R. W. Funk (ed.), *The Gospel of Mark: Red Letter Edition* (Sonoma: Polebridge, 1991) 29-52, esp. 30-35; the quotation is from p. 35.

[15] Such is, for example, the correction made to the interdependence proposed between the dissimilarity criterion and the criterion of coherence. According to Perrin (*Rediscovering*, 43), only material distinguished by means of the criterion of dissimilarity can provide an adequate basis for employing the criterion of coherence. This contention has rightly been rejected (see, for example, Borg, *Holiness*, 21-22; see n. 13 above).

[16] B. F. Meyer, *The Aims of Jesus* (London: SCM Press, 1979) 86. See also *idem*, "Objectivity," 547-48.

criterion should be applied.

MEYER'S CRITICISM OF THE REQUIREMENT OF DOUBLE DISSIMILARITY

Meyer writes:

> It has often been observed that Judaism in general is a possible source for the Jesus tradition. What has not been observed, however, is that the requirement of simultaneous discontinuity with Judaism and the post-paschal church errs by excess. That the community should gratuitously adopt from Judaism elements in discontinuity with its own concerns, practices, and tendencies simply does not make sense. Discontinuity with the post-paschal church is sufficient by itself to establish historicity.[17]

So, the logic—seemingly sound and balanced—necessitating the demand of double dissimilarity is: Only when it can be ascertained that a tradition derives *neither* from Judaism *nor* from Christianity can a claim for authenticity be put forward. For if dissimilarity can be established only in one direction, say to Christianity, the possibility still remains that the tradition in question actually derives from Judaism.[18] However, Meyer's assessment reveals this reasoning as specious. It is admittedly possible that the early Christians not only fabricated new ideas, but also adopted profoundly Jewish thoughts and attributed these to Jesus. But this they would not likely have done *against their own interests*. The line of thought is simple: The rationale "it is likely that the early Christians would not invent teachings of Jesus they themselves disagreed with" is true independently of the question whether the teachings discontinuous with the primitive Church's views were actually sustained by Judaism, Hellenism or any other religion or outlook on life. Therefore, dissimilarity to Christianity already suffices as an argument for authenticity. We do not need the double test of dissimilarity, that is, the *combination* of dissimilarity to Judaism and dissimilarity to Christianity.

But Meyer's observation is not only sound, it is even appealing. According to the observation, if dissimilarity to Christianity is

---

[17]   Meyer, *The Aims of Jesus*, 86.

[18]   So precisely, for example, W. Simonis, *Jesus von Nazareth: Seine Botschaft vom Reich Gottes und der Glaube der Urgemeinde* (Düsseldorf: Patmos, 1985) 27. Merkel ("Die Gottesherrschaft," 132), after quoting Simonis, concludes approvingly that logic speaks for the criterion.

detected, there is no need yet to survey the enormous bulk of Jewish thought, at least as far it is authenticity that is at issue. We may also summon the penetrating criticism of the dissimilarity criterion put forward by M. D. Hooker: One of the prerequisites of the criterion —as it is usually understood—is that the material regarded as authentic is to be dissimilar to Judaism. At the same time, however, there is the common (and reasonable) assumption that the material stemming from Jesus should be "'at home' in first-century Palestine."[19] This logical dead-end is an inevitable result of the demand of double dissimilarity, but is easily avoided by consenting to establishing dissimilarity to Christianity alone. Further, Hooker has called attention to the fact that in employing the criterion we are not dealing with two knowns (that is—according to the common view—Judaism and Christianity) and one unknown (teachings of Jesus), but actually with three incompletely discoverable entities.[20] In other words, our knowledge of Jesus traditions that would be dissimilar to Judaism and Christianity depends on our knowledge of precisely these two, Judaism and Christianity. When the distinction made by Meyer is acknowledged, at least the number of unknowns can be reduced by one, and the efforts may be centered on testing the putative dissimilarity to Christianity.[21]

---

[19]   Hooker, "Christology," 482.

[20]   Hooker, "Tool," 575; see also Meyer, "Objectivity," 554.

[21]   It is of course precarious to draw a clear-cut line between "Judaism" and "Christianity." To be sure, Jewish-Christians regarded themselves as representatives of Judaism. However, the use of the terms here is not generic, but denotes those behind the sources. The people responsible for our sources for Jesus we call Christians, and the religion—however heterogeneous and incompletely definable— in these sources Christianity, regardless of the people's possible generic affiliation or proximity to Judaism. If the sources then suggest something that is discontinuous to their wit, it can be—by definition—labeled as "dissimilar to Christianity." This is not to say that the Christian literature would display one consistent agenda only. Different groupings would probably have experienced different things as dissimilar to their theology. This problem is satisfactorily encountered by the statement of Polkow, "Method," 349: "We don't need to speculate as to the characteristic emphases [needed to be able to decide what is dissimilar] in Judaism, Christianity, and Gnosticism because we can actually see such emphases by how the evangelist . . . or the evangelists and/or writers . . . change or use a given Jesus saying or event for their own theological purposes." Now, there may of course have been forms of Christianity with agendas which are unknown to us simply because the sources we possess do not relate them. However, whatever specula-

Considering the clear logic and the apparent benefits of Meyer's disposal, it is surprising that the requisite of double dissimilarity is still upheld. In fact, the criticism of the double test has been ignored to a large degree.[22] It seems like only R. H. Stein and S.-O. Back have succeeded in noticing it.[23]

Moreover, as yet, all the consequences of Meyer's observation have not been recognized. In my estimation, the requirement of double dissimilarity is even more specious, and its endorsement by Jesus research more critical than would appear at first sight. The following sections try to specify what exactly in the application of the double test goes wrong and what are the issues that call for reconsideration. Firstly, the theoretical groundwork of the criteria needs to be elaborated.

THE CRITERIA AS MINIMUM REQUIREMENTS

To further the analysis, I would like to put into words an apprehension of the criteria not previously verbalized in the discussion about the authenticating methods but still expressing an idea always involved therein and simply elementary for understanding what the criteria are all about. This is the conception of the criteria as *minimum requirements*.

Now, each criterion of authenticity is based on a rationale that functions as legitimizing authenticity claims.[24] For example, the rationale "a consistent testimony of two or more independent witnesses can be trusted" allows the conclusion that because Q, Mark and the special sources of Luke and Matthew all maintain that Jesus preached the kingdom of God,[25] he most likely indeed did that.

---

tions can be advanced, we are but referred to the sources available no matter how incomplete a picture they convey of the varieties of early Christianity. Precisely this incompleteness was pointed out by Hooker.

[22]   See for example the scholars referred to in n. 8 above, all of whom advocate the double test of dissimilarity (Theissen and Winter [*Die Kriterienfrage*, 175-217] promote a double test of "plausibility"; see my comments in n. 106 below).

[23]   Stein, "The 'Criteria'," 242; S.-O. Back, *Jesus of Nazareth and the Sabbath Commandment* (Åbo: Åbo Akademi University Press, 1995) 18. However, though mentioning Meyer's view, Stein refrains from any comment thereon and apparently does not sustain it.

[24]   For the expression "claim for authenticity," see n. 7 above. Cf. also, for example, Perrin, *Rediscovering*, 32.

[25]   Mark 1:15; Luke 12:22-31; 17:20-21; and Matt 13:24-30, representing

Relying on rationales such as this, then, the various criteria state what is *at least* demanded from a tradition so that it could be regarded as having a claim for authenticity. The criterion of multiple attestation, the rationale of which was paraphrased above, dictates that if a certain piece of information is witnessed in *at least two* independent sources,[26] then it has a claim for authenticity. The criterion of coherence, again, states that if a certain tradition A is coherent with *a tradition B (or a number of traditions)*, the authenticity of which has already been determined, then the tradition A also has a claim for authenticity.[27]

Hence, the criteria make demands, and these demands can be characterized as *minimum requirements*. A criterion should then be so defined that it demands exactly the minimum required for legitimization of an authenticity claim, no less and no more. For if a criterion demands too little, the authenticity claim put forward would not be justified. If, again, it demands too much, it most likely bypasses a number of instances where an authenticity claim would in fact have been justified. Another thing is that a criterion can become fulfilled excessively without there being anything wrong in its definition. Say, a tradition is witnessed not only in two but in three independent sources. It is clear that such traditions exceeding the minimum requirement of the criterion of multiple attestation (namely two independent attestations) do exist.[28] But their very existence by no means indicates that the criterion ought to be redefined accordingly, that is, that *at least* three independent attestations should be demanded in order that an authenticity claim could be forwarded.

The term may now be used to illuminate the criterion of dissimilarity. What suffices as the minimum requirement is that a tradition can be found dissimilar to Christianity;[29] no less will do, no more should be demanded. When this requirement is fulfilled, a claim for authenticity already exists. Of course, it remains a fact that

---

Mark, Q, Lukan and Matthean sources respectively, and the last three featuring wisdom sayings, pronouncement stories and parables.

[26] And/or forms.

[27] It should again be noticed that failure to receive support from, *inter alia*, these criteria is in itself no indication of inauthenticity. Cf. France, "The Authenticity," 114.

[28] Cf. the attestations of Jesus' preaching of the kingdom of God referred to above.

[29] Precisely this was argued above in the previous section.

there are traditions which are indeed dissimilar to both Christianity and Judaism.[30] But this in no way invalidates dissimilarity to Christianity as a minimum requirement (cf. the example of the criterion of multiple attestation above). And I would stress the following point: There is nothing to hinder us to *observe* double dissimilarity and then draw every consequence we feel inclined to, but we should not *demand* it—as the prerequisite for a tradition to be regarded as having a claim for authenticity—because this means exceeding the correct minimum requirement. The error would be analogous to demanding three, not two, independent attestations as the minimum requirement of the criterion of multiple attestation, or consistence with more than one (say three) authentic traditions as that of the criterion of coherence.

Thus, double dissimilarity causes troubles when *demanded*. But to urge something as a criterion precisely means that a demand is made. Therefore the criterion of double dissimilarity is an indisputably erroneous conception. The flaws which emerge in its application will be the concern of the next section.[31]

THE DEFECTS OF THE CRITERION (EQUAL TO DEMAND) OF DOUBLE DISSIMILARITY

The incorrectly (namely too highly) placed minimum requirement of the criterion of double dissimilarity results in misjudgments on two different levels of the research of the authentic teaching of Jesus. In this research one usually begins with the individual traditions dealing with each of them at the time. But what in the long run is aimed at is an overall picture of Jesus as a historical figure, achieved by combining and systemizing the individual pieces of information gauged as trustworthy. Though these aspects, or levels, of course interact in the actual research process, they may now be treated separately in order to better grasp how the assessment of authenticity is influenced by the dubious logic of the double test.

(a) Evaluation of individual traditions

The occurrence of misjudgments on this level depends on the way

---

[30]   Or even multiply dissimilar, e.g. to Hellenism, Hinduism, Islam, etc.

[31]   Throughout, it should be noticed, we are talking about the *demand* of double dissimilarity as being erroneous, not about the mere fact that simultaneously dissimilar traditions exist.

in which the traditions evaluated are dissimilar. Traditions that pass the double test, i.e. are dissimilar to *both* Judaism *and* Christianity,[32] can of course be regarded as having a claim for authenticity because the correct minimum requirement of dissimilarity to Christianity is fulfilled. On the point of such simultaneously dissimilar traditions, the fallacies of the criterion of double dissimilarity are thus not yet revealed, but the results are correct and reliable. The same can be said about traditions which are dissimilar *neither* to Judaism *nor* to Christianity.[33] Then the criterion of dissimilarity, be it a double or a single test, cannot forward any judgment on the question of authenticity.

The problems in urging the criterion of double dissimilarity appear on the point of traditions that are dissimilar to Christianity *but not* to Judaism. Such instances are simply dropped from the agenda of the criterion, although, as has been shown above, they do indeed have a claim for authenticity.[34] This is precisely what can occur when demanding more than is actually exactly needed, i.e. more than is the minimum requirement: A number of instances where an authenticity claim would in reality have been justified are

---

[32]   As an example we may take Jesus' way of not practicing voluntary fast. Within contemporary Judaism such a dismissal was quite unique. Likewise, regularly fasting marked the behavior of the early Christians.

[33]   Say, Jesus' commitment to prayer, which coheres with the piety of both the Jews of his time and the subsequent Christians.

[34]   Jesus' prohibition of divorce (Matt 5:31-32 par.), for example, can be considered clearly dissimilar to Christianity, as we find Paul struggling with the strenuous command (1 Corinthians 7) and even Matthew including a clause of exception. But it has been claimed that the Qumran scrolls contain same kind of prohibition and that Jesus thus does not here appear clearly dissimilar to Judaism (so, for instance, J. A. Fitzmyer, "The Matthean Divorce Texts and Some New Palestinian Evidence," in Fitzmyer, *To Advance the Gospel: New Testament Studies* [New York: Crossroad, 1981] 79-111; cf., however, now T. Holmén, "Divorce in CD 4:20-5:2 and 11QT 57:17-18. Some remarks on the pertinence of the question," appearing in the first issue of the *Revue de Qumran* 1998). Quite regardless of the alleged lack of this dissimilarity, however, the question may be posed: Why would the early Church have fabricated such a strenuous proscription causing apparent difficulties and ascribed it to Jesus? Certainly the fact that the proscription was known in Judaism cannot function as an answer. But if we demand double dissimilarity, we should logically accept that answer and conclude that there is nothing here (namely, when it comes to the criterion of dissimilarity) to speak in favor of authenticity of the prohibition.

bypassed. Arriving at a correct estimation of such traditions' claim for authenticity then depends on whether some other criterion can be appealed to in favor of their authenticity or, eventually, on the question of which side *the burden of proof* is to be placed on.[35] In the worst case[36] a tradition, though found as dissimilar to Christianity, is discharged with nothing to speak for its authenticity.

Thus, in cases where traditions are found dissimilar only to Christianity, the results arrived at by using the double test of dissimilarity are no more reliable.[37] But there is a further inaccuracy to be pointed out.

(b) The aggregate of authentic traditions

As noticed above, the criterion of dissimilarity is restricted in the way that it can identify as authentic such traditions only where Jesus appears as distinct from what he is compared with. The points of continuity, which naturally also existed,[38] the criterion simply bypasses being incapable of verifying authenticity is such cases. Therefore the material assembled by means of the criterion—though it indeed has claims for authenticity—will always be one-sided and biased, a fact that necessitates the use of "balancing" criteria. This peculiarity, unavoidable since it is rooted in the rationale the criterion builds on, causes that demanding double dissimilarity has a deteriorating effect even in the long run.

When focusing on traditions which display dissimilarity *either* to both Christianity and Judaism *or* to Christianity alone—this is when sticking to the minimum requirement of dissimilarity to Christianity

---

[35]   There are all in all three options: The burden of proof lies (a) on the one who wants to show inauthenticity (so, for example, W. G. Kümmel, *Heils‐geschehen und Geschichte. Bd. 2.* [Marburg: N.G. Elwert Verlag, 1978] 187-190), (b) on the one who wants to show authenticity (so, for instance, W. Zager, *Gottesherrschaft und Endgericht in der Verkündigung Jesu: Eine Untersuchung zur markinischen Jesusüberlieferung einschließlich der Q-Parallelen* [Berlin and New York: de Gruyter, 1996] 47), or (c) on the one who in general tries to show something, either inauthenticity or authenticity (so, for example, Meier, *A Marginal Jew*, 183). It is not necessary to take a stand on this question here.

[36]   That is, if the burden of proof is considered to lie on showing authenticity and no other criteria can be appealed to in favor of a tradition's authenticity.

[37]   The fourth possibility, namely that a tradition is dissimilar only to Judaism, will be dealt with in the next section.

[38]   See n. 12 above.

—the inevitable bias of the material assembled will be towards detaching Jesus from his followers but not from Judaism, since material where Jesus appears to conform Judaism can be included here. But if one narrows the scope of the criterion so that it focuses only on traditions being simultaneously dissimilar but bypasses traditions which are dissimilar to Christianity alone—this, again, is when demanding double dissimilarity thus surpassing the correct minimum requirement—the bias of the material assorted will be towards detaching Jesus from both Christianity and Judaism.

Thus, the criterion of double dissimilarity increases the bias of the material assorted. In addition to points of continuity between Jesus and Christianity, we, demanding double dissimilarity, bypass even instances where Jesus agreed with Judaism. This is, however, not required for the sake of determining authenticity and could readily be avoided by staying at the correct minimum requirement of dissimilarity to Christianity. Gratuitously increasing the bias of the authentic material gathered is especially critical for the reason that the criteria that can be used to balance the bias are not particularly numerous.[39]

Hence, clear drawbacks are involved in the implementation of the criterion of double dissimilarity. Therefore, in my estimation, the double test is not merely superfluous or needless, but in fact harmful and should, accordingly, not be employed at all.

We now turn to consider the role left for evaluating dissimilarity to Judaism, *the* dissimilarity, which some scholars actually promote as the more significant part of the double test.[40]

THE RELEVANCE OF DISSIMILARITY TO JUDAISM TO THE QUESTION OF AUTHENTICITY

Being part and parcel with the criterion of double dissimilarity, dissimilarity to Judaism, as a principle, also has been regarded as relevant to the question of authenticity. Now that the sufficiency of dissimilarity to Christianity alone to legitimize claims for authenticity has been stated, it stands for reason to ask whether the role of dissimilarity to Judaism, too, needs reconsideration.

---

[39] See here n. 13 above.

[40] Cf. Becker, *Jesus*, 17: "Das Kriterium wird inkonsequent erweicht, wenn es voll gegenüber der späteren Gemeinde in Anwendung, gegenüber dem Frühjudentum jedoch nur abgeschwächt in Geltung gebracht werden soll."

We can scrutinize the bearing of dissimilarity on the question of authenticity by comparing the following slightly differing sentences:

(a) "A source that reports against *its own* agenda can, at least on that particular point, be considered trustworthy."

(b) "A source that reports against *somebody else's* agenda can, at least on that particular point, be considered trustworthy."

(c) "A source that reports against *its own and somebody else's* agenda can, at least on that particular point, be considered trustworthy."

These represent the varying rationales the different combinations of the two dissimilarities (to Christianity and to Judaism) may be seen to rely upon. "Own" denotes Christianity, "somebody else" Judaism. "Source," again, is to be understood to comprise all writings relating the Jesus tradition.[41]

Now, in (a) we have the rationale behind the form of the criterion of dissimilarity that in the present article has, assenting to Meyer, been argued as sufficient to indicate authenticity: dissimilarity to Christianity. The sentence seems to make perfect sense. But can we claim the same with regard to (b)? If Christian writings report something that is against the Jewish agenda, is this really an indication that the writings are, on the particular point, trustworthy? I would say not. However, as we shall see, in Jesus research it is actually quite common to regard a tradition's dissimilarity to Judaism (and to Judaism alone) to indicate its authenticity. As to (c), then, the words "somebody else's" could be dismissed without there being any difference in how the rationale functions. This is precisely what has been done when discharging the evaluation of dissimilarity to Judaism.

One might yet intervene by pointing out that the agendas of "own" and "somebody else" may sometimes converge[42] and that in such cases even the rationale (b) is sound. However, the statement "a source that reports against *somebody else's* agenda *congruent with its own* can, at least on that particular point, be considered trustworthy" is painfully tautological with the statement we already have in (a). In other words, the reasoning that dissimilarity to Judaism when dissimilar to Christianity may indicate authenticity has nothing to recommend itself. If it shows anything, it is the complete incapability

---

41   Cf. here n. 21 above.

42   Which, with respect to the role of Jewish-Christians within the early Church, is a plausible thought.

of dissimilarity to Judaism to bear, in itself, upon the question of authenticity.

We shall now consider in greater detail the use of a "criterion" based on the rationale (b), which, as maintained, keeps appearing in the investigation of authentic Jesus traditions. The use of this "criterion" is in fact an abuse of the criterion of double dissimilarity, a distortion comprising only the evaluation of dissimilarity to Judaism.

We can begin with a critical comment on how Meyer dealt with the issue. With his criticism of the demand of the double dissimilarity Meyer did not seek to nullify the importance of dissimilarity to Judaism. On the contrary, he thought that this dissimilarity could be used as an indication of authenticity on its own.[43] Thus, just as dissimilarity of a Jesus tradition to Christianity suffices as an indication of authenticity regardless of the tradition's possible resemblance to Judaism, so dissimilarity to Judaism functions autonomously, independently of the relation of the tradition to Christianity. Meyer, in a manner of speaking, divided the criterion of double dissimilarity into two distinct and independent criteria. According to him, dissimilarity to Judaism—now labeled as the "index [i.e. criterion][44] of originality"—could still be used for establishing authenticity.[45]

---

[43] Meyer, *The Aims of Jesus*, 86-87; *idem*, "Objectivity," 548.

[44] Meyer prefers "index" to "criterion." It is, of course, true that the word "criterion" may convey a sense of perfect certainty while "index" more clearly implies the relativity of the results reached by means of the various tools of authenticity. However, the use of "criterion" is traditional, and when emphasizing (as in n. 7 above) that we are dealing with a range of probabilities the old terminology needs not to be replaced by a new one.

[45] Meyer is, however, somewhat vague on this point. After claiming that "whereas such discontinuity [sc. dissimilarity to Judaism] is not requisite to historicity, it is a distinct and positive index to it," he states that "inasmuch as a given instance of originality [i.e. dissimilarity to Judaism] may be of post-paschal provenance, the degree of probability attaching to inferences of historicity on this basis will vary in accord with the particulars of the case." I take "the particulars" to suggest that Meyer presupposed dissimilarity to Christianity to be attested in order that dissimilarity to Judaism would be capable of indicating authenticity. This is at least how he in practice (see, for example, Meyer, *The Aims of Jesus*, 289-91) appears to use the criteria (or indices): "Discontinuity" and "originality" are not applied *in combination*, but they are applied together. Their co-appearance is required (for "originality" to be a valid index), but they are still utilized independently to suggest authenticity thus counting two indices instead of one as when pursuing the criterion of double dissimilarity. This is tantamount to assuming that

Here I disagree with Meyer. Dissimilarity to Judaism furnishes no argument for regarding a tradition as authentic.[46] We may remodel the rationale (b) referred to above as follows: "A Jesus tradition that is dissimilar to Judaism is unlikely to have been manufactured by the early Church." That this line of thought cannot legitimize an authenticity claim is, I think, clear. It is an untenable assumption that the early Church could invent and ascribe to Jesus sayings only in continuity with Judaism. Or are we to picture the early Christians as so selectively respectful that they were indeed well prepared to invent things Jesus actually never taught and freely attribute these to him, but only within the limits of being wary of not importing anything that would disagree with Judaism? No. Thus, dissimilarity to Judaism is inappropriate as a minimum requirement for forwarding authenticity claims. A source that reports against somebody else's agenda may very well be untrustworthy.

This note is by no means as trivial as it may seem. In accordance with—albeit hardly dependent on—Meyer's criterion of originality, Jesus traditions dissimilar to Judaism are often regarded as authentic on the grounds of this dissimilarity alone.[47] Below three examples will illustrate how this methodological miscalculation has misled the investigation and how the analyses should be rectified.[48]

(a) The prohibition of oaths – Matt 5:33-37

Within the antitheses of the Sermon on the Mount the prohibition

---

the rationale (b) phrased above becomes sound (in itself) when co-appearing with the rationale (a). We do not agree.

46   Calvert ("An Examination of the Criteria," 214) appears to make the same observation. However, this leads him to join dissimilarity to Judaism and dissimilarity to Christianity, in other words, to uphold the criterion of double dissimilarity.

47   See the authors referred to in the surveys of the three Gospel texts on the following pages.

48   The surveys of the three sayings below are not intended as full treatments. Nor is the argumentation of their authenticity by means of other criteria the primary concern. The question of authenticity of a Jesus tradition is usually too intricate to be decided on basis of one criterion only and without proper application of form, redaction, and tradition criticism (cf. n. 3 above). The focus here is, naturally, on the use of the criterion of dissimilarity. It should also be observed that in pointing out the inability of dissimilarity to Judaism to solve the question of authenticity, I do not wish to suggest that the sayings were in fact inauthentic. It is well possible that proper ways for verifying their genuineness may still be found. To search for these, however, lies beyond the scope of this article.

of oaths has commonly been counted among the primary ones, that is, among those whose antithetical form does not derive from the Matthean redaction.[49] The criterion of dissimilarity has been appealed to in favor of the authenticity of the prohibition, and thus scholars usually regard it as a genuine saying of Jesus.[50] However, skepticism has been voiced by G. Dautzenberg.[51] His arguments and those of his opponents now exemplify how dissimilarity to Judaism has been used for purposes it is not fitted to serve.

Dautzenberg argues, among other things, that the prohibition of oaths is in fact consistent with Judaism.[52] It readily coheres with Jewish criticism of swearing which was intended to protect the name of God from profanation. Even though there is a difference in that Jesus totally forbids taking oaths, the difference is not a matter of principle; it is not significant enough to justify the appeal to the criterion of dissimilarity.[53]

Just in passing, failure to appeal to the criterion of dissimilarity by no means indicates inauthenticity as Dautzenberg seems to think, but only annuls the possibility of developing an argument from dissimilarity *for* the authenticity.[54] But as regards our concerns now, it is interesting to observe that both in Dautzenberg's argument and in the subsequent discussion the criterion of dissimilarity is understood

---

[49] The common assumption is that as to their antithetical form only the first, second, and fourth of the antitheses in the Sermon on the Mount are pre-Matthean; see, for example, H. Merklein, *Jesu Botschaft von der Gottesherrschaft* (3rd ed., Stuttgart: Katholisches Bibelwerk, 1989) 105.

[50] For example, G. Strecker,"Die Antithesen der Bergpredigt (Mt 5, 21-48 par)," *ZNW* 69 (1978) 36-72, esp. 58-60, 70; J. Gnilka, *Das Matthäusevangelium: I. Teil* (Freiburg: Herder, 1986) 177; U. Luz, *Das Evangelium nach Matthäus. 1. Teilband Mt 1-7* (3rd ed., Zürich: Benzinger Verlag; Neukirchen-Vluyn: Neukirchener Verlag, 1992) 282.

[51] G. Dautzenberg, "Ist das Schwurverbot Mt 5,33-37; Jak 5,12 ein Beispiel für die Torakritik Jesu?" *BZ* 25 (1981) 47-66.

[52] Dautzenberg considers the ban on swearing also incoherent with Jesus' own way of speaking (though Dautzenberg does not use the technical term "incoherence," in effect it is this negative application of the criterion of coherence he appeals to. Incoherence is indeed a cogent negative criterion, but should be used with caution; see, for example, Riesner, *Lehrer*, 92). A third case speaking against the authenticity of the prohibition of making oaths would, according to Dautzenberg, evolve from its lacking *Wirkungsgeschichte* in early Christianity.

[53] Dautzenberg, "Schwurverbot," 56.

[54] See above section, What is the Criterion of Dissimilarity?

to consist of dissimilarity to Judaism only and the authenticity of the prohibition made dependent on whether or not this dissimilarity can be established. Typical is U. Luz's characterization: "Da das katego-rische Schwurverbot im Judentum singulär ist, stammt es wohl von Jesus." For him this is a classic case for the dissimilarity criterion.[55] Likewise A. Ito, who most extensively has opposed Dautzenberg, seems to be content with establishing "a fine distinction" between Jesus' prohibition and Jewish thought.[56] He indeed brings forth some hesitation, but only for the reason that the small distinction between Jesus and Judaism he makes is perhaps not "enough."[57] There is not a word about the prohibition's possible dissimilarity to Christianity, though Ito actually quotes the definition of the criterion of dissimilarity in its double form thus mentioning even this dimension! Eventually the whole case is dismissed "since the validity of the criterion of dissimilarity has been questioned."[58]

Now, I would actually concur with Ito (and others) in that there is indeed a distinction between Judaism's and the Gospel's teaching on taking oaths. And I would even say that the distinction is in no way to be discharged as meaningless. Dautzenberg's assertion that the difference between these opinions is not a matter of principle is untenable, because the case is quite the opposite. In the saying Jesus totally forbids taking oaths while Jewish reflections remain critical (only). There is indeed a difference in principle between criticizing, on the one hand, the abuse of a practice and, on the other, the practice itself. The total prohibition of oaths ascribed to Jesus—very much unlike the Old Testament and contemporary Jewish criticism of swearing falsely or loosely—implies criticism of the law itself. If

---

[55] Luz, *Matthäus*, 282.

[56] A. Ito, "The Question of the Authenticity of the Ban on Swearing (Matthew 5.33-37)," *JSNT* 43 (1991) 5-13, esp. 6.

[57] Ito, "Question," 7.

[58] Ito, "Question," 7 n. 3. If Ito derives this judgement of his from Stein's article to which he refers, he has apparently misread what Stein has written. Stein writes against abuses of the criterion, precisely like the one Ito escapes noticing when he takes the lack of dissimilarity to Judaism to indicate inauthenticity, that is, the negative use of the criterion. On the whole Stein's ("The 'Criteria'," 244) evaluation of the criterion of dissimilarity is as follows: "It [sc. the criterion of dissimilarity] may in fact be the single most valuable tool for authenticity, for if a saying or action of Jesus in the gospel tradition meets the demands of this criterion, the likelihood of it being authentic is extremely good."

swearing is wrong *in toto*, why is it allowed, even if discouraged, by the Scripture?[59]

So, I really think we can establish a clear dissimilarity to Judaism on this point. However—what does this consideration tell about the authenticity of the saying? Surely many fictive things have been claimed about Jesus by his followers, things that appear unique in comparison with profound Jewish thought. Yet, such dissimilarity in no way makes these innovations genuine teachings of Jesus. In other words, the prohibition may well be dissimilar to Judaism, but this in no way excludes its early Christian provenance because the early Church cannot be pictured as incapable of diverging from Judaism. Therefore, what should be considered is whether the prohibition can still be an early Christian production, something that is accomplished precisely by determining its similarity versus dissimilarity to Christianity. Even so, Ito, Strecker[60] and others[61] contemplate *exclusively* the uniqueness of the prohibition within the contemporary Jewish (and Hellenistic) world, working hard to affirm it.[62] Nobody seems to have been interested in whether this uniqueness perhaps should be seen as an early Christian innovation or if it rather is discontinuous with the views of the Church.[63]

(b) The command to love the enemy – Matt 5:38-48 = Luke 6:27-36

The command to love one's enemy is properly verbalized only in the Gospels of Matthew and Luke.[64] In pondering whether the

---

[59]   These reflections are mostly mine. Ito ("Question," 6-7) advances a set of comparable ideas.

[60]   Strecker, "Antithesen;" idem, *Die Bergpredigt: Ein exegetischer Kommentar* (2nd ed., Göttingen: Vandenhoeck & Ruprecht, 1985).

[61]   See, for example, Gnilka, *Matthäusevangelium*, 176-77; Luz, *Matthäus*, 282-83; Becker, *Jesus*, 370-71.

[62]   Dautzenberg is, of course, struggling to deny the uniqueness of the prohibition.

[63]   In a note Luz (*Matthäus*, 282 n. 16) contemplates the possibility that the prohibition was initiated by a Jewish-Christian community, as is proposed by Dautzenberg. Luz wonders whether such a community would produce a saying which would be neither Jesuanic nor Jewish. This is a step in the right direction, but on the whole the evaluation of dissimilarity to Christianity is regarded by Luz as irrelevant to the question of authenticity.

[64]   Other instances: 1 Thess 5:15; 1 Cor 4:12; Rom 12:14, 17-20; 1 Pet 3:9. On the question of their mutual relationship see, for instance, J. Piper, *'Love Your Enemies': Jesus' Love Command in the Synoptic Gospels and in the Early Christian*

traditional saying may go back to Jesus, scholars have compared it
with similar ideas stemming from Jesus' background. Corresponding
views are discernible in the Hellenistic world, especially in Stoic
thought.[65] But already in the Old Testament one is ordered to help
the enemy.[66] And later Jewish accounts also come close to the
teaching in the Gospels.[67] It is, then, clear that Jesus—if the teaching
derives from him—could attach to these ideas. Still, the tradition in
Matt 5:44-45 = Luke 6:27-28 + 35 has an angle which distinguishes it
from its background.

The comparable contemporary thoughts pertain more suitably to
the theme of retaliation. The goodness to be shown to the enemy
consists of individual and concrete things which tend to demand only
what is realistic, what reasonably can be required.[68] Likewise, the
aim of the goodness is often to induce the enemy to repent.[69]

In contrast, the Jesus tradition in Matt 5:44-45 = Luke 6:27-28 + 35
depicts no realistic model for peaceful co-existence, no guidance on
how to remain calm and composed when faced with the evil of this
world, nor does it try to play down the discrepancy between the bad
and the good in the sense "we are all brothers." The saying is realistic about the evil of the world and the people whom one can call

---

Paraenesis. A history of the tradition and interpretation of its uses (SNTSMS 38;
Cambridge: Cambridge University Press, 1979) 4-18. As evident from the comparison, the Matthean and Lukan pericopes are based on a common tradition. The
texts forward same ideas and also the wording is in many places identical.
However, it is equally clear that tracing the pericopes back to Q and reconstructing
the original text is far more complicated. Still, most commentators seem to promote
a common Q-text as the origin for both pericopes (see references in J. Sauer,
"Traditionsgeschichtliche Erwägungen zu den synoptischen und paulinischen
Aussagen über Feindesliebe und Wiedervergeltungsverzicht," *ZNW* 76 [1985] 1-
28, esp. 6 n. 17), although alternative solutions have also been presented (H.-D.
Betz [*The Sermon on the Mount* (Hermeneia; Minneapolis: Fortress, 1995) 299-
300] would distinguish between two differing texts of one common source, i.e. Q).

    65   L. Schottroff, *Befreiungserfahrungen: Studien zur Sozialgeschichte des
Neuen Testaments* (München: Kaiser Verlag, 1990) 19-27.

    66   Prov 25:21-22; Exod 23:4-5.

    67   H.-W. Kuhn, "Das Liebesgebot Jesu als Tora und als Evangelium: Zur
Feindesliebe und zur christlichen und jüdischen Auslegung der Bergpredigt," in H.
Frankemölle and K. Kertelge (eds.), *Vom Urchristentum zu Jesus* (Freiburg:
Herder, 1989) 194-230, esp. 224.

    68   Luz, *Matthäus*, 307.

    69   Strecker, *Bergpredigt*, 92.

enemies.[70] But it is plainly unrealistic about the actual accomplishment of the command to love the enemy. Matt 5:44-45 = Luke 6:27-28 + 35 is "a utopian standard."[71] There is no consideration of how this kind of wisdom could be lived up to, how life could continue this way. The saying actually presupposes *a change of realities*. As such it completely fits the eschatological outlook of Jesus' message of the kingdom of God, discernible in the Gospels.[72] Regardless of how the question of authenticity is solved, then, it indeed seems to be that the command is best understood and explained within this kind of framework.[73]

So, there have been attempts to resolve the historicity of the command to love the enemy on the grounds that it is slightly but still significantly different from the contemporary ideas, and from Judaism in the first place.[74] There actually seems to be a consensus about its authenticity relying on the argument developed from dissimilarity to Judaism.[75] The statement of H.-W. Kuhn is characteristic:

> Die relative Sicherheit, beim Gebot der Feindesliebe von Jesus selbst zu reden, ergibt sich nicht zuletzt von den Umwelttexten her, die vielfach in die Nähe des Gebots der Feindesliebe kommen, allerdings eben nur in die Nähe! Für die schroffe Formulierung, den "Feind" zu "lieben," gibt es keine Parallele in *zeitgenössischen Texten*.[76]

The "contemporary texts" are for Kuhn the Old Testament, early Jewish writings, rabbinic documents and Graeco-Roman literature.[77] In other words, the early Christian disposition to the command is not even considered to be relevant to the question of authenticity![78] And we may again pose the (rhetorical) question: Were the early Chris-

---

[70] For the meaning of ἐχθρός, see Strecker, *Bergpredigt*, 91.

[71] S. Zeitlin in foreword to G. Friedlander, *The Jewish Sources of the Sermon on the Mount* (New York: Ktav, 1969) xxv.

[72] Kuhn, "Liebesgebot," 226-27.

[73] See Strecker, *Bergpredigt*, 91-92.

[74] So, for instance, H. Merklein, *Die Gottesherrschaft als Handlungsprinzip: Untersuchung zur Ethik Jesu* (2nd ed., Würzburg: Echter, 1981) 229-31. See also the following note.

[75] See Sauer, "Erwägungen," 3 and nn. 3, 5, and 6. More recently for example Luz, *Matthäus*, 306-307.

[76] Kuhn, "Liebesgebot," 224. Emphasis added.

[77] Kuhn, "Liebesgebot," 224-26.

[78] And in Kuhn *particularly* to the authenticity (cf. n. 87 below).

tians indeed incapable of coming up with something new?

I now wish to elaborate upon the present saying in order to show how defenseless an authenticity claim based on dissimilarity to Judaism actually is, and to demonstrate that while concentrating on the prohibition's dissimilarity to Judaism, scholarship has remained totally inattentive to a possibility of developing a cogent argument for authenticity from dissimilarity to Christianity.

Recently J. Sauer has argued, against the consensus, that the saying is in fact inauthentic. Sauer points out that in comparison with the synoptic tradition, many New Testament letters are notably earlier.[79] He analyzes the clearest parallel to the synoptic texts about the command to love the enemy, namely Rom 12:9-21, and concludes that the Pauline passage is also traditio-historically earlier.[80] Because the teaching in Rom 12:9-12 is easily derivative from Hellenistic Judaism and Paul does not say that he is dependent on the teaching of the Lord, the command to love the enemy in the Gospels can be but secondarily ascribed to Jesus and thus inauthentic.[81]

Together with others I disagree with Sauer's traditio-historical delineation.[82] Still, what is intriguing to see is how the argument based on dissimilarity to Judaism has no defense against Sauer's claim that the command has developed from a Pauline (or early Christian) invention. If Paul in fact elaborates—as assumed by Sauer —the idea of love of the enemy, how does the idea's dissimilarity to Judaism prove that it does not derive from Paul but from Jesus? Are we to think that while Jesus could deviate from Judaism, Paul could not? Not a very long time ago things were pictured just the opposite way. These considerations do not, of course, indicate the command's inauthenticity. What they do show is that its dissimilarity to Judaism in no way solves to whom it should be ascribed—to Paul (or early Christianity) or Jesus.

However, Sauer's assumption that both the Gospels and Paul articulate the same command to love the enemy is incorrect. Although this does not change the incapability of dissimilarity to Judaism to save the command as genuinely Jesuanic, here lies the possibility yet

---

79   Sauer, "Erwägungen," 4-5.

80   Sauer, "Erwägungen," 17-25.

81   Sauer, "Erwägungen," 26-28.

82   See, for example, Kuhn, "Liebesgebot," 223; G. Schneider, "Imitatio Dei als Motiv der 'Ethik Jesu'," in H. Merklein (ed.), *Neues Testament und Ethik* (Freiburg: Herder, 1989) 71-83, esp. 82.

to develop a cogent argument for its authenticity.

Sauer has indeed erred in juxtaposing the exhortations in Paul with the command to love the enemy appearing in the two Gospels. The Pauline passage completely lacks the "utopian" and unrealistic idea characteristic of the Gospels' saying, an idea which is comprehensible only in an eschatological framework. We might also say: Romans 12 lacks the command to love the enemy. On the other hand, the Pauline teaching contains all the earmarks familiar from contemporary thought pertaining to retaliation and related issues, but, again, lacking from the synoptic accounts. It presupposes continuation of the world as it is and therefore seeks to come to terms with people (vv. 17-18), it has the utilitarian motive of the repentance of the enemy (vv. 20-21),[83] it is characterized by concretism and realism.

From this it becomes clear that neither the *idea* of the command to love the enemy nor its exact *form* are found in Romans 12.[84] Likewise, the subsequent early Christian literature attests that the "utopian standard" of the command to love the enemy in the Gospels actually developed into a more realistic piece of common wisdom. Texts advancing such an interpretation of the command are available from c. 100 to 250 CE.[85] They disclose the difficulties faced by the early Christians in dealing with the demanding words.[86] Only after 250 does the strict interpretation of the command to love the enemy reappear, now in apologetic connections: The Christians love even their enemies![87]

As maintained, the exact command to love the enemy with its unrealistic, utopian thrust is unique within the contemporary Jewish (and Graeco-Roman) world. Now, *this* dissimilarity in no way proves its authenticity. But while the early Church finds the utopian command useless until c. 250 CE it is well argued to speak about its

---

83 For the meaning of the metaphor in v. 20, see W. Klassen, *Love of Enemies: The Way to Peace* (Philadelphia: Fortress, 1984) 36-37, 120-21.

84 Sauer ("Erwägungen," 26) tries to obscure the issue by stating that Paul does not know the synoptic *form* of the command to love the enemy.

85 See Kuhn, "Liebesgebot," 196-98. See even H. Köster, *Synoptische Überlieferung bei den Apostolischen Vätern* (Berlin: Akademie-Verlag, 1957) 220-26.

86 Kuhn, "Liebesgebot," 197.

87 Kuhn, "Liebesgebot," 198. It is remarkable that while reporting this reception of the command in Christian literature Kuhn does not notice its relevance to the issue of authenticity. For him, too, only dissimilarity to Judaism has bearing on that question.

dissimilarity to Christianity, and the (rhetorical) question that now can be posed is: Why would the primitive Church invent an idea she was not particularly interested in and ascribe it to Jesus? But its existence in the early Christian tradition is explicable if professed by Jesus himself.[88]

(c) On defilement – Mark 7:15

Mark 7:15 may be treated as an isolated unit.[89] How are we to expound it as such?[90] We may first notice that it echoes many Old Testament passages, for instance Jer 7:22-23 and Hos 6:6. Its tone is clearly reminiscent of these and other prophetic oracles, which by stressing what is now urgently needed seemingly dismiss the opposite. I suppose it can be settled that these oracles do not aim at abolishing the sacrificial cult.[91] In them the importance of obedience or mercy is emphasized to the degree that a seemingly absolute statement concerning the sacrifice is made: "I did not command you to sacrifice." Still, what is meant is clearly "I do not so much want

---

[88]   I do not hereby mean that the authenticity of the command would thus be readily solved. The aim was only to show that the command's dissimilarity to Judaism offers no indication of its authenticity, while dissimilarity to Christianity, which perhaps can be established here, may indeed do that.

[89]   J. Riches, *Jesus and the Transformation of Judaism* (London: Darton, Longman & Todd, 1980) 136; H. Räisänen, "Zur Herkunft von Markus 7,15," in J. Delobel (ed.), *Logia: The Sayings of Jesus* (BETL 59; Leuven: Peeters and Leuven University Press, 1982) 477-84, esp. 478.

[90]   A short semantical analysis: The saying begins by referring to food (cf. H. Räisänen, "Jesus and the Food Laws: Reflections on Mark 7.15," in *The Torah and Christ: Essays in German and English on the problem of the law in early Christianity* [Helsinki: Raamattutalo, 1986] 219-41, here 223 n. 5: "The text says 'into', not 'upon'!"; see even J. Lambrecht, "Jesus and the Law: An investigation of Mk 7, 1-23," *ETL* 53 [1977] 24-79, esp. 75). The first part alleges that nothing that enters a man can defile him. Because "to defile" (κοινοῦν) has direct ritual connotations, the beginning thus rejects the distinction made between clean and unclean foods. It simply claims that no food can defile man. In the last part of the saying, however, the issue can no longer be cultic impurity resulting from unclean foods, but rather moral contamination (R. P. Booth, *Jesus and the Laws of Purity: Tradition History and Legal History in Mark 7* [JSNTSup 13; Sheffield: JSOT Press, 1986] 206-13).

[91]   F. I. Andersen and D.N. Freedman, *Hosea* (AB 24; Garden City: Doubleday, 1980) 430-31; D. Stuart, *Hosea – Jonah* (WBC 31; Waco: Word, 1987) 110; P. C. Craigie, P. H. Kelley, and J. F. Drinkard, *Jeremiah 1–25* (WBC 26; Dallas: Word, 1991) 124-25.

you to sacrifice as I want you to be obedient."[92] In the same manner the saying in Mark 7:15, a parallel as to both its form and its contents, is not a *programmatic* abrogation of the cultic laws of purity, but a *prophetic* summons to hear the will of God.[93] In interpreting it "we must be on guard against using a statement polemical in nature and paradoxical in expression to reconstruct anything like a systematic theology."[94] Grammatically speaking, Mark 7:15—as well as the Old Testament passages—may be understood as a "dialectic negation."[95] As a Semitic idiom the formula "not A, but B" (οὐ . . . ἀλλά) can be rendered "not so much A, but rather B."[96] The antithesis in the saying is then *relative* rather than *absolute*: "A man is not so much defiled by that which enters him from outside as he is by that which comes from within."[97] Thus, it seems clear that no more than the quoted Old Testament passages aim at abolishing the sacrifice cult does Mark 7:15 intend to abrogate the cultic laws of purity. It only relativizes them in stressing the importance of morality.

Now, obviously this reading of the saying puts forward an idea that is not particularly unique within Judaism.[98] It is conveniently in harmony with, for instance, the passage from Hosea referred to above. For those who champion dissimilarity to Judaism as the foremost indication of authenticity, this would mean that the saying cannot be saved as genuinely Jesuanic. However, the absolute interpretation gives better options. According to this, Jesus would have denied one of the fundamental presuppositions of Judaism, namely the distinction between the sacred and the secular.[99] Such a drastic

---

[92] H. Kruse, "Die 'dialektische Negation' als semitisches Idiom," *VT* 4 (1954) 385-400, esp. 391-92, 393-95.

[93] R. A. Guelich, *Mark 1-8:26* (WBC 34A; Dallas: Word, 1989) 376.

[94] S. Westerholm, *Jesus and Scribal Authority* (ConBNT 10; Lund: Gleerup, 1978) 83.

[95] Kruse, "Negation."

[96] Kruse, "Negation," 390. See even Westerholm, *Scribal Authority*, 83; J. D. G. Dunn, "Jesus and Ritual Purity: A study of the tradition history of Mk 7,15," in *À Cause de l'Évangile: Études sur les Synoptiques et les Actes* (Paris: Cerf, 1985) 251-76, esp. 274; Booth, *Laws of Purity*, 68-71. The Hosea passage would be rendered "rather A, not so much B."

[97] Westerholm, *Scribal Authority*, 83.

[98] See Booth, *Laws of Purity*, 100-107.

[99] Perrin, *Rediscovering*, 150. Moreover, J. Marcus has recently made a plausible case for seeing such a denial as also violating the Fourth Commandment

statement against the law would be unique in the Jesus tradition and, of course, unique within Judaism. So, understanding the saying as absolutely and radically as possible,[100] scholars have been able to appeal to the criterion of dissimilarity.[101]

We may now turn to the issue of dissimilarity to Judaism as an indication of authenticity. For the sake of the argument we adopt for a moment the absolute reading of the saying. Is the saying's authenticity assured, as is assumed by some scholars, on grounds of it being unique within Judaism in this way? Is it reasonable to argue that Jesus could indeed come upon a thought so radically deviating from contemporary Judaism, while his followers could not have fancied (or would not have dared to present) such an idea? I would say no. Interestingly, on the point of Mark 7:15 this methodological fallacy seems to result in an explicit anomaly.

There are especially good reasons to think that the early Christians were motivated to introduce a saying of Jesus which rejects the distinction between clean and unclean food. In authenticating its unique Gentile mission, the early Church would presumably have had no greater difficulty in creating sayings with equal uniqueness. Statements such as Mark 7:15—according to its absolute interpretation—would have proven extremely helpful. So, what indeed is the point in stressing that Mark 7:15 is "completely without parallel in either rabbinic or sectarian Judaism"[102] when it so perfectly fits the agenda of the missionary Church?[103]

Therefore, particularly on the point of Mark 7:15, the apprehen-

---

reflected in 7:10-12; see his "Scripture and Tradition in Mark 7," in C. M. Tuckett (ed.), *The Scriptures in the Gospels* (BETL 131; Leuven: Peeters and University Press, 1997) 177-95, esp. 187-90.

[100] For example Perrin, *Rediscovering*, 150; J. Lambrecht, "Jesus and the Law," 76; Kümmel, *Heilsgeschehen*, 129; R. Pesch, *Das Markusevangelium. 1. Teil* (5th ed., HTKNT 2.1; Freiburg: Herder, 1989) 383.

[101] Usually in principle drawing on the conception of double dissimilarity, but in practice paying attention to dissimilarity to Judaism alone. See the statement of W. Weiss, *"Eine neue Lehre in Vollmacht": Die Streit- und Schulgespräche des Markus-Evangeliums* (Berlin and New York: de Gruyter, 1989) 70-71: "Das Logion selbst gilt der Forschung meist als authentisches Jesuswort; allerdings vor allem unter der oben angewiesenen Prämisse, es setze generell die Reinheitstora außer Kraft."

[102] Perrin, *Rediscovering*, 150.

[103] However, things become more obscure if the attribute "missionary" is omitted.

sion of dissimilarity to Judaism as indicating authenticity leads to a paradoxical situation: The more we stress that Mark 7:15 is absolute, thus according to the very apprehension strengthening its authenticity claim, the more difficult it in fact becomes to think that Jesus was actually known to have uttered such a thing. For if Jesus explicitly rejected the distinction between clean and unclean, how can we explain the fact that communion with Gentiles proved so difficult for the early Church to approve? How can we explain that the Church in the disputes that emerged around these situations did not from the outset utilize such clear and helpful sayings of Jesus as Mark 7:15?[104]

The natural explanation for an emergence of an absolute abrogation of the distinction between clean and unclean would of course be that, while not existing at the beginning of the Gentile mission of the early Church, the saying was in the course of time introduced to legitimate decisions or to smoothen their making. Dissimilarity to Judaism in no way rules out this kind of profession of such a saying.

Hence, even if Mark 7:15 would totally abolish the purity laws and thus completely disagree with all forms of contemporary Judaism, it would not appear more authentic. On the contrary, it begins to look like a deliberate product of the missionary Church.[105] Dissimilarity to Judaism thus in no way saves the saying as Jesuanic, but in fact prompts that it is a secondary fabrication.

The purpose here (in (a) – (c)) has not been to decide on the authenticity of the sayings, but only to exemplify the fact that appealing to dissimilarity to Judaism for a tradition's authenticity proves nothing. This theoretical conclusion stands regardless of whether one agrees with the above interpretations of the texts. In my estimation, therefore, the concept of dissimilarity to Judaism should be deprived of the role it has been given in the discussion of the criteria of authenticity.[106] Note that I am not hereby claiming that

---

[104] Räisänen, "Herkunft," 479-80; Marcus, "Scripture and Tradition," 183 n. 23.

[105] Cf. B. Chilton ("A Generative Exegesis of Mark 7:1-23," in B. Chilton and C. A. Evans, *Jesus in Context: Temple, Purity, and Restoration* [AGJU 39; Leiden: Brill, 1997] 297-317, esp. 311-16) who correctly identifies this and related understandings as prompted by vv. 17-23 and ascribes these verses to circles which were already engaged in mission activity.

[106] Theissen's and Winter's (*Die Kriterienfrage*, 183-91) modification of dissimilarity to Judaism signifies no real improvement. The substitute criterion "Kontextplausibilität" consists of two principles: (1) "Je besser eine Überlieferung

Jesus traditions that appear dissimilar to Judaism would necessarily be inauthentic, nor that the authenticity of such traditions were impossible to determine. What I am proposing, is that we should not regard the mere fact that a tradition is dissimilar to Judaism as an indication of its authenticity.

CONCLUSIONS

To sum up: (1) Dissimilarity to Christianity alone suffices as an

---

in den konkreten jüdischen Kontext Palästinas und Galiläas paßt, um so mehr hat sie Anspruch auf Authentizität" (p. 183). As a matter of fact, this principle is a positive variant of one of the few *negative* criteria, non-Palestinian environment, which dictates that "a saying that reflects social, political, economic, or religious conditions that existed only outside Palestine or only after the death of Jesus is to be considered inauthentic" (Meier, *A Marginal Jew*, 180). It is true that in the *general* assessment of the value of the Gospels as sources for authentic teaching of Jesus, the positive guise of the criterion may have some importance: The realization that many of the Gospel stories are indeed plausible within Palestinian environment instills confidence in the *ancient origin* of the Jesus tradition related (cf. Evans, *Jesus*, 22-23). However, as regards individual traditions, this form of the criterion has no evidencing power: Jesus' Jewish followers were no doubt familiar with the world they lived in and could, consequently, depict historically plausible events in Jesus' life. Therefore, the fact that an individual Jesus tradition is plausible within the Judaism of Jesus' time cannot feature as an indication of its authenticity (see Meier, *A Marginal Jew*, 180). Now, Theissen and Winter are aware of this shortcoming and try to rectify their criterion with the help of the balancing second principle, which, however, rather makes the tool worse: (2) "Was innerhalb dieses jüdisches Kontextes ein eigenständiges Profil zeigt, werden wir eher Jesus als einem seiner jüdischen Anhänger zutrauen" (p. 183). To grasp "ein eigenständiges Profil" means searching for "individuellen Zügen Jesu." But this discloses a failure in methodological thinking. How do we know what the "individuellen Zügen Jesu" are? If we already knew that, we would not need any criteria of authenticity. As maintained, we endeavor to formulate methods that do not set out from (nor require) an *a priori* knowledge of what genuinely Jesuanic teaching looks like (see n. 14 above). Theissen and Winter do try to route entrance to this knowledge by defining three ways "zur Feststellung solcher individuellen Züge." These are (pp. 189-91) "profile of comparison" (Jesus compared with other religious figures and movements of contemporary Judaism), "indices of particularity" (*ipsissima vox Jesu*), and "individual complexity" (a plausible combination of separate elements of Jesus' individuality). All three "ways," however, involve the stumbling block of presupposing knowledge of what kind of person Jesus actually was. The amount of reliable information about Jesus needed for "Kontextplausibilität" to be useful, as it is revealed by these three ways, merits repeating the point made above: If all this is already ascertained, why bother?

argument for authenticity. To demand double dissimilarity in fact causes the method to deteriorate. For this reason, employing the criterion of double dissimilarity we not only miss the benefits attendant on consenting to establishing dissimilarity to Christianity alone,[107] but in all likelihood add to the number of misjudgments made in assessing the authenticity of the teaching of Jesus. (2) Dissimilarity to Judaism furnishes no indication of authenticity and has, as a principle, nothing to do with the question of authenticity.

These observations actually necessitate a restructuring of the criterion of dissimilarity. The rejection of the demand of double dissimilarity (most concretely: the need for establishing dissimilarity to Judaism) causes the basic idea of the criterion to alter. The criterion ought to be seen to consists of one principle only: Sayings or deeds of Jesus which are discontinuous with the views of the subsequent primitive Church have a claim for authenticity. In short, the criterion of dissimilarity is thus equal to dissimilarity to Christianity. As it happens, this kind of principle has been employed by some scholars *in addition* to the criterion of dissimilarity in its conventional dual form. J. Breech, J. P. Meier, and C. A. Evans include in their list of tools of authenticity both the criterion of dissimilarity and an allied criterion, namely that of *embarrassment*.[108] The criterion of embarrassment "focuses on actions or sayings of Jesus that would have embarrassed or created difficulty for the early Church."[109]

We easily see that the difference between this and the dissimilarity criterion—as it is now correctly understood as a "single" test of dissimilarity—is only a matter of emphasis. The criterion of embarrassment exhibits but a special case of this dissimilarity test, namely when a tradition's dissimilarity to Christianity is radical enough to have supposedly caused "embarrassment." The reason why Breech, Meier, and Evans can still think that there is actually two distinct

---

[107] See the second section above.

[108] J. Breech, *The Silence of Jesus: The Authentic Voice of the Historical Man* (Philadelphia: Fortress, 1983) 22-26; Meier, *A Marginal Jew*, 168-71; Evans, *Jesus*, 18-19.

[109] Meier, *A Marginal Jew*, 168. This is the principle behind P. W. Schmiedel's ("Gospels," in T. K. Cheyne and J. S. Black [eds.], *Encyclopaedia Biblica II* [London: A. & C. Black, 1901] 1761–1898, esp. 1881–83) famous pillar sayings.

criteria is that they urge the *double* dissimilarity.[110] In its traditional
dual form the criterion of dissimilarity, of course, bases on a
rationale different from that of the criterion of embarrassment.[111]
But if the demand for double dissimilarity should thus be rejected,
there is no more need to separate these two, dissimilarity and
embarrassment, but an account could be given to the fact that there
may indeed appear different degrees of dissimilarity. There are no
doubt traditions, of which the dissimilarity to Christianity is not
particularly notable and consequently, the claim for authenticity put
forward is not particularly strong. Traditions that supposedly were
experienced as embarrassing by the early Christians, again, would
exhibit the other end. Their claim for authenticity would be excep-
tionally compelling. Now, I do not mean that it is always possible to
make these kinds of distinctions, confidently or at all. On the
contrary, precisely because this is difficult I think that it is better to
distinguish between different degrees of certainty of one criterion
than to try to turn these degrees to a number of different criteria,
e.g. dissimilarity and embarrassment.

Hence, in the place of the criteria of double dissimilarity and
embarrassment and others like that[112] I propose the one criterion of
single dissimilarity, namely the test of dissimilarity to Christianity.
The question about the name of the criterion is actually only of
secondary importance, while it is the principle, the basic idea that
makes the difference.[113]

What then is the importance of this restructuring of the criterion

---

110 Breech, *Silence*, 9-10 (quite unclearly though); Meier, *A Marginal Jew*,
171-74; Evans, *Jesus*, 19-21.

111 Cf. Meier, *A Marginal Jew*, 188 n. 16: The criterion of embarrassment is
"allied, but not reducible to discontinuity."

112 E. P. Sanders and M. Davies (*Studying the Synoptic Gospels* [London:
SCM Press; Philadelphia: Trinity, 1989] 304-305) present a criterion characterized
with the pair of phrases: "Strongly against the grain; too much with the grain" of the
early Christian agenda.

113 The old term "criterion of dissimilarity" does not exclude the thought of a
double test of dissimilarity. It is thus not actually suitable for introducing a new
conception. "Criterion of single dissimilarity" would leave open the question of
which dissimilarity is aimed at. In view of the tendency to focus on dissimilarity to
Judaism alone, misinterpretations would certainly arise. "Embarrassment," again,
is, as shown in the text immediately above, a narrower concept than "dissimilarity,"
an unnecessarily narrow one. Therefore, for the sake of clarity (and simplicity), I
would propose the name "criterion of dissimilarity to Christianity."

of dissimilarity? Its effects on previous research depend on the way in which the dubious method of double dissimilarity has been pursued: (a) Consistently as a demand of a *double* test, or (b) inconsistently as a test of dissimilarity to Judaism alone.

(a) Misjudgments are perhaps not particularly grievous when account is given, not only to a tradition's dissimilarity to Judaism, but also to its dissimilarity to Christianity, that is, one is really urging a *double* test of dissimilarity. Then sayings or deeds of Jesus that could be argued as authentic on the grounds of their being dissimilar to Christianity are denied the argument if they cannot be shown to be dissimilar to Judaism too. Further, the material assembled by means of the criterion will have the added bias towards detaching Jesus from Judaism. However, at least the traditions that pass the double test really do have a claim for authenticity.

(b) The situation is much worse when the criterion is, at least in practice, understood to consist of dissimilarity to Judaism only. That a tradition, whose genuineness has been verified by this kind of "criterion," factually has a claim for authenticity is a pure stroke of luck. At least there seem to be single passages, where this distorted version of the double test of dissimilarity has occupied a conclusive position. I refer to the sayings analyzed above. I think that we are "lucky" here and that there yet may be also proper ways of arguing for their genuineness. Still, considering the weight of (for instance) these passages, Matt 5:33-37, Matt 5:38-48 = Luke 6:27-36, and Mark 7:15, with regard to the quest for the historical Jesus (and Christianity in general), it is justified to say that this methodological miscalculation has seriously misled the investigation. The argumentation of the Markan passage may even indicate that a tendency to interpret sayings of Jesus more sharply in contrast with Judaism than is actually needed has been called out.

If carried out systematically, then, the reliance upon dissimilarity to Judaism alone in questioning the authenticity of Jesus traditions is likely to lead to distortion of whole investigations. Exposed to this danger is, for example, the otherwise scrupulous and excellently argued study of H. Merklein: *Die Gottesherrschaft als Handlungsprinzip*.[114] Time after time dissimilarity to Judaism suffices for Merklein as an indication of authenticity (as well as affinity suggests

---

[114] See n. 74 above.

a non-jesuanic origin!).[115] Similarly J. Riches almost throughout the innovative book *Jesus and the Transformation of Judaism*[116] regards dissimilarity to Judaism alone as an indication of authenticity.[117] In chap. 7 particularly (Jesus' Theism) Riches, investigating a number of sayings deemed similar to Judaism by Bultmann, nearly pleads for interpretations that could establish them as dissimilar. At the same time affinity to Judaism leads him to deny a saying its authenticity.[118] W. Weiss also relies heavily on the ability of affinity to Judaism to indicate inauthenticity.[119] Let us pause to consider: If dissimilarity to Judaism is taken to indicate authenticity and similarity thereto, again, inauthenticity, what will the Jesus that survives this "logic" look like?

These notions are quite important for the objectivity of the whole quest for the historical Jesus. In the agenda of the quest the issue of Jesus' Jewishness is on the top: The "third quest"[120] particularly has emphasized that Jesus should be viewed and comprehended within Judaism.[121] And as noticed, the errors made in applying the criterion of dissimilarity, perhaps the most important tool of authenticity,

---

115 See Merklein, *Die Gottesherrschaft*, for instance 50-56, 66, 116, 125 (affinity —> inauthentic), 128-129, 129 (affinity —> inauthentic), 132 (affinity —> inauthentic).

116 See n. 89 above.

117 Though Riches allows for both parts of the double test when considering methodological issues (cf. Riches, *Jesus*, 44-61), all that matters in the actual application of the tool is establishing dissimilarity to Judaism (see, for instance, 91 and the pages referred to in the following note). The treatment of Mark 7:15 in chap. 6 is an exception. However, it should be noted that the dissimilarity test is not the only criterion Riches uses.

118 Riches, *Jesus*, 148-154.

119 Weiss, *Eine neue Lehre*, 48-50, 70-71, 91-92.

120 For this new phase in Jesus research see, for example, N. T. Wright, "Quest for the Historical Jesus," *ABD* 3 (1992) 796-802, esp. 800; B. Holmberg, "En historisk vändning i forskningen om Jesus," *STK* 69 (1993) 69-76, esp. 72; B. Witherington, *The Jesus Quest: The Third Search for the Jew of the Nazareth* (Downers Grove: InterVarsity, 1995). See, however, the scepticism of W. R. Telford, "Major Trends and Interpretive Issues in the Study of Jesus," in B. Chilton and C. A. Evans (eds.), *Studying the Historical Jesus: Evaluations of the State of Current Research* (NTTS 19; Leiden: Brill, 1994) 33-74, esp. 74. As the phrase implies, the era would be third in order. The previous phases have traditionally been named "die Leben-Jesu-Forschung" (end of the 19th century) and "die neue Frage" or "the new quest" (from 1950 onwards).

121 See J. H. Charlesworth (ed.), *Jesus' Jewishness: Exploring the Place of Jesus within Early Judaism* (New York: Crossroad, 1996).

especially affect the way we picture Jesus' relation to Judaism. In order to stand out from the previous phases, the "third quest" should indeed pay attention to the correctness of the criteria it uses.[122] If the adjustments indicated in the present article are made, the Jesus research of biblical exegesis is, as regards its basic methodology, again somewhat closer to commensurability with the general historiography.[123] For ordinary historians the principle behind the criterion of "single" dissimilarity has since long been a regular tool of internal criticism of the sources.[124] This is phrased already in E. Bernheim's classical[125] methodology:[126]

Der allgemeine Grundsatz, worauf unser Urteil über die Zuverlässigkeit beruht, entstammt der Erfahrung, daß kein Mensch die Thatsachen, welche er weiß, ohne Grund und Zweck falsch mitzuteilen pflegt . . . Die in echten Quellen mitgeteilten Thatsachen nehmen wir also erfahrungsgemäß für wahr an, halten wir für zuverlässig, wenn in dem Charakter der Quelle, den Verhältnissen des Autors u.s.w. keiner der mannigfachen Gründe der Entstellung erfindlich ist, welche wir in den vorhergehenden Abschnitten analysiert haben; . . . Angaben von Begebenheiten so einfacher, neutraler und ich möchte sagen monumentaler Art, daß Täuschung oder Mißverständnis des Berichtenden dabei unwahrscheinlich und irgend ein Motiv der Entstellung nicht absehbar ist, dürfen wir getrost für zuverlässig halten, und

---

[122] Cf. J. H. Charlesworth (*Jesus within Judaism* [2nd ed., London: SPCK, 1990] 26), who wants to distinguish this new phase of Jesus research from the previous ones which more or less, according to him, were grounded on dogmatic and theological interests.

[123] I do not mean that completely identical methodologies should be the goal. On the contrary, Jesus-of-history research and the research of the Gospels will always retain their characteristics ensuing not only from the particularity of the object of study but also from the scholarly tradition. However, keeping an eye on what methods historians in general utlize should guard us against altogether awkward and idiosyncratic conceptions.

[124] The criteria of multiple attestation and coherence also have their counterparts in the internal criticism of the source criticism of historiography.

[125] Cf. J. Rüsen, "Historische Methode," in C. Meier and J. Rüsen (eds.), *Historische Methode* (München: Deutscher Taschenbuch Verlag, 1988) 62-80, esp. 65: "Mit Bernheims *Lehrbuch der historichen Methode* gewinnt dann die um die historiographische Formungsoperation verkürzte Methodenkonzeption ihre kanonische Form."

[126] More recently, for example, H. C. Hockett, *The Critical Method in Historical Research and Writing* (7th ed., New York: Macmillan, 1964) 56; R. J. Shafer (ed.), *A Guide to Historical Method* (Homewood: Dorsey Press, 1974) 157.

solche hat man auch wohl nie verworfen.[127]

As we may notice, this is along the rationale (a) formulated in the beginning of the previous section: "A source that reports against *its own* agenda can, at least on that particular point, be considered trustworthy." That "somebody else's agenda"—Judaism's or whoever's—would somehow be relevant to the reasoning does not hold true.

---

[127] E. Bernheim, *Lehrbuch der Historischen Methode und der Geschichtsphilosophie* (3rd and 4th eds., Leipzig: Duncker & Humblot, 1903) 483.

HOW JESUS CHARGED LANGUAGE WITH MEANING:
A STUDY IN RHETORIC[1]

Ben F. Meyer

Beginning with the clash between Socrates and the Sophists "rhetoric" has often seemed to the cognoscenti to be a dangerous business, best kept strictly in its place. Philosophers blamed rhetoric for undermining the purity of the desire to know and turning seekers after truth into seekers after prizes. Poets blamed rhetoric, first, for pretending to be subtler and finer than poetry; second, for wrecking poetry by artifice. Theologians of our time blame their predecessors for allowing such logical and rhetorical ideals as clarity, coherence, and rigor to dress up static abstractions in the guise of eternal truths.

But if the word "rhetoric" comes to us trailing connotations of pretension and artificiality, of language trying too hard to do too much, it remains that in the present context and for present purposes rhetoric is the study of style, whether to bring one's own capacity for style into being or at least to understand how it works for others. Cicero, moreover, did have a point when (in the *De Oratore* 3.32) he deplored the Socratic split between the wise and the eloquent or, as he put it, between the heart and the tongue. For heart and tongue belong together, heart setting tongue in motion, tongue making heart understood.

In biblical tradition "heart" signified the whole of human intentionality which showed itself in bodily and facial expression, but above all in words. Authentic speech revealed the pure heart, skilled speech the wise heart. The "understanding" or "hearing" heart (*lēb šōmēᶜa*) that Solomon prayed for (1 Kgs 3:9) and that the Lord immediately conferred on him, was to set the speech of Solomon

---

[1]   This paper was originally delivered as the Presidential Address, Canadian Society of Biblical Studies, Québec, 29 May 1989. This address was, and is, dedicated to William L. Moran, who for me as for many others has been *magister in sacra pagina*. The paper was published in *SR* 19 (1990) 273-85 and later reprinted in my *Christus Faber: The Master Builder and the House of God* (Allison Park: Pickwick, 1992) 91-106; it has been slightly revised and updated for the present volume.

apart "so that none like you has been before you and none like you shall arise after you" (1 Kgs 3:12). But we are about to take up the speech of one who spoke in the consciousness that his words outstripped Solomon's (Matt 12:42 = Luke 11:31). Yet the same speaker spoke out of a consciousness of being "meek and lowly of heart" (Matt 11:29), who thanked his Father (Matt 11:25-26 = Luke 10:21) for reserving revelation to the "simple" (nēpioi/šabrîn). To advert from the start to this paradoxical consciousness—an abyss of riches, an abyss of poverty—is to offer a foretaste of the antitheses, paradoxes, and reversal that are the ipsissima vox Jesu. Here was one who without training, without writing, so charged language with meaning as to elicit, generation after generation, the disarming protest, "Lord, to whom shall we go? You have the words of eternal life" (John 6:68).

Ezra Pound specified three ways of charging language with meaning: by phanopoeia (or the evocation of sharp visual images), but melopoeia (or the orchestration of sound), and by logopoeia (or the exploitation of resonances latent in the listener's memory).[2] We shall act on this clue, inquiring into the practice of Jesus as phanopoeist, as melopoeist, and as logopoeist. Though the parables of Jesus exhibit his rhetorical art at its finest, and though we intend to take account of the visual imagery of the parables, we shall limit our treatment of texts to short sayings: proclamation of the reign of God; macarisms thematically parallel to the proclamation; proverbs given new point in function of a new coign of vantage and a new set of referents (both definable by eschatology inaugurated and in process of realization); aphoristic challenges to his disciples to steel them for imminent eschatological ordeal; and finally, prophetic words revealing his scenario of the future.

PHANOPEIA

We shall begin by surveying the repertory of visual images to be found in the words of the historical Jesus. These images first of all reflect the fields and villages among which he was nurtured: they are images of alternating sun and rain (Matt 5:45); of the hot sun scorching the tender shoot (Matt 13:6 = Mark 4:6; cf. Luke 8:6); of evening rain-cloud alternating with south wind blowing (Luke 12:54;

---

[2]   E. Pound, *The ABC of Reading* (London: Routledge; New Haven: Yale University Press, 1934).

cf. Matt 16:2-3); of the sky and its ravens (Matt 6:26; Luke 12:23); fields of wild grass (Matt 6:30 = Luke 12:28) and wild lilies (Matt 6:28 = Luke 12:27); the freshly ploughed field being sown, an image played off against the same field ready for harvest (Matt 13:1-9 = Mark 4:1-9 = Luke 8:4-8); the image of the tiniest seed (say) cupped in the hand, played off against that of the great bush that will have grown out of it (Matt 13:3-4 = Mark 4:31-32 = Luke 13:18-19). There is also the imagery of foxes and their lairs, birds and their nests (Matt 8:20 = Luke 9:58); the unwitting bird about to be snared (Luke 21:34); plentiful sparrows (Matt 10:29 = Luke 12:6); birds of prey circling over a carcass (Matt 24:28 = Luke 17:37). Other countryside images are the fruit tree and its fruit (Matt 7:16-19 = Luke 6:43-44; Matt 12:33); the fig tree as its leaves return (Matt 24:32 = Mark 13:28 = Luke 21:29); sowers and reapers (Matt 9:37 = Luke 10:2); sheep and wolves (Matt 10:16; Luke 10:3); dogs and swine (Matt 7:6).

The defining imagery, however, is that of village life: children playing "Wedding" with mimicry of flute music, or "Funeral" with breast-beating; grown-up weddings with proper bridesmaids (Matt 25:1-13) and real funerals with mourners and and flute-players (Luke 7:11-13; Matt 8:22 = Luke 9:60; cf. Matt 9:23). The village is made up mainly of single-roomed houses barred at night (Luke 11:7), a small oil-lamp flickering (Matt 5:15 = Luke 11:33). It is a village of rich and poor, farmers and fishermen, women and children, widows and judges.

There is also Jerusalem: the city set on a hill (Matt 5:14); the courts and buildings of the Temple (Matt 24:1-2 = Mark 13:1-2 = Luke 21:5); ceremony at the altar of holocausts (Matt 5:23). The city has a varied population: side by side, the very rich and the utterly destitute (Luke 16:19-21); notorious sinners and the famously pious praying in public places (Matt 6:5) and conspicuously fasting (Matt 6:16); a hereditary aristocracy and a meritocracy of scribes; tax-collectors and publicans; an underclass of thieves and beggars. In Jesus' speech villagers and city-folk alike come alive engaged in routine transactions or caught at critical moments of reward or punishment, sudden good fortune or catastrophic reversal.

The immediate world of Jesus was greatly expanded by popular and especially biblical lore. In the former we meet an imagery of great wealth: great houses administered by a numerous retinue; great transactions involving large sums of money; and festive parties. This world is gentile. Now and again we meet commonsense conceptions shared by gentile and Jewish world but foreign to us (the extramission theory of vision—if your eye is good it shows that your body is full of light [Matt 6:22 = Luke 11:24] or the anthropology that attributes hunger to the soul [Matt 6:25]).

The biblical world sometimes seems remote but in fact it is omnipresent in Jesus' speech. Again and again his words betray an acute awareness of biblical promise. Where, however, the classic biblical imagery of salvation recurs in Jesus' words it is shorn of its stately expression. Such charged images as the new wine (symbol of salvation) or the new cloak (renewal of the cosmos) occur with artless ease in the most ordinary figurative idiom (Matt 9:16-17 = Mark 2:21-22 = Luke 5:36-38) which nevertheless designates the present as fulfillment. This kind of affirmation likewise draws on the imagery of wedding (Matt 9:15 = Mark 2:19 = Luke 5:34), banquet (Matt 22:1-14 = Luke 14:16-24), and harvest (Matt 9:37 = Luke 10:2).

The deliberately toned-down exploitation of biblical symbol goes hand in hand with a generic trait: a pronounced simplicity and sobriety in the use of visual imagery. There seems not to be a single image dwelt on for its own sake, i.e. for even fleeting aesthetic effect. True, one might detect in Jesus' imagery of field and sky, bird and flower, a spontaneous affectivity towards nature; still, this affectivity is radically and pervasively theocentric (Matt 6:28-30 = Luke 12:26-28; Matt 10:29-30 = Luke 12:6-7). Deft use of the evocative visual image, which is what Pound meant by phanopoeia, does characterize the words of Jesus; but always the point was to turn a line memorable not for disinterested beauty but for didactic truth. And if the visual images that we have just surveyed do indeed belong to memorable parables and short sayings, they have all been made memorable for their suprapoetic usage.

MELOPOEIA

Melopoeia, or the orchestration of sound, is the stylistic factor least likely to survive translation. But *parallelismus membrorum*, which is found in 80 percent of the Synoptic units of Jesus' sayings material,[3] does survive translation, and in the Greek form of Jesus'

---

3   See R. Riesner, "Der Ursprung der Jesus-Überlieferung," *TZ* 38 (1982) 493-513, here 507. For comparison of Jesus with the Jewish teachers of late

sayings it is often an index to the original rhythm. This is among the lessons taught by two accomplished philologians, Gustaf Dalman (1855-1941) and Charles Fox Burney (1868-1925), both of whom have given us retroversions into Aramaic of the words of Jesus. Dalman, the founder of modern Aramaic studies, was the severest critic of the retroversions proposed by the late-19th century scholars. Burney allied himself with Dalman in identifying the linguistic wellsprings on which Jesus drew. The study of Aramaic has meantime progressed; Qumran Aramaic, for example, has been specified as the currently most appropriate linguistic control for reconstructing the Aramaic of Jesus.[4] Purists, ranging from the delicate to the fanatic, will find fault with the retroversions of Dalman and Burney even in their variously corrected forms; and it is true that these retroversions will always be subject to incidental correction. For my part, I expect such incidental correction and am not intimidated by the prospect of it.

The principal sound-factors are rhythm, particularly as measured by the number of accents per line, and tone-color: rhyme, assonance, consonance, alliteration, and onomatopoeia. Synoptic-sayings material exhibits lines of two beats, of three beats, of four beats and combinations, especially that in which a three-beat line is followed by a two-beat line (*qînâ* or dirge rhythm). The same material is rich in tone-color, especially rhyme, but with copious assonance and consonance, and not infrequent alliteration.

The two-beat line, though by no means commonplace, is well attested: "Bless your cursers / pray for your persecutors" (Luke 6:28),

> *barĕkûn lĕlātêkôn / ṣallôn ʿal radĕpêkôn.*[5]

Again, in the Our Father, "Let your name be hallowed / Let your reign come" (Matt 6:9b-10 = Luke 11:2),

---

antiquity, see idem, *Jesus als Lehrer: Eine Untersuchung zum Ursprung der Evangelien-Überlieferung* (WUNT 2.7; Tübingen: Mohr [Siebeck], 1981; 4th ed., 1994).

4   See J. A. Fitzmyer, "The Phases of the Aramaic Language," in Fitzmyer, *A Wandering Aramean: Collected Essays* (SBLMS 25; Missoula: Scholars Press, 1979) 57-84; E. M. Cook, "The Aramaic of the Dead Sea Scrolls," in P. Flint and J. C. VanderKam (eds.), *The Dead Sea Scrolls: A Comprehensive Assessment after Fifty Years* (2 vols., Leiden: Brill, 1998) 1.359-78.

5   C. F. Burney, *The Poetry of Our Lord* (Oxford: Clarendon, 1925) 169.

yitqaddaš šĕmāk / tē²tē² malkûtāk.[6]

Tone-coloring in the first of these two texts derives especially from· rhymes (*-kôn, -lôn, -kôn*) and consonance in *k*-sounds (*-kûn, -kôn, -kôn*). The second text displays end-rhymes (*-māk* and *-tāk*) and assonance in the *a*-sounds (*-qaddaš, -māk, māl-, tāk*). The terse two-beat line suggests urgency.

The three-beat line is far more common. Here is a distich in three-beat rhythm: "Blessed are the poor / for the reign of God is for them" (based on Matt 5:3 = Luke 6:20),

tûbêhôn miskĕnayyā² / dĕdilĕhôn malkûtā² dē²lāhā².[7]

First of all, we have rhyming here: *-hôn -hôn / -yā² -tā² -lāhā²*. Consonantal sound-texture is established by *m*-sounds: *mis- mal-*; by *h*-sounds: *hôn -hôn -hā*; and if, in our retroversion, we were simply to adopt the Lukan text ("Blessed are you poor, for the reign of God is for you") we would have consonance with four *k*-sounds:

tûbêhôn miskĕnayyā² / dĕdilĕhôn malkûtā² dē²lāhā².

Dalman gave us two retroversions of the aphorism "Many are called, but few are chosen" (Matt 22:14). First, a distich in two-beat rhythm:

saggî²în zemînîn / zē²ênîn bĕḥîrîn.[8]

Here all four words rhyme. Some years later Dalman gave us a more likely retroversion, a distich in three-beat rhythm, the usual rhythm of aphorisms:

saggî²în dē²innûn zĕmînîn / wĕṣibḥad dē²innûn beḥîrîn.[9]

The rhyming is somewhat less prominent; there is also, perhaps by chance, what we would call an anapestic accent pattern.

Another, quite different, three-beat distich: a lightly revised form of the last word of Jesus to the high priest, according to Luke: "Soon the Son of man/will be seated at the right hand of power" (Luke 22:69):

---

[6]   J. Jeremias, *New Testament Theology: The Proclamation of Jesus* (New York: Scribner's, 1971) 196.

[7]   Revised from Burney, *Poetry*, 166. With Burney here and with Jeremias, *New Testament Theology*, 24, we are positing two accents in *miskĕnayyā²*, namely, on the first and on the last syllables.

[8]   G. Dalman, *The Words of Jesus* (Edinburgh: T. & T. Clark, 1902 [German edition, 1898]) 119.

[9]   G. Dalman *Jesus-Jeshua* (London: SPCK, 1929) 228.

mikkĕʾan bar ʾĕnāšāʾ | yātēb min yammînāʾ digĕbûrĕtāʾ.[10]

Some examples of four beat rhythm: first, in the Greek test of "from the fullness of the heart the mouth speaks" (Matt 12:34 = Luke 6:45)—*ek perisseumatos tēs kardias to stoma lalei*—liquid consonants roll trippingly from the tongue. Likewise the Aramaic retroversion:

min môtĕrēh dĕlibbāʾ pummāʾ mĕmallêl.[11]

The proclamation formula, the reign of God is at hand, may be disputed. For Paul Joüon the formula is a three beat-line: *qĕrabat malkûtāʾ dišĕmayyāʾ*; for Dalman, a four-beat line: *qārîbâ malkûtāʾ dišĕmayyāʾ lĕmêtê.* More likely than either would be a three-beat *mĕṭāʾ malkûtāʾ dēʾlāhāʾ*, or, still more likely, in view of Greek *ēggiken*,

qĕrabat malkûtāʾ dēʾlāhāʾ.[12]

From among the instructions of disciples we have a distich in four beats followed by a half-line: "If anyone wishes to follow me, let him deny himself and take up his cross and (so) follow me (Matt 16:24 = Mark 8:34 = Luke 9:23):

kol man dibāʿê mĕhallākâ bātĕray
yikpōr bĕgarmēh wĕyiṭʿan ṣelîbēh
wĕyêtê bātĕray.[13]

We have here two sets of rhymes: *rime riche* in the repetition "after me," *bātĕray / bātĕray*, and *rime suffisant* in lines two and three:

---

10   Revised from Dalman, *Words of Jesus*, 311. With Burney (*Poetry*, 132, 142) and Jeremias (*New Testament Theology*, 23; cf. 282) I would find one or two beats in *bar ʾĕnāšāʾ*, depending on what seems to be required by the rhythmic pattern of the texts in which the words stand.

11   Jeremias, *New Testament Theology*, 22.

12   Jeremias (*New Testament Theology*, 97) points out that "'kingdom of heaven' appears for the first time in Jewish literature half a century after Jesus' ministry"; this rules out *malkûtāʾ dišĕmayyāʾ* proposed by both P. Joüon, "Notes philologiques sur les Évangiles," *RSR* 17 (1927) 537-40, at 538, and Dalman, *Words of Jesus*, 106. I am inferring from the synonymous parallelism of Mark 1:15 and sense of *ēggisen* in Matt 21:34 that the verb *qĕrab/qĕrêb* could signify "has arrived" and the adjective *qārîbāʾ* could signify "present, here." (Joüon ["Notes philologiques," 538] adduces Hebrew examples of *qārēb* = has arrived.) But however one settles the most likely retroversion of this text it is clear that in Jesus' teaching generally the *malkût* of God was *formaliter* future (e.g. Matt 10:23) and *virtualiter* present (e.g. Matt 12:28 = Luke 11:20).

13   Dalman, *Jesus-Jeshua*, 191.

bĕgarmēh / *ṣĕlîbēh* / *wĕyêtê*.

Qînâ rhythm (three beats/two beats) in Aramaic may be illustrated by the text addressed to followers: "Whoever wishes to save his life will lose it, and whoever loses his life for my sake will save it":

man dibĕʿāʾ lĕḥayyāʾ â napšēh / *môbēd yātah*
ûman dĕmôbēd napšēh bĕginnî / *mĕḥayyê yātah*.[14]

This saying comes to us in four forms, of which the first appears in two variants. I have cited the variant in Mark 8:35 and Luke 9:24 where the chiasmus runs: save / lose // lose / save. The variant form in Luke 17:33 reads: preserve / lose // lose / preserve. A second form, in Matt 10:39, reads: find / lose // lose / find; and there are mixed forms in Matt 16:25 and John 12:25.

This retroversion most obviously features assonance in *a*-sounds. As for consonance here is the *m*-sound: *man, mô-, -man, -mô, me*: an *n*-sound: *man, nap-, man, nap-, -ginnî*; an soft *b*-sound (v): *-be-, -bed, -bed*: and a *d*-sound: *dib-, bēd, dĕmôbēd*.

FOUR CONTEXTUAL FACTORS

Before considering some typical instances of logopoeia in the words of Jesus it may be in order to interject a clarification on charging words with meaning. Ezra Pound's analysis took the rudiments of discourse for granted. Phanopoeia, melopoeia, and logopoeia provide, not the substance of meaning, but its heightening or enhancement. Before considering how logopoeia heightens or enhances Jesus' words we should recall four factors that define the situations out of which he spoke.

First, the origins of his public career lay in the movement of John the Baptist who summoned all Israel to repentance, the confession of sins, and a rite of washing in the face of God's impending judgment. Second, Jesus, like John, addressed his message to all Israel; it was epitomized in the word, "The reign of God is at hand!" Third, Jesus, like John, conceived his mission and message in election-historical terms; that is, those who answered with yes were destined for acquittal and restoration; those who answered with no were destined for condemnation and ruin.[15]

---

14   Jeremias, *New Testament Theology*, 26.

15   See J. Jeremias, *Jesus' Promise to the Nations* (London: SCM Press, 1958; Philadelphia: Fortress, 1982) 50-51.

This third point has two corollaries, sometimes overlooked or otherwise rendered harmless. Corollary one: Inasmuch as Jesus, like John, understood his mission to derive from the God of Israel and to have an eschatological (climactic and definitive) bearing on Israel's election/ salvation, he can hardly have conceived his mission either in terms of political revolution or in terms of mere religious reform. This partly a priori observation is solidly confirmed by examination of the relevant data, which are copious and interlocking. Jesus understood himself as *fulfiller*: the agent chosen to announce and bring about the final restoration of Israel promised in the scriptures.[16]

Corollary two: since the election-historical terms in which he conceived his mission meant that on it hinged the standing of Israel before God, Jesus was necessarily aware of an enormous risk. Refusal by Israel would convert a ministry of acquittal and restoration and life into a ministry of condemnation and ruin and death. In any such situation of refusal, what could be done for the refuser? Jesus' answer, his response to the prospect of refusal, was the resolve to offer his life not only to seal the new covenant but as a ransom and expiatory sacrifice for Israel and the world.[17]

Fourth and last point: Jesus' prophetic scenario projected a drama in two acts. Act one was the eschatological ordeal. His own death would launch it. It would engulf his disciples and, indeed, the whole nation, its capital and temple. Act two was the resolution of the ordeal by the glorification of the son of man, the pilgrimage of the world to Zion, the judgment, the banquet of the saved.[18]

These four points, here given necessarily swift and jejune formulation, allow us to hear Jesus' words in dramatic context and to

---

[16]   The hallmark of this restoration was set of reversals having both a pragmatic and a symbolic dimension. God was on the point of enriching the poor, consoling the mourners, giving the hungry their fill. Already Jesus was giving sight to the blind, mobility to the crippled, release to the possessed. These effective reversals, together with his startling initiatives toward notorious sinners, were all charged with symbolic meaning: all depressed classes—the poor and the ill, the sinners and the ostracized, women and children, the unimportant, unpowerful, and unpromising—imaged the situation of Israel vis-à-vis God. Salvation, in a word was to show, not that Israel was good, but that God was good.

[17]   See R. Pesch, *Das Abendmahl und Jesu Todesverstandnis* (Freiburg: Herder, 1978) 103-109.

[18]   See B. F. Meyer, *The Aims of Jesus* (London, SCM Press, 1979) 202-206.

attend to their diversity of tone and diverse exploitation of biblical resonance.

LOGOPOEIA

To return, then, to sayings we have already seen and heard, but now looking for instances of language charged by implicit allusion: "The reign of God is at hand!" To many, at least, who first heard it *qĕrabat malkûtā° dĕ°lāhā°* could hardly have failed to recall the news of salvation capsulated in the cry, *mālak °ĕlōhāik,* "your God reigns!" (Isa 52:7). John Gray may well be right in urging a cultic origin for this word and its proclamation: the great Autumn festival remembered by Deutero-Isaiah (Isa 52:7) and attested for pre-exilic Israel by Nahum (Nah 2:1).[19] But Jesus' evocation of *mālak °ĕlōhāik* struck the apocalyptic note that the word *mēlak* had already acquired in the Synagogue. The voice of the Isaian *mĕbaśśēr/euaggelizomenos* (Isa 52:7; cf. 61:1), anointed (Isa 61:1) to break news of salvation to Israel, declared God's definitive triumph: the end of the old world, the birth of the new. The heart of the news was the advent of restoration, the day Israel had prayed for every Sabbath in the *Qaddiš.*[20] Jesus was summoning the children of Abraham to welcome God's climactic saving act, summoning them to the banquet with the patriarchs (see *kalesai* in Matt 9:13 = Mark 2:17b = Luke 5:32; cf. Luke 14:16-17 and Matt 8:11-12 = Luke 13:28-29).

Paul Joüon long ago established the probability, confirmed by synonymous parallelism in Mark 1:15 and by such parallels as Luke 4:17-21, that the proclamation of Jesus announced the *presence* of the reign of God.[21] Salvation was now. God was already comforting his people, already redeeming Jerusalem (cf. Isa 52:9b).

Just as Isa 61:1-3 takes up and carries forward themes from Isa 52:7-10 (the texts, it is worth noting, are brought together in 11QMelch, along with parts of Leviticus 25, the Jubilee passage), so too the Synoptic tradition—especially the Lukan account of Jesus at Nazareth (Luke 4:17-21), the Lukan form of the beatitudes (Luke 6:20-21; cf. Matt 5:1-3), and the account of himself that Jesus sent to John (Matt 11:5 = Luke 7:22)—join together the motifs of Isaiah 52

---

[19]   J. Gray, *The Biblical Doctrine of the Reign of God* (Edinburgh: T. & T. Clark, 1979) 6, 11.

[20]   Meyer, *Aims of Jesus,* 134, 138.

[21]   Joüon, "Notes philologiques," 537-40. See also B. D. Chilton, "Regnum Dei Deus Est," *SJT* 31 (1978) 261-70.

and Isaiah 61, namely, the reign of God (Isa 52:7), the news of salvation (Isa 52:7; 61:1), and the poor, the mourners, the captives as its beneficiaries (Isa 61:1-3). The latter parts of Isaiah resonate equally in Jesus' proclamation (*qĕrabat malkûtā᾽ dĕ᾽lāhā᾽*), in his "Happy the poor" (*tûbêhôn miskĕnayyā᾽, dĕdilĕhôn malkûtā᾽ dĕ᾽lāhā᾽*) and in the lyric staccato of his answer to John (Matt 11:5 = Luke 7:22).[22] But Jesus' *malkûtā᾽ dĕ᾽lāhā᾽* for the poor appealed to more than the isolated text of Isaiah 61; it evoked the entire ῾*ănāwîm* tradition that got under way with Jeremiah, Zephaniah, and the Psalms and lived on even when classical prophecy died out. In Jesus' words and acts in favor of the simple, the afflicted, and the outcast[23] global logopoeia of this kind was recurrent.

We go now to the called and the chosen: *saggî᾽în dĕ᾽innûn zĕmînîn wĕṣibḥad dĕ᾽innûn bĕḥîrîn*. This, of course, has long been a *crux interpretum*. In 1952 a French Benedictine, Edmond Boissard, offered a solution to the scandal that Jesus seems to say that only a few would be saved.[24] The positive forms "many" and "few," he argued, were played off against one another precisely so as to yield a comparative sense: "many" became "more" and "few" became "fewer." This semantic particularity may be illustrated by Gen 1:16, where the two "great lights," the sun and the moon, were "great" by comparison with the stars: they were the *major* lights, or "*greater* lights." Moreover the text went on to specify "the great light to rule the day" and "the small light to rule the night." Again, great and small were positive in form, comparative in sense: greater and smaller. This Semitic usage may be named the correlative comparative. If it is true that *polloi* and *oligoi* in Matt 22:14 represent this idiom, the hitherto baffling scandal of the text is dissipated. The "chosen," and hence saved, are simply "fewer" than the "called." As Boissard put it, "to be chosen, it does not suffice to be called," or again, "not all are chosen."[25]

If Boissard's solution has not been widely adopted it must be because he failed to illustrate the correlative comparative by the

---

[22]   Jeremias, *New Testament Theology*, 197-98. See also the good observation on Isaiah 61 in Matthew and Luke by D. C. Allison, Jr., "Jesus and the Covenant," *JSNT* 29 (1987) 57-78, at 77 n. 29.

[23]   See Meyer, *Aims of Jesus*, 171-72.

[24]   E. Boissard, "Note sur l'interprétation du texte 'Multi sunt vocati, pauci vero electi," *Revue Thomiste* 52 (1952) 569-85.

[25]   Boissard, "Note sur l'interprétation," 581.

precise words "many" and "few" (*rab* and *mĕ͏ʿaṭ* in Hebrew, *polus* and *oligos* in Greek). But since we do in fact have instances of this usage in Hebrew and in Greek translation (e.g. Num 26:52-56; LXX Num 26:54-56; see also Exod 16:17-18 in MT and LXX),[26] Boissard's solution is probably correct. Only one addition to it must be made: Joachim Jeremias's observation that here the referent of *polloi* is inclusive.[27] Accordingly the sense of Jesus' saying is: "All are called, but not all are chosen." And now what becomes clear is that we have to do with quite a different scandal. In Isa 48:12 Israel is "my called one" (*mĕqōrāʾî*); in Isa 49:7 the phrase "who has chosen you" is almost an epithet of the LORD. Judaism, selectively echoing the Law and the prophets, was entirely at home with: all Israel is called and chosen. By logopoeia with reverse English, Jesus said: called, yes, chosen, that depends. That depends on whether the response to this eschatological, i.e. climactic and definitive, mission is yes or no.

The tone is not sorrowful but severe. The word is a warning that recalls the Baptist's sharp admonition to Israel (Matt 3:9 = Luke 3:8); and it is richly paralleled, filled as the Synoptic tradition is with sharp warnings against the reigning soteriological optimism. See the "this generation" texts (e.g. Mark 8:12, 38; 9:19; Matt 11:16; 12:39; Luke 11:30, 50; 17:25); add thereto the words addressed to scoffers (Luke 17:26-27 = Matt 24:37-39); the images of the unwitting bird about to be snared (Luke 21:34), the salt that has lost its savor (Matt 5:13 = Luke 14:34), the barren fig tree (Luke 13:6-9).

As eschatological mission, heavy with consequence, to be accepted or rejected, defined Jesus' dramatic role: "that of mediator of God's final controversy with his people."[28] The prospect of rejection, the theme in which the Caesarea Philippi pericopes climax, entailed numerous consequences. One of the most deadly of them—potential desertion by his followers—prompted a new call to discipleship: "If anyone wishes to follow me, let him deny himself and take up his cross, and (so) follow me" (Matt 16:24 = Mark 8:34 = Luke 9:23).

---

[26] See my study, "Many (=All) are Called, but Few (=Not All) are Chosen," *NTS* 36 (1990) 89-97.

[27] J. Jeremias, "πολλοί," *TDNT* 6 (1968) 542.

[28] A. N. Wilder, "Eschatology and the Speech-Modes of the Gospel," in E. Dinkler (ed.), *Zeit und Geschichte* (R. Bultmann Festschrift; Tübingen: Mohr [Siebeck], 1964) 19-30, here 29.

First, we may take up line one: *kol man dibāʿê měhallākâ bātěray
. . .* To walk behind or follow after is a biblicism (*hālak ʾăḥēr*)
denoting allegiance. But perhaps we should recall here that the
Palestinian shepherd walked before his flock when taking the sheep
out to pasture.[29] "Come after" in the phrase "if anyone would come
after me" might accordingly suggest the correlation of this text with
those in which Jesus, drawing on the tradition of the messianic
shepherd in Ezekiel and Zechariah (Ezek 34:23-24; 37:24; Zech
13:7-9; cf. 12:10; 13:1-6), explicitly presented himself in the
shepherd image: "I was sent only to the lost sheep that are the house
of Israel" (Matt 15:24); or, I have "come to seek and save the lost
[sheep], (Luke 19:10; cf. 15:3-7); or, "You will all fall away, for it is
written, 'I will strike the shepherd and the sheep will be scattered'"
(Mark 14:27 = Matt 26:31) and, most significant parallel of all,
complementary to the preceding text and so evoking the shepherd
leading the previously scattered flock: "I will go before you into
Galilee" (Matt 26:32 = Mark 14:28; cf. John 10:4).[30] If there is a
submerged shepherd imagery here, its effect is simply to invest the
motif of the following of Jesus with messianic connotations.

Now consider lines two and three: the point of the present saying
is to name a new condition of discipleship in the face of the
impending ordeal: heroic willingness to accept expulsion from
society as the cost of discipleship. Such expulsion—a prospect for
disciples of a rejected Messiah—was caught perfectly in the image of
the condemned man at the moment when, taking the crossbar on his
shoulder to carry it to the place of execution, he turns to face the
contemptuous throng that has disowned him. The tone is one of
challenge. Are you ready for this? The second and third lines of the
saying,

yikpōr běgarmēh wěyiṭʿan ṣělîbēh	let him deny himself and take up his cross
wěyêtê bātěray	and (so) follow me

are unparalleled in biblical tradition.

The same generic situation is reflect in the *qînâ*-quatrain:

*man dibĕʿăʾ lěḥayyāʾ â napšēh / môbēd yātah
ûman děmôbēd napšēh běginnî / mēḥayyê yātah*

---

29   G. Dalman, "Arbeit und Sitte in Palästina VI," *BFCT* 2.41 (1939) 249-50,
253-55.

30   Jeremias, *New Testament Theology*, 297-98.

whoever is set on saying his life / will lose it
and whoever loses his life for my sake / will save it

This eschatological riddle (Mark 8:35 = Luke 9:24; cf. Luke 17:33; Matt 10:39; 16:25; John 12:25), seen in context, is a mystagogue: Jesus invites his disciples into the messianic mystery of his own death and life. The first half warns the disciples against apostasy under pressure. It too is without parallel in biblical tradition. And though, for that matter, there is no truly close parallel to the lapidary antithesis of the second half, its major premise—the blessing of life for the faithful—pervades the Law and the prophets. It is grounded in the theme of the living God (*'ĕlōhîm ḥayyîm*, Deut 5:26; Josh 3:10; 1 Sam 17:26, 36; 2 Kgs 19:4, 10; Isa 37:4; Jer 10:10; 23:36; Ps 84:3) who has life in himself and lives forever; from whom all life comes; who gives life to his people; and who is himself this life (Jer 2:13; 17:13; Ps 36:9).

In the Gospels the imposing themes of the Lord of life (Job 34:14-15; Ps 104:29-30) who made to live and who made to die (Deut 32:39) remained in the background (Matt 10:28 = Luke 12:5). But the field of meaning that implicitly, inauthentically defined and energized the mission of Jesus could only be made thematic by themes of life. Outside the ambit of his saving mission there was only death and the dead (Matt 8:22 = Luke 9:60). Themes of life were subjacent to the Gospels' language of "saving"[31] and would find adequate expression in Johannine theology as well as in the early community's description of Jesus as "prince (of life)" (Acts 3:15; 5:31) and "savior" (Luke 2:11; Acts 5:31; 13:23).

Jesus' word on saving one's life and losing it, losing it on his account and saving it, affirmed (in the new context of this age and the age to come) the age-old orthodoxy of life as God's blessing on the faithful. This held, said Jesus, even for the dreadful situation that would be produced by his death.[32] Those who persevered in their allegiance to him would not escape death—and still they would live! Here logopoeia in a broad sense lay in the act of setting the imminent ordeal under the sign of a great scriptural theme.

---

[31]   On the Aramaic substratum of gospel texts using the language of "saving/salvation," see P. Joüon, "Quelques aramaïsmes sousjacents au grec des Évangiles," *RSR* 17 (1927) 210-29, esp. 225-27.

[32]   Jeremias, *New Testament Theology*, 127-28, with reference especially to Luke 22:53; 23:28-31; also p. 241, with reference especially to Luke 22:35-38.

Finally, in words spoken by Jesus in his last week of his earthly
life his distinctive scenario of the future came to expression on
several occasions. These words drew on a wide range of biblical
resources. I shall cite only one of the them: the warning word of
Jesus to the High Priest, in its Lukan form, slightly revised:

mikkĕʾan bar ʾĕnāšāʾ / yātēb min yammînāʾ digĕbûrătā,[33]
Soon the Son of man / will be seated at the right hand of Power.

The word evoked judgment. Through *bar ʾĕnāšāʾ* and the motif of
judgment there shone the scene of Daniel 7. But in Luke 22:69
(contrast the parallels in Matt 26:64 and Mark 14:62) only the words
ho huios tou anthrōpou / bar ʾĕnāšāʾ reflect the wording of Daniel 7.
Having two facets, the saying strikes two notes: one of assurance, one
of warning. Here Jesus affirmed that *bar ʾĕnāšāʾ* would vindicate his
messianic mission; by the same words he warned that *bar ʾĕnāšāʾ*
would confront his judge as judge. This would happen *mikkʾān* or
min kaddûn—a word that the Lukan text renders by *apo tou nun*, but
the most obvious sense of which is "soon." Jesus would be vindicated
soon; his judges would meet judgment soon. This "soon" appears to
be unfulfilled prophecy;[34] for that very reason it savors strongly of
historical authenticity. The word yields a glimpse of how Jesus saw
the promise of Daniel 7: the triumph of God would subsume and
sublate the triumph of justice.

CONCLUSION

As rhetorician, Jesus was a moderate. He was a skilled but sober
phanopoeist. He was equally proficient and equally restrained as
melopoeist. Visual imagery and the orchestration of sound were kept
rigorously functional to a unique mission, covertly sublime, delicate
and dangerous. It was the mission of a prince sent to his people in the
guise of a commoner commissioned to fire their allegiances against
the day when he would be revealed and enthroned as their rightful
king.

---

[33]   If *min yammînāʾ* is a deliberate allusion to Ps 110:1 (and it probably is) this
text would offer a base from which to reconsider the historicity of Matt 22:41-46 =
Mark 12:35-37a = Luke 20:41-44.

[34]   On the issue of historicity in such cases, see Jeremias, *New Testament
Theology*, 2, 139-40. But, while acknowledging the evidential value for historicity
of "non-fulfillment," I would set the entire matter of seeming non-fulfillment in the
context of the traits of prophetic knowledge generally and of the prophetic knowledge of Jesus in particular. See Meyer, *Aims of Jesus*, 245-49.

The going-awry of this scenario was itself hidden piecemeal in the scriptures. The originality of Jesus as logopoeist lay less in implicit allusion as a technique than in the vision of things fashioned by his choice and articulation of biblical themes. True, the technique belongs to rhetoric; the vision does not. But rhetoric does give access to the vision. Only the Son knows the Father; and he has taken great pains, including rhetorical pains, to reveal him.

THE IMPLICATIONS OF TEXTUAL VARIANTS FOR
AUTHENTICATING THE WORDS OF JESUS

Stanley E. Porter and Matthew Brook O'Donnell

1. INTRODUCTION

Textual variants in the words of Jesus in the Synoptic Gospels are neglected in recent research regarding the historical Jesus. It is true that when various, specific passages are discussed in Historical Jesus research, there is usually reference to pertinent variants, such as in a kingdom saying or a parable or a pronouncement of Jesus. For example, in an article on Matt 23:39 = Luke 15:35b, Dale Allison notes in his first footnote that there is variation in wording in these verses, and cites manuscript evidence, returning to this later in his article.[1] This is only to be expected in exegetical work focusing upon the text of the New Testament. Almost inevitably, since they are confined to individual passages, these comments must be limited in what they say about a given variant, since the variant is not seen within any larger context, such as the patterns of variants in a manuscript. However, if dealing with pertinent variants in a single passage is important to doing Historical Jesus research then it would seem logical to think that exploration of the entire complex of the words of Jesus with regard to their textual variants would also be important. We will return to specific areas where such variants might play a particularly important role, but they would certainly seem to have relevance for many of the traditional criteria of authenticity, specifically that of multiple attestation (is a saying, including particular words or phrases, found in more than one independent source?).[2] We have chosen this criterion because it has a closer relation to the wording of the text than do others, such as

---

[1]   D. C. Allison, Jr, "Matthew 23.39 = Luke 13.35B as a Conditional Prophecy," *JSNT* 18 (1983) 75-84, repr. in C. A. Evans and S. E. Porter (eds.), *The Historical Jesus: A Sheffield Reader* (BibSem 33; Sheffield: Sheffield Academic Press, 1995) 262-70.

[2]   See J. P. Meier, *A Marginal Jew: Rethinking the Historical Jesus*. I. *The Roots of the Problem and the Person* (ABRL; New York: Doubleday, 1991) 168-75. We will return to the criterion regarding Aramaic elements, as well.

historical coherence, for example. So far as it can be determined from the pertinent secondary literature, however, this kind and degree of interest is not the case among contemporary Historical Jesus scholars.

To our knowledge, there is no systematic or extended study of how any given variant is to be seen within the context of all of the variants of the words of Jesus in the Gospels. For example, in the recent comprehensive study of Life of Jesus research by Craig Evans, there is no major study mentioned or described as devoting a sizable portion of its content to considering matters of textual variation.[3] Two sections of Evans's volume are of particular relevance for this topic. The historical survey of general discussion of Historical Jesus research does not mention any study that takes the variants in the words of Jesus as a central item of consideration. The section on special topics, with two pertinent sub-sections, one on criteria of authenticity and the other on the teaching of Jesus, reveals a similar situation, with no specific study devoted to this subject. Similarly, the cumulative bibliography on Markan research by Neirynck *et al.* has an index entry for textual criticism, with reference to numerous studies on specific Markan passages. However, under general studies, there is none mentioned that specifically addresses the question of textual variants in the words of Jesus.[4] This situation is further confirmed by two recent collections of essays on various dimensions of Historical Jesus research. In the important predecessor to the volume in which this essay appears, *Studying the Historical Jesus*, there is no single study of the variants of the words of Jesus, but there is at least one essay where one might at least expect to find the issue mentioned. The essay on "Major Trends and Interpretive Issues in the Study of Jesus"[5] is where one might reasonably expect to find mention of textual criticism of the words of Jesus as an issue in current research. Apparently it is not, since

---

3   C. A. Evans, *Life of Jesus Research: An Annotated Bibliography* (NTTS 24; Leiden: Brill, 2nd edn, 1996).

4   F. Neirynck *et al.*, *The Gospel of Mark: A Cumulative Bibliography 1950–1990* (BETL 102; Leuven: Peeters and Leuven University Press, 1992) esp. 628-29.

5   W. R. Telford, "Major Trends and Interpretive Issues in the Study of Jesus," in B. Chilton and C. A. Evans (eds.), *Studying the Historical Jesus: Evaluations of the State of Current Research* (NTTS 19; Leiden: Brill, 1994) 33-74.

Telford gives no significant mention to this topic.[6] A recent collection of essays extracted from the last twenty years or so of publication of a major journal in New Testament studies confirms this picture. There are essays on topics and exegetical issues. There is even a section on linguistic and stylistic aspects of Jesus' teaching, but apart from one essay (to which we will refer below), all of these essays confine themselves to a particular phrase or pericope.[7]

One of the few works to address the question of textual criticism in Jesus research is Norman Perrin's *Jesus and the Language of the Kingdom*. In it, he addresses the importance of textual criticism as the first step in the hermeneutical process: "we begin by establishing the text to be interpreted."[8] In his volume, he is concerned with language about the kingdom, and thus proceeds to analyze previous work in this regard, in each instance starting by summarizing what previous scholars have done in the area of textual criticism, before analyzing their use of historical criticism, in order to get to his area of major interest, literary criticism. In the area of parable research, he notes that work on textual criticism has been done, seeing this as the best possible arena for viewing "the problems and possibilities" of the hermeneutical approach that he is advocating. He first looks at Jeremias, concluding that "it is to Jeremias above all others that we owe our present ability to reconstruct the parables very much in the form in which Jesus told them."[9] Whereas Jeremias was, according to Perrin, the one to whom so much is owed in this regard, the same cannot be said of subsequent interpreters. Perrin concludes that, with regard to textual criticism, the New Hermeneutic of Fuchs, Linnemann and Jüngel "has little to offer,"[10] simply following the

---

[6]   Another essay where one might hope to find such an issue discussed is S. E. Porter, "Jesus and the Use of Greek in Galilee," in Chilton and Evans (eds.), *Studying the Historical Jesus*, 123-54. It is not discussed there.

[7]   Porter and Evans (eds.), *The Historical Jesus* (see above, note 1).

[8]   N. Perrin, *Jesus and the Language of the Kingdom: Symbol and Metaphor in New Testament Interpretation* (NTL; London: SCM Press, 1976) 2.

[9]   Perrin, *Jesus and the Language*, 101, citing J. Jeremias, *The Parables of Jesus* (New York: Scribners, 2nd rev. edn, 1972).

[10]   Perrin, *Jesus and the Language*, 120, citing E. Fuchs, *Studies of the Historical Jesus* (SBT 42; London: SCM Press, 1964); E. Linnemann, *Jesus of the Parables* (New York: Harper & Row, 1966); E. Jüngel, *Paulus und Jesus* (Tübingen: Mohr [Siebeck], 1962).

work of Jeremias, as did Funk and his metaphorical interpretation,[11] and Via.[12] It is with the work of Crossan, according to Perrin, that "the most important work since Jeremias" is done in "establishing the text to be interpreted."[13] Two comments may be made about Perrin's work. The first is that, on the basis of our research, it is exceptional in this regard. For example, two recent articles on the state of research regarding the parables of Jesus and the kingdom of God in Jesus research do not mention textual criticism as an area of concern or importance for the topic.[14] The second is that, even with Perrin's concern, what he seems to mean by textual criticism is the minimalist agenda of establishing the parameters of the extent of Jesus' words, such as whether he spoke Luke 16:9-13 in the Parable of the Unjust Steward.

In a recent study of the Life of Jesus in a handbook to exegesis, Craig Evans deals ably with source, form and redaction criticism, but does not treat textual criticism. This chapter on exegesis perhaps reveals the reason for neglect of this area. In his discussion of the practice of exegesis, Evans turns to linguistic aspects. He rightly states that "Linguistic study is closely tied to several, and perhaps in some cases all, of the dimensions of Jesus research." He also rightly notes that four languages were used in Palestine (Aramaic, Greek, Hebrew and Latin, in their order of usage among Jews), but states his judgment that Jesus' "mother tongue was Aramaic and that he could converse in Greek, but normally did not teach in it."[15] He then goes on to give examples of linguistic aspects, virtually all of which reflect an Aramaic retroversion, and how knowledge of Aramaic helps to understand a particular passage in the Gospels. When Evans turns to Jesus' teaching, he discusses parables, again noting how

---

[11]   Perrin, *Jesus and the Language*, 132, citing R. W. Funk, *Language, Hermeneutic, and Word of God* (New York: Harper & Row, 1966).

[12]   Perrin, *Jesus and the Language*, 153, citing D. O. Via, Jr, *The Parables: Their Literary and Existential Dimension* (Philadelphia: Fortress Press, 1967).

[13]   Perrin, *Jesus and the Language*, 166, citing J. D. Crossan, *In Parables: The Challenge of the Historical Jesus* (New York: Harper & Row, 1973).

[14]   See C. L. Blomberg, "The Parables of Jesus: Current Trends and Needs in Research," in Chilton and Evans (eds.), *Studying the Historical Jesus*, 231-54; and B. Chilton, "The Kingdom of God in Recent Discussion," in Chilton and Evans (eds.), *Studying the Historical Jesus*, 255-80.

[15]   C. A. Evans, "Life of Jesus," in S. E. Porter (ed.), *Handbook to Exegesis of the New Testament* (NTTS 25; Leiden: Brill, 1997) 447.

much Jesus' parables have in common with those of the rabbis; proverbs, where he begins with one that supposedly is found verbatim in the Babylonian Talmud (*b. Ber.* 8b); and prayers, where parallels with Jewish literature are drawn. In other words, when the linguistic dimensions of the words of Jesus are discussed among contemporary Historical Jesus scholars, the tendency is to discuss the Aramaic words of Jesus, not the Greek words. One can understand this tendency from Evans's analysis. If Jesus taught in Aramaic, not Greek, textual criticism can easily be dismissed or not even considered, since it is confined at best to variants in the translated words of Jesus, that is, the concepts represented by the words in Greek, though delivered in Aramaic.

This emphasis upon the Aramaic words of Jesus is consistent with one of the major criteria that has evolved in Historical Jesus research. For some time, the Aramaic hypothesis has clearly dominated the verbal dimension of Historical Jesus research. A quick overview of the history of this discussion might well be instructive, however. Many of the early proponents of the Aramaic hypothesis, that is, those who argued that Aramaic was a significant language of Jesus and merited study to understand his teaching, were not exclusively given to the Aramaic hypothesis. Such authors as Nestle, Wellhausen, Dalman and Blass discussed Aramaic retroversions and features of New Testament Greek within the context of the wider use of Koine Greek.[16] For example, Dalman puts the use of Aramaic within the context of widespread use of Greek in Palestine, both in Jerusalem and in Galilee. Even the next generation of proponents of a form of the Aramaic hypothesis, such as Torrey, who advocated the translation hypothesis, that is, that the Gospels and other portions of the New Testament were translated from Aramaic into Greek, gave due recognition to the place of Greek in relation to Aramaic, an approach also recognized to varying degrees by other scholars of the

---

[16]   See E. Nestle, *Philologica Sacra: Bemerkungen über die Urgestalt der Evangelien und Apostelgeschichte* (Berlin: Reuther & Reichard, 1896); F. Blass, *Philology of the Gospels* (London: Macmillan, 1898); J. Wellhausen, *Einleitung in die drei ersten Evangelien* (Berlin: Reimer, 2nd edn, 1911) esp. 7-32; G. Dalman, *The Words of Jesus: Considered in the Light of Post-Biblical Jewish Writings and the Aramaic Language* (trans. D. M. Kay; Edinburgh: T. & T. Clark, 1909); *idem, Jesus–Jeshua: Studies in the Gospels* (trans. P. P. Levertoff; London: SPCK, 1929).

time, such as de Zwaan.[17] Nevertheless, these two generations of scholars were criticized, even by those who later advocated an Aramaic hypothesis, for failing to be as rigorous or convincing as was methodologically desirable.

The third generation did not go as far into unbridled speculation as had some of the earlier generations, but the major shift was to an almost exclusive concentration upon the Aramaic language, to the virtual exclusion of Greek, in looking at the language of Jesus. This shift can be traced in a number of representative writers. For example, T. W. Manson, in his *The Teaching of Jesus*, makes the following telling remark, one which represents the resulting tradition:

> At this point a new problem—the linguistic—arises. Up to this point we are dealing with Greek Gospels . . . But the mother-tongue of our Lord and the Apostles was not Greek but Galilean Aramaic, so that, even if we could push the analysis of the Greek evidence to its farthest limit, we should be left with the hazardous enterprise of retranslation in order to get back to the *ipsissima verba* of Jesus; and, at the end, we should have no certainty that anything more than an Aramaic Targum of the Greek had been produced. More than that, it may be questioned whether the result would be worth the labour involved.[18]

Matthew Black's *An Aramaic Approach to the Gospels and Acts* became, in many ways, the standard authority in discussion of this issue. First published in 1946, and then supplemented with further essays in two later versions of 1954 and 1967, Black's work illustrates the change in perspective.[19] In chap. 1 on "Previous Work on the Aramaic of the Gospels and Acts," he begins with the assumption of the Aramaic hypothesis, citing the work of predecessors, especially Dalman. Although he mentions Greek in his second

---

[17]   C. C. Torrey, *Our Translated Gospels: Some of the Evidence* (Cambridge, MA: Harvard University Press, 1916); *idem, The Four Gospels: A New Translation* (New Haven: Yale University Press, 1958); J. de Zwaan, "The Use of the Greek Language in Acts," in F. J. Foakes Jackson and K. Lake (eds.), *The Beginnings of Christianity* II. (London: Macmillan, 1922) 30-65.

[18]   T. W. Manson, *The Teaching of Jesus: Studies of its Form and Content* (Cambridge: Cambridge University Press, 1939) 10-11. Note that after mentioning retranslation above, Manson cites Dalman's *The Words of Jesus* and *Jesus–Jeshua* on retranslation.

[19]   M. Black, *An Aramaic Approach to the Gospels and Acts* (Oxford: Clarendon Press, 1946; 2nd edn, 1954; 3rd edn, 1967).

chapter, his linguistic and textual approach is virtually entirely dedicated to discussion of Aramaic. His chapter on textual variants (chap. 8 in the first edition, chap. 9 in the third edition) is focused completely on Aramaic as a cause of these variants, of which he mentions four.[20] In his *New Testament Theology*, another hallmark work in the ongoing discussion of Jesus and his language, Jeremias goes so far as to speak of the Greek of the New Testament being so heavily Semiticized that it must have been felt to be "unattractive" and "in need of improvement" to readers in a Hellenistic setting.[21] Noting Dalman's demonstration of the Aramaic dialect of Jesus, Jeremias then discusses the words of Jesus in these terms. Thus, in the light of this palpable shift to Aramaic, as well as further discussion of who Jesus was, especially typifying him as a Galilean peasant,[22] it is not surprising that very recently Funk *et al.* state that:

> Accordingly, *if Jesus spoke only in Aramaic*, his original words have been lost forever. The words of Jesus recorded in the gospels are thus at best a translation from Aramaic into Greek or some other ancient tongue.[23]

One can readily understand the current neglect of attention to variants in the Greek words of Jesus in the Gospels, since there has been a progressive marginalization of Greek and elevation of Aramaic, despite the fact that the evidence itself has not changed, only the ideological and methodological framework in which the evidence is treated, with some of the earliest scholars who advocated consideration of Aramaic, yet within a context in which Greek also was seen to be important, being marshalled as support for what now amounts to an almost exclusive Aramaic hypothesis.[24] The result can only be that the Greek text of the New Testament, which has the

---

[20]   It is interesting to note that an example discussed by Black at the beginning of this chapter in the first edition (*Aramaic Approach*, 1st edn, 178-79) is deleted in the third edition (*Aramaic Approach*, 3rd edn, 244).

[21]   J. Jeremias, *New Testament Theology* (trans. J. Bowden; London: SCM Press, 1971) 3.

[22]   See J. D. Crossan, *The Historical Jesus: The Life of a Mediterranean Jewish Peasant* (San Francisco: HarperSan Francisco, 1992).

[23]   R. W. Funk *et al.*, *The Parables of Jesus: Red Letter Edition* (Sonoma, CA: Polebridge, 1988) 2, emphasis added.

[24]   For a history of this discussion, see S. E. Porter, "The Greek of the New Testament as a Disputed Area of Research," in S. E. Porter (ed.), *The Language of the New Testament: Classic Essays* (JSNTSup 60; Sheffield: JSOT Press, 1991) 11-38.

textual variants, is reduced in significance, since it is not the words of Jesus in this text that are being discussed, but the thoughts of Jesus that lie behind them.

In recent discussion, however, the Aramaic hypothesis has come into question among a number of scholars. For example, Meier has noted that it does not suffice as an adequate criterion for distinguishing the words of Jesus for two major reasons. The first is that other early Christians also spoke Aramaic, so that Jesus may have said something in Aramaic, but so may have others. Even those who claim that they can retrovert into Aramaic from Greek may still be left without a basis for authenticating words of Jesus. The second criticism is the question of retroversion itself. Whether a saying does or does not go easily into Aramaic actually says nothing about whether an Aramaic source lies behind a statement of Jesus in Greek.[25] This has been adequately demonstrated in an incisive essay by Larry Hurst, in his demonstration that translation is a far more complex process, and rarely relies on word for word equivalence between languages.[26] This criterion is further threatened by the evidence that Jesus himself may have used Greek in some of his teaching, and almost assuredly in some conversation. It is often forgotten in recent discussion of the Aramaic hypothesis that Dalman himself, for example, stated that:

> We have a perfect right to assume that Pilate, in putting the question to our Lord: "Art though the King of the Jews?", did not need to use an interpreter, and that our Lord answered him in the same language: "Thou sayest" (Mk. xv. 2 f.; Mt. xxvii. 11; Lk. xxiii. 3), even though the form of the answer emanates less from the Greek than from the Semitic idiom (cf. Mt. xxvi. 64).[27]

In addition, Manson states that, though Jesus' knowledge of Greek was perhaps minimal, the one occasion "when he may perhaps have spoken in Greek is in the trial before Pilate."[28]

---

[25] Meier, *Marginal Jew*, 1.178-79.

[26] L. D. Hurst, "The Neglected Role of Semantics in the Search for the Aramaic Words of Jesus," *JSNT* 28 (1986) 63-80, repr. in Evans and Porter (eds.), *Historical Jesus*, 219-36.

[27] Dalman, *Jesus–Jeshua*, 6.

[28] Manson, *Teaching*, 46. Cf., e.g., the significant article by J. A. Fitzmyer, "The Languages of Palestine in the First Century AD," in his *Wandering Aramean: Collected Aramaic Essays* (Missoula, MT: Scholars Press, 1979) 29-56, repr. in Porter (ed.), *Language*, 126-62; and D. Dormeyer, *The New Testament among the*

If this criterion is, therefore, under serious threat, it is perhaps legitimate to wonder if an investigation of the textual variants in the Greek words of Jesus in the Gospels might well bring others into needed question, in an attempt to clarify them and their use. Below we will look specifically at the criterion of multiple attestation below, since comparison of the Greek text is often involved in the use of this criteron.

2. CLASSIFYING THE VARIANTS IN THE WORDS OF JESUS

As noted above, there are a number of individual studies, as well as those within larger works such as commentaries, that note particular textual variants. However, there does not appear to be any inclusive study of the variants in the sayings of Jesus in the Synoptic Gospels. There are, of course, individual studies of particular text-critical phenomena, especially works written from the perspective of traditional textual criticism[29] and Metzger's important *Textual Commentary* on the UBSGNT, but these are not thorough, systematic or complete.[30]

In order to be able to generalize about variants in the words of Jesus, one must begin with a means of gathering all of these data together. Starting with Nestle and Aland's twenty-seventh edition of the Greek New Testament, we have coded each textual variant in the three Synoptic Gospels, along with the Greek witnesses to each variant. We realize that there are inherent limitations in this method, the primary one being that even the Nestle–Aland[27]'s thorough

---

Writings of Antiquity (BibSem 55; Sheffield: Sheffield Academic Press, 1997) 67-75.

[29] A sampling of major works includes G. D. Kilpatrick, *The Principles and Practice of New Testament Textual Criticism: Collected Essays* (ed. J. K. Elliott; BETL 96; Leuven: Peeters and Leuven University Press, 1990); J. K. Elliott, *Essays and Studies in New Testament Textual Criticism* (Estudios de Filología Neotestamentaria 3; Córdoba: Ediciones El Almendro, 1992); and E. J. Epp and G. D. Fee, *Studies in the Theory and Method of New Testament Textual Criticism* (SD 45; Grand Rapids: Eerdmans, 1993).

[30] B. M. Metzger, *A Textual Commentary on the Greek New Testament* (London: United Bible Societies, 1971; Stuttgart: Deutsche Bibelgesellschaft/United Bible Societies, 2nd edn, 1994). In some ways, this is understandable, since textual criticism of the New Testament documents is designed to study the manuscripts themselves, not to make distinctions between the kinds of material within these manuscripts, such as the words of Jesus versus narrative.

number of variants is far from complete in either the number of variants listed or the witnesses cited in the critical apparatus.[31] At this stage in text-critical research, however, it is the most complete and reliable source available. Nevertheless, we have come to realize in the course of our work with this edition that it does have a number of inhibiting inconsistencies and limitations, such as failure to be consistent in its cited witnesses, including presentation of the textual basis for what they have printed. We have also followed the Synoptic section numbers of the Huck–Lietzmann synopsis as revised by Cross, with the number given in parentheses following each reference (e.g. Matt 4:10 [8]).[32]

For each variant,[33] we have classified it according to the following set of categories: addition/insertion, subtraction/omission, lexical differentiation/replacement, morphological alteration (e.g. tense-form (aspect), mood, voice, case, number), and syntax, usually pertaining to word order, although other complex variants are included here as well. Each of these can be illustrated briefly.

1. Addition/Insertion

Addition or insertion occurs when one or more other manuscript witnesses add or insert a word or more to the text that is given in the Nestle–Aland[27] text.

(a) Matt 4:10 (8). Jesus is recorded as saying to Satan, ὕπαγε, σατανᾶ, read in ℵ B C*vid K P W Δ 0233 f[1, 13] 565 579* 700 892*vid. The variant, adding the words ὀπίσω μου after the verb, is found in C² D L Z 33 Majority text. There is no verbal equivalent in the parallel passage at Luke 4:8. There are two reasons for rejecting this variant, with the second apparently the one endorsed by the committee.[34] One is the inferior quality of the textual witness,

---

[31] A number of the places where the Nestle–Aland[27] fails to cite pertinent manuscripts are cited in S. E. Porter and W. J. Porter, *The New Testament Greek Papyri and Parchments: New Editions* (MPER 28; Vienna: Austrian National Library, forthcoming 1999).

[32] A. Huck, *Synopsis of the First Three Gospels* (rev. H. Lietzmann and F.L. Cross; Oxford: Blackwell, 9th edn, 1949).

[33] On how to define a textual variant, see E. J. Epp, "Toward the Clarification of the Term 'Textual Variant'," in Epp and Fee, *Studies*, 47-61.

[34] See Metzger, *Textual Commentary*, 2nd edn, 10. This reading received an A rating in the UBSGNT⁴, having received a B in all of the previous editions. On questions raised by the rating system of the UBSGNT, see K. D. Clarke, *Textual Optimism: A Critique of the United Bible Societies' Greek New Testament*

confined to Western and Byzantine readings, and the other is the parallel in Matt 16:23, which, according to the Nestle–Aland²⁷ apparatus, does not have variants but does include this phrase.

(b) Mark 3:3 (70). Jesus is recorded as telling the man with the withered hand to ἔγειρε εἰς τὸ μέσον. The variant adds the words καὶ στῆθι, found in D and at the parallel in Luke 6:8. Luke 6:8 is not listed as having a variant, thus making no attempt to omit any of the words of the fuller command. Nestle–Aland²⁷ apparently rejects this reading on the basis of the limited textual witness and the thought that this is an attempt at harmonization.

2. Subtraction/Omission

Subtraction or omission occurs when one or more other manuscript witnesses subtract or omit a word or more from the text that is given in the Nestle–Aland²⁷.

(a) Matt 5:16 (20). In the Sermon on the Mount, Jesus says that his hearers' light should shine so that people might see τὰ καλὰ ἔργα. The word ἔργα is omitted in B*. This variant is obviously rejected because of its limited textual witnesses, although Nestle–Aland²⁷ does not say specifically which texts do have the fuller reading.

(b) Mark 8:35 (123). Jesus reportedly tells his listeners that whoever loses his soul on account of ἐμοῦ καὶ τοῦ εὐαγγελίου will save it. The manuscripts that contain this reading are not metioned by Nestle–Aland²⁷, but, on the basis of other variants in the verse and the witnesses cited, perhaps include A B C. There are two variants in this verse that involve subtraction or omission. Some manuscripts omit ἐμοῦ καί (𝔓⁴⁵ D 28 700), while others omit καὶ τοῦ εὐαγγελίου (33 579). Both Synoptic parallels have simply ἐμοῦ (Matt 26:25; Luke 9:24), neither with variants listed. This variant is not discussed in Metzger's textual commentary, but the reading is perhaps one that could be called into question. The evidence of 𝔓⁴⁵ and D would tend to argue for omission of ἐμοῦ καί, while the parallels would tend to endorse omission of καὶ τοῦ εὐαγγελίου. The fuller reading is probably a conflation.

3. Lexical Differentiation/Replacement

Lexical differentiation or replacement involves the substitution of a different lexical item or items into the text, taking the place of an item or items that are already in the text. The substitution of

(JSNTSup 138; Sheffield: Sheffield Academic Press, 1997).

prepositions is fairly common as a textual variant in this category.

(a) Matt 5:39 (26). Jesus says regarding retaliation that if someone strikes you εἰς the right cheek, you are to turn to him the other, with ℵ* B W. The preposition ἐπί is used in ℵ² D L Θ f¹, ¹³ 33 Majority text. Nestle–Aland²⁷ apparently use εἰς because a secondary hand of Sinaiticus and the Western tradition indicate to them a later reading, and the parallel in Matt 6:29 uses ἐπί.

(b) Luke 6:49 (78). Jesus compares people, saying some are builders whose product immediately συνέπεσεν and results in great destruction, with this prefixed verb form read in 𝔓⁴⁵, ⁷⁵ ℵ B D L Θ Ξ f¹, ¹³ 33 579 700 892 1241 2542. Other manuscripts, however, have the simple verb form ἔπεσεν (A C W Ψ Majority text). The parallel in Matt 7:27 uses the unprefixed form, with no indication of any textual variant. The Nestle–Aland²⁷ committee apparently thinks that the Lukan variant arose from an attempt at harmonization, and is a later and more weakly attested reading compared to the text as printed.

4. Morphological Alteration

Morphological alteration involves changing the morphology of a word that is fixed in the tradition, such as changing the aspect, mood, voice, case, or number of a word.

(a) Matt 6:5 (29). In the Sermon on the Mount, Jesus reportedly tells his hearers whenever προσεύξησθε, οὐκ ἔσεσθε as the hypocrites, following ℵ² B Z f¹ 892. The singular προσεύξῃ, οὐκ ἔσῃ is found in ℵ* D L W Θ f¹³ 33 Majority text. There is no parallel for comparison. It is difficult to know the reasoning for rejection of this variant, since it would appear to be the more difficult reading but one that makes sense, in the light of the fact that most of the commands of this section are in the second person plural, even though the second person singular is used elsewhere in the context, and it is clearly better attested externally due to the strong Alexandrian and Western tradition, supported by the Byzantine.

(b) Mark 2:9 (52). Jesus asks whether it is easier to say your sins ἀφίενται, with ℵ B 28 565 2427. The variant asks whether it is easier to say ἀφέωνται, with A C (D) L Θ W 0130 f¹, ¹³ 33 Majority text (cf. Mark 2:5 for similar variants). This variant is discussed below in more detail.

5. Syntactical Word Order Variation

Syntactical word order designates instances where the ordering of words, or phrases, has been changed in the variants.

(a) Mark 7:13 (115). Regarding *corban*, Jesus concludes καὶ παρόμοια τοιαῦτα πολλὰ ποιεῖτε, read in A B (D) L Θ 33 2427 Majority text. There are several variants in word order here. One reads καὶ παρόμοια πολλὰ τοιαῦτα ποιεῖτε (ℵ f¹, ¹³ 579 700 1241), another reads καὶ παρόμοια πολλὰ τοιαῦτα (D), and another deletes the words altogether (W). There are no parallels. This decision is apparently decided on the strength of the witnesses, in both the Alexandrian and the later Western traditions, with Byzantine support.

(b) Luke 6:26 (74). This verse actually has two instances of the same type of variant. Jesus reportedly warns his followers regarding whenever ὑμᾶς καλῶς εἴπωσιν, read in 𝔓⁷⁵ B. The words are καλῶς ὑμᾶς εἴπωσιν in (D) Q W Θ Ξ f¹, ¹³ Majority text, and καλῶς εἴπωσιν ὑμᾶς in ℵ A L Ψ 33 579 892 (2542). Jesus attributes these words to πάντες οἱ ἄνθρωποι, with the evidence not specified in Nestle–Aland[27] but presumaby similar to the above. The words are, οἱ ἄνθρωποι πάντες in ℵ, and simply οἱ ἄνθρωποι in D L G Δ 892*.

6. *Syntactical Other Variation*

In a few instances we have given a special label to those variants where there is a complex of changes, usually including syntactical ordering, as well as other possible grammatical changes. This category is best treated as a separate category, even though it is closely related to that of syntactical word order.

(a) Matt 5:32 (24). In the Sermon on the Mount, Jesus speaks of πᾶς ὁ ἀπολύων, with Nestle–Aland[27] not noting the basis of this reading. There is a variant, however, with ὃς ἂν ἀπολύσῃ, read in D 0250 579. There are several parallel passages to this verse. Matt 19:9 reads the subjunctive construction, but without any note of textual variants. Mark 10:11 reads the subjunctive construction, with variants, but these variants are those of addition/insertion, not those that change the subjunctive reading. Luke 16:18 reads the participle construction, but with no notation of any textual variant. The Matthean reading is apparently accepted because of its being out of harmony with Mark, and the relatively weak textual attestation. The question of how Matthew and Luke got their common variant, and why Luke has no textual variants, is not easy to answer.

(b) Luke 6:37 (76). Jesus tells his followers not to judge "and you will not be judged (καὶ οὐ μὴ κριθῆτε)," and not to condemn, and "you will not be condemned (καὶ οὐ μὴ καταδικασθῆτε)," with Nestle–Aland[27] not noting the basis of their text. The construction is changed from καὶ οὐ μὴ to ἵνα μὴ in both instances, changing an emphatic negative to a negated purpose clause.[35] The first time the attestation is A D W Ψ and the second time D W*. Matt 7:1 reads the subjunctive (ἵνα μὴ κριθῆτε) in its parallel to the first sentence above, but with no textual variants.

These six categories provide a useful classificatory scheme for the variants that we have encountered in our coding of the text of the words of Jesus in the Synoptic Gospels. We encountered a number of variants for which two or more of the categories applied, and these variant readings were recorded in our database as belonging to multiple categories, and were included in our statistics as separate items, even though part of a single variant. For example, at Mark 2:22 (54) the Nestle–Aland[27] text has the words ῥήξει ὁ οἶνος τοὺς ἀσκούς. Washingtonianus reads διαρρήσσονται οἱ ἀσκοί, which is classified as a lexical replacement (διαρρήγνυμι for ῥήσσω), a subtraction (the lack of ὁ οἶνος) and a morphological alteration (the change of case and number, from τοὺς ἀσκοὺς to ὁ οἶνος). The apparatus of the Nestle–Aland[27] treats this as a single variant. It may, however, be better to mark each element of the variant reading separately, according to its category.

Even the relatively neutral examples presented above are provocative in the questions that they raise regarding establishing the words of Jesus, besides raising questions regarding the textual basis and its witnesses for the study of the words of Jesus through conventional printed editions.

3. DATA REGARDING TEXTUAL VARIANTS

1. General Figures Regarding Variants in the Words of Jesus in the Synoptic Gospels

Once one has access to the data regarding the words of Jesus and their textual variants, there are a number of intriguing conclusions that begin to emerge. Table 1 shows the number of words of Jesus in Mark's Gospel, the first 16 chapters of Matthew's Gospel and Luke 1:1–11:17.

---

35   On οὐ μή as an emphatic negative and the use of ἵνα with the subjunctive, see S. E. Porter, *Idioms of the Greek New Testament* (BLG 2; Sheffield: Sheffield Academic Press, 2nd edn, 1994) 226, 235-36, 283.

Number of:	Matthew 1–16		Mark		Luke 1–11:17	
Words without variant reading(s)	4519	(80%)	3470	(80%)	2415	(77%)
Words with variant reading(s)	1155	(20%)	832	(20%)	734	(23%)
Total words of Jesus in sample	**5674**		**4302**		**3149**	

Table 1 - Number of words of Jesus in Synoptics with and without variant readings in NA[27]

These figures illustrate the importance of considering the textual variants of the words of Jesus, graphically highlighting the serious omission in recent Historical Jesus research. In the samples we studied, capturing all the words of Jesus recorded in Mark and roughly half of those in the other two Synoptics, roughly 1 in 5 words of Jesus has a disputed reading. Of course, some of these disputes may be quite late, and of relatively little concern compared to others, but disputed they are, nonetheless. As such, these summary figures display the size of the problem.

It is also possible and useful to list the number of variant readings by category for each of the three samples noted above (see table 2). As might be expected, the most frequent type of variant is addition/insertion, although subtraction/omission, lexical differentiation/replacement and morphological alterations are all almost as frequent. Again, simply examining the numbers of each variant does not reveal the value of each variant, since many of them may be much later readings. However, these figures are still useful and provide direction towards more detailed study of particular manuscripts or groups of manuscripts.

CATEGORY	Matthew 1–16		Mark		Luke 1–11:17	
addition/insertion	142	(25%)	179	(28%)	100	(26%)
subtraction/omission	111	(19%)	130	(21%)	82	(22%)
lexical differentiation/ replacement	112	(20%)	136	(21%)	81	(21%)
morphological alteration	128	(23%)	115	(18%)	72	(20%)

syntactical word order	57	(11%)	72	(11%)	42	(11%)
syntactical other	10	(2%)	1		2	
TOTAL	**560**		**633**		**379**	

Table 2 - Number of variants of each category for Synoptic samples

It is further illuminating to investigate individual manuscripts with reference to these variant categories. This reveals where particular manuscripts have a tendency to vary from the eclectic text created by the Nestle–Aland[27]. Throughout this paper the Nestle–Aland[27] is the base text against which variation is disussed. The tables below (see table 3) show the 15 most frequent manuscripts to exhibit variants in the five main categories of variation (syntactical other change, the sixth category, has been left out because of its low frequency of occurrence). These figures cover the same samples from the Synoptic Gospels listed above. For instance, Θ is found as a witness of a variant of addition/insertion 165 times in Matthew 1–16, Luke 1:1–11:17 and Mark. Sinaiticus (ℵ) supports a variant reading exhibiting a morphological alteration from the base text 56 times.

It is also clear from these charts that there are certain manuscripts that are commonly found in the Nestle–Aland[27] as witnesses for variant readings and not as support for the base reading. Codex Bezae, for instance, contains the highest frequency of subtraction/ omission, lexical differentiation/replacement and morphological alterations. Because of the nature of apparatus of the Nestle–Aland[27], it is not possible to produce precise figures as to the number of times a particular manuscript supports the text reading compared to the number of times it is among those of a variant reading. There does not seem to be a consistent method for citing witnesses that support the text. From our sample, we found 419 readings with no witness information given and 446 with this information. So, only in roughly half of the instances is this information provided, which is surprising, given that it is necessary information in order to be able to make a decision on which reading to adopt.

add			sub			lex			morph			sntx WO	
Θ	165		D	148		D	118		D	122		f13	54
f13	154		W	80		Θ	86		W	98		Mj	50
D	153		B	55		Mj	78		Θ	92		A	46
Mj	149		ℵ	54		f13	74		Mj	91		W	44

W	122	fl	48	W	70	f13	86	D	41
33	115	f13	44	fl	55	L	78	fl	40
A	110	Θ	42	33	54	fl	73	ℵ	33
fl	100	L	40	L	52	A	64	Θ	33
C	96	700	39	A	48	33	56	33	30
L	83	Mj	30	ℵ	42	ℵ	56	L	28
Ψ	60	1424	28	C	39	C	54	C	26
ℵ	57	579	27	565	35	1424	32	892	15
565	47	Ψ	27	B	28	Δ	30	700	14
1424	46	565	26	700	28	565	29	Ψ	14
1241	35	A	25	2542	27	Ps	28	579	13

Table 3 - Fifteen most frequent manuscripts for each category of variation in the words of Jesus

From the 446 instances in which witness information is cited in support of the text reading, it is possible to state as a ratio the number of times a particular manuscript supports the text to the number of times it is found among the variant readings. Vaticanus (B), for instance, has a ratio of about 6:1, indicating that it is usually followed as a witness for the words of Jesus.[36] The tables above, showing the fifteen most frequent manscripts of each of our categories of variants, further show that B most frequently either omits words (55 times) or has a different word (28 times). It is not among the 15 most frequent manuscripts for addition/insertion, morphological alteration or syntactical word-order variation. Other manuscripts frequently supporting the Nestle–Aland[27] text of the words of Jesus and their ratio are: $\mathfrak{P}^{75}$ (4:1), ℵ (3:1), L (2:1), Δ (2:1), Ξ (3:1), Ψ (2:1), 892 (4:1), 2427 (6:1) and 1241 (2:1). Some of those found more frequently supporting variant readings are: A (1:2), D (1:2), Γ (1:2), 0233 (1:3), Family 13 (1:2), and the Majority text (1:3).

These figures serve simply to begin the investigation of specific types of variants in the words of Jesus or of particular manuscripts.

---

36 All ratio figures given are approximate, due the lack of precise information concerning Nestle-Aland[27]'s "*txt*" reading in the critical apparatus. The ratios have been calculated by taking the raw frequencies, dividing the variants reading in half (to compensate for the lack of textual witness data) and then rounding up or down the resulting ratios. For example, in our sample, B is cited supporting the text 361 times, and found amongst the variants 122 times, giving a ratio of 361:66 = 5.92:1.

There is much more that could be listed; however, sufficient general data have been presented above to illustrate a number of useful points: (1) The nature and size of the textual variation in the words of Jesus is just about one in five words. In other words, about 20% of the words of Jesus in our sample shows some variation on the basis of the textual evidence given in the Nestle–Aland[27] text. (2) Variation by addition/insertion is the most common type of variant in the words of Jesus, although subtraction/omission, morphological alteration and lexical differentiation/replacement are nearly as common in the sections of the Synoptics we examined. (3) Though somewhat imprecise, it is possible to identify certain manuscripts that either more frequently support the reading found in the Nestle–Aland[27] text or are more frequently among the witnesses for the variant readings. For instance, Codex Bezae is frequently found to exhibit addition/insertion, subtraction/omission, lexical differentiation/replacement, morphological alteration and syntactical word-order variation.

2. Variants in the Words of Jesus in Mark

In this paper, we wish to draw specific attention to variants in the Gospel of Mark. According to our findings, there are 4302 words of Jesus in Mark's Gospel. Of these, 3470 of the words do not have variants, which leaves 832 of Jesus' propertied words with variants. This means that roughly 1 in 5 words of Jesus in Mark's Gospel has a disputed reading. If we look at the number of variant readings according to the classifications presented above, we find that this is probably the kind of variation that one might reasonably expect (see table 2). For example, the largest single category of variant is one where there has been an addition/insertion to the text (179 instances). This, however, is followed fairly closely by lexical differentiation/replacement (136 instances) and subtraction/omission (130 instances). Morphological alterations comprise 115 instances, followed at the bottom by syntactical word-order variants (72 instances). We should first note that the manuscripts that constitute the basis of Mark's Gospel in the Nestle–Aland[27] critical edition, according to the criteria presented by Aland and Aland in their introduction to textual criticism, are: the early papyri (there are only three, $\mathfrak{P}^{45}$ with much of the Gospel, $\mathfrak{P}^{84}$ with Mark 2:2-5, 8-9; 6:30-31, 33-34, 36-37, 39-41 and $\mathfrak{P}^{88}$ with Mark 2:1-26), and four major codexes, Sinaiticus,

Vaticanus, Bezae and Washingtonianus.[37]

An analysis of these variants, according to the manuscripts that have them, presents some results that one might expect. However, there are also some surprises. For example, regarding addition/ insertions to the text, one might rightly expect Family 13 and the Majority text to have a significant proportion of addition/insertions, and they do, with 69 instances each. However, this is the same number of variants as Alexandrinus, just three more than Bezae with 66, and slightly more than Washingtonianus with 54. Sinaiticus itself has 32 variants that add words to the text. Of the most important early manuscripts, $\mathfrak{P}^{45}$ with much, though certainly not all, of the Gospel of Mark, has 10 addition/insertions and Vaticanus has 8. In terms of lexical differentiation/replacements, Bezae has by far the largest number, with 45, exceeding even that of Family 13 (35 instances) and the Majority text (29 instances). However, Washingtonianus also has 29 examples of lexical differentiation/ replacement, followed closely by Alexandrinus with 24, Sinaiticus with 18, and Vaticanus with 11. Even $\mathfrak{P}^{45}$ has six lexical differen- tiation/replacements, as does $\mathfrak{P}^{88}$ in its only 26 extant verses. Morphological alterations reveal that Alexandrinus and Bezae, with 37 variants each, have the largest number, followed closely by Washingtonianus and the Majority text, with 36 instances each. Sinaiticus also has 24 instances of morphological variation, followed somewhat further down by Vaticanus with 17. $\mathfrak{P}^{45}$ has only two morphological alterations. Concerning variants with subtraction/ omission, again Bezae has the largest number, with 57, followed by Washingtonianus, with 51. There is then a significant gap before Family 1 with 27 and Family 13 with 23. However, Vaticanus has 22 subtraction/omissions, and Sinaiticus has 20. In this instance, Alexandrinus has only 15 variants, and the Majority text only 11. $\mathfrak{P}^{45}$ has 5 variants. Finally, with regard to syntactical word-order variants, the Majority text and Alexandrinus (A) have 29 instances, followed closely by Washingtonianus with 24 instances, Bezae (D) with 19 instances, and Sinaiticus with 11 instances. Vaticanus has only 5 instances of syntactical variation, and the two papyri, $\mathfrak{P}^{45}$ and $\mathfrak{P}^{88}$, have 2 and 1 each, respectively.

---

37   K. Aland and B. Aland, *The Text of the New Testament* (trans. E. F. Rhodes; Grand Rapids: Eerdmans, 2nd edn, 1989) 104. None of the four early majuscules has the text of Mark.

These figures, as rough as they might be, do reveal a number of interesting features regarding textual variants in the words of Jesus in Mark's Gospel that should not be neglected. The first is that, even though the Aland's claim is that the text of the Gospels is established on the basis of four major codices, the early papyri (here quite limited for Mark, being only three), and the other four major majuscule texts (none of which has Mark's Gospel, and so none is cited), there is a significant amount of variation within even these manuscripts regarding the words of Jesus. The statistics indicate that some of the manuscripts with the largest number of variants come from this group, as well as some of those with the fewest number. As a result, it would appear that the text of the words of Jesus in Mark, as found in the Nestle–Aland[27] is a truly eclectic text, that is, a text that draws from a variety of manuscripts, rather than reflecting a single manuscript.

The second factor to notice, however, is that, for a variety of manuscripts, including a number with significant variation among themselves, there are definite patterns regarding which ones appear to be used or rejected in the Nestle–Aland[27] readings. $\mathfrak{P}$[45] and Vaticanus appear to form the basis of the words of Jesus of the text in Mark, from what can be gathered from the variants noted above, with Bezae and Washingtonianus being rejected in a vast number of instances. Sinaiticus is left somewhere in the middle. Even so, the figures above indicate that there are a number of instances where even $\mathfrak{P}$[45], Vaticanus and Sinaiticus are rejected by the Nestle–Aland[27]. This raises a number of important questions regarding the criteria by which these decisions are made. More important for this paper, however, is the question of whether such acceptance and rejection of readings in the major manuscripts has a bearing on the question of the authenticity of the teachings of Jesus and the criteria by which authenticity is evaluated. It is therefore necessary in the next section to examine specific examples of textual variants in Mark's Gospel.

4. STUDIES OF SELECT VARIANTS AND THEIR IMPLICATIONS FOR THE CRITERIA OF AUTHENTICITY

From the number of variants that we have uncovered through the course of gathering this material, several examples seem to merit further discussion for their programmatic implications regarding research into the words of Jesus.[38] In discussing several of these examples, we wish to raise questions regarding the criteria of authenticity suggested by these examples, especially that of multiple attestation, since it is the criterion that pays the closest attention to the wording of the text. As a result, in the Gospel of Mark we have counted 104 instances where there is diversity of opinion among the major manuscripts (not even considering the minor manuscripts). From a *prima facie* standpoint this has serious implications for Historical Jesus research, since it raises the question of to exactly which text the criteria of authenticity are being applied. Even if it does not cast doubt on the ultimate ability of scholars to determine whether Jesus uttered a particular statement or not, it requires a previous stage of investigation, namely deciding which statement it is that is being investigated. One of the widely neglected areas of textual criticism of the Jesus tradition (in the small number of cases where textual criticism is actually carried out at all) is that of knowledge of patterns of variants among manuscripts. This study begins to correct this pattern of neglect.

1. Mark 1:44 (45)

Jesus reportedly says in this verse ὅρα μηδενὶ μηδὲν εἴπῃς. This might seem like an insignificant example, but it has more to offer than is at first apparent. Virtually all commentators accept the text as written, with Taylor stating that "there can be no doubt that it is original."[39] This phrase is found in B C Θ f¹ 2427 and the Majority text, but the omission of μηδέν occurs in ℵ A D L W Δ 0130 f¹³ 33 565 700 892 1241 1424 2542 *l*2211. In spite of the superior quality of these manuscripts that omit μηδέν, Taylor accepts the fuller reading because he sees the asyndeton and double negative of the

---

[38]   In the light of the lack of attention given to variation in the Greek text of the words of Jesus in Historical Jesus, and the focus instead on the *concepts* of Jesus (see discussion in section 1), we have paid close attention to lexical differentiation/ replacement in the words of Jesus in the Gospel of Mark. It is in such instances that conceptual variation is most likely to be exhibited. The appendix contains a table showing all the occurrences of lexical differentiation/replacement in the major manuscripts cited by Nestle–Aland[27] as constituting the basis of Mark's Gospel (𝔓[45, 84, 84], ℵ, B, D, W) for the words of Jesus.

[39]   V. Taylor, *The Gospel According to St. Mark: The Greek Text with Introduction, Notes and Indexes* (London: Macmillan, 1959) 189.

verse as representative of Markan style.[40] The text-critical issue must
be treated first, before turning to the issues related to whether these
are the words of Jesus. From a text-critical standpoint, the negative
μηδέν should probably be rejected on two grounds. The first is the
very one that Taylor suggests, that is, it is too typical of Markan
style (although he provides no argumentation that this is typical of
Markan style), and the second is the manuscript evidence, which is
clearly inclined towards omitting the words. The apparent reason for
including the words is that it makes the Markan passage out of
harmony with Matt 8:4 and Luke 5:14, both of which omit the
second negative (without, unfortunately any textual variants being
noted in the Nestle–Aland[27] apparatus). So, in spite of the evidence
of what Taylor calls "important MSS," and perhaps a stylistic issue,
both of which support the omission of μηδέν, both he and the
Nestle–Aland[27] retain the word, μηδέν, in their texts.

This raises an important issue regarding the methodology, and
specifically the criteria, that serve as operational canons in both text-
criticial and Historical Jesus research. In a recent treatment of the
relevance and place of textual criticism in New Testament exegesis,
Epp discusses the role of the scribe in textual transmission. He
suggests that:

> Subtle influences such as parallel passages, especially in the Synoptic
> Gospels, or daily familiarity with liturgical forms of biblical passages led
> scribes to conform the texts they were producing to those more familiar
> parallel forms that were fixed in their minds.[41]

This scribal tendency is one of the reasons Epp sees for adopting his
eighth criterion related to internal evidence. The criteria are written
in such a way that, if they are met by a particular reading, then the
reading should be accepted as the most probable and closest to the
original. This criteron is stated as follows:

> A variant's lack of conformity to parallel passages or to extraneous items in
> the context generally. Scribes tend, consciously or unconsciously, to shape
> the text being copied to familiar parallel passages in the Synoptic Gospels or

---

40   He suggests that asyndeton is "a feature of Mark's style, sometimes in
narratives, but more frequently in sayings," and that, "in most cases the ommision
[of a conjunction] renders the style more rapid, and in consequence more
expressive" (*The Gospel According to St. Mark,* 189).

41   E. J. Epp, "Textual Criticism in the Exegesis of the New Testament, with
an Excursus on Canon," in Porter (ed.), *Handbook to Exegesis,* 60.

to words or phrases just copied.[42]

Similar statements can be found in the standard works on New Testament textual criticism.[43]

In contrast to the text-critical suspicion of agreement between parallel passages, because of the assumed scribal tendencies towards harmonization, Historical Jesus research places considerable weight upon the criterion of multiple attestation. For example, Meier states that:

> The criterion of multiple attestation (or "the cross section") focuses on those sayings and deeds of Jesus that are attested in more than one independent literary source (e.g., Mark, Q, Paul, John) and/or in more than one literary form or genre (e.g., parable, dispute story, miracle story, prophecy, aphorism).[44]

It is granted that this criterion is stated primarily as operational with regard to independent sources, and not neccessarily for the triple tradition, as in the case of Mark 1:44. However, it still seems to present a conflict, or at least the potential for a conflict, between the criteria of textual criticism and those of authenticity.

Out of the 104 instances of diversity of opinion among the major manuscripts in the text of Mark, according to the Nestle–Aland[27], there are 13 in which a variant reading is signified by the critical apparatus as being a reading from a parallel passage.[45] Without examining these in detail here, it seems likely that, in these cases at least, the fact that the reading is found in a parallel was at least one of the reasons why the Nestle–Aland[27] committee decided against that particular reading in favour of the one found in the text, perhaps eliminating instances of possible multiple attestation.

2. Mark 2:5, 9 (52)

In contrast to the example discussed in the previous section, Mark 2:5 and 2:9 represent examples where a reading from a parallel is not considered in the evaluation of the textual evidence. Nestle–

---

42   Epp, "Textual Criticism," 63.

43   E.g., see B. M. Metzger, *The Text of the New Testament: Its Transmission, Corruption, and Restoration* (Oxford and New York: Oxford University Press, 2nd edn, 1968) 197-98.

44   Meier, *Marginal Jew*, I.174. Cf. R. H. Stein, "The 'Criteria' for Authenticity," in R. France and D. Wenham (eds.), *Gospel Perspectives* (vol. 1; Sheffield: JSOT Press, 1980), 225-26.

45   Mark 1:44; 2:19, 26; 3:5; 8:17, 20; 9:19; 11:3; 12:15, 30; 13:23; 14:21, 38.

Aland[27] print ἀφίενταί σου αἱ ἁμαρτίαι in Mark 2:5, 9. Here there are textual variants, with the present form being read in B 28 33 565 1241 2427 *l*2211 in v. 5 and ℵ B 28 565 2427 in v. 9. The variant ἀφέωνται, the perfect indicative form, is read in 𝔓[88] ℵ A C D L Θ 0130 f[1, 13] Majority text in v. 5 and A C (D) L W Θ 0130 f[1, 13] 33 Majority text in v. 9. The manuscript evidence looks strongly in favour of the perfect form being read in v. 5, and quite possibly, if not likely, in v. 9. The Synoptic parallels present a mixed and provocative picture. Matt 9:2 reads ἀφίενται in ℵ B (D) *l*2211, and 9:5 reads ἀφίενται in ℵ(*) B (D), but with the variant ἀφέωνται in 9:2 in C L W Θ 0233 0281 f[1, 13] 33 Majority text, and in 9:5 in C L W Θ 0233 f[1, 13] 33 Majority text. Luke 5:20 and 23 read ἀφέωνται, but with no textual variants, according to the Nestle–Aland[27].

The explanation for the reading in the printed edition, which received a "B" rating in every edition of the UBSGNT, is given by Metzger:

> Although strongly supported in the manuscripts, the perfect tense (ἀφέων-ται) appears to be secondary, having been introduced by copyists from Luke's acount (Lk 5.20). Mark's use of the present tense (ἀφίενται) was followed by Matthew (Mt 9.2).[46]

This interesting textual situation raises a number of questions, although virtually none of them are addressed by commentators, especially on Luke. They are apparently content with the kind of explanation offered by Metzger.[47] However, Metzger's explanation does not actually explain the variation among the Gospels at this point. First, he must admit that the perfect tense-form is strongly supported in the manuscripts. Whether copyists introduced the perfect into Mark's Gospel begs the question of why Luke introduced it. However, it seems to us that the lack of any variation in Luke (if Nestle–Aland[27] is to be accepted at this point; if they are not it raises other questions regarding this edition)[48] would indicate that Luke

---

46 Metzger, *Textual Commentary*, 2nd edn, 66. The wording is identical in the 1st edn, 77.

47 It is questionable how Fitzmyer's observation that Luke has used "the Doric-Ionic dialectal form of the pf. pass." is cogent to this discussion. See J. A. Fitzmyer, *The Gospel according to Luke I–IX* (AB 28; New York: Doubleday, 1981) 583.

48 C. Tischendorf (*Novum Testamentum Graece* [vol. 1; Leipzig: Giesecke & Devrient, 1869] 470) does not list a textual variant with the present tense form here either, noting only the spelling variant ἀφέονται.

read the perfect verb form in his source. Otherwise, one might well expect a variant in which some scribe re-introduced the present tense to restore harmony with Mark's Gospel. The source that Luke would have read would have been either Mark, if Markan priority is assumed, or Matthew, if Matthew's place of pre-eminence in the early Church is followed. In either case, it would seem that perhaps the perfect tense is the better reading, for at least Mark, if not both Mark and Matthew.

This textual variant not only emphasizes the problems of dealing with Synoptic parallels, but also introduces the question of how the Markan hypothesis dominates and controls textual criticism, as well as Historical Jesus research.[49] Metzger's comments above, for example, are written from this standpoint, assuming that Matthew copied Mark.[50] Elliott has shown that there are numerous passages in the Synoptic Gospels where one's Synoptic priority theory influences one's results, where an alternative hypothesis may result in different choices regarding variants.[51] The implications regarding Historical Jesus research are equally significant. There is potential for many instances of text-critical decision-making to have the secondary effect of determining the words of Jesus. This of course raises doubt as to whether or not one can plausibly argue for or against their authenticity.

3. Mark 7:9 (115) and 4:24 (94)

A last example worth brief discussion is found in the combination of Mark 7:9 and 4:24. In Mark 7:9, this statement by Jesus, καλῶς ἀθετεῖτε τὴν ἐντολὴν τοῦ θεοῦ, ἵνα τὴν παράδοσιν ὑμῶν στήσητε, has been debated by scholars as to its authenticity and its redactional nature.[52] However, there is a textual variant in the verse that has a potential influence upon how this verse is interpreted. Several significant issues emerge out of consideration of this textual variant. The first considers which text scholars are reading here—the

---

49   See, for example, Evans, "Life of Jesus," 429-33.

50   Metzger states as much in the introductory comments to his *Textual Commentary* (1st edn, xxviii; 2nd edn, 14*).

51   Elliott, "The Relevance of Textual Criticism to the Synoptic Problem," in his *Essays and Studies*, 147-58.

52   See R. A. Guelich, *Mark 1–8:26* (WBC 34A; Dallas: Word Books, 1989) 368, for a summary of research. In Guelich's summary, the textual variant does not enter into discussion of authenticity.

decision is not an easy one. The variant in 7:9 with the word
τηρήσητε is read in ℵ A (B) L f¹³ 33 Majority text, while the
Nestle–Aland²⁷ bases its reading στήσητε on D W Θ f¹ 28 565 2542.
This variant presents a difficult choice. It has consistently received a
D rating in the UBSGNT, and, even with the increase in letter
ratings in the fourth edition, has retained this insecure status. As
Metzger states,

> It is most difficult to decide whether scribes deliberately substituted
> στήσητε ("establish") for τηρήσητε ("keep"), as being the more appropriate
> verb in the context, or whether, through inadvertence in copying and
> perhaps influenced subconsciously by the preceding phrase τὴν ἐντολὴν
> τοῦ θεοῦ, they replaced στήσητε with τηρήσητε. The Committee judged
> that, on the whole, the latter possibility was slightly more probable.[53]

The second significance of this variant is seen in its implications
for authenticating Jesus' words in this verse. The sense of these
lexical items is sufficiently different that one might well argue that
στήσητε implies a later Church addition, after division between the
Church and Judaism,[54] because it speaks of establishment or re-
establishment, implying that Christians and Jews had already parted
company. One might also argue that τηρήσητε implies that
Christianity and Judaism were still in relation, that Jesus himself may
even have been speaking as a Jewish teacher about acceptable or
unacceptable Jewish practice as a follower of certain of these
precepts.

We are less concerned to adjudicate this dispute than to see its
implications for other passages that have a bearing on the words of
Jesus. In his recent work on Mark and Q, Fleddermann argues for 28
passages that reflect overlap between Mark and Q.[55] The significance
of these overlaps is that they have the possibility of fulfilling the
criterion of multiple attestation, representing points of conceptual

---

53   Metzger, *Textual Commentary*, 2nd edn, 81. This is the same as the
statement in the 1st edition, p. 94.

54   There are several different models regarding the split between Christianity
and Judaism. Regardless of the model accepted, this variant would imply that
separation had occurred. Cf. S. E. Porter and B. W. R. Pearson, "Christians and
Jews by the 4th Century," in S. Mitchell and G. Greatrex (eds.), *Race, Religion,
and Culture in Late Antiquity A.D. 300–600* (2 vols; Swansea: Classical Press of
Wales, forthcoming 2000).

55   H. T. Fleddermann, *Mark and Q: A Study of the Overlap Texts* (BETL 122;
Leuven: Peeters/Leuven University Press, 1995); cf. Evans, "Life of Jesus," 442.

overlap, on the basis of verbal overlap, between what are held by most to be independent sources. Fleddermann posits that Mark 4:24d, with καὶ προστεθήσεται ὑμῖν, overlaps with Q 12:31, with its καὶ . . . προστεθήσεται ὑμῖν.[56] The only difficulty with this overlap is that the words in Mark are textually precarious, with all three words deleted in D W 565 579. One notices that the attestation for deleting these words is not unlike that for accepting the words of the text in Mark 7:9, cited above. Metzger claims that the variant here arose through an accidental mistake:

> The omission of καὶ προστεθήσεται ὑμῖν seems to have been accidental, owing to homoeoteleuton. The words τοῖς ἀκούσουσιν appear to be a gloss inserted to explain the connection of the saying with βλέπετε τι ἀκούετε.[57]

Homoeoteleuton may be an explanation of this variant, but the similarity in textual witness for deleting the crucial words in Mark 4:24 and for accepting the reading in Mark 7:9 makes one pause to think of the implications of accepting or rejecting these variants. One might well wish to argue on the basis of the character of manuscripts as seen over the whole of Mark that a reading attested as this variant is ought to be treated more consistently. If the variant is accepted as offering the more plausible reading in Mark 4:24, then it jeopardizes the overlap between Mark 4:24cd and Q 6:38c and 12:31, thereby possibly reducing the overlap passages between Mark and Q by one. If the variant is accepted for Mark 7:9, then it perhaps argues for words originating with Jesus and reflecting his situation within Judaism. One may not be able to have both. This instance, therefore, causes one to reconsider the importance of examining textual variants in the words of Jesus, both in terms of their function in a given variant unit, but also in terms of their tendencies over an entire Gospel. Whereas in many instances discussion avoids dealing with the specific Greek words of Jesus, in at least this instance, the criterion of multiple attestation can be seen to be dependent upon a specific variation in wording in the Greek New Testament.

---

[56] Fleddermann, *Mark and Q*, 85-87.
[57] Metzger, *Textual Commentary*, 2nd edn, 71-72. Cf. 1st edn, 83-84. This textual reading has always received an "A" rating in the UBSGNT.

CONCLUSION

A number of conclusions emerge from this study. The first is the need to take a second look at the state of affairs regarding research into the words of Jesus from the sources that we have. As was recounted at the beginning of this paper, there has been an evolution in critical thought regarding how the words of Jesus have been viewed with regard to their language of utterance and representation in Greek in the New Testament. Whereas earlier scholars accommodated a multi-lingual environment in which Jesus could well have spoken some Greek, later scholars have virtually eliminated this possibility, with the consequence that the actual words of Jesus as found in the Gospels have been neglected. As a result, there has not been very much specific attention to textual variants in these Greek words, ancertainly no large-scale or global study of these phenomena. We have therefore undertaken to examine and categorize all of these variants. In some ways, the words of Jesus, at least as they are represented in the Greek Gospels, seem far more precarious than they may have before this study, since there is an abundance of variants. The variants themselves, however, are not the crucial matter. The crucial matter is to examine the implications of these variants for establishing the authenticity of the words of Jesus. Several key examples show that there needs to be a rethinking of both the importance of these textual variants and the criteria of authenticity that are so dependent upon them. We hope that this short exploration of these variants in the words of Jesus will constitute a first step in this process of re-examination, since established conclusions regarding the words of Jesus can only be arrived at if they are erected on a firm foundation.

APPENDIX

LEXICAL DIFFERENTIATION/REPLACEMENT

IN THE WORDS OF JESUS IN MARK

Vs.	NA27	Witnesses	Variant	Witnesses
1:25	ἐξ αὐτοῦ	ℵ, A, B, C, f1, f33, Mj	ἐκ τοῦ ἀνθρώπου, πνεῦμα ἀκαράτον	D, W, (Θ), (565)
			ἀπ᾽ αὐτοῦ	L, 33, 565*, 579, 700, 892, 1424, 2427, l2211
1:38	ἐχομένας κωμοπόλεις		ἐγγὺς κωμὰς καὶ εἰ τὰς πόλεις	D
1:38	ἐξῆλθον	ℵ, B, C, L, Th, 33, 579, 2427	ἐλήλυθα	W, Δ, f13, 28, 565, 892, 1424
			ἀπεστάλην	2542
2:9	περιπάτει	A, B, C, W, Th, f1, f13, 2427, Mj	ὕπαγε	𝔓88, ℵ, L, Δ, 892
			ὕπαγε εἰς τὸν οἰκόν σου	D, (33)
2:19	μετ᾽ αὐτῶν		μεθ᾽ ἑαυτῶν	𝔓88, L, 2542
2:22	ῥήξει ὁ οἰς τοὺς ἀσκοὺς	𝔓88, ℵ, B, C*, D, L, Th, 565, 892, 2427	διαρρήσσονται οἱ ἀσκοί	W
2:22	ἀπόλλυται καὶ οἱ ἀσκοί	𝔓88, B, 892, 2427	ἐχεῖται καὶ οἱ ἀσκοί	L
2:26	τοὺς ἱερεῖς	ℵ, B, 892, 2427	τοῖς ἀρχιερεῦσιν	(Φ), 28, 579, 1241
3:4	ἀγαθὸν ποιῆσαι	ℵ, W	ἀγαποποιῆσαι	A, B, C, L, Θ, f1, f13, 2427, Mj

3:4	ἀποκτεῖναι	ℵ, A, B, C, D, 2427, Mj	ἀπολέσαι	L, W, Δ, Θ, f1, f13, 28, 565, 579, 700, 892, 1424, 2542, *l*2211
3:29	ἁμαρτήματος	ℵ, B, L, Δ, Th, 28, 33, 565, 892*, 2427	κρίσεως	A, C2, f1, (1424), Mj
			κολάσεως	348, 1216
			ἁμαρτίας	C*vid, D, W, f13
3:33	καὶ	ℵ, B, C, L, W, Δ, Th, f1, f13, 565, 892, 1241, 1424, 2427, 2542	ἤ	A, (D), K, 28, 33, 700
4:5	ὅπου		ὅτι	D, W
4:5	ἐξανέτειλεν		ἐξεβλάστησεν	f1, f13, 28, 700, 2542
			ἀνέτειλεν	W
4:8	ἕν		εἰς	ℵ, B2, C*vid, Δ, 28, 700, (2427)
			ἐν	f1, 33vid, Mj
4:8	ἕν		ἐν	f1, 33vid, Mj
4:8	ἕν		ἐν	f1, 33vid, Mj
4:11	ἔξω		ἔξωθεν	B, Σ, 1424, 2427
4:11	γίνεται		λέγεται	D, Θ, 28, 565, 2542
4:15	εἰς αὐτούς	B, W, f1, f13, 28, 2427, 2542	ἐν ταῖς καρδίαις αὐτῶν	D, Θ, 33, Mj
			ἀπὸ τῆς καρδίας αὐτῶν	A

			ἐν αὐτοῖς	א, C, L, Δ, 579, 892
4:18	ἄλλοι εἰσίν	א, B, C, (C2), D, L, Δ, 2427	οὗτοι εἰσίν	A, 33, Mj
4:18	εἰς	A, B, Δ, Λ, Ω, Th, f1, f13, 33, 2427, Mj	ἐπί	א, C, D, 579
4:19	αἰῶνος		βιοῦ	Δ, Ω, Θ, 565, 700, 1424
4:19	ἀπάτη		ἀγάπη	Δ
4:19	πλούτου		κόσμου	Δ
4·20	ἕν		ἐν	f1, f13, 33, Mj
4:20	ἕν		ἐν	f1, f13, 33, Mj
4:20	ἕν		ἐν	f1, f13, 33, Mj
4:21	ἔρχεται		ἅπτεται	D, (W), (f13)
4:21	ἐπί		ὑπό	א, B*, f13, 33
4:26	ὡς ἄνθρωπος	א, B, D, L, Δ, 579, 700, 892, 2427	ὥσπερ ἄνθρωπος	Θ, f13, 28, 565, 700, 2542
4:28	ϵι	(א1), A, B2, C, D, W, Th, 0107, 0167, f1, f13, 33, 2427, Mj	ἔπειτα	565
4:28	ϵι	(א1), A, B2, C, D, W, Th, 0107, 0167, 565, f1, f13, 33, 2427, Mj	ϵἴτεν	(א*), B*, L, Δ
4:30	αὐτὴν παραβολῇ θῶμεν	א, B, C*vid, L, (Δ), 28, (579), 892, 2427	παραβολὴ παραβάλωμεν αὐτήν	A, C2, D, Θ, 0107vid, 33, Mj
			ὁμοιώματι παραβάλωμεν αὐτήν	f1

			τὴν παραβολὴν δῶμεν	W
4:40	δειλοί ἐστε; οὔπω	ℵ, B, D, L, Δ, Th, 565, (579), 700, 892*, 2427	δειλοί ἐστε οὕτως; πῶς οὐκ	A, C, 33, Mj
			δειλοί ἐστε οὕτως	W
			οὕτως δειλοί ἐστε; οὔπω	𝔓45vid, f1, f13, 28(*), (892c) 2542
5:19	ἀπάγγειλον	ℵ, B, C, Δ, Th, 579, 2427	διάγγειλον	𝔓45, D, W, f1, f13, 27, 700, 2542
			ἀνάγγειλον	A, L, 0132, 33, Mj
5:19	ὁ κύριός σοι	(ℵ), B, C, Δ, Th, 579, 2427	σοι ὁ θεός	D, (1241)
5:41	ταλιθα κουμ	ℵ, B, C, L, f1, 28, 33, 892, 1241, 1424, 2427	ταβιθα	W
			ραββι θαβιτα κουμι	D
6:4	πατρίδι αὐτοῦ	B, C, D, W, f1, 33, 2427, Mj	πατρίδι ἑαυτοῦ	ℵ*, f13
			πατρίδι τῇ ἑαυτοῦ	Θ, 565
6:11	ὃ ς ἂν τόπος μὴ δέξηται	ℵ, B, L, W, Δ, f13, 28, 2427	ὅσοι ἂν μὴ δέξωνται	A, C2, D, Θ, 0167vid, 33, Mj
6:31	ὑμεῖς αὐτοὶ κατ' ἰδίαν		ὑπάγωμεν	D
7:6	τιμᾷ		ἀγαπᾷ	D, W
7:8	παράδοσιν		ἐντολήν	𝔓45
7:9	στήσητε	D, W, Th, f1, 28, 565, 2542	τηρήσητε	ℵ, A, L, f13, 33, Mj
			τήρητε	B, 247

7:12	οὐκέτι ἀφίετε	𝔓45, ℵ, A, B, L, W, Δ, Th, f1, f13, 28, 33, 565, 700, 892, 1241, 427, 2542, Mj	οὐκ ἐνάφειτε	D
7:18	οὐ		οὔπω	ℵ, L, Δ, f1, 700, 892
7:19	ἀφεδρῶνα		ὀχετόν	D
8:2	ἡμέραι τρεῖς προσμένουσίν μοι		ἡμέραι τρεῖς εἰσὶν ἀπὸ πότε ὧδε εἰσίν	D
8:3	ἥκασιν	ℵ, A, D, N, W, Th, f1, 28, 33, 565, 579, 700, 1241, 1424, 2542	εἰσίν	B, L, Δ, 0274, 892, 2427
			ἥκουσιν	0131, f13, Mj
8:12	ζητεῖ σημεῖον	ℵ, B, C, D, L, Δ, Th, f1, 28, 33, 565, 579, 700, 892, (1241), 2427, 2542	σημεῖον ἐπιζητεῖ	A, W, 0131, f13, Mj
			σημεῖον αἴτει	𝔓45
8:15	Ἡρῴδου		τῶν Ἡρῳδιανων	𝔓45, W, Θ, f1, f13, 28, 565, 2542
8:17	πεπωρωμένην ἔχετε τὴν καρδίαν ὑμῶν		πεπωρωμένην ὑμῶν ἐστιν ἡ καρδία	(D), Θ, (0143vid), 565
8:26	μηδὲ εἰς τὴν κώμην εἰσέλθῃς	ℵ, B, L, f1, 2427	ὕπαγε εἰς τὸν οἰκόν σου καὶ μηδένι εἴπῃς εἰς τὴν κώμην	D
8:34	εἴ τις	ℵ, B, C*, D, L, W, Δ, 0214, f1, f13, 28, 33, 565, 579, 700, 892, 2427, 2542	ὅστις	A, C2, Θ, Mj

8:34	ἀκολουθεῖν	𝔓45, C*, D, W, Th, 0214, f1, Mj	ἐλθεῖν	ℵ, A, B, C2, K, L, Γ, f13, 33, 579, 892, 1241, 2427, 2542
			ἐλθεῖν καὶ ἀκολουθεῖν	D
8:35	τὴν ψυχήν		ἑαυτοῦ ψυχήν	B, 28
8:35	τὴν ψυχὴν αὐτοῦ	ℵ, A, B, C*, L, Δ, 0214, f1, 33, 565, 892, 1241, 1424	τὴν ἑαυτοῦ ψυχήν	C3, K, W, f13, 28, 700, 2427, 2542
8:38	μετά		καί	𝔓45, W, 2542
9:12	ἀποκαθιστάνει	ℵ2, A, B, L, W, Δ, Ψ, f1, 33, 2542	ἀποκαταστήσει	C, Θ, 565, 579
			ἀποκαταστάνει	ℵ*, D, (28)
9:21	ὡς	ℵ*, A, C3, D, f1, Mj	ἕως	𝔓45, B, 2427
			ἐξ οὗ	ℵ2, C*, L, W, Δ, Θ, Ψ, 33, 565, 579, 892, 1241l 1424, l2211
			ἀφ' οὗ	N, f13
9:23	τὸ εἰ δύνῃ	ℵ, B, C*, L, N*, Δ, f1, 579, 892, 2427	τοῦτο εἰ δύνῃ	W
9:31	μετὰ τρεῖς ἡμέρας	ℵ, B, C*, D, L, Δ, Ψ, 579, 892, 2427	τῇ τρίτῃ ἡμέρᾳ	A, C3, W, Θ, f1, f13, Mj
9:37	ἕν		ἐκ	W, Θ, f13, 565, (2542)
9:37	τοιούτων παιδίων		παιδίων τούτων	ℵ, C, Δ, (Ψ)
9:40	ἡμῶν	ℵ, B, C, L, W, Δ, Θ, Ψ, f1, f13, 28, 565, 579, 892, 1241, 2427, 2542	ὑμῶν	A, D, Mj, X

9:40	ἡμῶν	ℵ, B, C, W, X, Δ, Θ, Ψ, f1, f13, 28, 565, 579, 892, 1241, 2427, 2542	ὑμῶν	A, D, Mj
9:42	τούτων		μου	W
9:42	πιστευόντων εἰς ἐμέ	A, B, C2, L, W, Θ, Ψ, f1, f13, 2427, Mj	πίστιν ἐχόντων	D
9:43	ἀπελθεῖν εἰς τὴν γέενναν, εἰς τὸ πῦρ τὸ ἄσβεστον		βληθῆαι εἰς τὴν γένενναν ὅπου ἐστὶν τὸ πῦρ τὸ ἄσβεστον	D
9:47	βληθῆναι		ἀπελθεῖν	D, f1, (1241), 1424
9:49	πᾶς γὰρ πυρὶ ἁλισθήσεται	B, L, Δ, 0274, f1, f13, 28*, 565, 700	πᾶσα γὰρ θυσία ἅλι ἁλισθήσεται	D
			πᾶς γὰρ πυρὶ ἀναλωθήσεται καὶ πᾶσα θυσία ἅλι ἁλισθήσεται	Θ
			πᾶς γὰρ ἐν πυρὶ ἁλισθήσεται καὶ πᾶσα θυσία ἅλι ἀναλωθήσεται	Ψ
10:6	αὐτούς	ℵ, B, C, L, Δ, 579, 2427	ὁ θεός	D, W
10:12	αὐτή	ℵ, B, C, L, Δ, Ψ, 579, 892, 2427	γυνή	A, D, (Θ), f13, Mj
10:12	ἀπολύσασα τὸν ἄνδρα αὐτῆς γαμήσῃ ἄλλον	ℵ, B, (C), L, (Δ), (Ψ), 892, 2427	ἐξέλθῃ ἀπὸ τοῦ ἀνδρὸς καὶ ἄλλον γαμήσῃ	D, (Θ), f13, (28), 565, (700)
10:25	κάμηλον		κάμιλον	f13, 28, 579
10:25	τρυμαλιᾶς		τρήματος	ℵ*
			τρυπήματος	f13
10:25	ῥαφίδος		βελόνης	f13
10:30	οἰκίας καὶ ἀδελφοὺς καὶ ἀδελφάς	B, Ψ, Mj		D

10:34	μετὰ τρεῖς ἡμέρας	ℵ, B, C, D, L, Δ, Ψ, 579, 892, 2427		A(*), W, Θ, f1, f13, Mj
10:40	ἀλλ' οἷς	B2, Θ, Ψ, f1, f13, 2427, Mj	ἄλλοις	225
10:42	μεγάλοι αὐτῶν		βασιλεῖς αὐτῶν	C*vid
			βασιλεῖς	ℵ
10:43	γενέσθαι		ει	D, W, f1, 565, 2542
			ἔστω	ℵ, C, Δ, 565, 2542
11:2	οὐδεὶς οὔπω ἀνθρώπων	B, L, Δ, Ψ, 892, 1844	οὐδεὶς πωπότε ἀνθρώπων	A, 1241
11:23	πιστεύῃ ὅτι ὃ λαλεῖ γίνεται, ἔσται		πιστεύσῃ τὸ μέλλον, ὃ ἂν εἴπῃ γενήσεται	D
12:3	καί	ℵ, B, D, L, Δ, Ψ, 33, 579, 892, 1424, 2427	οἱ δέ	A, C, W, Θ, f1, f13, Mj
12:6	ἔτι	ℵ, B, L, Δ, Ψ, f1, 33, 579, 892*, 2427	ὕστερον δέ	W, Θ, (f13), (28), (700), (2542), 565
12:6	αὐτόν	ℵ, B, L, Δ, Θ, 892*, 2427	καὶ αὐτόν	A, C, (Ψ), 33, Mj
			κακεῖνον	D
12:7	πρὸς ἑαυτοὺς ει ὅτι	ℵ, B, C, L, W, (Δ), Ψ, (f1), 33, 579, (892), 2427	θεασάμενοι αὐτὸν ἐρχόμενον ει πρὸς ἑαυτούς	Θ, N, f13, 28, 2542, 565, 700
12:29	ὅτι πρώτη ἐστίν	ℵ, B, L, Δ, (Ψ), 33, (579), 892, 2427, 2542	πάτων πρώτη	D, W, Θ, 28, 565, 700
			πρώτη πάτων	f1, 2542
12:36	ὑποκάτω	B, D, W, 28, 2542	ὑποδίον	ℵ, A, L, Θ, Ψ, 087, f1, f13, 33, 2427, Mj
13:7	θροεῖσθε		θοευβεῖσθε	D
13:15	ὁ δὲ	ℵ, A, L, W, Ψ, f1, f13, Mj	καὶ ὁ	D, Θ, 565, 700

13:22	γάρ	A, B, D, L, W, Θ, Ψ, 083, f1, f13, 2427, Mj	δέ	ℵ, C
13:22	δώσουσιν	ℵ, A, B, C, L, W, Ψ, 083, f1, 2427, Mj	ποιησούσιν	D, Θ, f13, 28, 565
14:24	ἐκχυννόμενον ὑπὲρ πολλῶν	ℵ, B, C, L, Ψ, 892	περὶ πολλῶν ἐκχυννόμενον	A, f1, Mj
14:25	οὐκέτι οὐ μὴ πίω	A, B, f1, f13, 2427, Mj	οὐ μὴ πρόσθω πεῖν	D, (Θ), (565)
14:36	οὐ τί ἐγὼ θέλω ἀλλὰ τί σύ		οὐκ ὃ ἐγὼ θέλω ἀλλ' ὃ σὺ θέλεις	D, (Θ), (f13), (2542), (L844), (565)
15:34	ἐλωι		ηλι	D, Θ, 059, 565
15:34	ἐλωι		ηλι	D, Θ, 059, 565
15:34	λεμα σαβαχθανι	ℵ, C, L, Δ, Ψ, 892	λαμα σαβαχθανι	Θ, 059
			λαμα ζαβαφθανι	B
			λιμα σαβαχθανι	f13, 33, Mj
			λιμα σαβακτανι	A
15:34	ἐγκατέλιπές με	ℵ, B, Ψ, 059	ὠνείδισάς με	D
16:17	ταῦτα παρακολουθήσει	C3, D, Θ, f1, f13, Mj	ἀκολουθήσει ταῦτα	C*, L, Ψ, 579, 892

PART TWO

AUTHENTICATING THE WORDS OF JESUS

THE LORD'S PRAYER IN SOCIAL PERSPECTIVE

Douglas E. Oakman

In the villages of Galilee, the Lord's Prayer was revolutionary "wisdom" and "prophetic" teaching . . . .[1]

INTRODUCTION

Much has been written about the Lord's Prayer during the modern era. It may seem as if everything has been said that could have been said. Learned disquisitions are available regarding the linguistic aspects (Greek, Aramaic, even Hebrew), the various forms of the Greek text and their relationship to Q, and the meaning of the Prayer or its individual petitions.[2] The voting of the Jesus Seminar has stimulated much discussion related to the words of Jesus generally, and the Lord's Prayer in particular.[3]

This essay is centrally concerned with the tradition history and social meaning of Jesus' prayer. It presumes or interacts with existing scholarship, but is not intended to offer anything dramatically new related to linguistic or textual issues. The Jesus Seminar's judgments are reviewed and in some ways endorsed, though it is argued that the Seminar incorrectly has assigned gray and pink. In their chromatic terms, we apportion red to אבא and the second table of Matthew (though pink in Luke), and pink or gray to the first table.[4] The canonical texts provide a starting point for inquiry into

---

[1]   D. C. Duling and N. Perrin, *The New Testament: Proclamation and Parenesis, Myth and History* (3rd ed., Fort Worth: Harcourt Brace, 1994) 25. Duling and Perrin offer an excellent discussion of methods that have been applied in the study of the Lord's Prayer, and a valuable beginning point for further study.

[2]   The recent bibliography compiled by Mark Harding includes over 250 items, scattered among some 2000 entries in J. H. Charlesworth, M. Harding, and M. Kiley (eds.), *The Lord's Prayer and Other Prayer Texts from the Greco-Roman Era* (Valley Forge: Trinity Press International, 1994) 101-257.

[3]   Results first appeared piecemeal in the journal *Forum*, then in R. W. Funk, B. B. Scott, and J. R. Butts (eds.), *The Parables of Jesus: Red Letter Edition* (Sonoma: Polebridge, 1988); and most fully in R. W. Funk and R. W. Hoover (eds.), *The Five Gospels: What Did Jesus Really Say?* (New York: Macmillan, 1993).

[4]   The (Lord's) Prayer, for the purposes of this study, is discussed formally in

the tradition history. The social meaning is considered *pari passu* with this history, since basic impulses in the tradition derive from. conflicting social interests. The meaning for the earliest Jesus movement is parsed essentially in the light of a significant "social problem" of Jesus' day, namely, the growth of indebtedness and the swelling of the ranks of those displaced from the land because of debt. As the Prayer passed into written forms, the interests of various scribes found their way, as it were by way of glosses, into the Prayer tradition. We consider two distinct *Sitze im Leben*—the village and town scribal settings of earliest Q in Galilee, and the Judean-oriented scribal concerns of later Q recensions. By the time the Prayer was incorporated into canonical Matthew, Luke, and indirectly John, Judean interests had come to predominate, and basic concerns of the original Jesus movement had been reworked in systematic ways.

BASIC SOCIAL MODELS OF THIS STUDY

The employment of explicit social models provides distinctive perspectives on the "trajectory" of the Prayer from Jesus up until inclusion in the canonical gospels and later Christian traditions. Since the meaning of a prayer depends significantly upon the social system and location of the petitioner, social-scientific criticism plays a prominent role in the formulation of this essay's approach, working hypotheses, exegesis, and conclusions.[5] The meaning of the text is perceived vis-à-vis a critically reconstructed social world. The approach is thereby dialectical, and if it gives a credible and reasonable accounting of the data, and can incorporate or rule out the major alternatives, it becomes persuasive.

Recent scholarship has strongly urged that religion was imbedded in politics in Jesus' Palestine.[6] Religion and theology were

---

terms of an address, two "tables" of two to four petitions each, and a concluding doxology or "ascription." Table 1 = Petitions 1-3; Table 2 = Petitions 4-7.

5   J. H. Elliott, *What Is Social-Scientific Criticism?* (Guides to Biblical Scholarship; Minneapolis: Fortress, 1993). Regarding the relation of meaning to social system, see B. J. Malina, *The Social World of Jesus and the Gospels* (London and New York: Routledge, 1996) 10, 17.

6   D. E. Oakman, "The Archaeology of First-Century Galilee and the Social Interpretation of the Historical Jesus," in E. H. Lovering, Jr. (ed.), *Society of Biblical Literature 1994 Seminar Papers* (SBLSP 33; Atlanta: Scholars Press, 1994) 220-51; R. A. Horsley, "Jesus, Itinerant Cynic or Israelite Prophet?" in J. A.

consequently bound up with certain kinds of socio-economic interests, and it is possible to recover some of those links through our extant textual traditions. The social model that supplies the primary working assumptions of this essay, thus, begins with the consideration that *Jesus' religion spoke to an immediate need in concrete terms.* As with peasants generally, Jesus had little concern for priestly mediations of the divine, or purity in the priestly sense, and was paramountly concerned with the changing of material circumstances and the institutions that controlled them.[7] He spoke out of an intense election consciousness: His experience of God was immediate and in little need of mediating institutions. This characteristic could be construed by later Judean tradents of the Jesus materials as evidence of Jesus' (messianic) authority and status. While Jesus' aims have been hotly debated, he did seem to want to articulate the meaning of Israel's core traditions, especially Moses (Passover) and the prophets (justice for the powerless), for the situation of early Roman Palestine.

Charlesworth and W. P. Weaver (eds.), *Images of Jesus Today* (Valley Forge: Trinity Press International, 1994) 80.

[7]   The abductive procedure here (see B. J. Malina, "Interpretation: Reading, Abduction, Metaphor," in D. Jobling, P. L. Day and G. T. Sheppard [eds.], *The Bible and the Politics of Exegesis: Essays in Honor of Norman K. Gottwald on His Sixty-Fifth Birthday* [Cleveland: Pilgrim, 1991] 259-60) depends upon peasant studies and readings of the Jesus tradition that are justified in the subsequent pages. For general concerns of peasant religion, see M. Weber, *The Sociology of Religion* (Introduction by T. Parsons; trans. E. Fischoff; Boston: Beacon, 1963) 80, 82; E. R. Wolf, *Peasants* (ed. M. D. Sahlins; Foundations of Modern Anthropology Series; Englewood Cliffs: Prentice Hall, 1966) 101; R. Redfield, "The Social Organization of Tradition," in J. M. Potter, M. N. Diaz, and G. M. Foster (eds.), *Peasant Society: A Reader* (The Little, Brown Series in Anthropology; Boston: Little, Brown, 1967) 26. Jesus of Nazareth, of course, came from the peasantry, but was not entirely limited in his own concerns to peasant horizons, as I have argued in D. E. Oakman, *Jesus and the Economic Questions of His Day* (SBEC 8; Lewiston and Queenston: Edwin Mellen, 1986) 175-98; and "Was Jesus a Peasant? Implications for Reading the Samaritan Story (Luke 10:30-35)," *BTB* 22 (1992) 117-25. Jesus' "brokerage" activities, moreover, had to do with transforming, not sustaining, the socio-economic order. For a very different view of Jesus' relationship to purity, see B. Chilton, *The Temple of Jesus: His Sacrificial Program Within a Cultural History of Sacrifice* (University Park: Penn State University Press, 1992), who claims (p. 133) that Jesus was concerned about fulfillment of the aims of Leviticus. Jesus was still in fundamental conflict with the priestly establishment (pp. 100-102).

Social conflicts were endemic in early Roman Palestine and are presumed as concomitants to the activity of Jesus as well as the development of the gospel traditions. Such conflicts should not be construed naively as "Jesus (or Christians) versus the Jews." The Herods or the Judean elites in Jerusalem were often the object of popular enmity, as not only the gospels, but also Josephus and later rabbinic traditions show. The socio-political conflict which is the initial frame for understanding the Lord's Prayer is analogous to social phenomena familiar to us from the Old Testament and Intertestamental Jewish writings. For instance, Micah's tirade against eighth-century Jerusalem (Mic 3:9-12) or Jeremiah's later judgment against the Jerusalem temple (Jer 7:8-15) provide suggestive social parallels (involving agrarian and village discontent) to the conflicts in Jesus' day. The traditions of 1 Enoch bespeak similar social discontent in the early Hellenistic period, and the revolt of the Maccabees, beginning in the village or town of Modein, certainly had agrarian overtones (1 Macc 2:23-30). The literature of Qumran attests for the late Hellenistic and early Roman periods that Jerusalem politics, overlaid by strong religious ideology, could become quite volatile. And Josephus amply documents the "banditry" and disorder that preceded the Judean-Roman War of 66-70 CE.[8] In striking Judean analogy to the peasant prophet Jesus of Nazareth, "Jesus son of Ananus" appeared in Jerusalem in 62 or 63 CE declaring that the temple was dishonored and the people bound for disaster.[9]

The earliest scribes of the Jesus tradition, working in villages and towns of eastern Galilee, produced the first translations of Jesus' Aramaic speech into Greek. For perceptions of the original meaning of the Lord's Prayer, some appeal must be made to the Aramaic behind the (likely) Q Greek. Nevertheless, the case made in this essay about original meaning does not depend upon a precise knowledge of the original words, but only upon probable linguistic elements conjoined with social considerations.[10] There would have been a close interface, although hardly an identity, between the early Q

---

[8]   Material discussed at length in R. A. Horsley and J. S. Hanson, *Bandits, Prophets, and Messiahs: Popular Movements at the Time of Jesus* (San Francisco: Harper & Row, 1985).

[9]   See Josephus, *Ant.* 6.5.3 §300-305.

[10]   Some of these ideas and issues were first sketched, much too simply, in D. E. Oakman, "Rulers' Houses, Thieves, and Usurpers: The Beelzebul Pericope," *Forum* 4.3 (1988) 109-23.

tradents' social interests and the interests of Jesus.[11] Q was originally compiled by Galilean scribes, probably within the Herodian adminis- tration (Mark 6:14; Luke 8:3; 13:31) and not overly sympathetic to scribal interests prevalent later in the Jesus tradition (Luke 11:39- 52).[12]

Once Jesus' Prayer had assumed written form, in the language of commerce and to some extent empire, other interests would become more significant than those of the originating context. "Social- textural" considerations (to use Vernon Robbins' language) are more important at an earlier stage, "intertextural" considerations come into play at later stages.[13] Whereas an illiterate Jesus was preoc- cupied with the immediate and concrete, *later tradents of the Jesus tradition become more concerned with theological (christological, eschatological) abstractions or the articulation of the Jesus material with Israel's great traditions.* Also, as the Prayer was uttered within other social locations, socio-political concerns were softened (but not completely obliterated) while socio-religious concerns came more to the fore.

In general, purity concerns and apocalyptic concerns emphasizing judgment are highly correlated; as Qumran clearly shows, apocalyp- tic Judean interests stood within priestly and temple concerns.[14] Similarly, apocalyptic New Testament images (Mark 13; 1 Corinthi- ans 5–6; Revelation) are filled with violence and conflict, reflecting the collision of incompatible principles. These interests are marked by a concern for God's magical intervention to rectify conditions of

---

[11]   I consider that Jesus was an illiterate peasant, for these reasons: (1) Jesus did not leave any written record that we know of; (2) Jesus was known through oral-speech forms (parable, aphorism); (3) generally, peasant artisans would have little opportunity for education (see D. E. Oakman, "Was Jesus a Peasant?" 117- 21). Some have urged that Jesus possessed at least Torah-education, e.g. J. Klausner, *Jesus of Nazareth: His Life, Times, and Teaching* (trans. H. Danby; New York: Macmillan, 1925) 234-5 (cf. p. 193), but this does not urge a literate education.

[12]   J. S. Kloppenborg ("Literary Convention, Self-Evidence and the Social History of the Q People," *Semeia* 55 [1991] 77-102) has been influential here.

[13]   V. K. Robbins, *Exploring the Texture of Texts: A Guide to Socio- Rhetorical Interpretation* (Valley Forge: Trinity Press International, 1996) 40, 71.

[14]   The author is aware that this generalization glosses over some of the fine distinctions in recent studies, for instance J. J. Collins, "Early Jewish Apocalyp- ticism," *ABD* 1.287. However, even Judean apocalyptic traditions that emphasize wisdom are probably still within the orbit of priestly interests.

impurity from the standpoint of priestly sensibilities. Apocalyptic "readings" of Jesus, Jesus' aims, or Jesus material will thus have depended upon Judean scribes standing within significant temple or priestly interests (late-Q, Paul, late Mark [i.e. 11–15]).

THE CANONICAL TEXTS OF THE LORD'S PRAYER

The fact that there are differing forms of the Lord's Prayer provides one of the key warrants for a tradition-critical analysis and for letting "social imagination" loose in dialectic between text and social models. It is necessary at the start to examine the textual basis for the study.

There is a modern "sociology of knowledge" issue reflected in defense of harmonistic texts, glossed understandings, or the printing of both the Matthean and Lukan versions in red in Red Letter Editions. This issue is well illustrated in the history of English versions. The King James Version offers the non-specialist with perhaps the easiest access to the shape of the Lord's Prayer according to the *textus receptus*, the Greek text most common during the Middle Ages that shaped the earliest printed Greek testaments, English versions, and liturgical traditions among English-speaking Protestants. The Matthean and Lukan versions of the Prayer are printed almost identically. Missing in Luke is the final doxology; heaven and earth are reversed in Luke 11:2b; Luke's "day by day" (11:3) replaces Matthew's "this day" (6:11); Luke's "sins" (11:4a) replaces Matthew's "debts" (6:12a), and the final clause of Luke 11:4a is longer than the Matthean version (6:12b). These similarities demonstrate the well known harmonistic tendencies of *textus receptus* (in light of numerous variants in the Greek manuscript tradition of the Prayer).

Following important textual discoveries and the critical work of scholars like Tischendorf and Westcott-Hort, the English revisions in the late-nineteenth and early twentieth centuries began to incorporate more critical readings.[15] Edgar Goodspeed's New American Translation was greeted with popular indignation based in ignorance of

---

15 The English Revised Version appeared in 1881–1885 and its American counterpart in 1901: see *The Holy Bible Containing the Old and New Testaments* (New York: Thomas Nelson, 1901). Westcott and Hort detailed many of the problems in their *Introduction to the New Testament in the Original Greek, With Notes on Selected Readings* (New York: Harper and Brothers, 1882).

scholarly progress in text critical work.[16] One editorialist even suggested that the Prayer that Jesus had prayed should be left unchanged:

> Nothing stops his [Goodspeed's] devastating pen. He has even abbreviated the Lord's Prayer, a petition not so long originally but that hustling, hurrying Chicagoans could find time for it, if they ever thought of prayer. It is a petition that in its present wording has been held sacred for nearly two thousand years, for the King James translators are said to have made no changes.[17]

Goodspeed justly observed that the *English Revised Version* (1881) together with its close relative the *American Standard Version* (1901), as well as Weymouth (1903), the *Twentieth Century New Testament* (1905), and Moffatt (1913), had all printed the shortened Lord's Prayer at Luke 11:2-4.[18] The shorter Lukan text, moreover, was adopted in the Revised Standard Version, and indeed in all modern versions based upon a critical Greek text. While at least one scholar has promoted a return to something like the *textus receptus*, his arguments have not proven persuasive.[19]

Turning to the Greek text itself, eight variant readings in the Lukan prayer stem from Matthean parallels, since early copyists were often tempted to harmonize. Typical of this type of variant would be the expansion of the address in Luke: Alexandrinus and several Western manuscripts (which tend to conflate readings) have "ours in heaven." Similarly, against the majority of Greek manuscripts, Alexandrian (especially $\mathfrak{P}^{75}$), Western, and pre-Caesarean types supply the Matthean third petition in Luke 11:2.[20]

---

[16]   E. J. Goodspeed, *The New Testament: An American Translation* (Chicago: University of Chicago Press, 1923).

[17]   E. J. Goodspeed, *As I Remember* (New York: Harper & Brothers, 1953) 176.

[18]   Goodspeed, *As I Remember*, 177.

[19]   J. van Bruggen ("The Lord's Prayer and Textual Criticism," *Calvin Theological Journal* 17 [1981] 78-87) argues the case and is generally skeptical about modern text criticism, but A. J. Bandstra ("The Original Form of the Lord's Prayer," *Calvin Theological Journal* 16 [1981] 15-37) provides a thorough refutation.

[20]   The other parallels: Aorist δός for δίδου and σήμερον for τὸ καθ' ἡμέραν in 11:3; τὰ ὀφειλήματα for τὰς ἁμαρτίας, ὡς καὶ ἡμεῖς for καὶ γὰρ αὐτοί, τοῖς ὀφειλέταις for παντὶ ὀφείλοντι ἡμῖν, and the insertion of ἀλλὰ ῥῦσαι ἡμᾶς ἀπὸ τοῦ πονηροῦ in 11:4.

The most interesting Lukan variant appears in 11:2: Several medieval manuscripts have for the second petition, "Let your holy spirit come upon us and cleanse us." This reading is attested in the East in the writings of Gregory of Nyssa and faintly in the West in Tertullian. Perhaps the reading entered the manuscript tradition out of Montanism in the second century CE and likely in connection with baptism.[21]

The longer Matthean version shows no variants of the harmonistic type. The most significant variant here is the doxology or ascription—"For thine is the kingdom, and the power, and the glory, for ever"—which also appears in the *Didache* (c. 125 CE) but not in the best manuscripts of the Alexandrian, Western, and pre-Caesarean types. (The manuscript tradition shows a number of interesting minor variations to this reading.) It would also seem to have crept into the Matthean Prayer as a gloss encouraged by liturgical usage.[22] There are numerous other minor variations between the two forms of the Prayer as well as within the manuscript tradition, but these will not be comprehensively itemized.

The manuscript tradition of the Prayer thus shows that its text was not immune to accretions or modifications. A critical Greek text, maintaining the striking differences between Matthew and Luke, must form the starting point for a consideration of the original form and meaning of the Prayer.[23]

TRADITION-HISTORY AND THE SOCIAL CONTEXTS OF
THE LORD'S PRAYER

The early tradition history of the Lord's Prayer must be reconstructed primarily through canonical New Testament materials (Q through Luke, Matthew; allusions in Paul, Mark).[24] *Didache* 8 provides a point of reference for Syrian tradition after the time of

---

21   B. M. Metzger, *A Textual Commentary on the Greek New Testament: A Companion Volume to the United Bible Societies' Greek New Testament* (3rd ed., London and New York: The United Bible Societies, 1971) 155-56.

22   Metzger, *A Textual Commentary*, 16-17; H. D. Betz, *The Sermon on the Mount* (Hermeneia; Minneapolis: Fortress, 1995) 414-15.

23   The NA[27] edition provides this basis.

24   G. J. Brooke traces allusions more extensively in Paul and John ("The Lord's Prayer Interpreted through John and Paul," *Downside Review* 98 [1980] 298-311). Compare the chart in J. L. Houlden, "The Lord's Prayer," *ABD* 4.357.

Matthew, but the Gospel of Thomas does not allude to the prayer or seem to offer additional insight. Several earlier stages or strata can be perceived through a tradition-critical analysis of the canonical materials. The penultimate stage corresponds with the latest form of the Q Prayer; developments from Jesus to the latest Q form are perceptible though somewhat dimly; and some proposals can be made about the form of the Prayer used by Jesus himself. We turn to an examination of these stages in reverse chronological order.

Stage 3: The Latest Setting in Q

Doubt persists as to whether the Lord's Prayer pericope belonged to Q.[25] Kloppenborg accepts the Prayer as early as Q[1], since he claims it formed the core of one of the sapiential speeches. Jacobson, however, sees the Prayer as a late addition to Q (with concerns similar to the Temptation) and follows Manson in thinking that it may have been "secret teaching" reserved for the mature. Betz also urges that the Prayer entered Q rather late in two different versions, and existed only in Greek.[26]

The most persuasive reasons for seeing a Q version behind Luke and Matthew reside in the verbatim identity of Petitions 1-2 and in the word ἐπιούσιον. In regard to the latter, it would be very difficult for two completely independent versions of the Prayer to convey the Aramaic by a word that turns out to be *hapax legomenon* in ancient Greek. This fact seems easier to account for by means of a common Greek origin for the canonical prayers. Departures from that common form have then to be accounted for more by the evangelists' redaction than by translation, but the divergences in their language still reflect to some extent uncertainties about meaning

---

[25]   Kloppenborg provides a helpful survey, *Q Parallels: Synopsis, Critical Notes, and Concordance* (Foundations and Facets Reference Series; Sonoma: Polebridge, 1988) 84.

[26]   J. S. Kloppenborg, *The Formation of Q: Trajectories in Ancient Wisdom Collections* (Studies in Antiquity and Christianity; Philadelphia: Fortress, 1987) 203-206; A. D. Jacobson, *The First Gospel: An Introduction to Q* (Foundations and Facets Series; Sonoma: Polebridge, 1992) 158-59; F. J. Botha, "Recent Research on the Lord's Prayer," *Neot* 1 (1967) 43. Betz, *Sermon on the Mount*, 371: "If the Lord's Prayer was part of Q, it must have become a part of it after the two versions of Q developed." He denies (p. 375) that the Prayer ever existed in Aramaic: "no evidence suggests that the Lord's Prayer as we have it was first composed in Aramaic or Hebrew and only then translated into Greek."

derivative from the Prayer's earlier history.

At the latest Q stage, before the Prayer was taken up and edited by. Matthew and Luke, the Q prayer had a form similar to this:[27]

	Address	Πάτερ
Table 1	Petition 1	ἁγιασθήτω τὸ ὄνομά σου
	Petition 2	ἐλθέτω ἡ βασιλεία σου
Table 2	Petition 4	τὸν ἄρτον ἡμῶν τὸν ἐπιούσιον δὸς ἡμῖν σήμερον
	Petition 5	καὶ ἄφες ἡμῖν τὰ ὀφειλήματα ἡμῶν καὶ γὰρ αὐτοὶ ἀφήκαμεν τῷ ὀφείλοντι ἡμῖν
	Petition 6	καὶ μὴ εἰσενέγκῃς ἡμᾶς εἰς πειρασμόν

Even given a Q Lord's Prayer, the view of Jeremias that an "original Aramaic form" lies behind the Greek retains strong plausibility because of the uncertainties regarding meaning manifest in Matthew's and Luke's diverging wordings:

> the Lucan version has preserved the oldest form with respect to length, but the Matthaean text is more original with regard to wording.[28]

Jeremias' reasons for giving priority to the Lukan length were fourfold: (1) The strict parallelism of Matthew's version, as well as (2) Matthew's greater elaboration, suggested to Jeremias the end product of liturgical usage. Furthermore, (3) Luke's simple address "Father," in contrast to Matthew's "Our Father in heaven" (well attested in Targums and later Jewish prayer forms), seems to reflect the Aramaic address of Jesus, אבא, also adopted by later Christians (Paul: Rom 8:15; Gal 4:6; *Didache* 8). Finally, (4) Jeremias noted the parallel between the Lucan version of the first two petitions of the Lord's Prayer and the *Qaddish* of the Jewish synagogue. The *Qaddish* begins (following Jeremias' arrangement):

> Exalted and hallowed be his great name in the world which he created according to his will. May he let his kingdom rule in your lifetime and in your days and in the lifetime of the whole house of Israel, speedily and

---

27   W. D. Davies and D. C. Allison, "Excursus: The Lord's Prayer: Matthew 6.9-13 = Luke 11.2-4," in *A Critical and Exegetical Commentary on the Gospel according to Saint Matthew*. Volume I: *Introduction and Commentary on Matthew I-VII* (ICC; Edinburgh: T. & T. Clark, 1988) 591. Duling and Perrin concur, *The New Testament*, 16.

28   J. Jeremias, *The Prayers of Jesus* (SBT 6; London: SCM Press, 1967) 93. Cf. J. A. Fitzmyer, *The Gospel According to Luke X–XXIV* (AB 28A; Garden City: Doubleday, 1985) 897.

soon. And to this, say: amen.[29]

On the other hand, Jeremias was forced to the anomalous conclusion that, in terms of the specific wording of the respective prayers, the Matthean version was at several points indicative of earlier understandings. What these observations imply is that a critical discussion of an "original Aramaic form" is still necessary, though in this task Jeremias' position requires some modifications. The changes and expansions evident between Luke and Matthew are along lines governed not only by a semitic linguistic sensibility, but also by social interests operant in the tradition.

It is important to have some definite, even though general, ideas about the social origins of the Q recensions. Kloppenborg has provided the most satisfying proposal so far about these matters. He notes that the wisdom interests manifested in the contents and composition of Q^1 (consequently, "Wisdom Q") would be appropriate to town or village scribes, "the 'petit bourgeois' in the lower administrative sector of cities and villages. It is plain from Egyptian evidence that it is precisely within these sectors that the instructional genre was cultivated."[30] Moreover, wisdom was usually the concern of royal administrative personnel. And Q^1's metaphorical preoccupation with an "alternate kingdom" would indicate this as well.[31] It goes a step beyond Kloppenborg, though he sparks the thought, to suggest that Herod Antipas' administrative personnel around the Galilean Lake probably provided the first Q draft (adumbrated by Matt 9:9?). Kloppenborg tantalizingly suggests that the transfer of Tiberias to Agrippa II (54 CE), and concomitantly the royal archives back to Sepphoris, left its mark in the Q tradition in the move to prophetic forms. It certainly makes sense, given that ancient recensions were frequently connected with changes in political fortunes, to connect the more heavily Judean character of Q^2 ("Deuteronomic Q") with the work of Sepphorean scribes.[32] These

---

[29] Jeremias, *Prayers*, 98.

[30] Kloppenborg, "Literary Convention," 85. Jacobson's reservations about "wisdom" (*First Gospel*, 257) are noted. He prefers to account for Q transformations by appeals to the diachronic experiences (p. 256) of a single group, while the proposal here assumes activity in different scribal spheres.

[31] Kloppenborg, *Formation of Q*, 317-20.

[32] R. B. Coote and M. P. Coote, *Power, Politics, and the Making of the Bible: An Introduction* (Minneapolis: Fortress, 1990). On the Judean character of Sepphoris, see S. S. Miller, *Studies in the History and Traditions of Sepphoris*

considerations would urge dating Q^1 somewhere between the late 20s and 54 CE, and Q^2 somewhere in the period 54-66 CE.[33]

Zahavy has lent insight into the sociology of scribalism around the time of the Judean-Roman War. In the immediate aftermath, he sees a struggle between scribes who focused their ultimate concerns and piety around the *Shema^c* and Deuteronomy and scribes whose interests congregated in the *Amidah*. As he sees the situation:

> In the crucial transitional period after the destruction of the Temple, the *Shema^c* emerged as the primary ritual of the scribal profession and its proponents. The *Amidah* . . . was a ritual sponsored mainly by the patriarchal families and their priestly adherents.[34]

Both of these scribal groups were involved in Jerusalem-Judean affairs, but Zahavy's "professional scribes" would have been less tied to Jerusalem than families associated with the temple and priesthood. Therefore, post-temple Judaism was to be (as Zahavy sees it) a compromise between these two scribal interests, attested in the combination of *Shema^c* and *Amidah* in the synagogue service. What Zahavy's work suggests about the Q tradents, assuming similar circumstances a quarter century or so before, is this: Q^1 was the product of Herodian scribes; Q^2 was the product of Judean scribes whose theological commitments were expressed through the *Shema^c*. A logical line from Q^1 to Q^2 and the later synoptic tradition (in strong argument with Pharisees and post-temple developments) can begin to be traced.

Stage 2: Between Jesus and Q^2

So within years of Jesus' death, if not during his lifetime, some intrepid collector or collectors began gathering his oral legacy and committing it to writing. It is perhaps appropriate to apply the second-century word of Papias to this stage, "Matthew collected the sayings in the Hebrew language, and each interpreted them as best he could."[35] Jesus' sayings existed originally in Aramaic (Papias'

(SJLA 37; Leiden: Brill, 1984).

[33] Jacobson (*First Gospel*, 251-55) indicates that the situation was probably more complicated than indicated in a two-stage development. For the purposes of this essay, however, identifying the two major contexts is sufficient.

[34] T. Zahavy, *Studies in Jewish Prayer* (Studies in Judaism; Lanham and London: University Press of America, 1990) 87.

[35] Eusebius, *Eccl. Hist.* 3.39.16. Kloppenborg is extremely skeptical

"Hebrew"), but were partially in Greek as early as Q[1].

Numerous attempts at retrotranslation (from Greek to Aramaic or Hebrew) have been made over the last century. Notable are the efforts of Dalman, Jeremias, Fitzmyer, and de Moor.[36] Whereas Dalman, Jeremias, and Fitzmyer had attempted to recover the "everyday" speech of Jesus, de Moor places the Prayer within the sphere of "literary Aramaic." Here is something like the Aramaic exemplar for Q[2] (following Fitzmyer):

	Address	אבא
Table 1	Petition 1	יתקדש שמך
	Petition 2	תיתי מלכותך
Table 2	Petition 4	לחמנא דימסתיא (דלמחר :Jeremias; פתגם יום :de Moor)
		הב לנה יומא דנה (ביומיה :de Moor)
	Petition 5	ושבוק לנה חובינא כדי שבקנא לחיבינא
	Petition 6	ולא תעלינא (איתינא :de Moor) לנסיון

Since various assumptions have to come into play, consensus about reconstruction has not been achieved. Variations in the modern retrotranslations appear especially in the second table (the underlined words). Fitzmyer aptly writes: "The reconstruction of the original Aramaic form of the 'Our Father' will always remain problematic, conditioned above all by our knowledge of the Palestinian Aramaic of Jesus' days."[37] Not only the Aramaic, but also the meaning of the Greek controlling the Aramaic retrotranslation is obscure. Though consensus may not be possible, certain details in the tradition reach higher salience, especially related to bread and debt.

The evidence of Paul and Mark with respect to the use of אבא

(*Formation of Q*, 51-54).

36 G. H. Dalman, "Anhang A: Das Vaterunser," in *Die Worte Jesu* (2nd ed., Leipzig: Hinrichs, 1930) 283-365; J. Jeremias, "The Lord's Prayer in Modern Research," *ExpTim* 71 (1960) 141-46; Fitzmyer, *The Gospel According to Luke X–XXIV*, 901; J. C. de Moor, "The Reconstruction of the Aramaic Original of the Lord's Prayer," in W. van der Meer and J. C. de Moor (eds.), *The Structural Analysis of Biblical and Canaanite Poetry* (JSOTSup 74; Sheffield: JSOT Press, 1988) 403 n. 17; B. D. Chilton, *Jesus' Prayer and Jesus' Eucharist* (Valley Forge: Trinity Press International, 1997). See Davies and Allison, "Excursus: The Lord's Prayer," 593. For an attempt to discover a Hebrew exemplar of the Prayer, see B. Young, *The Jewish Background to the Lord's Prayer* (Austin: Center for Judaic-Christian Studies, 1984). See also J. P. Meier, *A Marginal Jew: Rethinking the Historical Jesus* (ABRL 2; New York: Doubleday, 1994) 291-302.

37 Fitzmyer, *Luke X–XXIV*, 901.

supplies important information regarding this period of the Prayer's history. Since the Lord's Prayer inculcates an election consciousness that bespeaks immediacy with God, these two writers seem generally familiar with Jesus' characteristic understanding of God (Q = Luke 10:21-22; Rom 8:15-16; Mark 1:10-11; 14:36). Mark 11:25 and 14:36 also seem to echo the third and fifth petitions, but neither Paul nor Mark quotes the entire Prayer. How should its absence in their texts be understood?

As the Corinthian correspondence, Romans 15, and Acts make clear, Paul was widely traveled, and it would be difficult now to determine with precision where he came into contact with particular streams of early Jesus traditions. By a careful study of quotes and allusions, and keeping in mind Victor Paul Furnish's observation about Paul's rare use of Jesus in contrast to the Old Testament,[38] we can make the following observations:

> (1) Paul seems only fragmentarily to have known Q in its distinctive Galilean form (i.e. Wisdom Q). 1 Corinthians 9:14 and 10:27 allude to Luke 10:7-8 respectively. These seem to be the only places where Paul connects with Q^r. Perhaps one of the factions of Corinth possessed a copy, in view of the general concern for wisdom there. However, Paul's failure to mention the Prayer where it might be beneficial (e.g. 1 Corinthians 11 in reference to the communal difficulties surrounding the meal of association, when such a Prayer might be offered) seems to speak against this, or at least Paul's knowledge of it.

> (2) Paul otherwise is more familiar with "Judean" elements of the synoptics, as when he refers in 1 Cor 7:10-11 to something like Mark 10:11 or in 1 Cor 11:23-25 to something like Luke 22:17-19. Already in 1 Thess 5:2, 4 there is contact with Q = Luke 12:39 or Mark 13:35-36. Elsewhere (Rom 12:14, 17) Paul shows familiarity with traditions like Q = Luke 6:27, 29 = Matt 5:39-44 and in a fashion that would suggest concern for Antiochene Torah interpretation. Concerns with marital purity, Jerusalem traditions of the Last Supper, Torah interpretation, and apocalyptic timetables we would expect from a former Pharisee (Gal 1:14; Phil 3:5) who received significant elements of his knowledge about Jesus from the Jerusalem church (1 Cor

---

[38]   V. P. Furnish, *Theology and Ethics in Paul* (Nashville and New York: Abingdon Press, 1968) 55: ". . . one must concede the relative sparsity of direct references to or citations of Jesus' teachings in the Pauline letters. The argument that he could presuppose his readers' familiarity with these because he had already passed them on in his missionary preaching is not convincing. He could and does presuppose knowledge of the Old Testament, but this in no way deters him from constantly and specifically citing it in the course of his ethical teaching."

11:23; 15:3).[39]

Mark, while still remaining unfamiliar with the majority of Q's contents, had more substantial contact with them (how is unclear). This can be seen, for instance, in Mark's knowledge of Q = Luke 3:2-4; 3:16-17; 4:1-2; 10:4-11 (cf. Paul); 11:14-23; 13:18-19. As in Q[2], Mark also evinces a prophet christology (e.g. Mark 1:1, 8, 10; Q = Luke 6:23; 7:31-35), shows conflict with Pharisees (Mark 2:16; Q elements of Luke 11:39-52), a heightened concern with purity issues (Mark 7:1-2, 14-15; Q = Luke 11:39-41), and apocalyptic/eschatological preoccupations (e.g. "son of man" preoccupations as at Mark 14:62; Q = Luke 12:8). Paul was not familiar with the bulk of this material (absence of "son of man" material in Paul is particularly striking), so a time after Paul for Q[2] seems appropriate. Mark, however, clearly had contact with or at least shared interests with the later Q tradents.

Q[1], therefore, did not contain the Lord's Prayer, or contained the Lord's Prayer (Kloppenborg) which however remained unknown to Paul and Mark. These both were substantially linked to Jerusalem-Judean traditions. Paul remained largely ignorant of Galilean Jesus materials, though Mark had access to Galilean miracle stories and ideas similar to those of Q[2].[40] As the two-source hypothesis has long urged, extensive Jesus materials were mediated independently to Matthew, Luke, and John(?) through at least two separate lineages of Judean-oriented scribes (Mark, Q). Q was a Galilean source, but with Judean interests. Unless the "secret teaching" hypothesis is embraced, the Lord's Prayer would seem to have been largely unknown or only imperfectly known to Jerusalem-Judean sources (available to Paul and Mark) until the later first century.

Stage 1: The Setting of Jesus

The Lord's Prayer existed in a much simpler form in the context of Jesus and the earliest Jesus movement, and grew by certain measurable developments into the forms we have come to know today.[41] The differences in form are best accounted for by differing

---

[39]   Compare Betz's assessment of these issues, and additional bibliography (*Sermon on the Mount*, 6 and n. 12).

[40]   G. Theissen, *The Gospels in Context: Social and Political History in the Synoptic Tradition* (Minneapolis: Fortress, 1991) 99.

[41]   There are similarities between the approach of this essay and the views of

scribal traditions and interests.

Some further decisions are necessary about the form of the Prayer for Jesus. The uniformity of the first table in contrast to the second at the Q^2 stage suggests that the former was extremely conventional and perhaps extant only in Greek, while the latter offered difficulties of interpretation indicative of the earlier move from Aramaic to Greek. Besides uniformity in the Greek, various other considerations argue against the first table having belonged originally to the Prayer of Jesus; chief among them are linguistic, internal theological, and external social considerations. Linguistically, the first table adopts the more polite jussive, while the imperatives of the second table are coarse and direct. Theologically, there is great tension between Jesus' own *Abba*-consciousness and Petitions 1, 2, or 3; as well, the abstractions of the first table (God's name, kingdom, and will) militate against the concrete and mundane concerns in Jesus' Prayer. Sociologically, the first table stands in clear relationship to later synagogue prayer traditions and thus is an understandable accretion.

Taussig points out that אבא stands uneasily over against the first petition. He characterizes this tension as deriving from either Jesus or someone closer to Q: "The irony of an occasional juxtaposition of the familiar אבא with the next phrase 'May your name be holy' certainly could have been appreciated by a witty aphorizer."[42] A comparable tension, however, is evident between the second petition and the address. An immediate consciousness of God and concern for God's direct involvement in the moment (second table) are *both* difficult to reconcile with purity (Petition 1) and eschatology (Petition 2).

Jeremias a generation ago pointed out the connection between the Lord's Prayer and the *Qaddish*. He can be criticized today for a rather anachronistic employment of this material, since there is debate as to the antiquity of the prayer.[43] Jeremias argued that the

---

Lohmeyer, who distinguished a Galilean from a Jerusalem form of the Prayer. We work with a more developed relation of the Prayer to social context.

[42]   H. Taussig, "The Lord's Prayer," *Forum* 4.4 (1988) 33.

[43]   D. Baumgardt ("Kaddish and Lord's Prayer," *Jewish Bible Quarterly (Dor leDor)* 19 [1991] 165), who is dependent upon I. Elbogen, *Der jüdische Gottesdienst*, notes that the *Qaddish* is attested no earlier than the Byzantine period. De Moor ("The Reconstruction of the Aramaic Original of the Lord's Prayer," 405 n. 26) claims that the "antiquity of the prayer is recognized by all authorities" and appeals to *b. Ber.* 3a (R. Jose b. Halaphta, c. 150 CE) and *Sipre* §306 (132[b]). S.

form of the *Qaddish* validated the shorter Lukan form of the prayer, even though all three of Matthew's first-table petitions are contained within the *Qaddish*:

> *Exalted and hallowed be his great name* in the world which he created *according to his will.*

> May he let his *kingdom rule* (*etc.*)

> [Our Father who are in heaven, let your name be *sanctified*, let your *kingdom come*, let your *will be done* (*etc.*)]

Clearly the *Qaddish* is related to the late-synoptic forms of the Lord's Prayer. There are also perceptible links between the Lord's Prayer and the *Amidah* (or *Shemoneh Esreh*, "Eighteen Benedictions").[44] As Zahavy's discussion of the social origins of these materials indicates, Jerusalem-Judean interests are in view, with the implication that the Lord's Prayer was augmented at the Q^2 stage for better alignment with Judean scribal interests. Hence, the first table of the Lord's Prayer ought to be assigned pink, if not gray, in the scheme of The Jesus Seminar's *The Five Gospels*.[45]

However, whereas Taussig and the Jesus Seminar have tended to read Jesus too much in relation to Socrates, Jesus' concerns can with greater historical logic be seen to stand solidly within the orbit of Israelite tradition, have much more to do with Moses than Socrates, and define Jesus as a particular type of first-century "Jew." This is evident in a perceptible link between the Lukan beatitudes (the first sapiential compositional unit in Q^1) and the Aramaic beginning of the Passover Haggadah:[46]

Passover Haggadah	*Beatitudes*
The bread of poverty	Blessed are you poor
Let all who are hungry	Blessed are the hungry
This year we are here	Blessed are those who mourn

Likewise, the second discourse in Q^1 = Luke 10:4 contains a possible

---

T. Lachs ("The Lord's Prayer," in Lachs, *A Rabbinic Commentary on the New Testament* [Hoboken: Ktav, 1987] 118) considers that the *Qaddish* is too dissimilar to the Lord's Prayer to provide a convincing parallel and that the Tannaitic "short prayer" (תפיללה קצרה) provides a more appropriate genre.

44   Lachs, "The Lord's Prayer," 118, 123 n. 1. Davies and Allison, "Excursus: The Lord's Prayer," 595-97.

45   Funk and Hoover (eds.), *The Five Gospels*, 36-38.

46   A fuller statement about this connection is made in Oakman, "Archaeology of First-Century Galilee," 220-51.

(albeit negative) allusion to Exod 12:11. Ezekiel the Tragedian, of the second century BCE, already showed a concern for this text in the Hellenistic period:

> your loins girt up and shoes upon your feet, and in your hand a staff, for thus in haste the king will order all to leave the land. It shall be called "Passover."[47]

It is clear in comparing Mark's to Q's "discourses" that the respective traditions have situated these instructions within a less focused mission for the kingdom of God. Mark's tradition would thus seem to be closer to Jesus given an original Passover or Passover pilgrimage setting for the material. The injunctions about money, bag, food, and clothing suggest dependence upon hospitality along the pilgrim's way, perhaps reflecting trust that God will provide for the pilgrim. Galilean "Jews" seem to have been particularly attracted to the Passover pilgrimage. Jesus alluded to Exodus imagery in stating the meaning of his own healing activity (Q = Luke 11:20; cf. Exod 8:19). And Jesus' Last Supper (even if not a Passover meal) is clearly tied to the great festival within the synoptic tradition.

While this is not the place to develop a full-blown account of the "theology of Jesus," a few remarks will make intelligible the exegetical approach taken below toward the Lord's Prayer. Jesus' preaching of the kingdom is universally conceded by scholars to be the center of his historical message.[48] The interests of Jesus in Passover and Exodus, as well as the early prophet christologies, would suggest that he meant by "kingdom of God" something like the "lordship of God" over historical affairs and looked for something like an Exodus from "Egypt," representing what must have been felt to be oppressive circumstances of his first-century environment. Jesus was not a scripture specialist, however, and seemed to flesh out his theology as a kind of village wisdom preacher more with

---

47   *Exagōgē* 181-184, according to R. G. Robertson, "Ezekiel the Tragedian," in J. H. Charlesworth (ed.), *The Old Testament Pseudepigrapha 2: Expansions of the "Old Testament" and Legends, Wisdom and Philosophical Literature, Prayers, Psalms and Odes, Fragments of Lost Judeo-Hellenistic Works* (ABRL 14; Garden City: Doubleday, 1985) 816. Cf. Mark 6:8-9 which is closer to the injunction of Ezekiel.

48   J. Jeremias, *New Testament Theology 1: The Proclamation of Jesus* (New York: Scribner's, 1971) 96. N. Perrin (*Rediscovering the Teaching of Jesus* [New York: Harper & Row, 1976] 47) points to the close linkage between kingdom of God and the Prayer.

reference to the natural order of things.[49] Both aspects (concern with Moses and natural theological wisdom) allow us to understand how the peasant Jesus could inspire Wisdom Q as well as Deuteronomic Q and apocalyptic Mark.

This picture seems corroborated by indications of Josephus about typical, lower-class theological concerns around the Lake of Galilee. During the early phases of the Judean-Roman War, Jesus son of Sapphias had led an attack of the lower classes of Tiberias against Herod Antipas's palace, in which were animal representations.[50] Half a century earlier, Judas of Gamala had urged that payment of Roman taxes was a sign of servitude to alien gods.[51] If Judas of Gamala brought to expression the rage of at least some Galilean peasantry, who could be convinced that Roman Palestine might be a new Egypt, then Jesus of Nazareth operating in the vicinity naturally might have shared similar religious interests and orientations. His interests and concerns stand at the root of a complex of traditions, not only Q^1, but also Q^2, Paul, Mark, and even John. Elaborations of these traditions have to be kept in the discussion about Jesus' theological and social outlooks. The Lord's Prayer, nonetheless, can certainly be understood as an expression of familiarity with the God of Exodus.[52] Its meaning thus can be investigated within a developmental frame that expanded Jesus' concrete requests in definite directions.

THE SOCIAL MEANING OF THE LORD'S PRAYER

Three major stages of development of the Lord's Prayer have thus been suggested, now listed in chronological order: *Stage (1)* The form of the prayer in Jesus' own usage, consisting of the address + Petitions 4-6; *Stage (2)* the difficult-to-trace transition from oral-Aramaic to written-Greek forms of the Prayer; and *Stage (3)* the form of the Prayer reached by the latest stratum of Q (as seen in Luke), consisting of the address + Petitions 1-2 + Petitions 4-6. Matthew and *Didache*, indicative of late first-century Syrian tradition, subsequently carried things further by the addition of expanded address, Petitions 3 and 7, plus the doxology. These presumptions

---

49   Oakman, *Jesus and the Economic Questions*, 240-42.
50   *Life* 12 §65-7.
51   *J.W.* 2.8.1 §118; *Ant.* 18.1.1 §4.
52   R. F. Cyster ("The Lord's Prayer and the Exodus Tradition," *Th* 64 [1961] 377-81) provides a rather popular treatment of this idea.

now come into play in pursuit of the social meaning of the Lord's
Prayer, first for Jesus and then for the later tradents of the Jesus
traditions.

The Address

Luke's version of the address stands closest to the actual speech of
Jesus. The emphatic and simple address, in contrast to Matthew's
version which reflects more nearly the formal conventions of
synagogue prayer, is noteworthy.[53] Jeremias argued for the
uniqueness within Judaism, as well as the intimacy, of addressing
God as אבא, "Papa," but both claims are disputed today.[54]

Whether intimate or simply direct, the prayer addresses as *pater
familias*, "head of the household," the One who is also expected to
rule as King. The petitioner acts as a royal personage and heir, a part
of the royal household.[55] The generosity and benevolence of the
King are invoked, who acts as Patron. This assumption of the
graciousness and benevolence of God comes through at several other
points in the Jesus tradition. One thinks, for instance, of the Prodigal
Son/Father (L = Luke 15:11-32). There are also passages like M =
Matt 5:45; Q = Luke 11:11-13; 12:30; and Mark 10:30.[56] In Jesus'
context, the concern for God's patronage in relation to concrete need
was underscored by immediate transition to the petitions of the
second table.

Petition 4 of the Second Table

The general concern of Jesus and the early Jesus movement for the
hungry is manifest directly in the feeding narratives (e.g. Mark
6:34-44) and indirectly by a number of other gospel passages. For
instance, many of the people "healed" by Jesus were perhaps
suffering the effects of malnutrition. These were typically people
with skin ailments or eye problems (Mark 1:40-45; 10:46; cf. 5:43
and the Q saying Matt 6:22-23)—perhaps due simply to vitamin
deficiencies. Therefore, one must emphasize the therapeutic signifi-

---

53   Jeremias, *Prayers*, 96-97.

54   Davies and Allison, "Excursus: The Lord's Prayer," 601-602; J. Barr,
"Abba Isn't Daddy," *JTS* 39 (1988) 28-47.

55   This will have further implications in the discussion of the bread petition.

56   Kloppenborg, "Literary Convention," 89. See Malina, *The Social World of
Jesus and the Gospels*, 143-75.

cance, in a physical as well as a social sense, of table fellowship for the Jesus movement (Mark 2:15). This fellowship was probably the primary *Sitz im Leben* of the first petition of Jesus' Prayer, a table fellowship I have elsewhere argued was tied to Passover concerns.[57]

Interpreting the petition for bread has long been vexed by the question surrounding the meaning of the word ἐπιούσιος. Questions were already raised in the days of Origen, who believed the word was a neologism of the evangelists. On the basis of current philology, Origen's judgment appears to be correct.[58]

Four major solutions to the issue of meaning have been suggested over the centuries: (1) That of Origen, Chrysostom, and others tracing the etymology of ἐπιούσιος to ἐπί + οὐσία = "necessary for existence"; (2) that of Debrunner seeing an analogy with the phrase ἐπὶ τὴν οὖσαν [sc. ἡμέραν], "for the current day"; (3) that of Grotius, Wettstein, and Lightfoot connecting the adjective with the Greek phrase ἡ ἐπιοῦσα [sc. ἡμέρα], "the following day"; (4) finally, that of Cyril of Alexander, Peter of Laodicea, and others linking ἐπιούσιος with the verb ἐπιέναι "coming in the future."[59] There are subvarieties of these major solutions; all but (1) assume a temporal meaning of some sort.

The two somewhat different solutions proposed here build upon Origen's suggestion and basic interpretation. However, the meaning is not sought in the philosophical use of οὐσία, i.e. "being, existence, substance," but in the usages attested in many of the Egyptian papyri. The word οὐσία in the papyri often means "landed estate" or "large estate."[60] This is a concrete meaning rooted in the material realities

---

57   Oakman, "The Archaeology of First-Century Galilee," 243-44.

58   BAGD 297; BDF 66 §123. See, however, the cautionary remarks of A. Deissmann, *Light From the Ancient East* (Reprint; Grand Rapids: Baker, 1965) 78, whose experience with the papyri led him to suspect any "neologistic" approaches to biblical Greek. He offered a slightly different opinion in his *Bible Studies* (Reprint; Winona Lake: Alpha, 1979) 214. C. Hemer ("Epiousios," *JSNT* 22 [1984] 81-94) attempts to find a good Greek lineage for ἐπιούσιος. He follows Lightfoot and argues strenuously for Solution 3, "the following day." For a thorough discussion of previous philological solutions, see W. Foerster, "Ἐπιούσιος," *TDNT* 2 (1964) 590-99.

59   BAGD 297.

60   MM 242, s.v. ἐπιούσιος, and 467, s.v. οὐσία. J. Moulton once wrote (J. Moulton and W. F. Howard, *Grammar of New Testament Greek* [Edinburgh: T. & T. Clark, 1920] 313): "the only meaning quotable for this noun [sc. οὐσία] from NT and papyri is property or estate, which is not hopeful." Moulton could see no

of antiquity. If ἐπιούσιος is a neologism reflecting a semitic idiom, it makes sense to look for something in Aramaic incorporating the notion of "estate." The papyri, as purveyors of a more popular idiom, are more likely than Greek philosophy to give a clue to the meaning of ἐπιούσιος.

Warrant for this philological procedure is given by considering the New Testament *hapax legomenon* περιούσιος, a word linguistically near in kinship to ἐπιούσιος.[61] While περιούσιος clearly means "chosen" in Titus 2:14, its meaning in the Septuagint is tied more literally to the Hebrew word סגלה = "possession, property" and in very late Hebrew "treasure."[62] Thus, in Eccl 2:8 (LXX) "Solomon" talks about having gathered "gold and silver, and treasures (περιουσιασμούς) of kings and countries." In the Greek papyri, περιούσιος means "abundance, superfluity." An excellent example of the use of this word from approximately the same time as the prayer of Jesus was being translated from Aramaic into Greek is given by the famous rescript of Claudius to the Alexandrian Jewish community (c. 41 CE):

> I explicitly order the Jews not to agitate for more privileges than they formerly possessed . . . while enjoying their own privileges and sharing a great abundance [περιούσιος] of advantages in a city not their own . . .[63]

Περιούσιος in some cases in the Septuagint and in the secular usage

---

way to elucidate the meaning of ἐπιούσιος from the papyri. He did, however, recognize (p. 91) that the lack of elision between ἐπί and οὐσία would constitute no barrier to Solution 1: "The Hellenistic indifference to the confluence of vowels, due to the slower pronunciation which has been already noted, is well seen . . . This feature of the Κοινή makes it very plain that classical scholars of the last generation were yielding to their besetting sin when they ruled out (e.g.) etymologies of ἐπιούσιος that broke the laws of 'correctness' by allowing hiatus." Recently, Fitzmyer (*The Gospel According to Luke X–XXIV*, 900) has endorsed the use of Solution 1 with these words: "After long consideration, I have reverted to the explanation given by Origen . . ."

[61]   Titus 2:14, quoting Deut 14:2 (LXX). Origen already noted this parallel, observing the underlying material implications of both words in ordinary speech but arguing for the "spiritual" meaning of ἐπιούσιος in view of the use of περιούσιος in Titus.

[62]   BDB 688. M. Jastrow, *A Dictionary of the Targumim, the Talmud Babli and Yerushalmi, and the Midrashic Literature* (2 vols., New York: Pardes, 1950) 953.

[63]   A. Hunt and C. Edgar, *Select Papyri* (LCL 282; Harvard University, 1956) 2.87; MM 507.

of the papyri occurs in contexts reflecting material abundance. A
similar sphere of meaning can be suggested for ἐπιούσιος.[64]

Thus, the first proposal offered here is that ἐπιούσιος is simply a
synonym for περιούσιος as used in the papyri, which would lead to
the meaning for the fourth petition, "give us today bread in
abundance." The implication is that adequate bread is not available,
and the Divine Patron is approached for immediate redress. Since
several of the ancient Jewish apocalypses expected the end time to be
a time of great abundance, it is not difficult to see how this petition
might later (in Q) have connected with eschatological themes.[65]

A related inquiry (proposal two) might pursue some semitic idiom
behind the word ἐπιούσιος. Fitzmyer, presuming Origen's basic
view, cites Prov 30:8 חֻקִּי לֶחֶם, "the food I need." In the Aramaic
targum this is expressed לַחְמָא <דִּי> מִסְתִּי. Fitzmyer consequently
offers as a translation for his reconstruction of the Aramaic form of
the bread petition: "Give us this day our bread for subsistence."[66]
This concrete meaning (as opposed to Origen's abstraction of
"supersubstantial" bread) undoubtedly appealed to peasants. Again,
"peasant" included not only agriculturalists, but also their impoverished relatives eking out a living in lowly building trades or the
fishing syndicates by the lake.[67]

Perhaps there is yet another option related to this line of inquiry:
A correspondence might be established between ἐπί and the Aramaic
particle דִּי. Both the Greek preposition and the Aramaic particle can
serve to mark the genitive case in their respective languages.[68]

---

64   Ἐπί often means "in addition, above" [in a figurative sense], BAGD 287,
s.v. ἐπί II.1.b.b . Περί in περιούσιος is synonymous with ὑπέρ: J. Moulton and
W. F. Howard, *Grammar*, 321. The adverb ἐνούσιος also provides an analogy,
meaning "very rich"; LSJ 572, 1439.

65   E.g. *1 Enoch* 10; *2 Apoc. Bar.* 29:5.

66   Fitzmyer, *Luke X–XXIV*, 900-901.

67   Oakman, "Was Jesus a Peasant?" 117-18.

68   "A genuine Aram. idiom," according to BDB 1088. The corresponding
particle in late Hebrew is שֶׁ, which shows the influence of Aramaic: "in usage
limited to late Heb., and passages with N. Palest. colouring," BDB 979. Cf.
Jastrow, *Dictionary*, 1577, s.v. שֶׁל [= שֶׁ]. A literal equivalence would pair ἐπί with
Aramaic עַל = "upon." N. Turner (*A Grammar of New Testament Greek*
[Edinburgh: T. & T. Clark, 1963] 271) shows that during the New Testament
period ἐπί was fast becoming a marker of the accusative case rather than the
genitive case. The ratios for various bodies of literature (taken from Turner) are:
(Papyri) 4.5 [gen.] :: 2.5 [acc.], (NT) 1.2 :: 2, (LXX) 1.4 :: 3.8.

Hence, there may be nothing more than a simple possessive sense demanded by the ἐπί: "Belonging to the estate or property." In Dan 2:15, for instance, the Aramaic reads שַׁלִּיטָא דִּי־מַלְכָּא, "the king's captain." In the Septuagint, this is translated by a simple genitive case. However, in the case of ἐπιούσιος a very literal correspondence between the languages has evidently been maintained. It might also be an attempt to avoid ambiguities which would result from making a genitival adjective out of οὐσία, the stem of which ends in *iota*.

Such a wooden Greek translation may have signposted a meaning integral to Jesus' understanding of אבא: The patron made regular provision for those already on the estate ("the kingdom"). A suggestive late-Hebrew parallel is at hand in *Ruth Rab.* 5.6 (on Ruth 2:14). There reference is made to לחם שֶׁל מַלְכוּת, "bread belonging to the kingdom," or "the royal maintenance."[69] Οὐσία in the Egyptian papyri can signify an imperial estate. Ἐπιούσιος with this connotation would then give the following sense for the fourth petition: "Give us the bread of the kingdom today," or perhaps "Give us the royal bread ration today." An even more colloquial rendition, taken in conjunction with the suggested interpretation of the address, might be: "Give us today bread on the house." These are words spoken by the King's own children, addressed to their benevolent Father.

(Secondary: Petition 1 of the First Table)

Abundant or "estate-bread" was of immediate concern to Jesus and his disciples, but the Q tradition moved toward greater theological abstraction. If the Lord's Prayer belonged to Wisdom Q, then the concrete concerns above were still evident in Q = Luke 11:9-13 (better preserved at the end in Matt 7:11). A later concern about idolatry in Deuteronomic Q (Q = Luke 4:3-4, 7-8) pushed the meaning of the Prayer toward a concern for purity of the name (Q = Luke 11:2) and eventually the doing of God's righteous will on earth (Matt 6:10). Q and Mark would then align Jesus' interests more clearly with the prophetic traditions of Israel, and this also involved the purity and eschatological concerns evident in later first-century Jewish prayers.

A general distance, though clear connection, between Jesus and the

---

69   Jastrow, *Dictionary*, 704.

interests of Judean-Jerusalem scribes can be traced. Careful study of ἁγιάζειν, which appears in the New Testament in 1 Thessalonians, 1 Corinthians, Romans, Matthew, Luke, John, Acts, Ephesians, 1–2 Timothy, Hebrews, 1 Peter, and Revelation, shows that the word signifies New Testament materials with clear links to temple or Judean-Jerusalem interests (Paul, later gospels and Acts, Deutero-Paulines, Hebrews, and Revelation). The lack of such links in early Q (Q[1]), and the unlikelihood of such interests for peasant Galileans, is therefore worth note.[70]

The accretion of Petition 1 by the time of later Q (Q[2]) moves the Prayer more tightly into the orbit of Judean interests. What is meant by sanctification (ἁγιασθῆναι) of the name in early Judaism? Jeremias connects this petition (and the second) with the previously mentioned Jewish *Qaddish* prayer and believes that both prayers make entreaty for

> the revelation of God's eschatological kingdom . . . . They seek the hour in which God's profaned and misused name will be glorified and his reign revealed, in accordance with the promise, "I will vindicate the holiness of my great name, which has been profaned among the nations . . ." (Ezek 36:23).[71]

Jeremias' understanding, however, does not go far enough. For Jeremias and for many twentieth-century commentators, the first petition is only a prayer bidding God to sanctify his own name in an eschatological sense.

Yet even the *Qaddish* suggests a more extended significance: "Exalted and hallowed be his great name *in the world . . .*" *Who* it is who will "sanctify the name," and *where* this will happen, are the critical questions. The *Qaddish* implies that human, in addition to divine action, and actions in the world, are critical for the issue of sanctification.

This impression is borne out by a study of the idiom "sanctify the name" in rabbinic traditions.[72] The Piᶜel form of the Hebrew verb

---

70 Meier (*A Marginal Jew*, 295-98) notes that "The idea of hallowing (sanctifying, making holy) the name of God is totally absent from the rest of the Synoptic sayings of Jesus . . ."

71 Jeremias, *Prayers*, 99.

72 In addition to what is laid out here, see the material gathered in P. Billerbeck and H. L. Strack, *Kommentar zum Neuen Testament aus Talmud und Midrasch* (9th ed., Munich: Beck, 1986) 1.411-18 ("Menschen als Subjekt des Heiligens").

קדשׁ, just as the Paᶜel in Aramaic, can specify human activity as sanctification of the name. *B. Soṭa* refers to Joseph's sanctifying. deed; *Sipra* 18, §6 (339ᵃ) refers to Israel's obligation; and the third benediction of the *Amidah* enjoins such human activity without specifying precise content. Later midrash is rich in illustration. In *Genesis Rabbah* Abraham says, "I will go forth and fall [in battle] in sanctifying the name of the Holy One, Blessed be He."[73] The Levites were believed to have given their lives slaughtering the unfaithful to sanctify the name.[74] The suffering of the exile is an occasion for sanctifying the name.[75] God's name can also be sanctified when justice is accomplished in human affairs.[76] Most of these instances illustrate *in extremis* that fidelity unto death or punishment by death can sanctify the name. This observation is documented perhaps most completely by a midrashic passage about the martyrs at the time of the Bar Kochba revolt (132-35 CE):

> The Rabbis say: He [*sc.* God] adjured them by the generation of the great persecution. They are called *zebaoth* because they carried out My will (*zibyoni*) in the world and through them My will was executed; and HINDS OF THE FIELD because they poured out their blood for the sanctification of My Name . . . R. Hiyya b. Abba said: If one should say to me, "Sacrifice your life for the sanctification of God's name," I am ready to do so, on condition only that they slay me at once, but I could not endure the tortures of the great persecution.[77]

Other lesser human actions can sanctify the name of God. Blessing is one such action. In the Babylonian Talmud we read, "A

---

[73]   *Gen. Rab.* 43.2 (on Gen 14:14) [1.352]. (Numbers in brackets refer to the volume and page in H. Freedman and M. Simon [eds.], *Midrash Rabbah* [10 vols., London: Soncino, 1939]). Abraham in the fiery furnace, *Gen. Rab.* 63.2 (on Gen 25:19) [2.557]; *Lev. Rab.* 11.7 (on Lev 9:1) [4.144]; *Num. Rab.* 2.12 (on Num 2:32) [5.43]; *Eccl. Rab.* 2:14 §1 [8.64]. Jastrow, *Dictionary*, s.v. קדשׁ.

[74]   *Num. Rab.* 1.12 (on Num 1:47) [5.19-20]; *Num. Rab.* 4.6 (on Num 3:42) [5.100].

[75]   *Num. Rab.* 13.2 (on Num 7:12) [6.501]; cf. *Gen. Rab.* 98.14 (on Gen 49:17) [2.964].

[76]   David wipes out Saul's family: *Num. Rab.* 8.4 (on Num 5:6) [5.219]. Punishment of the unfaithful of Jerusalem by Nebuchadnezzar: *Lam. Rab.* 2:1 §3 [7.155].

[77]   *Cant. Rab.* 2:7 §1 [9.113]. Incidentally, the parallel between God's will and sanctification of the name is again established. On the date of the great persecution, see *Cant. Rab.* 2:5 §3 [9.106 n. 2]. However, compare *Cant. Rab.* 2:7 §1 [9.115] where "great persecution" refers to days before "Ben Koziba."

benediction which contains no mention of the Divine Name is no benediction."[78] The Passover Meal begins with a blessing of the name: "Blessed art thou, O Lord our God, creator of the fruit of the vine."[79] This connection between human blessing and divine sanctification is further cemented by the *Qaddish* at the beginning of the Sabbath service in the Jewish Prayer Book:

> Glorified and *sanctified* be God's great name throughout the world which he has created according to his will. May he establish his kingdom in your lifetime and during your days, and within the life of the entire house of Israel, speedily and soon; and say, Amen.

> May his great name *be blessed* forever and to all eternity. Blessed and praised, glorified and exalted, extolled and honored, adored and lauded be the name of the Holy One, blessed be he, beyond all the blessings and hymns, praises and consolations that are ever spoken in the world; and say, Amen.[80]

Many other such blessings—and the firm connection between blessing and God's name—can be seen throughout the devotional literature of the Jewish people. Furthermore, the Mishnah gives a rather detailed picture of the events and situations that elicit blessings.[81] Many of these blessings are connected with food and the meeting of material need.

The first petition of the first table is secondary, therefore, though in some senses it forms a logical development out of the bread petition. If the fourth petition prayed for the concrete situation that would evoke such blessings of the name, then blessing God for the reception of food can be one of the concrete meanings of "sanctifying the Name." This may indeed be one understanding of the tradition in the synoptics (heavily influenced by Judean-Jerusalem scribal interests), as evident in Jesus' words around bread-breaking (Matt 14:19; 26:26; and par.) and *Didache*'s association of the Prayer with the Lord's Supper. Q^2 played a significant role in these

---

[78] *B. Ber.* 40b, quoted in B. T. D. Smith, "Lord's Prayer," *IDB* 3 (1962) 155.

[79] A reading from Genesis is placed just before this blessing when Passover coincides with the Sabbath: See *The Passover Haggadah: With English Translation, Introduction, and Commentary*, based on the commentaries of E. D. Goldschmidt, edited by N. Glatzer (3d ed.; New York: Schocken, 1979) 17.

[80] *Daily Prayer Book*, translated and annotated with an introduction by P. Birnbaum (Hebrew Publishing Company, 1949) 50 [my emphasis].

[81] *M. Berakot* 6–9.

developed meanings of the Lord's Prayer, for while it does not directly mention a concern with the *Shema* (as Mark 12:29-30), it does show concern with Israel's integrity and fidelity to God (Q = Luke 3:8; 4:4):

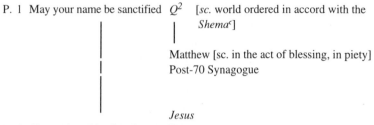

P. 1 May your name be sanctified Q^2 [*sc.* world ordered in accord with the *Shema*]

                  Matthew [sc. in the act of blessing, in piety]
                  Post-70 Synagogue

            Jesus
P. 4 Give us bread in abundance today *or*
      Give us the bread of the kingdom today   [patronage resulting from exclusive allegiance and the ground for blessing]

Petition 5 of the Second Table

The fifth petition of Jesus' Prayer gives a critical clue as to what brought about this situation of want and hunger (not to mention we surmise the cursing of God's name because of physical deprivation). An agrarian context in which indebtedness prevails is a social context that will be characterized by an increasing level of impoverishment and hunger. Lack of bread coupled with debt presented a familiar constellation for Jesus and his peasant contemporaries.

Agrarian debt was pushing peasantry of Jesus' day either entirely off the land (wage labor on estates) or into client-dependency relations on the land vis-à-vis the Roman overlord (e.g. Caesar's large estates in the Esdraelon Plain or the land controlled by Judean-Herodian aristocrats in Sepphoris-Tiberias). The insecurity of the tenant or wage laborer was evidenced in the increase in beggary and brigandage.[82] Brigands perhaps would have been more impressed by a zealot-like religious movement, but the ministry of Jesus, which clearly shows concern for the beggar and disadvantaged, sought alternate ways to resolve class tensions and reconcile class interests.[83]

The Jesus tradition reveals an intimate acquaintance and concern with debt in the first half of the first century CE.[84] Q material

---

82   See Horsley and Hanson, *Bandits, Prophets, and Messiahs*, 52-85.

83   Oakman, *Jesus and the Economic Questions*, 210, 215.

84   See also my "Jesus and Agrarian Palestine: The Factor of Debt," in K. H. Richards (ed.), *Society of Biblical Literature 1985 Seminar Papers* (SBLSP 24;

alluding to debtor's prison (Luke 12:58-59 = Matt 5:25-26), the story of the Unforgiving Servant (M = Matt 18:23-35), the parable of the Two Debtors (L = Luke 7:41-42), and the Widow's λεπτά (Mark 12:41-44) suggest this. The parables of the Talents (Q? = Luke 19:12-27 = Matt 25:14-30) and the Unjust Steward (L = Luke 16:1-8) relate the oppressiveness of the creditor.

Outside of the New Testament, historical data for a debt problem in early Roman Palestine are supplied by the so-called *prozbul* of Hillel and an important passage in Josephus. One of the first acts of the insurgents in 66 CE was the burning of the record office where debt contracts were kept:

> [The rebels] next carried their combustibles to the public archives, eager to destroy the money-lenders' bonds and to prevent the recovery of debts, in order to win over a host of grateful debtors and to cause a rising of the poor against the rich . . .[85]

In the same context, Josephus refers to such archives as the "sinews" (τὰ νεῦρα) of the city, a telling metaphor.

The precise significance of the *prozbul* is not easily established. The Mishnah indicates that Hillel's measure was supposed to make credit easier to obtain. Loans were not being given on account of the seventh-year release, so Hillel ostensibly permitted a practice that would alleviate the cash flow crisis. According to *m. Šeb.* 10:2 and *b. Git.* 37b, loan contracts "delivered to the court" are not canceled according to the seventh-year prescriptions of Deuteronomy 15. The "logic" behind this is that the letter of the law in Deut 15:3 demands, "your hand shall release," but if the bonds are with the court, the letter does not apply. The development of this legal maneuver apparently resulted in the interpretation "before the court" commonly placed upon *prozbul* in later rabbinic tradition.[86]

Work of Ludwig Blau years ago offered a different insight into the meaning of *prozbul*. The Hebrew in the Mishnah in fact is פרוזבול, sometimes פרוסבול.[87] Blau traced the etymology of the

---

Atlanta: Scholars Press, 1985); idem, *Jesus and the Economic Questions*, 72-77; and M. Goodman, "The First Jewish Revolt: Social Conflict and the Problem of Debt," *JJS* 33 (1982) 417-27.

[85]   *J.W.* 2.17.6 §427; translation by H. St. J. Thackeray, *Josephus II* (LCL 203; London: Heinemann; Cambridge: Harvard University Press, 1928) 491.

[86]   Again *b. Git.* 37b. Cf. L. Blau, "Der Prosbol im Lichte der griechischen Papyri und der Rechtsgeschichte" (Budapest, 1927) 111.

[87]   Jastrow, *Dictionary*, 1218.

word back to the Greek προσβολή, which according to Egyptian papyri was the "knocking down" of mortgaged property. Blau's view has recently been revived by Hans Kippenberg.[88] Furthermore, form-critical study of the Hillel legislation by Neusner has led him to believe that Hillel's name and scriptural warrants were only later attached to a legal institution firmly established prior to the second century CE. Debt documents from the Judean desert, for instance, show no knowledge of a stipulation along the lines of the later rabbinic view of the *prozbul*, but they do reveal that loans were secured by various kinds of property:

Murabbaᶜat Contract 18 (c. 55 CE):

[On . . . of the month . . . in] the second year of Caesar Nero in Siwaya, Absalom, son of Hanin, from Siwaya agreed that he borrowed from him in his presence: I, Zechariah, son of Johanan, son of . . . resident in Chessalon, have received the money [as a loan] of 20 denarii. I will repay it on . . . and if I do not restitute it by this term, then it will be paid to you with a fifth, and it will be completely repaid on this sabbatical year ([alternately] though a sabbath year intervene). And if I should not do it, there will be a substitute for you out of my goods, and to that which I shall acquire, you have right of appropriation.[89]

Murabbaᶜat Contract 22 (132 CE):

On the fourteenth of Marheschwan, Year One of the liberation of Israel . . . [the sum] of 50 [denarii] in coins according to the assessed valuation. This piece of ground of Chizqia is security for the payment [of the debt] to the value of . . .[90]

It can be concluded that the *prozbul* originally was a legal device whereby debts were secured by means of immovable property and

---

[88]   H. G. Kippenberg, *Religion und Klassenbildung im antiken Judäa* (Vandenhoeck & Ruprecht, 1978) 139. Cf. F. Preisigke, *Fachwörter des öffentlichen Verwaltungsdienstes Ägyptens* (Göttingen: Vandenhoeck & Ruprecht, 1915) 149. Also LSJ 1504.

[89]   J. T. Milik, "Reconnaisaance de dette, en Araméen," in P. Benoit et al. (eds.), *Les Grottes de Murabbaᶜat* (DJD 2; Oxford: Clarendon, 1961) 102; E. Koffmahn, *Die Doppelurkunden aus der Wüste Juda* (STDJ 5; Leiden: Brill, 1968) 80-81. Cf. J. Neusner, *From Politics to Piety: The Emergence of Pharisaic Judaism* (Englewood Cliffs: Prentice-Hall, 1973) 17 n. 2.

[90]   Milik, "Acte de vente de terrain, en Hébreu," in Benoit et al. (eds.), *Les Grottes de Murabbaᶜat*, 119; Koffmahn, *Doppelurkunde*, 158-59. J. S. Kloppenborg indicates (private communication) that the "execution clause" here was a standard feature of Greco-Roman legal contracts.

foreclosure accomplished through a court proceeding. This practice went against the letter of the Mosaic law, which viewed the patrimonial lands of the clan as a permanent trust (Lev 25:23). Any land that had to be sold had to be redeemed under the old Israelite law (Lev 25:25-28). If the *prozbul* measure was "good" for urban artisans like the Pharisees and later rabbis, it could not have been as sympathetically perceived by rural folk.[91]

The fact that a Greek legal institution is here in view suggests three possible "entry points" into the legal practice of early Judaism: Ptolemaic Palestine, the later Hasmoneans (perhaps Jannaeus), or Herod. This legal institution, in any view, was a part of the social fabric of Jesus' period. Passages like 1 Macc 14:8 and 14:12 seem to indicate that the Maccabees were "pro-peasant." The picture in *Aristeas* (esp. 107-120), if it is to be dated around 100 BCE, confirms the agrarian prosperity of the early Hasmonean years. If under the first Hasmoneans the ancient Jewish peasantry was in relatively good shape, by the second century CE its condition had deteriorated dramatically. There is evidence throughout the Mishnah of a large pool of "free" labor. Martin Goodman's book on Roman Galilee provides a start at analyzing the second-century social situation behind the Tannaitic material.[92]

Stresses on rural déclassés (including artisans and fishingfolk) were on the increase in turn-of-the-eras Palestine. In place of traditional peasants holding patrimonial land, tenants and wage-laborers were appearing, on the one hand, and large landed proprietors, on the other. For these social realities the parables of Jesus give ample evidence. One of the chief mechanisms fueling this process of agrarian destruction was the burden of debt. Roman taxation (including the building programs of the Herods) and population increase contributed to this problem.

In a milieu in which debt of one sort or another was compro-mising the viability of life for many, the fifth petition of Jesus' prayer takes on a special vibrancy and urgency. The meaning of the petition assumes a "horizontal" and a "vertical" aspect. The horizon-tal meaning is concretely perceptible in both the Matthean and the

---

[91]   Neusner, *From Politics to Piety*, 16: "Debtors . . . were here given a good motive to dislike Pharisees, who now rendered their debts into a perpetual burden."

[92]   M. Goodman, *State and Society in Roman Galilee, A.D. 132-212* (Totowa: Rowman & Allanheld, 1983).

Lukan versions of the second half of the petition:

> (Matt) as we have released (or forgiven) our debtors.
> (Luke) for we ourselves are releasing (or forgiving) everyone in debt to us.

The meaning "release" for ἀφίημι (Matt perfect tense, Luke present tense) in a literal or concrete sense is clearly attested by Deut 15:3 (LXX).

How is the vertical aspect to be understood? It must be noted that Matthew has "Forgive us our debts," while Luke has "Forgive us our sins." The literal or concrete material understanding of the petition is not thwarted, because in Aramaic the same word means sin or debt (חובה). Also, the dative plural ἡμῖν, "for us," can best be understood as the dative of advantage (indicative of the general thrust of the original Aramaic).

There were perhaps two concrete situations in which God might be petitioned to achieve debt forgiveness for the advantage of the petitioner: (1) A court-system, perhaps one in which the *prozbul* held sway, and (2) the temple debt-system. Q = Luke 12:58-59 likely refers to the courts within the jurisdiction of Herod Antipas. The passage makes clear that the debtor goes to court at a great disadvantage (ironically, petitioning the creditor as patron provides better "justice") and indicates that prisons stood ready to effect execution (cf. M = Matt 18:30, 34). Josephus and Philo show clearly how this mechanism worked: Debt prison forced the debtor's family to pay up![93]

The Temple also imposed indebtedness upon Jews. The Temple tax was levied on all Jewish males over twenty years of age. The *Mishnah* indicates that ability to pay was not considered:

> On the 15th thereof the tables [of the money-changers] were set up in the provinces; and on the 25th thereof they were set up in the Temple. After they were set up in the Temple they began to exact pledges.[94]

M = Matt 17:24-27 certainly depicts a post-70 CE situation (v. 27a), but the pronouncement of v. 26 likely goes back to Jesus himself and fits well with the notion of debt forgiveness. In such a case, then, the fifth petition could request of the "owner of the house" (i.e. the

---

93   Consider for instance the behavior of Albinus (*J.W.* 2.14.1 §273). Philo (*Spec. Laws* 3.30) recounts the depredations of an early first-century tax collector who laid hands on family members to force payment; see N. Lewis, *Life in Egypt Under Roman Rule* (Oxford: Clarendon, 1983) 161-62.

94   *Šeqal.* 1:3 (Danby translation).

Temple) for release from the onerous obligations requisitioned each year by Judean authorities.

Another significant index of a concern about debt appears in the attention Jesus gives to disadvantaged groups—children (Mark 9:36), women forced into degrading social situations for economic reasons ("impure," Mark 5:25; prostitutes, Matt 21:31; widows, Mark 12:41-44), and others economically marginalized.[95] The case of the widow in Mark 12:41-44 = Luke 21:1-4 is especially illuminating for the connection between economic marginalization and indebtedness. Why was the widow putting her money in the box at the Temple? And was Jesus praising her generosity or lamenting her misfortune?[96]

There is compelling evidence that the widow's deposit in the Temple was reason for lament. As Wright has convincingly observed, to think that Jesus praises the widow for depositing her "whole life" in the temple coffers directly contradicts Jesus' censure of the Pharisees over Qorban vows (Mark 7:11-12). The principle enunci-ated there by Jesus brings out the priority of human need over temple piety. The same logic can be expected to apply in the case of the widow's λεπτά. Whatever she may be doing for God by her temple sacrifice, she is thereby depriving herself and her orphaned children. Furthermore, Wright points out the significant connection in the synoptic tradition between this story and Jesus' saying immediately preceding it: "Beware of the Scribes . . . who devour widows' houses and for a pretext make long prayers" (Mark 12:38, 40).

Wright might have gone farther with this connection between "devouring widows' houses" and the widow's λεπτά. There may in fact be grounds for restoring to some extent an aspect of praise in Jesus' word, although lament will also remain apparent, for there is another legislative tradition attached to the name of Hillel that perhaps brings a direct light upon the widow's action in Mark 12:41-44:

> If a man sold a house from among the houses in a walled city, he may redeem it at once and at any time during twelve months. . . . Beforetime the

---

95 For a discussion of the connection between these groups and economic marginalization, see L. Schottroff and W. Stegemann, *Jesus von Nazareth—Hoffnung der Armen* (2nd ed., Stuttgart: Kohlhammer, 1981) 15-28.

96 A. Wright, "The Widow's Mites: Praise or Lament?" *CBQ* 44 (1982) 256-65.

buyer used to hide himself on the last day of the twelve months so that [the house] might be his for ever; but Hillel the Elder ordained that he [that sold it] could deposit his money in the [Temple] Chamber, and break down the door and enter, and that the other, when he would, might come and take his money.[97]

This tradition seems to pit Hillel against the scribes "who devour widows' houses," but it supplies a possible context for the widow's behavior and rationale for Jesus' observation as a mixture of lament and praise. The widow was demonstrating fidelity to her obligations to keep the house (which perhaps included land) in the family. Her deposit was, in this view, redemption money of some sort.

(Secondary: Petition 2 of the First Table)

In framing possible understandings of God's kingdom and will in the first table, emphases at the penultimate stage of the synoptic tradition indicate how Q and Markan prophetic understandings would flesh out the Prayer of Jesus. Q^2 held a general concern for Israel's prophets, and linked John the Baptist and Jesus with their fate. John had been active at one point in Batanea, within the tetrarchy of Philip.[98] John was also associated with Perea and Herod Antipas's territory. Elijah had originated from Gilead (1 Kgs 17:1), and an Elijah-John the Baptist association came to be made at least in Mark (Mark 1:6). Since the Elijah-Elisha traditions had also showed concern for miraculous feedings (1 Kgs 17:6,16) and demonstrated special concern for widows (1 Kgs 17:8; 2 Kgs 4:1-7), these aspects of Jesus' activity were also highlighted by Mark (Mark 6:15; 8:28; 9:4, 11-13) and later Luke (4:26).

The precarious legal position of the widow in the ancient Near East was long recognized, especially in the wisdom tradition and the promulgations of kings.[99] Unlike the Greeks, many peoples of the ancient orient believed that God or the gods and the powerful on earth had a special obligation toward widows and orphans. Thus, in the Old Testament:

---

97   M. ʿArak. 9:3-4. This tradition is discussed in detail by Neusner, *From Politics to Piety*, 18-19. On temples as depositories for money preserving redemption rights, see E. Ginzberg, *Studies in the Economics of the Bible* (Philadelphia: Jewish Publication Society, 1932) 62-63.

98   R. Riesner, "Bethany Beyond the Jordan," *ABD* 1.704.

99   Especially helpful in understanding the widow's plight is the article by G. Stählin, "Χήρα," *TDNT* 9 (1974) 440-65.

You shall not afflict any widow or orphan. If you do afflict them, and they cry out to me, I will surely hear their cry; and my wrath will burn, and I will kill you with the sword, and your wives shall become widows and your children fatherless.[100]

The Ugaritic story of Aqhat praises the wise man Daniel:

Straightway Daniel the Rapha-man, Forthwith Ghazir [the Harna]miyy— [man], *Is upr*ight, [sitting before the g]at[e, Un]der [a mighty tree on the threshing floor, Judging] the cause [of the widow, Adjudicating] the case [of the fatherless.][101]

Hammurabi boasts that he has protected the rights of widows and orphans.[102] In Egyptian wisdom tradition, the "Instruction for King Meri-Ka-Re" admonishes:

Do justice whilst thou endurest upon earth. Quiet the weeper; do not oppress the widow; supplant no man in the property of his father; and impair no officials at their posts.[103]

The connection of widow, property, and officials is significant. For, the "ancient oppression of widows at law may be seen in their frequent sale as slaves for debt," and "the main plight of widows was in the legal sphere."[104]

Much-later Jewish traditions continue to validate this picture quite precisely. The Judean Qumran material shows acute awareness of this problem:

Unless they are careful to act in accordance with the exact interpretation of the law for the age of wickedness: to separate themselves from the sons of the pit; to abstain from wicked wealth which defiles, either by promise or by vow, and from the wealth of the temple and from stealing from the poor of the people, from making their widows their spoils and from murdering orphans . . .[105]

Goods of orphans might be valued by a Jewish court to meet their

---

[100] Exod 22:22 (RSV).

[101] J. Pritchard, *The Ancient Near East* (Princeton: Princeton University Press, 1958) 126.

[102] Stählin, "Χήρα," 443 n. 31, for other ancient Near Eastern references.

[103] J. Pritchard, *Ancient Near Eastern Texts Relating to the Old Testament* (2nd ed., Princeton: Princeton University Press, 1955) 415.

[104] Stählin, "Χήρα," 443, 445, respectively.

[105] CD 6:14-17, according to F. G. Martínez, *The Dead Sea Scrolls Translated: The Qumran Texts in English* (2nd ed., Leiden: Brill; Grand Rapids: Eerdmans, 1996) 37.

father's debt.[106] The property of widows was similarly vulnerable. A widow's כתובה, her marriage contract, could be compromised if her husband dedicated his property to the temple. However, the rabbis stipulated that when the property was redeemed, the proceeds must go to meet the former contractual obligations of the husband to the wife. Debts and obligations, whether inherited from her former husband or forced upon her by circumstance, could seriously undermine the economic security of the widow in antiquity.

Num. Rab. 21.12 (on Num 27:5) relates that the inheritance of a woman changes hands only through judges.[107] The control of property in antiquity was a man's game. *Num. Rab.* 10.1 (on Num 6:2) tells how a widow is forced to bring suit against her own son, although the precise issue at law is not clear.[108] Undoubtedly, the dispute is over property or the widow's maintenance—which are also concerns of Tannaitic discussions.[109] *Exod. Rab.* 31.5 (on Exod 22:24) shows clearly that widows are oppressed by the lending at interest.[110]

The second petition now links Jesus' immediate and concrete concern for the oppressive affliction of little people with the sphere of royalty and the long-standing ancient Near Eastern traditions to place the weak under royal justice. As has been suggested on the basis of the *Qaddish*, the second petition for the coming of the kingdom of God emphasizes the (eschatological) hope for the manifestation of God's rule in the world. אבא and the direct, second-person imperatives of the second table of the Prayer indicate God's immediacy to the needs of the petitioners. Wisdom Q also shared a much stronger sense of God's presence in Jesus' context. This immediacy is compromised a bit by a stronger eschatological sense of kingdom, which develops in the decades prior to the Jewish-Roman War and is evident in Q^2 and Mark. Whereas Jesus and followers had requested release from immediate ties of indebtedness, eschatology might prolong the wait for release or convert literal debt into sin (e.g. Luke 12:33-34).

---

106   *M. ʿArak.* 6:1.
107   Freedman and Simon (ed.), *Midrash Rabbah*, 6.840.
108   Freedman and Simon (ed.), *Midrash Rabbah*, 5.333.
109   *Mishnah Ketubot.*
110   Freedman and Simon (ed.), *Midrash Rabbah*, 3.397.

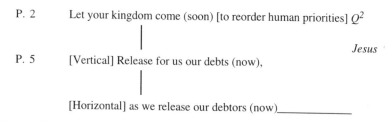

P. 2   Let your kingdom come (soon) [to reorder human priorities] Q^2

Jesus

P. 5   [Vertical] Release for us our debts (now),

[Horizontal] as we release our debtors (now)_____

To ask God to release debts is to ask in the name of God's rule that
human oppression through debt machinations cease. Many of these
machinations are abetted by the courts and other "legal" means. This
leads logically into Jesus' final petition.

Petition 6 of the Second Table

Most commentators consider the sixth petition in the light of
Jewish eschatology, as a request for the ultimate defeat of evil.[111]
This might be close to its meaning at the Matthean or Lukan stages of
redaction, but for Jesus the meaning of the sixth petition was far
more mundane and pertinent to the concerns being traced up to this
point. It brings into focus the subornation of justice for the weak and
appeals directly to God for redress.

The Unjust Judge parable (Luke 18:2-5) links nicely the situation
of the lowly, issues of indebtedness, and courts of law.[112] While
nothing directly states that the widow's cause pertains to debt, the
word used of her unnamed adversary at law, ἀντίδικος, appears in
another significant text, Q = Luke 12:58-59. The widow's opponent
at law is likely a creditor. This picture coheres with what we
previously learned about the plight typical of widows in antiquity.[113]

The twice-repeated phrase about the judge, who "neither feared
God nor regarded man" (vv. 2, 4 RSV), offers another key linkage.

---

[111] Typical are B. T. Viviano, "The Gospel According to Matthew," in R.
Brown, J. Fitzmyer, and R. Murphy (eds.), *The New Jerome Biblical Commentary*
(Englewood Cliffs: Prentice-Hall, 1990) 645 [42:39] on v. 13; and K. Stendahl,
"Matthew," in M. Black and H. Rowley (eds.), *Peake's Commentary on the Bible*
(Nashville: Thomas Nelson, 1962) 778-79. Cf. Billerbeck and Strack, *Kommentar*,
1.422.

[112] Helpful in reading this parable is J. D. M. Derrett, "Law in the New
Testament: The Parable of the Unjust Judge," *NTS* 18 (1971) 178-91. The parable
is prefigured in Sir 35:12-18. See also T. W. Manson, *The Sayings of Jesus*
(London: SCM Press, 1937; repr. Grand Rapids: Eerdmans, 1979) 305-308.

[113] Also see Derrett, "Law in the New Testament," 187.

The general meaning of the phrase is already suggested in 18:6 by "unjust judge," ὁ κριτὴς τῆς ἀδικίας. Fitzmyer translates the phrase. "neither feared God nor cared about human beings," citing a parallel from Josephus about King Jehoiakim, "neither reverent toward God nor fair toward human beings."[114] Irreverence captures only part of the issue. The first half of the description needs to be considered from the fact that "fear of God" for a Jew would imply doing what God wants, hence, doing the will of God: From the wisdom tradition of the Old Testament comes the sentiment, "The fear of the Lord is the beginning of knowledge" (Prov 1:7). Sirach explicitly connects fear of God, God's law, and wisdom:

> The man who fears the Lord will do this, and he who holds to the law will obtain wisdom.[115]

It is likely, then that the judge's problem in this story, and the source of his ἀδικία, is his lack of respect for the will of God. After all, he does not seem to take Exod 22:22 seriously.

What then might we make of the second part of this phrase, "does not regard or care for human beings." Perhaps all that needs to be said is that this expresses in concrete form how the judge lacks fear of God. He cares not for the widow's plight. On the other hand, this is a rather bland result for such a colorful expression. There is reason to suspect some sort of idiom, undoubtedly a semitic rather than a Greek idiom. Furthermore, we can suspect a synonymous parallelism to "not fearing God."

Some help seems afforded by a regular idiom in Old Testament Hebrew that is carried over into rabbinic usage. In the Old Testament "to lift up the face," פנים נשא is "to show favor, respect, or partiality to."[116] The Greek verb ἐντρέπομαι in Luke's text also means "respect."[117] In the Old Testament showing partiality in judgment was considered heinous. "Turning one's face to silver" (i.e. accepting gifts or bribes) was thought to be synonymous with thwarting justice (Prov 6:35). In later Jewish tradition we encounter what was undoubtedly typical:

---

114 Fitzmyer, *Luke X–XXIV*, 1178.

115 Sirach 15:7.

116 BDB 670; Jastrow, *Dictionary*, 937.

117 A study of the translation of the Greek verb ἐντρέπω in the Septuagint shows that on several occasions the underlying Hebrew text has an idiom involving "face" (e.g. Exod 10:3; 2 Kgs 22:19).

> The usual experience is: Two men go before a judge, one of them poor and the other rich; towards whom does the judge turn his face? Is it not towards the rich man?[118]

This idiom helps to understand ἐντρέπομαι, but the unjust judge is said *not* to show respect to human beings. Can we suspect here an ironic narrative device to emphasize the fact that the judge *does* show partiality to the more powerful cause? Jesus' audience could then be expected to laugh (bitterly) at the judge's self-deception in Luke 18:4. Perhaps there is double meaning, too, if the judge "neither feared God nor was partial to humane considerations." He shows partiality to the powerful who can pay, but the widow has nothing to offer except her obnoxious persistence. Sirach was aware of just this sort of situation:

> Do not offer him [sc. God] a bribe, for he will not accept it . . . for the Lord is the judge, and with him is no partiality. He will not show partiality in the case of a poor man . . . He will not ignore the supplications of the fatherless, nor the widow when she pours out her story. Do not the tears of the widow run down her cheek as she cries out against him who has caused them to fall?[119]

If in the *Sitz im Leben* of Jesus' own ministry the meaning of the Unjust Judge was to indict those who devour the houses of widows, then the final comment of Jesus (Luke 18:7) means something other than Luke thought (18:1). This story is not so much an example story encouraging prayer, as it is a warning to judges not to oppress the widow. Jesus promises that the God who shows great compassion for the fatherless and widow will be vindicating their cause quickly.

What then does the sixth petition mean? Its rather crude attribution of cause to God stands in good stead with previous comments about peasant sensibilities (immediacy, direct address). The *crux* of the matter has to do with the meaning of πειρασμός. Derived from a root περ-, with cognates in the Latin *experiri* and English "experience," this noun is extremely rare in non-biblical Greek.[120] Verbal forms appear with the basic senses of "to attempt" or "to put to the test." Since Homer, πεῖρα conveys the notion of "to test the value of something." In the Hellenistic-Roman period, the word can be

---

[118] *Lev. Rab.* 3.2 (on Lev 2:1) [4.37].

[119] Sirach 35:12-15. Cf. Prov 6:35.

[120] Appears only three times; BAGD 640; J. Seesemann, "Πεῖρα," in *TDNT* 6 (1968) 23.

associated with imperial or royal contexts in the sense of "loyalty test."[121] Πειρασμός translates an Aramaic noun נסיון from נסי, Hebrew נסה. Manifesting a field of meanings similar to the Greek πεῖρα, the biblical word, for instance, can refer to the testing of or attempting to use military equipment (1 Sam 17:39). Perhaps the most significant occurrence appears in biblical wisdom: Job 9:23-24 links the "trials" of the innocent (if indeed the root there is נסה) with the flourishing of the wicked and the "covering of judges' faces" (i.e. the denial of justice). In later rabbinic usage, the standard understanding of "temptation" comes to the fore.[122]

Matthew's seventh petition may confirm these tentative expositions if it is seen as "epexegetic" of the meaning of Petition 6. The "evil one," then, refers to the corrupt judge who presides over a court prejudiced toward the collection of debts and rigged in favor of royal or imperial interests. The sixth and seventh petitions vividly request deliverance from suborned legal proceedings before evil judges.

In light of this discussion of the second table, it is highly probable that Jesus' Prayer originally expressed a concrete and tight-knit integrity: It is a vivid request for deliverance from hunger, debt, and trials in rigged courts before evil judges. The social system of Roman Palestine, with debt relations reenforced by temple religion, had left many hungry and marginalized. Jesus' Prayer directly addressed their plight, and held out hope that God would hear their prayer as God had heard the cry of the Israelites in Egypt.

The presence of the kingdom's power (Q = Luke 11:20) has profound implications for human institutions and action. Many of the parables of Jesus refer to this reordering power. It is a power as effective as yeast (Q = Luke 13:20-21 parable of the Leaven) or a tiny seed to grow into a towering mustard shrub in a field (Mark 4:30-32 and par.). In terms of human affairs, the reign of God disorients and reorients like the sudden discovery of a priceless pearl (Q = Matt 13:46). The reign of God leads to surprising actions, perhaps foolish from the standpoint of conventional wisdom (the Good Samaritan, L = Luke 10:29-37; or the Prodigal Father, L = Luke 15:11-32). The third petition of the first table develops this line of understanding even further.

---

121 Egyptian papyri: MM 501, s.v. πεῖρα; Plutarch, *Brutus* 10.
122 Billerbeck and Strack, *Kommentar*, 1.422.

(Secondary: Petition 3 of the First Table)

The word "will" in "will of God," θέλημα τοῦ θεοῦ, often translates in the Septuagint (LXX) the Hebrew word for "pleasure" of
God, חפץ.[123] Another significant Hebrew word for "will" is רצון. In
either case, the emphasis in the semitic mind is upon the objective
ethical content of God's will and its concrete performance.[124] This
can be seen from a few of the Old Testament occurrences of either
word:

> [The Lord] says of Cyrus, "He is my shepherd, and he shall fulfil all my
> *purpose*.[125]

> The Lord loves him; he shall perform his *purpose* on Babylon . . .[126]

> I *delight* to do thy will, O my God; thy law is within my heart.[127]

The Psalmist brings together will and delight in the last quotation,
and the parallelism between "will" and "law" is particularly noteworthy. While many of the occurrences of חפץ (verb) and רצון are
in priestly or cultic contexts, there are also a significant number of
occurrences of חפץ (verb and noun forms) in contexts that emphasize that justice and mercy are qualities pleasing to God:

> . . . let him who glories glory in this, that he understands and knows me,
> that I am the Lord who practice steadfast love, justice and righteousness in
> the earth; for in these things I *delight*, says the Lord.[128]

> For I *desire* steadfast love and not sacrifice, the knowledge of God, rather
> than burnt offerings.[129]

Perhaps the most important passages from the Old Testament for
the purposes of this discussion lie in Malachi. Various words for
God's pleasure or displeasure occur frequently here. Furthermore,
the hope of the return of Elijah—which colors at a number of points
the gospel accounts of John the Baptist's and Jesus' ministries—is
brought to expression in this book. Finally, the critical stance of
Malachi toward the cultus suggests some striking parallels to the

---

[123] W. Schrenk, "Θέλημα," *TDNT* 3 (1965) 52-62. Cf. idem, "Βούλομαι,"
TDNT 1 (1964) 629-37. S. V. McCasland, "Will of God," *IDB* 4 (1962) 844-48.

[124] McCasland, "Will of God," 844-48.

[125] Isaiah 44:28 (RSV). "Purpose" = LXX θέλημα = חפץ.

[126] Isaiah 48:14 (RSV). "Purpose" = LXX βουλή = חפץ.

[127] Psalm 40:8 (RSV) = 40:9 (MT). "Will" = LXX θέλημα = רצון.

[128] Jeremiah 9:24 (RSV) = 9:23 (MT).

[129] Hosea 6:6 (RSV).

Jesus traditions:

> I have no *pleasure* (חפץ) in you, says the Lord of hosts, and I will not accept an offering from your hand.[130]

> You have wearied the Lord with your words. Yet you say, "How have we wearied him?" By saying, "Every one who does evil is good in the sight of the Lord, and he *delights* in them."[131]

> Behold, I send my messenger . . . the messenger of the covenant in whom you *delight* . . .[132]

> Then the offering of Judah and Jerusalem *will be pleasing* to the Lord . . .[133]

The "will" of God, that is, what is pleasing to God, is not only cultic in Malachi, but also ethical:

> For the lips of a priest should guard knowledge, and men should seek instruction (תורה) from his mouth, for he is the messenger of the Lord of hosts. But you have turned aside from the way; you have caused many to stumble by your instruction (תורה); you have corrupted the covenant of Levi . . . and so I make you despised and abased before all the people, inasmuch as you have not kept my ways but have shown partiality in your instruction (תורה). (2:7-9)

> I will draw near to you for judgment; I will be a swift witness against the sorcerers, against the adulterers, against those who swear falsely, against those who oppress the hireling in his wages, the widow and the orphan, against those who thrust aside the sojourner, and do not fear me, says the Lord of hosts. (3:5)

These passages are addressed to the sons of Levi (2:8; 3:3). They reflect old Israelite conceptions of the role of the Levites, who were both cultic figures and judges rolled into one (cf. תורה). Where might such traditions have been preserved? Malachi is generally dated to the early fifth century BCE—prior to the work of Nehemiah and Ezra.[134] The nature of the criticism of the cultus evident in the

---

130 Malachi 1:10 (RSV); cf. Mark 7:6-7; 12:32-34; Matt 9:13; 23:23.

131 Malachi 2:17; cf. Mark 3:4; Matt 23:27-28.

132 Malachi 3:1; cf. Mark 9:11-13; Matt 23:30, 34; Luke 4:18-19 (+ Isa 42:1).

133 Malachi 3:4; Mark 11:15-19.

134 For the historical situation of Malachi, see O. Eissfeld, *The Old Testament: An Introduction* (trans. P. Ackroyd; New York: Harper & Row, 1965) 442-43. Nehemiah's dates are fairly certain: 446-434 BCE Ezra's mission has been variously dated: The two most likely dates are 458 and 398 BCE (depending upon which Artaxerxes is meant in Ezra 7:1). F. M. Cross ("Reconstruction of the Judean Restoration," *JBL* 94 [1975] 14 n. 60) sees 458 BCE as the more likely date.

document suggests a writer among the priests, but not among the upper echelon. In the post-exilic situation, families descended from Aaron were the dominant figures in the Jerusalem cultus. Furthermore, the address in Malachi to the sons of Levi perhaps reveals the interest of the author in this second-class group of priests. The book of Ezekiel tells us that the Levites or families tracing their lineage back to Levi had fallen into disfavor during the period immediately after the exile (Ezek 44:10-31). Ezekiel in fact relates that the Aaronides, who supplant the Levites

> shall not marry a widow, or a divorced woman . . . They shall teach my people the difference between the holy and the common, and show them how to distinguish between the unclean and the clean. In a controversy they shall act as judges, and they shall judge it according to my judgments.[135]

These are the very issues that concern Malachi, so it is not entirely clear whether Malachi is thinking of the Aaronides under the more comprehensive designation "sons of Levi." In any case, Malachi is written from a critical, not sympathetic, point of view. The writing insists that the priests must attend both to cultic and covenantal concerns. Its author is probably a lower division priest knowledgeable regarding the Old Israelite legal traditions (which combined covenant-ethical and cultic concerns). As proof of this orientation, the figure of the Old Israelite charismatic prophet, Elijah the Tishbite, appears in the final chapters of Malachi.

The later tradition about Elijah presents fascinating material for study.[136] There are tantalizing glimpses of apparently widespread popular beliefs about Elijah. The impression given is of expectations forged in conformity with specific needs of diverse groups.

Thus, Mal 3:2 envisions the work of the Messenger (Elijah according to Mal 4:5) as "purification." Furthermore, as the passage quoted above indicates, Elijah will restore the integrity of judgment for those who are legally at a disadvantage (3:5-12). Mal 4:5 adds

---

Consult Eissfeld, *The Old Testament*, 554-55, for the opposing arguments.

[135] Ezekiel 44:22-24.

[136] J. Lightfoot, *A Commentary on the New Testament from the Talmud and Hebraica* (Grand Rapids: Baker, 1979) 2.243-247 (on Matt 17:10). J. Jeremias, "Ἠλ(ε)ίας," *TDNT* 2 (1964) 928-41 (+ bibliography). P. Billerbeck, "Der Prophet Elias nach seiner Entrückung aus dem Diesseits," Appendix 28 of the *Kommentar zum Neuen Testament aus Talmud und Midrasch* (5 vols., Munich: Beck 1986) 4.764-98.

that Elijah will "turn the hearts" of fathers to their children. Sirach
(c. 200 BCE) adds to this list the restoration of the tribes of Israel
(Sir 48:10). According to rabbinic tradition, Elijah will decide
disputed questions of law.[137] On the more popular side, and reflecting traditions of Northern Israel, Elijah will anoint the Messiah and
set up the symbols of the messianic age—the three bowls of manna,
purificatory water, and oil.

> Thus Elijah prepares the people of God for the last time. When peace has
> been restored, the community reconstituted, Antichrist overcome and killed
> and the Messiah anointed for His kingly office, then the great final age of
> grace begins.[138]

Elijah comes, therefore, to seal the eschatological will or pleasure
of God. The third petition of Jesus' Prayer came to evoke this matrix
of expectation, and in conjunction with the other petitions to ask for
the concrete observance of God's will among humankind. This point
is underscored by the expansion of the third petition's probably
original form in Matthew by "on earth as it is in heaven." This
parallel may have been intended to go with the entire first table
rather than just the third petition.[139] It certainly would be
appropriate as an explicit conclusion to what is implied in the other
petitions. Furthermore, there is latent in the third petition the
intimation that those who guarantee the observance of God's will—
the interpreters of the law or torah, i.e. priests, levites, scholars of
Q^2's day—must come in for blame. If God's will is not now being
observed as it should be, then the guarantors have failed (cf. Q =
Luke 11:52).

This petition articulates quite concretely what is implied already in
the sixth petition (and likely the seventh):

P. 3   Let your will be done Q^2 [May Elijah, who judges truly, come]

                                    Jesus

P. 6   Do not cause us to come into a trial [court] (Matt + Luke)
P. 7   but rescue us from the evil [judge (lit. one)] (Matt)

---

[137] Jeremias, "Ἠλ(ε)ίας," 934.
[138] Jeremias, "Ἠλ(ε)ίας," 934.
[139] Origen long ago suggested this; cf. Smith, "Lord's Prayer," 156.

Originally these latter petitions articulated the immediate concerns of people threatened with foreclosure or imprisonment through court action. These sentiments were also felt to be appropriate to the agony scene in Gethsemane. There Jesus prays words quite similar to the third petition. The prayer is offered up immediately before Jesus is arrested and taken to the suborned Sanhedrin. He is being arrested precisely because he has openly criticized in his teaching (Mark 12:40) and in his actions (Mark 11:15-17) the mechanisms proliferating debt and misery in Roman Palestine around 30 CE. For Mark, Jesus is about to suffer for doing the work of Elijah.

CONCLUSION

The Lord's Prayer, when viewed in its original connection to the work of Jesus, displays a concrete, immediate, and consistent this-worldly concern. While we may still speak (as older scholarship does) of its basic framework of meaning as "eschatological," in the sense that it hopes for ultimate and final changes in human affairs and conditions, nevertheless, the Lord's Prayer is surprisingly more concerned with specific problems and human welfare in the here and now than might have been suspected.

This essay has argued that Jesus' original prayer consisted in the distinctive אבא address and Petitions 4–6; the seventh petition repeats Petition 6 in synonymous parallelism. These petitions centered around the constellation of social problems bound up with court-enforced debt collections and resulting lack of adequate bread (whether substantial, subsistence, belonging to the estate, or "daily"). The first table of the prayer in the Q tradition elaborates on the basis of the great traditions of Israel, and reflects more abstract theological interests of these early scribes of the Jesus traditions.

The two tables of the Prayer, thus, are organically related and internally unified to a degree. Where the second table delves into specific human needs and expresses values peculiar to Jesus' Galilean movement, the first table articulates the general care of God and parameters of faithful human action. Each petition of the earlier second table correlates in some definite respect with the parallel member of the later first table:

	TABLE 2		TABLE 1
	Primary (Jesus, Q[1]?)		Secondary (Q[2], later evangelists)
P. 4	Petition for	P. 1	Sanctifying the name

	daily bread		in blessing
P. 5	Request for the removal of debt	P. 2	Request for the arrival of God's kingdom
PP. 6-7	God to deliver from rigged courts and evil judges	P. 3	God's will to be done

Central to the concerns of Jesus' original Prayer was the reality of oppression, indebtedness, hunger, and social insecurity. When early Christian groups moved out of the immediate context of such social realities, the concrete and immediate meaning of Jesus' prayer was led in the direction of theological abstractions and aligned with Israelite traditions and early Jewish forms of prayer. Late, twentieth-century Christian communities might reflect on the meaning and consequences of that transition as they confront social and economic crises at the threshold of a new millennium.[140]

SELECT BIBLIOGRAPHIC LISTING

Bandstra, A. J. "The Original Form of the Lord's Prayer." *Calvin Theological Journal* 16 (1981) 15-37.

Barr, J. "Abba Isn't Daddy." *JTS* 39 (1988) 28-47.

Baumgardt, D. "Kaddish and Lord's Prayer." *Jewish Bible Quarterly (Dor leDor)* 19 (1991) 164-69.

Betz, H. D. *The Sermon on the Mount.* Hermeneia Commentary Series. Minneapolis: Fortress Press, 1995.

Bindemann, W. "Das Brot für morgen gib uns heute: Sozialgeschichtliche Erwägungen zu den Wir-Bittendes Vaterunsers." *BTZ* 8 (1991) 199-215.

Black, M. "The Aramaic of *ton arton hemon ton epiousion* (Matt vi.11=Luke xi.3." *JTS* 42 (1941) 186-89.

Blau, L. "Der Prosbol im Lichte der griechischen Papyri und der Rechtsgeschichte." Budapest, 1927.

Botha, F. J. "Recent Research on the Lord's Prayer." *Neot* 1 (1967) 42-50.

Brooke, G. J. "The Lord's Prayer Interpreted through John and Paul." *Downside Review* 98 (1980) 298-311.

Bruggen, J. van. "The Lord's Prayer and Textual Criticism." *Calvin Theological Journal* 17 (1981) 78-87.

Charlesworth, J. H. "A Caveat on Textual Transmission and the Meaning of *Abba*: A Study of the Lord's Prayer." In *The Lord's Prayer and Other Prayer Texts*

---

[140] I am grateful to Jerome H. Neyrey, Dennis C. Duling, and John S. Kloppenborg for astute comments on earlier drafts of this study. They, of course, cannot be held responsible for the views promoted here.

from the Greco-Roman Era, edited by J. H. Charlesworth, M. Harding, and M. Kiley, 1-14. Valley Forge: Trinity Press International, 1994.

Chilton, B. *The Temple of Jesus: His Sacrificial Program Within a Cultural History of Sacrifice*. University Park: The Pennsylvania State University Press, 1992.

Cyster, R. F. "The Lord's Prayer and the Exodus Tradition." *Theology* 64 (1961) 377-81.

Dalman, G. H. "Anhang A: Das Vaterunser." In *Die Worte Jesu*, 2d ed., 283-365. Leipzig: Hinrichs, 1930.

Davies, W. D., and D. C. Allison. "Excursus: The Lord's Prayer: Matthew 6.9-13 = Luke 11.2-4." In *Matthew*, 590-617. International Critical Commentary. Edinburgh: T. & T. Clark, 1988.

de Moor, J. C. "The Reconstruction of the Aramaic Original of the Lord's Prayer." In *The Structural Analyhsis of Biblical and Canaanite Poetry*, edited by W. van der Meer and J. C. de Moor, 397-422. JSOTSup 74. Sheffield: JSOT Press, 1988.

Debrunner, A. "Epiousios." *Glotta* 4 (1913) 249-53.

—. "'Epiousios' und kein Ende." *Museum Helvetica* 9 (1952) 60-62.

Deissmann, A. *Light From the Ancient East*, trans. by L. R. M. Strachan. New and completely rev.ed. Grand Rapids: Baker, 1965.

—. *Bible Studies*, trans. by A. Grieve. Reprint. Winona Lake: Alpha Publications, 1979.

Dorneich, M., ed. *Vater-Unser Bibliographie—The Lord's Prayer, a Bibliography*. 3d ed. Freiburg i. Breisgau: Herder, 1988.

Duling, D. C., and N. Perrin. *The New Testament: Proclamation and Parenesis, Myth and History*. 3d ed. Fort Worth: Harcourt Brace College Publishers, 1994.

Elliott, J. H. *What Is Social-Scientific Criticism?* Guides to Biblical Scholarship. Minneapolis: Fortress Press, 1993.

Evans, C. F. *The Lord's Prayer*. London: SPCK, 1963.

Evans, C. A. *Life of Jesus Research: An Annotated Bibliography*. Rev. ed. NTTS 24. Leiden: Brill, 1996.

Fitzmyer, J. A. *The Gospel According to Luke*. AB 28-28A. Garden City: Doubleday, 1981-85. 2 vols.

Foerster, W. "Ἐπιούσιος." In *Theological Dictionary of the New Testament*, vol. 2, edited by G. Kittel, 590-99. Grand Rapids: Eerdmans, 1964. [= *TDNT*]

Funk, R. W., B. B. Scott, and J. R. Butts. *The Parables of Jesus: Red Letter Edition*. Sonoma: Polebridge, 1988.

Funk, R. W., R. W. Hoover, and The Jesus Seminar. *The Five Gospels: What Did Jesus Really Say?* San Francisco: HarperSanFrancisco, 1993.

Ginzberg, E. *Studies in the Economics of the Bible*. Philadelphia: Jewish

Publication Society, 1932.

Goodman, M. "The First Jewish Revolt: Social Conflict and the Problem of Debt." *JJS* 33 (1982) 417-27.

—. *State and Society in Roman Galilee, A.D. 132-212*. Totowa: Rowman & Allanheld, 1983.

Hemer, C. "'*Epiousios'*." *JSNT* 22 (1984) 81-94.

Horsley, R. A. "Jesus, Itinerant Cynic or Israelite Prophet?" In *Images of Jesus Today*, edited by J. A. Charlesworth and W. P. Weaver, 68-97. Valley Forge: Trinity Press International, 1994.

Horsley, R. A., and J. S. Hanson. *Bandits, Prophets, and Messiahs: Popular Movements at the Time of Jesus*. San Francisco: Harper & Row, 1985.

Houlden, J. L. "The Lord's Prayer." In *The Anchor Bible Dictionary*, vol. 4, edited by D. N. Freedman, 356-62. New York: Doubleday, 1992.

Jacobson, A. D. *The First Gospel: An Introduction to Q*. Foundations and Facets Series. Sonoma: Polebridge Press, 1992.

Jeremias, J. "The Lord's Prayer in Modern Research." *ExpTim* 71 (1960) 141-46.

—. "Ἡλ(ε)ίας." In *Theological Dictionary of the New Testament*, vol. 2, edited by G. Kittel, 928-41. Grand Rapids: Eerdmans, 1964.

—. *New Testament Theology*, vol. 1, *The Proclamation of Jesus*, trans. by J. Bowden. New York: Charles Scribner's Sons, 1971.

—. *The Prayers of Jesus*, trans. by J. Bowden and C. Burchard. Studies in Biblical Theology. Philadelphia: Fortress, 1978.

—. *The Lord's Prayer*, trans. by J. Reumann. Philadelphia: Fortress Press, 1980.

Kiley, M. "The Lord's Prayer and Other Prayer Texts from the Greco-Roman Era: A Bibliography." In *The Lord's Prayer and Other Prayer Texts from the Greco-Roman Era*, edited by J. H. Charlesworth, M. Harding, and M. Kiley, 101-257. Valley Forge: Trinity Press International, 1994.

Kippenberg, H. G. *Religion und Klassenbildung im antiken Judäa*. Vandenhoeck & Ruprecht, 1978.

Klausner, J. *Jesus of Nazareth: His Life, Times, and Teaching*, trans. by H. Danby. New York: Macmillan, 1925.

Kloppenborg, J. S. *The Formation of Q: Trajectories in Ancient Wisdom Collections*. Studies in Antiquity and Christianity. Philadelphia: Fortress, 1987.

—. *Q Parallels: Synopsis, Critical Notes, and Concordance*. Foundations and Facets Reference Series. Sonoma: Polebridge, 1988.

—. "Literary Convention, Self-Evidence and the Social History of the Q People." *Semeia* 55 (1991) 77-102.

Lachs, S. T. "The Lord's Prayer." In *A Rabbinic Commentary on the New Testament*, 117-24. Hoboken: Ktav, 1987.

Lohmeyer, E. *"Our Father."* New York: Harper & Row, 1965.

Luz, U. "Das Unservater (6,9-13)." In *Das Evangelium nach Matthäus*, vol. 1, 332-53. Evangelisch-Katholischer Kommentar zum Neuen Testament. Neukirchenen-Vluyn: Neukirchener Verlag, 1985.

Malina, B. J. "Interpretation: Reading, Abduction, Metaphor," *The Bible and the Politics of Exegesis: Essays in Honor of Norman K. Gottwald on His Sixty-Fifth Birthday* (ed. D. Jobling, P. L. Day and G. T. Sheppard; Cleveland, OH: Pilgrim Press, 1991) 253-66.

—. *The Social World of Jesus and the Gospels*. London and New York: Routledge, 1996.

Manson, T. W. *The Sayings of Jesus*. London: SCM Press, 1949.

—. *The Teaching of Jesus: Studies of Its Form and Content*. Cambridge: Cambridge University Press, 1959.

McCasland, S. V. "Will of God." In *Interpreter's Dictionary of the Bible*, vol. 4, edited by G. Buttrick, 844-48. Nashville and New York: Abingdon, 1962. [= *IDB*]

Metzger, B. M. "How Many Times Does 'Epiousios' Occur Outside the Lord's Prayer?" *ExpTim* 69 (1957) 52-54.

Neusner, J. *From Politics to Piety: The Emergence of Pharisaic Judaism*. Englewood Cliffs: Prentice-Hall, 1973.

Oakman, D. E. "Jesus and Agrarian Palestine: The Factor of Debt." In *Society of Biblical Literature 1985 Seminar Papers*, vol. 24, edited by K. H. Richards, 57-73. Atlanta: Scholars Press, 1985.

—. *Jesus and the Economic Questions of His Day*. Studies in the Bible and Early Christianity, vol. 8. Lewiston and Queenston: Edwin Mellen Press, 1986.

—. "Rulers' Houses, Thieves, and Usurpers: The Beelzebul Pericope." *Forum* 4.3 (1988) 109-23.

—. "Was Jesus a Peasant? Implications for Reading the Samaritan Story (Luke 10:30-35)." *BTB* 22 (1992) 117-25.

—. "The Archaeology of First-Century Galilee and the Social Interpretation of the Historical Jesus." In *Society of Biblical Literature 1994 Seminar Papers*, vol. 33, edited by E. H. Lovering, Jr., 220-51. Atlanta: Scholars Press, 1994.

Redfield, R. "The Social Organization of Tradition." In *Peasant Society: A Reader*, edited by J. M. Potter, M. N. Diaz, and G. M. Foster, 25-34. The Little, Brown Series in Anthropology. Boston: Little, Brown, 1967.

Riesner, R. "Bethany Beyond the Jordan." In *The Anchor Bible Dictionary*, vol. 1, edited by D. N. Freedman, 703-05. New York: Doubleday, 1992.

Robbins, V. K. *Exploring the Texture of Texts: A Guide to Socio-Rhetorical Interpretation*. Valley Forge: Trinity Press International, 1996.

Schrenk, W. "βούλομαι." In *Theological Dictionary of the New Testament*, vol. 1, edited by G. Kittel, 629-37. Grand Rapids: Eerdmans, 1964.

—. "θέλημα." In *Theological Dictionary of the New Testament*, vol. 3, edited by

G. Kittel, 52-62. Grand Rapids: Eerdmans, 1965.

Seesemann, H. "πεῖρα." In *Theological Dictionary of the New Testament*, vol. 6, edited by G. Kittel and G. Friedrich, 23-36. Grand Rapids: Eerdmans, 1968.

Smith, B. T. D. "Lord's Prayer." In *Interpreter's Dictionary of the Bible*, vol. 3, edited by G. Buttrick, 155. Nashville and New York: Abingdon, 1962.

Stählin, G. "χήρα." In *Theological Dictionary of the New Testament*, vol. 9, edited by G. Bromiley, 440-65. Grand Rapids: Eerdmans, 1974.

Strecker, G. "The Lord's Prayer." In *The Sermon on the Mount: An Exegetical Commentary*, 105-28. Nashville: Abingdon, 1988.

Taussig, H. "The Lord's Prayer." *Forum* 4,4 (1988) 25-41.

Wolf, E. R. *Peasants*. Foundations of Modern Anthropology Series. Englewood Cliffs: Prentice Hall, 1966.

Wright, A. "The Widow's Mites: Praise or Lament?" *CBQ* 44 (1982) 256-65.

Young, B. *The Jewish Background to the Lord's Prayer*. Austin: Center for Judaic-Christian Studies, 1984.

Zahavy, T. *Studies in Jewish Prayer*. Studies in Judaism. Lanham and New York: University Press of America, 1990.

THE LORD'S PRAYER
SECOND THOUGHTS ON THE FIRST PETITION

Norman Metzler

INTRODUCTION

No portion of the Bible is more familiar than the Lord's Prayer, and few have been studied more than this model prayer given to the Christian Church by its Lord. As the quintessential prayer taught by Jesus himself, it has been analyzed, dissected, expounded, interpreted and devotionally uttered more often than any other of the words of Jesus. It is unquestionably the most beloved and memorized of Jesus' words.[1]

In recent time the Jesus Seminar has critically questioned the authenticity of this prayer, along with all the sayings attributed to Jesus in the Scriptures; yet even this very sceptical group of scholars allows that at least some of the words of the prayer are likely the actual words of Jesus himself.[2] Most scholars have been inclined to see some version of the whole prayer as the authentic teaching and words of Jesus.

While the myriad of studies of the Lord's Prayer has attempted to discern the structure and logic of the prayer, to grasp its development of thought or emphases, to describe its parallels in expression and intent, one aspect of the prayer has remained fairly constant and basic—the understanding of the "petitions" or requests expressed in the prayer by Jesus. One may debate whether the Matthean or Lukan version is more original.[3] One can discuss

---

[1] See for example J. Fuellenbach, *The Kingdom of God* (Maryknoll: Orbis, 1995) 275.

[2] R. W. Funk and R. W. Hoover (eds.), *The Five Gospels: The Search for the Authentic Words of Jesus* (Sonoma: Polebridge Press; New York: Macmillan, 1993) 148. The Jesus Seminar prints "Our Father" in red letters, signifying Jesus "undoubtedly said this," and "your name be revered. Impose your imperial rule" (i.e. "Hallowed be thy name. Thy Kingdom come") is printed in purple, indicating that Jesus "probably said something like this." Our present study will generally use the familiar King James Version of the Lord's Prayer.

[3] See for example the translations and rationales in R. H. Gundry, *Matthew:*

whether Jesus meant for us to pray for the coming day's bread today, or just to pray for each day's sustaining bread. But it is universally accepted among scholars that Jesus' prayer in Matthew consists of an introduction and seven petitions; in Luke, an introduction and five petitions.[4]

Christian teaching concerning the Lord's Prayer has maintained this understanding of the petitions down through the centuries. Martin Luther for example, in his *Small Catechism* of 1529, treats the Christian faith according to a number of major articles, one of them being the Lord's Prayer as the model for all prayer.[5] In that treatment of the Lord's Prayer, Luther divides his commentary according to the traditional designation of the portions of the Lord's Prayer as "petitions." His analysis of the Lord's Prayer divides it into the traditional seven petitions with an introduction and conclusion. In his original Small Catechism, the introduction was "Our Father, who art in heaven" and the conclusion was the "Amen." Later editions of his Small Catechism added the doxological ending before the "Amen" as part of the conclusion of the prayer.[6]

The seven petitions, then, begin with "hallowed be thy name." The idea that "hallowed be thy name" is the first petition of the Lord's Prayer—indeed, that it is a petition—is reflected in catechisms of the whole spectrum of denominations beside Luther's Catechism, and remains the general assumption of commentaries to this day.

A Commentary on His Literary and Theological Art (Grand Rapids: Eerdmans, 1982); and J. A. Fitzmyer, *The Gospel according to Luke X–XXIV* (AB 28A; Garden City: Doubleday, 1985).

4   If the last two petitions, "lead us not into temptation" and "but deliver us from evil," are taken as two parts of one petition, then the Matthean version consists of six petitions with an introduction or address.

5   See T. G. Tappert, *The Book of Concord* (Philadelphia: Muhlenberg Press, 1959) 346-48.

6   In modern traditional usage, this doxological ending is added to the Matthean version: "for thine is the Kingdom and the power and the glory forever. Amen." While this ending does not appear in the best manuscripts of either Gospel (see F. W. Beare, *The Gospel according to Matthew* [San Francisco: Harper & Row, 1981] 171), Jewish prayers of Jesus' time often ended with such a doxology; it is understandable, therefore, that the early Christians may have added this phrase. After dropping out of liturgical usage already in the early Church, it has been reintroduced in Protestant liturgies since the Reformation. See Tappert, *Book of Concord*, 348; also Gundry, *Matthew*, 109; and N. T. Wright, *The Lord and His Prayer* (Grand Rapids: Eerdmans, 1996) 81.

A number of factors, however, have caused us to dare to question this universal assumption. One is a longstanding interest in the Kingdom of God as the leitmotif of Jesus' proclamation and ministry. Another is considered reflection on the phrase "hallowed be thy name," and its similarity to the common semitic usage which we shall call the doxological honorific qualifier. This reflection was stimulated by a conversation with a Muslim student who, in his references to the prophet Mohammed, would immediately follow the mention of the name with a parenthetical doxological phrase like "may his name be praised."

Perhaps the phrase "hallowed be thy name," upon such reflection, is not really a petition at all, asking that God may make his name to be hallowed or holy among us; rather, it may be a qualifier of the address "Our Father who art in heaven," similar to the Muslim student's usage. This would make the petition "thy Kingdom come" the first actual petition of Jesus' prayer, consistent with his ministry's priority on the coming Kingdom.

Further study and reflection have convinced us that this is indeed the case. In this chapter we will attempt to make the case for revising the common understanding of the Lord's Prayer, so that the phrase "hallowed be thy name" is shown to be a doxological honorific qualifier of the address, and that the phrase "thy Kingdom come" is the first actual petition of the prayer. We will then further discuss the significance of this revision for grasping Jesus' focus on the Kingdom of God as the top priority of his whole ministry, and its possible ramifications for understanding the remainder of his most famous prayer.

I

It should be acknowledged at the outset that the Gospels do in fact contain two versions of the Lord's Prayer: the longer, more familiar version from the Gospel of Matthew, traditionally used in Protestant worship; and the shorter version in the Gospel of Luke. F. W. Beare argues that these variations show that Jesus' prayer was not memorized verbatim, but somewhat freely adapted.[7] It seems generally agreed that both Gospels draw from the Q source, but that Luke is closer to the original, since Matthew tends to add phrases to the words of Jesus, and Luke would not likely have removed some of

---

[7]   Beare, *Matthew*, 171.

our Lord's words.[8]

It is also possible that Matthew inherited the prayer in its longer form from an earlier liturgical tradition. The concluding doxology does not appear in the earliest manuscripts of Matthew or Luke, but first in the second-century text of the prayer in the *Didache*, which follows the Matthean version. The Latin Vulgate excludes the doxology, as does Roman Catholic liturgical tradition following the Vulgate.[9] Matthew's version gives the prayer a more Jewish cast than Luke's, in line with the phrasing of rabbinical prayers. In any case, for our purposes the two versions are consistent, using the exact same greek wording of the traditional first and second petitions.

Commentators on the prayer, both in the Matthean and Lukan versions, treat the phrase "hallowed be thy name" as a petition.[10]They may accentuate certain aspects of the petition to elaborate upon its meaning—expounding on the import of "hallowed" (ἁγιασθήτω) (so Marshall) or the significance of "name" (so Danker or Gundry)—but they agree in considering it a petition of some sort, a specific prayer to God the Father.

These commentators typically continue with an interpretation of the significance of the first set of petitions, the "thy" petitions, directed toward God. Beare, for example, understands the first three petitions, according to Matthew, to be closely related:

> The sanctifying of God's name is one significant aspect of the coming of his Kingdom, and it is when his Kingdom is fully established—his sovereignty universally accepted—that his will is to be done on earth as it is in heaven.[11]

Marshall observes, in commenting upon the Lukan version,

> After the address come two sets of petitions. The first set, composed of two parallel requests, is concerned with the establishment of God's purposes on a cosmic scale, while the second set, composed of three petitions, is concerned with the personal needs of the disciples. Thus the prayer begins with a theocentric attitude.[12]

---

8   Fitzmyer, *Luke X–XXIV*, 897.

9   Beare, *Matthew*, 171.

10   So for example Martin Luther, "The Small Catechism," in Tappert, *The Book of Concord*; Beare, *Matthew*; Gundry, *Matthew*; I. H. Marshall, *Commentary On Luke* (Grand Rapids: Eerdmans, 1978); Fitzmyer, *Luke X–XXIV*; F. W. Danker, *Jesus and the New Age* (Minneapolis: Fortress, 1988).

11   Beare, *Matthew*, 172.

12   Marshall, *Luke*, 457.

He also points out the parallelism of the first and second petitions, as do various other commentators. Even Wolfhart Pannenberg, whose theology strongly emphasizes the priority of the Kingdom of God in the mission of Jesus, follows the traditional assumption in considering the phrase "hallowed be thy name" to be the first petition, closely linked with the second "thy kingdom come."[13]

It is interesting to note that Fitzmyer in his commentary on Luke does seek to indicate a certain distinctiveness of the first petition by suggesting that it is of a doxological nature. Commenting on the first two petitions of the prayer in the Lukan version ("hallowed be thy name, thy kingdom come") Fitzmyer observes, "the two wishes express a form of praise of God which the Christian community utters in its capacity as children of the Father."[14] His view is that the petitions toward God are not the same as the petitions directed toward human need; the former are more in the nature of "wishes," and serve to express a form of praise to God.

The significance of Fitzmyer's observation is that he recognizes a difference in this petition from some of the other petitions; indeed, he acknowledges that the petition is somehow also doxological. At the same time, he supposes a parallelism between the first petition concerning hallowing God's name, and the second petition, dealing with the coming of God's kingdom. In so doing, he essentially equates the nature of the two petitions "may your name be sanctified" and "may your kingdom come." Fitzmyer therefore fails to identify a doxological quality that is unique to the first petition.

Gundry, in his commentary on Matthew, breaks with other commentators by proposing a structural distinction of this petition from the others.[15] In his analysis of the prayer, Matthew adds to the Lukan version in order to make the prayer form three couplets:

– the first is	(a)	Your kingdom come,
	(b)	your will come to pass on earth as also [it comes to pass] in heaven.
– the second is	(a)	give us the coming day's bread today,
	(b)	and forgive us our debts as we also have forgiven our debtors.

---

13   W. Pannenberg, *Systematic Theology*, vol. 1 (Grand Rapids: Eerdmans, 1991) 399. Similarly Fuellenbach, *The Kingdom of God*, 284.

14   Fitzmyer, *Luke X–XXIV*, 898.

15   Gundry, *Matthew*, 105.

– the third is   (a)   And bring us not into temptation,

                   (b)   but deliver us from the evil one.

One may or may not see merit in this attempt to find a liturgical logic or flow in the prayer as formulated by Matthew. For our purposes, what is noteworthy is that in order to develop his three-couplet approach, Gundry must construe Matthew as "taking the first petition, 'hallowed be your name' with the address; i.e. 'Father' is the name to be hallowed."[16] Intriguingly, Gundry even goes on to bring in the idea of an honorific phrase at this point—although in his view it is the phrase "who are in heaven" that serves as the honorific addition by Matthew. He also closely links the first petition with the address in observing that "your name" in this construction matches "Father." "That name is to be hallowed, i.e. reverenced as a revelation of God's relation to Jesus' disciples."[17]

Gundry also points out that it is left indeterminate who is to hold in reverence the name; and this is in fact an interpretive issue for those treating the prayer. Is it to be interpreted that only God can bring about the hallowing or sanctifying of his name, just as only God can bring about his Kingdom?[18] Or as Martin Luther explains it in his Small Catechism, does this petition mean that God's name should be holy among us, and the emphasis is to be upon our human reverencing of God's name when we pray this petition?[19] Or does one attempt to include both, like Marshall, who says, "the passive form of the verb "be hallowed" may be a circumlocution for naming God himself as the subject: the prayer is for God to act in such a way as to lead to the hallowing of his name by men."[20] Different commentators arrive at different solutions to this interpretive problem; but whatever their solution, as long as they view this phrase as a genuine petition, they must understand someone to be doing the hallowing.

For purposes of our discussion, the significance of Gundry's treatment of the Lord's Prayer lies in the fact that he separates the first petition from the second, and links it closely with the opening address. It is interesting to note that some translations of the Lord's

---

[16]   Gundry, *Matthew*, 105.

[17]   Gundry, *Matthew*, 106.

[18]   Gundry, *Matthew*, 106.

[19]   Luther, "Small Catechism," in Tappert, *The Book of Concord*, 346.

[20]   Marshall, *Luke*, 457.

prayer in Matthew, for example the King James and RSV versions, grammatically link the address and first petition by placing a comma after "Our father who art in heaven," and a period after "hallowed be thy name." In these versions "thy kingdom come" begins or is itself a new sentence.

Another significance of Gundry's treatment is that while he resolves the issue in his own way, he does surface clearly the fact that the subject of the hallowing—who is to hold in reverence or honor or sanctify the name—is in the first instance indeterminate within the prayer itself. This at least hints at a problematic in the traditional understanding of the phrase as the first petition.

Despite the value of their scholarship, neither Fitzmyer nor Gundry is led by their insights to what seems to be an obvious and much more natural explanation of the phrase "hallowed be thy name."

Various commentators on the Lord's Prayer point out the likely relationship between Jesus' prayer and Jewish prayers, particularly the "Qaddish" and the "Prayer of the Eighteen Benedictions."[21] Indeed, a study entitled *The Lord's Prayer and Jewish Liturgy*, edited by Jakob Petuchowski and Michael Brocke, contains a number of essays examining the relationships between Jesus' prayer and the liturgical traditions of rabbinic Judaism.[22] One form of the Qaddish, a prayer originally uttered after the sermon in synagogue worship, begins:

> Exalted and hallowed be His great name
> in the world which He created
> according to His will.
> May He establish His kingdom
> in your lifetime and in your days,
> and in the lifetime of the whole household of
> Israel, speedily and at a near time.[23]

One can hardly miss the similarity of the phrasing here to the phrases "hallowed be thy name" and "thy kingdom come" in the

---

[21]   So for example E. Schweizer, *The Good News according to Matthew* (Atlanta: John Knox Press, 1975) 151-52; also Marshall, *Luke*, 457; Gundry, *Matthew*, 104.

[22]   J. J. Petuchowski and M. Brocke (eds.), *The Lord's Prayer and Jewish Liturgy* (A Crossroad Book; New York: Seabury, 1978).

[23]   Petuchowski and Brocke (eds.), *The Lord's Prayer*, 37. This is taken from the "Half Qaddish."

Lord's Prayer. This is not surprising, since Jesus prayed and taught his disciples to pray in the context of the Jewish prayer tradition. Within this tradition one finds numerous doxological expressions such as "hallowed be His great Name," "may Your Name be praised," or "may His great Name be praised." These might be understood as a type of petitionary form when they stand on their own within a prayer, for example in the "Half Qaddish," "May His great Name be praised forever and unto all eternity."[24] Upon closer scrutiny, however, these phrases seem to be lacking in petitionary force, in that the subject is indeterminate, and they have more of the character of exclamations of praise to God rather than requests that God or someone may cause his name to be praised.

But there are some instances in which the doxological phrase is even more obviously a qualifier of the mention of God, as in the following portion of the Qaddish:

> Blessed and praised,
> glorified and exalted,
> extolled and honoured,
> magnified and lauded
> be the Name of the Holy One, *praised be He*—
> although He is beyond all blessings and hymns,
> praises and consolations
> which may be uttered in the world.[25]

Or again, from the "Burial Qaddish:"

> Exalted and hallowed be His great Name
> in the world which He will renew,
> resurrecting the dead,
> and raising them up to eternal life.
> He will rebuild the city of Jerusalem,
> and establish His temple in its midst.
> He will uproot idolatry from the earth,
> and restore the worship of God to its place.
> The Holy One, *praised be He*, will reign
> in His sovereignty and in His glory.[26]

In both of these instances we have the name of God spoken, immediately followed by a unique parenthetical phrase, which we are

---

[24] Petuchowski and Brocke (eds.), *The Lord's Prayer*, 37.

[25] Petuchowski and Brocke (eds.), *The Lord's Prayer*, 37. Emphasis added.

[26] Petuchowski and Brocke (eds.), *The Lord's Prayer*, 38-39. Emphasis added.

calling a doxological honorific qualifier, and then the prayer continues. It is important for the purposes of our study to note that the terms "hallowed" (qōdeš), "praised" (hallel), and "blessed" (barûch), are functionally equivalent in Jewish doxological usage.

A similar construction is to be found in Paul's letter to the Romans (1:25), where Paul is talking about how humankind has become estranged from God and reflects in its behaviors this separation. Paul observes:

> they exchanged the truth of God for a lie, and worshiped and served created things rather than the Creator—who is forever praised. Amen. Because of this, God gave them over to shameful lusts . . .[27]

The parenthetical phrase "who is forever praised. Amen." is a qualifier of the mention of God as Creator. In speaking of the perversion of the human race, it seems as if Paul is almost compelled to break in with this doxological honorific qualifier.

In fact, the Sanday and Headlam commentary on Romans, in its translation of this phrase, specifically sets it aside in parentheses, thus:

> Reprobates, who could abandon the living and true God for a sham divinity, and render divine honours and ritual observance to the creature, neglecting the Creator (Blessed be His name for ever!).[28]

Their commentary on this phrase notes:

> Doxologies like this are of constant occurrence in the Talmud, and are a spontaneous expression of devout feeling called forth either by the thought of God's adorable perfections or sometimes (as here) by the forced mention of that which reverence would rather hide.[29]

A quotation from the Talmud will serve to illustrate the truth of this observation. The Palestinian Talmud, commenting on boldness and humility in prayer, makes the observation, "However much you bother Him, the Holy One, blessed be He, will receive you."[30] Again, that parenthetical phrase "blessed be He," serves as a doxological honorific qualifier of the reference to God as "the Holy One." As

---

[27]   New International Version translation.

[28]   W. Sanday and A. C. Headlam, *A Critical and Exegetical Commentary on the Epistle to the Romans* (ICC; Edinburgh: T. & T. Clark, 1895; 5th ed., 1902) 4.

[29]   Sanday and Headlam, *Romans*, 46.

[30]   *Y. Ber.* 9 (p. 13b), as cited in Petuchowski and Brocke (eds.), *The Lord's Prayer*, 84.

was mentioned earlier, one finds this kind of spontaneous doxological honorific qualifier, following the name of God or even of a
revered loved one, still present in semitic usage today.

If one looks at the phrase "hallowed be thy name" in the Lord's
Prayer in this light, it seems very natural to see it as a similar
parenthetical phrase, a doxological honorific qualifier of the address,
"Our Father who art in heaven." In the instances cited above, the
third person rather than the second person is more frequently used.
Jesus, on the other hand, may well have used the second person
because he was teaching his disciples the importance of praying to
God in a more personal, intimate fashion. One can surmise that in
another context Jesus might just as well have prayed, "Our Father in
heaven—blessed be his name . . ." There seems to be no evidence
indicating that the second person rather than the third person detracts
from our argument. An example of the use of the second person
noted above from the Prayer of the Eighteen Benedictions ("may
Your Name be praised") appears very similar to Jesus' usage.[31]

Jesus thus teaches his disciples to address God as "Abba" (possibly
with the connotation of "daddy" or "pappa," though in recent years
this has been disputed), in a very warm, personal way. He then
qualifies and intensifies closeness and familiarity by adding the
doxological honorific qualifier "hallowed be thy name." As an
obedient and loving child of God, Jesus cannot keep from breaking
into a spontaneous exclamation of praise when he speaks the name of
his heavenly Father. His traditional Jewish liturgical heritage and
sensibilities simply break through, even when he is otherwise
criticizing the longwinded prayers of the pagans by teaching his
disciples how to pray simply and to the point.

A grammatical investigation of the Greek original of the Lord's
Prayer appears to lend further credence to our contention. Careful
examination reveals that the verbs for "hallowed" and "Thy kingdom
come" and "Thy will be done" do not offer the neat parallelism
suggested by the commentators and by those translations which try to
emphasize the supposed parallelism by using a wording such as "may
your name be hallowed," "may your kingdom come" and "may your
will be done."[32] An important grammatical observation is that the

---

31   Petuchowski and Brocke (eds.), *The Lord's Prayer*, 34.
32   So for example J. B. Phillips, *The New Testament in Modern English*
(New York: Macmillan, 1958); also Beare, *Matthew*, 172, as well as Fitzmyer's

verb for "may your name be hallowed" (ἁγιασθήτω) is aorist passive imperative, while "may your kingdom come" (ἐλθέτω) is aorist active imperative, and "may your will be done" (γενηθήτω) is a deponent verb, having only a passive form in Greek but having an active meaning.[33] Indeed, all the verbs in the Lord's prayer are grammatically active in intent except "be hallowed" (ἁγιασθήτω), further reinforcing our contention that this phrase is different in kind from the other phrases in the prayer. Thus there is nothing to be discerned in the text which demands that "name be hallowed," "kingdom come" and "will be done" be construed as parallel petitions.

The latter two phrases, as opposed to the first, may well be seen as genuine petitions. When they are separated from the truly doxological nature of the first phrase "hallowed be thy name," they do not need to be construed as somehow addressing God's glory, over against the petitions concerning our human needs in the second part of the prayer.[34] This kind of forced interpretation arises because of the failure to distinguish the doxological qualifying phrase from the first actual petitions. These first two petitions are closely related and extremely relevant in putting our focus in prayer, as in life, on the Kingdom of God, and on living a life that befits God's Kingdom (may your will be done on earth as it is in Your Kingdom). Jesus is teaching his disciples to plead fervently for the coming of God's kingdom, indeed for its inbreaking in our present lives as we seek to do his Kingdom will.

The second part of Jesus' prayer then asks God to provide the essentials of our present life as we live for that Kingdom. Give us the bread, that is, the essential things we need for each day, so that we

---

treatment of the prayer as found in Luke (*Luke X–XXIV*, 896).

33   We must differ with Fuellenbach, *The Kingdom of God*, 284, in his treatment of the Lord's Prayer, when he states, "The mood in 'hallowed be' has the same force as in 'come' and 'be done'; therefore, petition, not praise, is expressed." He maintains that this is a real petition.

34   So for example the note in the *Oxford Annotated Bible*, commenting on Matt 6:9-13. The *Oxford Annotated* even tries to reinforce the parallelism of the first three petitions by claiming that the phrase "on earth as it is in heaven" should be read with each of the three petitions, not just with "Thy will be done." This idea might provide some interesting material for homiletical treatments, but it certainly does violence to the integrity of the doxological honorific qualifier, and seems rather nonsensical or at best quite forced when added to "thy kingdom come."

are not distracted by petty daily needs as we live for the Kingdom. Continually forgive us as we live in forgiveness toward others, that we might leave the weight of the past behind as we live our lives directed toward the coming Kingdom. And protect us from being entrapped by further sin and evil which could detract from our focus on that heavenly Kingdom.

Our basic line of argumentation, therefore, is that "hallowed be thy name" is not in fact a petition at all, parallel to the other petitions of the Lord's Prayer. Rather, we have argued that it is a parenthetical phrase serving as a doxological honorific qualifier of the address, similar in style and function to the other doxological honorific qualifiers mentioned above. The Lord's Prayer so understood might be more appropriately read and prayed in this way:

> Our Father in heaven—hallowed be thy name!—
> Thy Kingdom come!
> Thy will be done on earth as it is in heaven.

II

If our argument has merit, then the first actual petition of the Lord's prayer is the phrase "thy kingdom come" and not the traditional "hallowed be thy name." That Jesus would teach his disciples to put top priority on praying for the coming of God's kingdom is totally congruous with his whole mission and ministry, which proclaimed and anticipated the coming of that heavenly Kingdom. Indeed, the various commentators are quite consistent in recognizing the eschatological character of the whole prayer. To quote from Anton Vögtle's essay in *The Lord's Prayer and Jewish Liturgy*:

> As, above all, a comparison with the prayer of the Eighteen Benedictions shows, Jesus has placed the main concerns of the Kaddish prayer emphatically at the beginning of his instruction for prayer by means of his significantly formulated Thou-petitions. In view of the basic theme of his preaching of God and his Kingdom, his proclamation of the eschatological acts of God indicated by his speech and action leads us to expect nothing else; in other words, the final revelation of God, understood as the essence of salvation, is the primary concern of Jesus; and this concern determines, too, the remaining contents of the prayer as enumerated by him. One may, therefore, presume from the beginning that each of the following We-

petitions must have an "eschatological" reference.[35]

It was only in the last century that Albrecht Ritschl gave appropriate place to the concept of the Kingdom of God in the life and teaching of Jesus, by making it the central theme of his own constructive theology.[36] While Ritschl's understanding of that Kingdom as an ethical, developing reality in our present history was not an adequate reading of the New Testament witnesses, it did rightly bring forward the Kingdom thematic as pivotal to the whole mission and ministry of Jesus. Ritschl's work prompted scholars like Johannes Weiss and Albert Schweitzer to undertake more discerning investigations into the nature of the Kingdom proclaimed by Jesus, resulting in important critiques of Ritschl's approach. While they themselves could not see the relevance for today of their own biblical findings, scholars in this century have applied their insights in more positive constructive ways.[37]

Most notably the work of Wolfhart Pannenberg and Jürgen Moltmann has demonstrated the relevance of Jesus' living for and looking forward fervently to the imminent coming of his heavenly Father's Kingdom. In developing a futurist or hope theology, they and others have shown that the proclamation of the Kingdom was the leitmotif of Jesus' whole ministry—his preaching, his parables, his miracles. As Pannenberg expresses it:

> In the New Testament, however, Jesus' message of the imminent Kingdom
> of God precedes every Christology and every new qualification of human

---

[35]   A. Voegtle, "The Lord's Prayer: A Prayer for Jews and Christians?" in Petuchowski and Brocke (eds.), *The Lord's Prayer*, 102. J. Jeremias (*The Lord's Prayer in the Light of Recent Research* [London: SCM Press, 1977]) treats this prayer as an eschatological prayer. More recently, Fuellenbach (*The Kingdom of God*, 274), in his extensive study of the Kingdom of God in the message of Jesus, affirms the eschatological nature of this prayer throughout.

[36]   See my dissertation *The Ethics of the Kingdom* (Ann Arbor: University Microfilms, 1974) for a fuller explication of this emergence of the Kingdom of God motif in modern theology.

[37]   Metzler, *The Ethics of the Kingdom*. It is interesting to note that while Weiss and Schweitzer properly critiqued Ritschl's interpretation of the biblical concept of the Kingdom of God, they could see no relevance of Jesus' approach for today. Weiss in effect conceded that, given the non-arrival of the parousia as Jesus and the early church expected it, Ritschl's ethicizing of the Kingdom concept is perhaps the best we can do to make the idea relevant for our time. Schweitzer turned to a kind of Christ mysticism as the continuing relevance of Jesus for today.

existence and thus becomes the foundation of both. Christological and anthropological interpretations cannot be imposed upon the preaching of the Kingdom, but must themselves be judged in the light of the Kingdom. This resounding motif of Jesus' message—the imminent Kingdom of God—must be recovered as a key to the whole of Christian theology.[38]

In light of the expectation of that Kingdom, Jesus prayed, according to Matthew, that the power of that coming Kingdom would be evident already in the present world by the doing of God's will on earth. While this second petition of Matthew's version is certainly a fitting and appropriate prayer for Christians seeking to live in accordance with the will of God whose Kingdom is coming soon, the more brief and stark petition in the Lukan version of the prayer, "Thy Kingdom come!", if it is indeed more original, focuses even more single-mindedly on the priority of the Kingdom for Jesus. The whole first or "thy" part of Jesus' prayer according to Luke deals solely with the coming Kingdom, while the last three (or four, according to Matthew) petitions, the "us" petitions, address the fundamental things we need as we live for and await that coming Kingdom. In any case, whether one prefers the Matthean or Lukan version, the centrality of the Kingdom vision and expectation provides the key to understanding how Jesus intended for his disciples to pray.

Clement of Alexandria affirms the desire of Jesus that his disciples keep focused on the important or "great things" in their prayer life, "the Kingdom of God and its righteousness," and not get distracted by the "little things:"

> Ask for the great things—for God's almighty glory and kingdom, and that God's great gifts, the bread of life and the endless mercy of God, may be granted to you—even here, even now, already today. That does not mean that you may not bring your small personal needs before God, but they must not govern your prayer, for you are praying to your Father. He knows all. He knows what things his children have need of before they ask him, and he adds them to his great gifts. Jesus says: Ask ye for the great things, so God will grant you all the little things. The Lord's Prayer teaches us how to ask for the great things.[39]

---

[38]　W. Pannenberg, "The Kingdom of God and the Church," in *Theology and the Kingdom of God* (Philadelphia: Westminster, 1977) 52-53. Pannenberg's whole theological project is based upon the reality of the coming Kingdom of God as proclaimed by Jesus, and the power of that eschatological reality as the real dynamic of history.

[39]　Clement of Alexandria, as cited in Jeremias, *The Lord's Prayer*, 33.

The later addition of the doxological ending, "for Thine is the Kingdom, and the power, and the glory, forever and ever. Amen" proves to be consistent with the Kingdom thematic and priority at the beginning of the Lord's Prayer. Like the first "petition," this ending is not a petition, but rather a doxological expression. Gordon Bahr proposes that the Lord's Prayer, following what he sees as the praise-petition-praise tripartite formula for prayer similar to the Eighteen Benedictions of Jewish tradition, actually was used by the primitive church in the same way as the contemporary synagogue used the Eighteen Benedictions.[40] While this writer disagrees with Bahr's assumption that the whole first part of the prayer is praise or doxology, our proposal can be understood as consonant with this tripartite style. It may well be, as Bahr argues, that the Lord's prayer did in fact take the place of the Eighteen Benedictions for the early Christian community.

III

If this proposal concerning the Lord's Prayer has validity, then it will exercise at least a fourfold impact on the theology and practice surrounding these most beloved and authentic words of Jesus:

1. It sheds new light on the way in which Jesus himself prayed and taught his disciples to pray. It provides a new insight into the style of Jesus' prayer, and reinforces the argument for his continuity with Jewish and semitic prayer and linguistic patterns which persist in some circles even to this day.

2. It strengthens and authenticates the theological argument for the centrality of the imminent Kingdom of God in the life and teaching of Jesus, and the importance of understanding his whole ministry in terms of this Kingdom priority. And if Jesus' teaching is the permanent touchstone for Christian faith, then it reaffirms the crucial role of the Kingdom for all of Christian theology.

3. It suggests a practical effect upon the way in which the Lord's Prayer is treated in the life of the Church. The phrase "hallowed be thy name" will be intoned more appropriately in the manner of a parenthetical semitic doxological expression, rather than as the first of a series of petitions. Hymnals, prayer books, and other liturgical and prayer materials will more helpfully print this phrase in a clearly parenthetical fashion, so that readers and prayers will speak it in the way in which Jesus himself intended.

---

40   G. J. Bahr, "The Use of the Lord's Prayer in the Primitive Church," in Petuchowski and Brocke (eds.), *The Lord's Prayer*, 149-55.

4. Given our Lord's own teaching and modelling, it reaffirms the importance of the doxological dimension in all Christian prayer, worship, and life.

This proposal in no way seeks to denigrate the practical meaning and value of the traditional ways in which this first "petition" has been understood and used. Christians may certainly pray that God's name might be kept holy and honored and reverenced in our lives, as a sign of the inbreaking power of the Kingdom into a world that is so unholy and irreverent and dishonoring of God.

Our contention is simply that this specific type of petition is not what Jesus was teaching in his splendidly simple and pointed prayer. He was addressing his heavenly Father in a personal yet honoring way, and the parenthetical phrase "hallowed be thy name" rolled off his tongue naturally and spontaneously as part of his prayer life as a pious Jew. And in Jesus' whole life, as we know, his heavenly Father was indeed supremely reverenced and holy.

If this proposal is taken seriously, then we will pray Jesus' prayer more closely in tune with the style and spirit in which he first taught it. And the chief emphasis in our prayers, as in Jesus' prayer, will be on God's coming Kingdom and on our relationship to it.

THE SILENCE OF JESUS
THE GALILEAN RABBI WHO WAS MORE THAN A PROPHET

Eckhard J. Schnabel

Whatever else his contemporaries thought of Jesus, they saw him as a teacher.[1] Both outsiders and his followers addressed him as ῥαββί,[2] usually translated as διδάσκαλος.[3] Jesus saw himself as a teacher. This is evident not only in his self-designation as teacher in Mark 14:14 (= Matt 26:18 = Luke 22:12) and in logia which imply a teacher-pupil relationship (Matt 10:24-25; 23:8; Luke 6:40) but also in the character of his public ministry: he lived with "students" (μαθηταί) who wanted to learn from him, he taught in synagogues, he discussed with other rabbis (γραμματεῖς), he answered theological questions posed by ordinary people.

Jesus evidently always gave an answer when question were posed to him, even when the people asking the questions did not take him seriously, or were openly hostile, and were thus not personally interested in the answer he might give. There is only one exception to Jesus' readiness to explain what he did and what he taught: Jesus remained silent at crucial points during the legal proceedings which were carried out both by the Jewish authorities and by the Roman

---

[1] On Jesus as teacher, see S. Byrskog, *Jesus the Only Teacher. Didactic Authority and Transmission in Ancient Israel, Ancient Judaism and the Matthean Community* (ConBNT 24; Stockholm: Almqvist & Wiksell, 1994); D. Dormeyer, "Jesus as Wandering Prophetic Wisdom Teacher," *HervTS* 49 (1993) 101-17; M. Karrer, "Der lehrende Jesus: Neutestamentliche Erwägungen," *ZNW* 83 (1992) 1-20; P. Perkins, *Jesus as Teacher* (Understanding Jesus Today; Cambridge: Cambridge University Press, 1990); R. Riesner, *Jesus als Lehrer: Eine Untersuchung zum Ursprung der Evangelien-Überlieferung* (3rd ed., WUNT 2.7; Tübingen: Mohr [Siebeck], 1988); V. K. Robbins, *Jesus the Teacher: A Socio-Rhetorical Interpretation of Mark* (Philadelphia: Fortress, 1984).

[2] Followers: Mark 9:5; 11:21; 14:45; Matt 26:25,49 (Judas Iscariot); John 1:38,49; 4:31; 9:2; 11:8; cf. ῥαββουνί in Mark 10:51; John 20:16. Outsiders: John 3:2; 6:25.

[3] Followers: Mark 4:38; 9:38; 10:35; 13:1; John 1:38; 20:16. Outsiders: Matt 8:19; 12:38; 19:16; 22:16, 24, 36; Mark 9:17; 10:17, 20; 12:14, 19, 32; Luke 7:40; [8:49]; 9:38; 10:25; 11:45; 12:13; 18:18; 19:39; 20:21, 28, 39; 21:7; John 3:2; 6:25.

governor. All of the four Gospels report this extraordinary fact for various stages of the trial: Mark 14:60-61, 65; 15:3-4; Matt 26:62, 63, 67-68; 27:12, 14; Luke 23:9; John 19:9).

In order to understand this exceptional silence of Jesus,[4] I propose (1) to assess Jesus' reactions to questions as described by the Gospel writers, (2) to analyze his reaction to questions put to him during the trial, before (3) evaluating Jesus' silence in the trial.

JESUS' REACTION TO QUESTIONS

In order to be able to assess the silence of Jesus in the Gospel accounts of the trial, we will discuss each of the Gospels individually in order to be able to determine whether Jesus' silence is a literary device used by the evangelists.

Jesus' Reaction to Questions in the Gospel of Mark

1. Jesus' followers ask (ἐρωτᾶν and ἐπερωτᾶν) about the meaning of parables and puzzling sayings (Mark 4:10; 7:17), about their inability to cast out an evil spirit (9:28), about acceptable grounds for divorce (10:10), about securing eternal life (10:17), about eschatological questions (9:11; 13:3-4), about the one who would

---

4   It seems surprising that only a couple of studies have been devoted to the silence of Jesus during the trial: J. Schreiber, "Das Schweigen Jesu," in W. Wegenast (ed.), *Theologie und Unterricht: Über die Repräsentanz des Christlichen in der Schule* (H. Stock Festschrift; Gütersloh: Mohn, 1969) 79-87 = J. Schreiber, *Die Markuspassion. Eine redaktionsgeschichtliche Untersuchung* (2nd ed.; BZNW 68; Berlin: de Gruyter, 1993 [1970]) 260-72 [Nachtrag: 269-72]; M. L. Soards, "The Silence of Jesus Before Herod: An Interpretative Suggestion," *Australian Biblical Review* 33 (1985) 41-45; cf. also J. D. Crossan, *The Cross That Spoke. The Origins of the Passion Narrative* (San Francisco: Harper & Row, 1988) 174-87. See also the work of the Toronto philosopher P. W. Gooch, *Reflections on Jesus and Socrates: Word and Silence* (New Haven: Yale University Press, 1996). The study of J. C. O'Neill ("The Silence of Jesus," *NTS* 15 [1968-69] 153-67) does not discuss Jesus' silence during the trial but Jesus' silence about his Messiahship, which he regards as "absolute" (p. 162), despite the fact that he thought that he was Messiah which can be established on the basis of several key events in his ministry (pp. 163-64); O'Neill argues that Jesus' silence about his Messiahship is part of his messianic role, as his Jewish contemporaries would have understood that "the Messiah would not be able to claim Messiahship for himself, but must wait for God to enthrone him" (p. 165). This theory does not explain Jesus' silence during the trial, as Jesus *does* respond to the questions both of the Sanhedrin and of Pilate whether he claims to be Messiah or king of the Jews, respectively.

betray him (14:19: λέγειν).

Jesus always gives an answer. He clarifies his pronouncement which elicited the question (9:12-13; 10:11-12), even though his explanation may be enigmatic (4:11-12; 7:18-23); he explains the power of exorcism (9:29); he quotes Scripture (10:19); he points with sovereign authority to the critical significance of his own person (10:21); he explains at length eschatological issues (13:5-37). And he is prepared to point out the follower who would betray him (14:20-21).

2. When evil spirits ask (λέγειν) Jesus a question (1:24; 5:7) he responds: he tells them to be silent (1:25) or he asks their name and grants their request of being allowed to enter into pigs (5:9-13). When the people of Gerasa heard the story of the demon-possessed pigs they asked Jesus to leave their area (5:17: παρακαλεῖν)—Jesus grants their request and thus accepts their rejection of himself.

3. In Capernaum scribes ask themselves whether Jesus is blaspheming as he pronounced a paralytic's sins forgiven (2:7). The Pharisees and scribes ask (ἐπερωτᾶν) Jesus about the unclean lifestyle of his students (7:5), about the unorthodox sabbath observance of his disciples (2:24), about the issue of divorce (10:2), about his table fellowship with tax collectors and sinners (2:16: λέγειν). The Sadducees ask Jesus about the issue of resurrection (12:18: ἐπερωτᾶν). The Jerusalem priestly aristocracy asks Jesus about the nature of his authority (11:28: λέγειν).

Jesus always replies to queries from his opponents. He often quotes (2:25-26; 7:6, 10; 10:7-8) or interprets Scripture (10:3-12; 12:24-27); he explains his provocative behavior (2:17); he attacks premises of their position (7:7-9, 11-14). He honors questions, albeit in an indirect manner (in good rabbinic fashion), which are hardly asked for the sake of information (thus evidently in 11:27-33) but are rather meant to embarrass him or expose him as an imposter[5] and/or to gather ammunition which could be used against him.[6] And he answers questions that people who are sceptical are not prepared to voice publicly: he addresses the charge that he violates God's majesty as he pronounces sins to be forgiven, thus causing the scribes in

---

5   Cf. R. H. Gundry, *Mark: A Commentary on His Apology for the Cross* (Grand Rapids: Eerdmans, 1993) 657.

6   Cf. R. Pesch, *Das Markusevangelium* (5th/4th ed., HTKNT 2.1-2; Freiburg: Herder, 1989/1991 [1976/1977]) 2.210.

Capernaum to wonder whether he indeed has the authority to forgive sins (2:8-12).

4. In 3:1-6 Mark relates a miracle of healing in the antagonistic presence of Pharisees who had already warned him against violating the sabbath (2:24). Despite their malevolent scrutiny (note in 3:2 παρετήρουν linked with the final clause ἵνα κατηγορήσωσιν αὐτοῦ) Jesus starts the proceedings which eventually lead to the healing of the man with a withered hand. He deliberately ignores the earlier warning of the Pharisees. His action shows audacious aggressiveness:[7] Jesus provocatively raises the issue of permissibility and, with strong language—reversing the traditional order of the antithetical pairs "good and evil" and "life and death" (cf. Sir 33:14 and Deut 30:15, 19 LXX) in order to end on the climactic contrast between life and death—sets out alternatives in human behavior which leaves the opponents speechless (3:4b: οἱ δὲ ἐσιώπων).

As regards the issue of "doing good and saving a life" the Pharisees would have agreed that saving a life was a legal possibility and constituted halakhic priority over the laws of sabbath observance; as regards the issue of "doing evil and killing [a life]" the Pharisees could have argued that a crippled hand did not threaten the life of the man and that a healing could wait for the day after the sabbath. Their silence thus does not demonstrate the halakhic persuasiveness of Jesus' answer.

The powerful contrast which Jesus draws between saving life and killing is variously interpreted. Most recent interpreters place the alternative of "killing" in the context of the antagonism of the Pharisees and take it as an allusion to their murderous intentions.[8] Others take it to mean "not to heal" and place Jesus' question and the response of the Pharisees in the context of the broader scope of Jesus' proclamation of the presence of God's redemptive rule where healing was a question of life and death as it brought the healed person the benefits of God's restoring power (see the healing in 2:1-

---

7   Cf. Gundry, *Mark*, 153, 155.

8   Cf. E. Lohmeyer, *Das Evangelium des Markus* (8th ed., MeyerK 1.2, Göttingen: Vandenhoeck & Ruprecht, 1967 [1937]) 68; V. Taylor, *The Gospel According to St. Mark* (2nd ed., Thornapple Commentaries; Grand Rapids: Baker, 1981 [1966]) 222; Pesch, *Markusevangelium*, 1.192; J. Gnilka, *Das Evangelium nach Markus* (EKKNT 2.1-2; Zürich: Benziger; Neukirchen-Vluyn: Neukirchener, 1978/1979) 1.127; Gundry, *Mark*, 151, 153.

12 and Jesus' fellowship with sinners in 2:13-17).[9] Either way, the silence of the Pharisees does not signify their defeat, on the contrary: they conspire with the Herodians to destroy Jesus (3:6).[10] Their silence indicates that they were not willing to enter into a genuine dialogue about the person and the ministry of Jesus who announced and claimed to effect the realization of God's promised (messianic) activity in history. On another occasion a response by Jesus causes the scribes to refrain from asking further questions (12:34b: καὶ οὐδεὶς οὐκέτι ἐτόλμα αὐτὸν ἐπερωτῆσαι).

5. As is well known, the historicity of Jesus' command for silence is linked with one of the great debates of New Testament scholarship that began with William Wrede.[11] Wrede regarded narratives which spell out or imply the conception that Jesus was the Messiah as editorial interpolation into the non-messianic account of the life of Jesus by means of the messianic secret motif, manifestly in the *Schweigegebote*. Today many scholars doubt the validity of Wrede's theory,[12] not only because it has become increasingly clear that there is no evidence of such a pre-Markan theory but also, and more importantly, because the assumption of non-messianic Jesus traditions is untenable.[13] Several scholars link the motif of Jesus' silence during

---

[9] Cf. R. A. Guelich, *Mark* (WBC 34; Dallas: Word 1989) 1.136.

[10] On the authenticity of 3:6 and the assumption of an original connection of 3:1-6 with 2:23-28, see Gundry, *Mark*, 155-56.

[11] W. Wrede, *Das Messiasgeheimnis in den Evangelien. Zugleich ein Beitrag zum Verständnis des Markusevangeliums* (4th ed., Göttingen: Vandenhoeck & Ruprecht, 1969 [1901]); ET: *The Messianic Secret* (Cambridge: Clarke, 1971); see J. L. Blevins, *The Messianic Secret in Markan Research, 1901–1976* (Washington: University Press, 1981); C. Tuckett (ed.), *The Messianic Secret* (Philadelphia: Fortress, 1983).

[12] Cf. more recently H. Räisänen, *Das "Messiasgeheimnis" im Markusevangelium* (SFEG 28; Helsinki: Suomalainen Tiedeakatemia, 1976); ET: *The 'Messianic Secret' in Mark* (Edinburgh: T.& T. Clark, 1990); Pesch, *Markusevangelium*, 2.36-37; G. Strecker, *Theologie des Neuen Testaments* (Berlin: de Gruyter, 1994) 362-71; see also H. Hübner, *Biblische Theologie des Neuen Testaments* (Vol. 3; Göttingen: Vandenhoeck & Ruprecht, 1995) 67.

[13] Cf. J. D. G. Dunn, "The Messianic Secret in Mark," in Tuckett (ed.), *Messianic Secret*, 116-31; B. Witherington, *The Christoloy of Jesus* (Minneapolis: Fortress, 1990); C. A. Evans, *Jesus and His Contemporaries. Comparative Studies* (AGJU 25; Leiden: Brill, 1995) 437-56; N. T. Wright, *Jesus and the Victory of God* (Christian Origins and the Question of God, vol. 2; Minneapolis: Fortress, 1996) 477-539; P. Stuhlmacher, *Biblische Theologie des Neuen Testaments. Band*

his trial with the Marcan "messianic secret."[14]

I cannot see a uniform "silence motif" in Mark[15] for the following reasons. (1) The rebuking of the wind with the command to be silent (σιώπα, πεφίμωσο) in 4:39 emphasizes the power of Jesus by echoing passages in the Scriptures concerning God's power to rebuke and still the sea (Job 26:11-12; Ps 65:8; 66:6; 107:9; 107:29-30; Nah 1:4) as well as the accounts of exorcisms. (2) In shutting up demons (Mark 1:25, 34; 3:12; 9:25) Jesus again shows his greater power as he stops the attempt by the unclean spirits to use their knowledge of Jesus in self-defense or to gain control over Jesus.[16] Jesus commands only the unclean spirits to keep silent, not the people who were healed. (3) In the passages where Jesus shuts up demons the verb σιωπᾶν does not occur (1:25, 34 have φιμοῦμαι), and a command to shut up may be lacking altogether (cf. 5:6-13). (4) The strong rebuke to remain silent in 3:12 may perhaps be interpreted (in the context of the large multitude which threatens to crush Jesus; cf. 3:9-10), without allusion to deeper theological purposes, simply in terms of "crowd control": Jesus attracts so large a multitude "that he must have a boat ready and insist that the unclean spirits not publicize him as God's Son lest the throngs crush him."[17] (5) The command which Jesus issued to the disciples to keep his messiahship private (8:30) is to be explained on the background of contemporary Jewish hopes of a coming agent of God who would be king, fighting with success Israel's battles against her enemies, restoring the Temple and the

---

1: Grundlegung. Von Jesus zu Paulus (2nd ed., Göttingen: Vandenhoeck & Ruprecht, 1997) 107-17; M. Hengel, *Studies in Early Christology* (Edinburgh: T. & T. Clark, 1995) 41-58, 63-72, 217; see also G. Theissen and A. Merz, *Der historische Jesus: Ein Lehrbuch* (Göttingen: Vandenhoeck & Ruprecht, 1996) 467-70. Many scholars would of course disagree with this argument.

14   Cf. T. A. Mohr, *Markus- und Johannespassion: Redaktions- und traditionsgeschichtliche Untersuchung der markinischen und johanneischen Passionstradition* (ATANT 70; Zürich: Zwingli Verlag, 1982) 256, 287.

15   Pace Gnilka, *Markusevangelium*, 1.128 n.18.

16   Thus the interpretation of Gundry, *Mark*, 76, 84, 88, who asserts: Mark's "emphasis on the wide publication of Jesus' miracles and the comparative infrequency of commands to silence about miracles of healing weaken the argument that those commands will interpret the shutting up of unclean spirits in terms of a messianic secret rather than apotropaically" (p. 84).

17   Thus Gundry, *Mark*, 159; see p. 163, for a discussion of the view that Jesus did not want people to think of him as God's Son apart from the crucifixion and resurrection which had yet to take place.

nation—hopes which were so powerful that they could cause large crowds to follow leaders who believed themselves to be messiahs into battle against Roman legions. In the words of Tom Wright: "Once Jesus was thought of as a potential or would-be Messiah, the movement would swiftly attract attention of the wrong sort."[18] (6) When Jesus orders the three disciples to keep silent about what they saw on the mountain (9:9), this can be explained in the context of 8:31-38: "a premature publicizing of the Transfiguration would counteract both the teaching that the son of man must suffer and the general summons to cross-taking."[19] (7) The silence of the disciples in 9:34 (οἱ δὲ ἐσιώπων) is neither theologically motivated nor of special interest to Mark who leaves the reason for their silence unidentified. (8) Similarly the attempt of "many" (πολλοί) to silence Bartimaeus who calls out to Jesus "son of David" (10:48) should be explained without reference to a Marcan or pre-Marcan messianic secret: the crowds want to stave off unwelcome disturbance from a blind beggar.[20]

The contexts in which Mark refers to or implies silence are diverse, as is the rationale for rebukes to keep silent. Each pericope in which the issue of "silence" occurs must be interpreted on its own terms. However, nobody disputes that Jesus always responded when people asked questions, whether sympathizers or opponents, friends or hostile religious or political leaders. This makes his silence during the trial all the more striking.

Jesus' Reaction to Questions in the Gospel of Matthew

1. Jesus' disciples inquire (λέγουσιν) whether Jesus realized that he had offended the Pharisees (Matt 15:12); they ask questions (ἐπερωτᾶν) about eschatological issues (17:10: ἐπερωτᾶν), about hierarchy in God's kingdom (18:1: λέγοντες), about the sudden withering of the fig tree (21:20: λέγοντες), about which of the

---

18   Wright, *Jesus*, 529.

19   Gundry, *Mark*, 462.

20   Cf. Gnilka, *Markusevangelium*, 2.110; pace Pesch, *Markusevangelium*, 2.172, who assumes that people who accompany Jesus, "am ehesten Jünger," attempt to silence the beggar who declares Jesus to be the son of David because they are afraid of political misunderstanding. In the larger context of the story, the rebuke of the crowd also functions as providing an obstacle which magnifies the faith of Bartimaeus.

disciples would betray him (26:22: λέγειν). John the Baptist sends his disciples with the question whether Jesus is the Messiah or not, considering the fact that he did not bring judgment on the unrighteous (11:3). A potential follower inquires about what he must do in order to gain eternal life (19:18, 20). A trusting Roman officer implores to heal his servant (8:5-6: παρακαλῶν . . . λέγων).

Jesus always gives an answer. He tells the disciples of John to assess his ministry and come to their own conclusions about whether he fulfills messianic prophecy or not (11:4-6). He affirms with strong words had his criticism of the Pharisees was both fundamental and intentional (15:13-14); he explains how he understands the prophetic hope of the return of Elijah (17:11-12); he provocatively rejects their notion of the importance of status (18:2-5); he responds by quoting Scripture (19:18-19). Answering the question about the requirements for participation in God's kingdom Jesus goes beyond the traditional answers which pointed to obedience to God's commandments to demand that one must follow him and be prepared even to give away one's wealth to the poor (19:21). He honors the "somewhat irrelevant question"[21] of the disciples concerning how Jesus had made the tree wither so suddenly and gives an answer (21:21-22). He is willing to point to Judas as the disciple who would betray him (26:23-25). He heals the son of the Roman officer (8:7-13).

2. When evil spirits come with a request (λέγειν) Jesus responds (8:31), granting their plea to be allowed to enter a herd of pigs. And he grants the request of the people living in the nearby city who ask him to leave (8:34: παρακαλῶν).

3. Matthew's version of the story of the Gentile woman who asks Jesus to expel a demon from her daughter includes the remark that Jesus reacted, at first, with silence (15:23: ὁ δὲ οὐκ ἀπεκρίθη αὐτῇ λόγον). Most interpreters to not comment on the silence of Jesus. Davies and Allison are an exception, offering this explanation: "He is either turning her down or trying her faith."[22] Jesus explains his lack

---

21   D. A. Hagner, *Matthew* (2 vols., WBC 33; Dallas: Word, 1993-95) 1.606.

22   W. D. Davies and D. C. Allison, *A Critical and Exegetical Commentary on the Gospel According to Saint Matthew* (3 vols., ICC; Edinburgh: T. & T. Clark, 1988-97) 2.549; they regard v. 23 as redactional, as do many other commentators. An argument in favor of inauthenticity is the fact that Jesus regularly answers requests of people, even if they are spurious. On the other hand, the very particularism of a silence of Jesus as "answer" to a genuine request may be taken to

of response by pointing to the fundamental thrust of his mission which is directed to the covenant people (15:24).

4. Scribes who witnessed Jesus' forgiving the sins of the paralyzed man question in their mind whether Jesus is blaspheming (9:3). Pharisees ask (ἐπερωτᾶν) Jesus, with dishonest intentions, whether the law allows healing on the sabbath (12:10). One of their scribes asks Jesus, with hostile intentions (ἐπηρώτησεν ... πειράζων αὐτόν), which is the most important commandment (22:35-36)—a critical question since the answer to it "will establish whether Jesus belongs to some radical fringe group or within the piety of mainstream Judaism."[23] They try to trap him with a question regarding his view on justifiable grounds for divorce (19:3: πειράζων αὐτόν ... λέγοντες). Together with Sadducees they request Jesus (ἐπερωτᾶν) to give them a sign in or from the heavens—a heavenly voice? or some eschatological cosmic sign?—which would need no interpretation and thus compel them to believe in him (16:1). Together with partisans of the Herodian family the Pharisees ask (λέγει) Jesus about his view on paying imperial taxes (22:15-17), trying to trap him (v. 15: συμβούλιον ἔλαβον ὅπως αὐτὸν παγιδεύσεσιν ἐν λόγῳ). The Sadducees ask (ἐπερωτᾶν) Jesus about his view of the resurrection hope, attempting to show the absurdity of his belief with a bizarre case study (22:23-28).

The priestly aristocracy in Jerusalem together with Temple scribes ask Jesus whether he was not upset when children in the Temple who had observed healings of some blind and lame people chanted to him "Hosanna to the Son of David" (21:16: λέγειν), implying that any claim of Jesus to this title could have no truth.[24] Together with

---

support the authenticity of the remark. The response of the disciples in v. 23b (ἀπόλυσον αὐτήνν, ὅτι κράζει ὄπισθεν ἡμῶν), if understood in the sense of "send her away with her request granted"—which is likely, as v. 24 states the case not for sending her away but for not helping her—also supports authenticity (unless the request of the disciples, understood in this way, is explained by their annoyance *and* the assumption that Jesus would be willing to use his healing powers simply to get rid of an inconvenience). If the possibility that Jesus made the statement in 15:24 cannot be excluded (Davies and Allison, *Matthew*, 2.551), the same may be said for 15:23, particularly if v. 23 "serves primarily to set the stage for the declaration in v. 24" (p. 549). D. A. Carson ("Matthew," *EBC* 8 [Grand Rapids: Zondervan, 1984] 353-55) defends the authenticity of the dialogue in vv. 23-25.

23   Hagner, *Matthew*, 2.644.

24   Cf. Hagner, *Matthew*, 2.602. The episode in Matt 21:14-17 is usually

representatives of the Sanhedrin the chief priests ask (λέγειν) Jesus about the nature and the source of the authority which he presumed to underlie his actions and his teaching (21:23).

Jesus always gives an answer. He responds to the charge of blasphemy and challenges the scribes in Capernaum to draw conclusions from the fact that he was able to heal the paralytic and infer that he can also forgive sins (9:5). He responds even in cases where the questioners do not honestly seek an answer but attempt to elicit a response which might be used in court against him (12:10: ἵνα κατηγορήσωσιν αὐτοῦ; also 21:23-25), or which are aimed at discrediting him as a conservative Jewish teacher and at gathering information that might prove useful in future legal proceedings against him (22:18-21),[25] or which are specifically designed to make him appear ridiculous (22:29-32). Jesus honors questions even in instances (16:1-4) where petitions are challenges of unbelief (note πειράζοντες in 16:1). He answers questions concerning halakhic issues in a way which seems to challenge the authority of Moses (19:4-9).

His answers demonstrate a fearless sovereignty, whether he is confronted by ordinary Pharisees or by their scribes, by Sadducees or by Herodians, by the priestly aristocracy of Jerusalem or by representatives of the Sanhedrin. And he has no qualms to unmask his opponents as "hypocrites" (22:18). Jack Dean Kingsbury has described Matthew's presentation of the last great confrontation between Jesus and the religious leaders which took place in the Temple in Jerusalem and lasted for two days in the following

---

regarded as due to Matthean redaction; cf. J. Gnilka, *Das Matthäusevangelium* (2nd ed., HTKNT 1.1-2; Freiburg: Herder, 1988) 2.206; U. Luz, *Das Evangelium nach Matthäus* (EKKNT 1.1-3; Zürich: Benziger; Neukirchen-Vluyn: Neukirchener, 1985-96) 3.179-80. But why would a Christian author try to expose the theological ignorance of the Scripture experts in the Temple by making Jesus quote a Scripture passage which necessitates the redactional introduction of children into the story? There is no reason why Matthew should include a quotation from Ps 8:3. If the messianic interpretation of Jesus' arrival in Jerusalem by the crowd which accompanies Jesus is accepted as authentic (cf. e.g. Pesch, *Markusevangelium*, 2.187-88; Gundry, *Mark*, 623-34, who correctly comments that "lack of historical imagination can distort critical judgment as badly as historical credulity can distort it" [p. 632]), it is not impossible to assume that children (perhaps of pilgrims who entered Jerusalem with Jesus) mimicked the chant they had heard earlier, maybe "in all good fun" (thus Hagner, *Matthew*, 2.602).

25   Cf. Hagner, *Matthew*, 2.634.

manner: the tone of these controversies is acutely confrontational (cf. 21:16, 23; 22:15-17, 23, 34-36), the issues which are debated are all of critical importance for the Jewish religious and political leadership (21:15-16, 23; 22:42-45), the controversies continue virtually unabated for two days (cf. 21:15, 23; 22:16, 23, 3, 5, 41), and the atmosphere is one of profound hostility (cf. 21:15-16, 45-46; 22:15-17, 35). In none of the debates the Jewish leaders and law experts are able to outdo or to outmaneuver Jesus. At the end of this climactic confrontation, they are reduced to silence, as the narrator comments: "And no one was able to answer him a word (οὐδεὶς ἐδύνατο ἀποκριθῆναι αὐτῷ λόγον), nor from that day did any one dare to ask him any more questions" (22:46).[26] All the more surprising is Jesus' silence during his trial which was secured and carried out by the same people.

Jesus' Reaction to Questions in the Gospel of Luke

1. Jesus' followers ask (ἐρωτᾶν, ἐπερωτᾶν) for healing (Luke 4:38), they ask about the meaning of the parable of the sower (8:9) and about the signs which would signal the imminence of the destruction of the Temple (21:7). Sympathetic Pharisees ask Jesus to share a meal in his house, probably after the synagogue service on the Sabbath (7:36; 11:37).[27] Peter asks whether the call to be alert is directed only to those disciples who have responsibilities of leadership or to disciples at large: he finds the imagery which Jesus had used ambiguous (12:41).[28] Later the disciples ask about the location of the judgment which accompanies the visible coming of God's kingdom (17:37a).

John the Baptist sends two of his disciples who inquire whether Jesus is the Coming One or whether they have been mistaken in believing this (7:18-20). A leading man of society asks Jesus how he can be sure that he will be saved in the final resurrection (18:18). A Roman officer asks Jesus to come and cure his slave (7:3).

Jesus answers all of these questions. He heals Peter's mother-in-law

---

26 J. D. Kingsbury, *Matthew as Story* (2nd ed., Philadelphia: Fortress, 1986) 6-7, 122-23.

27 Cf. I. H. Marshall, *The Gospel of Luke* (NIGTC; Exeter: Paternoster, 1978) 308, 493-94.

28 Cf. Marshall, *Luke*, 540; D. L. Bock, *Luke* (2 vols., BECNT; Grand Rapids: Baker, 1995-96) 2.1178.

(4:39); he heals the centurion's slave (7:6-10); he interprets the parable of the sower (8:10-15); he accepts invitations from Pharisees. to share a meal (7:36; 11:37); he tells John's disciples to evaluate his ministry of miraculous healing and come to the appropriate conclusions (7:21-23); he answers Peter's request to clarify what he meant when he talked about being prepared for the master's return (12:42-48); he tells the rich ruler to do God's will in being wholly committed to Jesus and sell his possessions (18:19-22); he explains to the disciples the coming judgment will be visible, universal, and permanent (17:37b); he warns his disciples against false prophets and against misunderstanding catastrophes such as wars or natural disasters as signs of the end (21:8-11).

2. When evil spirits ask him to be allowed to enter a herd of swine (8:32: παρακαλεῖν), Jesus grants their request. When the Gerasene people ask Jesus to leave after they witnessed the healing of the possessed man and the destruction of the swine (8:37: ἐρωτᾶν), Jesus fulfills this request: he accepts that they reject him (8:38c).

3. Scribes and Pharisees in Capernaum ask whether Jesus is not aware that only God can forgive sins (5:21). A scribe challenges him with the question what requirements must be fulfilled in order to receive eternal life (10:25: λέγειν). Pharisees ask when the kingdom of God is coming (17:20a: ἐπερωτᾶν). A deputation of members of the priestly aristocracy and of scribes asks whether it is permitted by the law for God's people to pay taxes to the Roman emperor (20:22: ἐπερωτᾶν). Sadducees ask a question regarding the resurrection hope (20:27: ἐπερωτᾶν). Leading aristocratic representatives of the Sanhedrin and scribes ask Jesus about the nature and source of his authority, evidently to trap him (20:2: λέγειν).

Jesus always gives answers. He answers the scribes and Pharisees in Capernaum by trying to make them wonder, on account of a stunning miracle which he performs in front of their eyes, whether his declaration of forgiveness does not indeed result from the power of God (5:22-26). He answers questions put to him indirectly, via his disciples, about eating with tax-collectors and sinners (5:30-32). He answers the question of the scribe about the reception of eternal life by discussing Torah and by illustrating the fundamental requirement of love for God with a provocative parable (10:26-37). When scribes and Pharisees who had shared a meal with Jesus and who had heard his accusations and his harsh condemnation of hypocrisy crowded around him, pressing hostile questions (δεινῶς ἐνέχειν) and examin-

ing him closely and trying to catch him in things he says (ἀποστομα-
τίζειν has been translated both ways), lying in ambush and trying to
catch him (11:53-54: ἐνεδρεύοντες αὐτὸν θηρεῦσαι), Jesus evidently stood his ground: the aspect of the verbs and the term περὶ
πλειόνων hint at a prolonged discussion.[29]

Jesus tells the Pharisees that God's kingdom is not accompanied by
supporting signs, it is present in their midst (17:20b-21). He takes up
the issue of authority which official envoys of the Sanhedrin raise
and implies with his answer that the source of his authority is the
same as that of John the Baptist: heaven, i.e. God himself (20:3-8).[30]
Despite the hypocritical flattery of the influential priests who
claimed to accept his teaching when they asked about taxes, wanting
to find incriminating evidence which they could use against him
before the governor, Jesus gives them an answer, even though he
recognized their ruse (20:23-25). He answers the Sadducees even
though they evidently wanted to ridicule his belief in the resurrection: he attacks the basis of their case which assumed the continuation
of ordinary human relationships and then positively defends the
doctrine of the resurrection by reference to the nature of God
(20:34-38).[31]

The evidence in Luke corresponds to what we have found in
surveying Mark and Matthew: Jesus invariably responds to questions,
whether they are genuine or deceitful, amiable or hostile, direct or
indirect, religious or political in nature, innocuous or dangerous if
answered.

Jesus' Reaction to Questions in the Gospel of John

1. When Jesus tells his disciples that he has food of which they
know nothing, they do not understand that he wants to teach them a
lesson: they speculate whether someone else has brought him food
(4:32-33). This is one instance of many where statements of Jesus in
the Fourth Gospel are misunderstood, by the disciples, the crowds or
opponents alike, prompting questions which Jesus always answers. He
tells the disciples that doing the will of the Father is the real ground

---

[29]   J. Nolland (*Luke* [3 vols., WBC 35; Dallas: Word, 1989-93] 2.669) defends
the possibility that Luke may be following his source in 11:53-54.

[30]   Cf. Bock, *Luke*, 2.1582.

[31]   Cf. Marshall, *Luke*, 737-38.

of his life and the source of his power (4:34).[32]

The disciples ask (ἐρωτᾶν[33]) Jesus about the cause of the blindness of a man born blind (John 9:2); they want to ask him what he meant when he said that "in a little while" they will not see him any more and "then again in a little while" they will see him (16:16-19). Peter asks Jesus whether he really wants to wash his feet (13:6: λέγειν). Peter prompts the disciple "whom Jesus loved" to inquire (πυνθάν-ομαι) from Jesus whom he meant when he had said that one of them would betray him (13:24), and the disciple puts the question to Jesus (13:25: λέγειν). Peter asks Jesus what he meant when he said that he won't be with them much longer (13:36a: λέγειν) and why he cannot follow him (13:37: λέγειν), and Thomas asks for directions in order to find the way to where Jesus is going (14:5).

Jesus always gives an answer. He tells his disciples that the question is not who is the cause of the blindness of the man who was born blind but what is God's purpose in his blindness (9:3). Jesus answers the question of the disciples about the meaning of what would happen "in a little while" before they had asked it, talking about his death and resurrection (16:20-23);[34] on that day, when their joy has been renewed, they will have "no more questions" to put to Jesus (16:23). He responds to Peter's indignant objection when he wanted to wash his feet (13:7,8b). He answers the question about the disciple who would betray him (13:26). He replies to Peter's questions about where he will go, although his answer can be understood fully only later (13:36b,38), and he answers Thomas' question by explaining

---

[32]   Cf. A. Schlatter, *Der Evangelist Johannes* (4th ed., Stuttgart: Calwer, 1975) 130.

[33]   In John 4:31, 40, 47 ἐρωτᾶν (see further 14:16; 16:26; 17:9) is used as synoym for αἰτεῖν in the sense of "to ask for something": the disciples ask Jesus to eat; people of Samaria ask Jesus to stay with them; a Roman officer in Capernaum asks Jesus to come and heal his son. Jesus always fulfills the request.

[34]   Thus T. Zahn, *Das Evangelium des Johannes* (repr. Wuppertal: Brockhaus, 1983 [orig. 1921]) 595-96; R. Schnackenburg, *Das Johannesevangelium* (6th/5th ed., HTKNT 4.1-3; Freiburg: Herder, 1986 [1965-75]) 3:175-76; U. Wilckens, *Das Evangelium nach Johannes* (NTD 4; Göttingen: Vandenhoeck & Ruprecht, 1998) 253-54. Augustin, *Tractatus in Joannem* CI,5-6 (CC 592-594) interpreted in terms of the parousia. Some have interpreted in terms of the descent of the Paraclete (cf. 14:23), see C. K. Barrett, *The Gospel According to St. John* (2nd ed., London: SPCK, 1978 [1955]) 494. Some commentators understand 16:16-24 to imply double or treble references; cf. R. E. Brown, *The Gospel According to John* (AB 29; New York: Doubleday, 1966-70) 729-30.

that he represents the way to get to the Father (14:6-7).

2. In conversations with sympathetic listeners, Jesus answers their questions, often prompting them with ambiguous statements. When Nicodemus asks, incredulously, how a new birth could be possible (3:9: λέγειν), Jesus gives a sharp retort, blaming him as a teacher who lacks understanding (3:10). The Samaritan woman at the well asks, surprised by Jesus' request, why he as a Jew wants to have a drink from her (4:9: λέγειν). In the course of the ensuing conversation Jesus explains that the old distinctions between Jews and Samaritans do not count any longer.

3. The crowds ask Jesus how long he had been on the other side of the lake (6:25: λέγειν). Jesus does not answer their question directly, but he responds, questioning their motives in looking for him (6:26). When they ask (λέγειν) "what must we do in order to work the works God requires?" (6:28), i.e. about works they can do, Jesus sets them straight by putting the emphasis on faith, which means submission to God's work in Jesus.[35] The crowd responds by asking (λέγειν) for a sign which would validate Jesus' authority, something equivalent to God's provision of manna (6:30-31). Jesus responds by telling them that the manna in the desert was not the true bread from heaven but only a foreshadowing of the true bread from heaven which is Jesus himself (6:32-35). During the feast of Tabernacles people in Jerusalem ask with amazement how someone who had not studied in one the rabbinical schools could carry on learned disputations with such a command of Scripture (7:15).[36] Jesus responds by stating that he draws his teaching from his Father (7:16).

The Pharisees react to a statement Jesus had made about his unique relation with his father, by misunderstanding him as they think in purely human terms, and they ask Jesus who his father is (8:19a: λέγειν). Jesus responds with the accusation that they know neither him nor his father (8:19b), which leads to a discussion about the origin and departure of Jesus and of his parentage and that of "the Jews" (8:21-58). When Jesus asserts that he will go away to a place where they cannot come, they suggest they he may contemplating suicide (8:22)—probably not a misunderstanding[37] but meant to scoff

---

35   Cf. Brown, *John*, 265.

36   Pace Barrett (*John*, 317) I cannot see why this question of the Jerusalem crowd is "scornful."

37   Thus most commentaries; cf. Barrett, *John*, 341; Brown, *John*, 351.

at the apparent nonsense of what he is saying,[38] or perhaps suggesting that the content of Jesus' teaching and his skirmishes with the
Jerusalem authorities constitute a provocation of death which
amounts to suicide.[39] Jesus reacts by declaring that they belong to the
realm of fallen creation whereas he comes from the realm of God
himself (8:23). When he asserts that men must believe that he comes
from above with the power of the forgiveness of sins and that he
therefore is ἐγώ εἰμι (8:23-24), the crowds fail to grasp the real
force of Jesus' implicit claim to divinity and ask who he is (8:25a:
λέγειν). Jesus answers by pointing out (8:25b) that "from the
beginning, from his very first discourse with Nicodemus, he has
claimed to be from above and to be uniquely representative of the
Father."[40] And he tells them that he has "much to say" (8:26): he is
anything but reluctant to speak![41] As Jesus continues to talk about
truth which liberates, a truth which is linked with commitment to
Jesus and the revelation he brings (8:31-32), the audience grasps that
Jesus implies that they are currently slaves. This they deny, affirming that they are the children of Abraham and thus possess "inward
freedom of soul."[42] Jesus answers their question "what do you mean"
(8:33: λέγειν): he explains what he means by freedom and slavery
(8:34-36), he asserts that they are falsely claiming Abraham as their
father (8:37-44) and he reasserts his own unique authority which can
alone guarantee eternal life (8:45-51). When opponents crassly
misinterpret the assertion of Jesus that Abraham rejoiced to see his
day, implying that Abraham's hopes find fulfillment in his person
and ministry, they contentiously ask whether Jesus claims to be
Abraham's contemporary (8:57: λέγειν). Jesus' response "before

---

[38]   Cf. Zahn, *Johannes*, 410, who suggests that the assumption that Jesus may
consider suicide is not meant seriously; also Wilckens, *Johannes*, 144.

[39]   Thus E. Haenchen, *Das Johannesevangelium: Ein Kommentar* (Tübingen:
Mohr [Siebeck], 1980) 368.

[40]   Cf. Brown (*John*, 350), who considers the wisdom tradition (Prov 8:22;
Sir 24:9) to provide additional background for Jesus' answer in 8:25b.

[41]   Cf. D. A. Carson, *The Gospel According to John* (Leicester: Inter-Varsity
Press; Grand Rapids: Eerdmans, 1991) 344.

[42]   Barrett, *John*, 345; cf. Carson, *John*, 349; pace Brown (*John*, 363), who
interprets the reaction of the audience as a misunderstanding in political terms and
as evidence of "nationalistic pride." The boast of Eleazar to the besieged Jews at
Masada (Josephus, *J.W.* 7.8.6 §323) is irrelevant here since the Zealots attempted
to throw of the bondage of Roman power—unsuccessfully, as it turned out.

Abraham was born, I am" provoked the Jews to pick up stones to kill him (8:59).

As Jesus brings out the underlying theological meaning of the miracle which he had just performed on the man born blind, talking about those who do not see but receive sight and about those who see but become blind (9:39), some Pharisees ask (λέγειν) him whether he considers them to be blind as well, expecting him to answer in the negative (9:40: μὴ καὶ ἡμεῖς). Jesus replies that since they claim to be βλέποντες, making confident pronouncements to the effect that Jesus is not the Messiah but a sinner (9:16, 22, 24, 29, 34), but refuse to acknowledge the light of revelation that Jesus brings, claiming that they have sufficient illumination as they have the law (9:28-29), they become incurably blind since they deliberately reject the only cure for blindness.[43]

During the feast of Dedication Jews surround Jesus in Solomon's Colonnade in the Temple precincts and ask him (10:24: λέγειν): "How long are you going to keep us in suspense? If you are really the Messiah, tell us so in plain words." If the question, "Εως πότε τὴν ψυχὴν ἡμῶν αἴρεις; means in effect "How long are you going to annoy us?"[44] the "Jews" are opponents who attempt to procure a clear statement from Jesus which they could use against him. Jesus did not do them this favor to publicly declare himself to be the Messiah, but he does give them an answer which points in this direction (10:25-30): he reminds them of his ministry in words and deeds, he tells his opponents that they do not belong to the sheep of the flock (i.e. God's people) and that only those have eternal life who listen to his teaching and commit themselves to himself who is one with the Father. The Jews understand this statement to meet the criteria of blasphemy, they want to execute him by stoning (10:31, 33).

After Jesus' triumphal entry into Jerusalem, when he spoke about being "lifted up," the crowd asks how he can claim that the Son of Man must be lifted up since the Scriptures state that the Messiah would remain forever: "Who is this Son of Man?" (12:34). The crowd knew that Jesus referred to himself as "Son of Man" and evidently interpreted the circumstances of his entry into Jerusalem as

---

[43] Cf. Barrett, *John*, 366.

[44] Cf. Barrett, *John*, 380; Carson, *John*, 392.

a messianic gesture.[45] Jesus does not answer the questions of the crowd directly; he summaries his ministry with the terminology of light and darkness, he warns of the impending judgment which is associated with the Son of Man, and he urges the crowd to trust him as he is the light of the world as the power of darkness is closing in for the final struggle (12:35-36). "Thus, Jesus ends his ministry to the Jews on a note of challenge."[46]

JESUS' REACTION TO QUESTIONS IN THE TRIAL

We have seen that Jesus is described as consistently answering questions, whether they were put to him by friends or adversaries, by followers or strangers, by simple people or by theological experts, by priests or by Roman soldiers. He answered questions no matter what the motives of those asking them. His answers could be direct or enigmatic, favorable or provocative, "traditional" or "broad-minded." This makes the silence during his trial unexpected. Of course Jesus did not maintain complete silence. He did respond to questions during his trial. In order to be able to understand his silence, we must first assess the narratives of the cross-examination.[47]

The Cross-Examination in the Gospel of Mark

Mark begins the story of the trial against Jesus with the High Priest (Caiaphas)[48] and the leading members of the Sanhedrin seeking

---

45   Cf. Brown, *John*, 478.

46   Cf. Brown, *John*, 479.

47   In the following remarks we will concentrate on the meaning conveyed by the extant Gospel narratives, disregarding literary critical issues. On the question of historicity see the commentaries, with regard to the trial of Jesus see notably August Strobel, *Die Stunde der Wahrheit: Untersuchungen zum Strafverfahren gegen Jesus* (WUNT 21; Tübingen: Mohr [Siebeck], 1980); also B. Corley, "Trial of Jesus," in: J. B. Green, S. McKnight, and I. H. Marshall (eds.), *Dictionary of Jesus and the Gospels* (Leicester and Downers Grove: InterVarsity Press, 1992) 841-54. Hypercritical is the recent study of W. Reinbold, *Der älteste Bericht über den Tod Jesu: Literarische Analyse und historische Kritik der Passionsdarstellungen der Evangelien* (BZNW 69; Berlin: de Gruyter, 1994), who regards the entire trial scene before the Sanhedrin and the dialogue between Jesus and Pilate as unhistorical.

48   Mark mentions no High Priest by name in his gospel. Pesch (*Markusevangelium*, 2.425) assumes that the narrative of the passion account took shape in the Jerusalem community at such an early date that the High Priest was still in office

evidence which would allow them to condemn Jesus over the issue of
the threat that he posed to the Temple; they want his execution (Mark
14:53-59). The question of the High Priest: "Have you nothing at all
to answer to what these are testifying against you?" (Mark 14:60:
Οὐκ ἀποκρίνῃ οὐδέν τί οὗτοί σου καταμαρτυροῦσιν;) implies that
Jesus evidently listened in silence (I) to the accusations brought forward by the witnesses. The High Priest seeks to obtain a deposition
from Jesus about the Temple which would compensate the lack of
agreement in the witnesses. But Jesus stays silent (II) and answers
nothing at all (14:61: ὁ δὲ ἐσιώπα καὶ οὐκ ἀπεκρίνατο οὐδέν).

The High Priest was persistent (πάλιν): since the testimony about
Jesus' views on the Temple did not move the proceedings any
further, "he tries another tactic to see if he can get Jesus to speak."[49]

---

and thus didn't need to be identified. A perhaps more straightforward explanation
may be seen in the assumption that the Christian readers of the Gospel knew that
Jesus died during the long administration of the High Priest Caiaphas—his rule of
eighteen to nineteen years (18–36 CE) was by far the longest of the nineteen High
Priests in Jerusalem in the 1st cent. CE; on Caiaphas, see R. E. Brown, *The Death
of the Messiah: From Gethsemane to the Grave. A Commentary on the Passion
Narratives in the Four Gospels* (2 vols., ABRL 7; Garden City: Doubleday, 1994)
1.409-11.

[49]   Brown, *Death*, 465. The link between the inadmissible testimony of the
witnesses and the question of the High Priest whether Jesus is "the messiah, the
Son of the Blessed One" can be discussed on the tactical level as follows (see
Gundry, *Mark*, 908-909, who thinks the third option to be the more likely): (1) The
High Priest asks the question out of frustration at the Sanhedrin's failure to convict
Jesus of a capital offense—assuming that not only the office of "messiah" but also
the phrase "the Son of God" (understood in the sense of divine appointment) were
understood in human terms. In this case the High Priest lowered the stakes: the
discussion about destroying the Temple and building the Temple seems to entail the
charge that Jesus arrogated to himself a divine role, as only God (rather than the
messiah, in pre-rabbinic Jewish literature!) was portrayed as destroyer (Jer 7:12-15;
26:4-6, 9; *1 Enoch* 90:28-29) and builder (Exod 15:17; *1 Enoch* 90:28-29; *Jub.*
1:17; 11QTemple 29:8-10; 4QFlor 1:3, 6) of the Temple. The High Priest asks
whether Jesus claims the office of messiah—the subject of a new Temple might
have prompted the High Priest to think of the messianic age—a high but still only
human office. Jesus does the High Priest an unforeseen favor: he provides a
statement which implies a claim that fulfills the criteria of blasphemy. (2) The High
Priest asks the question out of determination to follow up on the arrogation of
divine activity implied in the claims of Jesus to destroy and rebuild the Temple—
assuming that the phrase "the Son of God" is understood as implying divine nature,
rather than (only) divine appointment. In this case the High Priest does not lower

He puts the question to Jesus (ἐπηρώτα αὐτὸν): "Are you the Messiah, the Son of the Blessed?" (14:61b: Σὺ εἶ ὁ Χριστὸς ὁ υἱὸς τοῦ εὐλογητοῦ;). Jesus answers (III) in the affirmative: "I am" (14:62a: Ἐγώ εἰμι), and elucidates: "and you (plural) will see the Son of Man sitting at the right of the Power and coming with the clouds of heaven" (14:62bc: καὶ ὄψεσθε τὸν υἱὸν τοῦ ἀνθρώπου ἐκ δεξιῶν καθήμενον τῆς δυνάμεως καὶ ἐρχόμενον μετὰ τῶν νεφελῶν τοῦ οὐρανοῦ).[50] The question which Jesus had turned by with a counter-question in 11:27-33 and to which he replied only indirectly in 12:1-9, is now answered with decisive lucidity. When the High Priest hears Jesus' claim that he will share in heavenly glory at God's right hand and that he will return as heavenly judge,[51] he tears his

---

the stakes, but demonstrates the determination of a skilled interrogator. Jesus does the High Priest the favor he is looking for: he asserts that he possesses divine status and that he will fulfill divine functions. (3) The High Priest asks the question as an attempt to put to test claims of Jesus to be the messiah—assuming that he was aware of such claims, which is likely given the circumstances of Jesus' recent entry in Jerusalem and the reaction of the people accompanying him, and given the possibility that Judas Iscariot may have told Sanhedrin members that Jesus had accepted the title of messiah from his disciples (thus C. E. B. Cranfield, *The Gospel according to Saint Mark* [CGTC; Cambridge: Cambridge University Press, 1959] 443). Or he may have introduced the subject of messiahship after the witnesses talked about claims of Jesus to build a new temple, which may have prompted him to think of the messianic age. The scene where members of the Sanhedrin cover the face of Jesus and challenge him to prophesy who had hit him (Mark 14:65; Luke 22:63-64; Matt 26:67-68) might have been a messianic test (which then turned into a repudiation of blasphemy). Jesus provides the High Priest with a statement which can readily be interpreted in terms of the capital charge of blasphemy—much more easily than a conviction as a messianic pretender who is a false prophet.

50   Cf. O. Betz, "Probleme des Prozesses Jesu," *ANRW* II.25.1 (1982) 565-647, esp. 634-35, who regards the second part of 14:62c as redactional. The authenticity of 14:62 is defended by Pesch, *Markusevangelium*, 2.437-39, 443; Gundry, *Mark*, 912-14; and C. A. Evans, "In What Sense 'Blasphemy'? Jesus Before Caiaphas in Mark 14:61-64," in E. H. Lovering, Jr. (ed.), *Society of Biblical Literature 1991 Seminar Papers* (SBLSP 30; Atlanta: Scholars Press, 1991) 215-34; rev. and repr. in Evans, *Jesus and His Contemporaries*, 407-34.

51   G. Vermes (*Jesus the Jew: A Historian's Reading of the Gospel* [2nd ed., London: Collins, 1983 (1973)] 147-49, 183-84) regards the entire answer of Jesus in Mark 14:62 to be redactional, since elsewhere in the gospel Jesus is reticent about messiahship. Apart from the necessity to qualify the earlier reticence of Jesus as regards the claim to be messiah, it should be noted that the circumstance of

garments, states that the offense of blasphemy has been committed, and prompts the Sanhedrin to issue a death sentence (14:63-64).[52] No response of Jesus (IV) to the following abuse by members of the Sanhedrin is reported.

After being handed over to the Roman prefect Pontius Pilate (15:1), he questions Jesus (ἐπηρώτησεν αὐτόν) whether he is the king of the Jews (15:2a: Σὺ εἶ ὁ βασιλεὺς τῶν Ἰουδαίων;), suggesting political accusations by the Jewish leadership against Jesus who evidently was charged with being a revolutionary with monarchical pretensions. Jesus answers (V) with σύ λέγεις, a formulation which should very probably be understood as evasive.[53] When the chief priests seize on the ambiguity of this answer they press their case with many other accusations (15:3: πολλά), evidently following up on the issue of his claims to kingship. But Jesus does not defend himself (VI), as Pilate notices with amazement (15:3: Οὐκ ἀποκρίνῃ οὐδέν;), pointing out that to keep silent in the face of so many accusations is dangerous.[54] But Jesus answers nothing (VII) (15:4: ὁ

Jesus' trial make it perfectly clear that an uprising under the leadership of Jesus is no longer a threat, that a political reading of his ministry is no longer an option—which means that there is no further need for Jesus to buy time with silence regarding the question whether he is the messiah (see Gundry, *Mark*, 913).

[52]   The question what exactly established the offense of blasphemy is disputed. See the commentaries and Brown, *Death*, 520-47. The most plausible options are (1) Jesus' words and attitude toward the Temple; (2) the charge that Jesus was a false prophet; (3) Jesus's claim to be the Son of Man sitting at God's right hand coming with the clouds of heaven.

[53]   Cf. Pesch, *Markusevangelium*, 2.457-58; Gundry, *Mark*, 932-33; K. Haacker, "Wer war schuld am Tode Jesu?" *TBei* 25 (1994) 23-36, esp. 34 n. 49. Pace D. R. Catchpole, "The Answer of Jesus to Caiaphas (Matt. xxvi.64)," *NTS* 17 (1970-71) 213-26, who argues against evasiveness, followed by Brown, *Death*, 488-89, 733, who interprets in terms of an answer which is "affirmative in content, and reluctant or circumlocutory in formulation." The decisive arguments are the following: (1) The σύ is emphatic; (2) if Jesus wanted to give an affirmative answer, he could have given the same answer which he gave to the very similar quesiton of the High Priest in 14:62; (3) if Pilate had heard an affirmative answer, he would have taken it as challenge to the authority of the emperor, and thus would have responded accordingly (both historically and on the narrative level!); (4) Mark 15:3 records no response of Pilate but further accusations of the chief priests; (5) Pilate points out to the crowd that *they* call Jesus the king of the Jews (15:12), he does not say that *Jesus* claimed the title. (6) The parallels in Luke 22:70 and John 18:34-37 support this interpretation.

[54]   Cf. Brown, *Death*, 734, who points out Pilate's fairness. Origen (*Contra*

δὲ Ἰησοῦς οὐκέτι οὐδὲν ἀπεκρίθη).

The Cross-Examination in the Gospel of Matthew

Matthew's narrative closely follows that of Mark. Jesus does not respond (I) to the contradictory accusations which focus on his views on the Temple (Matt 26:62: Οὐδὲν ἀποκρίνῃ;). And he does not respond (II) to the challenge of Caiaphas to comment on these accusations (26:63a: ὁ δὲ Ἰησοῦς ἐσιώπα). When the High Priest charges Jesus under oath (26:63b: Ἐξορκίζω σε κατὰ τοῦ θεοῦ τοῦ ζῶντος) to tell truthfully whether he considers himself to be "the Messiah, the Son of God" (26:63c: εἰ σὺ εἶ ὁ Χριστὸς ὁ υἱὸς τοῦ θεοῦ), Jesus answers (III) with a qualified affirmative: "You have said it" (Σὺ εἶπας)[55] and continues by invoking the image of the Son of Man coming in judgment: "Yet I say to you (plural), 'From now on you will see the Son of Man sitting at the right of the Power and coming on the clouds of heaven'" (26:64: πλὴν λέγω ὑμῖν, ἀπ' ἄρτι ὄψεσθε τὸν υἱὸν τοῦ ἀνθρώπου καθήμενον ἐκ δεξιῶν τῆς δυνάμεως καὶ ἐρχόμενον ἐπὶ τῶν νεφελῶν τοῦ οὐρανοῦ). The Sanhedrin reacts with the charge of blasphemy and the death sentence. The mockery and abuse by members of the Sanhedrin elicit evidently no response from Jesus (IV).

In the trial before Pilate, the prefect asks Jesus: "Are you the king of the Jews?" (27:11b: Σὺ εἶ ὁ βασιλεὺς τῶν Ἰουδαίων;). Jesus responds (V): "You say (so)" (27:11c: Σὺ λέγεις). Even though most interpreters understand this answer as a (qualified) affirmative,[56] it should probably be taken as evasive.[57] The chief priests and leading

---

Celsum, Preface 2) believes that Pilate would have released Jesus immediately had he chosen to defend himself, which he would have done effectively.

55   Brown, *Death*, 489-91; Hagner, *Matthew*, 799; Gnilka, *Matthäusevangelium*, 2.429. Gundry, *Mark*, 932, thinks that the formulation in Matt 26:64 "avoids the terms of an oath under which Matthew's Jesus would otherwise have answered in contradiction of his own, uniquely Matthean prohibition of oath-taking."

56   Cf. T. Zahn, *Das Evangelium des Matthäus* (repr. Wuppertal: Brockhaus, 1984 [1922]) 710; D. Hill, *The Gospel of Matthew* (NCBC; Grand Rapids: Eerdmans, 1972) 350; R. T. France, *The Gospel According to Matthew* (TNTC; Leicester: Inter-Varsity Press, 1985 [1989]) 388-89; Carson, *Matthew*, 568; Hagner, *Matthew*, 818; Gnilka, *Matthäusevangelium*, 2.455; Brown, *Death*, 733, 736.

57   Note the following arguments: (1) Pilate seems to know that Jesus is not really the threat to the political stability he was charged to represent (thus correctly

members of the Sanhedrin continue to bring charges against Jesus (27:12a), evidently on the issue of his claims to kingship, but Jesus gives no answer (VI) (27:12b: οὐδὲν ἀπεκρίνατο). When Pilate points out that it is dangerous to refuse to answer their accusations, Jesus continues to be silent (VII) and responds "to not even one charge" (27:14a: καὶ οὐκ ἀπεκρίθη αὐτῷ πρὸς οὐδὲ ἓν ῥῆμα), so that Pilate is astonished.

The Cross-Examination in the Gospel of Luke

Luke begins the account of the trial before the Sanhedrin (Luke 22:54, 63-71) with the blindfolding and mocking of Jesus during the night. The depiction of the morning session of the Sanhedrin (22:66) moves right into the central question: "If you are the Messiah, tell us!" (22:67a: Εἰ σὺ εἶ ὁ Χριστός, εἰπὸν ἡμῖν). Jesus responds (I) by refusing to answer their demand: "If I tell you, you will not believe ('Εὰν ὑμῖν εἴπω, οὐ μὴ πιστεύσητε); if I ask, you will not answer. But from now on the Son of Man will be seated at the right hand of the power of God" (22:67b-69). According to Luke Jesus avoids a positive answer, as he is certain that the members of the Sanhedrin would not believe him whatever answer he would give, and he knows that they would not be willing to answer a question if he asked one.[58] The remark about questions he might ask himself "begins to shift

---

Hagner, *Matthew*, 818—but not "despite Jesus' answer"!); (2) on the historical level, as regards the sense in which Pilate presumably understood the title "king of the Jews," Jesus could hardly affirm the charge of such a political claim (thus correctly France, *Matthew*, 388); (3) it seems not very likely that Jesus would answer a political question, asked by the Roman prefect, in terms of spiritual fulfillment of prophecies of Scripture; (4) Matthew reports neither a cross-examination after Jesus' answer nor an immediate verdict by Pilate, but further accusations from the chief priests and leading members of the Sanhedrin (27:12-13) —which is strange if Jesus just confessed that he was "the king of the Jews"; (5) the symbolic washing of hands and Pilate's comment "I am innocent of the blood of this one" (27:24) show that the Roman prefect found no reason to be worried about Jesus claiming to be king—which is less likely if Jesus would have directly affirmed his question whether he claims to be king of the Jews.

58   Bock (*Luke*, 1796) insists that Jesus' response in Luke 22:67-69 makes much sense in a second trial in the morning in which the chief priests under the leadership of Caiaphas, who had found Jesus guilty of blasphemy during a meeting held at night, sought to obtain official sanction from the Sanhedrin: Jesus "knows that this 'official' meeting is not for the purpose of trying to get a fair hearing, but to formalize the earlier inquiry . . . Jesus is refusing to engage the council directly."

Jesus over from being defendant to being judge who prosecutes with questions."[59] The last part of his answer (22:69) is affirmative: as. Messiah (= Son of God) he is exalted as the Son of Man—he will go directly into God's presence and sit at his right hand, ruling as judge from his side. Thus Jesus gives the council members more than they expected: a statement which can be used to indict him of a capital offense, as he profaned the Shekinah, the incommensurateness and unity of God.

The question of the interrogators: "Are you, then, the Son of God?" (22:70a: Σὺ οὖν εἶ ὁ υἱὸς τοῦ θεοῦ;) shows that the Jewish leaders correctly infer Jesus' status claimed by him to be that of the Messiah.[60] Jesus responds (II) to this question by saying: "You yourself are saying that I am" (22:70b: Ὑμεῖς λέγετε ὅτι ἐγώ εἰμι). The drift of Jesus' basic statement in 22:67-68 suggests that Jesus avoids an affirmative answer:[61] the council members are not prepared to face and answer his identity and ministry as Messiah, they just want to elicit a confession which can be used for a capital verdict.

The official charges of the Sanhedrin against Jesus which are put before Pilate (23:2) claim that he misleads the nation (as a false prophet), that he instigates people not to pay taxes to the emperor and that he claims to be the messianic king (of the Jews). When Pilate asks Jesus: "Are you the king of the Jews?" (23:3a: Σὺ εἶ ὁ βασιλεὺς τῶν Ἰουδαίων;), Jesus replies (III): "You have said so" (23:3b: Σὺ λέγεις)—a statement which in the absence of further cross-examination by the Roman prefect who, rather, states that he finds no chargeable offense in Jesus, is (again) evasive.[62]

---

[59]   Brown, *Death*, 487.

[60]   Cf. J. B. Green, *The Gospel of Luke* (NIC; Grand Rapids: Eerdmans, 1997) 796; pace Nolland (*Luke*, 1112), who thinks that for the council members "all remains ambiguous."

[61]   Nolland (*Luke*, 1111) punctuates the Greek phrase as a question: "Do you say/are you saying that I am?" Pace Brown, *Death*, 493; Marshall (*Luke*, 851) speaks of a "grudging admission."

[62]   If Jesus' answer is taken to be evasive, there is no need to declare the link between 23:3 and 23:4 to be "poor," as Nolland (*Luke*, 1117) does ("innocence inferred from an [equivocal] confession of 'guilt'"). An affirmative answer hardly fits into the "fundamental historicity of Pilate's skepticism about the charges against Jesus laid before him by Jewish leaders" that Nolland argues for (1116-17)—unless we must assume (what nobody does) that Jesus explained his claim to messiahship as non-political, at least as not threatening for the Roman empire.

Pilate sends Jesus to Herod Antipas (23:6-12) who tries for some
time to question him (23:9a: ἐπηρώτα δὲ αὐτὸν ἐν λόγοις ἱκανοῖς),
but Jesus refuses to respond (IV) to his queries: "but he would not
answer him at all" (23:9b: αὐτὸς δὲ οὐδὲν ἀπεκρίνατο αὐτῷ).

The Cross-Examination in the Gospel of John

John narrates an interrogation of Jesus by the former High Priest
Annas (John 18:12-24) and a trial before Pontius Pilate (18:28-
19:16). Annas cross-examines Jesus about his disciples and about his
teaching (18:19). These questions may reflect, on a theological level,
the concern of the religious leaders that Jesus was a false prophet,
and on a political level, the question whether his growing movement
was likely to cause an uprising.[63] Jesus responds (I) with defiant self-
assurance (18:20-21) by pointing to the fact that he has "spoken
openly to the world" ('Εγὼ παρρησίᾳ λελάληκα τῷ κόσμῳ), both in
synagogues and in the Temple, that he spoke nothing "in secret" (ἐν
κρυπτῷ ἐλάλησα οὐδέν), and that he should not try to force a
convicting answer from him (τί με ἐρωτᾷς;) but should ask witnesses who heard him teach. Either Jesus is demanding a proper trial
with witnesses, or he accuses the Jewish leadership of having made
up their minds without evidence (or both).[64] Jesus' sovereign attitude
toward Hannas results in an insulting rebuke and a slap by an aide, to
which Jesus replies (II), equally unafraid, that he should produce
evidence if he said anything wrong, asking for a fair trial (18:23).

Pilate cross-examines Jesus about the charge of the Jewish authori-
ties that he was guilty of a capital civil offense (18:31) and asks him:
"Are you the King of the Jews?" (18:33: Σὺ εἶ ὁ βασιλεὺς τῶν
Ἰουδαίων;). Jesus answers (III) with a counter-question,[65] asking him

---

[63]   Cf. Brown, *John*, 835; Brown finds "no clear Johannine theological motive
that would explain the invention of the Annas narrative"; for questions regarding the
historicity of the scene, see also Brown, *Death*, 404-408. Many commentators have
grave doubts; however, cf. Schnackenburg, *Johannesevangelium*, 3.263-64,
refering to A. Dauer, *Die Passionsgeschichte im Johannesevangelium: Eine traditionsgeschichtliche und theologische Untersuchung zu Joh 18,1-19,30* (München:
Kösel, 1972) and F. Hahn, "Der Prozeß Jesu nach dem Johannesevangelium,"
EKK Vorarbeiten (Heft 2; Neukirchen-Vluyn: Neukirchener Verlag, 1970) 23-96.

[64]   Cf. Brown, *John*, 826, 836; *Death*, 415-16.

[65]   Brown (*John*, 868) notes that "the accused criminal asks questions as if he
were the judge." Brown's suggestion that in 18:34 the "Johannine Jesus first
distinguishes between 'king' used in a political sense which the Romans would

to clarify the origin and thus the nature of the charge implicit in the question (18:34: Ἀπὸ σεαυτοῦ σὺ τοῦτο λέγεις ἢ ἄλλοι εἶπόν σοι περὶ ἐμοῦ;). When Pilate replies that he was just reiterating what he has been told by the "Jewish nation" and the High Priest, asking him bluntly what he has done (18:35: τί ἐποίησας;), Jesus answers (IV) by defining his kingdom in a way which shows that it poses no threat for the Roman empire (18:36: Ἡ βασιλεία ἡ ἐμὴ οὐκ ἔστιν ἐκ τοῦ κόσμου τούτου . . .).

Pilate has not understood what Jesus' statement means and presses for clarification: "So then, you are a king?" (18:37a). Jesus gives an evasive answer (V) (Σὺ λέγεις ὅτι βασιλεύς εἰμι), spelling out the distinctive nature and the extent of his reign which reveals the truth (of God, of his son, of judgment), a fact which is grasped by those who belong to the truth (8:37b: ἐγὼ εἰς τοῦτο γεγέννημαι καὶ εἰς τοῦτο ἐλήλυθα εἰς τὸν κόσμον, ἵνα μαρτυρήσω τῇ ἀληθείᾳ· πᾶς ὁ ὢν ἐκ τῆς ἀληθείας ἀκούει μου τῆς φωνῆς). The last remark may imply a test of Pilate, challenging him to hear Jesus' voice and to establish that he knows the truth. In this case Pilate's response "What is truth?" (8:38a: Τί ἐστιν ἀλήθεια;) echoes "the imperiousness of the Roman when challenged."[66] As Pilate allows the trial to continue, we must conclude that he either took Jesus' answer to the question whether he is a king to be negative or he did not take his claim to kingship seriously.[67]

When Pilate had scourged Jesus and sought to release him, convinced of his innocence, "the Jews" confront him again with the demand that Jesus must be executed since he made himself God's Son. Pilate begins the ensuing second interrogation of Jesus with the question: "From where are you?" (19:9a: Πόθεν εἶ σύ;). He evidently realizes that the identity of Jesus is the real issue, rather then what Jesus has done. Jesus (V) refuses to give an answer (19:9b: ὁ δὲ Ἰησοῦς ἀπόκρισιν οὐκ ἔδωκεν αὐτῷ).

Pilate reacts surprised, or irritated, and threatens Jesus by pointing to the fact that he possesses (for provincials who were not Roman

---

understand and 'king' in the Jewish sense with religious implications," is not very helpful since early Jewish tradition does not know an a-political "religious" king— this is a feature of the (later) Christian view of Jesus.

66   Cf. Brown, *Death*, 752, who remarks: "the judge is being judged."

67   Cf. J. B. Green, *The Death of Jesus: Tradition and Interpretation in the Passion Narrative* (WUNT 2.33; Tübingen: Mohr [Siebeck], 1988) 287.

citizens) final judicial authority as a consequence of the *imperium* (ἐξουσία) which the emperor had given to him (19:10). Jesus responds (VI) by asserting that the power over Jesus' life—indeed the entire turn of events, particularly the betrayal which "gave" (δεδομένον) Jesus into the hands of Pilate[68]—was given to him by God (Οὐκ εἶχες ἐξουσίαν κατ᾽ ἐμοῦ οὐδεμίαν εἰ μὴ ἦν δεδομένον σοι ἄνωθεν), and that his sin is less than the guilt of the one who handed Jesus over to him—prominently Caiaphas, presumably all of "the Jews" (19:11: διὰ τοῦτο ὁ παραδούς μέ σοι μείζονα ἁμαρτίαν ἔχει). On hearing this statement, Pilate seeks to release Jesus but is pressured by "the Jews" to condemn Jesus to death by crucifixion.

The evidenve of the four Gospel narratives with regard to the response of Jesus to questions put to him during the interrogation by Hannas, the Sanhedrin trial, the Herod Antipas scene and the trial before Pilate can be summarized as follows:

MARK	MATTHEW	LUKE	JOHN
			Annas: Question (disciples and teaching)
			Jesus (I): *Answer* (defiant self-assurance)
			Annas' aide: Abusive insult
			Jesus (II): *Answer*
Witnesses: Charges (Temple)	Witnesses: Charges (Temple)		(challenge)
Jesus (I): *Silence*	Jesus (I): *Silence*		
High Priest: Request for comment	High Priest: Request for comment		
Jesus (II): *Silence*	Jesus (II): *Silence*		
High Priest: Question (claim to messiahship)	High Priest: Question (claim to messiahship)	Sanhedrin: Question (claim to messiahship)	
Jesus (III): *Answer* (affirmative: heavenly glory and judge)	Jesus (III): *Answer* (qualified affirmative)	Jesus (I): *Answer* (refusal to respond; affirmative addition)	
High Priest: Conclusion	High Priest: Conclusion	Sanhedrin: Question	

---

[68]   Cf. Carson, *John*, 601-602.

(charge of blasphemy)	(charge of blasphemy)	(Jesus as Son of God)	
		Jesus (II): *Answer* (evasive)	
Sanhedrin: Abuse	Sanhedrin: Abuse		
Jesus (IV): *Silence* (inferred)	Jesus (IV): *Silence* (inferred)		
Pilate: Question (claim to be king)	Pilate: Question (claim to be king)	Pilate: Question (claim to be king)	Pilate: Question (claim to be king)
			Jesus (III): Question (denial and clarification)
			Pilate: Question (Jesus' actions)
Jesus (V): Answer (evasive)	Jesus (V): Answer (evasive)	Jesus (III): Answer (evasive)	Jesus (IV): Answer (political defense)
			Pilate: Question (clarification of kingship)
Chief priests: Accusations	Chief priests: Accusations		Jesus (V): Answer (theological defense: challenge)
Jesus (VI): *Silence*	Jesus (VI): *Silence*		
Pilate: Warning	Pilate: Warning		
Jesus (VII): *Silence*	Jesus (VII): *Silence*		
		Herod Antipas: Questions	
		Jesus (IV): *Silence*	
			Pilate: Question (Jesus' identity)
			Jesus (V): *Silence*
			Pilate: Threat (as prefect he has *imperium*)
			Jesus (VI): Answer (theological explanation)

JESUS' SILENCE IN THE TRIAL

Why did Jesus refrain from defending himself? This question is critical precisely because the trial was not the first time that Jesus stood in front of religious and political leaders who were determined to find incriminating evidence which would warrant a death penalty. For three years Jesus had to defend himself against all sorts of accusations. In the controversies which the Gospel writers relate we encounter a Jesus who needs no help to defend himself. Jesus can use arguments which remind us of (later) Rabbinic argumentation. He can use logic. His answers may leave people wondering what he meant. Or they make people understand only too well, leaving them behind seething with active hostility, eager even to destroy this Galilean teacher. Jesus is never reduced to silence, he always has something to say.

The Evidence

In their narration of the cross-examination of Jesus during the trial, the Gospel writers portray Jesus as responding to critical questions and as being silent at crucial occasions. The evidence as follows:

Responses by Jesus:
1. When the former High Priest Annas questions him about his disciples and about his teaching, Jesus responds (John 18:20-21).
2. When one of the aides of Annas slaps Jesus on the face, Jesus asks for a fair trial (John 18:23).
3. When the High Priest Caiaphas asks whether he claims to be "the Messiah, the Son of God," Jesus responds (Mark 14:62; Matt 26:64; Luke 22:67).
4. When the members of the Sanhedrin seek confirmation whether he claims to be the Son of God, Jesus responds (Luke 22:70).
5. When the Roman governor Pilate asks whether he claims to be king, Jesus responds, apparently in an evasive manner (Mark 15:2; Matt 27:11; Luke 23:3; John 18:34, 36, 37).
6. When Pilate threatens Jesus with his *imperium* which gives him the power to pronounce the death sentence which would lead to execution on a cross, Jesus responds (John 19:11).

Silence of Jesus:
7. Jesus does not interact with accusations of witnesses who report about his views on the Temple (Mark 14:59, 60; Matt 26:62).
8. Jesus does not respond to the High Priest's challenge to discuss

his views on the Temple (Mark 14:61; Matt 26:63).

9. Jesus evidently does not respond to the blindfolding and abuse by the members of the Sanhedrin who mock him with what is possibly a messianic test (Mark 14:65; Matt 26:68).

10. Jesus stays stubbornly silent when the chief priests accuse him before Pilate with regard to claims to be king (Mark 15:4; Matt 27:12).

11. Jesus does not respond when Pilate suggests that he should answer the accusations of the chief priests and elders (Mark 15:5; Matt 27:14).

12. Jesus refuses to answer the questions put to him by Herod Antipas (Luke 23:9).

13. Jesus refuses to answer Pilate's question "From where are you?" (John 19:9).

We note the following observations: (1) Jesus never replies to accusations, whether they are articulated by witnesses at the beginning of the Jewish trial (no. 7) or by the chief priests and leading members of the Sanhedrin in the crucial Roman trial (nos. 10, 11). (2) Jesus refuses vis-à-vis the chief priests to clarify his convictions about the Temple (nos. 7, 8). (3) Jesus refuses vis-à-vis the members of the Sanhedrin to defend himself in the context of their mocking test of his messiahship (no. 9). (4) Jesus refuses vis-à-vis the chief priests to clarify his convictions about his kingship (nos. 10, 11). (5) Jesus refuses to interact with Herod Antipas (no. 12). (6) Jesus refuses to answer when Pilate inquires about his true identity (no. 13)—an issue which he was prepared to address when (according to Luke) the members of the Sanhedrin pressed him to clarify his messiahship (no. 4; note the πάντες in Luke 22:70). (7) Jesus responds to the crucial questions: to Annas' questions about his followers and about his teaching, to the chief priests and the members of the Sanhedrin when they question him directly on the issue of his claim to be Messiah and Son of God, to Pilate when he asks him whether he claims to be king (nos. 1, 3, 4, 5).

We may summarize the evidence as follows: Jesus is silent with regard to accusations brought against him by the Jewish leadership, but is prepared to respond to the question whether he is "the Messiah, the Son of God." Jesus is prepared to answer the questions of the Roman governor, but is silent when he solicits information about his true identity. Before we probe the reasons for Jesus' silence, we must briefly look at possible parallels in Greco-Roman or Jewish trials which might explain Jesus' behavior during the trial.

Analogous Scenes in Jewish, Greek, or Roman Trials?

The Old Testament stories depicting a conflict between a prophet and a king, varying widely in details, exhibit the following similarities: (1) The impetus for confronting the king comes from the "word of the Lord," i.e. from outside the prophet. (2) Prophets who are brought before kings deliver an oracle of judgment which condemns the behavior and the attitudes of the king and spell out consequences. (3) During the confrontation the prophet may perform miracles which authenticate his credentials as messenger of the Lord and establish the efficacy of the word of the Lord. (4) The accusation, oracle, threat or miracle usually triggers a hostile response from the king who refuses to listen.[69] This pattern surfaces in the conflicts between Moses and the Pharaoh (Exodus 5–11), Samuel and Saul, Nathan and David, an unnamed seer and Jeroboam (1 Kgs 13:1-10), Elijah and Ahab (1 Kgs 18:18; 21:20-26), Micaiah ben Imlah and Ahab (1 Kgs 22:8; 22:17), Jeremiah and Jehoiakim (Jer 34:1-7; 37:3-10; 37:17). Even though the narrators sometimes point out weaknesses of the prophets—Elijah flees from Ahab and Jezebel, Micaiah ben Imlah falsifies his message in order not to upset Ahab—the prophets never seem to choose to be silent in the presence of the king. In climactic confrontations between prophet and king, the messenger of God proves to be the ruler's superior in some way.

The contrast to Jesus' behavior during his trial is self-evident: Jesus does not perform miracles (even though Herod Antipas asks for "signs"), he does not establish superiority over the Jewish leaders or the Roman governor, he does not proclaim a message of God (apart from reference to himself as heavenly judge).

The Greco-Roman version of the Jewish "prophet versus king" narratives are scenes in which a wise man, usually a philosopher, confronts a tyrant. It seems that "the portrait of the *vir bonus et sapiens* resisting the tyrant became a stock motif in the rhetorical and philosophical schools, especially in the Roman period."[70] The following features are present: (1) The philosopher invariably exhibits

---

[69] Cf. J. A. Darr, *On Character Building: The Reader and the Rhetoric of Characterization in Luke-Acts* (Louisville: Westminster/Knox, 1992) 155-58.

[70] For the following see Darr, *Character Building*, 151-55; quotation on p.155 from H. Musurillo, *The Acts of the Pagan Martyrs* (Oxford: Clarendon, 1972) 239.

the (Cynic and Stoic) ideals of self-sufficiency (αὐτάρκεια), self-control and boldness (παρρησία). (2) The wise man responds to threats by the tyrant with witty answers, or he expounds his philosophy, or he demonstrates preternatural gifts. (3) The impetus for confronting the ruler came from the sage. The model of the traveling philosopher confronting local rulers had become a cliché by the first century that "no self-respecting sage could afford not to confront the nearest tyrant."[71] An often quoted example was Diogenes of Sinope (cf. Dio Chrysostom's "Diogenes, or, On Tyranny"); Epictetus wrote an essay on "How ought we to bear ourselves toward tyrants?" The influence of the "philosopher versus tyrant" pattern shows itself in Jewish hellenistic literature, notably in the narrative of Eleazar and the seven sons who oppose Antiochus (4 Macc 5:1–17:6). When the king ordered the instruments of torture to be brought forward and tried to entice the seven brothers to eat unclean food forbidden by Jewish law, they "not only were not frightened but even resisted the tyrant with their own philosophy, and by their right reasoning brought down his tyranny" (8:15).

Again, while there are parallels to Jesus' behavior during his trial—he is not intimidated by his accusers, he also has αὐτάρκεια and παρρησία—there are no parallels with regard to Jesus' refusal to respond to questions and accusations.

In Josephus' descriptions of legal proceedings self-defense of the defendants is the norm. The defense may be ingratiating or rigorous. When Pilate threatens to execute the Jews who protested against his bringing the Roman standards into Jerusalem if they would not stop their protests, they cast themselves prostrate and declare that "they had gladly welcomed death rather than make bold to transgress the wise provisions of the laws"; as Pilate saw "the strength of their devotion to the laws" he removed the standards (*Ant.* 18.3.1 §57-59). When the leaders of a Samaritan delegation went to Ummidius Quadratus, governor of Syria, to initiate legal proceedings because of a Jewish attack against some of their villages, the Jews defend themselves vigorously: they accuse not only the Samaritan villagers but also Ventitius Cumanus, procurator of Judaea, to be responsible for the fighting as he had accepted bribes by the Samaritans (*Ant.* 20.6.2 §125-133).

In his description of legal proceedings of the Sanhedrin against the

---

71   Darr, *Character Building*, 151.

young Herod, Josephus implies that humility, fearfulness and mercy-seeking of the defendant before a judge were normal expectations. When the Sanhedrin was overawed by Herod's appearance before the council so that there was silence (ἦν ἡσυχία) and nobody knew what to do, a certain Samaia, a δίκαιος ἀνήρ, reminds the Sanhedrin that whoever came before this assembly for trial, "has shown himself humble (ταπεινὸς παρίσταται) and has assumed the manner of one who is fearful (σχήματι δεδοικότος) and seeks mercy from you (ἔλεον θηρωμένου παρ' ὑμῶν) by letting his hair grow long and wearing a black garment" (*Ant.* 14.9.4 §172).

The story of Jesus bar Ananias (Josephus, *J.W.* 6.5.3 §300-309) is often quoted as parallel for the silence of Jesus.[72] This prophet of doom, "a rude peasant" (τῶν ἰδιωτῶν ἄγροικος), began in the autumn of the year 62 CE, on the Feast of Tabernacles, to announce the destruction of Jerusalem and of the Temple, prophesying not only in the Temple but going about "all the alleys with this cry on his lips." Some of the "leading citizens" (ἐπιστήμων) arrested and abused him. Josephus continues: "But he, without a word on his own behalf (ὁ οὔθ' ὑπὲρ αὐτοῦ φθεγξάμενος) or for the private ear of those who smote him, only continued his cries as before (ἃς καὶ πρότερον φωνὰς βοῶν διετέλει)" (§302). The magistrates (οἱ ἄρχοντες) assumed that the man spoke on account of a supernatural impulse (δαιμονιώτερον τὸ κίνημα τἀνδρός) and brought him before the Roman governor Albinus who had him scourged. But the prophet "neither sued for mercy (οὔθ' ἱκέτευσεν) nor shed a tear, but, merely introducing the most mournful of variations into his ejaculation, responded to each stroke with 'Woe to Jerusalem!'" (§304). When Albinus questioned him about his identity and his motivation "he answered him never a word" (πρὸς ταῦτα μὲν οὐδ' ὁτιοῦν ἀπεκρίνατο) but continued "unceasingly" to reiterate his dirge over the city "until Albinus pronounced him a maniac (καταγνοὺς μανίαν) and let him go" (§305). However, differences to the behavior of Jesus during the trial are apparent: (1) Jesus bar Ananias obviously made no claims about his own person. (2) Nothing is reported of large crowds becoming "followers" of this prophet. (3) The message of Jesus bar Ananias posed no direct threat for the

---

72   Cf. C. A. Evans, "Jesus in non-Christian Sources," in B. Chilton and C. A. Evans (eds.), *Studying the Historical Jesus: Evaluations of the State of Current Research* (NTTS 19; Leiden: Brill, 1994) 443-78, here 475-76.

Romans (Jerusalem was not the residence of the Roman prefects), except in the sense of potentially instigating public disorder. (4) The Jewish authorities became convinced that this "peasant" spoke under divine inspiration; there is no corresponding "positive evaluation" of Jesus of Nazareth by the Sanhedrin. (5) It is not entirely clear whether Josephus implies that there were Jewish legal proceedings against Jesus bar Ananias before the Sanhedrin; as the magistrates brought him before Albinus they evidently hoped that he would be willing to silence him. (6) The Jewish authorities wanted him silenced, but they did not bring false accusations against him; evidently they were able to tolerate his predictions of a future destruction of Jerusalem and of the Temple for seven years. (7) The silence of Jesus bar Ananias with regard to personal questions is absolute, whereas Jesus of Nazareth finally did respond to questions about his identity. (8) The silence of Jesus bar Ananias was not consistent as such: he "unceasingly reiterated his dirge over the city," which led Albinus to the conviction that the man was deranged. In contrast, Jesus of Nazareth gives what we may call contextually relevant answers to questions from both the High Priest and Pilate.

Another account of a trial scene in Josephus which has been claimed as parallel to Jesus' silence is the reference to the silence of Mariamme, the wife of Herod the Great, before her execution in 29 BCE (*Ant.* 15.7.4-5 §218-236]).[73] Herod gave to Mariamme the benefit of a trial (κρίσις) when he heard of intimacies with Soemus, whom he had executed immediately; the assembly of the people "who were closest to him" were terrified as Herod was "intemperate in speech and too angry to judge (calmly)" and thus condemned her to death (§229). After the trial it occurred to Herod that Mariamme "ought not to be done away with so hastily" (§230), so he put her away in one of his fortresses. But Salome and her friends pressured the king to get rid of her, and "that is how Mariamme came to be led to execution" (§231). As Alexandra, Mariamme's mother, feared to be implicated in the matters with which her daughter had been charged, she "sprang up and in the hearing of all the people cried out," accused her daughter and shouted that the pending execution was a just punishment, pulling Mariamme's hair. Those present disapproved of her play-acting (§234: ἡ κατάγνωσις ἦν τῆς ἀπρεπούς προσποιήσεως), especially (μᾶλλον δέ) the condemned Mariamme

---

73   Cf. Soards, "Silence," 41-45.

"who spoke not a single word (οὔτε γὰρ λόγον δοῦσα τὴν ἀρχήν) nor did she show confusion as she watched her mother's disgusting behavior, but in her greatness of spirit she did make it plain that she was indeed greatly distressed by her offense in behaving in this conspicuously disgraceful manner" (§235). Josephus concludes by praising Mariamme who went to her death "with a wholly calm demeanor and without change of color, and so even in her last moments she made her nobility of descent very clear to those who were looking on" (§236). It seems obvious that this narrative cannot be used to explain Jesus' refusal to give answers showing "nobility of silence":[74] (1) Josephus includes no account of Mariamme's behavior during the actual trial. (2) Mariamme is silent in a situation where she has already been condemned to death. (3) Her silence is directed not against her accusers in a legal setting but against her mother who amplifies her death wishes for her daughter with theatrical behavior.

The most famous trial scene in Greek literature involves the legal proceedings against Socrates.[75] He was accused of being guilty "of refusing to recognize the gods recognized by the state and introducing other, new divinities" and of "corrupting the youth," leading his accusers Meletus, Anytus and Lycon to demand the death penalty (Xenophon, *Memorabilia* 1.1.1). The accusers spoke first, then Socrates answered the indictment. Plato's account of the trial in *The Apology of Socrates* is devoted almost exclusively to (allegedly) repeating the very words Socrates spoke at his trial—nearly a thousand lines in the Eigler-Schleiermacher edition,[76] whereas Meletus is allowed only a few brief answers at one point in the proceedings. Socrates explains and defends his philosophical activity at length in order to establish his innocence, he proposes a series of penalties, and in his closing words he addresses the jury. Socrates is not prepared to do everything in his power to secure acquittal (*Ap.* 35c): he disparages appeals to pity, he does not work on the emotions of the jury since he cannot wish to be exonerated except under the conditions of justice and the divine will. Socrates silences Miletus,

---

74   The "nobility" that Josephus mentions is Mariamme's nobility of descent!

75   For the following see Gooch, *Reflections*, 81-106.

76   Platon, "ΑΠΟΛΟΓΙΑ ΣΩΚΡΑΤΟΥΣ: Des Sokrates Verteidigung," in G. Eigler (ed.), *Platon: Werke in acht Bänden. Griechisch und Deutsch* (Übersetzung von F. Schleiermacher; Darmstadt: Wissenschaftliche Buchgesellschaft, 1990 [orig. 1973]) 2.1-69.

the only voice other than Socrates' which Plato allows us to hear
(*Ap.* 24d: ὁρᾶς, ὦ Μέλητε, ὅτι σιγᾶς καὶ οὐκ ἔχεις εἰπεῖν;)..
Socrates requests other voices—reported voices like the words
between Chaerophon and the oracle at Delphi, construed voices such
as the murmurings from the jury—not to interrupt him, to let him
say things which they may find surprising or difficult. Nonetheless
he does interact with the accusations of people who are not present,
even though this is like fighting with shadows (*Ap.* 18d: ὥσπερ
σκιαμαχεῖν ἀπολογούμενον). The later traditions (six centuries
after Socrates' death in 399 BCE) which state that Socrates said
nothing in his own defense (Appian; Maximus of Tyre; Philostratus)
can perhaps be linked with Plato's *Gorgias* where he has Callicles
attack philosophy as linguistically impotent, as the words of the
philosopher make no difference in the real world (*Gorg.* 485e, 486a,
508a); Socrates acknowledges that he will not make speeches at a
trial in order to gratify the listener—in a situation analogous to the
trial of a doctor who is charged by a cook in front of a jury of
children, he "won't know what to say in court" (*Gorg.* 521e: οὐχ ἕξω
ὅ τι λέγω ἐν τῷ δικαστηρίῳ). "It is not that he is unable to speak;
rather, because of the condition of the listeners, he cannot be
heard."[77]

When we compare the behavior of Socrates and Jesus during their
trials, we note that both are unwilling to save their lives at all costs
using whatever means would prove effective. But the differences are
more significant. Socrates silences all accusing voices, Jesus becomes
silent himself. Socrates defends himself, Jesus incriminates himself
by going beyond the High Priest's question about his messiahship
when he claims to possess the heavenly divine status of the Son of
Man.

This survey of analogous conflict narratives which use the Jewish
"prophet versus king" pattern or the Greco-Roman "philosopher
versus tyrant" pattern, and of apparently parallel trial scenes, allows
us—in the context of the evidence of the narrative strategy of the
authors of the Gospels which we traced earlier—to answer the
question whether the narration of Jesus' silence in the trial can claim
historical authenticity.[78] The answer must be yes, at least for the

---

77   Cf. Gooch, *Reflections*, 93.

78   Among critics who reject the authenticity of Jesus' silence in Mark 14:60,
61a and 15:4-5 as due to Markan redaction are the following: Schreiber, "Silence,"

following reasons: (1) None of the authors of the Gospels has prepared his readers for the possibility that Jesus could choose not to answer questions put to him. (2) In analogous scenes in both Greco-Roman and Jewish literature, philosophers and prophets defend themselves, speaking out for themselves or delivering oracles of judgment. (3) Jewish martyrs who stood before a tyrannical interrogator, surrounded by insistent accusers, usually gave a defiant speech in their defense, explaining at length their convictions and actions (2 Macc 6:23-28; 7:2, 9, 11; 4 Macc 5:14-38; 9:1-9; 11:1-9).[79] (4) In analogous scenes in early Christian literature, followers of Jesus always defend themselves during interrogations (Acts 4:8-12; 5:29-32; 7:2-53; 16:37-38; 18:14-15; 21:40–22:21; 22:25-30; 23:1-6; 24:10-21; 25:8-11; 26:1-29; cf. *Mart. Pol.* 9-11).[80] (5) When later Christian authors refer to the silence of Jesus or of persecuted Christians, it is usually[81] a silence during torture (cf. *Odes of Solomon* 31:8-13;[82] Dionysius of Alexandria;[83] *GPet.* 4:10;[84] *Mart. Pol.*

---

[79] (= *Markuspassion*, 260); D. Dormeyer, *Die Passion Jesu als Verhaltensmodell: Literarische und theologische Analyse der Traditions- und Redaktionsgeschichte der Markuspassion* (NTAbh 11; Münster: Aschendorff, 1974) 163-64, 177; W. Schenk, *Der Passionsbericht nach Markus. Untersuchungen zur Überlieferungsgeschichte der Passionstraditionen* (Gütersloh: Mohn, 1974) 239, 245; Mohr, *Markus- und Johannespassion*, 255-56, 286-87; Crossan, *Cross*, 186-87.

[79] This argument was used already by K. L. Schmidt, *Der Rahmen der Geschichte Jesu. Literarkritische Untersuchungen zur ältesten Jesusüberlieferung* (2nd ed., Darmstadt: Wissenschaftliche Buchgesellschaft 1969 [1919]) 306 n. 1; R. H. Lightfoot, *History and Interpretation in the Gospels* (London: Hodder & Stoughton 1935) 145; V. Taylor, *Jesus and His Sacrifice* (London: Macmillan 1937) 157.

[80] It is therefore not entirely surprising that some ancient copyists were disturbed by Jesus' silence and thus proceeded to make emendations: the old Syriac MS Curetonianus adds "as if he were not present," and the old Latin MS Colbertinus adds "as if he did not hear." Cf. Brown, *Death*, 772 n. 17.

[81] Exceptions are Justin, *Dial.* 102-103; John Chrysostom, *Homilies on the Gospel of St. Matthew*, 86.1 (on Matt 27:11-12); Origen, *Contra Celsum*, Preface 1-2. Origen begins his introduction to his eight books against Celsus by pointing out that "our Saviour and Lord Jesus Christ" remained "silent" (ἐσιώπα) when false testimony was brought against him, that he "answered nothing" (οὐδὲν ἀπεκρίνετο) when accusations were brought against him.

[82] *Odes Sol.* 31:8-13: "And they condemned me when I stood up, me who had not been condemned. Then they divided my spoil, though nothing was owed them. But I endured and held my peace and was silent, that I might not be disturbed by them. But I stood undisturbed like a solid rock, which is continuously pounded by columns of waves and and endures. And I bore their bitterness because of humility,

2:2[85]). (6) When the authors of the Gospels narrate sayings of Jesus which relate to behavior during trials, they always imply defense, promising the supernatural help of the Holy Spirit who would teach the followers of Jesus during cross-examinations what to say (Mark 13:11; Matt 10:19-20; Luke 12:11-12; 21:12-15; cf. John 15:26-27). Christian missionaries are passive in the sense that they do not resist arrest and imprisonment, but they are active in the sense that they defend themselves verbally: "Their only action is speaking."[86] As the authors of the Gospels describe Jesus as possessor and vehicle for God's Spirit,[87] it is not likely that they invented a Jesus who, during his own trial, would sometimes speak and sometimes be silent.[88]

---

that I might save my nation and instruct it. And that I might not nullify the promises to the patriarchs, to whom I was promised for the salvation of their offspring" (translation from *OTP* 2.763).

[83]   "Blows, spittings, scourgings, death, and the lifting up in that death, all came upon Him; and when all these were gone through, he became silent (ἐσιώπα) and endured in patience unto the end, as if He suffered nothing, or was already dead" (*ANF* 6.118).

[84]   *Gos. Pet.* 4:10: "And they brought two malefactors and crucified the Lord in the midst between them. But he held his peace (αὐτὸς δὲ ἐσιώπα), as if (ὡς) he felt no pain" (translation from E. Hennecke and W. Schneemelcher [eds.], *New Testament Apocrypha* [Philadelphia: Westminster, 1963] 1.184). The passage does probably not reflect docetism (explaining Jesus' silence by the fact that he did not really suffer at all; here ὡς would be translated by "because") but "underlines the silence of Jesus despite the pain" (Crossan, *Cross*, 180).

[85]   *Mart. Pol.* 2:2: "For some were torn by scourging until the mechanism of their flesh was seen even to the lower veins and arteries, and they endured so that even the bystanders pitied them and mourned. And some even reached such a pitch of nobility that none of them groaned or wailed (ὥστε μήτε γρύξαι μήτε στενάξαι τινὰ αὐτῶν), showing to all of us that at the hour of their torture the noble martyrs of Christ were absent from the flesh, or rather that the Lord was standing by and talking with them." On this passage and the early Christian concept of μάρτυς, see now G. Buchmann, *Das Martyrium des Polykarp* (Kommentar zu den Apostolisch-en Vätern 6; Göttingen: Vandenhoek & Ruprecht, 1998) 92-105.

[86]   Davies and Allison, *Matthew*, 2.185, with regard to Matt 10:19.

[87]   Mark 1:10; Matt 3:16; 12:18, 28; Luke 3:22; 4:1, 14, 18-19; John 1:32-33; 7:37-39; 14:15-26.

[88]   Even Mohr (*Markus- und Johannespassion*, 287-88), who takes Mark 14:60; 15:4-5 as redactional, is forced to admit that the redaction-critical verdict on the purpose of the *Schweigemotiv* must not prevent us from accepting that Jesus factually remained silent during several stages of the trial. This *caveat* prompts the question why one should resort to redaction-critical assumptions about the introduc-tion of a "silence motif" into a traditional passion account if the latter already

We conclude, therefore, that the complete lack of self-defense of Jesus during his trial, part of which is his refusal to respond to questions, has no genuine analogies. The Gospel writers' reference to Pilate's astonishment is a historical reminiscence utterly intelligible in an ancient setting, whether Jewish or Greco-Roman, whether non-Christian or Christian. The silence of Jesus is not a traditional topos, on the contrary, it surprised the readers of the Gospel narratives.[89]

Reasons for Jesus' Silence

In our effort to understand Jesus' silence we will first survey proposed solutions which work on the literary level of the Gospel narratives as understood by readers in the first century.

1. Kerygmatic explanation: Jesus as the Suffering Servant. As the intended readers of the Gospels have usually been assumed to be Christians whose understanding of tradition was controlled by the literary categories of the Old Testament and early Jewish literature —even in the case of Gentile Christians most of whom were either former proselytes or God-fearers—it has frequently been suggested that the silence of Jesus corresponds to silence on the part of the Suffering Servant in Isa 53:7 with whom Jesus is thus identified.[90]

---

reported the fact of Jesus' repeated silence. Crossan (*Cross*, 185-86) asserts that "it is not at all clear that Mark is primarily or even secondarily interested in Jesus' silence in terms of passion prophecy. He may be much more interested in giving a model to his community for reaction under interrogation and trial"—a model which says that Christians should "answer questions of confessional identity but to ignore questions of false accusation." This position is untenable for the following reasons: (1) Mark's text is a narrative of Jesus' life rather than a community manual, a fact which suggests that Mark is indeed interested in details of Jesus' behavior, particularly during his final days. Even when Mark intends Jesus to be a model for discipleship, this does not obliterate historical interests. (2) The "false accusations" that Jesus refused to respond to were false because they were contradictory. Would Mark want his Christian readers to "learn" from this that they should abstain from clarifying contradictory accusations which their persecutors might throw against them? (3) The answers of Jesus cannot uniformly be interpreted in terms of a model for "confessional" acknowledgments, since Jesus' answer to the decivise question of Pilate whether he is the king of the Jews is elusive at the least, and thus surely not meant as a model for confessing Christians.

89   Thus the conviction of Origen, *Contra Celsum*, Preface 2, and "people with average intelligence" in the third century CE (ibid., see below n. 105).

90   Cf. Carson, *Matthew*, 554, 568; Gnilka, *Matthäusevangelium*, 2.427; Hagner, *Matthew*, 799, 819; Lohmeyer, *Markus*, 335; Pesch, *Markusevangelium*,

This has been disputed, however. (1) There are no linguistic parallels between the Isaianic text and the Gospel narratives.[91]

Matt 26:62 καὶ ἀναστὰς ὁ ἀρχιερεὺς εἶπεν αὐτῷ, Οὐδὲν ἀποκρίνῃ;
Matt 26:63 ὁ δὲ Ἰησοῦς ἐσιώπα
Matt 27:12 καὶ ἐν τῷ κατηγορεῖσθαι αὐτὸν ὑπὸ τῶν ἀρχιερέων καὶ πρεσβυτέρων οὐδὲν ἀπεκρίνατο
Matt 27:14 καὶ οὐκ ἀπεκρίθη αὐτῷ πρὸς οὐδὲ ἓν ῥῆμα, ὥστε θαυμάζειν τὸν ἡγεμόνα λίαν
Mark 14:60 καὶ ἀναστὰς ὁ ἀρχιερεὺς εἰς μέσον ἐπηρώτησεν τὸν Ἰησοῦν λέγων, Οὐκ ἀποκρίνῃ οὐδέν;

2:435; Marshall, *Luke*, 856 ("probably"); Nolland, *Luke*, 1123; Green, *Luke*, 805; Brown, *John*, 861, 878; Haenchen, *Johannesevangelium*, 539; Soards, "Silence," 41-45; Green, *Death*, 71, 276; Brown, *Death*, 734 n. 13; E. Linnemann, *Studien zur Passionsgeschichte* (FRLANT 102; Göttingen: Vandenhoek & Ruprecht, 1970) 131-32; Mohr, *Markus- und Johannespassion*, 257, 287; D. J. Moo, *The Old Testament in the Gospel Passion Narratives* (Sheffield: Almond, 1983) 148-51; J. Schreiber, *Der Kreuzigungsbericht des Markusevangeliums: Mark 15,20b-41. Eine traditionsgeschichtliche und methodenkritische Untersuchung nach William Wrede (1859-1906)* (BZNW 48; Berlin: de Gruyter, 1986) 208 n. 1 (one of several explanations); Reinbold, *Bericht*, 152, 200; J. T. Carroll and J. B. Green, *The Death of Jesus in Early Christianity* (Peabody: Hendrickson, 1995) 53 with n. 46.

[91]   Cf. H. Kosmala, "Der Prozess Jesu," *Saat auf Hoffnung* 69 (1932) 24-39, here 28; H. W. Wolff, *Jesaja 53 im Urchristentum* (4th ed., Giessen: Brunnen, 1984 [1942]) 75-76; Brown, *Death*, 464, 840 ("secondary at most"); Gnilka, *Markus*, 2.281, is also uncertain, referring to *T. Benj.* 5:4, where the pious shows mercy for those who revile him "and is silent" (σιωπᾷ). See Gundry (*Mark*, 908, 933) who stresses that the phraseology does not carry over; he points out that the reference to Pilate's marveling at the silence of Jesus (Mark 15:5) does not reflect Isa 52:13-15 since there the astonishment is not related to the silence of the Servant (in 53:7) but to kings. M. D. Hooker (*Jesus and the Servant: The Influence of the Servant Concept of Deutero-Isaiah in the New Testament* [London: SPCK, 1959] 88-89) argued that it is not necessary to assume an influence of Isa 53:7 on the silence motif in the passion narratives (1) since the silence motif forms a definite pattern, in terms of an authentic feature, of Jesus' behavior during the trial, and (2) since the allusion is not made more explicit by the Gospel writers. Moo (*Old Testament*, 150) is correct in arguing that one cannot deny a correspondence of Jesus' silence during the trial with Isa 53:7 on the grounds that the allusion gives no evidence of an awareness of Jesus that he was fulfilling the same purpose as that of the Servant. Still, the linguistic parallels should be stronger in order to be certain of a link with Isa 53:7. The recent study of B. Janowski and P. Stuhlmacher (eds.), *Der leidende Gottesknecht. Jesaja 53 und seine Wirkungsgeschichte* (FAT 14; Tübingen: Mohr [Siebeck], 1996) does not relate Isa 53:7 to the passion story (except in passing; Stuhlmacher, p. 101).

Mark 14:61 ὁ δὲ ἐσιώπα καὶ <u>οὐκ ἀπεκρίνατο οὐδέν</u>
Mark 15:4 ὁ δὲ Πιλᾶτος πάλιν ἐπηρώτα αὐτὸν λέγων, <u>Οὐκ ἀποκρίνῃ οὐδέν;</u>
Mark 15:5 ὁ δὲ Ἰησοῦς <u>οὐκέτι οὐδὲν ἀπεκρίθη</u>, ὥστε θαυμάζειν τὸν Πιλᾶτον
Luke 23:9 ἐπηρώτα δὲ αὐτὸν ἐν λόγοις ἱκανοῖς, αὐτὸς δὲ <u>οὐδὲν ἀπεκρίνατο</u>
αὐτῷ
John 19:9 καὶ λέγει τῷ Ἰησοῦ, Πόθεν εἶ σύ; ὁ δὲ Ἰησοῦς <u>ἀπόκρισιν οὐκ ἔδωκεν</u>
αὐτῷ

Isa 53:7 (LXX):
καὶ αὐτὸς διὰ τὸ κεκακῶσθαι <u>οὐκ ἀνοίγει τὸ στόμα·</u> ὡς πρόβατον ἐπὶ σφαγὴν
ἤχθη καὶ ὡς ἀμνὸς ἐναντίον τοῦ κείροντος αὐτὸν ἄφωνος οὕτως <u>οὐκ ἀνοίγει</u>
<u>τὸ στόμα αὐτοῦ</u>

Isa 53:7 (MT): נִגַּשׂ וְהוּא נַעֲנֶה וְלֹא יִפְתַּח־פִּיו כַּשֶּׂה לַטֶּבַח יוּבָל

וּכְרָחֵל לִפְנֵי גֹזְזֶיהָ נֶאֱלָמָה וְלֹא יִפְתַּח פִּיו

The Servant in Isa 53:7 does not even open his mouth, which
underlines the quiet submission of the Servant which is expressed in
the language of slaughter (יבל, גזז, ענה, טבח) in this passage. He did
not verbally accuse or retaliate, despite physical abuse, but trusted in
God for his vindication as his suffering is part of God's plan (cf.
53:4, 6, 10).[92] It has been claimed that this lack of linguistic parallels
is less important than "the presence of multiple points of contact
between Luke's portrayal of Jesus in his passion and the Isaianic
Servant of the Lord."[93] While we do not want to dispute the latter
claim,[94] and while we recognize that Luke includes a quotation from
Isaiah 53 in his passion narrative (Luke 22:37, during the Last Supper, in the context of Jesus' last discourse in the Third Gospel), we
plead for caution in using a general portrayal of Jesus in terms of the
Servant of God for linking specifics of Jesus' behavior during the

---

92 Cf. J. A. Thompson and E. A. Martens, *NIDOTTE* 3.585; V. P. Hamilton,
NIDOTTE, 3.717; and H.-J. Hermisson, "Das vierte Gottesknechtslied im deutero-
jesajanischen Kontext," in Janowski and Stuhlmacher, *Gottesknecht*, 1-25, here
15.
93 Green, *Luke*, 805 n. 50.
94 Cf. J. Jeremias, "παῖς θεοῦ," *TDNT* 5 (1967) 713; D. P. Seccombe, "Luke
and Isaiah," in G. K. Beale (ed.), *The Right Doctrine from the Wrongs Texts?*
(Grand Rapids: Baker, 1994) 248-56; J. B. Green, "The Death of Jesus, God's
Servant," in D. D. Sylva (ed.), *Reimaging the Death of the Lukan Jesus* (BBB 73;
Frankfurt: Hain, 1990) 1-28, 170-73; R. T. France, "Servant of Yahweh," in J. B.
Green, S. McKnight, and I. H. Marshall (eds.), *Dictionary of Jesus and the
Gospels* (Downers Grove and Leicester: InterVarsity Press, 1992) 746; M. L.
Strauss, *The Davidic Messiah in Luke-Acts: The Promise and its Fulfilment in
Lukan Christology* (JSNTSup 110; Sheffield: Sheffield Academic Press, 1995).

trial (such as Jesus' silence mentioned in Luke 23:9 and the other passages) to Isa 53:7.[95] (2) The statement in Isa 53:7 does not refer to or imply accusers of the Servant but is related to physical violence to which the Servant offered no verbal resistance; it is concerned with the fact that animals go with blind subjection whatever the destination, whereas the Servant goes with knowing submission to what awaits him, and this leads him to maintain self-imposed silence as he goes into death. (3) Jesus was not consistently silent during the trial, and it is therefore not surprising that the Gospel writers make nothing of a possible correspondence between the silence of the Suffering Servant in Isa 53:7 and the silence of Jesus during his trial.[96]

The picture of the Suffering Servant going silently into (sacrificial) death might perhaps provide the hermeneutical background for Jesus' general refusal to defend himself, and more specifically for his presumed silence during the mocking and abuse by the members of the Sanhedrin who had just condemned him to death (Response IV in Mark/Matthew).[97] But it seems wise not to generally link Jesus' silence during his trial with Isa 53:7 as the Gospel writers do not hint

---

[95]   It is correct that Luke presents a formal citation from Isaiah 53 ("and he was numbered among the lawless"; Isa 53:12, in Luke 22:37), introduced by the formula "this which is written must be fulfilled in me" and followed by the affirmation "for what is [written] about me has its fulfillment." We note, however: (1) Luke's quotation is the only formal citation from Isaiah 53 in the Synoptic Gospels; (2) the point in Luke 22:37 is the assertion of Jesus that he will die a shameful death between criminals; (3) Luke cites Isaiah 53 "as a text that prophetically anticipates the fulfillment Jesus brings" (Bock, *Luke*, 1749); (4) Luke, as some have argued, has ignored Mark's allusions to the suffering Servant in the passion story, cf. H. Schürmann, *Jesu Abschiedsrede, Luke 22,21-38* (NTA 19.5; Münster: Aschendorff, 1957) 126-28; (5) the contrast inherent in Luke's narrative between Jesus and his accusers (Luke 23:9-10) does not link Jesus' silence in Luke 23:9 with Isa 53:7 (pace Soards, "Silence," 41-45).

[96]   The fact that the silence of Jesus during the trial cannot easily be explained as reflecting Isa 53:7 leads to the conclusion that the silence of Jesus cannot be regarded as invention based on prophecy (even assuming influence of Isa 53:7 on the way the Gospel writers' narration of Jesus' silence, the inauthenticity of the latter would not follow, since all Gospels consistently portray Jesus as being prepared to respond to any questions put to him).

[97]   Cf. Crossan (*Cross*, 174), who links Isa 53:7 with Jesus' "silence under suffering," who appropriately points out that it is easier to find allusions to silence under suffering than there are parallels to silence under interrogation. This fact underlines the necessity to seek differentiated explanations for the silence of Jesus during his trial.

at such an allusion more explicitly.

Other scholars suggest that the silence of Jesus corresponds to the silence on the part of the righteous sufferer (Ps 38:14-16; 39:10).[98] This view is not very likely either, since the suffering psalmists remain silent out of penitence for their own sins: "They are suffering, but they are not righteous."[99] Again, the vocabulary of silence in these passages is not the same as in the passion narratives.[100]

In a similar vein, it has been suggested[101] that the silence of Jesus is a fulfillment of Ps 22:16: "My strength dried up like a potsherd, and my tongue was fused to my jaws, and you deposited me in death's dust." Even though Psalm 22 is used by the Gospel writers to describe Jesus' passion (Mark 15:29, 34; Matt 27:39, 46), it should be recognized that the description of Jesus' silence does not borrow from Psalm 22. And Ps 22:16 does not refer to silence, but (in the context of vv. 15-16) to the "fear evoked by enemies who are waiting and watching for death to come."[102] To be sure, Psalm 22 refers to silence—but to the silence of God (22:3) which the sufferer bemoans as he feels deserted by God despite the fact that he is sick and feels death approaching and is spurned by fellow human beings.

2. Reader-oriented explanation. It has been suggested that Greek and Roman readers may have been able to regard Jesus' silence as an "expression of admirable self-control, perhaps even nobility."[103] However, as Jesus's silence must be linked both with his refusal to defend himself against accusations and with his extraordinary confession to be the heavenly Son of Man, this does not seem likely. (1) In narratives of trial scenes the defendant is exactly that: an accused

---

[98]   Cf. Pesch, *Markusevangelium*, 2.436; Gnilka, *Matthäusevangelium*, 2.427; Hagner, *Matthew*, 799; Reinbold, *Bericht*, 152.199-200; cf. Strobel, *Stunde*, 96. Some link this motif with the notion of the Suffering Servant of Isa 53:7. On the Righteous Sufferer in general, see L. Ruppert, *Der leidende Gerechte: Eine motivgeschichtliche Untersuchung zum Alten Testament und zwischentestamentlichen Judentum* (FB 5; Würzburg: Echter Verlag, 1972); K. T. Kleinknecht, *Der leidende Gerechtfertigte: Die alttestamentlich-jüdische Tradition vom 'leidenden Gerechten' und ihre Rezeption bei Paulus* (2nd ed., WUNT 2.13; Tübingen: Mohr [Siebeck], 1988).

[99]   Thus Gundry, *Mark*, 908.

[100]   Cf. Brown, *Death*, 464.

[101]   Justin, *Dial.* 102-103.

[102]   P. C. Craigie, *Psalms 1–50* (WBC 19; Waco: Word, 1983) 200.

[103]   Thus Green, *Luke*, 805.

person who defends himself. (2) In the literary scenes of conflict
between teacher and ruler the former demonstrates his self-control
in the way in which he conducts his defense, never in refusing to
fend for his survival, or in the way in which he accepts the
punishment (which may well have been a death sentence). (3)
Without doubt Jesus displayed—in the eyes of readers who are used
to these terms of Cynic-Stoic values—remarkable αὐτάρκεια and
παρρησία during his trial. But self-control is a feature of the entire
narrative of the trial, beginning with the arrest in Gethsemane and
ending with his last words on the cross, and therefore not a specific
quality of his silence.

3. *Rhetorical explanation.* Can Jesus' silence during his trial be
explained by reference to the "rhetoric of silence" which can be
traced in Greco-Roman poetry, theater, literature and historiography? According to Pseudo-Longinus (*On the Sublime* 9.2) and
Quintilian (*Institutio Oratoria* 2.13.12-13) the virtue of not telling
everything, of leaving things unsaid, of narrative suspense, intends to
solicit the imagination of the reader and to lead him to supply the
outcome of the story through his own reflection.[104] It is not clear,
however, how the reader of the passion narratives would "complete"
the story, especially since Jesus breaks his silence at different stages
of the trial. For example, the silence of Jesus vis-à-vis the charges
regarding his views on the Temple could hardly be expected to be
"completed" in a way which results in his subsequent claim to be the
heavenly Son of Man. If Jesus' silence serves a rhetorical function all
we can say is that (1) his silence startled readers in the Greco-Roman
world who would expect any defendant to defend himself in a trial
where the issue is life and death,[105] (2) his silence would make
readers think that Jesus had given up and was prepared to die, (3) his
silence serves to highlight his responses which he gave during the
trial, i.e. on his claim to be the messianic heavenly Son of Man.

4. *Sapiential explanation.* A further possibility could be to explore

---

[104] Cf. D. Marguerat, "The End of Acts (28.16-31) and the Rhetoric of
Silence," in S. E. Porter and T. H. Olbricht (eds.), *Rhetoric and the New Testament* (JSNTSup 90; Sheffield: JSOT Press, 1993) 74-89, esp. 75-82.

[105] Cf. Origen, *Contra Celsum*, Preface 2, who asserts that even people with
average intelligence (παρὰ τοῖς μετρίως φρονεῖν δυναμένοις) must have been
astonished that the accused, who was threatened by false testimony, would not
defend himself, even though he was perfectly able to do so and demonstrate his
complete innocence, his glorious life and his wonderful deeds.

Jesus' silence as reflecting his portrayal as a sage or teacher of wisdom.[106] In the wisdom tradition silence is linked with wisdom: "If you would only keep silent, that would be your wisdom" (Job 13:5 LXX: εἴη δὲ ὑμῖν κωφεῦσαι, καὶ ἀποβήσεται ὑμῖν εἰς σοφίαν). Qohelet knows that "there is a time to be silent and a time to speak" (Qoh 3:7: καιρὸς τοῦ σιγᾶν καὶ καιρὸς τοῦ λαλεῖν). Proverbs repeatedly speaks of or implies silence as sign of wisdom (Prov 11:13; 15:23; 20:19; 23:9; 30:32-33). Similarly Ben Sira links silence and wisdom: "There is one who by keeping silent is thought to be wise" (Sir 20:5: ἔστιν σιωπῶν εὑρισκόμενος σοφός). In his teaching on silence (Sir 20:1-8)[107] Ben Sira condemns not only waste of words in talkativeness, but emphasizes on a more positive note two motives for silence: silence for want of knowledge and silence in wait for the proper time (καιρός) to speak in order to be effective. Motives for silence are (1) prudence, lest somebody pass on wrong information because he speaks without sufficient insight (5:12), (2) staying loyal to one's friends (19:5-12), (3) perplexity or embarrassment in not knowing the proper answer one needs to give (20:5), and, most importantly, (4) waiting for the propitious time to speak with maximum effectiveness (20:6-7). Granted that there are numerous features in Jesus' teaching and behavior which can be correlated with the wisdom tradition,[108] it is difficult to see how the sapiential silence motif could be relevant for explaining Jesus' silence during his trial: he did not have to be careful so as not to pass on wrong information, he didn't have to cover for his friends, he surely cannot have been perplexed by the questions which his accusers asked, and

---

106 Cf. F. W. Danker (*Jesus and the New Age: A Commentary on St. Luke's Gospel* [rev. ed., Philadelphia: Fortress, 1988] 355-56), who refers to Diogenes Laertius 3.19; 9.115, for occasions where the accused is silent. See also Bock (*Luke*, 1819-20), who refers to Sir 20:1 for the silence of the sage when reproof is not required.

107 For an analysis, cf. J. I. Okoye, *Speech in Ben Sira with Special Reference to 5,9-6,1* (EUS 23.535; Frankfurt: Lang, 1995) 151-67.

108 Cf. M. J. Suggs, *Wisdom, Christology, and Law in Matthew's Gospel* (Cambridge: Harvard, 1970); J. M. Robinson, "Jesus as Sophos and Sophia: Wisdom Tradition and the Gospels," in R. L. Wilken (ed.), *Aspects of Wisdom in Judaism and Early Christianity* (Notre Dame: University of Notre Dame, 1975) 1-15; R. A. Piper, *Wisdom in the Q-Tradition: The Aphoristic Teaching of Jesus* (SNTSMS 61; Cambaridge: Cambridge University Press, 1989); H. von Lips, *Weisheitliche Traditionen im Neuen Testament* (WMANT 64; Neukirchen-Vluyn: Neukirchener Verlag, 1990).

he certainly didn't just wait for a more propitious time to speak. And consistent silence such as is narrated with regard to the interrogation before Herod Antipas (Luke 23:9) would indicate stubbornness or even arrogance rather than wisdom.[109]

5. *Other suggestions* include the opinions that (1) Jesus proves by his silence that he is in command of the scene,[110] (2) Jesus shows that he is the eschatological judge before the final verdict,[111] (3) Jesus shows his contempt for the hostile proceedings,[112] (4) Jesus accepts his pending death as the will of the Father.[113] It appears that these explanations, while most likely correct for some contexts, or in general terms, or on a theological level, do not suffice as explanation since Jesus does not remain silent throughout the trial, and because Jesus' refusal to answer is "intimately related to the context in the storyline."[114]

6. *Historical explanation.* It is precisely in this context of the

---

[109] Pace Danker (*Jesus*, 355-56) and Bock (*Luke*, 1819-20), who relate Jesus' silence in Luke 23:9 to the wisdom tradition.

[110] Fitzmyer, *Luke*, 1480.

[111] Cf. Schreiber, "Schweigen," 81-85 (= *Markuspassion*, 262-65), assuming that Jesus' silence is a redactional motif.

[112] Brown, *Death*, 464, 841. Jesus' silence before Pilate can hardly explained in terms of contempt, as Pilate alerts Jesus about the danger of keeping silent, which gives an impression of fairness; cf. Brown, *Death*, 734 (who claims on p. 841 that Pilate understands "that by not answering Jesus is somehow looking down on him"; I cannot detect such a nuance in John 19:9-10).

[113] Cf. Gundry, *Mark*, 886; Hagner, *Matthew*, 799.

[114] Brown, *Death*, 841. This "inconsistent" silence of Jesus is the reason why other explanations are not compelling, such as the view of Schreiber, "Schweigen," 82 (= *Kreuzigungsbericht*, 208 n.1), who wishes to correlate the silence of Jesus with the eschatological "primeval silence for seven days" of 4 Ezra 7:30; the further suggestion that Jesus as the "stranger" does not want to disclose his identity before satanic powers or sinnners, is not helpful either; see similarly (?) *Odes Sol.* 31:8-13 where Jesus' silence during his suffering is explained theologically by "that I might not be disturbed by them," i.e. that he may elude the powers which control Sheol so that he can descend into Sheol and release the holy ones of Israel. The tradition-historical suggestion by J. Weiss (*Das Evangelium nach Markus* [Schriften zum Neuen Testament I; Göttingen: Vandenhoek & Ruprecht, 1907] 214) that "die Überlieferung hatte kein Wort Jesu," is consistent in attempting to explain the references to Jesus' silence, but hardly convincing. We note that P. Billerbeck (*Kommentar zum Neuen Testament aus Talmud und Midrasch* [9th ed., München: Beck 1986] 1.1005, 1031, 2.51, 263, 572) provides no parallels to Jesus' silence during the trial from rabbinic literature.

narration of Jesus' behavior during his trial that we must keep in mind two facts. First, the references to Jesus' silence in the four Gospels appear in different contexts and therefore necessitate individual explanations. Second, both Greco-Roman and Jewish readers of the narrative of Jesus' cross-examination would have been disturbed by Jesus' lack of self-defense, culminating in his silence. "The Roman criminal courts were more familiar with the absentee accuser than with the defendant who would not defend himself."[115] These two facts taken together require that we look for an explanation which moves beyond the purely literary level and which seeks to understand the Jesus of history who stands before accusers as defendant in a criminal trial and who refuses to defend himself and who is repeatedly silent during cross-examination. We will treat the various instances for which the Gospel writers narrate that Jesus remained silent and attempt to provide an explanation that takes the respective contexts seriously.

(1) *Mark 14:59:60 = Matt 26:62* (Response I in Mark/Matthew): Jesus does not interact with accusations of witnesses who report about his views on the Temple. The view that, legally, Jesus's silence stopped the Sanhedrin from using the testimony of the witnesses[116] is not convincing because Jesus remains silent when the High Priest questions him about his refusal to respond to the witnesses (on this view he could have explained his silence without putting himself in jeopardy), and because he responds when questioned about his messiahship. Does Jesus' silence show contempt for his accusers?[117] The context in both passages does not allow a definite answer. Perhaps Jesus remained silent because, at least according to later Jewish law, it was improper to have an accused person convict himself;[118] however, it cannot be demonstrated that this principle was in effect in the first century.

The narratives simply report that Jesus refuses to defend himself: evidently he is willing to put up with any sentence to which the legal proceedings might lead—which could hardly be less than the death

---

[115] A. N. Sherwin-White, *Roman Society and Roman Law in the New Testament* (Grand Rapids: Baker, 1992 [orig. 1963]) 25.

[116] Thus J. Blinzler, *The Trial of Jesus* (Westminster: Newman, 1959) 101-102.

[117] Thus Brown, *Death*, 463.

[118] Brown, *John*, 826, referring to Maimonides.

sentence, judging both from the circumstances of his arrest and
cross-examination during the night of a festival, and from the critical
subject matter of Temple destruction. Jesus' lack of self-defense
appears to signal his willingness to die. His silence evidently shows
an acceptance of his passion as the will of the Father (cf. Mark
14:36, 39 par Matt 26:39, 42 par Luke 22:42, cf. John 12:27; cf. also
Mark 8:31 par; 9:31 par; 10:32-34 par; 10:45).[119]

(2) *Mark 14:61 = Matt 26:63* (Response II in Mark/Matthew):
Jesus does not respond to the High Priest's challenge to discuss his
views on the Temple. Jesus remains silent because the testimony of
the witnesses is contradictory and is leading nowhere, which is
recognized by the priests who conduct the cross-examination. It is
unnecessary for him to answer acknowledgedly contradictory accusations. Some see Jesus' silence as "a contemptuous rebuke for the low
quality of the charade."[120] However, the context of the reference to
Jesus' silence, again, gives no clues that Jesus regarded the members
of the Sanhedrin with contempt. Others suggest that Jesus' silence
before Caiaphas was probably understood by the High Priest as consent to the truthfulness of the charge: "Jesus submits to the faulty
reasoning of his accusers and opponents in order to accomplish the
will of God and so fulfill the scriptures."[121] Since we are not certain
what the reasoning of the witnesses with their contradictory testimony was, it is difficult to speculate on a "submission" by Jesus to
his accusers.

More likely is the explanation that Jesus refuses to assist the High
Priest who is determined not to discover the truth about Jesus' claims
but, rather, to destroy him[122]—a fact which evidently was known in

---

[119] Cf. Gundry, *Mark*, 886; similarly already Schreiber, "Schweigen," 80-81
(= *Markuspassion*, 262; as motif of the redaction).

[120] Brown, *Death*, 463.

[121] Hagner, *Matthew*, 799; cf. his comment on Matt 27:12-13: "It is not the
silence of defeat or confusion but of a triumphant resolution."

[122] Cf. John Chrysostom, *Homilies on the Gospel of St. Matthew* 86.1 (on
Matt 27:11-12): "Wherefore then did he not bring forward these things, it may be
said, at that time, when accused of usurpation? Because having the proofs from His
acts, of His power, His meekness, His gentleness, beyond number, they were
willfully blind, and dealt unfairly, and the tribunal was corrupt. For these reasons
then He replies to nothing, but holds His peace, yet answering briefly (so as not to
get the reputation of arrogance from continual silence) when the High Priest adjured
Him, when the governor asked, but in reply to their accusations He no longer saith

the circle of Jesus' friends (cf. Mark 14:1, 10). The aorist middle voice of the phrase οὐκ ἀπεκρίνατο οὐδέν, which is rare in the New Testament, has been interpreted on the background of evidence in papyri as a "technical legal term for response": the phrase describes "Jesus' failure to cooperate with the high priest."[123] The unique doubling of Jesus' refusal to answer (Mark 14:61: ὁ δὲ ἐσιώπα καὶ οὐκ ἀπεκρίνατο οὐδέν) can be seen as emphasizing "Jesus' strength in withstanding the attempt to browbeat him into an admission of guilt."[124] Again, Jesus silence evidently shows his acceptance of suffering and impending death as the will of God. This becomes evident in Mark 14:62 = Matt 26:64 where Jesus breaks his silence— not to defend himself but to make a "deposition" which speaks of his divine authority as heavenly judge, a statement which must lead to the death sentence.[125]

(3) *Mark 14:65 = Matt 26:68* (inferred Response IV in Mark/ Matthew): Jesus evidently does not respond to the blindfolding and abuse by the members of the Sanhedrin who mock him with what is possibly a messianic test. Jesus has never been willing to provide an objective demonstration of his mission, and therefore refuses to yield to the brutal demand for a sign.[126] And what is probably more important, as Jesus had, in a way, "asked" for the death sentence by claiming to be the heavenly Son of Man who possesses divine glory

---

anything; for He was not now likely to persuade them" (*NPNF* 1 10.511). This explanation is more appropriate with regard to Jesus's silence during the Sanhedrin trial, less so during the interrogation by Pilate. See also Origen, *Contra Celsum*, Preface 1, who suggests that Jesus remained silent since he was convinced (πειθό- μενος) that his entire life and his deeds were more powerful evidence testifying for him than any discourse which attempted to refute the false testimony could ever be.

[123] Brown, *Death*, 464, referring to J. H. Moulton and G. Milligan, *The Vocabulary of the Greek Testament Illustrated from the Papyri and other Non- literary Sources* (Grand Rapids: Eerdmans, 1982 [ori. 1930]) 64. The referent of an aorist middle of ἀποκρίνομαι is not automatically a legal context, however. More likely is the possibility that the middle voice adds a note of solemnity to Jesus' silence, cf. M. Zerwick (*Biblical Greek* [Rome: Pontifical Biblical Institute, 1963] 229), who points out that the passive deponent ἀποκρίνομαι "answer" is common in Hellenistic Greek and that the middle voice adds a note a solemnity. See Gundry, *Mark*, 885.

[124] Gundry, *Mark*, 885.

[125] Cf. Schreiber, "Silence," 81 (= *Markuspassion*, 262): "Erst Jesu vollmächt- iges Wort von 14,62 ermöglicht das Todesurteil (14,63f)."

[126] Cf. Betz, "Probleme," 639.

and divine functions, he cannot expect—in the first century—restrained behavior of the people who just condemned him to death. As he had not defended himself during cross-examination, he would not defend himself now.

(4) *Mark 15:4 = Matt 27:12* (Response VI in Mark/Matthew): Jesus stays stubbornly silent when the chief priests accuse him before Pilate with regard to claims to be king. As he had been silent during the cross-examination at the night session of the Sanhedrin members, he could hardly begin defending himself against accusations from the Jewish leaders at this stage of the proceedings.[127]

(5) *Mark 15:5 = Matt 27:14* (Response VII in Mark/Matthew): Jesus does not respond when Pilate suggests that he should answer the accusations of the chief priests and elders. Some interpret Jesus' silence again as his showing contempt for the accusations which were hurled against him by the authorities. The context does not help us to determine whether this is the case: Jesus is simply silent, he does not review his treatment by the Sanhedrin. Others suggest that when Jesus refuses to respond to the many accusations of the chief priests, after he had affirmed that he indeed claims to be "king of the Jews," the narrators—and why not Jesus himself?!—emphasize the fact "there is only one real question and that is the theme of the whole trial; beyond the King issue the many other things are subordinate and irrelevant, and that is why Jesus answers to them nothing at all."[128]

Assuming that Jesus wanted to die, in fulfillment of what he knew to be God's will for him, we may ask whether his silence intended to force Pilate to condemn him. This seems to be a correct appraisal of the situation, generally speaking, since Jesus' refusal to defend himself warranted Pilate's judgment of guilt, as he would be bound to condemn him: in the Roman legal system both a verdict and a regular *quaestio* became unnecessary if the accused admitted his guilt or if he abandoned defending himself (*defensionem relinquere*) which indicated renunciation of his claim to be innocent and relinquishing to demand from the plaintiff to prove his guilt.[129] Who

---

[127] Cf. J. A. Bengel, *Gnomon Novi Testamenti* (8th ed., ed. P. Steudel; Stuttgart: Steinkopf, 1887 [orig. ed. 1773]) 162: "Accusatoribus nil novi proferentibus silentium Jesu eorum quae jam dixerat, confirmatio subinde fuit."

[128] Brown, *Death*, 734.

[129] Cf. W. Kunkel, "Prinzipien des römischen Strafverfahrens," *Kleine*

thus confesses to be guilty brings the trial to an end: *confessus pro iudicato est*.[130]

(6) *Luke 23:9* (Response IV in Luke): Jesus refuses to answer the questions put to him by Herod Antipas. Does Jesus' silence show contempt for Herod?[131] I cannot detect a nuance of contempt in the

---

Schriften: Zum römischen Strafverfahren und zur römischen Verfassungsgeschichte (Weimar: Hermann Böhlaus Nachfolger, 1974) 11-31, here 19; P. Garnsey, "The *LEX IULIA* Appeal under the Empire," *JRS* 56 (1966) 167-89, here 173: "According to the *lex Rubria* (XXI, *de pecunia certe credita*), the *confessus*, the *non respondens*, and the *indefensus*, were all *iudicati*, or '*iure lege damnati*'." Cf. Haacker, "Schuld," 34-35. Of course the defense would depend heavily on the response of the defendant; cf. Sherwin-White, *Roman Society and Roman Law*, 25-26; referred to by Carson, *Matthew*, 568. The more specific version of this view, that silence means admission of guilt, cannot be defended, however: the principle *Qui tacet, consentire videtur*, i.e. "The one who is silent is considered to have consented," cannot be traced back beyond c. 1200 CE. In everyday encounters the silence of a person who is accused of something often is indeed a sign of guilt and embarrassment, thus the proposition of Euripides: "Silence itself constitutes your admission" (*Iphigenia in Aulis*, 1142). But a court of law "requires more than impressions," and the principle "silence means consent" does not explain Pilate's amazement with regard to the fact that Jesus does not defend himself; cf. Brown, *Death*, 735; pace Haacker, "Schuld," 34.

130 See Kunkel, "Prinzipien," 19-20, for evidence regarding the Roman legal system. With regard to the trial of Jesus Kunkel states: "Wenn Christus nach Matth. 27,11ff auf die Frage des Pilatus, ob er der Juden König sei, antwortete: 'du sagst es' (was 'ja' bedeutet), *und wenn er auf die Anschuldigungen der Juden nicht antwortete* [italics mine], so war er ein *confessus*. Eines auf Schuldfeststellung gerichteten Verfahrens bedurfte es nicht mehr. Vielmehr war Pilatus, wenn die Ankläger darauf bestanden, genötigt, die Strafe zu verhängen, und zwar die Todesstrafe, die für einen Nichtbürger, der sich das Königtum anmaßte, allein in Betracht kam" (pp. 20-21). Jesus' refusal to defend himself is seen in the fact that he does not invoke means which assert circumstances which are favorable for him (lat. *praescriptio*), such as prescribed periods of time (*praescriptio temporis*), absence of prerequisites for the trial such as lack of jurisdiction, or procedural flaws. On the *praescriptio* in criminal and private law, see M. Kaser, *Das römische Zivilprozeßrecht* (Handbuch der Altertumswissenschaft X.3.4; München: Beck, 1966) 385-86.

131 Thus Brown, *Death*, 841; cf. Nolland, *Luke*, 1124 (with some reservation); similarly Schreiber, "Schweigen," 84 (= *Markuspassion*, 266), who thinks that the silence of Jesus in Luke 23:9 signals Jesus' superiority. W. Radl, "Sonderüberlieferungen bei Lukas? Traditionsgeschichtliche Fragen zu Luke 22,67f; 23,2 und 23,6-12," in: K. Kertelge (ed.), *Der Prozess gegen Jesus. Historische Rückfrage und theologische Deutung* (2nd ed., QD 112; Freiburg: Herder, 1989) 131-47, esp.

context. Jesus' silence may signal his awareness of the fact that Herod is not seriously interested in establishing the truthfulness of the accusations which must have been reported to him. He evidently has no interest at all to somehow impress Herod and gain him as intercessor before Pilate. He does not defend himself and he does nothing which might at least delay the trial. Jesus seems determined to let the trial run its course—a course which would in all probability lead to a death sentence since the entire Jewish leadership is determined to do away with him. Thus, if Jesus saw indeed his death as part of the mission which his Father had given to him, he remained silent because he accepted God's will which was his death.[132]

(7) *John 19:9* (Response VI in John): Jesus refuses to answer Pilate's question about his identity as God's son. He has just affirmed that the charge of the Jewish authorities is correct, that he is king of the Jews, but he had started to clarify the nature and the extent of his reign which poses no threat to Pilate's *imperium* but is concerned with the truth of God, of his son and of judgment, and with those people who belong to the truth and listen to his teaching. In this context Jesus' silence may reflect a "recognition that Pilate, who could not understand when Jesus explained about his being a king, will never understand his origins from above,"[133] as the Roman governor is only interested in uncovering a political agenda.[134]

139, thinks that Luke 23:9 is secondary, derived from Mark 14:60, 61, and Mark 15:4-5. This assumption would be a possibility only in the case that we could demonstrate (and not just postulate) that Mark used a *Schweigemotiv* which Luke found necessary to introduce into the Herod scene.

[132]   Similarly Nolland, *Luke*, 1124, as "perhaps" best idea.

[133]   Brown, *Death*, 841.

[134]   R. Baum-Bodenbender, *Hoheit in Niedrigkeit: Johanneische Christologie im Prozess Jesu vor Pilatus (Joh 18,28-19,16a)* (FB 49; Würzburg: Echter, 1984) 150, suggests that the silence of Jesus in John 19:9 is consistent from the narrator's point of view since he had stated in 18:36-37 that the βασιλεία of Jesus is not "of this world," therefore a second answer to the πόθεν of Jesus is superfluous. However, the second question of Pilate as to the πόθεν of Jesus is not simply a repetition of his first question, and it is by no means "erzählerisch konsequent" for a narrator of a trial scene with a defendant being interrogated by a Roman prefect to simply be silent. C. Diebold-Scheuermann (*Jesus vor Pilatus. Eine exegetische Untersuchung zum Verhör Jesu durch Pilatus (Joh 18,28-19,16a)* [SBB 43; Stuttgart: Katholisches Bibelwerk, 1996] 62-63, 277-78) thinks that Jesus' silence in John 19:9 is a literary device meant to achieve a dramatic effect, used by the

Pilate was amazed at the persistent silence of Jesus (Matt 27:14: ὥστε θαυμάζειν τὸν ἡγεμόνα λίαν). He must have wondered—as any reader of the passion narratives would wonder—what kind of man Jesus was. Who would refuse to defend himself in a criminal trial where the accusers demand the death sentence? (1) The accused knows that the accusers have made up their mind and that he has no chance at all to get away with his life. This could have been Jesus' frame of mind in the Sanhedrin trial—even though it should be noted that the Sanhedrin trial was no sham: the testimony of the witnesses was thrown out of court because it was conflicting and thus "false," i.e. the witnesses were not manipulated, which seems to imply that Jesus could have had a chance if he chose to defend himself. This sense of total resignation would probably not have been Jesus' frame of mind during the Roman trial, since Pilate is not portrayed as being on the side of the accusers—on the contrary, he seems intent in releasing Jesus (if only to provoke the Jewish leadership, as he did on other occasions).[135] (2) Or the accused has been totally broken, by the massiveness of the accusations and/or by torture, so that he is not able to say anything. This was not the case in Jesus' trial, either before the Sanhedrin or before Pilate. (3) Or the accused knows that he is "guilty" of the charges brought against him—as determined by the accusers, who are at the same time the judges, on the basis of their own prepositions—but has no strong convictions about his deed and thus is not interested in making it public.[136] This option does not account for Jesus' silence either since nobody doubts that Jesus had strong convictions about his mission and his teaching and could have defended the purpose of his mission as Messiah. (4) This seems to leave only two options: either the accused knows that he won't be able to make himself understood because the accusers would not be able to grasp the true nature of his claims and actions, or the accused

---

author to carry on the dialogue. However, this is not plausible since the dialogues in the Fourth Gospel never included the feature of "silence" which, therefore, should not be regarded as merely a literary device.

[135] Cf. the description of his rule by Josephus (*J.W.* 2.9.2–4 §169-177; *Ant.* 18.3.1–4.2 §55-89), and Philo (*Legatio ad Gaium* 299-310). On Pilate and his tactics, see Strobel, *Stunde*, 99-130.

[136] In contrast to the Jewish and the later Christian martyrs who were "guilty" of the "crimes" they were accused of but insisted that their behavior was correct and proper in the context of their convictions, and who gave a courageous defense of their views when given the opportunity.

intends to die—or both. It is precisely in this combination of factors that the silence of Jesus in view of his impending condemnation to death confirms (for himself to start with) both the claims to divine dignity[137] and the inevitability of his death.

CONCLUSION

The mystery of Jesus' identity and mission could be grasped only after his resurrection. According to the Gospel narratives not even his closest followers were able to understand what he meant when he talk about his coming suffering, death and resurrection. Jesus' silence was a sovereign silence. He had come as obedient Son to accomplish the will of his heavenly Father,[138] in fulfillment of the prophecies of old, to bring blessing to the spiritually poor, to bring comfort to those who mourn, to bring satisfaction to those who hunger and thirst for righteousness, to bring those who were willing to receive a pure heart and who had repented into the real—and in the end visible —presence of God. He knew himself to be the messianic Son of Man, whose mission as Son of God was the giving of his life as a ransom for the many.[139]

Jesus went to Jerusalem not just to preach, but to die, so that the promised new covenant could become a reality. He had enacted this mission of his in the Temple and in the Upper Room: he had

---

137   A. Sand (*Das Evangelium nach Matthäus* [RNT; Regensburg: Pustet, 1986] 550) wants to move this implied confirmation from the historical to the theological level. I am not sure whether Jesus or his first followers or the Gospel writers would have made such a distinction, believing in Jesus' divine dignity as a (mere) "metahistorical reality."

138   P. Egger (*"Crucifixus sub Pontio Pilato": Das "crimen" Jesu von Nazareth* [NTAbh 32; Münster: Aschendorff, 1997] 198, 209) has correctly pointed out that the intimate, exclusive relationship which Jesus claimed to have with God—as his authorized representative, establishing his kingdom as reality in his own ministry— was the basic cause of the progressing opposition against him, leading eventually to his arrest, trial and execution.

139   On the authenticity of Mark 10:45, see Stuhlmacher, *Theologie*, 120-21, 127-30; recent attempts to refute Stuhlmacher's arguments by W. Zager ("Wie kam es im Urchristentum zur Deutung des Todes Jesu als Sühnegeschehen? Eine Auseinandersetzung mit Peter Stuhlmachers Entwurf einer Biblischen Theologie des Neuen Testaments," *ZNW* 87 [1996] 165-86) are not convincing. On Jesus' prediction of his own death, and the essential meaning of that death in the context of his mission, see Wright, *Jesus*, 540-611, for a fresh, integrative line of argumentation; cf. ibid., 609-10, for the following remarks.

indicated that the present experience of God and his mercy had come
to an end, that he is the Messiah through whom the God of Israel,
who is the God of all the world, would save Israel and thereby the
nations, and that all this would come about through his own death.
Jesus must have known that these actions and the accompanying
message, after all the opposition that he had attracted during the past
three years, finally would very likely get him put on trial as a false
prophet and messianic pretender leading the people astray. Jesus was
willing to die. Therefore he did not defend himself against the
charges with which the Jewish leaders accused him during the cross-
examination in his trial. He was willing to speak to the charges that
he claimed to be the Messiah and the Son of God. He was evasive
with regard to the Messiah charge because he had no immediate
political agenda and because he knew the possible misunderstanding
concerning the messianic role. Jesus reserves the right to "define his
terms."[140] But he was adamant about his identity as Son of God,
claiming much more than a rhetorical dignity. But this could not be
understood during the trial, before his death—and vindication—had
taken place. Thus Jesus maintained silence.

---

[140] Green, *Death*, 286.

(THE) SON OF (THE) MAN, AND JESUS

Bruce Chilton

PART ONE
THE MEANING AND APPLICATION OF THE ARAMAIC IDIOM

A. The meaning of the Phrase

An Aramaic idiom, "(the) son of (the) man" (a rendering to be explained) has recently received renewed attention, as providing a possible antecedent of the characteristically dominical expression, "the son of the man" (as a slavish translation of ὁ υἱὸς τοῦ ἀνθρώπου would have it). In Aramaic, the phrase essentially means "human being," and the issue which has emerged in the study of the Gospels centers on whether Jesus used the phrase with that broad, non-messianic reference. Amongst recent contributors, Geza Vermes has perhaps been the most conspicuous exponent of the view that the Aramaic idiom is the only key necessary for understanding Jesus' preaching in regard to "the son of man."[1] His own particular generalization, that the phrase is a circumlocution for "I," has rightly been attacked:[2] the fact is that "(the) son of (the) man" in Aramaic is generic, in the sense that, insofar as it is self-referential, the speaker is included in the class (or a class) of human beings, but the class normally refers to mortal humanity (or a group of people), not to one human being alone.[3]

---

[1]   See Vermes, *Jesus the Jew: A Historian's Reading of the Gospels* (London: Collins, 1973) 160-91; idem, "'The Son of Man' Debate," *JSNT* 11 (1978) 19-32.

[2]   See J. A. Fitzmyer, "Another View of the 'Son of Man' Debate," *JSNT* 14 (1979) 58-68; idem, "The New Testament Title 'Son of Man' Philologically Considered," in Fitzmyer, *A Wandering Aramean: Collected Aramaic Essays* (SBLMS 25; Missoula: Scholars, 1979) 143-60, esp. 153-55.

[3]   See J. W. Bowker, "The Son of Man," *JTS* 28 (1977) 19-48; B. D. Chilton, *The Isaiah Targum: Introduction, Translation, Apparatus, and Notes* (ArBib 11; Wilmington: Glazier; Edinburgh: T. & T. Clark, 1987) lvi-lvii. B. Lindars (*Jesus, Son of Man: A fresh examination of the Son of Man Sayings in the Gospels in the Light of Recent Research* [Grand Rapids: Eerdmans, 1983] 24) refers to "the idiomatic use of the generic article, in which the speaker refers to a class of persons, with whom he identifies himself." I would prefer to describe the

One of the passages cited by Vermes, from Talmud Yerushalmi (*Šeb.* 9.1), should have made the last point entirely plain to him:

> Rabbi Simeon ben Yoḥai made a hide-out in a cave thirteen years, in a cave of carobs and dates, until his flesh came up mangy. At the end of thirteen years, he said, If I do not go forth to see (*sic!*) what the voice of the world is . . . . He went forth and sat at the mouth of the cave. He saw one hunter, hunting birds, spreading his net. He heard a *bath qol* saying, "Release," and the bird was saved. He said, "A bird apart from heaven will not perish, how much less (the) son of (the) man!"

Quite evidently, the syllogism (such as it is) cannot function unless both "bird" and "(the) son of (the) man" are understood as classes of being, not particular entities. The point is that the divine care for animals demonstrates by analogy that human beings are not left hopeless, and Simeon goes on to leave the cave. The genre of being which is described by "(the) son of (the) man" obviously includes Simeon, since otherwise he could not reach the conclusion, and undertake the action, which he does. But the genre is no mere circumlocution for Simeon, since otherwise the class could not be compared to that of which the bird in the narrative is an instance, not the entire set.[4]

The generic quality of the phrase is even more apparent when an ordinary feature of Aramaic grammar is taken into account: the determined state of "man" was not held to equate to the usage of the definite article in English. As it happens, *bar naš* ("son of man") and *bar naša'* ("the son of the man") are closely related in usage, and the line of demarcation between them is subject to dialectical variation;[5] there was an increasing tendency for the determined state to be used with an indefinite sense as the language developed. By the time of Jesus, the form was probably *bar 'enaša'*: the prosthetic 'aleph (meaningless though it is) is more securely attested than is the usage or the precise meaning of the determined state.[6] That is the reason

---

usage as "generic" with or without the article, in order to refer to people globally or to certain people under some set of circumstances. See P. M. Casey, "General, Generic, and Indefinite: the Use of the Term 'Son of Man' in Aramaic Sources and in the Teaching of Jesus," *JSNT* 29 (1987) 21-56.

4 See Casey, "Use of the Term 'Son of Man' in Aramaic Sources," 25.

5 Casey, "Use of the Term 'Son of Man' in Aramaic Sources," 30-31.

6 See Fitzmyer, "Another View," 62; idem, "The New Testament Title," 149-51. For a characterization of the debate between Fitzmyer and Vermes, See J. R. Donahue, "Recent Studies in the Origin of 'Son of Man' in the Gospels," *CBQ* 48

for the parenthetical qualification of "the" in renderings from Aramaic here. Nonetheless, the generic force in the usage to hand is obvious. If God cares for birds, and his care for humans can be inferred therefrom, Simeon has grounds for assurance; if his resolve to leave the cave is based solely on his observation of a single bird's illustration of his own destiny, his thinking is wishful, not positively forceful.

The function of the *bath qol* is similar to what may be observed in other stories: the heavenly voice requires earthly explication. As in the case of the *bath qol* in respect of Hillel,[7] where a message concerning his fitness to receive the holy spirit is given, a new language is used, but in the case of Simeon the language is Latin, "Release" (*dimissio*), rather than Aramaic.[8]

Given the setting of the story, in the hard period subsequent to the revolt of Bar Kokhba, when the Roman Imperium exerted its power definitively over Palestine, the language of the voice is apposite. A version of the story with slightly more by way of setting occurs in *Gen. Rab.* 79:6 (on Gen 33:18); in that case, Simeon also sees a bird taken when the voice cries "Spekula" (that is, "executioner," a loan-word from Latin [*speculator*] which also traveled into Greek). Even more clearly than in Yerushalmi, the narrative concerns a genre of being, which is comparable to the class of humanity, not to a particular bird, in that Simeon decides that both he and his son should leave the cave. Unfortunately, Vermes does not observe this aspect of the story, which is also found (substantively) in *Eccl. Rab.* 10:8 §1. All these versions are presented, neatly laid out, in Hugh Odeberg's *The Aramaic Portions of Bereshit Rabbah*,[9] from which Vermes drew his examples.[10]

The fact is also worth mentioning, since it has been overlooked, that Odeberg called attention as well to the value of the story concerning Simeon for understanding the Gospels.[11] Vermes's

---

[7]   See *t. Soṭa* 13.3; y. *Soṭa* 9.13; b. *Soṭa* 48b.

[8]   The choice of language is not beside the point. Simeon goes forth to "see" what he calls "the voice of the world," and he hears a *bath qol* ("the daughter of a voice") in Latin, the tongue of the new oppression.

[9]   H. Odeberg, *The Aramaic Portions of Bereshit Rabbah* (Lunds Universitets Arsskrift 36.3; Lund: Gleerup, 1939) 92, 154-57.

[10]   See Vermes, *Jesus the Jew*, 257 n. 26.

[11]   Odeberg, *The Aramaic Portions of Bereshit Rabbah*, 154.

assertions of originality have been so exaggerated as to suggest that
he for the first time identified the various versions of the haggadah,
and for the first time related them to the Gospels.[12] Neither
suggestion is tenable. In addition to providing the fullest citation of
the versions available (even today), Odeberg makes specific mention
of Matt 10:29, where Jesus insists that the very sparrows which are
bought cheaply do not fall to earth apart from the father's will. By
analogy, people ought to take comfort (v. 31). Odeberg observed
that "apart from your father" in Matt 10:29 is substantively equivalent to "apart from heaven" in Genesis Rabbah (and, one might add,
Yerushalmi and Ecclesiastes Rabbah). His observation may also be
applied to "before God" in the Lukan equivalent of the saying (12:6-
7). (Luke 12:6 envisions sparrows being "forgotten," not falling, and
they are cheaper than Matthew's birds; otherwise, the agreement
with Matt 10:29 is striking, albeit not verbatim.) It would appear that
essentially the same observation of nature is employed by Jesus and
Simeon. In the case of Jesus, the observation seems to urge careless-
ness upon disciples, in view of providence; in the case of Simeon, the
lesson derived from the bird is courage in view of providence, and
the observation is explicitly directed to Simeon himself (with his son,
as relevant), although the very transmission of the haggadah
intimates that there is also a wider application.

Odeberg's comparison of the passages may be pressed further; it
becomes evident that his laconic citation of a single verse from
Matthew is an invitation to see the power of a theologoumenon as it
unfolds in texts of differing periods and circumstances. For just as
the haggadah of Simeon is directed to the circumstances of
persecution, when the Romans prowled for followers of a failed
revolt, so the haggadah of Jesus is couched in the form of advice to
those who confront the punishing power of civil rulers (who "kill the
body, but are not able to kill the soul," Matt 10:28; see Luke 12:4.)
Underlying the sayings of Jesus and of Simeon, despite their evident
independence from a genetic point of view (be it at the level of
literary or of oral influence), is a common, metaphorical transposi-
tion. The target of the saying (disciples or Simeon) is compared to
birds which may perish (by natural causes or hunting), but then the
divine care for such humble creatures is used to assure the target. In
just this application of assurance, Simeon's saying is aesthetically

---

12   See Vermes, "'The Son of Man' Debate," 19-32.

superior to Jesus', because the image of the bird ensnared is far more evocative (from the established perspectives of both sayings) than that of the bird as fallen or (worse still) forgotten.

A striking feature of a comparison of Jesus' saying and Simeon's (again, passed over in silence by Odeberg—consciously or not—in his laconic citation), is that Jesus does *not* here employ the theologoumenon "(the) son of (the) man" in any form. That is, Jesus' saying performs a meaning comparable to Simeon's, by means of the same, essentially generic contrast between birds and those people who are in circumstances of persecution, but it does so without reference to the phrase which concerns Vermes. In itself, the question of the origins of the dominical usage "the son of the man," in all its complexity, cannot be adequately answered here. That is (still) a suitable subject for monographic treatment. But it might be noted immediately how Vermes's omission to cite Odeberg fully has distorted the course of recent research. Vermes has been able to argue for an analogy between Jesus' and rabbinic usage which is so perfect as to approach identity, but only by ignoring evidence of obvious disanalogy. Everyone who has ever read Odeberg knows (1) that the usage is well and truly generic (not circumlocutional, as Vermes would have it) and (2) that Matt 10:29-31 (with Luke 12:6-7) represents a tendency *not* to employ the usage when essentially the same meaning as in Simeon's dictum is at issue. But because Vermes failed adequately to cite Odeberg, in his pretension to originality, it has required considerable discussion (and several contributions from J. A. Fitzmyer) to establish the first point, and scholars continue to be misled in respect of the second.

In his recent and otherwise excellent study of "the son of the man" in the Gospels, Barnabas Lindars[13] cites Vermes's collection of haggadoth concerning Simeon, and he also accepts the analogy posited by Vermes with Jesus' usage. Had sound scholarly technique stood behind Vermes's treatment, Lindars would have been encouraged to include Odeberg's analysis, in which it becomes evident that "the son of the man" is not used generically in a saying of Jesus (namely, Matt 10:29-31; Luke 12:6-7), when the comparison with the haggadah of the cave might lead us to expect that the phrase would be employed. In the event, Luke 12:8-9 has Jesus refer to "the son of the man" immediately after his remark concerning sparrows (see Matt 10:32-

---

13   Lindars, *Jesus, Son of Man*, 228-31.

33);[14] it emphatically refers, not generically, but particularly, to a specific figure in the heavenly court. That fact is explicit within the Gospel.

As has already been suggested, no solution can yet be offered definitively to the perplexing question of what the dominical phrase, "the son of the man," refers to. Essentially, the question has only been obfuscated by the issue of authenticity (as will be discussed below). Clarity is only possible when we impute the spectrum of meanings to the phrase which is appropriate to the sphere of language in which it was spoken on any given occasion by any speaker. The advantage of a comparative analysis is that it helps texts mutually to define their spheres of discourse. Our initial attention must therefore focus on a feature of the comparison of the materials attributed to Simeon and Jesus, a feature which is a regular phenomenon of textual comparison. In other studies, I have treated of texts in which a single tradition (be it of Yoḥanan and the problem of the Levites in Numbers 3 or of Jesus and the problem of divorce) occasioned construals of that tradition which were mutually explicable; the synoptic relationship among common construals of single traditions—whether instanced in the Gospels or Rabbinica—is first of all an invitation to observe meanings unfold, not a puzzle to be deciphered.[15] The same opportunity obtains in the case of a haggadah concerning such a teacher: the transfiguration and the story of Hillel and the *bath qol* were considered from that point of view.[16] But in the latter case, we also encountered alternative developments within traditions which went beyond what we might ordinarily refer to as "construal." Within Yerushalmi, the additional instances of *bath qol* which are cited tend to shift the emphasis, from the exaltation of Hillel to the phenomenon of *bath qol* generally. Even more dramatically, the story of Jesus and the *bath qol* in John 12 is so distinctive a version of the haggadah of his transfiguration in the

---

[14]   The Matthean reference is to Jesus in the heavenly court, implicitly as "the son of the man" (with whom he is emphatically identified, see v. 23), as analogous to the "men" before whom one has confessed or denied him.

[15]   See B. D. Chilton, *Profiles of a Rabbi: Synoptic Opportunities in Reading about Jesus* (BJS 177; Atlanta: Scholars Press, 1989) 49-75. The relevant texts are *b. Bek.* 5a; *y. Sanh.* 1.4; *Num. Rab.* 4.9 (on Num 3:46); and Matt 19:3-12; Mark 10:2-12; Luke 16:18.

[16]   See *t. Soṭa* 13.3; *y. Soṭa* 9.13; *b. Soṭa* 48b; and Matt 17:1-13; Mark 9:1-13; Luke 9:28-36; Chilton, *Profiles of a Rabbi*, 77-89.

Synoptics as to call for the designation of "transformation," rather than "construal." But now, as we compare the haggadoth concerning Jesus and Simeon, it is perfectly plain that we are dealing with neither construals nor transformations of a common tradition, for the simple reason that no common tradition evidently lies behind them.

The force of these observations is to the effect that Odeberg put his finger on an order of relationship between texts which does not demand the supposition of their genetic dependence upon the same tradition. "Simeon" and "Jesus" (or whichever speakers are represented by Yerushalmi, Genesis Rabbah, and Ecclesiastes Rabbah on the one hand, and by Matthew and Luke on the other hand)[17] simply use a similar topos of the comparative value of the human and ornithological in order to provide assurance of divine care in the midst of real or potential persecution. Notably, their similarity in the conveyance of a cognate meaning by a comparable topos does not extend to the usage of the theologoumenon, "(the) son of (the) man." Simeon and Jesus are comparable—and better understood in one another's light—in respect of the meaning performed within haggadoth attributed to them: they urge similar things by a single topos developed distinctively. But what they perform—as far as presently can be seen—are not the traditions of others (that would be construal or transformation), but their own insights within the theological language available to them. In other words, for all that their sayings are comparable, Simeon and Jesus have no need of a *tertium quid*, a yet more ancient dictum, to explicate for us why they say what they say.[18] They simply speak, and traditions are generated which are

---

[17] For the immediate purpose, issues of "authenticity," which are themselves often invoked in an inexact manner, are not of concern: the focus here is upon describing the relationships of texts and their meanings. Part 2 will represent an adjustment of focus.

[18] During a meeting of the Seminar on the Aramaic Background of the New Testament, within the *Studiorum Novi Testamenti Societas* (Dublin, 25 July 1989) the suggestion was made by Prof. Otto Betz that Amos 3:5 constitutes precisely such a *tertium quid*. There is no question but that proverbial reasoning from the fate of birds and other wildlife to the condition of humanity before God is a feature of the Hebrew Scriptures, and as such one of the elements of early Judaism. But the members of the Seminar were not convinced by the argument of any particular dependence of the dominical saying upon Amos. From the point of view of the idiom under discussion, Eccl 9:12 in any case presents a closer analogy.

then subject to haggadic construal and/or transformation. They are performers, not tradents. For the purposes of creating these sayings, they required only a language, eyes, ears, and a mouth; appeal to some prior tradition (in the absence of evidence to that effect) only distracts us from our appreciation of the distinctive performances.

Indeed, it should be emphasized that our distinctions among performances, transformations, and construals are heuristic, in respect of readers' cognition: they appear sensible given the lay of texts at a given moment. A "performance" is not necessarily something actually said (or, for that matter, not said) by Simeon or Jesus at some time; it is a distinctive, autonomous conveyance of meaning within the language of early Judaism. A "transformation" is not necessarily a tradent's attempt to alter a performance, any more than a "construal" is necessarily a deliberate effort at nuance; they are simply the names we might use to describe greater or lesser degrees of congruence in that promulgation of performance which is known as tradition. "Simeon" and "Jesus" are, in the first instance, nothing more than names given to performances, just as "Yerushalmi," "Genesis Rabbah," "Ecclesiastes Rabbah," "Matthew," and "Luke" are, in the first instance, nothing other than names given to transformations and construals by anonymous tradents (orally and/or in writing) of such performances.

B. A Distinctive Application within the Gospels

The relative absence of Simeon's theologoumenon, "(the) son of (the) man," from Jesus' saying should by itself alert us to the possibility, already mentioned, that the phrase carries a different significance within the sayings attributed to Jesus. Precisely that possibility comes evidently to the fore in a saying in which "the son of the man" is employed, again in the material known as "Q" (Matt 8:19-20 = Luke 9:57-58):

> One scribe came forward and said,
>   "Teacher, I shall follow you wherever you go away to."
> And Yeshua says to him,
>   "Foxes have holes and the birds of heaven nests,
>   But the son of man does not have a spot to lay his head."

The saying explicitly addresses the issue of discipleship in both Gospels. The famous dictum, "Let the dead bury their own dead!" follows in each case (Matt 8:21-22 = Luke 9:59-60).

Moreover, the same issue is developed within the construals of each Gospel. In Matthew, a scribe is the interlocutor, and such figures in the first Gospel might be "trained for the kingdom" (13:52); that is evidently the understanding here, because the next interlocutor is described as "another of his disciples" (v. 21). The story of the stilling of the storm follows (vv. 23-27), a paradigmatic instance of discipleship.

The Lukan construal attains a cognate presentation of the saying, by its own means, as can be traced by observing the usage of the verb, "to travel" (πορεύεσθαι), within this complex of material. Jesus is said programmatically to "set his face to travel to Jerusalem" in 9:51, and he sends messengers before him (v. 52a). They proceed to "travel" (v. 52b), but do not manage to prepare a welcome for him in a village of Samaritans "because his face was traveling to Jerusalem" (v. 53). Jesus rebukes the manifestly odd suggestions that fire be called down from heaven (vv. 54-55); rather, "they traveled to another village" (v. 56). It is, then, "While they were traveling on the way" that an unnamed interlocutor appears and says what is attributed to a scribe in Matthew (v. 57). But there is an addition to the Lukan complex. Just as Jesus' disciples had suggested they call down fire from heaven, in the manner of Elijah (see 2 Kgs 1:10, 12), so the Lukan Jesus closes this group of sayings with the observation that no one who exercises domestic responsibility, by putting his hand to the plough, even in the manner of Elisha (1 Kgs 19:20), is worthy of the kingdom (vv. 61-62). The following material concerns the commissioning of seventy disciples, who promulgate precisely that kingdom (10:1-12, esp. vv. 9, 11).

There is an evident adjustment of meaning involved as the reader moves from the Matthean to the Lukan construal of Jesus' saying in respect of foxes, birds, and the son of the man. What is in the former case a paradigm of scribal discipleship is in the latter case a paradigm of peripatetic discipleship. Nonetheless, Matthew and Luke share the understanding that "the son of the man" is christologically redolent, and that the issue of the saying is discipleship in respect of precisely that "son of man." Nothing intrinsic to the saying, within the language of early Judaism, requires such a presentation of it. "Son of man" need mean no more than "person," and generally should not be pressed for more meaning without warrant. Within that sense of the phrase, it is hardly natural to understand the saying in reference to discipleship. The exigencies of human life are, perhaps, more plausibly at issue:

> Foxes[19] have dens and birds their nests:
> only man has nowhere to lay his head.[20]

If such a gnomic (if cynical) sense is held to have been the performed meaning of the saying,[21] then what we see in Matthew and Luke are two construals of a single and fundamental transformation of that meaning, into the new keys of christology and discipleship.

PART TWO
JESUS' APPLICATIONS OF THE PHRASE

The question naturally arises, whether the performed meaning posited in the last paragraph should be ascribed to Jesus. At just this point, a note of caution needs to be sounded. "The historical Jesus," who was bequeathed to us by the liberal theology of the last century, was an empirically knowable figure, who transcended the doctrines of Christianity. His epitaph was written by Albert Schweitzer and William Wrede. Schweitzer, for all his evident inadequacies,[22] did demonstrate that whatever Jesus said, thought, and did, was—historically speaking—conditioned by doctrinal constraints and religious perspectives no less compelling than those which influence Christians (and other religious people) generally. What has alienated many readers of Schweitzer is his perfectly sensible observation that the constraints and perspectives in the case of Jesus were not Christian in any definable sense, but Jewish and eschatological. Rather more profoundly, Wrede[23] demonstrated that to search for

---

[19]   P. M. Casey ("The Jackals and the Son of Man (Matt. 8.20//Luke 9.58," *JSNT* 23 [1985] 3-22, esp. 8) suggests an alternative reading, but M. H. Smith ("No Place for a Son of Man," *Forum* 14.4 [1988]) 83-107, esp. 89) replies that "foxes regularly dwell in burrows, while jackals seek such shelter only to bear young."

[20]   See the observation of R. Simeon b. Eleazar in *b. Qidd.* 82b, that he had never seen a fox keeping a shop; discussion in Casey, "The Jackals and the Son of Man," 9.

[21]   See Smith, "No Place for a Son of Man," 98-100.

[22]   See B. D. Chilton, *The Kingdom of God in the Teaching of Jesus* (IRT 5; Philadelphia: Fortress, 1984) 8-9; A. Schweitzer, *The Quest of the Historical Jesus: A Critical Study of its Progress from Reimarus to Wrede* (London: Black, 1954).

[23]   See W. Wrede, *Das Messiasgeheimnis in den Evangelien: Zugleich ein Beitrag zum Verständnis des Markusevangelium* (Göttingen: Vandenhoeck &

data concerning Jesus (as distinct from christological interpretations of him) in the Gospels is as sensible as looking for objectivity in an apologetic discourse. Attempts to revive the sort of historical Jesus liberal theology required, an archaeological datum which might refute modern dogmatism, are fashionable only among those who have remained unmoved by developments during this century.[24] Among Christians, certain conservatively inclined Evangelicals[25] continue to treat the Gospels as if they were concocted as puzzles which contain all the necessary facts of history, provided they are re-arranged cleverly. Among certain Jewish interpreters of Jesus, an equally astonishing naïveté is apparent. Harvey Falk[26] has recently represented the attitude that the Gospels are to be taken as relaying Jesus' *ipsissima verba*, and Vermes[27] claims such data can be gleaned, provided the texts are shorn of their hellenistic accretions.

Aside from "the historical Jesus" of liberal Protestantism (and his ghost among badly informed contributors), no other contenders have clearly emerged as viable. "The new quest of the historical Jesus" was hailed from time to time in the period since the war, but its claims have never been realized. It was an attempt to discover the dialectic between Bultmann's "eternal Logos, the Word,"[28] who required a decision for or against himself in the texts as they stand, and Bultmann's messianic prophet, the Judaic teacher who could be investigated by historical means.[29] In order to be successful, "the

---

Ruprecht, 1901); ET: *The Messianic Secret* (Cambridge and London: James Clarke, 1971).

[24] Sadly, the representation of this group includes some publications of "The Jesus Seminar," although the actual discussions which went into those works was more sophisticated than the popularization makes it seem. See R. W. Funk and R. W. Hoover (eds.), *The Five Gospels: The Search for the Authentic Words of Jesus* (San Francisco: HarperCollins, 1993); R. W. Funk (ed.), *The Acts of Jesus: The Search for the Authentic Deeds of Jesus* (San Francisco: HarperCollins, 1998).

[25] See J. W. Wenham, *Do the Resurrection Stories Contradict One Another?* (Exeter: Paternoster, 1984); M. Green, *The Empty Cross of Jesus* (The Jesus Library; London: Hodder and Stoughton, 1984).

[26] See H. Falk, *Jesus the Pharisee: A New Look at the Jewishness of Jesus* (New York: Paulist, 1985).

[27] See G. Vermes, *Jesus and the World of Judaism* (London: SCM Press, 1983) 85.

[28] R. Bultmann, *Jesus Christ and Mythology* (New York: Scribner's, 1958) 80.

[29] See R. Bultmann, *Jesus and the Word* (New York: Scribner's, 1934).

new quest" required grounding in the sources of Judaism, but its
practitioners were even less skilled in that regard than Bultmann
himself was. Instead, "new questers" of the 'fifties and 'sixties (and
their successors) turned to "the new hermeneutic" (see Fuchs),[30]
Gnosticism (see Robinson),[31] doctrinal interests (see Keck),[32] or
some other arena in which Jesus as an object of faith, in consequence
of the Gospels, rather than Jesus as the subject of faith, informing the
Gospels, is the principal concern. In other words, "the new quest"
became—and remains—so utterly bound up with ideological programs, that it would be truer to say that it has never really been
tried, than to say it has failed.

The suggested itinerary of "the new quest" may have been revived
in what has been called "The Third Quest of the Historical Jesus."[33]
Whether or not it has been, something needs to be done about the
question of Jesus in order for the Gospels to be understood at all.
For that present purpose, the question is not to be investigated in its
strictly historical or theological dimensions, since the essentially
literary issue of how the Gospels unfolded, and how the meaning of a
particular phrase evolved, is our purview. It is no doubt the case that
one's address of the literary issue will influence one's historical
and/or theological judgment, and vice versa, but such influence is not
our interest here; such questions can only be confused by muddling
them, as tends to be the case in "the new quest." Our concern is
simply: what do we need to posit, as performed meaning within early
Judaism, in order to explain how the Gospels came to say what they
do? The answer to that question is the generative, literary figure
called Jesus, insofar as that figure can be known. (Once that figure is
collated with historical evidence and reason, it may itself be claimed
to be historical. But any such claim is not an immediate part of our
present inquiry.) To a significant extent, that figure is a cipher, an
inference from texts. And yet the inference is not idle, since without

---

30   See E. Fuchs, *Studies of the Historical Jesus* (SBT 42; London: SCM
Press; Naperville: Allenson, 1964).

31   See J. M. Robinson, *A New Quest for the Historical Jesus and Other
Essays* (Philadelphia: Fortress, 1982).

32   See L. E. Keck, *A Future for the Historical Jesus: The Place of Jesus in
Preaching and Theology* (Nashville: Abingdon, 1971).

33   See W. R. Telford, "Major Trends and Interpretive Issues in the Study of
Jesus," in B. D. Chilton and C. A. Evans (eds.), *Studying the Historical Jesus:
Evaluations of the State of Current Research* (NTTS 19; Leiden: Brill, 1994) 33-74.

that figure, the texts have no center, and cease to mean anything: they point to Jesus, not only denotatively, as their necessary precedent, but generatively, as the informing source of what they mean. To this extent, it is sensible to speak of Jesus as a figure of literary history, whatever one might think of "the historical Jesus."

If Jesus' performance of the saying concerning foxes, birds, and the son of the man itself focused on the twin issues of christology and discipleship, that would certainly seem to explain the presentations of Matthew and Luke. But two considerations make that apparently straightforward explanation appear improbable. First, although there is a consensus between Matthew and Luke that the saying issues a call to discipleship grounded in christology, their respective understandings of both discipleship and christology are—as we have seen— distinctive. (Another, less probative, consideration within the same vein is that the context of log. 86 in the *Gospel according to Thomas* is somewhat different.[34]) Were Jesus' performance explicitly geared to specific views of such central matters, greater fidelity to his perspective might be expected. Second, the reference to "the son of the man," cognate with that of Simeon ben Yoḥai, contrasts the genre of humanity with animate creation; such a usage is scarcely a straightforward vehicle of christology (or of messianic claims). The point of the imagerial contrast pivots around the axis which separates people from animals, not disciples from others.

The performance of Jesus seems rather to have focused on how people are more rootless than animals. It inverts the logic of Simeon, his near contemporary. Where Simeon invoked the contrast between people and birds to show how much more God would care for humanity, and therefore Simeon himself, Jesus used the same contrast to show how much more difficult life was for people, and therefore for Jesus himself, than it was for animals. The point and purpose of the saying, of course, is found among those who commit themselves

---

34 Smith, "No Place for a Son of Man," 84-86. Smith (p. 85) sees the Thomaean context purely in terms of human mortality. I have argued elsewhere, however, that *Thomas* is framed by means of an interlocutory structure (see B. D. Chilton, "The Gospel according to Thomas as a Source of Jesus' Teaching," in D. Wenham [ed.], *The Jesus Tradition outside the Gospels* [Gospel Perspectives 5; Sheffield: JSOT Press, 1985] 155-75, esp. 161). That structure makes discipleship the leading theme since §61b, so that I would not agree with Smith's description of "Thomas' haphazard logic," nor would I characterize the Thomaean context as radically different from the Synoptic context.

to the rootlessness of Jesus,[35] and to that extent the transition to the issue of authority and discipleship in the Synoptics is predictable. But the transformation of that performance in Matthew and Luke only makes sense if (a) "the son of the man" is taken christologically, and (b) rootlessness is related to discipleship in particular. In other words, their transformation of Jesus' aphorism, a generalizing—if somewhat cynical—epigram, is only tenable within the confessional and sociological environment of primitive Christianity.

The recovery of Jesus' performance, as an inference from the Gospels and within the Gospels, is perfectly practicable, provided certain criteria are observed. To justify a characterization as "performance," a saying must proceed from an initiating figure of literary history, such as Simeon or Jesus, and that speaker must use the language of his milieu distinctively. In the present instance, their statements about "(the) son of (the) man" must be mutually intelligible, as they indeed are, but not merely repetitious. The very existence of texts attests that significantly literary figures are held by the literatures which refer to them to say and do things which are understood to be notable. They say and do surprising things, which influence the perceived course of events and traditions, and neither the performers nor what they performed would be recalled otherwise. Of course, Jesus performed within early Judaism, as did Simeon; but neither can be reduced to a repetition of the other. And the irony is, that neither performance is accessible directly from a source of early Judaism, although both are located in tributaries thereof (Christianity and Rabbinic Judaism): Jesus' saying is conveyed in Gospels, Simeon's in Talmud and Midrash.

The particular innovation which lies to hand concerns "(the) son of (the) man," and the appearance that Jesus' usage is to be distinguished from Simeon's. That impression is strengthened when one takes into consideration Luke 12:8-9. It has already been observed that 12:6-7 are striking in their non-use of the idiom, at least when the story of Simeon is read comparatively. In vv. 8-9, however, that non-use becomes not only striking, but also seems to be part of a conscious understanding (within the present, Lukan context) of the meaning of the phrase. In the latter two verses, "the son of the man" is manifestly *not* a generic person, but an angelic figure, who is in a

---

35   See Casey, "The Jackals and the Son of Man," 10-13, 15.

position to muster the angels of the heavenly court.[36] Such a figure, of course, is reminscent of the one like a son of man in Dan 7:13; 10:16, 18; and *1 Enoch* 46:2-4; 48:2; 60:10; 62:5, 7, 9, 14; 69:27, 29; 71:17. The Danielic imagery is taken up within the New Testament, in order to refer to Jesus' future coming in an anticipated apocalypse, but within Daniel itself, the figure is essentially an agent of redemption and disclosure within the heavenly court.

Since the contribution of Rudolf Bultmann, the tendency has been to take Luke 12:8-9 as referring to an apocalyptic figure, expressed in language redolent of Daniel 7.[37] The transition Bultmann postulated was from Jesus' expectation of a distinct "messiah" to the belief of the early Church that Jesus spoke of his own *parousia*.[38] In his recent study of the influence of Daniel upon the New Testament, Maurice Casey[39] concludes that Jesus' use of "(the) son of (the) man," generically understood,[40] prompted the use of Daniel 7 as a reference to his *parousia*.[41] It may be accepted that Casey's redefinition of the Bultmannian consensus, chiefly in order better to account for the Aramaic evidence, is a satisfactory explanation of most types of idiom within the New Testament. The Jesus of literary history, as here characterized, would therefore speak generically, while his followers—after his resurrection—would construe his speech in reference to his present authority and/or his future coming

---

[36] See D. R. Catchpole, "The Angelic Son of Man in Luke 12:8," *NovT* 24 (1982) 255-65, esp. 260. Catchpole himself argues against a legal construction (pp. 256-50), but his remarks are too limited to philological concerns to be fully convincing. It is the son of the man's confession or denial before the angels of God which invokes the imagery of the divine court, not the usage of any particular words. See also F. H. Borsch, *The Christian and Gnostic Son of Man* (SBT 14; Naperville: Allenson, 1970) 16-18, and his exegetical and conceptual comments in *The Son of Man in Myth and History* (Philadelphia: Weswtminster, 1967) 353-64.

[37] See M. Black, "Jesus and the Son of Man," *JSNT* 1 (1978) 4-18, esp. 7.

[38] R. Bultmann, *The Theology of the New Testament* (New York: Scribner's, 1951) 26-32.

[39] See P. M. Casey, *Son of Man: The Interpretation and Influence of Daniel 7* (London: SPCK, 1979).

[40] See Mark 2:10, 28; Matt 8:20 = Luke 9:58; Matt 11:19 = Luke 7:34; Matt 12:32 = Luke 12:10; Luke 22:48; Mark 10:45; 14:21a-b; and (to a less straight-forward extent) Luke 12:8b; Mark 8:38; Mark 8:31 = 9:31 = 10:33-4.

[41] Casey, *Son of Man*, 234-35; cf. Mark 13:26; 14:62 and Mark 8:38; Matt 10:23; 16:26; 24:44 = Luke 12:40; Matt 25:31; Luke 18:8; and the review of W. O. Walker, in *JBL* 100 (1981) 643-45.

(as may be seen in the comparison between Luke 12:8 and Matt 10:32). Such a solution, although commendably neat, fails to account. for two sorts of evidence.

The first sort of evidence has already been indicated: the simple fact of the matter is that Jesus' use of "(the) son of (the) man," even when it is generic, is not to be understood, without qualification, as identical to that of Simeon ben Yohai. The dominical usage is both applied and not applied distinctively, in a manner which tends to emphasize the negative predicament of ordinary humanity, and of Jesus as one of its number.

The second sort of evidence, which casts doubt upon the consensus in its neatest form, is of quite a different nature. As the saying in Luke 12:8-9 stands, Jesus is presented as invoking "the son of the man" in the context of angelic advocacy. It fits neatly neither with those sayings which refer to Daniel 7 in a parousial construal, nor with those which are generic. Of course, it might be taken as simply invoking Jesus' authority as "the son of the man," and therefore classed as secondary; it is possible to avoid the manifest sense of the passage by collapsing the meaning of "the son of the man" into a merely Lukan designation of Jesus.[42] But if the community responsible for the formation sanguinely conceived of Jesus' authority as invoked by the use of the phrase, why should there be the added paraphernalia of the heavenly court? No matter whether Luke 12:8, 9 be seen as dominical or ecclesial, the odd phenomenon, so far unaccounted for, is the emphatically angelic aspect of the usage.

The reader of Daniel 7:13 is scarcely perplexed by the association of angelic imagery with the phrase *bar ʾenaša*.[43] One who is described as *kebar ʾenaš* is presented (by angels, presumably) to the ancient of days within the heavenly court. Daniel clearly identifies the agent of final judgment as being human, "one like a son of man" (Dan 7:13-14):

> I saw in visions of the night, and behold,
> with clouds of heaven one like a son of man was coming
> and he approached the Ancient of Days [that is, God himself],
> and they [the angels in the divine court] presented him before him.
> And to him was given dominion and glory and kingdom,

---

42   See D. R. A. Hare, *The Son of Man Tradition* (Minneapolis: Fortress, 1990) 62.

43   See Catchpole, "The Angelic Son of Man," 262-65.

that all peoples, nations, and languages should serve him;
his dominion is an everlasting dominion
   which shall not pass away,
and his kingdom one that shall not be destroyed.

Here, an angelic figure is said to be "like a son of man," in the sense
of "like a human being." The natural understanding of 10:16, 18
(which refer to the likeness and appearance of the "sons of man" and
of "man") would link that figure with the angelic interpreter of chap.
10, who struggles with the angel Michael on behalf of Daniel's
people (vv. 20-21; see vv. 12-14). Some modern critics have read
Daniel, and therefore those of Jesus' sayings which refer to Daniel,
as referring symbolically to a pattern of humiliation and exaltation
on the part of God's people.[44] That overtly literary apprehension
does no justice to the obviously angelic construal of the language in *1
Enoch*; 4 Ezra 13; and Rev 1:13; 14:14. Side by side with the generic
usage, an angelic reference is also possible.

Indeed, the generic usage and the angelic usage are complementary. *Kebar ʾenaš* in Daniel is no technical reference, or title, but a
descriptive designation of an unusual, human angel. This visionary
passage appears at the literary heart of the book of Daniel, and its
meaning is plain. The kingdoms of the lion, the bear, the leopard,
and the beast of the terrible horns are all to be removed (7:1-12).
(The probable reference is to the Assyrian, Babylonian, and Persian
empires, followed by the multiple "horns" of Alexander the Great

---

44   See C. F. D. Moule, *The Birth of the New Testament* (New York: Harper
& Row, 1962) 63. Moule elsewhere refers to such analysis as a "British school of
thought," "Neglected features in the problem of the Son of Man," in Moule, *Essays
in New Testament Interpretation* (Cambridge: Cambridge University Press, 1982)
75-90, 76-77, 79, 89. On pp. 80-81, Moule attempts to refute the angelic reading
here defended; he can only do so by taking chap. 7 in isolation from chap. 10. As a
matter of fact, Moule appears not to exclude an angelic reading completely later in
his article, when he states, "then it is also conceivable that he (sc. Jesus) applied it
(sc. the phrase) not only to some transcendental figure, but to his authority
wherever it was exercised in his capacity as the focus of God's dedicated people"
(p. 84). He explicitly proceeds to affirm that "on occasion, he used it, as *though* of
someone other than himself, when he wished to stress the ultimate, eschatological
character of the final vindication" (p. 84). A more adequate understanding of Daniel
7 in its literary and historical context would remove the italicized qualification: Jesus
sometimes used the phrase, not "as *though* of someone other," but simply as of
someone another.

and his successors.[45]) The one like a son of man, Israel's heavenly counterpart of the beasts, is alone to receive a kingdom which stands forever. After his vision, Daniel seeks interpretation from one of the angels in the heavenly court, "one of those who standing there" (Dan 7:16), constantly at the ready to serve the Ancient of Days. The angel was among those who had just presented the one like a son of man at the divine throne, and therefore was in an ideal position to know the significance of the vision. Daniel is told that the four beasts are four kings, and that when the son of man is presented to the ancient of days, "the saints of the most high shall receive the kingdom, and possess the kingdom for ever" (Dan 7:17-18).

Just as the visionary angels of the previous kingdoms are beasts, the visionary angel of the final kingdom is "one like a son of man." God's will is that he, the angelic figure in the heavenly court, is to be the guarantor of the rule of the saints of the most high. The final chapter of Daniel refers explicitly to the resurrection; the events unfold when the archangel Michael arises from his place in the heavenly court (Dan 12:1-3). As described in the book of Daniel, "one like a son of man" is clearly identified as the messianic and angelic redeemer of Israel, a truly heavenly redeemer known to Israel as the archangel Michael.

The image of the messianic and angelic son of man in Daniel was a powerful development within the eschatological hopes of early Judaism and Christianity. In the book of Enoch, the phrase "the son of man" is used, in order to refer to a prominent figure in the heavenly court, privileged in his position near the throne of God (see *1 Enoch* 46:1-4):

> At that place, I saw the one to whom belongs the time before time. And his head was white like wool, and there was before him another individual, whose face was like that of a human being. His countenance was full of grace like that of one among the holy angels. And I asked the one—from among the angels—who was going with me . . ., "Who is this . . . ?" And he answered me and said to me, "This is the son of man to whom belongs righteousness, and with whom righteousness dwells. And he will open all the hidden storerooms; for the Lord of the Spirits has chosen him, and he is destined to be victorious before the Lord of Spirits in eternal uprightness. This son of man whom you have seen is the one who will remove the kings and the mighty ones from their comfortable seats and the strong ones from their thrones.

---

[45]   See J. J. Collins, *Daniel* (Hermeneia; Minneapolis: Fortress, 1993).

Clearly, "the son of man" was a well known designation by the time
the book was composed. The reference was to the Son of Man whom
Daniel had spoken of, and the imagery of the passage in *1 Enoch* 46
simply develops what is already in Daniel 7. But it is not certain that
the usage is pre-Christian; the portion of the book of Enoch which is
concerned has not been found at Qumran (although other sections
have been) and may date from a period well after Jesus. Similarly,
the vision of "one like a son of man" in Rev 1:12-20 is a way of
depicting Jesus after his resurrection by speaking of his heavenly
status in terms borrowed from Daniel 7. But that obviously does not
prove how Jesus himself used the phrase. Still, a development of
usage which is best described as angelic seems evident.

The generic usage is the best background to presuppose in that
development. Moreover, it would greatly ease our appreciation of
the arthrous phrase, ὁ υἱὸς τοῦ ἀνθρώπου, in the Gospels, to see in
the definite article prior to υἱός (after which the second articular
usage follows naturally) that a reminiscence of a specific figure (not
a title) was in mind. To see the redundantly arthrous usage merely as
an echo of the determined state in Aramaic is problematic: why
should the article appear consistently, if an occasional mistranslation
is at issue?[46] Moule has suggested that the arthrous usage is a deliberate reminiscence of the Danielic figure: although his corporate
(rather than angelic) reading of that figure has been refuted here,
that Daniel's image is evoked by the arthrous usage[47] is far to be

---

[46]   See Casey, "Use of the Term 'Son of Man' in Aramaic Sources," 31-34.
He argues that some of the usages are the result of literal rendering, and others
introduce articles "to make clear that a particular person was referred to" (p. 32).
The consistency of the pattern, however, may be said to vitiate such inherently
probabilistic arguments.

[47]   See Moule, *Essays*, 77, 82-85, 89; and idem, *The Origin of Christology*
(Cambridge: Cambridge University Press, 1977) 14. To an extremely limited
extent, an analogy may be posited between a reference to Daniel 7 in "the son of
man" and the reference to Ezekiel 1 in the phrase "the chariot" and the reference to
Exodus 3 in the phrase "the bush." What limits such an analogy is that the rabbinic
phrases are generally used to refer to the passages, not figures in the passages. See
M. Jastrow, *A Dictionary of the Targumim, the Talmud Babli and Yerushalmi, and
the Midrashic Literature* (2 vols., New York: Pardes, 1950).
Another usage constitutes a closer analogy, in terms of both substance and
chronology, when the figure of a man in 4 Ezra 13 harkens back to Daniel 7,
without special qualification. The anarthrous usage (in the predicative position) in
John 5:27 may permit us to see that the phrase *bar ᵓenaša* alone, without

preferred to the weak explanation that somehow the determined state in Aramaic was misunderstood (by translators who, after all, proved themselves capable of meeting far greater challenges in the ordinary course of transmission). In other words, the arthrous usage, which has long been seen as at the center of the dilemma, may be taken to support the argument that *bar ʾenašaʾ* in Jesus' teaching is ordinarily generic, but sometimes angelic in application (as the specific link with Daniel would suggest). The angelic reference was formalized by the usage of the article in Greek during the course of transmission.

Generally speaking, scholarly discussion has tended to distinguish among three categories of the usage, "the son of the man," within the Gospels. Sayings of Jesus are viewed as referring to his present authority (as a special envoy or as a human being),[48] to his suffering,[49] and/or to his advent as an eschatological judge.[50] Reliance upon an Aramaic approach to the phrase has helped us to see that there is a sense in which the phrase might be used generically, and that has enriched our understanding of Jesus as presented within the Gospels.

A more comprehensively Aramaic approach would help us to see that Jesus is also distinctive in his non-use of the phrase, a non-use which reinforces the innovation of placing, side by side with the

---

specifically Danielic associations, might have referred to an agent of angelic judgment under some circumstances. But the more common, arthrous usage is more plausibly taken as a conscious, titular reference to Dan 7:13 (which—taken in itself, outside the Danielic context—is not titular; see Fitzmyer, "Another View of the 'Son of Man' Debate," 154-55).

[48]   A list might include Matt 8:20 = Luke 9:58; Matt 9:6 = Mark 2:10 = Luke 5:24; Luke 6:22; Matt 11:19 = Luke 7:34; Matt 12:8 = Mark 2:28 = Luke 6:5; Luke 9:56; Matt 12:32 = Luke 12:10; Matt 12:40 = Luke 11:30; Matt 13:37; Matt 16:13; Matt 17:9 = Mark 9:9; Matt 18:11 = Luke 19:10; Matt 20:28 = Mark 10:45. For an argument for a wider understanding of the category, somewhat as is also reflected here, see C. Tuckett, "The Present Son of Man," *JSNT* 14 (1982) 58-81.

[49]   A list might include Mark 8:31 = Luke 9:22; Matt 17:12 = Mark 9:12; Matt 17:22-23 = Mark 9:31 = Luke 9:44; Matt 20:18-19 = Mark 10:33-34 = Luke 18:31-33; Matt 26:2; Matt 26:24 = Mark 14:21 = Luke 22:22; Luke 22:48; Matt 26:45 = Mark 14:41; Luke 24:7.

[50]   A list might include Matt 10:23; 13:41; 16:27-28; Mark 8:38 = Luke 9:26; Luke 12:8; 17:22; Matt 24:27 = Luke 17:24; Luke 18:8; Matt 24:30-31 = Mark 13:26-27 = Luke 21:27; Luke 21:36; Matt 24:37 = Luke 17:26; Matt 24:39 = Luke 17:30; Matt 24:44 = Luke 12:40; Matt 25:31; Matt 26:64 = Mark 14:62 = Luke 22:69.

generic meaning, reference to "(the) son of (the) man" as an angel of advocacy in the divine court. These two dominical performances of meaning have fed the construals which resulted in three sorts of usage in the Gospels. The texts as they lie to hand, of course, thoroughly represent that transformation which is characteristic of the Synoptic catechesis, but relatively few usages appear purely christological.[51] More usually, the sayings of Jesus reflect a generic *bar ʾenaša*,[52] its angelic analogue,[53] and possibly both.[54] It is a matter of course that the present categories are provisional, since they evolve out of a somewhat fresh perspective of analysis.

The present discussion has been anticipated by previous work in regard to a hypothesis of angelic meaning.[55] But the present suggestion would posit that the literarily historical Jesus performed sayings in which *bar ʾenaša* features as a generic and/or angelic reference.[56] The angelic reference is predicated upon the understanding of a close analogy between people and angels, which is well established within the Hebrew Scriptures (see Genesis 18; Josh 5:13, 14; Judg 13:2-20; Zech 1:7-11), and is still discernible in Matt 9:6 = Mark 2:10 = Luke 5:24; Matt 16:27 = Mark 8:38 = Luke 9:26; Luke 12:8; Matt 19:28;

---

[51] So Luke, perhaps, 6:22 (if it is not generic); 9:56; Matt 12:40 = Luke 11:30; Matt 13:37; Matt 16:13; Matt 17:9 = Mark 9:9; Matt 18:11 = Luke 19:10.

[52] See Matt 8:20 = Luke 9:58; Matt 11:19 = Luke 7:34; Mark 8:31 = Luke 9:22; Matt 17:12 = Mark 9:12; Matt 17:22-23 = Mark 9:31 = Luke 9:44; Matt 20:18-19 = Mark 10:33-34 = Luke 18:31-33; Matt 20:28 = Mark 10:34; Matt 26:2; Matt 26:24 = Mark 14:21 = Luke 22:22; Luke 22:48; Matt 26:45 = Mark 14:41; Luke 24:7.

[53] Matt 9:6 = Mark 2:10 = Luke 5:24; Matt 10:23; 13:41; Mark 8:38 = Luke 9:26; Matt 16:27-28; Luke 12:8; Matt 19:28; Luke 17:22; Matt 24:27 = Luke 17:24; Luke 18:8; Matt 24:30-31 = Mark 13:26-27 = Luke 21:27; Luke 21:36; Matt 24:37 = Luke 17:26; Matt 24:39 = Luke 17:30; Matt 24:44 = Luke 12:40; Matt 25:31; Matt 26:64 = Mark 14:62 = Luke 22:69.

[54] See Matt 12:8 = Mark 2:28 = Luke 6:5; Matt 12:32 = Luke 12:10.

[55] Catchpole ("The Angelic Son of Man in Luke 12:8," 260) refers to Luke 12:8-9 and Matt 18:10 by way of support, and cites Tobit 12:15; *1 Enoch* 104:1; Luke 1:19 as "an individualizing of the old idea of an angelic ruler for each nation" (see Dan 10:12; 12:1; Sir 17:17). On p. 261, he argues that his reading "dovetails" with Matt 24:27, 37, 39 = Luke 17:24, 26, 30; Matt 25:31-46. The thesis of an angelic meaning might also illuminate Acts 7:56 (see P. Doble, "The Son of Man Saying in Stephen's Witnessing," *NTS* 31 [1985] 68-84, esp. 83, although Doble presupposes an identification with Jesus), and—of course—John 1:51.

[56] Again, see Borsch, *The Son of Man in Myth and History*, 360.

25:31; Matt 26:64 = Mark 14:62 = Luke 22:69; John 1:51; Acts 7:56. Subsequently, both types of reference were transformed within the literary construals of the Synoptic Gospels, so that "the son of the man" referred to Jesus as the disciples' authority, their paradigm of suffering, and eschatological judge.

CONCLUSIONS

Taken in aggregate, the evidence of Daniel, Enoch, and the Revelation of John demonstrates the hope that God's final judgment would be accomplished with "one like a son of man." Just such a figure of final judgment (commonly and rightly rendered, "the son of man") is in view when Jesus warns his hearers in a well-known saying (Mark 8:38):

> Whoever is ashamed of me and of my words in this adulterous and sinful generation, the Son of Man will be ashamed of him, when he comes in his father's glory with his holy angels.

That saying appears in Mark, and likely derives from the tradition of Peter, which was shaped into the form of gospel by the time Peter met Paul in the year 35 CE (so Gal 1:18-20). That early attestation of the saying is joined by the source of Jesus' sayings known as "Q," which was circulating in Aramaic at the same time. "Q" presents a similar (but distinct) form of the saying which has already been considered (best represented in Luke 12:8-9, but also reflected in a different form in Matt 10:32-33). Here Jesus himself picks up the image of the Son of Man as found in the book of Daniel. That Son of Man, he says, will finally and definitively insist upon the truth of Jesus' own teaching. The saying is attested in the three Synoptic Gospels, in sources which take us back to within a few years of the crucifixion and resurrection of Jesus.[57]

The only possible argument against accepting the authenticity of the saying is that Jesus can not have claimed so much authority for himself. A publication of the "Jesus Seminar" makes that assumption:

> The identification of Jesus with the son of Adam almost certainly excludes the possibility of tracing this saying back to Jesus.[58]

---

[57]   On identifying and dating these cycles of tradition, see B. D. Chilton, *A Feast of Meanings: Eucharistic Theologies from Jesus through Johannine Circles* (NovTSup 72; Leiden: Brill, 1994) 146-58.

[58]   See Funk and Hoover (eds.), *The Five Gospels*, 80.

In other words, a preconceived view of what Jesus could have said about himself has determined the judgment of what he did say about himself. Several of us who have participated in the "Jesus Seminar," although we have appreciated the experience, have criticized our colleagues for voting along what seem to be ideological lines. Historical judgments should be based upon an analysis of how traditions concerning Jesus developed, not on global assumptions regarding what he should have said or could have said. A much more likely historical finding is that Jesus himself referred to the Son of Man of Daniel 7, and that the memory of that reference echoes through our sources.

The question really is not *whether* there is a reference to Daniel 7 within some of Jesus' sayings concerning the Son of Man, but rather: what does the reference mean? Rudolf Bultmann called attention to the fact that, in Mark 8:38, Jesus refers to himself and to the Son of Man as distinct figures. It was his idea (already discussed) that Jesus referred to the Son of Man of Daniel 7 as the divine confirmation of his teaching by a heavenly figure, the Danielic "one like a son of man." What we have proposed here is a change of key in Bultmann's proposal: the Danielic Son of Man is angelic, rather than apocalyptic (in the strictly futuristic sense of "apocalyptic" in Bultmann's suggestion). When Jesus refers to the Son of Man, he does not only have himself in mind, but is also thinking of the figure in the heavenly court described in Daniel. That Son of Man, Jesus said many times, would vindicate his teaching.

There is not doubt but that Jesus did use the Aramaic idiom, "son of man," in its usual, generic sense, as may be seen from our analysis of Luke 9:58; Matt 8:20; *Thomas* §86):

Foxes have dens and birds their nests:
only man has nowhere to lay his head.

The saying applies in context, not simply to Jesus (as a circumlocution would), but to homeless disciples generally, and it carries with it a resonant sympathy for homeless people as a whole. "The son of man" here can not mean "me, myself, I: and no one else." Others are included with the speaker, as in Ps 8:4.

At least, we can now suggest that a proper understanding of Aramaic usage links Jesus' experience with the experience of those who would follow him. That would explain one of the recognized categories of the usage of the phrase in the Gospels: the treatment of the Son of Man, and his suffering. But after so many years of intense discussion, that seems scant progress. The crucial point is: how can. we understand both the generic and the angelic/messianic meanings of "the Son of Man?"

The solution is to be found by becoming more precise than much discussion has been. Jesus is actually not quoted as referring to "son of man" in general, but to "the Son of the Man." Although the usage has sometimes been described as barbaric, it is in fact straightforward Greek. C. F. D. Moule, one of the finest exegetes and grammarians of the New Testament which Great Britain has produced this century, has pointed out that specifying "the Son of Man" simply refers to a well known usage of the phrase.[59] The phrase "the Son of Man" works much the way we say "the White House": in theory, there might be many sons of men and white houses, but only the one White House, the one Son of Man is at issue.

"The Son of Man" at issue must be the figure of Daniel 7, Israel's advocate in the heavenly court, the angel identified later in the book as Michael. Jesus' reference to the Son of Man, insistently with the word "the," indicates that the angelic figure of Danielic usage was very much a part of his own idiom. There is no reasonable way of denying that Jesus spoke of the Son of Man in this way.

But the angelic/messianic reference of the Son of the Man does not easily explain Jesus' generic usages of the phrase. The old dilemma has returned to haunt us: one solution takes account of a messianic meaning, and leaves the generic aspect unexplained, while another solution reduces the generic sayings to banal truisms, while dismissing messianic sayings as Christian inventions. If one of these solutions (or their many variations) could claim to accord with the history of the evolution of the traditions within the Gospels, that would lend it some support. But both the usages are early (as we have seen), and both die out of frequent usage after the period of the New Testament. Simply put: it seems Jesus was smart enough to use the phrase in both ways, and scholars have not yet figured out how to put the two together.

For most of critical scholarship, Jesus is a rational teacher, who wished to convey a single, prosaic meaning. The current debate is between "conservatives" who want to see the Son of Man as only messianic and "liberals" who want to see him as only generic. In fact,

---

[59]   See Moule, "Neglected Features," 75-90.

both adhere to the nineteenth century, liberal presupposition of rationality as the primary motivation in human affairs. Their disagreement is a side-show, compared to the basic question: can we understand Jesus at all, if we make the liberal assumption that he was rational by our standards of rationality? The sayings concerning the Son of Man answer that question clearly and unequivocally. We simply can not understand them if we assume Jesus' meaning was prosaic.

The passage in John 12:34, where the crowd expresses its exasperation (and perhaps ours), actually points to the need to see Jesus' usage as more than prosaic. When Jesus speaks of the exaltation of the Son of Man, the crowd replies impatiently:

> We have heard from the law that the messiah lives forever, and how do you say that the Son of the Man must be exalted? Who is this, the Son of the Man?

They understand "messiah" and they understand "Son of Man," and *for that reason* they do not understand the messianic Son of Man. John's Gospel is here showing us what is difficult to grasp about the Son of Man, and how to get over our confusion. The crowd assumes (as do liberal critics) that the Son of Man must be either generic or messianic, while Jesus uses the phrase in both those dimensions. He operates in the realm of poetry, not of prose.

Jesus was a master of the parable, the comparison (*matlaᶜ* in Aramaic). Comparative speech was his particular strength; he could portray the kingdom of God in terms of growing seed, a woman making bread, or a merchant out to close an attractive deal. The point of his parables was that you could understand the kingdom in terms of such realities, and that such ordinary activities found their true meanings in the reality of the kingdom. Jesus' characteristic activity was to eat with people, and those meals were themselves enacted parables: celebrations of the festivity of the kingdom of God. Basic human activities were intimately connected with the ultimate kingdom of God: that was the theme of Jesus' ministry, and he defined the purity of Israel in terms of people's readiness to respond to the opportunities of the kingdom.

If we appreciate that Jesus genuinely related his own activity and the activities of those around him to the kingdom of God, then we are in a position to appreciate his sayings concerning the Son of the Man. Who can have insight into the ways of the divine king, seated

upon his heavenly throne? To anyone who took Daniel 7 seriously as
a depiction of that throne, the answer would be that the Son of the
Man of that vision provides access to the mystery of the divine
kingship. When Jesus preached that the kingdom of God was
celebrated by his ministry, he claimed to have an insight into the
ways of heaven. That insight, Jesus went on to claim, is to be
warranted by the Son of the Man in heaven, "when he comes in his
father's glory with his holy angels" (Mark 8:38). He and that Son of
Man together were the agents of God's final intervention in human
affairs.

Because Jesus, a son of man on earth, saw himself as paired with
the Danielic Son of Man in heaven, there is a sliding scale of
reference. Sometimes he thinks more of the one, at other times more
of the other. This combined, poetic usage is Jesus' own invention: the
Son of the Man as human and heavenly. Sometimes Jesus referred
more to himself as the Son of Man, as when he complained that he
(and others, including his followers) had no place to lodge, while
foxes and birds did. At other times, he referred more to the majesty
of the Danielic vision, when he thought of the final judgment in
which the Son of the Man was to be the agent. But at every point, the
two references illuminated one another, because the Son of Man was
for Jesus both human and heavenly. The reality of the kingdom was
attested in heaven and on earth, in both cases by the Son of Man.

When Jesus is permitted to cease being a rational teacher of
reasonable truth, and to become the paradoxical, poetic rabbi he
more truly was, his message becomes clearer. His teaching is more
challenging when it is so understood, and it may be unbelievable to
many people, but it is none the less clearer within its historical
context. Jesus asserted that God was acting as king, and he implicitly
claimed that he alone knew how. His teaching and his activity were
designed to make his announcement concerning the kingdom as
public as possible. That desire to act in public on behalf of the
kingdom is what caused Jesus to send his disciples out in his name
and to challenge conventional worship in the Temple, the aspects of
his ministry which seems to make him unlike other rabbis of his
period.[60]

Jesus' reference to "the Son of the Man" makes explicit what his

---

[60]   See B. D. Chilton, *Pure Kingdom: Jesus' Vision of God* (Studying the
Historical Jesus 1; Eerdmans: Grand Rapids; London: SPCK, 1996).

preaching about the kingdom of God always implied. He claimed that he, a person (a *bar ʾenaša*ʾ) like any other, enjoyed access to the heavenly court through the angelic figure who was like a person (*kebar ʾenaša*ʾ). The Son of Man of Daniel 7 confirmed the words of the Son of Man who spoke to his disciples. Jesus' claim was not that he was identical with the Son of Man, but that he was intimate with the Son of Man. It was a claim which was no more and no less audacious than his assertion that the kingdom of God had arrived with his ministry. The Jesus of history is not what the old liberalism would desire, a skilled interpreter of timeless truth, but a demanding poet, seized by a prophetic vision which overcame him and those around him with its power.

The two themes, the kingdom of God and the Son of Man, imply one another. The kingdom is the public theme of Jesus' ministry, what was spoken of openly and fully to anyone who would hear. The Son of Man was the esoteric theme, the explanation to those who responded to the message of the kingdom of how Jesus could know what he did. Many rabbis spoke of the visionary reality of God's throne, which they usually referred to as the "chariot," in the manner of Ezekiel 1.[61] The vision of Daniel 7 is in part inspired by the passage in Ezekiel, which even speaks of a human appearance with the throne (Ezek 1:26). Jesus claimed that access to the heavenly Son of Man gave him, as human Son of Man, the insight which he displayed into the throne of God.

Jesus offered his contemporaries new insight into God as king, on the basis that his teaching concerning the kingdom would be confirmed by the Son of the Man in heaven. That special relationship between Jesus and the Son of the Man permeates Jesus' teaching, and helps to account for the large number of sayings concerning the Son of the Man in the Gospels.

Of course, the insight into heaven which Jesus taught was not just a repetition of what any rabbi might have taught. His teaching about the kingdom of God and the Son the Man was distinctive. He explained why he knew about such matters, while other rabbis did not (Matt 11:27; Luke 10:22):

Everything has been entrusted to me by my Father, and nobody is familiar

---

61   See M. Idel, *Kabbalah: New Perspectives* (New Haven: Yale University Press, 1988); E. R. Wolfson, *Through a speculum that shines: Vision and Imagination in Medieval Jewish Mysticism* (Princeton: Princeton Univeristy Press, 1994).

with the Son except the Father, and nobody is familiar with the Father
except the Son, and the one to whom the Son chooses to reveal him.

This "Son" knows about the kingdom of God and is specially
associated with the Son of Man who sits by the throne of God. This
"Son" is uniquely related to God on the basis of what the Father
reveals to him: he is the Son of God by virtue of that revelation.
Jesus' claim to divine Sonship is part and parcel of his teaching
concerning the kingdom of God and the Son of the Man.

Jesus' death grievously disappointed the hopes of those who
responded to his message of the kingdom. But the disappointment
was momentary for some of them. The resurrection produced a
conviction among the disciples that Jesus was alive, that he had been
vindicated by God. He had been exalted to the heavenly throne of
which he had spoken.

An early authority who was crucial in the development of that
conviction was James, Jesus' brother. He was a key witness of the
risen Jesus according to the testimony of Paul, the earliest writer to
speak of Jesus' resurrection (see 1 Cor 15:7). The New Testament
itself does not record an appearance to James, but the *Gospel to the
Hebrews* does. There, Jesus assures his brother that "the Son of the
Man has been raised from among those who sleep."[62] The authority
of James, it seems, was a key force in the complete identification
between Jesus and the figure of Daniel 7 after the resurrection. Once
that identification was made, it was natural for Jesus' own sayings to
be recast to speak consistently of his own authority, of his own
treatment and suffering, of his own vindication. But his original,

---

[62] Cited by Jerome, *Liber de Viris Illustribus* 2. It is notable that, in his treatment
of James, Jerome cites the *Gospel according to the Hebrews* alongside the New
Testament, Hegesippus, and Josephus. Because he valued it (as did Origen, he
says), he translated it into Greek and Latin. See also E. Hennecke, *New Testament
Apocrypha* (ed. W. Schneemelcher; London: SCM Press, 1963) 165. The passage
as a whole is worth considering:

*Dominus autem cum dedisset sindonem servo sacerdotis, ivit ad Jacobum et
apparuit ei. Juraverat enim Jacobus se non comesturum panem ad illa hora quia
biberat calicem Domini, donc videret cum resurgentem a dormientibus. Rursusque
post paululum: Afferte, ait Dominus, mensam et panem. Statimque additur: Tulit
panem et benedixit ac fregit, et dedit Jacobo Justo et dixit et: Frater, comede panem
tuum, quia resurexit filius hominis a dormientibus.*

See J. Martianaie, *Sancti Eusebii Hieronymi 2* (Patrologiae Latinae 23; Paris:
Garnier, 1883) 641-44.

parabolic speech still shines through the texts as they have been received.

The challenge of understanding the Gospels involves making reasoned inferences in regard to the teaching of Jesus and the interpretations of his first followers. By tracing them, we can understand how meanings interweaved with one another, in order to generate the texts which are open before us. The fabric of the Gospels was produced by the distinctive faiths of those who were involved in composing them. "The Son of the Man" is a thread which starts with Jesus: originally, Jesus developed an intriguing juxtaposition between his own humanity and the heavenly person at God's right hand. Woven together with the faith in Jesus' resurrection, the fabric of the Gospels presents Jesus' himself as that heavenly figure, the messianic agent of final vindication.

Q 12:51-53 AND MARK 9:11-13 AND THE MESSIANIC WOES

Dale C. Allison, Jr.

It is the purpose of this essay to establish that both Q 12:51-53 and Mark 9:11-13 rest upon things Jesus said. I shall begin by seeking the earliest obtainable form and wording of Q 12:51-53. Next, an interpretation of that form and wording will be offered. Thirdly, the fundamental content of Q 12:51-53 will be traced back to Jesus himself. Finally, a comparison of Q 12:51-53 with Mark 9:11-13 will reveal that if the former preserves teaching of Jesus, so almost certainly does the latter.

THE TEXT OF Q 12:51-53

Both Matt 10:34-36 and Luke 12:51-53 consist of three main parts. Each opens with a denial that Jesus has brought peace on the earth, follows with an affirmation that he has instead brought a sword (Matthew) or division (Luke), and concludes with a paraphrase of Mic 7:6. Within this general agreement, however, are numerous differences in wording. These should be set down to the evangelists' alterations of Q.

The opening denial. Matthew has Jesus open with an imperative: "Think not that I have come (μὴ νομίσητε ὅτι ἦλθον) to cast peace on the earth" (βαλεῖν εἰρήνην ἐπὶ τὴν γῆν). In Luke we find a question: "Do you think that I have come (δοκεῖτε ὅτι . . . παρεγεν-όμην) to bring peace on the earth (εἰρήνην . . . δοῦναι ἐν τῇ γῇ)?" Because it was Matthew's tendency to eliminate questions from Jesus' speech[1] and because there is no evidence that it was Luke's wont to create them,[2] the interrogatory form is likely to be original. Further, Matthew's μὴ νομίσητε is probably editorial, for the redactional 5:17 opens the same way.[3] But δοκέω[4] + ὅτι[5] is without parallel all

---

[1]   The questions in Mark 5:9, 30; 6:38; 8:12, 23; 9:12, 16, 21, 33; 10:3; and 14:14 have all been omitted or altered.

[2]   H. J. Cadbury, *The Style and Literary Method of Luke* (Cambridge: Harvard University Press, 1920) 81-82.

[3]   It remains possible, however, that Q 12:51 (in Matthew's form) was the

four times it appears in Luke and is obviously redactional in 19:11, so on the matter of the opening verb we cannot reach a firm verdict.

For the rest Matthew is probably closer to Q than Luke. For παραγίνομαι[6] is a Lukan favorite, and εἰρήνην δοῦναι instead of Matthew's βαλεῖν εἰρήνην and δίδωμι + ἐν[7] for βαλεῖν ἐπί are editorial improvements.[8] Moreover, Luke 12:49 (ἦλθον βαλεῖν ἐπὶ τὴν γῆν), which comes right before 12:51, is the perfect parallel to Matthew's expression. Whether or not Luke 12:49 stood in Q (a debated issue; it has no synoptic parallel), the verse shows knowledge of the form of expression in Matthew, and it helps account for some of Luke's changes in 12:51: the evangelist did not like the mechanical repetition of Semitic parallelism.[9] One is, then, led to suppose that Q 12:51 opened with something close to the following question: δοκεῖτε (?) ὅτι ἦλθον βαλεῖν εἰρήνην ἐπὶ τὴν γῆν;[10]

The affirmation. Does Matt 10:34b (οὐκ ἦλθον βαλεῖν εἰρήνην ἀλλὰ μάχαιραν) or Luke 12:51b (οὐχί, λέγω ὑμῖν, ἀλλ' ἢ διαμερισμόν) bring us closer to Q? Matthew's fondness for parallelism[11] might have led him to make the second clause resemble the first. The parallel in 5:17 points in this direction, for here Matthew follows μὴ νομίσητε ὅτι ἦλθον καταλῦσαι with οὐκ ἦλθον καταλῦσαι ἀλλά. On the other hand, οὐχί . . . ἀλλ' is on J. C. Hawkins' list of Lukanisms,[12] and commentators are generally agreed that Luke's "division" is a softening of Matthew's more difficult "sword."[13] Did Q have (λέγω ὑμῖν) οὐκ εἰρήνην ἀλλὰ μάχαιραν?

---

model for Matt 5:17.

[4]   Which appears elsewhere in Q: Matt 24:44 = Luke 12:40.

[5]   Matthew: 2; Mark: 1; Luke: 4 (three times in questions).

[6]   Matthew: 3; Mark: 1; Luke: 8; Acts: 20.

[7]   Matthew: 0; Mark: 0; Luke: 1; Acts: 2.

[8]   Cf. Cadbury, *Style* 183.

[9]   Cadbury, *Style*, 83-89.

[10]   Cf. the text of the International Q Project: *JBL* 113 (1994) 499.

[11]   W. D. Davies and D. C. Allison, Jr., *A Critical and Exegetical Commentary on the Gospel according to Saint Matthew* (3 vols., ICC; Edinburgh: T. & T. Clark, 1988-97) 1.94-95.

[12]   J. C. Hawkins, *Horae Synopticae*, 2nd ed. (Oxford: Clarendon, 1909) 21, 45. Cf. 13:2-3 and 4-5, where it twice follows δοκεῖτε ὅτι.

[13]   G. W. H. Lampe, "The Two Swords (Luke 22:35-38)," in E. Bammel and C. F. D. Moule (eds.), *Jesus and the Politics of his Day* (Cambridge: Cambridge University Press, 1984) 338. Although διαμερισμός is a Lukan *hapax*, Luke is fond of the verb διαμερίζω (Matthew: 1; Mark: 1; Luke: 6; Acts: 2).

The paraphrase of Scripture. Matt 10:35-36 and Luke 12:52-53 agree in taking up Mic 7:6, but in different ways.

Micah MT

כי

בן מנבל אב

בת קמה באמה

כלה בחמתה

איבי איש אנשי ביתו

Micah LXX

διότι

υἱὸς ἀτιμάζει πατέρα

θυγάτηρ ἐπαναστήσεται ἐπὶ τὴν μητέρα αὐτῆς

νύμφη ἐπὶ τὴν πενθερὰν αὐτῆς

ἐχθροὶ ἀνδρὸς πάντες οἱ ἄνδρες οἱ ἐν τῷ οἴκῳ αὐτοῦ

Matthew

ἦλθον γὰρ διχάσαι

ἄνθρωπον κατὰ τοῦ πατρὸς αὐτοῦ

καὶ θυγατέρα κατὰ τῆς μητρὸς αὐτῆς

καὶ νύμφην κατὰ τῆς πενθερᾶς αὐτῆς

καὶ ἐχθροὶ τοῦ ἀνθρώπου οἱ οἰκιακοὶ αὐτοῦ

Luke

ἔσονται γὰρ ἀπὸ τοῦ νῦν πέντε ἐν ἑνὶ οἴκῳ διαμεμερισμένοι

τρεῖς ἐπὶ δυσὶν καὶ δύο ἐπὶ τρισίν

διαμερισθήσονται πατὴρ ἐπὶ υἱῷ καὶ υἱὸς ἐπὶ πατρί

μήτηρ ἐπὶ τὴν θυγατέρα καὶ θυγάτηρ ἐπὶ τὴν μητέρα

πενθερὰ ἐπὶ τὴν νύμφην αὐτῆς καὶ νύμφη ἐπὶ τὴν πενθεράν

Regarding Matthew's text, διχάσαι is not his because διχάζω is a Matthean *hapax legomenon* and because in Q the word formed a catchword link with Q 12:46 (διχοτομήσει). But, beyond this, one suspects the evangelist's hand has been quite active. For, as compared with Luke, his shorter text—shorter despite the addition of a whole line[14]—is closer to Mic 7:6 in several respects, and it was Matthew's habit both to abbreviate[15] and to assimilate Gospel texts to the Tanak.[16] Matthew's agreements with Malachi over against Luke are

---

14   Matthew has twenty-seven words, Luke forty-four.

15   W. C. Allen, *A Critical and Exegetical Commentary on the Gospel according to S. Matthew*, ICC, 3rd ed. (Edinburgh: T. & T. Clark, 1977) xvii-xix.

16   R. H. Gundry, *The Use of the Old Testament in St. Matthew's Gospel*

four. (i) Luke 12:52, which has no parallel in Micah, also has no Matthean parallel (and would in any case be redundant in view of Matthew's conclusion). (ii) Luke's chiastic structures are missing from Mic 7:6 as well as Matthew. (iii) Matthew's αὐτῆς (*bis*) matches Mic 7:6 LXX. (iv) Matthew's concluding line (with its verbal link to 10:24-25—οἰκιακούς/οἰκιακοί) is from Micah.

Luke's text, as compared with Matthew, is distinguished by three particulars. First, v. 52 is without parallel.[17] Secondly, the entire unit features chiasmus—three against two and two against three, father against son and son against father, etc. Thirdly, in two minor respects Luke is closer to the LXX (υἱός instead of ἄνθρωπον and ἐπί instead of κατά). The increased nearness to the LXX might be put down to Luke's hand, for he sometimes conforms to that source.[18] It is, however, slightly more probable that Matthew substituted ἄνθρωπον (a word he is fond of) to create an *inclusio* with the end of his redactional v. 36,[19] and that he substituted κατά for ἐπί, as in 12:25 diff. Mark 3:24-25.[20] On the other hand, there are signs of Lukan activity in v. 52, for the verse uses the editorial διαμεμερισμένοι (cf. v. 51 diff. Matt 10:34), and the periphrastic conjugation (here ἔσονται . . . διαμεμερισμένοι) is often Lukan.[21] Further, the statistics on ἀπὸ τοῦ νῦν—Matthew: 0; Mark: 0; Luke: 5; Acts: 1—are telling.

What about the chiastic structures? Joachim Jeremias attributes the chiasmus in v. 53 to Luke's hand.[22] But he offers no justification; and while it is true that Luke does use chiasmus to order large units,[23] one can cite no evidence that he did this with small units.

(NovTSup 18; Leiden: Brill, 1967).

[17] And so many, including S. Schulz, *Q. Die Spruchquelle der Evangelisten* (Zürich: Theologischer Verlag, 1972) 258-59, and the International Q Project, do not assign it to Q.

[18] On Luke's use of the LXX see T. Holtz, *Untersuchungen über die alttestamentliche Zitate bei Lukas* (Berlin: de Gruyter, 1968).

[19] R. H. Gundry, *Matthew: A Commentary on his Literary and Theological Art* (Grand Rapids: Eerdmans, 1982) 199; Alexander Sand, *Das Evangelium nach Matthäus* (RNT; Regensburg: Pustet, 1986) 231.

[20] Cf. also Matt 12:32 diff. Luke 12:10.

[21] J. A. Fitzmyer, *The Gospel according to Luke* (2 vols., AB 28; Garden City: Doubleday, 1981-85) 1.122-23.

[22] J. Jeremias, *Die Sprache des Lukasevangeliums* (MeyerK; Göttingen: Vandenhoeck & Ruprecht, 1980) 224.

[23] C. H. Talbert, *Literary Patterns, Theological Themes and the Genre of*

Further, there is another consideration which, to my knowledge, has heretofore escaped notice.

Luke's chiastic pattern has its parallel in non-Christian paraphrases of Mic 7:6. For example, the allusion in *b. Sanh.* 97a takes this form:

> the young will shame the old
> and the old will rise up before the young
> daughter will rise up against her mother
> daughter-in-law will rise up against her mother-in-law.[24]

Mishnah *Soṭa* 9:15 offers something very similar:

> the young will shame the old
> and the old will rise up before the young
> for the son dishonors the father
> the daughter rises up against her mother
> the daughter-in-law against her mother-in-law
> and a man's enemies are the men of his own house.

As we shall see below, both *b. Sanh.* 97a and *m. Soṭa* 9:15, like Q 12:51-53, use Mic 7:6 to depict the tribulations of the latter days. All this would be interesting enough, but it is all the more intriguing because still earlier, in *Jub.* 23:19, the depiction of the eschatological tribulation includes this line: "Some of these will strive with others, youths with old men and old men with youths." While there is no clear verbal contact with Mic 7:6, the parallel with the rabbinic texts is striking. Here again we find, in a portrait of the latter days, a chiastic line concerning conflict between young and old and old and young. The same is true of *Sib. Or.* 8:84 ("Neither will parents be friendly to children nor children to parents") and the Armenian of 4 Ezra 5:9 ("And men shall fight with one another, sons with fathers and fathers with sons, mothers and daughters opposed to one another . . .").[25] When one finds the very same thing in Luke, coincidence cannot be the explanation. We obviously have here a traditional motif: a chiastic line about conflict between young and old was repeatedly used to depict one aspect of eschatological strife, and sometimes (as in Q 12:51-53; 4 Ezra 5:9 arm; *m. Soṭa* 9:15; and *b. Sanh.* 97a) such a line was linked with a citation of or allusion to Mic 7:6.

Luke-Acts (SBLMS 20; Missoula: Scholars Press, 1974) 51-65.

[24]   Cf. the paraphrases in *Pesiq. R.* 15.14/15; *Pesiq. Rab. Kah.* 5:9; and *Song of Songs Rab.* 2:13 §4.

[25]   See M. E. Stone, *Fourth Ezra* (Hermeneia; Minneapolis: Fortress, 1990) 113. This alludes to Mic 7:6.

The analysis of Matt 10:34-36 and Luke 12:51-53 indicates that Q included something close to the following:

(ἔσονται?/εἰσιν?)[26] πέντε ἐν ἑνὶ οἴκῳ
τρεῖς ἐπὶ δυσὶν καὶ δύο ἐπὶ τρισίν
ἦλθον γὰρ διχάσαι
πατὴρ ἐπὶ υἱῷ καὶ υἱὸς ἐπὶ πατρί
μήτηρ ἐπὶ τὴν θυγατέρα καὶ θυγάτηρ ἐπὶ τὴν μητέρα
πενθερὰ ἐπὶ τὴν νύμφην αὐτῆς καὶ νύμφη ἐπὶ τὴν πενθεράν

This analysis gains support from Mark 13:12: "And brother will deliver brother up to death, and the father his child, and children will rise against parents and have them put to death." The verb translated "rise against" is ἐπαναστήσονται. Commentators regularly regard this as an allusion to Mic 7:6 LXX, where ἐπαναστήσεται is used.[27] But the dependence upon Mic 7:6 runs deeper, for, as Lars Hartman saw, Mark's ἐπαναστήσεται is preceded and followed by themes that appear in the targum on Mic 7:6. Whereas the targum has "a man delivers up his brother to destruction" and ends with "those who hate a man are the men of his own house," Mark 13:12 opens with a reference to brother being delivered over, and Mark 13:13 announces that disciples will be hated. It is further no accident that whereas in Mark 13:13b we read that "the one enduring (ὑπομείνας) unto the end will be saved (σωθήσεται)," in Mic 7:7 the prophet declares, "I will wait (LXX: ὑπομενῶ) on the God of my salvation (σωτῆρι)." Obviously Mark's verse takes up exegetical traditions attached to Mic 7:6.[28]

---

26 Given that Luke 12:52 has no Matthean parallel and that the verbal construction is Luke's, one can only conjecture the pre-Lukan form. But what I have printed is formally very similar to Q 17:34-35. See Klaus Beyer, *Semitisches Syntax im Neuen Testament*, Band I (SUNT 1; Göttingen: Vandenhoeck & Ruprecht, 1962) 237 n. 1.

27 J. Gnilka, *Das Evangelium nach Markus (Mark 8,27-16,20)* (EKKNT 2.2; Zürich: Benziger; Neukirchen-Vluyn: Neukirchener, 1979) 191.

28 L. Hartman, *Prophecy Interpreted: The Formation of some Jewish Apocalyptic Texts and of the Eschatological Discourse Mark 13 Par.* (ConBNT 1; Lund: Almqvist & Wiksells, 1966) 168-69. See also C. A. Evans, "Mishna and Messiah 'in Context': Some Comments on Jacob Neusner's Proposals," *JBL* 112 (1993) 267-289; repr. in B. D. Chilton and C. A. Evans, *Jesus in Context: Temple, Purity, and Restoration* (AGJU 39; Leiden: Brill, 1997) 109-44. Evans traces the lines of continuity between the Synoptic saying(s) and the rabbinic interpretation of Mic 7:6.

What does this have to do with Q 12:51-53? Mark 13:12 appears to be a loose variant of the Q text.[29] Seemingly under the impact of events in the '60s, Mark or a predecessor rewrote the unit more faithfully preserved in Q 12:51-53, assimilating it to Mark 13:9-11 and expanding the theme beyond families to more general persecution and hatred.[30] As Vincent Taylor wrote, "Mark xiii.12 is a secondary form which appears to reflect the conditions which obtained during the Neronian persecution."[31] Now if indeed Mark 13:12 is, as so many have thought, a variant of Q 12:51-53, then it may be observed that Mark 13:12 shows traces of the very same pattern found in *m. Soṭa* 9:15 and the other texts examined above. In Mark too we find Mic 7:6 used to depict the strife of the latter times, and there is an a^1 b^1 b^2 a^2 pattern:

παραδώσει . . . πατὴρ τίκνον
καὶ ἐπαναστζησονται τέκνα ἐπὶ γνοεῖς.

So Mark's form seemingly testifies to the antiquity of Luke's chiastic arrangement in connection with the evangelical unit.[32]

---

29   By this I mean that Q 12:51-53 and Mark 13:12 take up the same oral Jesus tradition, not that Mark knew the written Q.

30   Pertinent considerations are found in M. Hengel, *Studies in the Gospel of Mark* (Philadelphia: Fortress, 1985) 21-28 (although he does not examine the relationship between Mark's text and Q) and G. Theissen, *Lokalkolorit und Zeitgeschichte in den Evangelien* (NTOA 8; Göttingen: Vandenhoeck & Ruprecht, 1989) 166-67.

31   V. Taylor, *The Gospel according to St. Mark* (2nd ed., New York: St. Martin's Press, 1966) 509. Cf. C. H. Dodd, *The Parables of the Kingdom* (rev. ed., New York: Scribner's, 1961) 50.

32   My analysis has not taken into account the variant in *GThom.* §16. This is because, against S. J. Patterson, "Ipsissima Vox Jesu in Q 12:49, 51-53?," *Forum* 5/2 (1989) 127-30, it appears to be secondary. (i) *GThom.* §16 refers to "divisions" (*hnpōrd*), which matches Luke's redactional διαμερισμόν. But "sword" (*sēfe*), the Matthean variant, also appears. Surely such agreement with both Matthew and Luke betrays synoptic influence. (ii) The lines about daughter and mother and daughter-in-law and mother-in-law are missing. This distancing from the Tanak is characteristic of *Thomas*. (iii) The closing line, "and they will stand as solitaries," is obviously a late feature. The mistaken conviction that *GThom.* is an independent witness to the tradition behind Q 12:51-53 skews the reconstruction of Philip Sellew, "Reconstruction of Q 12:33-59," in K. H. Richards (ed.), *Society of Biblical Literature 1987 Seminar Papers* (SBLSP 26; Atlanta: Scholars Press, 1987) 646-53.

INTERPRETATION

We shall in what follows seek the meaning of Q 12:51-53 as an isolated unit. Scholars have sometimes argued that vv. 52-53 are a secondary addition and that they and v. 51 should thus be treated separately.[33] The latter, however, remains too enigmatic ever to have stood alone.[34]

We begin with the use of the Mic 7:6, for there is a consistent use of this lament in Jewish and Christian literature.

(a) Although Mic 7:6 ostensibly portrays turmoil in the prophet's own day, both *b. Sanh.* 97a and *m. Soṭa* 9:15, as already observed, use it to foretell events that preface the Messiah's coming. For these two sources Mic 7:6 is a prophecy of eschatological tribulation.

(b) The targum prefaces Mic 7:6 with the words, "in that time" (בעדנא ההוא). This is an eschatological expression that moves the verse from the days of the prophet to the future.[35] Presumably the targum presupposes the interpretation found in *b. Sanh.* 97a and *m. Soṭa* 9:15.[36] The date of the targum is unfortunately unknown.

(c) The application of Mic 7:6 to the distress of the latter days in the rabbinic corpus and the targums has its parallel in the New Testament. The variant of Q 12:51-53 now found in Mark 13:12 is placed right in the middle of Mark's "little apocalypse" and belongs to a section which recounts the "birthpangs" (13:8) of the new age. In Luke, the Q unit is prefaced—was this so already in Q?—by Luke 12:49-50, where Jesus talks about casting fire on the earth and undergoing a baptism. The images are best understood as representing the divine judgment that is about to overtake the world. If John the Baptist spoke of a coming baptism of fire (Q 3:16), here Jesus anticipates going through that eschatological baptism himself.[37] In

---

[33]   O. L. Cope, *Matthew: A Scribe Trained for the Kingdom of Heaven* (CBQMS 5; Washington: Catholic Biblical Association, 1976) 78.

[34]   U. Luz, *Das Evangelium nach Matthäus* (2 vols., EKKNT 1.1-2; Zürich: Benziger; Neukirchen-Vluyn: Neukirchener Verlag, 1985, 1990) 2.135: "Ich neige dazu, die Einheitlichkeit zu vertreten, weil das rätselhafte Wort vom 'Bringen des Schwertes' von vornherein einer Erklärung bedarf, die in V 35f gegeben wird."

[35]   D. L. Büchner, "Micah 7:6 in the Ancient Old Testament Versions," *JNSL* 19 (1993) 159-68.

[36]   Büchner ("Micah 7:6," 159-68) argues that the targumic reading is the basis for the rabbinic texts.

[37]   See further D. C. Allison, Jr., *The End of the Ages has Come: An Early Interpretation of the Passion and Resurrection of Jesus* (Philadelphia: Fortress,

Matthew, Q 12:51-53 (along with Mark 13:9-13) is moved into the missionary discourse (Matt 10:34-36). There, beside other eschatological texts (e.g. 10:22-23), it serves to interpret the Christian mission as a manifestation of the birth pangs which herald the *parousia*.[38] So although the synoptics put the one saying of Jesus in three different contexts, each time the logion functions similarly, to typify the discord of the latter days.

(d) Among the Qumran finds are portions of a pesher on Micah. Sadly only a few pieces and fragments have been preserved, so we do not have the commentary on 7:6. But fragments 20-21 refer to "the men [of] his [hou]se," the last words of that verse. Further, following the text of 6:15-16 are these words: "The interpretation of it] concerns the [l]as[t] generation."[39] This raise the strong presumption, reinforced by the eschatological interests of the Scrolls in general and the sect's belief, otherwise attested, that familial friction was an eschatological expectation,[40] that Mic 7:6 was interpreted at Qumran as in the New Testament and in the *Mishnah*.

(e) The eschatological interpretation of Mic 7:6 may already be attested in the Hebrew Bible itself. The very last verse of Malachi, which is usually reckoned a late addition, foretells the coming of Elijah, who will turn the hearts of fathers to their sons and the hearts of sons to the fathers (4:6). Pierre Grelot, among others, detects in this an intertextual echo of Mic 7:6[41] and so offers an inner-biblical interpretation of Malachi's conclusion: Elijah will come and undo the sad situation prophesied by Mic 7:6, where the son treats the father with contempt.[42] He is probably correct. This means in turn that we

---

1985) 124-28.

   [38]   J. Gnilka, *Das Matthäusevangelium 1. Teil* (HTKNT 1.1; Freiburg: Herder, 1986) 395; Luz, *Matthäus*, 2.139.

   [39]   M. P. Horgan, *Pesharim: Qumran Interpretations of Biblical Books* (CBQMS 8; Washington: Catholic Biblical Association, 1979) 58.

   [40]   See O. Betz, "Jesu heiliger Krieg," *NovT* 2 (1957) 130 (interpreting the use of Deut 33:8-11 in 4Q175).

   [41]   One should keep in mind that Micah was a well-known text. Recall e.g. the quotation of 3:12 in Jer 26:18 and see further W. L. Holladay, *Jeremiah 2* (Hermeneia; Minneapolis: Fortress, 1989) 50-51.

   [42]   P. Grelot, "Michée 7,6 dans les évangiles et dans la littérature rabbinique," *Bib* 67 (1986) 375. The link between the two texts is also remarked upon by B. Reicke, "Liturgical Traditions in Mic. 7," *HTR* 60 (1967) 359, who in turn refers to J. Lindblom's commentary on Micah, which I have not seen.

likely have already in the late (Hellenistic?) addition to Malachi the
sequence implicit in 4 Ezra 6:24-28 and explicit in later rabbinic
texts: the last generation will witness great conflicts, even among
neighbors and within families, as Micah prophesied; but then Elijah
will come, Israelites will change for the better, and God will redeem
his people.[43]

Two important results follow for our purposes. First, if Mal 4:6
holds an intertextual allusion to Mic 7:6, the Hebrew Bible already
gives us the eschatological interpretation found later in the New
Testament and the rabbis, for Mal 4:6 plainly has to do with the
situation immediately before the "great and terrible day of the Lord"
(4:5). Secondly, if the ancients recognized that Malachi was commenting on Micah, we would have an explanation for the recurrent
chiastic pattern that, as already observed, appears in old texts citing
or alluding to Mic 7:6. For Mal 4:6 presents us with a chiastic line
about young and old: fathers—sons—sons—fathers. These words
presume that, before Elijah comes, father and son are not reconciled,
which is the picture of Mic 7:6. One may suggest, then, that because
Mic 7:6 and Mal 4:6 were traditionally associated, the chiastic
arrangement of the latter fostered chiastic paraphrases of the
former.[44]

Whatever one makes of these conjectures about Mal 4:5, the
evidence is more than sufficient to prove that before and after the
first-century Mic 7:6 was widely understood as an eschatological
prophecy—and there is no evidence that it was ever understood as
anything else. This fact is fundamental for the interpretation of Q
12:51-53.

If the citation of Mic 7:6 in Q 12:53 associates Jesus with eschatological discord, Q 12:51 dissociates him from eschatological peace.[45]

---

43   Cf. *Pirqe R. El.* 43. The notion that Israel will repent before the end is also
known apart from the Elijah texts; see e.g. Acts 3:19-21; *T. Dan* 6:4; *T. Sim.* 6:2-7;
T. Zeb. 9:7-9; *T. Jud.* 23:5; *As. Mos.* 1:18; *2 Bar.* 78:7; *Apoc. Abr.* 29; *Sipre
Deut.* §41 (on Deut 11:13); *b. Sanh.* 97b; *b. Šabb.* 118b; *b. Yoma* 86b.

44   Note that whereas in Mark 13:12 the chiastic allusion to Mic 7:6 employs
πατήρ and τέκνον, the allusion to Mal 4:6 in Luke 1:17 uses πατέρων and τέκνα.

45   A. Schlatter, *Der Evangelist Matthäus* (Stuttgart: Calwer, 1948) 151: here
Jesus refers to a messianic expectation "die aus dem messianischen Gedankenkreis
entstand." It should be noted, however, that our saying does not require that Jesus
is "the Messiah." For although there are texts that associate a future royal Davidid
or Messiah with peace (Isa 9:6-7; 11:1-10; Zech 9:9-10; *2 Bar.* 73:1), eschatologi-

It hardly seems necessary to argue that expectation of a final state of peace was standard fare in ancient Judaism. The very fact that so many ancient texts portray the time before the redemption as filled with war and destruction is proof enough:[46] all the terror serves as a foil for the tranquility that follows it. In the end God will make a covenant of peace with Israel (Ezek 34:25; cf. 37:26). His people will "abide in a peaceful habitation" (Isa 32:18). They will not learn war any more, and swords will become plowshares (Isa 2:4). The wolf will live with the lamb (Isa 11:6).[47]

In Q 12:51-53, however, Jesus denies that he has come to bring peace. This disavowal, which reminds one of passages in which Jeremiah (6:14; 8:11; 12:12; 28:9; 30:5) and Ezekiel (7:25; 13:10, 16) rebuke those who proclaim a premature peace, does not deny the eventual reality of eschatological šālôm. Disavowing the presence of peace is rather a way of saying that the new age has not yet come, and that it is not coming without tribulation. Jesus comes not in the time of eschatological peace but, as the use of Mic 7:6 indicates, in the apocalyptic time of trouble.[48]

Jesus also announces that he comes to bring a sword.[49] This affirmation likewise directs us to eschatological prophecies. For talk

---

cal peace was also associated with other figures (see Isa 52:7; Mal 4:6; 11QMelch 2:16; Sir 48:10) and with eschatology in general.

[46] Isa 19:2; Dan 7:21; 9:26; 11:5-45; Zech 14:3; 4Q244; 1QpHab 2:12-14; 3:1; *1 En.* 100:1-2; *Jub.* 23:13, 20; *Ps. Sol.* 15:7-8; *Rev* 6:4; *4 Ezra* 5:5, 9; 6:24; 9:3; 13:31; *2 Bar.* 27:3-5; 70:2-6; *Sib. Or.* 3:635-51; *Apoc. Abr.* 30:6; *Gk. Apoc. Ezra* 3:13; *b. Sanh.* 97a; *b. Meg.* 17b; etc.

[47] See further Isa 11:6-9; 60:17; 66:12; Mic 5:5; Zech 9:10; *1 En.* 5:7; 10:17; 11:2; 58:4; 71:15, 17; 4Q245; *Sib. Or.* 3:780.

[48] Cf. the interpretation of R. Bultmann, *History of the Synoptic Tradition* (rev. ed., New York: Harper & Row, 1963) 154-55 (although he wrongly attributes the saying to the community). Sometimes this apocalyptic interpretation is viewed as one possibility which is then set over against understanding the persecution "concretely with reference to the rejection and violence experienced by the members of the community itself." So J. S. Kloppenborg, *The Formation of Q: Trajectories in Ancient Wisdom Collections* (Philadelphia: Fortress, 1987) 152. But why these two interpretations are antithetical instead of complementary—as they are in Daniel, the *Testament of Moses*, and *m. Sota* 9:16—is not said. Bultmann got it right: here Jesus prophesies "the time of terror" which the community has "experienced . . . in its own life."

[49] Sword and peace are natural antitheses; note Rev 6:4; *Sib. Or.* 3:780-81; *2 En.* 52:14.

of the sword within prophecies of eschatological affliction or judgment was widespread.[50] So the meaning is: "With the coming of Jesus the ultimate age of peace has not yet dawned, but instead the last struggle has broken out."[51] As in Rev 6:4, the absence of peace and the presence of a sword are features of the great tribulation.

Is the sword of Q 12:51-53 to be understood literally?[52] This is unlikely, even though many of the prophecies about the latter days depict literal warfare and the variant in Mark 13:12 refers to killing. Luke 12:51 turns "sword" into "division," and this is a a proper interpretation. For Q's "to halve (διχάσαι) son against father, etc." already betrays a metaphorical understanding of μάχαιραν, and figurative meanings for "sword" are otherwise well attested.[53] Q 12:51-53 itself interprets the sword in terms of Mic 7:6: the time of the sword is the time of familial conflict when there are diverse religious loyalties within the same household. So even if the author of Luke 12:51 expected a literal end-time war (as in 1QM), the force of our saying is elsewhere.[54]

To sum up our results so far: Q 12:51-53 declares that Jesus' coming does not coincide with the establishment of eschatological peace. On the contrary, his terrible time is that prophesied in Dan 12:1 and elsewhere, the time (to use the later technical term) of the "messianic woe" (heblô šel māšîaḥ), the time when the bitter prophecy of Mic 7:6 will come to pass.

Q 12:51-53 AND THE HISTORICAL JESUS

We should with confidence assign the original composition of Q 12:51-53 to Jesus himself. For, on the one hand, three of its features seem uncharacteristic of the church while, on the other, at least four of them harmonize with what we otherwise know of Jesus.

---

50 E.g. Isa 66:16; Ezek 38:21; *Jub.* 9:15; *1 En.* 62:15; 63:11; 90:19; 91:11-12; 4QpIsa[b] 2:1; 4QPsDanA[a]; *Ps. Sol.* 15:8; *Sib. Or.* 3:797-99; 4:174; Rev 6:4; *2 Bar.* 27:6; 40:1.

51 F. Hahn, *The Titles of Jesus in Christology* (New York: World, 1969) 153.

52 So G. W. Buchanan, *The Gospel of Matthew* (Mellen Biblical Commentary 1; Lewiston: Mellen, 1996) 466-67.

53 For μάχαιρα: Eph 6:17; Heb 4:12. For ῥομφαία: Luke 2:35; *Sib. Or.* 3:316. Recall the common comparison of word to knife or sword (Ps 57:4; Wis 18:15-16; Heb 4:12; Aḥiqar 2:18 [100b]).

54 See further M. Black, "'Not Peace but a Sword': Matt. 10:34ff; Luke 12:51ff," in Bammel and Moule (eds.), *Jesus and the Politics of his Day*, 287-94.

(a) Q 12:51-53 and its relative in Mark 13:12 draw upon Mic 7:6, a prophetic text otherwise not cited or alluded to in Christian literature of the first century. Indeed, the book of Micah is not even discussed in C. H. Dodd's survey of those blocks of Scripture most used by the early church.[55]

(b) If in Q 12:51-53 Jesus denies that he is the bringer of peace, this is a function he nonetheless fulfills in early Christian literature. In John 14:27 Jesus leaves "peace" with his disciples (cf. 16:33; 20:19, 21, 26). According to Acts 10:36, God preached "peace by Jesus Christ." Paul in Rom 5:1 declares, "We have peace with God through our Lord Jesus Christ." According to Eph 2:14-18, Jesus "is our peace," and he "proclaimed peace to those who were far off and peace to those who were near." We read in Col 1:20 that Jesus "made peace through the blood of his cross." Paul, or whoever penned 2 Thess 3:16, describes Jesus as the "Lord of peace." Is it likely that the Christian community, for which peace was "nearly synonymous w[ith] messianic salvation,"[56] a community which knew that Jesus had enjoined love of enemies, would have constructed a saying in which he distances himself from peace? Commentators have from a very early time experienced some difficulty in harmonizing Matt 10:34 = Luke 12:51 with what they have otherwise believed about Jesus.[57]

(c) Franz Mussner is right to affirm that, "in view of the tendency, especially observable in Acts, to present Christianity as politically harmless, [the possibility that] the *machaira*-saying is a product of the Christian community appears to be excluded. Such 'misleading sayings' go back to Jesus himself."[58]

(d) On the assumption that Jesus spoke Aramaic, it is significant that Q 12:51-53 may reflect a Semitic original. βαλεῖν εἰρήνην is a striking Semitism which means "to bring peace"[59] (and one which is,

---

[55]   C. H. Dodd, *According to the Scriptures* (London: Fontana, 1965).

[56]   So BAGD, s.v., εἰρήνη.

[57]   See e.g. Tertullian, *Adv. Marc.* 3:14; Chrysostom, *Hom. on Matt.* 25:1; *Ps.-Clem. Rec.* 2.26-31. I note that my ten-year old daughter, who regularly asks me questions about the Bible, recently read Matthew 10 and had only one query— How could Jesus say he did not come to bring peace?

[58]   F. Mussner, "Wege zum Selbstbewusstsein Jesu," *BZ* 12 (1968) 166.

[59]   See Schlatter, *Matthäus*, 349; SB 1.586. For possible Aramaic equivalents, see H. Arens, *The ΗΛΘΟΝ–Sayings in the Synoptic Gospels: A Historico-Critical Investigation* (OBO 10; Göttingen: Vandenhoeck & Ruprecht, 1976) 84; and for an Aramaic translation of the opening line, see W. F. Albright and C. S. Mann,

interestingly, associated in some rabbinic texts with reconciliation within families[60]). νύμφη with the sense "daughter-in-law" (as often in the LXX) is another Semitism (cf. Heb. כלה, Aram. כלתא), and the asyndeton could be.[61] Moreover, there are no significant agreements between our reconstructed Q text and Mic 7:6 LXX over against the MT.

(e) Q 12:51-53 harmonizes with other hard sayings of Jesus about the family. Q 14:26 speaks of disciples hating their parents. According to Mark 10:29, following Jesus can mean leaving brother and sister and mother and father and children. In Q 9:59-60, the decision to follow Jesus comes before the obligation to bury one's father.[62]

(f) The suggestion that Q 12:51-53 is an authentic saying of Jesus that links his ministry with the messianic woes is greatly strenthened by the fact that scholars have found this link elsewhere in the tradition.[63] According to Norman Perrin, the cryptic saying about the kingdom and violence in Q 16:16 "evokes the myth of the eschatological war between God and the powers of evil and interprets the fate of John the Baptist, and the potential fate of Jesus and his disciples, as a manifestation of that conflict."[64] In the view of Jeremias, the final line of the Lord's Prayer (Q 11:4) envisages not the trials or temptations of everyday life but the final time of trouble

---

Matthew (AB 26; Garden City: Doubleday, 1971) 130.

[60] See e.g. *Mek.* on Exod 20:25 (*Baḥodeš* §11): "throws peace . . . between a man and his wife"; and *Sipre Num* §16 (on Num 5:16-28): "to throw peace between a man and his wife."

[61] M. Black, *An Aramaic Approach to the Gospels and Acts* (3rd. ed., Oxford: University Press, 1967) 55-59.

[62] Cf. also perhaps the eschatological separation in Q 17:34-35.

[63] See e.g. A. Schweitzer, *The Quest for the Historical Jesus* (New York: Macmillan, 1961) 361-72; R. Otto, *The Kingdom of God and the Son of Man* (rev. ed., London: Lutterworth, 1943) 60; R. H. Fuller, *The Mission and Achievement of Jesus* (SBT 12; London: SCM Press, 1954) 105-106; O. Cullmann, *Salvation in History* (London: SCM Press, 1967) 229-30; H. Braun, *Jesus of Nazareth: The Man and his Time* (Philadelphia: Fortress, 1979) 38-41; B. F. Meyer, *The Aims of Jesus* (London: SCM Press, 1979) 202-209. The doubts of M. de Jonge (*Jesus, the Servant-Messiah* [New Haven: Yale, 1991] 58-62) are ineffectually argued.

[64] N. Perrin, *Jesus and the Language of the Kingdom* (Philadelphia: Fortress, 1976) 46. Cf. R. H. Hiers, *The Kingdom of God in the Synoptic Tradition* (Gainesville: University of Florida Press, 1970) 36-42, and G. R. Beasley-Murray, *Jesus and the Kingdom of God* (Grand Rapids: Eerdmans, 1986) 95-96.

which precedes the renewal (cf. Rev 3:10).[65] Vincent Taylor believed that the saying about fire in Mark 9:49 means that "in the eschatological situation in which His [Jesus'] disciples stood every man would be tried and purified by the fires of persecution and suffering."[66] James D. G. Dunn made the case that the saying about fire and baptism in Luke 12:50-51 illustrates "that Jesus *did* see his death in dogmatic terms, in terms of the 'dogma' of the messianic woes . . .".[67] Eduard Schweizer supposed that the related saying in Mark 10:38-39 may mean that Jesus is to assume "the eschatological sorrow as part of his own destiny."[68] It is more than suggestive that so many different exegetes have found the idea of the messianic woes in so many different sayings, and in fact in sayings with a good claim to authenticity. Jesus, like others before and after him,[69] apparently interpreted the ills around him as harbingers of the final redemption.

(g) In Q 12:51-53 Jesus seems, at least on the surface, to distance himself from a scripturally grounded expectation, and one might even understand him to be setting Scripture (Mic 7:6) against Scripture (the prophetic promises of peace). Although unsettling, the outcome of the juxtaposition is not to uncover an unresolvable contradiction but to force hearers to ruminate upon two eschatological expectations that are not obviously harmonious with each other and to discover the deeper concord for themselves.[70]

---

[65]   J. Jeremias, *New Testament Theology: The Proclamation of Jesus* (New York: Scribner's, 1971) 201-202. Cf. R. E. Brown, *New Testament Essays* (New York: Doubleday, 1968) 314-19.

[66]   V. Taylor, *The Gospel according to St. Mark* (2nd ed., New York: St. Martin's, 1966) 413. Cf. D. E. Nineham, *Saint Mark* (Philadelphia: Westminster, 1963) 256.

[67]   J. D. G. Dunn, "The Birth of a Metaphor–Baptized in Spirit (Part I)," *ExpTim* 89 (1978) 138. Cf. J. Jeremias, *The Parables of Jesus* (2nd rev. ed., New York: Scribner's, 1972) 163-64.

[68]   E. Schweizer, *The Good News according to Mark* (Atlanta: John Knox, 1976) 221. Cf. Dunn, "Birth of a Metaphor."

[69]   See Allison, *The End of the Ages*, 5-25; G. Scholem, *Sabbatai Sevi: The Mystical Messiah* (Princeton: University Press Press, 1973) 92-93; idem, *Major Trends in Jewish Mysticism* (New York: Schocken, 1961) 247.

[70]   Keen interest in apparently conflicting Scriptures appears in the rabbis and even earlier in Paul; see N. A. Dahl, *Studies in Paul* (Minneapolis: Augsburg, 1977) 159-77. Such interest in fact can be seen in the Tanak itself; see M. Fishbane, *Biblical Interpretation in Ancient Israel* (Oxford: Clarendon, 1985); consult the Index, s.v., "Legal contradictions."

The tension in Q 12:51-53 may be regarded as typical, for Jesus characteristically said and did things which put himself or his reading of Scripture in seeming conflict with the Tanak. His purpose was not to undermine tradition by contesting it or showing it to be contradictory. Rather, a bit like Abelard in *Sic et non*, it was Jesus' custom to stimulate, through creative juxtapositions, reflection and maybe even doubt for the sake of the truth. Thus Mark 10:2-9 plays Gen 1:27 and 5:2 off against Deut 24:1-4.[71] And Matthew's mis-named "antitheses," the first two of which probably go back to Jesus,[72] cite Scripture only to better it. Again, Mark 10:45a says that the Son of man came not to be served but to serve—a line often thought to turn on its head Dan 7:13-14, where people serve the one like a Son of man.[73] Q 9:58 ("Foxes have holes, and birds of the air have nests, but the Son of man has nowhere to lay his head") apparently alludes to Psalm 8, where God puts the Son of man over the beasts of the field and the birds of the air. If so, the saying ironically reverses Scripture: the Son of man does not rule creation but has even less than the birds and beasts.[74] And the cryptic Mark 12:35-37, whose yet-to-be-resolved obscurity is reason enough not to exclude some pre-Easter basis, highlights a tension between David's "son" and David's "lord." One may add to all this that Jesus some-times (as in his Sabbath healings) acted in vexing ways which from the beginning have made people wonder about his attitude to Moses[75] —and yet the evidence that he actually intended to undo the law is not compelling.[76] He appears to have sought to be provocative without flatly contradicting the Torah and prophets (which partly

---

[71]   Regarding the origin of this tradition, the Torah itself allows divorce, so Jesus could never have disallowed it with an unsupported, blunt declaration; and because the appeal to the primeval state coheres with his eschatological outlook (*Urzeit = Endzeit*), Mark 10:2-9 probably preserves his justification.

[72]   So rightly Luz, *Matthäus*, 1.249.

[73]   P. Stuhlmacher, *Reconciliation, Law, and Righteousness* (Philadelphia: Fortress, 1986) 21. On the possible but uncertain authenticity of this line, see Davies and Allison, *Matthew*, 3.99-100.

[74]   M. H. Smith, "No Place for a Son of Man," *Forum* 4.4 (1988) 83-107.

[75]   See recently A. Watson, *Jesus and the Law* (Athens: University of Georgia, 1996).

[76]   E. P. Sanders, *Jewish Law from Jesus to the Mishnah* (London: SCM Press, 1990); G. Vermes, *The Religion of Jesus the Jew* (Minneapolis: Fortress, 1993) 11-45.

explains the confusion of early Christians *vis-à-vis* the law).[77]

Our conclusion should be that Q 12:51-53, which sets Mic 7:6 against the scripturally grounded hope of eschatological peace, is one example of a larger pattern and that it rests upon something Jesus said.[78] Those who have thought otherwise have invariably claimed that the christological ἦλθον is a decisive sign of a community formulation.[79] But the Psalmist could speak of Moses and Aaron as having been "sent" (105:26; cf. Mic 6:4); Jeremiah could ask, "Why did I come forth from the womb to see toil and sorrow and spend my days in shame?" (Jer 20:18; cf. 1:7); Obadiah could say of himself, "a messenger has been sent among the nations" (Obad 1); and the author of *2 Baruch* had Baruch say, "O Lord, my Lord, have I therefore come into the world to see the evil things of my mother?" (3:1). The Teacher of Righteousness at Qumran (on the assumption that he composed portions of 1QH), moreover, manifestly exhibited a *Sendungsbewusstsein*,[80] and Josephus tells us that he addressed Vespasian with the words, ἐγὼ δ' ἄγγελος ἥκω σοι μειζόνων.[81]

If Jesus thought himself a prophet, and if he could say "John the

---

[77]   We should probably relate this to what John A. T. Robinson once called Jesus' "challenging use of Scripture," that is, his use of the Bible "to pose rather than prove." See his "Did Jesus Have a Distinctive Use of Scripture?," in R. F. Berkey and S.A. Edwards (eds.), *Christological Perspectives: Essays in Honor of Harvey K. McArthur* (New York: Pilgrim, 1982) 54-57.

[78]   Mussner ("Weg," 165-67) pleads for authenticity, and J. D. Crossan (*The Historical Jesus: The Life of a Meditteranean Jewish Peasant* [San Francisco: Harper Collins, 1991] xvi, 439) thinks the unit goes back to Jesus. Luz (*Matthäus*, 2.135, 138-39) is undecided. Arens (*The ΗΛΘΟΝ–Sayings in the Synoptic Tradition*, 76, 83-86) maintains that an origin with Jesus is possible but not quite as likely as a post-Easter origin.

[79]   See e.g. Patterson, "Fire and Dissension," 137-38.

[80]   G. Jeremias, *Der Lehrer der Gerechtigkeit* (SUNT 2; Göttingen: Vandenhoeck & Ruprehct, 1963) 334-36. See further Fitzmyer, *Luke*, 2.995-96, who draws attention to the (apparent) self-testimony of the Teacher of Righteousness in 1QH 2:11-12, 14-15, and 2:32-33.

[81]   See O. Michel, "'Ich komme' (Jos. Bell. III,400)," *TZ* 24 (1968) 123-24. When Patterson, without explanation, writes that Q 12:51 "presupposes the kerygmatic claim that Jesus is the descending/ascending redeemer who has come from God" ("Fire and Dissension," 137), what basis can he have for saying this? There is probably no pre-existence anywhere else in the synoptic tradition, and certainly not in Q. Why not then interpret the "I came" of Q 12:51 in accord with Q's express conviction that Jesus is a prophet?

Baptist has come" (Q 7:33), and if the only objection to the authenticity of some "I came" sayings is that they are "I came" sayings, then
surely R. H. Fuller was right to "postulate an original nucleus of
ἦλθον ('I came') and ἀπεστάλην ('I was sent') sayings which formed
the model for the later church formations."[82] Q 12:51-53 belongs to
that original nucleus.

THE PARALLEL IN MARK 9:11-13

Although the fact has not, to my knowledge, been explored before,
Q 12:51-53 is very closely related to Mark 9:11-13. This last is a
notoriously perplexing passage. The commentaries customarily
describe it as "problematic," "confused," "difficult," "broken," "unintelligible." Following a question, "Why do the scribes say that Elijah
must come first?," Jesus answers with two questions of his own and
an assertion: "Is Elijah indeed coming first to restore all things?" (v.
12a).[83] "How then is it written about the Son of man that he is to
suffer and be treated with contempt?" (v. 12b). "Elijah has come,
and they did to him whatever they pleased, as it is written about him"
(v. 13).

Bultmann argued that v. 12b is a post-Markan gloss.[84] Others have
thought it an awkward Markan insertion.[85] Still others have surmised
that the half-verse is displaced (maybe it followed v. 10).[86] But Joel
Marcus (as in n. 83) has convincingly shown that Mark's sequence is,
if difficult, yet intelligible as it stands. His argument, supported by
parallels from the *Mekilta*, is that Mark 9:11-13 is an example of the
sort of juxtapositioning of scriptural contradictions one often finds in
the rabbis. According to Malachi, Elijah is to heal human relations
before the Messiah comes.[87] But this stands in tension with the

---

[82] R. H. Fuller, *The Foundations of New Testament Christology* (London:
Fontana, 1965) 128. One wonders, however, in view of Mark 2:17; 10:45; and Q
12:51-53, whether we should not rather think of a core of "I came *not*" sayings.

[83] On the reasons for punctuating this as a question, see Joel Marcus, "Mark
9,11-13: 'As It Has Been Written,'" *ZNW* 90 (1989) 47-48.

[84] Bultmann, *History*, 124-25, 332.

[85] This was once my opinion; see Davies and Allison, *Matthew*, 2.711.

[86] So M. Black, "The Theological Appropriation of the Old Testament by the
New Testament," *SJT* 39 (1986) 9-10, following C. H. Turner. See further C. C.
Oke, "The Rearrangement and Transmission of Mark ix, 11-13," *ExpTim* 64
(1953) 187-88.

[87] Cf. Sir 48:10; Luke 1:16-17; *4 Ezra* 6:26; *m. ʿEd.* 8:7; *Pirqe R. El.* §43;

scriptural prophecy that the Son of man (= Jesus the Messiah) is to suffer. Mark's text is an attempt to reconcile the conflict through an "implicit syllogism." Because Jesus is a suffering Messiah, his forerunner (the Baptist) must be a suffering Elijah.

Marcus is surely right that the clue to Mark 9:11-13 is that it confronts us with two opposing scriptural expectations. My only question concerns his straightforward equation of "the Son of man" with Jesus. Marcus correctly observes that "the identity of the sufferer as the 'Son of Man' probably brings into view at least Daniel 7 and perhaps Psalm 80 as well.[88] In the former, the 'one like a Son of Man' is identical to or at least linked with 'the people of the saints of the Most High' who undergo tribulation before their final, eschatological vindication (Dan 7,13-14.18.21.25.27). In the latter, the Son of Man, Yahweh's right-hand man, is linked with Israel, the plundered vine (Psalm 80,14-17)."[89] I should like to raise the possibility that the collective understanding of "Son of man" is still present in Mark 9:11-13. Several ancient and many modern commentators have identified Daniel's "one like a son of man" with the persecuted saints,[90] and some important exegetes have found a collective dimension in some of Jesus' words about "the Son of man."[91] If one equates the Son of man in Mark 9:12 not with Jesus alone but with the suffering saints of Daniel 7, then the argument clarifies itself and the logic becomes explicit rather than implicit. Jesus is asked why the scribes, in accordance with Malachi, say that Elijah will come first.[92] Jesus responds by asking if Elijah is indeed

---

Yalqut Shim'oni §771. The idea must also have been known to the Qumran sect, but the relevant evidence is very fragmentary; see 4Q521 frag. 2 iii (an allusion to Mal 4:6) and 4Q558 ("thus I will send Elijah be[fore] . . ."). Note also that Elijah was identified with Phineas (cf. already *LAB* 48:1), with whom God made a "covenant of peace" (Num 25:12; cf. Mal 2:5).

[88]   Isaiah 53:3 has also had influence here; see Black, "Theological Appropriation," 11-12. This is intriguing because Sir 48:10 uses Isa 49:6 of the returning Elijah and *Sipre Num* §131 (on Num 25:1) applies Isa 53:12 to Phineas (often identified with Elijah). Do we have here traces of an application of servant language to Elijah?

[89]   Marcus, "Mark 9,11-13," 44.

[90]   M. Casey, *Son of Man: The Interpretation and Influence of Daniel 7* (London: SPCK, 1979) 51-70.

[91]   E.g. M. D. Hooker, *The Son of Man in Mark* (Montreal: McGill University Press, 1967).

[92]   I once argued, against M. Faierstein, "Why Do the Scribes Say that Elijah

coming first to restore all things—a comment that, like those cited on p. 304, makes one wonder whether Jesus is questioning Scripture itself. He then goes on to say that the saints, as the Bible (Daniel 7) indicates, will suffer in the end time. It follows that if Elijah comes in the end time, he will suffer—as has happened to John the Baptist.[93] "They did to him whatever they pleased."[94]

Whether or not this tentative suggestion about the collective dimension of the Son of man in Mark 9:12 has merit, Marcus' observation that Mark 9:11-13 juxtaposes conflicting scriptural expectations remains valid. The point for us is that Q 12:51-53 likewise juxtaposes conflicting eschatological expectations grounded in Scripture. Indeed, the two texts deal with precisely the same issue. If in Q 12:51 Jesus counters the view that eschatological peace has appeared, in Mark 9:11-13 he queries the idea that the eschatological Elijah brings peace and makes reconciliation.[95] And if in Q 12:52-53

Must Come First?," *JBL* 100 (1981) 75-86, that Mark 9:11-13 is good evidence for a first-century Jewish belief in Elijah as the Messiah's precursor; see "Elijah Must Come First," *JBL* 103 (1984) 256-58. Although unpersuaded by the retort from J. A. Fitzmyer, "More about Elijah Coming First," *JBL* 104 (1985) 295-96, I am now less certain about this. If one interprets Mark 9:11-13 in isolation, the meaning is probably, "comes first, before the great and terrible day of the Lord" (cf. Mal 4:6). That is, Jesus is asked, in view of the imminence of the end, where Elijah the peacemaker is (cf. Bultmann's suggestion that Mark 9:11-13 once followed 9:1: *History* 124). There need be no connection with the Messiah. It is nevertheless true that, in Mark's narrative context, "comes first" probably means "comes first, before the Messiah," in which case we would still have evidence for the idea, attested in the rabbis, that Elijah will be the Messiah's precursor. See Marcus, "Mark 9,11-13."

93   One inevitably thinks of the tradition, of uncertain date and origin, of the eschatological martyrdom of Elijah; see R. Bauckham, "The Martyrdom of Enoch and Elijah: Jewish or Christian?," *JBL* 95 (1976) 447-58; A. Zeron, "The Martyrdom of Phineas-Elijah," *JBL* 98 (1979) 99-100.

94   This expression appears three times in Daniel (8:4; 11:3, 16). Does this not strengthen the proposal that John himself (under the symbol of the Son of man) is being associated with Daniel?

95   It is worth observing that Mal 4:6 ends with the words, "lest (פן) I come and smite the land with a curse." This can be taken to envisage the possibility of the failure of Elijah's mission, a failure which seems presupposed in Mark 9:11-13. Thus, although the Markan text–like others Marcus examines–does not spell out how to find harmony between its two conflicting scriptural expectations, one can achieve concord by taking seriously the contingent nature of Malachi's closing words: Malachi itself reveals that the eschatological Elijah may not achieve his goal.

Jesus cites Micah for the purposes of saying that his hearers are up against the messianic woes, in Mark 9:11-13 he links his hearers' present (which has witnessed John's execution) with Daniel 7, where the saints suffer the tribulation that immediately precedes the kingdom of God. In both cases the message is: the reign of eschatological peace and reconciliation is not at hand; rather, this is the time of final tribulation prophesied by Scripture.[96]

If there is a convincing correlation in content between Mark 9:11-13 and Q 12:51-53, there is also a scriptural link. For, as observed above, Mal 4:6, the text behind Mark 9:11-12, seems to allude to Mic 7:6, the text cited in Q 12:53. Even if that is not the case, we have found reason to believe that both Mic 7:6 and Mal 4:6 were read in the light of one another and that this explains the chiastic formulation in Q 12:53 (cf. Mark 13:13). It is also interesting to note that commentators on Matt 10:34-36 and Luke 12:51-53 have sometimes been put in mind of the apparent conflict between the synoptic passage and Mal 4:6.[97]

What does all this add up to? Q 12:51-53 and Mark 9:11-13 are, at first glance, very different texts. Close attention, however, reveals that they say very much the same thing—this is not the time of reconciliation but of eschatological suffering—and that they both say it by means of what Marcus calls a "refutational form"—by setting one scriptural text or expectation against another—, and further that the two Scriptures cited are probably intertextually related and have in any case been read together in exegetical history. So despite the

---

It is interesting that Christians who have seen Mal 4:5-6 fulfilled in the first advent have often taken "lest etc." to be a realized prophecy: the people rejected John and Jesus and suffered accordingly (see e.g. Calvin, *ad loc.*, and C. F. Keil, *Minor Prophets* [Grand Rapids: Eerdmans, n.d.] 473-74); others, however, have thought of Mal 4:5-6 as yet to be fulfilled; so e.g. Chrysostom, Theophylact, and Bengel in their comments on Matt 17:10-13.

[96]   If one assumes that John = Elijah, then my interpretation of Mark 9:11-13 produces precisely what Perrin found in Q 16:16: John's fate is a manifestation of the eschatological woes.

[97]   E.g. A. H. McNeile, *The Gospel according to St. Matthew* (London: Macmillan, 1915) 147 (who observes that Jesus could have been denying that he was Elijah); T. W. Manson, *The Sayings of Jesus* (London: SCM Press, 1949) 121; D. Hill, *The Gospel of Matthew* (London: Oliphants, 1972) 194; R. A. Horsley, *Jesus and the Spiral of Violence: Popular Jewish Resistance in Roman Palestine* (San Francisco: Harper & Row, 1987) 234 (who unconvincingly seeks to remove Q 12:51-53 from an apocalyptic scenario).

fact that they share no significant vocabulary and come from two different sources, Q 12:51-53 and Mark 9:11-13 exhibit profound agreements.

Now there is, as argued above, every reason to believe that Q 12:51-53 reflects something Jesus said. It would seem to follow that Mark 9:11-13, despite much doubt to the contrary, does also. The present conversational form and much of the wording of Mark 9:11-13 are presumably due to the community. Nonetheless, if Q 12:51-53 rests upon dominical tradition, one can hardly resist the inference that Mark 9:11-13 has a similar foundation. In other words, authenticating one complex has in this instance led us to authenticating another.

---

98   The implications of ascribing the original composition behind Mark 9:11-13 are large—e.g. Jesus used "Son of man" with reference to Daniel 7 and identified John with Elijah (cf. Q 7:27)—but cannot be unfolded here.

JESUS: A GLUTTON AND DRUNKARD*

Howard Clark Kee

SOME CURRENT APPROACHES TO ANALYSIS OF Q 7:18-35

The familiar but somewhat puzzling designation of Jesus as "a glutton and a drunkard" comes at the end of a sequence in the Q tradition which contrasts the respective roles of Jesus and John the Baptist.[1] Perceptions of the force and import of this appellation are linked with the context in which one understands it to have been uttered. A currently vocal scholarly contingent of those engaged in the study of Q insists that the section which runs from Luke 7:18 to 7:35 is composed of a random assemblage of pericopes of various types, including chriae, parables, commentaries thereon, and random sayings. There is said to be neither a coherent representation of John and Jesus in Q as we have it, nor a consistent evaluation of their respective roles.

But this understanding in what might be termed deconstructive exegesis ignores not only a number of features of this Q section as a cluster, but also the fact that this body of Q material is located in contexts in both Matthew and Luke where the roles of John the Baptist and Jesus are contrasted with respect to significant and distinctive elements in each of these Gospels.[2] In Matthew (11:2-19) this Q material serves to launch the third major section of that Gospel's account of Jesus' public ministry, as is shown by the favorite Matthean transitional phrase, "When Jesus had finished . . ." (Matt 11:1), following the commissioning of the Twelve. In Luke

---

* An earlier form of this paper appeared in *NTS* 42 (1996) 374-93 and makes its appearance in the present volume with the kind permission of Cambridge University Press.

[1] This pericope in Q is seen by Ben Witherington as marking the conclusion of the first main section of Q, which he describes as beginning with the announcement of the "sage's coming" (Luke 3:2-9, 15-17) and concluding with his rejection by "this generation." See Witherington, *Jesus the Sage: The Pilgrimage of Wisdom* (Edinburgh: T. & T. Clark; Minneapolis: Fortress, 1994) 219.

[2] As see in Matt 11:2-19 = Luke 7:18-35. In what follows, all references to Q are given in terms of Lukan versification.

(7:18-35) the transition from the Sermon on the Plain to the differentiation between the roles of John and Jesus is marked by a pair of miracle stories in which Jesus defies ethnic and cultic purity laws when he heals the slave of a Roman military officer, and then touches the bier and restores to life the son of the widow of Nain (Luke 7:1-10, 11-17).[3] It is such actions of Jesus, with their challenge to the norms of ritual purity, which implicitly raise for John the Baptist the crucial question articulated in this Q section as to whether Jesus is really the agent of renewal promised by God and awaited by his people. As John formulates the question, "Are you the one who is to come, or should we wait for another?" Central for our purposes is the recognition that there are two basic and closely linked issues involved which pervade this entire section of Q material (7:18-35): (1) the qualifications of Jesus as God's agent of renewal, and (2) the criteria for sharing in this renewal.[4]

Failure to recognize the dialectic between the two issues just noted —Jesus as agent of renewal, and the identity of those who share in the new community—leads some scholars to make what I believe are unwarranted distinctions and to claim stages of evolutionary development which run counter to the evidence. We shall also see that the Q sayings which are kindred to this section, but which are variously located in Matthew and Luke, are in fact compatible with the overall thrust of 7:18-35 as Luke has preserved it.

This observation as to consistent themes in the Q source runs contrary to one of the most detailed efforts to deconstruct the Q tradition as a whole, and specifically in considering the differences between Jesus and John found there. This project is that of John Kloppenborg, whose analysis of Q has been adopted as virtually normative by some scholars.[5] He regards Q 7:18-35 as a random

---

[3]   The healing of the centurion's slave derives from Q (Matt 8:5-13 = Luke 7:1-10), but the story of the widow's son comes from Luke's own source (Luke 7:11-17).

[4]   The section of Q dealing with Jesus and John differs in the Matthean and Lukan versions in several details: Matthew places 7:29-30 as the conclusions to his distinctive Parable of the Two Sons (Matt 21:28-32). Matthew includes in the section on Jesus and John a saying (Matt 11:12-13) located by Luke at 16:16 in a triad of sayings, two of which deal with obedience to the Law (16:17-18). Matthew also adds a declaration about the identity of John and Elijah, which is repeated in 17:9-13, where he is drawing on Mark (9:9-13).

[5]   J. S. Kloppenborg, *The Formation of Q: Trajectories in Ancient Wisdom*

collection of material, which has in common the theme of wisdom, and which he compares with Q 11:49-51. But he ignores the clearly apocalyptic dimensions of the latter passage, with its warning of divine judgment that will fall on those who reject God's messengers. The first pericope (Q 7:18-35) is treated as a pronouncement story, a post-Easter creation, aimed at luring former followers of John "into the Christian fold." No link is seen between the prophecies of Isaiah which are here depicted as being fulfilled and "traditional Jewish expectation about the messiah."[6] On the basis of the prior assumptions of those engaged in this approach to Q, the fact that there are miracles reported and eschatological predictions recounted is in itself sufficient proof that these are late developments of the tradition. Q 7:18-23, as well as 7:24-26, are treated as "responsorial chriae," which are defined as "short, pithy sayings" reported because of interest, not in Jesus' miracles, but in his pronouncements "occasioned by them."[7] It is the failure of most in Israel to respond to "John, Jesus and the Q preachers as the envoys of Sophia" which is the occasion for these pronouncements of "judgments and condemnation," rather than an authentic feature in the Jesus tradition.[8]

Jesus' estimate of John the Baptist in Q 7:24-26 is taken as authentic, however, on the basis of appeal to two norms: because of a pronouncement by Bultmann, and because it appears in the Gospel of Thomas, which is declared to antedate the other Gospels and Q, because it lacks apocalyptic and miraculous features! Verse 28 with its high praise of John ("among those born of women there is none greater than John") is regarded as "perhaps a dominical saying." But the two words immediately preceding and following are seen as later commentary: First, 7:27, "I am sending my messenger ahead of you, who will prepare the way before you," which is a composite of Exod 23:20 and Mal 3:1, as in Mark 1:2, and which assigns to John the role of Elijah (made explicit in the Matthean addition 11:14).[9] Second, a sharp contrast is perceived between on the one hand Q 7:28a ("none greater than John") and 7:27, where John is "Elijah

---

Collections (Philadelphia: Fortress, 1987).

6   Kloppenborg, *The Formation of Q*, 107-108.

7   Kloppenborg, *The Formation of Q*, 168.

8   Kloppenborg, *The Formation of Q*, 169.

9   An expanded version of this identification is present in Mark 9:9-13, which is reproduced in Matt 17:9-13, and which is probably reflected in the Matthean addition (11:14).

redivivus," and hence on the other hand Q 7:28b ("he who is least in the kingdom is greater than [John]"), which is said to relegate his function to an era prior to the kingdom.[10]

Not discussed by Kloppenborg is Luke 7:29-30, which does have a rough parallel in Matthew's Parable of the Two Sons (Matt 21:32), but which in fact points to a similarity between the responses to John and—implicitly—to Jesus. This response is favorable on the part of moral and social outsiders, and negative on the part of the religious leaders. Matthew includes here in his version of Q (11:12) a saying (Q 16:16) which predicts that violence will accompany the coming of the kingdom and differentiates between (1) the epoch of the law and the prophets, which culminates in the role of John, and (2) his role in relation to the proclamation of the kingdom (Luke) or its coming (Matthew). Kloppenborg is convinced that the Lukan form of this pericope has been thoroughly redacted, and was not part of the John the Baptist group of sayings in 7:18-28, 31-35. He regards the Matthean version (11:12b) as the more original form of the saying, which he understands in the words of Schrenk's paraphrase, "The Kingdom of God is contested, attacked and hampered by contentious opponents."[11] The inference is that, rather than marking the end of an era, John should be seen as inaugurating the end time.[12]

Turning to the second pericope, Q 7:31-35, which is the major focus of this paper, Kloppenborg once more describes the composite nature of the material. Here there is said to be a parable of the children playing in the market place (7:31-32), which is followed by an explanation. He asserts that there is no competition or tension depicted here between Jesus and John, since "wisdom is justified by all her children." The basic unity of the parable and the explanation of it lies in their common role in relation to wisdom, which is of course the central value for the International Q Project.[13] There are said to be no apocalyptic features, but rather it is Wisdom who is instigating the call to repentance. Appeal for this interpretation is made to Proverbs (1:10-33; 8:1-21), where the warning of judgment and the summons to repent are depicted, which is then juxtaposed with Wisdom's role in enabling to become "friends of the prophets"

---

10   Kloppenborg, *The Formation of Q*, 109.

11   G. Schrenk, "βιάζομαι," *TDNT* 1 (1964) 610-11.

12   Kloppenborg, *The Formation of Q*, 114-15.

13   Sponsored by the Society of Biblical Literature.

those who heed her call (Wis 7:26-28). The confirmation for this interpretation is said to be given in Q 11:49-51, where Wisdom is sent to call Israel to repentance. Passed over, however, is the climactic note in that Q pericope, where, in a manner consonant with apocalyptic, Wisdom announces the judgment that is to fall on the present generation because of their rejection and the death of the one whom God has sent to prepare his people for divine renewal.[14] Kloppenborg infers that both Jesus and John experienced the violence of those opposed to the coming of the Kingdom of God, but he treats these conflicts in terms of timeless wisdom, rather than as predictions of cosmic struggle in the manner of apocalyptic wisdom.

JESUS CONTRASTS HIS ROLE WITH THAT OF JOHN

In spite of this eager contemporary effort to fit the Jesus of the Q tradition into the dubious construct of timeless wisdom, the section under analysis here seems to me to define the relationships and roles of Jesus and John in ways which shed direct historical light on Christian origins when the passage is perceived in terms of redefining the people of God, and Jesus as the agent of divine renewal. In Judaism of the post-exilic period the twin questions concerning the definition and identity of God's people focused primarily on the role of the divine agent (or agents) of covenant renewal and the criteria for participation in the renewed community.[15] It is precisely these twin issues which are central in the Dead Sea Scrolls, where the leadership and the community requirements are contrasted with those in effect in the priestly establishment. Awaited in the Qumran community are the divinely appointed royal and priestly agents, the messiahs of Aaron and Israel, whose coming is foretold in the Rule of the Future Community (1QSa). Directly relevant for our investigation is the fact that in Daniel the same concerns are central. Primary attention has been paid by New Testament interpreters of Daniel 7 to the question of the identity of the "one like a human being" or more

---

[14]   Kloppenborg also thinks that Matthew's version of the saying about violence that will accompany the coming of the kingdom (Matt 11:12-13) is more original than Luke 16:16. But he ignores the apocalyptic dimensions of this prophecy as well.

[15]   The major models of community operative in this period are traced in my study, *Who Are the People of God? Models of Community in Judaism and Early Christianity* (New Haven and London: Yale University Press, 1995).

commonly, "like a son of man" to whom God ultimately gives "dominion and glory and kingship." But there is no mistaking that a major role in the ultimate sovereignty over the "kingdoms under the whole heaven" is promised as well "to the people of the holy ones of the Most High" (Dan 7:27). The implications of this linking of the Son of Man and the kingdom given to the "holy ones" as well as to "the people of the holy ones" have not—in my opinion—received adequate attention from many New Testament scholars. To put the issue succinctly and in the traditional terminology of our field, one cannot detach christological from ecclesiological issues.

John J. Collins has addressed the matter of relationship between Son of Man and the people of God with great insight in his study, *The Apocalyptic Imagination* and more recently in his superb commentary on Daniel.[16] He distinguishes between (1) the "holy ones" who in Dan 7:18 are said to "receive the kingdom," and to whom he identifies as angels, and (2) "the people of the holy ones," who are members of the human community to whom the everlasting kingdom is given (7:27).[17] In the *Similitudes of Enoch*, which he dates to the latter part of the first century BCE,[18] the Son of Man is to be the staff for the "holy ones" on earth, to whom he has been revealed (48:4-5). They will one day dwell and eat with him (62:14), but now he is the heavenly counterpart of the faithful earthly community, which is identified as "righteous" and the "chosen," rather than in political terms as a nation.[19] At the end of Daniel (12:6-13) there is a promise that the power or the powerful figure which had seemingly shattered the "holy people" (that is of course, Antiochus Epiphanes) will be destroyed, and the ultimate vindication of the faithful community will take place.[20] In Daniel and the subsequent apocalyptic tradition,

---

[16]   J. J. Collins, *The Apocalyptic Imagination: An Introduction to the Jewish Matrix of Christianity* (New York: Crossroad, 1987); idem, *Daniel* (Hermeneia; Minneapolis: Fortress, 1993).

[17]   Collins (*Daniel*, 313-17) notes that in a few texts "holy ones" refers to the people of Israel (Ps 34:9; 1QM 10:10), but that in most of the passages in which the term occurs, it means "angels" (Dan 4:10, 14, 20; 8:13; *1 Enoch* 14:22-23).

[18]   The basis for assigning this date includes the reference to the Parthian invasion (which took place about 40 BCE) and the allusion to the hot springs, which probably reflects Herod's effort to achieve healing for himself (cf. Josephus, *Ant.* 17.6.5 §171).

[19]   Collins, *Apocalyptic Imagination*, 148-50.

[20]   Collins (*Daniel*, 399) proposes a slight emendation of the MT here, but

therefore, the role of "one like a son of man" is linked directly with the destiny of the faithful community. With this bi-polar feature in view, we return to our analysis of Q 7:18-35.

John's question to Jesus as to whether he is "the one who is to come" clearly looks backward as well as forward: back to the promises in the scriptural tradition of the coming of an agent of God to renew his people, and forward to the fulfillment of that hope. John's urgent concern for the covenant renewal is expressed in Q 3:7-9, where the emphasis is on repentance in view of the impending divine judgment: "Even now the axe is laid to the root of the trees"; that is, judgment will fall on those who do not bear the fruits of repentance. The tone is actually denunciatory and condemnatory toward the "snakes," as though John would prefer that they did not repent. It is a radical change of lifestyle by these disobedient and misguided people that is called for, if they are to have any right to their claim to be "children of Abraham." The pericope ends with no word of hope, but rather with expectation of doom through fiery judgment on the wicked. It is this stringency of demand that lies behind Jesus' characterization of John as one whose ethical and cultic standards for participation in God's people are epitomized as "eating no bread and drinking no wine" (7:33). The primary issues in the Q account of the debate between Jesus and John, therefore, are two: What are the norms for sharing in the covenant community? and what is the role of the one through whom it will be established?

In Q 7:21 the activities of Jesus are summarized in response to the question of Jesus' eschatological role as "the one who is to come." It includes not only healings but also exorcisms, which in the Q addition (11:19-20) to Mark's account of the Beelzebub controversy (Mark 3:22-27) are highlighted as evidence of two features: (1) the source of this power is audaciously traced to "the finger of God," which of course echoes the action of God in delivering Israel from enslavement in Egypt (Exod 8:19); (2) Jesus' victory over the powers of evil is claimed to be demonstrating the inbreaking of God's rule. This report in Q of Jesus' response to John clearly puts his activity in the same framework of meaning as what is found in the Q version of the Beelzebub pericope. The same perspective on eschatological fulfillment is continued and amplified in the pastiche of prophetic

---

either reading of the text points to the destruction of Antiochus Epiphanes and the resulting liberation of God's faithful people.

quotations which Jesus offers to the questioners from John as justification for his acts of healing and renewal which they have observed him performing, and of which they have heard reports. The details of Jesus' description of his activities employ phrases which echo the clearly eschatological sections of Isaiah: the restoration of sight to the blind; the lame enabled to walk; the deaf can hear (Isa 29:18; 35:5-6; 42:18; 61:1). Whatever modern designation may be appropriate for *lepros*, Jesus' having touched those with this disease is perceived by his Jewish contemporaries to have been a violation of ritual regulations (Leviticus 13–14).[21] Even the resurrection of the faithful dead is announced in the post-exilic prophecies included in Isaiah to which Jesus here alludes (Isa 26:19). The good news to the poor here also echoes the promise of their blessedness in the first of the beatitudes (6:20), which of courses recalls the eschatological promise of Isa 61:1-2, as Luke makes explicit in his distinctive and extended account of Jesus' sermon in Nazareth (Luke 4:18-21).[22]

The force of the final verse in this section (7:23) should not be overlooked: "Blessed is the one who takes no offense at me." What Jesus is here depicted as saying and doing is highly controversial, since it is a direct challenge to the widespread concern among Jews of this period for maintenance of ritual and ethnic purity. The purity mode of defining God's people was shared by groups that differed on details but had a major commitment to such ritual criteria for participation in the covenant people. Groups with this mode of group identity included priests, Pharisees, Sadducees, Essenes, as well as John the Baptist and his followers. John's critique of his contemporaries, as we have noted, was not based on their ritual or ethnic exclusivism, but rather on the inconsistencies and inadequacies in their use of such criteria for sharing in the people of God. To one who promulgated and was committed to such a program and point of view as attributed in Q to John the Baptist, Jesus was inescapably and potently offensive.

It is essential also to consider the details of Jesus' depiction of John in Q 7:24-28 and elsewhere. Matthew (3:1) and Luke (3:2-3) both

---

21   See discussion by J. A. Fitzmyer, *The Gospel according to Luke I–IX* (AB 28; Garden City: Doubleday, 1981) 373-74.

22   One must now take into account the remarkable parallels found in 4Q521. See J. J. Collins, "The Works of the Messiah," *DSD* 1 (1994) 98-112; idem, *The Scepter and the Star: The Messiahs of the Dead Sea Scrolls and Other Ancient Literature* (ABRL 10; New York: Doubleday, 1995) 117-22.

supplement the Markan tradition about John the Baptist by identifying the "wilderness" where John was preaching and baptizing as "the wilderness of Judea," located in "the region around the Jordan," the river where Mark describes the baptizing as having taken place (1:5). Specific features of that wilderness are referred to in Q 7:24-26. It is important to keep in mind the peculiar terrain of the Jordan Valley at the lower end. The area immediately adjacent to the river or watered by it through irrigation channels is verdant, but even now the parts of the valley east and west of the river, although close to its banks, are barren and rocky, with only tiny, scattered patches of vegetation where moisture gathers. The "reed shaken by the wind" would by sight and sound offer no more than a minor contrast to the lonely realm of the barren desert, so the analogy with John does not fit. Equally inappropriate is the implied comparison of John with another feature of the lower Jordan Valley: the grand palace complex developed by Herod west of Jericho. It was a royal estate, with a generous supply of water channelled in from the river, swimming pools, irrigated gardens, pavilions, and baths. Excavations have shown that just the main wing of the palace occupied 10,000 square meters, with elaborate bath houses, frescoed walls, and decorated ceilings. It served as a winter retreat for the Jerusalem aristocracy.[23] Anyone eager to see such splendor could seek access to the "king's courts" in the Jordan Valley, but need not—would not—look there for John the Baptist. The point of Jesus' declaration becomes clear: the future for God's people does not depend on good relations with the puppet rulers, such as King Herod, who are the instruments of Roman power in the land of Judea, superficially attractive as the royal palace in the Jordan Valley and the "soft clothing" of those who gathered there may be. Instead, one must give heed to those individuals who are instruments in the hands of God for preparing and establishing his kingdom on earth: John the Baptist and Jesus.

The comparison of Jesus with John also concerns his role as one who is "more than a prophet." Earlier, Luke (3:4-6) like Matthew (3:3) has followed Mark (1:2-3) in linking John with the prediction in Second Isaiah about the one "crying in the wilderness," whose role is to "prepare the way of the Lord" (Isa 40:3). Although Matthew and Luke do not follow Mark by going on to quote Mal 3:1 concerning "my messenger before thy face" when John launches his

---

[23] Details are provided by E. Netzer, "Roman Jericho," *ABD* 3.737-39.

baptizing activity (Luke 3:4; Matt 3:3), they both use the Q version
of this quotation (Q 7:27) to identify John with his unique prophetic
role as the one who prepares the way for God's agent to establish his
rule in the world. Only Luke among the synoptic Gospels extends the
quotation of Isaiah 40 at the initial appearance of John at 3:5-6 in
such a way as to include the promise that "all flesh shall see the
salvation of God" (Luke 3:4-6).[24]

Returning to the Q material proper, we see that there (7:28) John
is depicted as in the top category of all humanity ("those born of
women") down to the time of the inbreaking of the Kingdom of God:
"none is greater than John." As we noted earlier, the Q tradition
(16:16) pictures John as standing at the crucial point of transition
between the present age and the coming of the kingdom: "The law and
the prophets were in effect until John came: since then, the Kingdom
of God is proclaimed." We saw that some interpreters[25] read this Q
text as including John in the same era as Jesus, but the clear intent of
the saying seems to be rather that, though John is the admirable
culmination of the former epoch, he remains outside the new
community whose "least" member is "greater than he." This is the
explicit thrust of Q 16:16, as is made clear by the contrast between
the age of the law and the prophets which extends "until John" and
the new epoch in which the Kingdom of God is now being proclaimed. The difference between the Matthean and Lukan versions of
the Q sayings about the violence that accompanies the coming of the
kingdom are significant, and probably to be accounted for on the
basis of the different perspectives of each of these Gospels.[26]
Throughout his Gospel Matthew highlights the conflict that the new
community and its messengers are experiencing, as is most evident in
the unique cluster of anti-Pharisaical polemics found in Matthew 23,
where blame is placed on them for scourging, persecuting, and
crucifying the true scribes, prophets, and wise men whom God is
sending to proclaim and interpret the message of Jesus. By contrast,
in Luke's version of Q 16:16 those who enter the kingdom are

---

24   Luke alone develops the motif of the inclusion of "all flesh" in God's saving
action. This is done by extending the quotation from Isaiah 40 at John's initial appearance to include all humanity (Luke 3:4-6), and by picturing John as baptizing
Roman soldiers and tax-collectors (Luke 3:11-14).

25   Kloppenborg et al. cited above.

26   In his article on βιάζομαι, Schrenk (*TDNT* 1 [1964] 609-13) seeks to
demonstrate that Matthew's is the more original version of the saying.

simply warned to be prepared for conflict. Indeed, the force of βιάζεται in this saying as recorded by Luke could be that everyone who enters the kingdom does so either with burning zeal, or with triumphant force. Both such meanings imply that the announcement of God's kingdom is to be heard as "good news" beyond the impending struggles, in contrast with Matthew's use of the saying in such a way as to highlight the vehemence of those hostile to Jesus' proclamation of the coming Kingdom of God, while seeking to show that Jesus had the proper understanding of the Law.[27]

The Q Parable of the Children in the Marketplace and the interpretation of it offered by Jesus offer not only a contrast between the respective roles of John and Jesus but also differentiate the kind of participation in community which each of them evokes. The contemporaries of John and Jesus are clearly referred to in the hard-to-please children here pictured as "sitting in the marketplace." They respond negatively to two sharply different kinds of invitation: a call to take part in joyful activity (piping and dancing) or a summons to share in mourning (wailing and weeping). The interpretation of this parabolic picture which follows involves a shift of imagery based on contrasts: from different modes of play to different means of sharing in a common life, either by ascetic restraint ("eating no bread and drinking no wine") or by joyous participation ("eating and drinking"). The majority of the contemporaries of John and Jesus follow one or both of these models of the peevish children: They reject the stringency of John's message and his norms for repentance in preparation for the renewal of God's people, and/or they reject the one who opens participation in God's people to those who are ethnically, occupationally, culturally, ritually beyond the traditional boundaries of God's people. That is, they reject Jesus. The force of this contrast is a significant factor in the whole of this Q pericope.

It is in Q, rather than in Mark, that we have access to the most detail about the message of John and his program of preparation for covenant renewal. Indeed, the very first pericope in the Q tradition, Q 3:7-9, consists of a report concerning John's denouncing the

---

[27] Detailed and convincing analyses of Matthew as the product of a community in conscious and vicious competition with emergent rabbinic Judaism in the period after the destruction of the Temple have been offered by J. A. Overman, *Matthew's Gospel and Formative Judaism* (Minneapolis: Fortress, 1990), and by A. J. Saldarini, *Matthew's Christian-Jewish Community* (Chicago and London: University of Chicago Press, 1994).

wickedness of his contemporaries and declaring the falsity of their claim to be children of Abraham, and therefore members of the covenant community. The climactic feature of this pericope is the redefining of God's people. God will act to establish his people in ways that these false claimants cannot foresee. What is foretold is primarily the doom that is about to fall on this morally fruitless generation of those who mistakenly consider themselves to be the people of God. When the Q tradition goes beyond the Markan account of John's prediction of the "mightier one" who is coming (Mark 1:7), it describes in vivid detail what the coming one will do: he will gather his "wheat [that is, of course, his people] into his granary," but also will burn "the chaff [that is, the false claimants to covenantal identity] . . . with unquenchable fire." Luke alone adds to his fiery prediction of the doom of the wicked the ironic remark: "So, with many other exhortations, he preached good news . . ." (Luke 3:18). In this Q pericope, however, the emphasis is not at all on good news but is emphatically on moral irresponsibility and the fires of judgment which will fall on the unrepentant and unresponsive.

These pericopes about John not only fit well with the characterization of him in Q 7:33 as ascetic, "eating no bread and drinking no wine," but they also convey powerfully a picture of the Coming One as an agent of judgment. Q 3:16 involves the addition of a significant phrase to John's prediction about the Coming One: he will baptize not only "with the Holy Spirit," as in Mark 1:8, but also "with fire!" The function of that fire is then made explicit: to consume the worthless and unfit, thereby preventing them from sharing in the life of God's people. The response that John's message and demands elicited from most of his contemporaries, according to Q 7:33b, is that John "has a demon." The same charge of being involved with demons is, of course, made against Jesus in the Q version of the Beelzebub controversy (Q 11:14-20), to which Jesus responds with the claim that his power to expel demons is a sign of the inbreaking of God's kingdom. Once again, this reinforces the contrast we have noted in Q 7:28 between John as herald of the one through whom the kingdom comes and Jesus as the agent in whose words and works the kingdom has already dawned. While John is reportedly accused in Q of *having* a demon, Jesus is the one through whom the demons are being routed.

The crucial and, for many, the most problematic texts are those that follow. The term Son of Man, as we have noted, is linked in Daniel with the major factors which are operative in these pericopes:

(1) The defeat of the demonic powers, who are deprived of the dominion that they have exercised in this world in the era of evil (Dan 7:12).

(2) The kingdom is given by God to "one like a human being," or literally, "like a son of man." In Daniel he is the agent through whom God's rule is established in the world. That kingdom is universal in its scope and everlasting in its duration (Dan 7:14).

(3) In the interpretation of the visions of Daniel (7:15-27), the beneficiary of God's bestowal of the kingdom is not merely a messianic type of individual, but "the people of the holy ones of the Most High." In this vision of Daniel, therefore, of equal significance with the agent through whom God's rule is established is the depiction of the new people of God who share in it, and to whom the whole of humanity is to be become servile and obedient. It is precisely these three factors which are operative in Q 7:31-35.

Before turning to our exegesis of this Q passage, however, it may be useful to engage in a rapid analytical survey of the phrase, "son of man" as it is used more broadly in the Q tradition. It occurs ten, or possibly eleven times in the Q material.[28] In every case, a primary factor is the defining of the community of God's people.[29] We shall examine the Son of Man sayings in Q in the Lukan order and in the context of the pericope in which each is found, bypassing Q 7:34 until after we have analyzed the others.

6:20-23 opens the so-called Sermon on the Plain, where the address is in the second person plural, and there is a repeated contrast between "now and the future time of fulfillment.[30] It is to the poor, the hungry, the weeping, those who are hated, excluded, reviled, and their names "cast out" that the promise is extended of blessedness in "that day" (6:23) when they share in the "kingdom of God." The cause of their rejection and sorrow is their association with "the Son of Man." The rejection which they will experience is

---

28   A. Polag (*Die Christologie der Logienquelle* [Neukirchen: Neukirchener Verlag, 1977] 102) includes Matt 19:28, where "Son of Man" appears but is lacking in the Lukan parallel (22:28-30). The latter text is discussed below, however.

29   Seriously inappropriate is the traditional scholarly classification of Son of Man sayings: (1) present, (2) future, and (3) suffering Son of Man in the Q tradition.

30   "Now" occurs twice in 6:21 and twice in 6:25.

analogous with that which the prophets experienced in the past at the hands of those who regarded themselves as the "fathers" of God's covenant people. The contrast between the self-styled people of God and the authentic covenant community is clear, and the criterion which differentiates the two is the combination of the person and the role of the Son of Man.

Analogous to this experience of rejection by the leaders of the traditional community is the necessity for those who join the followers of Jesus to forfeit the security of the natural family and to abdicate domestic obligations (9:57-62). It is Jesus as Son of Man who is the model for this manner of life and the consequent experience of a socially alien existence. In the longer Lukan form of this pericope, it is made explicit that the major focus and value of the life of his followers are to be the coming kingdom of God and the task of proclaiming it. But the radical break with family has as its model in the unmistakably Q material here the shattering of family links and security as one enters the life of the new community by becoming a follower of Jesus.

In Q 11:29-32 another dimension of the community that is being established by the Son of Man is indicated. In response to the skeptics' demand for a sign from Jesus that God is behind his enterprise and conveying his message through him, Jesus points to the two modes by which that message is being sent forth: a call to repentance, and wisdom. These are epitomized respectively by Jonah and Solomon, both of whom had success in communicating their respective modes of truth to non-members of the people of Israel: the Ninevites and the Queen of the South. The people of Nineveh repented, and the queen came "from the ends of the earth" to hear God's wisdom through Solomon. They symbolized the outsiders who are to hear God's message for his people through Jesus, the one who is "greater than Jonah" and "greater than Solomon." Participation in the new community is not to be limited by ethnic or hereditary or socio-cultural criteria. The sole requirement is readiness to hear God's message through his chosen agent, the Son of Man.

In Q 12:2-12 there is a mixture of imperatives and warnings to the messengers of the gospel. What they have proclaimed in private will become public. They are to beware of those who will not only martyr the witnesses to the good news but will also try to destroy their integrity as followers of Jesus, with the result that they will forfeit their place in the kingdom and end up in the fires of hell.

Countering this is the assurance of God's protection of his people. Those who confess their trusting relationship to "the Son of Man" will be confirmed by him in the presence of God, while those who denounce him and the power of the Spirit that it is at work through him and his people will never be forgiven. The destiny of the covenant people is inextricably bound up with the role and vindication of the Son of Man.

The role of the faithful as obedient servants is depicted in Q 12:35-40 on the analogy of the master whose return from a marriage feast is eagerly and diligently awaited by his household staff. The returning master will—astonishingly—serve them! They must be ready no matter when he returns, but they have no more of a clue when that will be than any householder has as to when a thief will break in and plunder the house. The community of faithful followers must be always ready for the unpredictable coming of "the Son of Man." The fidelity and wisdom of the effective member of the new community is then further compared with the steward who performs his duties, unlike the irresponsible servant who uses the absence of his master to give vent to cruelty and debauchery (12:42-46). The absence of the Son of Man is here depicted in an extended parabolic form in order to arouse consciousness within the community of their ongoing obligations as his servants.

Similar solemn warnings to the community are offered in Q 17:23-37. In the Lukan version there are three references to "the day(s) of the Son of Man." The first concerns the debate within the community as to the time when the Son of Man will be in control (v. 22); the second declares that the coming of the Son of Man will be as sudden and unpredictable as a flash of lightning (v. 24). The "days of the Son of Man," or his "coming" in Matthew's version (Matt 24:37-41) are apparently a reference to the final days before the Son of Man is revealed—days during which humanity goes about its normal routines, as oblivious of the crisis that is about to occur with the appearance of God's agent, the Son of Man, as were the contemporaries of Noah and the people of Sodom. The judgment will fall when the "Son of Man is revealed." What is called for here, and in the material associated with these sayings by both Matthew (24:42-51) and Luke (17:31-37) is the absolute necessity for the community to be obedient, diligent, and ready for the crisis which is about to occur.

In the Matthean version (Matt 19:28) of Q 22:28-30, the role of the community in judging the tribes of Israel is predicted to occur at the renewal of the creation (παλιγγενεσία) when "the Son of Man shall sit on his glorious throne." The Lukan version identifies the community as those "who have remained faithfully with [Jesus] throughout the testings" he has been experiencing. To them is "covenanted a kingdom," just as the Father covenanted a kingdom with Jesus. The analogy with the bestowal of the kingdom upon the Son of Man and the "saints of the Most High" in Daniel 7 is unmistakable in this Q passage. The shared meal here anticipated underscores the communal dimensions of the fulfillment of this promise.

Careful analysis of the 53 pericopes which comprise Q shows that only five or six of them can be construed as primarily instructions for individuals,[31] although even these personal ethical instructions make most sense when seen as part of the structuring and constituting of the new community. The vast majority of the Q pericopes, on the other hand, deal with the defining of the new community. The images are consistently corporate: family, flock, feast, harvest, household, kingdom. The issues discussed in this material are the open membership in the community. For example, ritual and ethnic limits (Q 14:16-24 [Parable of the Eschatological Feast]; 11:29-32 [the Sign of Jonah]; 7:2-3, 6-10 [Healing the Centurion's Slave]); warnings of persecution (12:4-5, 11-12), shattering of the family (12:49-53); martyrdom and divine judgment for those who abandon or betray their commitments within the community (13:25-29). Of paramount concern is behavior within the community, as the Parable of the Returning Nobleman exemplifies (Q 19:12-13, 15-26).

Ben Witherington, in *Jesus the Sage: The Pilgrimage of Wisdom*, offers a persuasive case for the thesis advanced by Gerd Theissen that in Q Jesus is both wisdom teacher and prophet.[32] Witherington concludes that "in the arguably authentic [Q] material there is an irreducible amount of both sapiential, prophetic, and eschatological material. Q has faithfully reflected this fact."[33] Richard Horsley rejected the notion that one should make a distinction in Q between sapiential wisdom at the formative stage and later apocalyptic

---

[31]   The most likely candidates for the category of instructions for individuals are 11:24-26, 33-36; 12:33-34; 16:13, 17-18. The inappropriateness of declaring sapiential wisdom in aphoristic mode of expression as characteristic of Q is self-evident.

[32]   G. Theissen, *The Gospels in Context: Social and Political History in the Synoptic Tradition* (Minneapolis: Fortress, 1991) 205.

[33]   Witherington, *Jesus the Sage*, 226.

material.[34] Richard Edwards noted that in Q the expectation of Jesus' return to carry out God's judgment of the world "led to a heightened, intense interest in the present time and its circumstances." He concludes that the Q community expected the imminent return of Jesus, who was still active within the community by the prophets he inspired, calling the faithful to obedience and warning of persecution.[35] The potent factor of community definition is abundantly evident.

It is against the wider background of the importance for Q of defining the community of God's people that we must now examine the concluding verses of our Q passage (7:34-35). The open, inclusive attitude on the part of Jesus toward fellowship and participation in the life of the new community is characteristic of all the Gospel tradition, including Q, as we have noted. This is affirmed symbolically in Jesus' characterization of himself ("the Son of Man") as one who comes "eating and drinking." The open basis for participation is dramatically specified in Jesus' characterization of himself as "a friend of tax collectors and sinners"—those excluded from social contact by the norms of the legally strict, the ritually pious, and the nationalistically zealous.

As we have seen, in several essays on the Q source Horsley has dismissed as arbitrary the claim of Kloppenborg, Koester, Robinson, and others that there is a radical distinction between sapiential wisdom (which is asserted to have been what was embodied in the early stage of Q) and apocalyptic wisdom, which was inserted into Q at a later stage.[36] Careful analysis of Q shows, I believe, that these

---

34   R. A. Horsley, "Questions about Redactional Strata and Social Relations Reflected in Q," in D. J. Lull (ed.), *Society of Biblical Literature 1989 Seminar Papers* (SBLSP 28; Atlanta: Scholars Press, 1989) 186-203.

35   R. A. Edwards, *A Theology of Q: Eschatology, Prophecy, and Wisdom* (Philadelphia: Fortress, 1976) 147-49.

36   Horsley's critique is offered in a pair of essays, "Wisdom Justified by All Her Children: Explaining Allegedly Disparate Traditions in Q," in E. H. Lovering, Jr. (ed.), *Society of Biblical Literature 1994 Seminar Papers* (SBLSP 33; Atlanta: Scholars Press, 1994) 733-51. But among early champions of a non-apocalyptic tradition is H. Koester, for example, who earlier advanced the thesis that the *Gospel of Thomas* was the original version of Q, which was later converted by the insertion of apocalyptic features ("Apocryphal and Canonical Gospels," *HTR* 73 [1980] 105-30). He has subsequently retreated somewhat from this position, asserting that the original Q did mix sapiential wisdom and eschatological statements, but he still assumes that a later editor imposed apocalyptic features on

distinctions are purely arbitrary and artificial. Horsley affirms the
conclusion of Adela Yarbro Collins that Son of Man sayings are to
be found at every stage of the formation of Q.[37] Above all, for our
purposes, Horsley rejects Kloppenborg's proposal which assigns to
the later redactional level all the passages in Q which project the
inclusion of those who would be regarded by ritual and ethical
standards as outsiders.[38] He sees the critique of Israel as a challenge,
rather than a rejection of Israel and a consequent appeal primarily to
Gentiles. The critique in Q is of the scribes and Pharisees, not of
Israel as a whole. Further, Horsley is persuaded that the prophetic
sayings in Q are not later additions, but are integral to the discourses.
He sees a contrast between Daniel and the outlook of Q, in that in
Daniel the future restoration of God's people is in response to an
attack by a foreign power (the Seleucids), but in Q the renewal has
already begun, and is a threat to the domestic rulers who are
collaborating with the pagan power.[39] It is the oppressed and
powerless for whom the hopes of liberation and renewal are here
articulated. "This generation," which is frequently criticized in Q,
refers to the leadership group within Israel and their retainers, but
by no means the people as a whole. The aim of Jesus as the prophet
of the coming kingdom of God in Q, according to Horsley, is to
renew the covenantal community. He finds this theme especially clear
in the section of Q which we have been examining (i.e. 7:18-35).[40]

That the issue of community definition is indeed the central
concern here is implicit in a crucial phrase, the implications of which
have been largely overlooked in exegesis of this passage: namely, the
denunciatory designation which Jesus here apparently borrows from
his opponents with reference to himself: "a glutton and drunkard."

---

this tradition. He attributes to later tradition (1) the announcement of judgment on
this generation; (2) the apocalyptic expectation of Jesus' return; and (3) the demarcation between Jesus and John the Baptist (cf. Koester, *Ancient Christian Gospels:
Their History and Development* [London: SCM Press; Philadelphia: Trinity Press
International, 1990] 150, 162).

[37]   A. Y. Collins, "The Son of Man in the Sayings Source," in M. P. Horgan
and P. J. Kobelski (eds.), *To Touch the Text: Biblical and Related Studies in
Honor of Joseph A. Fitzmyer, S.J.* (New York: Crossroad, 1989) 369-99.

[38]   Horsley, "Wisdom Justified," 741.

[39]   Horsley, "Wisdom Justified," 748.

[40]   R. A. Horsley, "Q and Jesus: Assumptions, Approaches, and Analyses,"
Semeia 55 (1991) 175-209.

The verbal links of this phrase with Deut 21:20 have been noted and discussed[41] but not adequately explored. The fact that the phrase in Q (φάγος καὶ οἰνοπότης) differs sharply from the LXX (συμβολοκοπῶν οἰνοφλυγεῖ) can be used to argue for the authenticity of the saying, since a direct quotation from the LXX, even its wording, would be a likely sign of a later addition to the Q tradition. What has been largely overlooked is the context in which the phrase occurs in Deuteronomy (21:18-21) and the implications which this carries with it for the use of the phrase in the Jesus tradition. The passage in Deuteronomy outlines the procedure for dealing with a "stubborn and rebellious son," who refuses to obey his parents. More is at stake than relations within the family, however. He constitutes a threat to the welfare of the community as a whole, as is evident in the court of appeal to which the case is to be referred and the agents through whom the legally prescribed punishment is to be carried out. The problem is not to be resolved by the parents alone. Instead, the charge against the rebel is to be brought to the town council: to the elders gathered at the town gate. The execution of the rebel is to be by stoning, and is to be carried out by all the adult males of the community.

In the setting of the ministry of Jesus, his aggressive practice of welcoming aliens and the excluded into the community which he is shaping can only be regarded as rebellion and sedition by strict adherents to ritual, cultic, and ethnic limits for participation in those who see themselves as the people of God. What is implicit in Jesus' use of this term, "glutton and drunkard"—which he borrowed from or attributed to the severe critics of his open and inclusive definition of the community of God's people—is that he is prepared for execution. Historically, of course, his execution was not by Jewish authorities on the basis of his alleged violation of Jewish laws, but by the Romans on the political charge that he aspired to "king of the Jews," as the inscription over the cross attests. The Pauline tradition of the Eucharist (1 Cor 11:23-25), which reports Jesus as interpreting the breaking of bread as symbolizing his "body which is broken for you," fits better the experience of death by stoning than by

---

41   J. Jeremias, *The Parables of Jesus* (New York: Scribner's, 1963) 160. Fitzmyer, however, in his monumental commentary (*Luke I–IX*, 681) dismisses the proposal of a connection, since the Greek of Q differs from the LXX of Deuteronomy.

crucifixion. It is conceivable that this was indeed the way by which
Jesus expected to die, but the important feature for our purposes is as
follows: Jesus' radical redefining of the people of God and of the
grounds for participation in this community he perceived to be
providing the basis for a plot to destroy him.

This interpretation of Q 7:31-35 fits well with Q 11:47-51 where
the scribes and Pharisees are denounced for having taken their place
in the deplorable tradition that resulted in the killing of the prophets
and messengers that God sent to his people Israel. This kind of
response to those sent by God is discernible throughout the biblical
tradition from Genesis ("the blood of Abel") to 2 Chronicles ("the
blood of Zechariah").[42] It is perhaps significant that the latter was
executed by stoning. Indeed, later rabbinic tradition says that Cain
murdered Abel by crushing his skull with a stone.[43] Although no
source for the apparent quotation in Q 11:49 has ever been
established,[44] it links Wisdom with the role of the prophets, and with
prophetic predictions of an apocalyptic flavor about the suffering
and martyrdom that God's messengers have experienced and will
experience. Although these Q texts pointing to the death of Jesus and
of his followers are very different from the explicit predictions of
the passion found in Mark (8:31; 9:31; 10:33-34), they demonstrate
the links between wisdom, prophecy, and the death of those who
speak for God to this people.[45] In this Q passage, Jesus' confrontation

---

[42]   Cf. 2 Chr 24:20-22. He is wrongly identified in Matt 23:35 as "son of
Barachiah," which fits the prophet Zechariah (Zech 1:1).

[43]   In the last part of a greatly expanded Gen 4:8, Targum Pseudo-Jonathan
reads: "And Cain rose up against Abel his brother *and drove a stone into his
forehead*" (M. Maher, *Targum Pseudo-Jonathan: Genesis* [ArBib 1B; Collegeville:
Liturgical Press, 1992] 33). The italics indicate the part that has been added to the
biblical text. A similar tradition is found in *Gen. Rab.* 22.8 (on Gen 4:8): "The
Rabbis said: 'He killed him with a stone.'" G. Reim ("Targum and Johannesevangelium," *BZ* 27 [1983] 1-13, esp. 9) and N. A. Dahl ("Der Erstgeborene
Satans und der Vater des Teufels (Polyk. 7.1 und Joh 8.44)," in U. Eickelberg et
al. [eds.], *Apophoreta* [E. Haenchen Festschrift; BZNW 30; Berlin: Töpelmann,
1964] 70-84, esp. 78) believe that John 8:59, where Pharisees threaten to stone
Jesus, may actual allude to an early form of this rabbinic tradition.

[44]   As Fitzmyer notes (*The Gospel according to Luke X–XXIV* [AB 28A;
Garden City: Doubleday, 1985] 950), the saying was attributed to some of the
patristic writers to Jesus, as the embodiment of divine wisdom.

[45]   The pattern of the prophet's death at the hands of the recalcitrant Israelites
was pointed out by O. H. Steck, *Israel und das gewaltsame Geschick der Propheten*

with the authorities which is expected to lead to his death is by no means a commitment to a philosophical or conceptual point of view, but constitutes direct action on the part of Jesus which challenges the prevailing norms for participation in the covenant community. It is Jesus' radical redefinition of the people of God which arouses the hostility toward him and his enterprise (Q 14:16-23). Subsequently, it is not his disciples' intellectual persistence but their willingness to share in the severe testings through which he and they must pass which is the ground of their future share in the kingdom (Q 22:28-30). One can be a μαθητής of Jesus only by making a radical break with the social *status quo*: it is this which will result in one's taking up the cross (Q 14:26-27) and the consequent death one must be prepared to suffer.

The final line in the Q pericope which has been the center of our inquiry appears with different details in Luke and Matthew. Luke says, "Wisdom is justified by all her children," while Matthew has "by her deeds." Both of these terms mean "what is produced," but the Lukan form is personal: wisdom's children. The children of Wisdom are depicted in Prov 8:32-36 and Sir 4:11 as receiving instruction as to how they are to live. But Wisdom is here seen in Q as striving to achieve her purpose in the world: first through John, who came to challenge his contemporaries and to articulate the promise that God would raise up a new community: the true children of Abraham. Subsequently, Jesus has actually founded that new community, which builds on the promise to Abraham that through him "all the families of the earth" would share in God's blessing.

For those who continue to define God's people in terms of ethnic and ritual requirements, Jesus could be perceived only as a threat to their tradition and their expectations. He is to be denounced and dispatched, as were the historical gluttons and drunkards—the rebellious and law-breaking children—according to the precepts of Deuteronomy. But the Wisdom of God, the agent powerfully at work to accomplish God's purpose in the world, will be vindicated by the results of Jesus' activity, as is evident in the new community which

---

(WMANT 23; Neukirchen: Neukirchener Verlag, 1967). Wholly unsuitable is the theory of the Jesus Seminar and others that in this Q passage Jesus is affirming the supposedly Cynic-Stoic attitude toward death. The principle, allegedly based on Socrates, that "nothing can prevent one from holding fast to what is right" and that, by dying, one exemplifies "the true student of philosophy," is now attributed to Jesus. So D. Seeley, "Jesus' Death in Q," *NTS* 38 (1992) 222-34.

he has inaugurated in defiance of the limits and restrictions operative in other covenant traditions of his Jewish contemporaries. It is this radical reconstituting of the covenant people which is the issue behind the demeaning designation of Jesus by his tradition-oriented critics as "glutton and drunkard." But the Wisdom of God will justify his activities, or "works," as well as the new people ("children"), whose qualifications are so different from those of prevailing Jewish piety. The new covenant people is in process of formation through the one who designates himself as "Son of Man" and acknowledges his contemporaries' attacking him because he embodies and fosters what they see as a threat to their definition of the covenant community. Hence, they denounce him as "a glutton and drunkard."

QUESTIONING AND DISCERNMENT IN GOSPEL DISCOURSE
COMMUNICATIVE STRATEGY IN MATTHEW 11:2-19

J. Ian H. McDonald

Apart from brief periods of reaction, the question of the historical Jesus has preoccupied scholarship for almost two centuries. Critical tools have been fashioned and sharpened over the same period.[1] At the end of the twentieth century, there is yet another boom in the *Leben Jesu* industry. The variety of characterisations is at least as great now as it was at the end of the twentieth century. Jesus is portrayed as a charismatic or exorcist, a wonder worker or magician, a political revolutionary, a distinctive sort of rabbi or prophet, a visionary or humane apocalypticist, a sage or wisdom teacher—and this is by no means a comprehensive list.[2] It is even more disquieting to observe that—apart from a few areas, such as parables—relatively little attention has been paid to Jesus as communicator. This is not a plea for yet another entry in the Jesus picture gallery, already oversubscribed. It is to reflect that unless we are able to penetrate into the dynamics of his ministry, none of the above characterisations is more than impressionistic sketch-work.

This brief article cannot pretend to make good the alleged deficiency. What it attempts to do is to probe one aspect of Jesus' communicative strategy, which in general was designed to enable his hearers to discern truth. Such an aim is not achieved without a sharing and exploring of horizons[3] with his audience and an attempt to push back the limits of these horizons until new perspectives on truth—or the way things are—emerge more clearly. The interaction

---

[1]   I reviewed this sweep of scholarship in "New Quest—Dead End? So what about the Historical Jesus?" in E. A. Livingstone (ed.), *Studia Biblica 1978. II: Papers on the Gospels* (JSNTSup 2; Sheffield: JSOT Press, 1980) 151-70.

[2]   Cf. W. R. Telford, "Major trends and Interpretive Issues in the Study of Jesus," in B. Chilton and C. A. Evans (eds.), *Studying the Historical Jesus* (NTTS 19; Leiden: Brill, 1994) 33-74, esp. 53-55.

[3]   Cf. B. F. Meyer, "The Relevance of 'Horizon'," *Downside Review* 112 (1994) 1-14.

might involve a strengthening of communion or an element of confrontation, involving alienation. The parables of Jesus were, undoubtedly part of his communicative enterprise, usually containing sufficient indirection to tease the mind and subvert defences.[4] In this article, however, we limit ourselves to probing one fundamental aspect of Jesus' method, namely his use of questioning to promote discernment. The focal passage in this connection is Matt 11:2-19, which comprises three main sections, each of which is introduced by a question or series of questions. What dynamics of communication does such a passage entail?[5]

It would be naive to assume that one could address this passage without appropriate critical rigour. After all, the interrogative form of the passage may have been devised by some church teacher or by an editor or compiler who opted for it as an effective presentation in rhetorically satisfying format. Let us then first review briefly the access to Jesus' world afforded by a selection of critical tools applied to this passage.

CRITICAL APPROACHES TO MATTHEW 11:2-19

1. The Question of Sources

T. W. Manson may be taken to epitomise the source critical approach, which had been given definitive expression in the work of B. H. Streeter (1924).[6] A careful comparison of Matt 11:2-6 and Luke 7:18-23 (the embassy of John's disciples to Jesus) suggests that Luke 7:18-20 is close to Q, Matthew tending to offer an abbreviated form. Luke 7:21 is editorial; Luke spells out what the messengers of John actually did see. The question "Are you he that is to come . . ." arises from the contrast between John's proclamation of judgement and Jesus' preaching of mercy and lovingkindness, the latter amounting virtually to "the falsification of John's predictions." The catena of passages from Isaiah (Luke 7:22-3; Matt 11:4-6) is presented as essentially poetic, reinforcing the emphasis of Jesus'

---

4   The subject has been much discussed. For a recent discussion, see G. Shillington, "Engaging with the Parables," in Shillington (ed.), *Jesus and His Parables* (Edinburgh: T. & T. Clark, 1997) 1-20.

5   See J. W. Carey, *Communication as Culture* (London and New York: Routledge, 1992) 13-36.

6   See T. W. Manson, *The Sayings of Jesus* (London: SCM Press, 1949) 66-71.

ministry. Manson takes the final beatitude to mean, "Do not be distressed if things are not turning out according to your plan."

The section on Jesus' testimony to John (Matt 11:7-11, 16-19 = Luke 7:24-35) evinces close verbal agreement and is thus Q material. The initial question "What did you go out into the wilderness to see?" seems to have no more force than that of an introduction to Jesus' justification of John to the people.[7] The issue in the Q material is the status and role of John. He is more than a prophet; he is an actor in the drama—he is the Baptist! Luke has an additional passage suggesting that although the 'Pharisees and the lawyers' rejected John, the common people and the tax collectors were justified in the sight of God. The final parable (Matt 11:16-19 = Luke 7.31-5) underlines "the unresponsiveness of men to any sort of high religious appeal" and contrasts with the assurance that the wisdom of God was nevertheless justified by results.

The assumption is that Q is as close as we can get to Jesus' teaching. The connected nature of the three pericopes, however, suggests that Q was more than a collection of detached sayings. It consists of material abstracted from Jesus' teaching ministry, but with its emphasis on content it does not give us any real insight into Jesus as communicator. It does not open up—to the extent we might expect—the horizons of Jesus' world or those of his hearers. Manson's treatment is surprisingly lacking in socio-historical depth. The concern is largely with *theologoumena*, and with presenting theological perspectives on Jesus' ministry and that of John. It is well to remember that all sayings of Jesus were originally grounded in the narrative and setting of his ministry. There is thus a significant gap between sayings collections and the genesis of the traditions themselves.[8]

---

[7]   According to Manson (*Sayings*, 66-71), Matt 11:12-15—on the critical role of the Baptist in ushering in the new age—may come from M. The saying about the Kingdom paralleled in Luke 16:16 may be connected with Q but did not stand in Q at this point It is also likely that Matt 11:10 = Luke 5:27—the gloss on Mal 3:1, reflecting Exod 23:20 LXX—was probably also absent from Q.

[8]   For more recent perspectives on Q, see J. S. Kloppenborg, *The Formation of Q* (Philadelphia: Fortress, 1987); D. R. Catchpole, *The Quest for Q* (Edinburgh: T. & T. Clark, 1993); R. A. Piper (ed.), *The Gospel Behind the Gospels: Current Studies on Q* (NovTSup 75; Leiden: Brill, 1994); C. M Tuckett, *Q and the History of Early Christianity* (Edinburgh: T. & T. Clark, 1996).

2. The Question of Form

Formgeschichte, literally the history of the forms and formation of the tradition, centred on the *Sitz im Leben* or life setting of the churches. In its heyday, this approach was characterised by considerable historical scepticism. Thus Bultmann took the first main unit of our passage (11:2-6: John the Baptist's question) as an apophthegm (or pronouncement story[9]) composed by the community around Isaianic prophecy and reflecting disputation with the followers of John: "in all probability the Baptist's question is a community product and belongs to those passages in which the Baptist is called as a witness to the Messiahship of Jesus."[10] The second section (11:7-11a: Jesus' question about the Baptist) also bears all the signs of polemic, but part of the material, Bultmann concedes, derives from the early Palestinian church, and a genuine saying of Jesus may well be preserved in it, although the precise criterion is not spelled out. The parable in the final section (11:16-18) may also be ancient—does he imply the criterion of coherence (with other parables)?—but the interpretation in Matt 11:18-19 is a product of the Hellenistic church.[11] As Bultmann's successors in the 'new quest' recognised, further advance in locating the historical Jesus depended on the development and application of precise criteria that would identify the historical substratum of tradition.[12] Generally speaking, the influence of dialectical theology and Bultmann's programme of existential interpretation ensured that priorities lay with the interpretation of the Word today rather than with the dynamics of communication in Jesus' ministry.

3. Questions of Redaction and Composition

Studies in the redaction and composition of the tradition (cf. *Redaktionsgeschichte*) place much emphasis on the creative role of the authors. The re-engagement of redaction critics with the quest of the historical Jesus was intrinsic to their theological concern, and with their emphasis on the criterion of dissimilarity (i.e. between the

---

[9]   See V.Taylor, *The Formation of the Gospel Tradition* (London: Macmillan, 1964) 63-87.

[10]   R. Bultmann, *The History of the Synoptic Tradition* (Oxford: Blackwell, 1968) 23.

[11]   Bultmann, *The History of the Synoptic Tradition*, 172.

[12]   See Telford, "Major Trends and Interpretive Issues," 66-68.

world of the evangelists and the world of Jesus) they tended to exaggerate rather than bridge the gap between the respective horizons.[13] But other approaches to the question of redaction and composition are possible. Thus, a distinctive interpretation of our passage is given by Michael Goulder, who argued that the material was written and edited for use in connection with the synagogue lectionary.[14] Our passage, which coincides with the beginning of Mark and the work of the Baptist, related to the 'new year' theme. The question which the imprisoned John raises through his emissaries anticipates the issue of Jesus' messiahship, as the string of messianic prophecies from Isaiah suggests. Goulder, who does not recognise Q, comments: "There seems no reason to posit a pre-Matthaean source."[15] Similarly, the three-fold question which Jesus puts to the crowds—Matthew likes triple formulae—is ironic in its allusion to reed-grass and soft clothing (which his captors wore); but the third question reflects Mark 6. The popular view of Jesus was that he was "a prophet, like one of the prophets of old" (Mark 6:16), or that he was Elijah (Mark 6:15). Herod's view was that he was John *redivivus* (Mark 6:14). Skilfully, Matthew weaves all these elements together in his discourse, even to the "rising up" of no one greater than the Baptist—the same phrase that Mark used of John *redivivus*. Goulder concludes: "The doctrine, and much of the words, of the paragraph, are thus a restatement of the Marcan passages on John."[16] To end with a similitude is an old scribal trick and is characteristically Matthaean.

Goulder's exegesis is ingenious, complex and controversial, not only raising the problem of lectionaries but also assaulting the bastion of Q. His general approach supplies an element missing in the Q hypothesis, namely the importance of a basic narrative substratum.

---

13   Particularly significant were J. M. Robinson, *A New Quest of the Historical Jesus* (SBT 25; London: SCM Press, 1959); G. Bornkamm, *Jesus of Nazareth* (London: Hodder & Stoughton; New York: Harper & Row, 1960); G. Bornkamm, G. Barth and H. J. Held, *Tradition and Interpretation in Matthew* (London: SCM Press; Philadelphia: Westminster, 1963). The issue is helpfully discussed in M. J. Borg, "Reflections on a Discipline," in Chilton and Evans (eds.), *Studying the Historical Jesus*, 12-16.

14   M. D. Goulder, *Midrash and Lection in Matthew* (London: SPCK, 1974) esp. 353-59.

15   Goulder, *Midrash and Lection*, 355.

16   Goulder, *Midrash and Lection*, 357.

It emphasises, however, the freedom with which Matthew composed his story from mainly Markan sources. Yet Goulder has a greater awareness than many others of the use to which questions can be put in the extending of horizons. What he found was a Matthaean elaboration of earlier tradition; but might it not be that Jesus was as skilled as Matthew in interpreting his own mission and that of John? The answer to that question depends on a historical assessment of Mark, but as is common in redactional studies this matter is not given priority.

4. The Question of the Unconventional Sage

A remarkable development in North America in recent years has been the emergence of what Marcus Borg has described as a consensus on Jesus as a wisdom teacher rather than an eschatological prophet. "Two streams of the early Christian movement—Q and early *Thomas*—point to communities whose traditions about Jesus portrayed him primarily as a teacher of an unconventional wisdom."[17] While much turns on definitions ("eschatology," "wisdom" and "sage" are cases in point), to put so much emphasis on hypothetical documents such as Q and "early *Thomas*," to the neglect of narrative tradition, is rash in the extreme. To be sure, parables can be described as sapiential, and Borg is surely correct to say that the genre is not so much about announcing the Kingdom as about enabling people to see things in a new way. But religious communities express their identity not so much through adherence to sayings or logia but through story. And story can also help people see things in a new way. Mark + Q is a much stronger foundation than Q + "early *Thomas*"!

Nevertheless, several attempts have been made to derive the story of John's emissaries from a basic gnomic statement. Thus, G. W. Buchanan points to a chiastic statement underlying the Matthaean

---

[17] M. J. Borg, "Reflections on a Discipline," 19. Caution must be exercised over "consensus" claims. In so far as such claims relate to Q, it should be noted that "large parts of Q are dominated by ideas of a futurist eschatology": Tuckett, *Q and the History of Early Christianity*, 163; cf. 139-63. To derive a non-eschatological stratum from such a source is hazardous indeed. To base a case on the hypothesis of an early *Thomas* is also to press conjecture very far. Moreover, the ground on which claims for "consensus" are based requires scrutiny. In so far as it involves a process of counting heads or majority voting, its epistemological presuppositions are open to question.

elaboration:[18]

> Tell John what you *hear*   and *see*
> the blind *see* again   and deaf *hear*

The whole section is an elaboration of this structure, not unlike a chreia or rhetorical exercise.[19] Ron Cameron presented a full account of Hermogenes *On the Chreia* in order to demonstrate that our passage was an elaboration of the question in Matt 11:3 = Luke 7:19 and the reply in Matt 11:6 = Luke 7:23.[20] The resultant gnomic utterance is as follows:

> *Question* (vs.19)
> Are you / the one who is to come / or should we expect another?
> *Rejoinder* (vs. 23)
> Whoever / is not offended by me / is blessed.

The picture emerges of John as a Cynic philosopher rather than a biblical prophet. This, however, is a totally different chreia from the one tentatively identified by G. W. Buchanan. At this rate, almost any narrative could be regarded as an elaboration of a chreia! It should also be pointed out that Matt 11:2-15 is explicitly concerned with prophets and prophecy, in which wisdom or gnomic utterances play a secondary role. Attempts to present them as basically sapiential are inevitably reductionist. Memory retains awareness of the sequence of events and the nature of the interaction at least as well as what was said. Without denying that Jesus was both sagacious and unconventional, it is doubtful if his ministry can be adequately represented by wisdom sayings alone.

Amidst all this creative interpretation, can we find authentic echoes of Jesus, the communicator? Can we recover the quality of his interaction with those with whom he came in contact? For this purpose, the questions he asked give a particularly valuable insight into the interactive mode of his communication. A noteworthy feature of the discourse in Matt 11:2-19 is the fact that all three main sections are introduced by questions. It is time now to move beyond

---

[18]   G. W. Buchanan, *The Gospel of Matthew* (Mellen Biblical Commentary 1.1; Lewiston and Queenstown: Mellen Biblical Press, 1996) 478.

[19]   Buchanan, *Matthew*, 468. The specific points of likeness are (i) the identification of the speaker; (ii) the indication of situation; and (iii) the response. But the same could hold true of much narrative tradition.

[20]   R. D. Cameron, "'What Have You Come Out To See?' Characterizations of John and Jesus in the Gospels," *Semeia* 49 (1990) 35-69, esp. 50-61.

the failed attempts of the past and focus more particularly on the role of questioning in communication and discernment in biblical discourse.

QUESTIONING AND DISCERNING IN BIBLICAL DISCOURSE

1. Introduction

In some ways it is unfortunate that the interrogative category most familiar to readers of the New Testament is the rhetorical question. As everyone knows, such questions do not seek information nor do they require an explicit response. For that reason, they are often dismissed as mere rhetorical devices. Even students of linguistics have been known to contrast them unfavourably with "real" questions. "Questions seeking information are generally perceived as real and genuine unlike, for instance, rhetorical questions, which do not require an answer . . ."[21] But there is much more to the rhetorical question than meets the eye. For example, it presupposes common ground, shared horizons.

Take, for example, Matt 5:13: "If the salt has lost its saltiness, how can it be made salty again?" True, no direct answer is possible. The truth of the implied proposition is self-evident. But, as Kennedy[22] and others have pointed out, the proposition could be argued—admittedly at greater length and with less effect—as an enthymeme or short syllogism characteristic of deliberative rhetoric.[23] The implicit steps would require to be identified—for example, "any active substance can lose its effectiveness"—and a general conclusion could be induced ("man can lose his effectiveness"; "you can lose your effectiveness"). In fact, rhetorical questions have several functions. They maintain audience contact and enable the speaker to identify with the hearers (cf. 1 Thess 2:19); and they suggest irresistible conclusions (cf. Matt 5:46-47), even in a confrontational setting (cf. Rom 2:21-23).

---

[21]   A.-B. Stenstrom, *Questions and Responses in English Conversation* (Lund: Gleerup, 1984) 1.

[22]   Cf. G. Kennedy, *New Testament Interpretation through Rhetorical Criticism* (Chapel Hill: University of North Carolina Press, 1984) 27, 53.

[23]   "Enthymeme" is Aristotle's term for the syllogism in rhetoric; cf. R. B. Vinson, "A Comparative Study and Use of Enthymemes in the Synoptic Gospels," in D. F. Watson (ed.), *Persuasive Artistry: Studies in New Testament Rhetoric in Honor of George A. Kennedy* (JSNTSup 50; Sheffield: JSOT Press, 1991) 119-41.

New perceptions can be achieved only through interactions based on shared or overlapping horizons. As Bernard Lonergan put it, horizons "are the structured resultant of past achievement and, as well, both the condition and limitation of further development."[24] Learning is not simply adding data to previous learning "but rather an organic growth out of it."[25] There are possibilities of failure in communication because people are too enclosed within their individual world. Horizons may be dialectically opposed. It is the skill of the communicator to establish points of concurrence (in rhetorical language, *ethos*), and through interaction initiate "a new sequence that can keep revealing ever greater depth and breadth and wealth. Such an about-face and new beginning is what is meant by conversion."[26]

It is commonly recognised that there are four modalities at the disposal of the communicator: the assertive, the injunctive, the interrogative, and the optative.[27] Each modality plays a specific role in communication. For our present purposes, it may be useful to view the interrogative mode in terms of three distinctive goals: communion with the audience, confrontation, and discernment. Finally, we will point out the prominent place it holds in prophetic discourse.

2. Communion with the Audience

Questioning is of considerable importance both in general communication and in rhetorical practice. "A question presupposes an object to which it relates and suggests that there is agreement on the existence of this object. To answer a question is to confirm this implicit agreement."[28] Questions—rhetorical and otherwise—are thus tools by which the speaker may establish and preserve a sense of

---

24   B. J. F. Lonergan, *Method in Theology* (London: Darton, Longman & Todd, 1972) 237.

25   Lonergan, *Method*, 237.

26   Lonergan, *Method*, 238.

27   C. Perelman and L. Olbrechts-Tyteca, *The New Rhetoric: A Treatise on Argumentation* (Notre Dame and London: University of Notre Dame Press, 1969) 158. For recent studies of rhetoric, see S. E. Porter and T. H. Olbricht (eds.), *Rhetoric and the New Testament: Essays from the 1992 Heidelberg Conference* (JSNTSup 90; Sheffield: JSOT Press, 1993); S. E. Porter (ed.), *Handbook of Classical Rhetoric in the Hellenistic Period 330 B.C.–A.D. 400* (Leiden: Brill, 1997).

28   Perelman and Olbrechts-Tyteca, *The New Rhetoric*, 159.

communion based on values shared with the audience. In Matt 5:43-48, for example, Jesus cites the popular interpretation which combined loving your neighbour and hating your enemy; and he proceeds to counter it with the command, Love your enemies (this is the "injunctive" mode of communication). His argument, however, takes the form of an enthymeme in which he utilises the interrogative mode. By a sequence of four questions, he leads his audience to see that expressing love only within reciprocating relationships does not get us very far in resolving the problem of enmity. Any common or garden taxgatherer, any uninstructed Gentile will act like that! The audience can only concur. The critical concept is expressed in the "what more?" of Jesus' third question. His series of questions induces his audience to assent to his original counter-proposal, that we should love our enemies, and even to accept a final injunction, to look towards obeying God's will in its entirety. Communion with the audience has been maintained throughout.[29]

3. Confrontation

Questions can be used as part of a confrontation with an audience with whom the speaker has an element of common ground but from whom he or she is diverging sharply in other respects. Kennedy has observed that the rhetoric of Jesus as presented by Matthew is highly confrontational.[30] A striking example is found in Matt 21:23-27 (cf. Luke 20:1-8; Mark 11:27-33). In the Temple, the worship, organisation and ethos of which Jesus has outspokenly challenged, Jesus is questioned about the source of the authority on which he acts. As Rollin Grams has observed, the *stasis* or basic issue is, in fact, one of jurisdiction.[31] The speakers have to pay attention to engaging and holding the sympathy of the audience (*ethos*), which they do largely through *logos*, the ability to answer questions. Avoiding a direct or dogmatic answer which would have provoked hostility no matter how it was presented, Jesus' way of handling the matter was to pose a counter-question relating to John the Baptist's authority. It would be wrong to see this merely as evasion. The tactic of his hostile ques-

---

[29]   See Kennedy, *New Testament Interpretation*, 57.

[30]   Kennedy, *New Testament Interpretation*, 60. The same can be said of John's Gospel: e.g. John 5:47; Kennedy, *New Testament Interpretation*, 113.

[31]   R. Grams, "The Temple Conflict Scene: A Rhetorical Analysis of Matthew 21-23," in Watson (ed.), *Persuasive Artistry*, 53-54.

tioners was to rest secure on the institutional validation of their authority while implying that the lack of such validation brought into question the status and authenticity of Jesus' ministry. But the authority inherent in the ministries of John and Jesus had to be discerned from the quality of their actions. It was a matter of insight and judgement, not of validation by institutional authority. Jesus demonstrated effectively that his opponents were in fact unable to answer *stasis* questions concerning John's authority. Consequently, they could not refute Jesus' authority, for it was common knowledge that John had testified to Jesus. Further comment on discernment is offered below. Meanwhile, it may be observed how close this kind of confrontation is to violence. As the writers of *The New Rhetoric* have shown, to engage in argument is to attempt to modify a pre-existing state of affairs. The person who initiates debate may be compared to an aggressor, but "the use of argumentation implies that one has renounced resorting to force alone."[32] Equally, the response to confrontation may be violent. In the Temple Jesus did not use force, although his words and acts were clearly forceful. The authorities' reaction, however, was violent and brutal. A further example is found in the sermon at Nazareth (Luke 4:16-30), which ends with at least threatened violence.

4. Discernment

The relationship between questioning and discernment is an important area.[33] While the assertive mode of expression depends on statements and propositions, the injunctive on imperatives and the optative on desired standards, the interrogative mode lends itself to the discerning of truth and error. It is therefore also a highly interactive and inductive mode. This can be illustrated from Luke's story of the boy Jesus in the Temple: "sitting among the teachers, listening to them and asking them questions; and all who heard him were amazed at his understanding and his answers" (Luke 2:46-7). As we noted in the previous discussion of Jesus' confrontation with the Temple authorities, Jesus confronted them with the need to *discern* the source of authority in the case of John's work and, of

---

32   Perelman and Olbrechts-Tyteca, *The New Rhetoric*, 55; cf. 54-59.

33   Relevant here is Lonergan's discussion of the basic patterns of operations, or insight; cf. *Method in Theology*, 6-13; cf. also his work, *Insight: A Study of Human Understanding* (London: Darton, Longman & Todd, 1983 [orig. 1957]).

course, his own. In the section of Matthew's narrative discussed below, John's disciples and, indeed, John himself, are not given a direct or 'assertive' answer by Jesus but inducted by questioning into an interpretive and discerning frame of mind (Matt 11:2-6). "Blessed are those who take no offence at me" (11:6)—for to them the road to discernment is open. The focal unit in the passage shows Jesus leading his audience by a series of questions to the point where they can recognise John as "more than a prophet" (11:7-9).

Religious rhetoric, like sophistic rhetoric, is concerned to present a persuasive case but, unlike the sophists, its exponents address the question of truth as the overriding priority. This presupposes a willingness to be open to new possibilities. Awareness of truth comes in the meeting of minds; the denial of the truth question—such as Pilate's "What is truth?"—closes the mind (cf. John 18.38). Jesus is frequently portrayed as using a dialectical method to open up issues. The questions, "Who do people say I am?" and "Who do you say I am?" (Mark 8.27-29 par.), occur at the turning-point in Mark's narrative. They serve to lead the disciples (and the readers) forward towards a new understanding of the course of Jesus' ministry. Again, the essentially participative nature of parabolic discourse involves posing questions to the audience—"Whose image and superscription is this?" (Mark 12:16 par.); "What will the owner of the vineyard do?" (Mark 12:9 par.); "Which of these three proved neighbour to the man who fell among the robbers?" (Luke 10:36)—thus not only teasing the mind into active thought but stimulating the thought processes towards discerning some aspect of truth. "He that has ears to hear, let him hear" (cf. Matt 11:15) is an invitation to penetrate beyond the surface or literal level and discern a deeper level of meaning. Lonergan describes this kind of dynamic operation as "not blind but open-eyed":

> It is attentive, intelligent, reasonable, responsible; it is conscious intending, ever going beyond what happens to be given or known, ever striving for a fuller and richer apprehension of the yet unknown or incompletely known totality, whole, universe.[34]

5. Questions in Prophetic Discourse

Finally, a wide range of questions characterises prophetic discourse. In Isaiah 40, where the leading concern is with restoring

---

[34]   Lonergan, *Method in Theology*, 13.

communion with God and confidence in him through forgiveness and reconciliation, the prophet uses a series of rhetorical questions to demonstrate the incontrovertible greatness of God (cf. 40:12-13, 18, 21, 25, 27-28). A different example of communion through questions is the presentation of a summons or invitation to service, as in the case of Isaiah's calling as a prophet (Isa 6:8). Isaiah also uses a series of questions concerning farming to present a parable designed to subvert the contention of his hearers and to help them discern the wisdom of God (Isa 28:23-29). Much prophetic questioning, however, has to do with disputation and confrontation. In Mic 2:6-11, the prophet's questions are directed against those who are forbidding him to preach. As Claus Westermann has noted, questions thus directed take the disputation close to the announcement of judgement against Israel.[35] Jeremiah offers a number of examples, including the image of Israel as the faithless wife divorced from her husband and seeking in vain an easy way back to his favour (Jer 3:1-5). In Amos 3:3-8, the prophet seems to answer a question about his authority by juxtaposing counter questions, as the Jesus of the Gospels did when his authority was challenged.

We turn now to consider our selected test passage. Can it take us beyond Matthew and his sources to the world of Jesus, to the horizons he shared at least in part with his hearers, and to a demonstration of his skill as a communicator? We begin with the observation that it cannot do so without effort on the part of the modern interpreter. If we are to appreciate such possibilities, we must accept guidance from specialist studies that will enable us to appreciate the horizons of Jesus' audience, whether environmental, political or religious, and see how he helped his hearers to discern more deeply the events in which they were involved.

QUESTIONING AND DISCERNING IN MATTHEW 11:2-19

1. Introduction

Matthew 11:2-19 is recognisable as a rhetorical structure, on which Matthew has left his stamp. As Goulder comments inimitably, "*Inclusio* and the gnomic paragraph-closer (arcetic) are alike *spécialités de la maison.*"[36] The structure may be outlined as follows:

---

35 C. Westerman, *Basic Forms of Prophetic Speech* (London: Lutterworth, 1967) 201.

36 M. Goulder, *Midrash and Lection*, 358.

I. Editorial preface (11:2)

II. *Exordium* (11:3-6)
    A. Question
    B. *Florilegium*
    C. Beatitude

III. *Probatio* (11:7-15)
    A. Questions
    B. Answer as affirmation
    C. *Florilegium*
    D. Solemn reaffirmartion
    E. Enthymeme
    F. Further clarification
    G. Exhortation to 'hear'

IV. *Peroratio* (11:16-19b)
    A. Question
    B. Parable

V. Closure (11:19c).[37]

Matthew's case is that Jesus is the Christ (11:2) and that his deeds encapsulate divine wisdom (11:19c). Such an appeal to wisdom is perfectly compatible with prophetic discourse. One can see an emerging pattern in John's question about Jesus, Jesus' evaluation of John, and the general indifference to both of them! Matthew's conclusion affirms that wisdom does not rest with such indifference but with Jesus' actions. Much of the Gospel story is condensed in this rhetorical unit. To make his case, however, Matthew (whether or not in heavy reliance on Q) brings together three disparate pieces of tradition. The first piece comes from an early stage in Jesus' ministry, when John is in prison and still very much alive. The second seems to presuppose a later perspective, John now being a figure of the past. The third involves a retrospective look at the ministry of John and Jesus, and thus assumes at least a later point in Jesus' ministry.

2. The Questioning of Jesus by John's Disciples (Matt 11:2-6)

Matthew doubtless records Jesus' discussion of John for his own (or for church) reasons. In doing so, he helps the church recollect its own beginnings. But the nature of the material takes the reader

---

[37]   In addition to the works on rhetoric already cited, see also W. Wuellner, "Where is Rhetorical Criticism Taking Us," *CBQ* 49 (1987) 448-63. On "enthymemes," see above, n. 22; and on *florilegia*, see below, n. 41.

retrospectively into the world in which John and Jesus moved: a world of eschatological expectation, in which the scriptures reached fulfilment and end-time figures were wonderingly discerned. In such a context, horizons are capable of extension by a skilled communicator who shares sufficient common ground with his hearers to make discernment possible. The use of questions is of particular significance.

The first is posed by, or on behalf of, John. His disciples are sent to ask whether Jesus is "the one who is to come" or whether they should "look for another" (Matt 11:2 = Luke 7:19). The question presupposes an eschatological code, to which the modern reader is not entirely privy. "He who is to come," for example, could relate to "the prophet like Moses" (Deut 34:10-12), which would carry messianic overtones, or to the return of Elijah (cf. Mal 3:1; 4:5), or to the fulfilment of John's own proclamation (Mark 1:7-8 par.).[38] Indeed, Jewish expectation often invoked the coming of two messiahs—a priestly or Aaronic messiah and a royal or Davidic messiah.[39] But this was dangerous territory. Jewish religion had strong political overtones, and messianic claims were politically sensitive in the tensions of the Roman occupation. This doubtless explains the resort to a coded formula. To anyone who "takes no offence at me" (11:6), Jesus' reply suggests messianic import. At this stage, however, Matthew—having given assurance of the christological solution—is content to let these possibilities tease the minds of the readers.

Our concern is not so much with the kinds of issues which have occupied commentators, ancient and modern—how, for example, John's apparent doubt may be reconciled with the firm witness the Baptist had already given to Jesus in Matthew's Gospel (and even more strongly in the Fourth Gospel), or whether John was enquiring for his disciples' sake (as the Fathers suggested), or whether John was by this time in serious decline (as Tertullian thought)[40]—as with the way Jesus handled the question put to him. His first response is an injunction or imperative: "Go and tell John what you see and hear…"

---

[38] Cf. W. D. Davies and D. C. Allison, Jr., *The Gospel according to Saint Matthew* II (ICC; Edinburgh: T. & T. Clark, 1991) 244-46; J. D. G. Dunn, *Jesus and the Spirit* (London: SCM Press, 1975) 59.

[39] Cf. Buchanan, *Matthew*, 479.

[40] Cf. Davies and Allison, *Matthew*, 241.

(Matt 11:4; cf. Luke 7:22). An empirical element is presupposed here; Jesus' words and deeds are public knowledge, and the Baptist's disciples are assumed to be aware of that fact. "What you hear and see" (11:4) relates by chiasmus to "the blind receive their sight and the lame walk" (11:5; cf. Isa 29:18), and it may be that these acts refer to the questioners' immediate awareness of Jesus' ministry. The most striking feature of the encounter, however, is that Jesus' reply is couched in biblical terms familiar to a Scripture-oriented community. Since biblical prophecy reaches fulfilment in messianic times, the prophet's words relating to the transformation of Israel (Isa 28:18-20) are juxtaposed with Jesus' own ministry and thereby made to interpret it. As G. W. Buchanan has observed, such collections of scriptural testimony—known as *florilegia*—constituted a well known phenomenon in Jesus' time and were used by, among others, the covenanters of Qumran (cf. 4Q521 2+4 ii 12).[41] The text Jesus cited "was sufficiently well known that Jesus had only to allude to it for John and his messengers to understand his intended message."[42] Thus horizons are extended, perceptions sharpened and understanding enriched. Let no genuine enquirer take offence, but rather reflect on whether the identification is valid. Discernment does not come through the heteronomous imposition of another's views. John and his disciples must finally *discern* the answer to their own question.

To round off this discussion, three distinctive responses to this passage may be singled out and assessed briefly in terms of questioning and discernment.

(i) *A community view.* The passage may be regarded as a product of the Christian communities. Kloppenborg took it as Christian propaganda designed to appeal to the followers of John. Bultmann saw it as a community product recording John's witness to Jesus. But, as Robert Webb has pointed out, John is not really a witness here, but rather a questioning seeker or even a disillusioned sceptic.[43] The "community view" is thus divided.[44] Its only alternative to the

---

[41]   Buchanan, *Matthew*, 478, 480.

[42]   Buchanan, *Matthew*, 478.

[43]   Cf. Kloppenborg, *The Formation of Q*, 107; Bultmann, *History of the Synoptic Tradition*, 23; R. L. Webb, *John the Baptizer and Prophet* (JSNTSup 62; Sheffield: JSOT Press, 1991) 281.

[44]   Cf. Bultmann, *History of the Synoptic Tradition*, 164.

"witness" emphasis is to ascribe the passage, equally unconvincingly, to anti-John propaganda. In propaganda, the question ascribed to John ceases to be a real one. It is merely the prelude to a definitive answer.

(ii) *A question from an old mentor.* Steve Mason has put forward a startling version of the relations between John and Jesus. John was an apocalyptic preacher, imaging judgement as rivers of fire. Jesus initially identified with John, but while John continued his independent course Jesus' ministry developed in a different direction. This passage, therefore, "seems to preserve an early tradition that the Baptist had once enquired about Jesus on the basis of reports about his wonders and that Jesus had responded positively to the enquiry."[45] This view relates to the notion that a shift took place in the ministry of Jesus, which was characterised by growth and development.[46] The Baptist's position, however, did not change. The questioning came from a defended position, and while the citing of the *florilegia* was intended to prompt reflections on Jesus' healing ministry as messianic, it did not sit easily with the kind of apocalyptic emphasis embraced by John. The questions and answers were therefore confrontational, at least in part, and there is no evidence that they prompted John to further discernment.

(iii) *An urgent question from John's disciples.* Let us take seriously Matthew's indication that John was in prison (Matt 11:2; cf. Mark 1:14; Matt 4:12). The question put by the Baptist's disciples on behalf of their master was an urgent one. In their extremity, they wondered if Jesus might indeed be "the one who is to come" and, if so, when they might expect to see appropriate action. Their immediate concern was to secure the release of John from prison, and as they read the scriptures (to what else would they turn?) they believed that the coming one would accomplish this end. Was it not explicit in Isa 61:1 and a reasonable deduction from Isa 29:18-21?[47] They had therefore an ulterior motive in putting the question. Their question sprang from the perspective in which they viewed their world and

---

45   S. Mason, "Fire, Water and Spirit: John the Baptist and the Tyranny of Canon," *SR* 21 (1992) 176.

46   Cf. R. L. Webb, "John the Baptist and his Relationship with Jesus," in Chilton and Evans (eds.), *Studying the Historical Jesus*, 223-29.

47   Cf. Buchanan, *Matthew*, 481. Isaiah 29:21 might seem to have a peculiar aptness to John's predicament.

had its own frame of reference. The coming one will set the prisoners free! Jesus' response was to use the *florilegium* from Isaiah, to suggest a range actions which related to what they heard and saw, but which did not include specific mention of release from prison (in contrast to Luke 4:18, which however is given a different context). Let John hear that the scriptural picture of the "day" of the Lord (cf. Isa 29:18) was being fulfilled in the present, and let him keep faith and not take offence at Jesus (Matt 11:6).

It is possible that the answer suggested to John that he would soon be released from prison. Such a view strengthens the conclusion that this passage owes little or nothing to christological speculation in the churches. What it does afford is insight into the fluid and dynamic nature of Jesus' style of communication, which placed a premium on discernment while coping with the restrictions and dangers of his times. It clearly served Matthew's purpose to incorporate this unit of tradition into his discourse to demonstrate the unfolding of Jesus' messianic mission in the pressurised context of first century Palestine.

3. Jesus' Questioning of the Crowds about John (Matt 11:7-11)

With this passage we reach the main body of the discourse and seem to be close to the bedrock of Gospel tradition. Bultmann, for example, took most of it to derive from the early Palestinian Church and to be a contender for the status of a genuine saying of Jesus.[48] The exceptions are the intrusive proof text (Matt 11:10 par.) and 11:11b ("he who is least in the kingdom . . ."), which he took to be Christian commentary, although it is cited in a variety of sources. Any passage relating to the Baptist is liable to a degree of Christian interpretation for apologetic reasons, but it is difficult to avoid the suspicion that Matt 11:10 par. represents an ancient tradition. Indeed, as we shall see, it is only one of the *testimonia* that interpret the passage. And our recognition that we touch on the bedrock of the tradition here is dependent not so much on form critical methods as on strong environmental indicators that afford admission into the world of Jesus' hearers.

Jesus, addressing a mixed audience ("the crowds"), poses an opening question: "What did you go out into the wilderness to see?" To respond to Jesus' questions involves an act of memory. It involves

---

48   Bultmann, *History of the Synoptic Tradition*, 165.

reflection on the time spent with John, and on the expectations aroused and the impressions left by that ministry by the Jordan. Indeed, the way the questions are put is itself evocative. Could they recapture some of the people's thoughts as they made their exodus into the wilderness?[49] Their purpose was certainly not to admire the reeds, flourishing as they did in the southern Jordan Valley (a banal thought, calculated to arouse indignant rejection). Was it to welcome the return of Elijah, the southern Jordan valley being the focus of popular expectation in this respect? Was it to plunge into the Jordan and so enter again into the promised land? To raise such questions is not simply to be fanciful. At their lowest, they sketch the connotation of John's ministry by the Jordan; and elements in the connotation could be dramatically activated to become powerful religious symbols breaking into contemporary meaningfulness. To go into the wilderness was an act of courage as well as faith. The prophet Hosea had spoken of Yahweh, God of Israel, leading her into the wilderness, restoring her vineyards there and "turning the valley of Achor into a gate of hope"; and Israel will know again the wonder of the exodus from Egypt (Hos 2:14-15). Were they going to repeat the experience at the *Yam Suf*, the Sea of Reeds, or find a new Moses in the bulrushes? Yet what was the reality? John was arrested and imprisoned. People congregating in the wilderness sent danger signals to the Romans. This was where rebellion started (cf. Josephus, *Ant.* 20.5.1 §97-98). A leader of such a movement was immediately suspect, as were those associated with him.[50] How could the crowds recapture once more the expectations of that time, now that John was in prison and the outlook so bleak? Jesus questions are designed to clear away this blockage.

Jesus' technique is worthy of attention. After the opening question, we find two supplementary negative suggestions. Did they go out to see a reed blowing in the wind? Or a man dressed in soft apparel? A rhetorical progression can be sustained by several negatives, particularly when the audience is able to play along with the train of thought and the suggestions are ridiculous enough in themselves to evoke humour. The humour acquires another dimension if there is a sub-text, recognised by the audience even if somewhat less obvious to later generations of readers. Once again, we are faced with coded

---

49   Cf. Davies and Allison, *Matthew*, 247.

50   Cf. Buchanan, *Matthew*, 483.

language.

We limit our discussion to three possibilities. The first represents suggestions favoured by older commentators and is the least likely. The reed blown in the wind is taken to symbolise either weakness or flexibility. The text may then refer negatively to John's vacillation (did you expect to see a broken reed?) or positively to the need to readjust one's expectations in the light of events as they unfold. The latter suggestion seems to owe more to theological speculation than to the context, while the former may be tinged with anti-John propaganda. Neither is convincing.[51]

The second looks to the religious tradition of Israel, encapsulated in the Baptist. "The Lord will strike Israel, until it is like a reed swaying in the water" (1 Kgs 14:15). Judgement is about to overtake disobedient Israel. The large scale pilgrimages are movements of repentance. Perhaps salvation will come to the faithful, as it did at the Sea of Reeds (Exodus 14–15). Perhaps they will see the Messiah in all his kingly glory. As we have seen, there is evidence in Josephus (*Ant.* 20.5.1 §97-99) that such movements did take place. This interpretation pays more heed to the context, but a messianic interpretation of "a man clothed in soft raiment" lacks cogency.[52]

The third possibility is grounded not only in the physical environment but also in the religio-political life of Israel. It also reckons with the unspoken assumption that the crowds went out to encounter a man of power. Jesus contrasts the kind of power evident in the ascetic John with worldly power reflected in the luxury loving courtier (the Herodians, or Herod himself?) whose ambience is king's palaces.[53] Gerd Theissen has pointed out that the crowds would have recognised the reed as the symbol on Herod's coins.[54]

---

[51]   Cf. W. F. Albright and C. S. Mann, *Matthew* (AB 26; Garden City: Doubleday, 1971) 136; E. Schweizer, *The Good News according to Matthew* (London: SPCK, 1976) 260.

[52]   Contra K.Stendahl, "Matthew," in M. Black and H. H. Rowley (eds), *Peake's Commentary on the Bible* (London: Nelson, 1962) 783; cf. Davies and Allison, *Matthew*, 247. Nor are attempts to refer it to zealots or Essenes any more persuasive: cf. C. Daniel, "Les Esseniens et 'Ceux Qui sont dans les Maisons des Rois'," *RevQ* 6 (1967-68) 261-77.

[53]   According to J. E. Taylor, *The Immerser.John the Baptist within Second Temple Judaism* (Grand Rapids: Eerdmans, 1997) 301: "The reference to soft clothing reflects an awareness that John was dressed in anything but nice clothes."

[54]   G. Theissen, *The Gospels in Context* (Edinburgh: T. & T. Clark, 1992) 28-

The "reed" is part of a sub-text, the meaning of which was known to the hearers. What we have is therefore a disparaging reference to Herod, in sharp contrast to the image the Baptist presented. But what relevance would such taunts have for Jesus' purpose, which was not to mock Herod but to evoke the memory of John at his peak? A convincing answer is found if we assume that the images of the reed and the sybarite were well known taunts with which John himself had baited Herod. The fatal antagonism between John and Herod is attested by all sources—not least, by Josephus. In his mighty denunciations of the king, John had not only mocked him for the effete extravagance of his life-style but—doubtless to the delight of the crowds—John had also used his own symbol of the reed to deride his character. Hence, when Jesus used the "old chestnuts" of the reed blown by the wind and the luxuriant courtier, his audience no doubt roared with laughter at the recalling of the joke,[55] and that very act of recollection took them in imagination back to Jordan's banks and the preaching of the Baptist. Then, in high good humour, they could face the question of what they really saw when they encountered John. The evocative questions brought them to the key issue of John's significance.

The term "prophet" was probably offered by the audience in answer to Jesus' questioning. It thus represents an evaluation of John as the crowds saw him. "Prophet," of course, could denote a wide range of figures, from soothsayers and diviners to messengers of Yahweh and oracular prophets of salvation and judgement in the latter day socio-political scene.[56] "Prophet" thus acquired eschatological overtones, whether as the embodiment of Elijah or the prophet like Moses. To recognise a prophet was therefore to "see" or discern some features of his message as a (final) message from God. Jesus affirms the attribution of "prophet" to John and extends its meaning. To describe John as "more than a prophet" is not to demean the prophetic role; the phrase suggests that John fulfils a particular role in the purpose of God for his people. Many prophets spoke of the end time, but John was himself part of the outworking of the end

42.

[55]   Joan Taylor at least recognises that Jesus used "ridiculous images that may have been designed to make people laugh" (*The Immerser*, 301).

[56]   Cf. Davies and Allison, *Matthew*, 248-49; R. A. Horsley, "Popular Messianic Movements around the time of Jesus," *CBQ* 46 (1984) 471-95.

time. Thus Jesus acknowledges the greatness of John (Matt 11:11a = Luke 7:28a)—probably the most authentic indication we have of how. Jesus estimated John. The statement is a reaffirmation of John as "prophet and more" (11:9b). This is not only accepted rhetorical practice but also reflects skilled communication, where repetition is a proper form of reinforcement.

4. Discerning Further Implications of the Questions

The process of discerning does not cease with the immediate situation. It continues wherever people reflect on the material and recall the tradition. Hence, it is proper to see early Christian interpretation not as an obstacle to recovering the "real meaning" of events but as a continuation of the process of interpretation, reflection and discernment which the original discussion was designed to provoke. Salient instances are found in our passage.

(a) Discerning the witness of Scripture (Matt 11:10 = Luke 7:27). In an extension of the *florilegium* principle, Scripture is cited here as an endorsement of "more than a prophet." The logic of the discourse could be expressed in the form of an *enthymeme*: "John is greater than a prophet, for this is he . . ." As already noted, the interpretation of scripture was the leading formal method of discernment in Judaeo-Christian discourse. Put at its baldest, it consisted of reading (or reciting) the scriptures in the light of contemporary events, and reading contemporary events in the light of the scriptures. It combined respect for the text while effecting a "merging of horizons." The nub of the issue was the question of specific religious role and identity, as in John's question to Jesus: "Are you he . . . ?" In fact, "This is . . ." or "This is he . . ." was a common way of identifying scriptural text and contemporary figure.[57] It was an approach designed to generate particular insights into the ways of God with his people at a perceived crisis in their understanding of their world. Indications of dependence on the Hebrew text rather than the LXX might link the interpretation to the Palestinian milieu, if not to the Palestinian synagogues.[58] Two levels should be distinguished. One is the identification of John with Mal 3:1, glossed with Mal 4:5-6. It is entirely possible, in view of his

---

57   Cf. Acts 2:16 and F. F. Bruce's comments on it in his *Commentary on the Book of Acts* (London and Edinburgh: Marshall, Morgan & Scott, 1954) 67-69.

58   Cf. Albright and Mann, *Matthew*, 136.

high estimate of John, that Jesus made, or at least suggested the possibility of, the identification of John with Elijah (cf. 11:14). At the very least, he is the eschatological prophet of Yahweh. The second level involved an elaboration of the textual evidence within the believing community—a process otherwise known as "intertextuality." Not only does Mark testify to the importation of Isa 40:3 into the equation, but Mal 3:1 was readily associated in the Jewish mind with Exod 23:20: "Behold, I send an angel before you . . ." This has prompted the second person "before you" in Matt 11:10 = Luke 5:27, instead of the first person as in Mal 3:1. On the basis of Exod 23:20, this second person address refers to the people of God. John is the emissary of God who will lead them into the new age. A further development would take "before you" to refer to Jesus. John, as Elijah (cf. Matt 11:14), prepares the way for Jesus, the Messiah. This, however, represents the end, rather than the early stages, of the hermeneutical process in question.

(b) Discerning the significance of violent times (Matt 11:12-15). "What did you go out to see . . . ?" was the trigger for even more radical questions. How realistic was it to discern the reality of the Kingdom of God (or of heaven, as Matthew prefers) in John's mission when (as everyone knows) John himself was the victim of a violent death and the violence has continued ever since? Evidence from Qumran suggests that the βιαζεται in Matt 11:12 may be identified with the "violent men" of the Thanksgiving Psalms. The decades leading up to the Jewish Revolt (66-70 CE) represented "a long, bloody period, when pious militaristic Jews continued the conflict with the Romans, hoping always to overcome this dominant power."[59] The saying itself is clearly post-Baptist ("From the days of John the Baptist until now . . ."), reflecting on the crucial significance of his work which endures in spite of his death. It is suggested that John marks the end of the era when prophecy looked forward and law spoke from the past (11:13). The suggestion is controversial. It may be a response to Pharisaic objections that John undermined the stable pattern of law and prophets, with the result that law and order has broken down. Jesus turns their complaint into an endorsement of John's epoch making importance.[60] What we see now

---

[59]   Buchanan, *Matthew*, 489.

[60]   Cf. F. W. Danker, "Luke 16:16—An Opposition Logion," *JBL* 77 (1958) 231-43, which is cited by W. Wink, *John the Baptist in Gospel Tradition*

is the deadly struggle between good and evil that constituted the eschatological woes of prophetic discourse. Matthew's discourse presupposes at least a version of the eschatological world view of Judaism and early Christianity, relieved only by the affirmation of John as the long expected Elijah (11:14). Matthew's logion (11:12) is thus to be taken *ad malem partem.*[61] The discerning (11:15) recognise the eschatological woes as messianic (cf. 11:2). In the continuing attempts to answer the question of John's deeper significance we find the outworking of Christian eschatology and the germ of christology.

(c) *Discerning the possibilities of the new age (cf. Luke 16:16).* The debate continues. The law and the prophets characterised the previous era,[62] but (according to Luke) now is the age of gospel preaching and "everyone forces his way into it." Here Luke shows that βιάζεται can be used in the Middle voice, although it is inappropriate to construe it thus in Matthew's text. Luke's version is optimistic: *ad bonam partem.* He conceives of the evangelisation of the world, and the nations streaming into the Kingdom. Although his interpretation of the tradition is different from Matthew's, he agrees that John marks the boundary of the new age. The context in which he places the logion is that of controversy with the Pharisees, whose observation of the law is seen as mere accommodation to worldly standards. It is precisely in the context of the gospel that the wholeness of the law is recognised (cf. Luke 16:14-15, 17). In spite of echoes of earlier forms, Luke's orientation is that of Christian mission.[63]

(d) *Discerning the original logion?* Both evangelists record Jesus' affirmation of John's greatness and his eschatological importance. Both recognise that a mighty transition had been effected by the power of God. This is reflected in the question, What did you go out to see? They went out to see an important event in the religious

---

(SNTSMS 7; Cambridge: Cambridge University Press, 1968) 21. Danker's interesting suggestion has even more force if related to Matthew's logion rather than Luke's, although Luke provides the context of disputation with the Pharisees.

61   Cf. P. S. Cameron, *Violence and the Kingdom: The Interpretation of Matthew 11.12* (ANTJ 5; Frankfurt am Main: Lang, 1984).

62   Luke 16:16a is parallel to Matt 11:13 and in some respects may echo an earlier form of the logion.

63   For a discussion of this passage in the light of the christology of Q, see Tuckett, *Q and the history of Early Christianity*, 211, and, more generally, 209-37.

history of Israel—a "turning to God" (*teshuvah*), a new God-centred movement. The tradition, therefore, records Jesus working with his audience (as the compiler of Q and the evangelists are working with theirs) to help his hearers discern the finger of God in their own history and experience (cf. Exod 8:19; Luke 11:20; or "Spirit of God," Matt 12:28). The overtones of the Exodus story suggest both deliverance and judgement by the power of God. Jesus' reply to John's emissaries is relevant here. The mighty works are evident in Jesus' ministry for those who have eyes to see—that is, for those who crack the code. The task was to discern the presence and power of God in John's work and in that of Jesus himself. Their roles are distinguished by their perspectives. Within the framework of the eschatological world view, John pointed forwards to the imminence of God's judgement and salvation, while Jesus enacted the Kingdom—gave reality to God's dynamic rule—in his words and actions. The Kingdom remains transcendent; it never becomes a human creation; but it can be encountered in Jesus' enactment of it, which represents, in Bruce Chilton's words, "a conscious performance of fresh meaning . . . which also invited his hearers to the sort of activity that was consistent with [his] vision."[64]

What then of the logion that may underlie Matt 11:12-13a = Luke 16:16? It is likely to have stated that the law and the prophets anticipated the Kingdom until John (thus far, following Luke), and then to have expressed the notion of the Kingdom as a powerful, compelling force.[65] Precise reconstruction is, I think, beyond us.[66] What we have, in Matthew and Luke, are interpretations of the logion in different contexts—echoes of the dialogue within the early Christian communities. For them, the truth of the Kingdom was not set in stone but was, indeed, among them (cf. Luke 17:21), to be

---

64   B. D. Chilton, "The Kingdom of God in Recent Discussion," in Chilton and Evans (eds.), *Studying the Historical Jesus*, 264.

65   Cf. B. D. Chilton, *God in Strength: Jesus' Announcement of the Kingdom* (SNTU 1; Freistadt: Plöchl, 1979; repr. BibSem 8; Sheffield: JSOT Press, 1987); idem, *Pure Kingdom: Jesus' Vision of God* (Studying the Historical Jesus; London: SPCK; Grand Rapids: Eerdmans, 1996); B. D. Chilton and J. I. H. McDonald, *Jesus and the Ethics of the Kingdom* (London: SPCK; Grand Rapids: Eerdmans, 1987) 59-60 .

66   Wink comments, "The history of the tradition shows we are dealing with a very primitive tradition, already unintelligible by the time of the Evangelists" (*John the Baptist*, 20).

discerned and performed. The sense of newness raised questions about the perspectives of law and prophets, now that the gospel held centre stage (so Luke) or now that the Kingdom was the centre of contention (so Matthew). These are precisely the kinds of questions that were canvassed in the early Christian communities. In view of the complexities in the scriptural tradition and the empirical situation of first century Jewish religion, it is not surprising that interpretations showed a certain ambivalence. Engagement with scripture was itself a search, a questing for truth, rather than a treasury of assured answers; and what was discerned was a mighty power at work in a new age.

(e) Discerning true greatness. The question of greatness (cf. Matt 18:1-4; 23:11; Mark 9:34; Luke 9:46, 22:24, 26; *Gospel of Thomas* §46) was raised explicitly by Jesus' evaluation of the Baptist (Matt 11:11; Luke 7:28), which was something of an embarrassment to some in the churches. As we have seen, John is undervalued when rated as a prophet. Among human beings to date he is pre-eminent.[67] He inaugurated the messianic age without seeing its full glory. What concerns us here is not the determined attempt to set such estimation in christological or apologetic context—either by insisting that the superiority of the "least" in the Kingdom is a downgrading of John,[68] or by suggesting that Jesus in his humility held himself to be "least" in the Kingdom,[69] or by exempting Jesus from the equation by suggesting that he is not to be counted "among those born of women."[70] Rather, the question is: in what sense is John great, for Jesus clearly attributes greatness to him. Again, discernment is the key, and it involves the combination of the empirical and scriptural and eschatological evaluation. John's greatness is to be seen in the way he fulfilled his vocation. In all respects he fulfilled the role of servant—indeed, the servant of God—and so met Jesus' criteria for greatness in the Kingdom.[71]

---

[67] Cf. D. R. Catchpole, "The Beginning of Q: A Proposal," *NTS* 38 (1992) 209.

[68] Cf. Buchanan, *Matthew*, 487-88.

[69] Cf. G. Vermes, *Jesus the Jew* (London: Collins, 1973) 32-33, notes that in Aramaic and Hebrew "the least one" may designate "the youngest" or last person in a series. Hence the phrase is a claim for Jesus' pre-eminence, although he came later.

[70] The phrase is a Semitism; cf. Davies and Allison, *Matthew*, 250-51.

[71] Jesus might well have used a pun on "least" as "youngest" in age and as

5. *Discerning the Condition of "this generation"*

The parable is introduced by a question, "To what shall I compare this generation?" (in Luke, by a double question) which, as Bultmann recognised, "is very likely original."[72] It is also typically Matthaean![73] With this parable the discourse takes a subversive form, comparing 'this generation' to children sitting in the market places (community gathering points) complaining that others will not act as they wish them to do.[74] The image is Palestinian and may well constitute the original parable. If so, its application owes much to continuing reflection and interpretation. It highlights the refusal of "this generation" to give a positive response to either John or Jesus, although they represented radically different life-styles. John's life-style—"neither eating nor drinking"—was ascetic in that he strictly observed dietary laws yet he was rejected as demon possessed. Jesus' much more sociable life-style[75] was castigated for over indulgence and for friendship with "tax collectors and sinners" (Matt 11:16-19; Luke 7:31-35). His was not, of course, a life of profligacy but an alternative strategy for the fulfilment of his mission. The point of the parable, however, revolves around the audience's refusal to become involved. It does not explicitly commend Jesus' way as superior to John's and thus does not represent Christian apologetic directed against John's disciples. Its target is clearly contemporary society, which ignores the claims of John and Jesus by refusing to discern where wisdom lies. The *peroratio* thus calls for decision.

The proverb which rounds off the passage—"Wisdom is justified by her deeds" (Matt 11:19b)—points once again to the empirical

---

"child/servant" (cf. Luke 9:48). The youngest will, of course, live to participate in the great coming events, but Jesus also had a concern for the quality of service in the Kingdom. This is picked up, for its own purposes, by *Gospel of Thomas* §46. Relevant also is the revelation to "babes" (Matt 11:25).

72   Bultmann, *History of the Synoptic Tradition*, 172; cf. 199. J. Jeremias presents a more elaborate case, which is not wholly convincing in spite of his vivid exegesis of the parable (*Parables of Jesus* [London: SCM Press, 1954] 121, including n. 75); cf. Goulder, *Midrash and Lection*, 357.

73   Cf. Goulder, *Midrash and Lection*, 357.

74   It is often noted that there is a male/female motif here: the girls play at mourning and the boys at wedding-dances (Goulder, *Midrash and Lection*, 98, 357).

75   "Son of man" here seems to reflect the Aramaic periphrasis for the first person singular.

baseline and picks up "the deeds of the Christ" from Matt 11:1. Luke underlines the fact that wisdom, like truth, is self-authenticating in the lives of those who follow her (Luke 7:35). In either case, wisdom cannot be known except through discernment and commitment.

CONCLUSION

Our study will have served its purpose if it has illustrated the centrality of questioning, communication and discernment in Gospel tradition. In pursuing the quest of the historical John and Jesus, an important concern—allied to contextual considerations—is to establish the *communicative situation* in which they could have operated. They were not solitaries—not even John. They related to people; their ministry was realised through interaction with others. They did not simply proclaim; they invited response. Jesus in particular led his audience forward towards insight and discernment by means of questions, promptings and parables. Even the much lamented secondary layers of tradition testify to the continuing process of interpretation and discernment. Truth is approached dialectically, through interaction. We must at least qualify the notion that Jesus' discourse consisted of theologoumena which have to be teased out of traditional complexity. He was not a gnostic redeemer, bringing hidden wisdom from above. Truth is to be found—or at least pursued—in the present world, where God works. There is therefore point in Otto's contention that it is not Jesus who brings the Kingdom but the Kingdom that brings Jesus.[76] John and Jesus articulated the reality that encompassed them—the nearness and power of God bringing into sharp focus the crisis of the times for Israel. With the articulation went *praxis*—the performance of the Kingdom as each was led to give expression to it. Underpinning it was the awareness that reality revealed itself to the childlike. Shortly after the passage considered in this article, Matthew records the revelation of the Father to "babes" (Matt 11:25).

Discernment was therefore the key to understanding, and communication and questioning the essential condition for enabling discernment. As Matthew indicates, christology—the wisdom of the Christ—was the goal of discernment which the churches attained.

---

[76]   R. Otto, *The Kingdom of God and the Son of Man* (London: Lutterworth; Boston: Starking, 1938) 97-107. Cf. Chilton, "The Kingdom of God in Recent Discussion," 264; idem, *Pure Kingdom*, 8.

Eschatology led to christology. Church communication had perforce to use catechetical methods, which tended to give formulated answers. Within the framework of the churches' christology, Matthew (11:2-19) leads us back to the real questions that were asked and to the communication, the dialogue and interaction that were central to the disclosure of truth. Only thus can we discern the signs of the times. He leaves us with the thought that the task of interpretation is never simply the exegesis of ancient Scripture but the reading of Scripture with a view to understanding the presence and purpose of God in the world. We too must discern the signs of the times.

PUBLIC DECLARATION OR FINAL JUDGMENT?

Matthew 10:26-27 = Luke 12:2-3 as a Case of Creative Redaction

Scot McKnight

Embedded in the Jesus traditions Matthew brought together to form his second discourse (Matt 9:36–11:1) is a Q tradition (10:26-33) exhorting Matthew's community (1) not to fear "them" (10:26a) and (2) to make known publicly what they have learned from Jesus in private (10:26b-27). The exhortation is then legitimated (1) by recognizing the overwhelming superiority of God over "them" (10:28), (2) by appealing to the innate superiority of the community over the natural realm (10:29-31), and (3) by threatening the community with judgment if it fails to confess Jesus (i.e. making his private words public) or promising the same with acceptance if it confesses Jesus in public (10:32-33).

The author of the Third Gospel, whom I shall refer to as Luke according to academic tradition, however, includes the same Q tradition (12:1-9) to exhort his community to avoid the fundamental sin of the Pharisees: hypocrisy (12:1b).[1] His legitimating apparatus proceeds as follows: Hypocrisy needs to be avoided (1) because whatever is done in private will become public when God acts to judge the community—whether at the End or, as would be typical for a Jewish prophet like Jesus, through the purgations of persecution which anticipate that End (12:2-3); (2) fear of the public/ Pharisees must not be permitted to dictate one's behavior and, since God is so much more powerful, the community needs to fear him

---

[1]   For an excellent statement as to the meaning of hypocrisy, see J. B. Green, *The Gospel of Luke* (NICNT; Grand Rapids: Eerdmans, 1997) 480-81: "Jesus' point is not that they are play-acting, but that Jesus regards them as misdirected in their fundamental understanding of God's purpose and, therefore, incapable of discerning the authentic meaning of the Scriptures and, therefore, unable to present anything other than the impression of piety." He extends here the important brief analysis H. Giesen, "ὑπόκρισις, κτλ," *EDNT* 3.403-404. A similar conclusion was reached independently by D. E. Garland, *The Intention of Matthew 23* (NovTSup 52; Leiden: Brill, 1979) 91-123. The older view can be seen in G. B. Caird, *Saint Luke* (WPC; Philadelphia: Westminster, 1977) 160.

(12:4-5); (3) God cares for his little flock and so will protect them (12:6-7); and (4) they need to live publicly in a manner consistent with their privacy (cf. 12:2-3) and if they so confess Jesus they will be finally approved by God (12:8-9).[2]

Exegesis of the various portions of this tradition provokes much discussion. In particular, heavy work has been done on the confessional logion (Matt 10:32-33 = Luke 12:8-9) with no emerging consensus in view. Not as much has been made of the "object" of fear in Matt 10:28-29 = Luke 12:4-5 or of the argument from God's providential care (Matt 10:29-31 = Luke 12:6-7) but, for some reason, the opening logion has been nearly totally neglected in scholarship.[3] Apparently, scholars have either avoided to compare the two separate uses of the logion or have simply failed to see the implications of what has been done to a logion in an instance of what may profitably be called "early Christian *Vergegenwärtigung*." It is this logion, the logion on public declaration, that concerns us in this paper. In what follows I shall examine the logion tradition-critically and then sketch the outlines of a tradition-history for the logion, explaining both the Matthean and Lukan forms of the logion.[4]

THE FORMS OF THE TRADITION

PUBLIC DECLARATION AND FINAL JUDGMENT

The Greek traditions, with my own numbered lines and short commentary, are as follows:

Matthew	*Luke*
1. Μὴ οὖν φοβηθῆτε αὐτούς·	
2. οὐδὲν γάρ ἐστιν κεκαλυμμένον	οὐδὲν δὲ συγκεκαλυμμένον ἐστὶν

---

2   On Luke 12:2-9, see Green, *Luke*, 478-85.

3   Cf. J. S. Kloppenborg, "The Q Sayings on Anxiety (Q 12:2-7)," *Forum* 5 (1989) 83-98; see also his *The Formation of Q: Trajectories in Ancient Wisdom Collections* (SAC; Philadelphia: Fortress, 1987), 206-16; D. Lührmann, *Die Redaktion der Logienquelle* (WMANT 33; Neukirchen-Vluyn: Neukirchener, 1969) 49-52; S. Schulz, *Q: Die Spruchquelle der Evangelisten* (Zurich: Theologischer Verlag, 1972) 461-65; R. Laufen, *Die Doppelüberlieferungen der Logienquelle und des Markusevangeliums* (BBB 54; Bonn: Peter Hanstein, 1980) 156-73; E. C. Park, *The Mission Discourse in Matthew's Interpretation* (WUNT 2.81; Tübingen: Mohr [Siebeck], 1995) 145-48.

4   I shall assume the Q conclusions of J. S. Kloppenborg, *Q Parallels: Synopsis, Critical Notes, and Concordance* (FFRS; Sonoma: Polebridge, 1988), 116-17. If I differ from Kloppenborg's "consensus" conclusions, I shall acknowledge the difference.

3. ὃ οὐκ ἀποκαλυφθήσεται   ὃ οὐκ ἀποκαλυφθήσεται
4. καὶ κρυπτὸν ὃ οὐ γνωσθήσεται.   καὶ κρυπτὸν ὃ οὐ γνωσθήσεται.
5. ὃ λέγω ὑμῖν ἐν τῇ σκοτίᾳ   ἀνθ' ὧν ὅσα ἐν τῇ σκοτίᾳ εἴπατε
6. εἴπατε ἐν τῷ φωτί,   ἐν τῷ φωτὶ ἀκουσθήσεται,
7. καὶ ὃ εἰς τὸ οὖς ἀκούετε   καὶ ὃ πρὸς τὸ οὖς ἐλαλήσατε ἐν
                              τοῖς ταμείοις
8. κηρύξατε ἐπὶ τῶν δωμάτων.   κηρυχθήσεται ἐπὶ τῶν δωμάτων.

(1) Matthew alone has the introductory Μὴ οὖν φοβηθῆτε αὐτούς as an introductory clause and, though it has an analogous rendering in 10:28 (= Luke 12:4) and could be derived from that line, is probably Matthean redaction (cf. Matt 9:8; 17:6, 7; 27:54; 28:5).[5]

(2-3) The second line begins to bring to the fore the distinctiveness of each rendering of this Q logion, even if at first glance the wording is so similar. Thus, both record that Jesus said to his disciples that "there is nothing concealed", even if Luke's word is compounded (συγκεκαλυμμένον). Surface appearances, however, retreat when one asks about the meaning of the words for, in Matthew, the term "concealed" refers to "what Jesus has divulged to them in private" while in Luke the term "concealed" refers to "the private practices of the disciples." Divulged secrets, the content of Jesus' teaching of the mysteries of the Kingdom, are to be made public through declaration of the Kingdom; on the other hand, private practices will become known to all when God enacts the final judgment. The differences are notable. One suspects as well that the passive voice in line 3 has a different referent in each tradition: for Matthew it is the disciples who make the divulged secrets known while in Luke it is God who will publicly declare in judment the private sins of the disciples.

(4) Line 4 forms a synonymous parallelism with lines 2-3 and is to be understood similarly: "what is hidden will become known" means, for Matthew, that the disciples are to make known publicly the secrets Jesus divulges while, for Luke, it means that the disciples are to be aware that what they do in private should be checked by the final searching judgment of God since that final act of God will make public what is done secretly.

(5-6) Lines 5 and 6 reveal the fundamentally different renderings of the tradition for each Evangelist. Thus, for Matthew the verb

---

εἴπατε belongs in line 6 while in Luke it belongs in line 5: "what I say to you in darkness, *you are to say* in the light" vs. "whatever *you. say* in darkness, will be heard in the light." To be sure, the world of the New Testament writers did not have commas, but the presence of the comma in English grammar prior to εἴπατε in Matt 10:27a reveals the whole traditional difference: Matthew converts the meaning of the verb "to say" from "private conversation" to "public evangelism" (or vice versa for Luke: Luke converts the term from "public evanglism" to "private conversation"). In addition, in so reading the logion Matthw has turned the indicative into an imperative. To facilitate this conversion of language, Matthew adds a subject clause: ὃ λέγω (Matt 10:27a). This further requires that Luke's ἀκουσθήσεται be dropped.

(7-8) Again, these lines are in synonymous parallelism with lines 5-6 and reveal the same redactional tendencies: first, for Matthew, what the disciples hear in their ears is the divulged secrets of Jesus pertaining to the mysteries of the Kingdom and they are exhorted to declare these secrets from housetops; second, for Luke, what the disciples speak privately to the ears of others will be declared (passive: God will declare) publicly at the final judgment. The evidence of lines 7-8 support the observations made about lines 5-6 and show a consistent hand for each rendering of the tradition.[6]

This brief survey of the data in this Q tradition leads to the following conclusion: what is for Luke an exhortation to live private lives in light of a final, searching judgment by God is for Matthew an exhortation for the missionaries to declare publicly what Jesus has made known to them privately.[7] And all of this takes place within the context of using nearly the same words! A comma before εἴπατε, perhaps simply a misunderstanding on the part of some tradent,

---

[6]   Some have argued that the separate lines here represent stages of missionary work (Jesus in v. 27a, and the Church in v. 27b; cf. Schulz, *Q*, 462) but simple Semitic synonymous parallelism is probably at work. Thus, the lines do not concern themselves with stages of mission so much as with two ways of looking at the mission of the early Christians of Matthew's community. I do not mean to suggest, however, that two mission periods are visible here (Jesus, the Matthean community), but I do not think they are talked about on separate lines. Cf. D. A. Hagner, *Matthew* (2 vols., WBC 33; Dallas: Word, 1993–95) 1.285.

[7]   For an excellent survey of the literary shape and flow of Matthew's text, see D. J. Weaver, *Matthew's Missionary Discourse: A Literary Critical Analysis* (JSNTSup 38; Sheffield: JSOT Press, 1990) 107-12.

converts the whole logion and tradition into a missionary injunction. As I. H. Marshall, when commenting on the changes in Matthew, has understatedly expressed it: "Some alterations of the wording to suit new contexts appear to have been made."[8] In spite of this obvious objective perception of the data (even if some might want to explain the data as Luke's use of Matthew or Matthew's use of Luke, such use would not alter the data themselves), some have argued for a common, more generalized background logion that gave rise to two different particular logia now found at Matt 10:26-27 and Luke 12:2-3. For instance, this seems to lurk behind the statement of M. E. Boring, when he says,

> As taken up by the Q community in conjunction with the other prophetic words of this sayings cluster, however, the sayings would be a word of prophetic assurance ("upbuilding and encouragement and consolation," 1 Cor 14:3) to the Q community that the hardly noticed beginnings of its proclamation will be revealed to the whole of Israel and the world because God himself will bring it about (divine passives "be revealed, be made known").[9]

My suggestion here is that such generic exegesis, though attractive in its own way, does not stand up to a more intense scrutiny of the text when compared to its parallels and then seen in its own particular context.

I propose that we ask how Matthew (or Luke) arrived at this interpretation but to do this we need first to sketch, however briefly, the shape of the underlying Q tradition which both Matthew and Luke inherited. When this has been done we can ask how it is that Matthew arrived at his interpretation. To do this we must also record the various renderings of the logia and potential significant parallels.

To begin with, we need to note the substantial parallel at Mark 4:22 = Luke 8:17.

---

[8]   I. H. Marshall, *The Gospel of Luke* (NIGTC; Grand Rapids: Eerdmans, 1978) 510.

[9]   M. E. Boring, *The Continuing Voice of Jesus: Christian Prophecy and the Gospel Tradition* (Louisville: Westminster/John Knox Press, 1991) 217. See also D. A. Carson, "Matthew," in F. E. Gaebelein (ed.), *Expositor's Bible Commentary* (vol. 8, Grand Rapids: Zondervan, 1984) 254, for a similar generic logion that attempts to cover both the Matthean and Lukan forms: "The truth must emerge; the gospel and its outworkings in the disciples may not now be visible to all, but nothing will remain hidden forever. And if the truth will emerge at the End, how wise to declare it fully and boldly now."

Mark 4:22	*Luke 8:17*
οὐ γάρ ἐστιν κρυπτὸν	οὐ γάρ ἐστιν κρυπτὸν
ἐὰν μὴ ἵνα φανερωθῇ,	ὃ οὐ φανερὸν γενήσεται
οὐδὲ ἐγένετο ἀπόκρυφον	οὐδὲ ἀπόκρυφον
	ὃ οὐ μὴ γνωσθῇ
ἀλλ' ἵνα ἔλθῃ εἰς φανερόν.	καὶ εἰς φανερὸν ἔλθῃ.

While the logion of Mark 4:22 is ostensibly the source for Luke 8:17, the two renderings are not identical. In particular, Luke has an extra line (8:17d) and the specific grammar of each varies. Thus, Mark's ἀλλ' ἵνα (4:22d) becomes the simpler εἰς in Luke (8:17e). If Luke's rendering can be explained as Luke's typical refinement of Markan syntax,[10] the logion is nonetheless presented with the same meaning in each tradition as it emerges in each from the same context: the parable of the sower and the need to sow the Word. Its essential orientation then is similar to that of Matt 10:26-27 as compared with Luke 12:2-3.

Both the *GThom* and POxy confirm a tradition somewhat like what is found in both Mark 4:22 = Luke 8:17 but especially that tradtion now found Matt 10:26-27 = Luke 12:2-3, with special tendencies that characterize Luke 12:2-3:[11]

GThom §5	*POxy 654 (lines 27-31)*
Jesus said, "Recognize what is in front of your face and what is concealed from you	Jesus says . . . before your eye and . . .
will be revealed to you.	from you will be revealed . . .
For there is nothing hidden	is hidden
which will not be disclosed."	that will not be manifest
	and buried that will not be . . .

GThom 6	*POxy 654 (lines 32-40)*
His disciples asked him, "Do you want us to fast?	. . . ask him . . . say, "How shall we fast . . .
How shall we pray, and shall we give alms, and	pray and . . . and what shall we observe . . .
what diet shall we keep?" Jesus	Jesus says . . .
said, "Do not lieand do not do what	do not do what you . . .
you hate, because all things are	truth . . .
revealed in the sight of Heaven.	

---

10   See R. A. Guelich, *Mark 1–8:26* (WBC 34A; Dallas: Word, 1989) 230.

11   I use the translation and text of J. K. Elliott, *The Apocryphal New Testament* (Oxford: Clarendon, 1993), since it provides a synopsis of the two separate traditions. I have adjusted the synopsis lines for ease in comparison.

For nothing is hidden that shall
not be revealed,and nothing is
covered that shall remain without
being uncovered."

hidden . . .

GThom 33
Jesus said, "What you hear with
your ear,
preach in others' ears from your
house-tops. For no one lights a
lamp and puts it under a bushel
nor does he put it in a hidden place,
but he sets it on a lampstand so
everyonewho comes in and out
may see its light."

POxy 1 (lines 41-42)
Jesus says, "You hear in one of your
ears . . ."

The lines surviving from the 3d and 4th century POxy, while
interesting, provide only fragmentary support for the logion in Mark
(and perhaps Q in POxy 1.33). Consequently, not much can be made
of these lines. On the other hand, the logia surviving from *GThom*
find substantial parallel in the Q and Markan logia cited above.
Logion §5, though somewhat obscure, probably moves in the tradition now found in the Lukan rendering of Q (Luke 12:2-3) in that its
concern is with revelation though in Luke it is sin that is revealed
while in *GThom* it seems truth is promised to be revealed to the
quester for wisdom. Logion §6, however, is clearly in the stream of
tradition that is found in Luke 12:2-3: the second half of the *GThom*
logion concerns God's final disclosure of one's personal (private)
behaviors. If these observations on logia §5 and §6 be accurate, the
GThom uses the wisdom saying "For there is nothing hidden . . ."
with two senses: God will reveal the truth to the wise (§5) and God
will disclose even private behavior (§6). In no case, however, does
he use the wisdom saying as it is found in Matt 10:26-27, though he
does show use of Matt 10:27 at *GThom* §33.

THE ORIGINAL Q SHAPE OF THE LOGION

General observations lead to the conclusion that we have before a
genuine Q tradition.[12] First, the overlaps between the two

---

12   Kloppenborg (*Q Parallels*, 118) observes that "most authors" see the tradi-
tion as stemming from Q. Recent commentaries assign the tradition to Q: A. Sand,
Das Evangelium nach Matthäus (RNT; Regensburg: Pustet, 1986) 227; J. Gnilka,
Das Matthäusevangelium (HTKNT 1.1-2; 2 vols., Freiburg: Herder, 1986) 1.384-

Evangelists is substantial: an impression gained from a colored synopsis reveals that the two are similar enough to suggest a common source or, if one is so inclined, the use of one by the other. For example, Matt 10:26, if one disregards the the introductory command (10:26a), is identical to Luke 12:2 except for Matthew's use of γάρ. Second, the connections between the logia in this tradition, and there are four of them (Matt 10:26-27 par; 10:28 par; 10:29-31 par; 10:32-33 par), are not as obvious as one might think, leading several scholars to think that the logia were at one time independent logia.[13] Thus, Mark 4:22 has a parallel at Luke 8:17 but not in Matthew; Matt 10:26 has a parallel in Luke 12:2 and in *GThom* §5 as well as POxy 654 §5; Matt 10:27 has a parallel in Luke 12:3 and *GThom* §33 as well as in POxy 654 §6 (1.33). If one argues for their original independence, one is providing at the same time evidence for the use of a common source since it is nearly impossible for both Matthew and Luke to have independently combined these various logia into one whole cloth—and to have done so with different meanings.

In my judgment, however, the logical connection in Luke from 12:2-3 to 12:4-5 is far from clear,[14] leading me to think that the two were united prior to Luke and not by Luke. Thus, being aware of the hypocrisy of the Pharisees (12:1) does not lead easily to the need for fear of God rather than a fear of the Pharisees (or possibly Satan— which would make the connection even more obtuse!). R. Bultmann and J. S. Kloppenborg have both argued that Luke 12:2 and 12:3 were originally independent of one another and deserve more than a hearing than can be offered at this point.[15] However, just because a tradition is quoted as separate logia (as can be seen for Luke 12:2

86; W. D. Davies and D. C. Allison, Jr., *The Gospel according to Saint Matthew* (ICC; 3 vols., Edinburg: T. & T. Clark, 1988–97) 2.201-202 (with concessions to Griesbach proponents); D. A. Hagner, *Matthew* (WBC 33; 2 vols., Dallas: Word, 1993–95) 1.284. The exception is D. Hill, *The Gospel of Matthew* (NCB; Grand Rapids: Eerdmans, 1972) 192, who is followed by Carson, "Matthew," 254.

13   E.g. R. A. Piper, *Wisdom in the Q-tradition: The Aphoristic Teaching of Jesus* (SNTSMS 61; Cambridge: Cambridge University Press, 1989) 52, who sees three traditions: Q 12:2-3, 4-7, 8-9.

14   See Kloppenborg, *Formation*, 207 (esp. n. 148).

15   See Bultmann, *History*, 83, 97 (a secular wisdom saying transformed by inclusion in Christian tradition); Kloppenborg, *Formation* , 206-207, 210 (see 206-14).

and 12:3) does not mean that originally they were independent of one another. Methodologically, all that can be inferred from separate citation is that the logion was capable of being separated and cited separately. What we have are isolable dimensions of a logion or tradition, not necessarily originally separate logion. What (supposedly) gave them impetus to be joined by a redactor may have been what gave them unity to begin with. It is not unsual for separate dimensions of various logia to be given separate citation at a later date.

Third, the distinctive elements of each text can be given a fairly reasonable explanation on the basis of redaction as opposed to a tradition behind the Evangelists. For example, the use of tidier parallels in Matt 10:28 and the use of characteristic ideas and terms by Luke in 12:4-5 account for the wording better than suggesting that Luke and Matthew are each using a different tradition.[16]

D. Hill, however, has revived an older argument that the tradition now in Matt 10:26-33 is not from Q. I shall respond to his suggestions *seriatim*. First, he contends that the Matthean text contains four logia "which probably circulated separately before being brought together in a thematic unity (the word-link being 'fear not')."[17] I would not contest the observation that the four logia here were possibly originally independent; that, however, would not support the non-use of Q because the question here is not about original setting but "where did Matthew/Luke get the tradition"? That four independent logia found themselves together in two separate Gospels strains credulity. Second, Hill contends that though Luke 12:2-9 forms a "significant parallel" the "context is different."[18] That the contexts are different hardly proves that the Evangelists were not using the same source: difference of context may simply prove that the Evangelists both had different motives for using the same tradition. For example, few doubt that Matthew used the so-called apocalyptic discourse material of Mark 13 when he composed his

---

[16]   E.g. J. Gnilka, *Matthäusevangelium* , 1. 384-85; Davies and Allison, *Matthew*, 2.205-207; J. Fitzmyer, *The Gospel According to Luke X–XXIV* (2 vols., AB 28; Garden City: Doubleday, 1985) 2.956-58.

[17]   D. Hill, *Matthew*, 192. This statement is a virtual translation of P. Bonnard, *L'Évangile selon Saint Matthieu* (CNT 1; 2nd ed., Paris: Delachaux & Niestlé, 1970) 150.

[18]   D. Hill, *Matthew*, 192. Again, Hill is heavily dependent here, in vocabulary and idea, on Bonnard, *Matthieu*, 150. The same is argued by D. Bock, *Luke* (BECNT 3; 2 vols., Grand Rapids: Baker, 1996) 2.1135.

missionary discourse (cf. Mark 13:9-13 and Matt 10:17-22). That the same tradition is found in a different context does not suggest, however, that Matthew is not using Mark. The examples of this can in fact be multiplied in the Synoptic tradition so frequently that we are led to think that different context, if not the rule, is hardly exceptional. Finally, Hill then contends that parallels to Matt 10:26-33 in other strands in the Jesus traditions (he points to Mark 4:22; Luke 8:17; 21:18; Matt 8:38 and Luke 9:26) shows that "the literary connection between this section an Lk. 12.2ff is more complex than is suggested by the affirmation that at this point both evangelists are drawing on Q material."[19] Few would contest the observation that our pericope has other parallels or that these other parallels suggest a complex relationship but one observation remains sure: the fundamental nature of the parallels in Luke 12:2-9, the use of four supposed independent logia together, as well as the rather insignificant "other parallels" lead me to conclude that, though the tradition may well have a complex oral and literary history, it makes far more sense to see in these two traditions in Matthew and Luke the common use of one tradition, namely a Q tradition.[20]

Can we know which context is more likely to have been the original for the logion now found in Matt 10:26-27 = Luke 12:2-3? The assumption of an original missionary context (as is found in Matthew) for this tradition deserves, and is here given, a challenge as it is all too frequently asserted with no or little argumentation.[21] One

---

[19]   Hill, *Matthew*, 192. The same observation applies with respect to the use of Bonnard.

[20]   Carson ("Matthew," 245) adds a further argument: "most of the individual sayings are brief, easily memorized, and usable again and again." But there is simply no evidence that the sayings were used "again and again" unless use in both Matthew *and* Luke means "again and again." Assertion of memorization here is a bogey man: the logia show enough divergence that memory is not the issue. What needs to be explained is how four rather independent logia find themselves tucked into one another with different meanings but similar wording—in the same order in different Gospels!

[21]   For the division of scholarship, see Kloppenborg, *Formation*, 207 n. 148. The majority of the major Q scholars in Germany favor Lukan originality here and a Matthean redaction of Q (e.g. S. Schulz, *Q*, 462 with n. 444). An exception is Laufen, *Die Doppelüberlieferungen*, 160-63, who however does not deal with enough significant arguments for the originality of the Lukan form of Q. Laufen assumes a fundamental coherence for Q 12:1-12 in his argument for Matthean priority. If, however, one argues that there are inherent tensions in the flow of the

recent attempt to defend the Matthean presentation as more primitive has been offered by W. D. Davies and D. C. Allison, Jr.[22] They offer four arguments: (1) Matthew fits better with the larger block since 10:32-33 deal with fearless confession; (2) Luke's wording could be an attempt to assimilate the tradition to Luke 12:1; (3) the doublet of Matt 10:26 at Mark 4:22 reveals that these kinds of words suggest that apocalyptic revelation was traditionally associated with the preaching of the gospel, that is, a missionary situation; and (4) if, in Q, Matt 10:27 was already about missionary work, then we have an adequate basis for seeing why Matthew shaped the block for his missionary discourse. I think their first argument is a good argument and not to be set aside lightly especially if it can be shown, on other than assertional grounds, that 10:32-33 is concerned with missionaries and their need for confession. If the logion applies more generally to disciples and their need to stand firm for Jesus in the midst of opposition, as Luke so presents the logion, then no serious argument is being presented. How do the other arguments stand up? Argument two begs the question: arguing that 12:2-3 assimilates to 12:1 is what we need to discover, not what we need to assert. Luke's wording in 12:2-3 may be what it is because that is what Q was: that

---

text one starts with a completely different set of criteria that need to be met in order to determine the original shape of Q. Put differently, a smoother reading of the whole text (in this case, from Matt 10:26 to 10:33) is more likely to be a later rather than earlier form of the text. Matthew's is smoother than Luke's; therefore, on the basis of this criterion Luke would be more primitive. In my estimation, Laufen (*Die Doppelüberlieferungen*, 163) assumes the Matthean shape and rejects the Lukan form for the precise reason I would see it as more primitive. His critical statement is as follows: "Der Logienquelle geht us zweifellos (?) um das Bekenntnis zu Jesus *vor den Menschen*, um das *öffentliche* Zeugnis des Glaubens." As has been shown with other scholars in this regard, this statement assumes the Matthean missionary context as the primitive context when it is precisely the context that is under question.

Kloppenborg, who surely represents the emerging North American viewpoint (but see the independent line of Hagner, *Matthew*, 1.284), sees the original Q best represented in Matt 10:27 and in harmony with Mark 4:22 and that Luke redacted the logion. His view, however, is not defended. Piper (*Wisdom*, 57-58) argues recently for Luke's rendition as the more primitive. See further at n. 23 below. Two recent Lukan scholars, however, have argued for Matthean redaction and for Lukan primitivity: cf. J. Nolland, *Luke 9:21–8:34* (WBC 35; 3 vols., Dallas: Word, 1989–93) 2.677; Marshall, *Luke*, 510-13.

[22] Davies and Allison, *Matthew*, 2.201-204.

is, 12:1-3 formed one whole cloth about the danger of hypocrisy. The key words here are "may be"; what we need to know is what is most probable and saying that 12:2-3 "may be" assimilation will not stand the scrutiny of a serious argument. Argument three stands firm in this: Mark 4:22 does show that apocalyptic revelation and early Christian proclamation could be tied together but the important question is not here answered: what is the relation of Mark 4:22 to Matt 10:26-27? And, to go even further, there is no reason to think that revelation is not also tied into the final judgment of God (as Luke's tradition is shaped); we have adequate context for thinking that either form of the logion would make sense within the world of Jesus and the early Christian tradents. Finally, argument four is a circular argument; the words they use reveal the problem: "If in Q 10.27 was already about missionary proclamation . . ." Then to conclude that such a view explains why 10:26-31 was placed in a missionary context is circular. The issue is whether 10:27 in Q was originally missionary; the evidence needs to be presented. What I would observe here is that these kinds of arguments are mounted for arguing for the original Q being best represented in Matt 10:26-27 because many, on other grounds (I assume), already think so but the evidence deserves to be examined once again before we proceed further.

I would suggest that at least three factors point to the Matthean missionary context as secondary to the mission of the disciples during the life of Jesus. First, the forensic tones of Matt 10:26-33, implicit in 10:26-27, probably to be deduced from 10:28, and emergent in 10:32-33, are without parallel in the earliest traditions about the mission of the followers of Jesus (10:17-23 are from a different setting) and, therefore, belong to a later level of the tradition. From Mark 6:13, 30, we can infer that the followers of Jesus were not put on trial during the mission. If we agree that Luke 12:2-3 is the most primitive form of the tradition (as will be presented below), then the forensic stuff in the Matthean rendering is secondary and probably to be assigned to the level of Matthean redaction. Second, a warning about death for involvement in the mission is clearly anachronistic for the mission of the first followers of Jesus. While it may be the case that Jesus inferred from John's death that he too might die, and therefore he could have inferrred that those associated with him could also die, the sayings of Jesus pertaining to this theme suggest rather that he would die before they did and their suffering was further into the future (cf. e.g. Mark 6:17-29 par; 10:45 pars; Matt 5:11-12 = Luke 6:22-23; Mark 2:20 pars; 6:1-6 par; 8:24 pars; 13:9-13 pars; Matt 10:34-36 = Luke 12:51-53). To infuse the mission of the Twelve with notions of martyrdom is to impart a sense that the original mission did not have. Such traditions must stem from another context. Finally, the emphasis of Jesus' message has been demonstrably proven to revolve around Kingdom of God, that is, it was a *theo*centric message. However, the force of the tradition before us is decidedly *christo*centric and this suggests once again a focus that does not pertain orginally to the missonary activity of the first followers of Jesus. That message was Kingdom of God and its works (cf. Matt 10:1-2 pars; 10:7 = Luke 9:2; 10:9). These three pieces of evidence then suggest that the material of Q 12:2-9 reflects conditions after the historic mission of the disciples or that it is Matthew who has brought a Q tradition into the context of the mission and has reworked that Q material to adjust it to its new home. In addition, I would concur with R. A. Piper when he suggests that Luke's intense interest in the missionary implications of the Jesus traditions would most likely have led him to maintain such connections.[23]

In addition, analysis of the overall Matthean pattern of redaction confirms the view that Matthew's text reflects a redactional application of the Q material to a mission context. First, the use of Μὴ οὖν φοβηθῆτε αὐτούς is clearly Matthean redaction and sets the stage for Matthew's use of the whole block of material (cf. 9:8; 17:6, 7; 27:54; 28:5).[24] Second, his intent to use the tradition in the context of mission calls forth the ὃ λέγω ὑμῖν (10:27a), the relocation of εἴπατε (now with the clause that follows), the use of ἀκούετε and the change to the second person in κηρύξατε.[25] Third, redactional tendencies are also found throughout the rest of the block but they cannot detain us here.[26] These observations lead to the conclusion that, as observed

---

23 Piper, *Wisdom*, 58. On the other hand, Luke's use of Pharisaic traditions, assuming that such was already present in Q, would have been ready material for Matthew's theology as well.

24 Cf. Schulz, *Q*, 461, who finds tension created when Matthew adds this introductory clause.

25 Cf. R. H. Gundry, *Matthew: A Commentary on His Literary and Theological Art* (Grand Rapids: Eerdmans, 1982) 196, 645.

26 See S. McKnight, *New Shepherds for Israel* (unpublished Ph.D. dissertation; University of Nottingham, 1986) 122-24, 256-57.

above, not only does the content of this block of material fit into the historical mission of the disciples but also its content has been significantly shaped by Matthean redaction: Matthew, then, has edited the material from Q so that it will fit into the mission context.

Slight confirmation of this conclusion can be gained from considering the later traditions which bear some relation to our logion at Matt 10:26-27 = Luke 12:2-3. In particular, as mentioned above, the Lukan interpretation of the matter was taken up, if slightly extended, in *GThom* §5–6 and perhaps in POxy. parallels. There is some confirmation of the Matthean rendering in *GThom* §33. Thus, the parallels at *GThom* have a stronger resemblance to the Lukan material than to the Matthean shape. Jewish parallels to Matt 10:26 = Luke 12:2-3 are more in the line with the Lukan rendering as well (cf. *Tg.* Eccl 12:13-14; *m.* *ʾAbot* 2:4). Thus, *m.* *ʾAbot* 2:4: "And do not say anything which cannot be heard, for in the end it will be heard."

The material in Luke shows both a contextual flow (Luke 12:1-3) as well as some indications of contextual dislocation:[27] (1) the logical connection between the minatory sayings in 12:1-3 and the wisdom traditions 12:4-7[28] is unclear; (2) the call to acknowledge Jesus publicly further complicates the logic of the tradition as it appears here; and (3) the various logia, with apparently no firm relation to what precedes, now found at 12:10 and 12:11-12 reveal that what Luke 12:1-12 is a resting spot for some tired logia with no other place for their head. Thus, we cannot postulate that the Lukan context for the larger tradition of Matt 10:26-33 = Luke 12:2-9 is any more appropriate; in fact, I would argue that the Lukan context does not provide any context for any of the logia except the first one where Luke seems constrained to place the logion in the context of Pharisaic hypocrisy.[29] From that point on Luke has simply added Q logia that were together prior to his Gospel.

---

[27]   So Marshall, *Luke*, 510; cf. also S. Schulz, *Q*, 462.

[28]   On the wisdom nature of Luke 12:4-7, which anchors his major thesis, see Kloppenborg, *Formation*, 208-10. Unfortunately, Kloppenborg *assumes* the missionary nature of the tradition and never seems to question the assumption; cf. 207 n. 148, 210. The same assumption can be found in Lührmann, *Redaktion*, 49; Piper, *Wisdom*, 60, 69, who does not permit the particularity of each text have full sway. See also D. C. Allison, Jr., *The Jesus Tradition in Q* (Harrisburg: Trinity Press International, 1997) 21.

[29]   See Marshall, *Luke*, 513.

But, since that first set of logia is our concern, we can ask whether the Lukan context is appropriate. If the reconstruction of Q that is suggested below be admitted, we can reasonably conclude that Luke's context is historically appropriate: not only does the logion relate a typical concern of Jesus with hypocrisy, its sense is entirely appropriate to the ministry of Jesus. The evidence that Luke composed Luke 12:1 is far from obvious and it better is assigned to Q or L,[30] with the logion of Jesus in 12:1b perhaps even more securely from Q. That is, followers of Jesus need to be aware that hypocrisy will be found out in God's searching final judgment.[31] Though not an original insight, recently A. D. Jacobson has argued that in the original Q, Q 12:2-3 was connected to Q 11:52, a woe saying. If this argument be granted, the original Q provided Luke (or some other editor) grounds for redacting a transition in the manner now found at Luke 12:1. Regardless of any attempt to rediscover the pedigree for Luke 12:1, the conclusion remains that Q would, in this view, have had a Pharisaic (or Pharisaic-type) context for Q 12:2-3.[32]

I conclude then that, while Matthew's context puts considerable stress on the logia when placed in the context of Jesus' sending out of the Twelve, Luke's own context, much less redacted and smoothed over, allows the logion of warning about the final judgment to have an adequate and historically reasonable context.

Without getting into an extensive, word-by-word analysis of the Q text itself, I suggest then the following as the shape of the Q text to which Matthew and Luke had access:

οὐδὲν . . . ἐστιν κεκαλυμμένον ὃ οὐκ ἀποκαλυφθήσεται καὶ κρυπτὸν ὃ οὐ γνωσθήσεται. ὅσα ἐν τῇ σκοτίᾳ εἴπατε ἐν τῷ φωτὶ ἀκουσθήσεται,[33] καὶ ὃ εἰς (πρὸς) τὸ οὖς ἐλαλήσατε (ἐν τοῖς ταμείοις) κηρυχθήσεται ἐπὶ τῶν δωμάτων.[34]

---

30   See Fitzmyer, *Luke*, 2.953, with Marshall, *Luke*, 510, 511-12.

31   See now M. Reiser, *Jesus and Judgment* (Minneapolis: Fortress, 1997).

32   See A. D. Jacobson, *The First Gospel: An Introduction to Q* (Sonoma: Polebridge, 1992) 184-86, 249. See also T. W. Manson, *The Sayings of Jesus* (London: SCM Press, 1949) 105-106.

33   Kloppenborg, *Formation*, 211, sees the second half of this Q text to be originally closer to Matthew than Luke (but see above). He assumes this view and offers very little, if any, argument for the primitivity of Matthew in comparison to Luke.

34   Apart from minor variations, my conclusions concur with a slight revision of Luke and with the conclusions of A. Polag, *Fragmenta Q: Textheft zur*

Because the original shape of the context for Q is not as important to us we can limit our concern to this logion alone. Thus, we do not need to explore the issue of which level found these four logia together but can limit our concern to whether or not this logion reflects an authentic word of Jesus and how it was that Matthew was able to convert the logion about final judgment into an exhortation to missionary activity.

AN AUTHENTIC LOGION?

Even if at times it seems appropriate to use the so-called criteria of authenticity,[35] I am of the view that the criteria themselves are substantive, but secondary, crystallizations of what historians do when they dig around and find things deemed worthy of keeping and recording. For instance, though I would argue that double dissimilarity is at times a useful criterion for making a solid historical judgment, I would also argue that I don't look first to see if things are doubly dissimilar. To illustrate: that Kingdom is largely absent from both Judaism at the time of Jesus and from the characteristic vocabulary of the earliest followers of Jesus counts with me as a valuable historical argument. On the other hand, just because Abba is found in some early Christian texts does not disqualify it as historically invaluable because other judgments count in its favor. (How else did it become so characteristic of early Christian prayer?) Accordingly, determining historical reliability of a logion putatively from Jesus is the result of art and careful judgment, not the result of some scientifically neutral application of supposedly rigid, neutral

---

Logienquelle (2nd ed., Neukirchen: Neurkirchener, 1982) 58 n. 37; Laufen, *Die Doppelüberlieferungen*, 156. I have used the Matthean word order of the copula in line one, ὅσα instead of ὅ in line 3, and included ἐν τοῖς ταμείοις on the fourth line.

35 The best survey of the criteria, along with the most rigorous use of the criteria, can now be found in J. P. Meier, *A Marginal Jew* (ABRL 3, 9; 2 vols., New York: Doubleday, 1991–94) 1.167-95. The method I mention here overlaps with the following Jesus scholarship: E. P. Sanders, *Jesus and Judaism* (Philadelphia: Fortress, 1985), though I am not so skeptical about the sayings of Jesus; B. F. Meyer, *The Aims of Jesus* (London: SCM Press, 1979); J. Becker, *Jesus von Nazaret* (New York: de Gruyter, 1996); N. T. Wright, *Jesus and the Victory of God* (Minneapolis: Fortress, 1996). I have utilized this approach in my *A New Vision for Israel: The Teachings of Jesus in National Context* (Studying the Historical Jesus; Grand Rapids: Eerdmans, forthcoming).

criteria. What counts for me most is sense and historical context: does the logion fit into the overall picture of Jesus that best explains how he interacted with the Judaisms he faced? Can the individual logion, especially if it is on a rather ancillary theme, be reasonably placed into the overall message and mission of Jesus to Israel? Since I take these observations as axiomatic I would also argue that historical judgment varies from case to case and no one set of criteria can be applied in some hierarchy to every logion. Rather, the historian's judgment comes into play for each logion. No matter how appealing the rigors of science may be, history involves the historian in a manner that precludes the discipline from being "simply scientific."

This logion coheres essentially with the historical Jesus and I shall attempt now to make the argument clear.[36] We can preface our arguments with the conclusion of M. E. Boring who analyzes the possible early Christian prophetic sayings in the Gospels and, about Q 12:2-3 says:

> The neatly structured form is in fact appropriate to a prophetic figure, as are the themes of the eschatological reversal and the revelation of secrets of human hearts. However, there is nothing that clearly points to a post-Easter setting, nor is there sufficient evidence to compel a Christian prophetic origin for the sayings, so in their original form they may have been part of the authentic teaching of Jesus.[37]

First, it is a well-known axiom of historical Jesus studies that the so-called divine passive is characteristic of how Jesus spoke and taught.[38] The Q logion as reconstructed above shows a divine passive in each line: each is an instance of God's name being avoided (due to

---

[36]   Kloppenborg ("Q 12:2-7," 85-86) finds 12:2 as early and "it might be regarded as a generalizing aphoristic conclusion generated from sayings and parables which can more securely be attributed to Jesus." Thus, it appears that he sees 12:2 as related to authentic stuff but only derivately authentic itself. On the other hand, Q 12:3 coheres with Jesus to the degree that Jesus sent out disciples on a mission (p. 88). If, however, we argue that the original context was one of warning about hypocrisy his argument falls apart; but, to muddy the water, I could use the same logic: to the degree that Jesus warned about hypocrisy the logion is authentic! See also Laufen, *Die Doppelüberlieferungen*, 158.

[37]   Borg, *Continuing Voice*, 217.

[38]   An original statement to this effect was that of J. Jeremias, *New Testament Theology: The Proclamation of Jesus* (New York: Scribner's, 1971) 9-14; but see now the fundamental challenge of Reiser, *Jesus and Judgment*, 266-73. Because I think Reiser has overstated his challenge, I continue to use the grammatical category though, I trust, in a more chastened sense.

Jewish piety) but implied; each is also an instance of the final judgment.[39] That is, God's name is avoided but more importantly the indeterminacy of the final judgment of God is the issue at hand: that a final judgment will take place shapes the call for this passive voice. Second, it is this theme of eschatological judgment that also frames the logion as historically reasonable: if Jesus was anything he was a Jewish prophet who called Israel to its knees and to its covenant senses in light of the coming judgment of God on the nation.[40] Jesus' baptism at the hands of John and the latter's thunderous message of a coming judgment confirms the point (cf. Q: Matt 3:7-10 par): the prospect of a final judgment dominated Jesus' horizon. To threaten his followers (along with the Pharisees) with the final judgment as a day in which hypocrisy will be revealed for what it is coheres then substantively with the mission and message of Jesus.

Third, while it may be theologically fashionable to think of the final judgment in terms of some heavenly, ethereal coutroom, such was not the case for Jesus. Jesus envisioned a final judgment coming soon (within a generation) and that judgment was to be earthly, not ethereal. Thus, the logion is to be understood not as some hope for final vindication on the part of the disciples nor as a threat about what will happen in "heaven". Rather, Jesus' warning about the Pharisees (Luke 12:1) and to the disciples (12:2) is envisioned as something about to happen: if they want to enter the Kingdom they need to rid themselves of hypocrisy right now! The urgency of the logion then fits admirably into the *Sitz im Leben Jesu* .

Fourth, a warning about hypocrisy is not only characteristic of Jesus, but an exaggerated warning about final damnation for practicing it is also a feature of Jesus' themes and style of expression (Matt 7:5 = Luke 6:42; Mark 12:15 = Matt 22:18; Matt 23:1-31[41]).

---

[39]   Reiser sees the fundamental historical instance being an "eschatological passive" (*Jesus and Judgment*, 271-72), rather than "divine passive," God is not so much the concern as is the indeterminacy of the future.

[40]   See esp. McKnight, *A New Vision for Israel*; Wright, *Jesus and the Victory of God*; K. H. Tan, *The Zion Traditions and the Aims of Jesus* (SNTSMS 91; Cambridge: Cambridge University Press, 1997). This understanding derives from G. B. Caird; cf. L. D. Hurst, *New Testament Theology* (New York: Oxford, 1994).

[41]   Even though the vocative ὑποκριταί is distinctively Matthean redaction in chap. 23, the notions behind it (conscious pretence and abuse of didactic authority) are at the bedrock of the tradition and Jesus' polemic with Jerusalem leadership. Cf. also Matt 6:1-18 par.

The relationship of Jesus with Jewish leadership is complex and beyond the scope of this paper but we are confident that Jesus ran aground on the shores of Jewish-based Jerusalem leadership. This conflict, as so many controversy stories show (cf. e.g. Mark 2:1-3:6), frequently concerned a different interpretation of what constituted true Jewish piety and how the will of God for Israel was to be understood. An accusation of hypocrisy adequately fills the need for knowing what Jesus accused the leaders of.

Finally, several other minor arguments count in favor of the logion being authentic. For instance, the use of bipolar oppositions (e.g., hidden-revealed; secret-known; darkness-light; whispers-public announcements) characterize Jesus' speech.[42] There are Semitisms in the logion now found in Matt 10:26-27 par in addition to its general parallelistic symmetry.[43] In addition, the parallel of the logion with Mark 4:22 counts in its favor since the logion's substance is witnessed in more than one putative source of the synoptic tradition.

In conclusion: I would argue that the Q logion behind Matt 10:26-27 = Luke 12:2-3 is substantially reliable and can be reasonably authenticated by historical method. However, in order best to put a logion into its fullest context we need also to ask how it was that Matthew came to the interpretation he used when he recorded the logion. As stated above, Matthew converted a logion concerning a warning about the final judgment into a logion about public declaration of the secrets of the Kingdom divulged by Jesus to the disciples.

THE GENESIS OF MATTHEW'S REINTERPRETATION

We ask, "How did Matthew get from the Q logion to his formation of the logion?" I want to suggest the following: that Matthew inherited the Q logion in virtually the same form as is now found in Luke (or as reconstructed above) but that he re-read the logion in light of Mark 4:22 so that a hybrid text, composed completely of the

---

42   See the alteration of E. Käsemann's viewpoint. In "The Problem of the Historical Jesus," in Käsemann, *Essays on New Testament Themes* (SBT 41; London: SCM Press, 1964) 41, Käsemann sees the contrasted pair as characteristic of Jesus; but later in his "The Beginnings of Christian Theology," in Käsemann, *New Testament Questions of Today* (Philadelphia: Fortress, 1969) 99, he attributes the logion to early Christian prophets. See also Boring, *Continuing Voice*, 217. Boring believes the logion may well be authentic.

43   Davies and Allison, *Matthew*, 2. 203-205.

words of Jesus, results.[44] Thus, our sketch of the history of this
logion is diagrammed as follows:

Stage I (Jesus)	Stage II (Q)	Stage III (Gospels)	Stage IV
Mark 4:22	Mk + Q =		GThom 5-6, 33
and	Matt 10:26-27		POxy 1, 654
Luke 12:2-3	Luke 12:2-3 + 12:4-9	Q + Luke 12:1	

Mark 4 contains the justly famous story of the Parable of the
Sower/Soils (Mark 4:13-20), attached to which are comments about
Jesus conveying the importance of comprehending what he is saying
(4:21-25). The logia found in 4:21-25 may well be another instance
of logia having nowhere else to lay down; if so, the logia could be
simply free-floating traditions that are used here and there by early
Christians in ways that are suitable.[45] However, the Sower is for the
Christian community a parable exhorting the followers of Jesus to
spread the word, to preach the gospel, and to annouce the Kingdom
of God publicly. Mark 4:21 exhorts the community to let one's lamp
be visible to others and so fulfill its purpose of exposing and
revealing. Mark 4:22 reads: οὐ γάρ ἐστιν κρυπτὸν ἐὰν μὴ ἵνα
φανερωθῇ, οὐδὲ ἐγένετο ἀπόκρυφον ἀλλ᾽ ἵνα ἔλθῃ εἰς φανερόν.
What has been hidden,[46] namely the presence of the mystery of the
Kingdom, will become public, though it is not clear in Mark just
when this publicity is to take place.[47] What is clear, however, is that
Matthew sees the publicity of the Kingdom to be an activity for his
community in the present.

The following observations are pertinent to our study: (1) the
same bipolar oppositions that are found in the Q logion (Matt 10:26-
27 par Luke 12:2-3) emerge in this logion; (2) the context of
spreading the Word suggests that what is "hidden" and "buried" is
the secrets of the Kingdom of God; and (3) what the disciples are

---

[44]   See Schulz, Q, 157-58, 463; H. Conzelmann, "Σκότος, κτλ," TWNT
7.442 (n. 157). I am unconvinced that we can know to any reasonable degree of
probability that some generic logion, of secular origin, formed the foundation of
this logion. See Schulz, Q, 463-64; this line of thinking probably derives from
Bultmann, History, 83-84, 97. For such an argument to be convincing more
concrete evidence of a secular logion needs to be provided.

[45]   See Laufen, Die Doppelüberlieferungen, 165-66.

[46]   Mark's use of this logion clearly states a present "hiddenness" of the
(mystery of the) Kingdom. Its publicity is still future to Mark's rendering of the
logion.

[47]   So Guelich, Mark, 232.

exhorted to do through this riddle is to make known the mysteries of the Kingdom. Now even if the logion here exhorts through the impersonal form ("except that it will be manifest," "except that it will come into the open"), the clear implication of the logion is that this sort of thing is supposed to happen as a divine necessity. That is, the logion here uses the language now found in the Q logion in an explicitly missionary sense.

This logion then provides for us a middle text for perceiving how it was that Matthew arrived at his interpretation of the Q logion. What concerned the publicity of final judgment in Q was interpreted, in the sense of *Vergegenwärtigung*, in light of another logion of Jesus on missionary work and the result was a third text, not stated by Jesus but filled with the words of Jesus, reexpressing the Q logion in missionary terms. I am suggesting then that Matthew derived his interpretation, not by fanciful midrashic redaction of a Q tradition that would not dance to his music, but rather by permitting the Q logion's terms to convey the meaning of the Markan tradition. Thus, κρυπτόν in Luke 12:2 no longer means for Matthew what it does in Q (actions done in secret) but what it does in the Markan tradition at 4:22 (secrets divulged by Jesus). The synonymous parallelism of both the Q logion and Mark 4:22 permits this kind of interpretation as does the negative form of the logion.

Perhaps it will be argued that it is unlikely that Matthew backed up in his copy of Mark to read the logion. I would not argue that Matthew stopped his writing to find the Markan parallel but rather that Matthew had become accustomed to the Markan rendering of this poetic form, the negation of the hidden and the affirmation of revelation in a missionary sense, and that he naturally read the Q logion in the same manner. I am not suggesting copying but rather oral or memory associations.

THE AUTHENTICITY OF THE COMMAND:
"LOVE YOUR ENEMIES"

William Klassen

The question of "authenticity" or genuineness is very much in the discussion these days and has lead to much controversy in the realm of art and even music. What is one to do, for example with a work of art, demonstrably not by the master but in no way inferior to that one's work? Or, in the case of a saying of Jesus from the cross, "Father forgive them for they know what they do," which rests on slim manuscript evidence (Luke 23:34)[1] but is in some ways the fullest expression of what Jesus did in his life and taught his disciples?

The efforts of the Jesus Seminar to try to establish a firm foundation for our understanding of Jesus through their "Search for the Authentic Deeds of Jesus" and for "the Authentic Words of Jesus" is symptomatic of this discussion and its relevance to the history of religion.[2] But especially in the field of New Testament studies, in the

---

[1]   So the commentaries hesitate: N. Geldenhuys, *Commentary on the Gospel of Luke* (NICNT; Grand Rapids: Eerdmans, 1951) 608: "in perfect agreement with Luke's predilection throughout his Gospel"; J. A. Fitzmyer, *The Gospel according to Luke X-XXIV* (AB 24A; Garden City: Doubleday, 1985) 1503: "the question is raised whether they really formed part of the original text of Luke"; "The suffering upright one obtains [sic!] forgiveness from his Father for those who make him suffer both physically and mentally" (p. 1504). I. H. Marshall (*The Gospel of Luke* [NIGTC; Grand Rapids: Eerdmans, 1978] 868) after extensive discussion concludes, "the balance of evidence . . . favours acceptance of the saying as Lucan." A. Schlatter (*Das Evangelium des Lukas* [Stuttgart: Calwer, 1960] 446) suggests the immediate context and the woe of Jerusalem's fate made it awkward to leave the intercession here and thus he votes for authenticity.

[2]   R. W. Funk and R. W. Hoover (eds.), *The Five Gospels: The Search for the Authentic Words of Jesus* (Sonoma: Polebridge Press; New York: Macmillan, 1993); and R. W. Funk (ed.), *The Acts of Jesus: What Did Jesus Really Do? The Search for the Authentic Deeds of Jesus* (San Francisco: HarperCollins, 1998), have that subtitle. In connection with our saying Funk writes, "The Fellows of the Jesus Seminar, along with countless other scholars, have ranked the admonition to love enemies very close to the heart of the teaching of Jesus" (*Honest to Jesus: Jesus for*

study of the historical Jesus, it has become a dominant obsession.[3] With almost messianic passion we are told about how the gospel has disappointed people but how they were liberated once they left the "faith" and encountered Jesus in a new and living way. What in effect they have done is mainly to tailor Jesus to their own likes and then they find him more palatable.[4]

My bias is solidly in favor of the quest for the historical Jesus. My faith in the Christ is strengthened by the conviction that everything he is reported to have said and everything he is reported to have done invites us to a historical quest of the highest order. I find it perplexing that he once apparently cursed a fig tree (Matt 21:18-19; Mark 11:12-14) because it bore no fruit during a time of the year when fig trees normally did not (Mark 11:13c); I find it unhelpful that he was reported to have walked on water (Matt 14:22-33; Mark 6:45-52; John 6:16-21), for it makes it more difficult to focus discussion on the true miracle of the God of love conquering over hate through the life of Jesus.

On the sayings of Jesus I ask: Could it be that he said that unless a person "hates father, mother, wife, husband and child, yes, even one's own life" one cannot be a disciple (Luke 14:26-27)? I believe it

---

a New Millennium [San Francisco: HarperCollins, 1996] 200). For him it is an "oxymoron of the first order" and "loved enemies a contradiction in terms" (ibid.).

3   The bibliography is endless and need not be repeated here except for some seminal essays which also provide the bibliographies: N. J. McEleney, "Authenticating Criteria and Mk 7:1-23," *CBQ* 34 (1972) 431-60. Noteworthy also are the articles by B. F. Meyer on Jesus Christ, especially the sections on "Indices to Historicity and Nonhistoricity" (*ABD* 3.776-777), and by J. K. Riches on "The Actual Words of Jesus" (*ABD* 3.802-804). R. H. Stein, "The 'Criteria' for Authenticity," in R. T. France and D. Wenham (eds.), *Studies of History and Tradition in the Four Gospels* (Gospel Perspectives 1; Sheffield: JSOT Press, 1980) 225-63.

4   E.g. Funk, *Honest to Jesus*. He "weeps that he spent thirty-five years in the classroom . . . to have had so little lasting impact on students . . . and the American mind" (p. 5). He "agonizes over the slavery in contrast to my freedom" so many followers of modern evangelists have (p. 18). The longing for intellectual freedom drove him out of the Seminary to the secular university (p. 5). While Funk acknowledges the significance of treating Jesus as a Jew, he cannot stand (nor understand) apocalypticism and therefore calls for a Christianity without it (p. 314). It would thus appear that "the aim of the quest for the historical Jesus is [not only] to set Jesus free, to liberate him from prevailing captivities" (p. 21) but also to free him from some shackles of Jewish apocalypticism!

quite possible and for me it becomes more likely when I recall that this invitation to "hate" one's nearest and dearest appears in ancient Greek (e.g. Tyrtaeus) invitations to war,[5] was a standard part of Cynic-Stoic invitations to follow their path to wisdom and goodness,[6] and is cited by Philo as part of the call to become a Levite.[7] If Jesus knew of even one of these, as he likely did, he was saying that his call to join the Kingdom is at least as demanding as the call to war, the call to the good life of the Hellenistic philosophers and religious vocation in Judaism. When Matthew tampers with or takes Luke's version of this saying in a different direction and substitutes, "loves more than" (compare Luke 14:26 with Matt 10:37-38) then the quest for the authentic word of Jesus becomes even more interesting. The startling statements, often an intensification of the Torah, seem to bear the stamp of Jesus' arresting style. It certainly is not difficult to imagine that a Jesus who said what Luke attributes to him about severing family relationships, who proclaimed that a person's life does not consist of possessions—a commonplace recognized by all, except by those who live for money—could also have said on several occasions: Love your enemies (Matt 5:44; Luke 6:27, 35).

Moreover, an ethical bombshell "which sets Jesus' ethic of love apart from other 'love ethics' of antiquity and best shows what kind of love is commanded by him"[8] also needs some illustration, some clarification. I fail to see why these had to be invented by the gospel writers, just as I fail to see why Jesus could not have used allegory as a teaching device on occasion if he so chose.

For our purposes we shall assume that the command of Jesus to "love your enemies" which in turn has also generated a great deal of discussion is genuine, historical and authentic. That is, Jesus spoke those words in either Greek or Aramaic and he urged his disciples to follow this command.[9] Since the command appears verbatim in Luke

---

5   J. Denney, "The word 'hate' in Luke 14:26," *ExpTim* 21 (1910) 41-44.

6   Epictetus, *Discourses* 3.3.5; cf. also 2.22.

7   Cited by B. F. Westcott, *The Epistle to the Hebrews: The Greek Text with Notes and Essays* (2nd ed., London: Macmillan, 1892; repr. Grand Rapids: Eerdmans, 1973) 173, but possibly from an inauthentic Philonic source.

8   V. P. Furnish, *The Love Command in the New Testament* (Nashville: Abingdon, 1972) 66-67.

9   W. Swartley (ed.), *The Love of Enemy and Nonretaliation in the New Testament* (Louisville: Westminster, 1992). This book contains thirteen essays on the application of this teaching. Not one of them seems to be interested in the

and Matthew in identical form but these two gospels differ somewhat in the illustrations they present from Jesus on "how" one loves one's enemies, I believe with greater certainty that the command comes from Jesus than I do that the illustrations do. In any case the illustrations appear first in Paul's letter to the Romans (12:14-21) and have an abundant attestation before the time of Jesus.[10]

Contrary to the argument of Bultmann who thought the command to love your enemies to be genuine because it was novel and deviated from Judaism, we will argue that precisely because it is Jewish and Jesus was a Jew it has the ring of authenticity about it. We accept the general consensus that the ethical ideal of benevolence towards one's enemies flourished in Diaspora Judaism or Hellenistic Judaism but suggest that Jesus was not immune to influences of popular Hellenistic moralists in Galilee and could therefore have derived the idea from either Jewish wisdom literature, the Hellenistic moralists or indeed from the Qumran group.[11] We do not need to specify where the idea originated in order to establish its authenticity.

Many scholars who have stressed the Jewishness of Jesus have tended to accept many of the New Testament sayings of Jesus as genuine. Symptomatic is David Flusser who asserts that "the early

---

question of authenticity and simply assumes that it is genuine. In my essay on the current status of research I argue that it is time to reopen the question (ibid., 8). The bibliography provided by Swartley cannot be improved upon.

10   In the book *Love of Enemy* this point was demonstrated and the suggestion made that we use the commandments Paul gives in Romans 12 as the framework for "loving the enemies" where the dominical command is understood to be well-known and therefore did not need to be spelled out.

11   Thus D. Flusser (*Jesus* [rev. ed., Jerusalem: Magnes Press, 1997] 88) argues that Jesus "broke the last fetters still restricting the ancient Jewish command-ment to love one's neighbor." He attributes influence from "semi-Essene circles" who had reached similar conclusions from different presuppositions. But, of course influences do not explain everything. He sees Jesus as leading the way further to unconditional love even of one's enemies and of sinners (p. 92). But he could not, or at least did not without the matrix of Judaism which bore him and nurtured him. There is clearly a "non-resistance" at Qumran inspired not by hope for future vengeance but by the imitation of God's love. I consider it highly doubtful that one can conclude that it is "only outwardly like that advocated in Matthew. It is over-shadowed and robbed of its moral grandeur by an eschatology of vengeance which Jesus, if not the primitive church, seems to have rejected" (W. D. Davies, *The Setting of the Sermon on the Mount* [Cambridge: Cambridge University Press, 1964] 248).

Christian accounts about Jesus are not as untrustworthy as people today often think."[12] He does not hesitate to attribute "creative inventions" to Mark, such as the quote from Ps 22:2 in Mark 15:34, but the tradition that Jesus' family considered him daft and sought to take him away for his own good (Mark 3:21) he designates an "unreliable report,"[13] while at the same time he gives credence to the tensions that existed between Jesus and his family, indeed considers that it was that "psychological fact" which was a determining factor powerfully contributing to his decision to depart from Nazareth.[14]

On the other extreme we have John Gager. Most likely mainly his own graduate students will follow Gager's radical skepticism which appears to begin with the assumption that a saying is not genuine, or rather a creation of the church, unless there are overriding arguments to the contrary.[15] Those who argue thus must have had experience with creative communities which have passed me by. It has been my experience that individuals create, communities restrain, modify, and inhibit.

The purpose of this paper is to address primarily the question: Did Jesus command his disciples to love their enemies? The question of authenticating the words of Jesus is, of course, complicated and we will need to come to terms with the many criteria, much discussed and commonly accepted by colleagues.[16] The saying, "love your enemies," brief as it is, has particular importance in the discussion of

---

12   Flusser, *Jesus*, 20. He concludes, moreover, that "The Jesus portrayed in the Synoptic Gospels is, therefore, the historical Jesus, not the 'kerygmatic Christ'" (ibid.). "When studied in the light of their Jewish background, the Synoptic Gospels do preserve a picture of Jesus which is more reliable than is generally acknowledged" (p. 21) "Luke and Matthew together provide the most authentic portrayal of Jesus' life and teaching" (p. 22).

13   Flusser, *Jesus*, 34.

14   Flusser, *Jesus*, 35. On the point, see the masterful discussion by J. W. Miller, *Jesus at Thirty* (Minneapolis: Fortress, 1997).

15   J. Gager, "The Gospels and Jesus: Some Doubts about Method," *JR* 54 (1954) 244-72.

16   Among others see Stein, "The 'Criteria' for Authenticity," 225-63, who lists eleven criteria. In addition, J. Breech (*The Silence of Jesus: The Authentic Voice of the Historical Man* [Philadelphia: Fortress, 1983]) lists the criterion of embarrassment. For a recent critical review of the criteria, see J. P. Meier, *A Marginal Jew: Rethinking the Historical Jesus*. Volume One: *The Roots of the Problem and the Person* (ABRL 3; New York: Doubleday, 1991) 167-95 (see Appendix A).

the historical Jesus.[17] Once we have dealt with the question of
authenticity, we may go on to ask the question: What are the.
implications of this teaching today?

Throughout the history of humankind various approaches to the
question of dealing with one's enemies have been proposed. In
biblical literature this is a recurrent theme and biblical scholars have
searched for a correct understanding of it with as much energy as
they have any other. Moreover, we may speak with a certain
confidence about the contribution of this idea of loving enemies to
this critical aspect of human relations. One can draw up an
impressive list of personal triumphs of love over hate, by now even
international triumphs where doing good to an enemy has resolved
conflicts of many years standing. I would certainly reject the notion
that it is through political alliances that peace is made *and not*
through the church![18]

It is apparent, moreover, that biblical specialists have spoken on
the issue with special urgency, even though with perhaps less
objectivity. Such discussion has not been limited to obscure scholars.
In New Testament studies the question of the authenticity of Jesus'

---

[17]   The background of the excellent article by D. Lührmann on this topic was
the Historical Jesus Seminar in the SNTS; see Lührmann, "Liebet Eure Feinde"
ZTK 69 (1972) 412.

[18]   So M. Honecker, "Themen und Tendenzen der Ethik," *TRu* 63 (1998) 119-
21 (*Friedensethik*). He refers to his previous essay, "Die Diskussion um den
Frieden," *TRu* 49 (1984) 372-411, and in regard to a book he is reviewing by
Führer says: "Nicht durch die Kirche, sondern durch politische Vereinbarung wird
der Friede gestiftet" (p. 318), adding: "F. hat recht" (p. 120). What does he make
of the miracles which truth, reconciliation, and forgiveness based in faithfulness in
following Jesus have wrought in South Africa? He could profit from D. Johnston
and C. Sampson (eds.), *Religion: The Missing Dimension of Statecraft* (Oxford:
Oxford University Press, 1994). In the Foreword President Carter comments on
the fact that both Begin and Sadat were deeply religious men. To have overlooked
that would have been a failure that "could have had a pervasive and incalculable
impact" (p. vii). There is a persistent temptation to change Jesus from the renewal
prophet he was, and thus an instructor of popular ethics and morality, to a lofty
philosopher. We are on the one hand urged to accept Jesus' teaching in this realm
as "something like [Luther's] two kingdom teaching," although not as systematic,
and on the other hand to reject the notion that Jesus provided a formula for "the
management of conflict" (so N. Walter, "'Nicht Frieden, sondern das Schwert?'" a
lecture first given in 1982 and published in W. Kraus and F. Wilk, [eds.],
Praeparatio Evangelica [WUNT 98; Tübingen: Mohr (Siebeck), 1997] 172, 175).

saying on loving enemies has been accepted ever since Bultmann, because it is believed that no Jew could have said that. "If anywhere we can find what is characteristic of the preaching of Jesus" it is in this saying, he declared.[19] If we accept that we cut Jesus off drastically from his roots and demand a fantastic level of "originality" from him.[20] We also denigrate Judaism and close our eyes to the evidence which exists in Judaism prior to and contemporary with him.

Thus Dieter Lührmann describes as "foolish" any one who denies the authenticity of this saying and most scholars would agree.[21] At the same time it has forced us to come to terms with the Judaism of the time of Jesus. It is impossible to accept the conclusions of John Piper that "Jesus' command to love the enemy as well as the friend contained the seed for the dissolution of the Jewish distinctive."[22]

In the field of Old Testament studies, to cite only one illustration, Hermann Gunkel used Old Testament literature to demonstrate that the Israelites had no place for a teaching of enemy love. They had war heroes and a definite war piety which had specific relevance for Germany during the first World War. There is no difference between religious and national heroes in Israel, he maintained, and Israel fought both aggressive and defensive wars. The history of Israel is seen by Gunkel as a result of her heroic ability to fight bloody battles. Her wars were more bloody, more wild, and filled with more hatred than those of the present. Without the heroes of

---

[19]   R. Bultmann, *The History of the Synoptic Tradition* (Oxford: Blackwell, 1972) 105. W. Bauer and H. Braun also declare it as genuine, and D. Lührmann ("Liebet Eure Feinde," 414) concludes: "It can be affirmed with the greatest certainty available to exegesis that these words belong to Jesus himself." For fuller documentation see W. Klassen, *Love of Enemies: The Way to Peace* (Philadelphia: Fortress, 1984) 102 n. 2.

[20]   W. Klassen, "The Novel Element in the Love Commandment of Jesus," in W. Klassen (ed.), *The New Way of Jesus* (Newton: Faith and Life Press, 1980) 100-114.

[21]   Lührmann, "Liebet Eure Feinde," 414: "Hier überhaupt zu fragen, ob dieser Satz auf den historischen Jesus zurück geht, scheint töricht."

[22]   J. Piper, *"Love Your Enemies." Jesus' Love Command in the Synoptic Gospels and the Early Christian Paraenesis: A History of the Tradition and Interpretation of its Uses* (SNTSMS 38; Cambridge: Cambridge University Press, 1979) 91-92; cf. 204, n. 83. Because of this widespread misinterpretation I devoted over half of my book, *Love of Enemies*, 27-73, to Jewish sources. For my response to Piper and Nissen, see *Love of Enemies*, 43, 66-67.

Phinehas and the Maccabees the religion of Israel could not have endured.

What then are we to make of Jesus, a Jew? He explains the attitude of Jesus by the loss of the strength of the Jewish religion in which one cultural layer, a more pacifist one took the upper hand. "To us, for whom war has become the solution for the problems of today, this book (the Old Testament) can become a source of strength. Our people also will remain invincible if we know both: the heroism of the sword and the heroism of faith."[23]

The reason the New Testament does not follow this line, says Gunkel, is that the Jews had become exhausted through defeat. He asserts that the New Testament was born among oppressed provincials, people who neither could nor would fight. Because of this preachers must during war years refrain from using New Testament texts and rather turn to the Old Testament. For on almost every page the war cry resounds in the Old Testament and there we find an intimate union between religion and war. The reader is urged to extract from the Old Testament not those elements that speak of meekness but rather those that have eternal validity. Israel was warlike until she was knocked down brutally by stronger nations. The book of Judges clearly teaches that a nation which is at peace will follow after Baal, and this should be a warning to us. "What war can do to the religious piety of a nation," says Gunkel confidently, "has been experienced in World War I."[24]

American and British scholars[25] likewise have felt that the Bible speaks to human conflict. There should be no doubt that in spite of

---

[23] H. Gunkel, *Israelitisches Heldentum und Kriegsfrömmigkeit im alten Testament* (Göttingen: Vandenhoeck & Ruprecht, 1916) 2-3.

[24] Gunkel, *Israelitisches Heldentum*, 23, 25.

[25] C. H. Dodd, not only in his courageous lecture on "The Theology of Christian Pacifism" delivered in 1937 and published in 1938 but in his commentary on Romans (*The Epistle of Paul to the Romans* (The Moffat New Testament Commentary; 2nd ed., London: Hodder & Stoughton, 1947] 201) refers to Paul's teaching on love of enemies as an "admirable summary of the teaching of the Sermon on the Mount about what is called 'non-resistance,' and it expresses the most creative element in Christian ethics." At another place he notes that the love commandment and "the imitatio Christi had more to say in the selection of incidents from the life of Jesus for record in the Gospels" than is generally noted; cf. C. H. Dodd, *The Johannine Epistles* (The Moffat New Testament Commentary; London: Hodder & Stoughton, 1946) 85.

the fact that these studies strongly reflect the nationalism of the scholars we can only commend them for their desire to allow the Scriptures to speak to the specific situation in which the Church found itself.

With this in mind it is the purpose of this essay to look anew at the question: Did Jesus teach his disciples how to deal with enemies? Who, indeed, are these enemies? What aspects of this approach does Christianity share with contemporary Judaism or with Greek thinkers prior to and contemporary with the emergence of the Church? The detailed application of this question to the modern scene must be left to others. But before looking at the precise saying it may be useful to rehearse the most recent history of research.[26]

In the literature surveyed there exists something of a consensus in asserting that the concept of "the enemy" cannot be narrowed down; but that it includes personal, national and religious enemies.[27] Love for the neighbor definitely includes the enemy if indeed in Christ's teaching it does not yield to love for the enemy (parable of the Good Samaritan). Is it not on the Cross that we see most clearly that enemies cannot be changed by hatred but only by nonviolent action driven by love, and that the demonic circle of vengeance and hatred cannot be broken by anything but loving sacrifice? Thus we may never be content with "knowing the enemy." We are invited to allow ourselves to be instruments of God's love toward the enemy.

The command to love enemies is found only three times in the Gospels and not at all in the epistles. Indeed it is not found at all in

---

[26]   This attempts to carry forward the history of the research presented in my essays, "'Love Your Enemy': A Study of NT Teaching on Coping with an Enemy," in P. Peachey (ed.), *Biblical Realism Confronts the Nation* (Nyack: Fellowship, 1963) 153-83; "'Love Your Enemies': Some Reflections on the Current Status of Research," in Swartley (ed.), *Love of Enemy and Nonretaliation*, 1-31; and *Love of Enemies*.

[27]   H.-W. Kuhn ("Das Liebesgebot Jesu als Torah und also Evangelium: Zur Feindesliebe und zur christlichen und jüdischen Auslegung der Bergpredigt," in H. Frankemölle and K. Kertelge (eds.), *Vom Urchristentum zu Jesus: Für Joachim Gnilka* (Freiburg and Basel: Herder, 1989) 194-230, here 229) states: "Die Weisung ist grenzenlos. Der religiöse, der politische und der persönliche Feind sind gemeint (The directive is without boundaries. The religious, the political, and the personal enemy are all meant)." K. L. Yinger ("Romans 12:14-21 and Nonretalia-tion in Second Temple Judaism: Addressing Persecution within the Community," *CBQ* 60 [1998] 74-96) seeks to overthrow the consensus arguing that Paul addresses the issue of "persecutors" as within the community.

any other source prior to the Gospels. The relevant texts are as follows:

Matt 5:44   ἐγὼ δὲ λέγω ὑμῖν, ἀγαπᾶτε τοὺς ἐχθροὺς ὑμῶν καὶ προσεύχεσθε ὑπὲρ
τῶν διωκόντων ὑμᾶς,

Luke 6:27   Ἀλλὰ ὑμῖν λέγω τοῖς ἀκούουσιν, ἀγαπᾶτε τοὺς ἐχθροὺς ὑμῶν, καλῶς
ποιεῖτε τοῖς μισοῦσιν ὑμᾶς,

Luke 6:33   καὶ [γὰρ] ἐὰν ἀγαθοποιῆτε τοὺς ἀγαθοποιοῦντας ὑμᾶς, ποία ὑμῖν
χάρις ἐστίν; καὶ οἱ ἁμαρτωλοὶ τὸ αὐτὸ ποιοῦσιν.

Luke 6:35   πλὴν ἀγαπᾶτε τοὺς ἐχθροὺς ὑμῶν καὶ ἀγαθοποιεῖτε καὶ δανίζετε
μηδὲν ἀπελπίζοντες· καὶ ἔσται ὁ μισθὸς ὑμῶν πολύς, καὶ ἔσεσθε υἱοὶ
ὑψίστου, ὅτι αὐτὸς χρηστός ἐστιν ἐπὶ τοὺς ἀχαρίστους καὶ
πονηρούς.

Only seldom has its authenticity been questioned. Furthermore it is recognized that the idea is found in the epistles without the precise commandment. It was the most frequently cited saying of Jesus in the second century[28] especially by the Apologists as evidence that the early Christians were not haters of humankind.[29] As early as the second century however, to modern times the idea has been either relegated to the personal realm or more frequently confined to a select group of Christians in religious communities, either in monastic orders or, since the Reformation, to people generally dismissed as "enthusiasts."

This century has however experienced a wave of interest in the teaching. Through the work of Hans Haas[30] and Michael Waldmann[31] it was demonstrated to be far from unique in Jesus and what had begun in this century as an attempt to show that enemy love was even found in the natural realm[32] soon became a deadly earnest pursuit during the first world war when scholars began seriously to study the idea of enemy love within Judaism and its uniquely Christian aspect was explored.[33] Moreover, the history of the idea and the

---

28   H. Koester, *Synoptische Überlieferung bei den apostolischen Vätern* (TU 65; Berlin: Akademie, 1957) 44, 76.

29   E. Osborn, "The Love Command in Second Century Christian Writings," *SecCent* 1 (1981) 223-43.

30   In 1927, see my "'Love Your Enemy'."

31   M. Waldmann, *Die Feindesliebe* (Wien: Mayer, 1902).

32   S. Randlinger, *Die Feindesliebe* (Paderborn: F. Schöningh, 1906; E. Bach, *Die Feindesliebe* (Kempten: J. Köselschen, 1914).

33   Compare, F. Kattenbusch, "Über die Feindesliebe im Sinne des Christen-

extent to which it was practiced by the early martyrs was analyzed.[34]

It was not, however, until the coming of the second world war and the threat which international enmity now posed to human civilization that scholars were drawn more deeply into the discussion and devoted much research to the theme. Nevertheless the subject has so far brought forth only two book-length English contributions dealing with the Biblical texts by Biblical scholars. One proposes that the ultimate source of the idea, although not in commandment form, can be traced to ancient Greek wisdom but above all to Judaism from whence Jesus derived it and that it has fundamental relevance for guidance on how to live today; thus he sees it fundamentally as Torah.[35]

The other, John Piper derives the idea directly from Jesus and sees it as a radical departure from Judaism.[36] Like Nissen,[37] his understanding of Judaism makes it impossible to see enemy love as mandatory within that religious framework. He is, however, able to follow his teacher, Leonhard Goppelt, and find in the text support for resisting wrong for the sake of his neighbor. As long as this is done without hatred, from which faith will free, this will accord with the Sermon on the Mount. How this is derived from the text itself is not clear; but the shades of Luther's two-kingdom view, now largely discredited, are obvious.

The argument for its genuineness, based by Bultmann and others on its discontinuity with Judaism, must now be rejected. Indeed it has

---

tums," *TSK* 89 (1916) 1-70; and P. Fiebig, "Jesu Worte über die Feindesliebe im Zusammenhang mit den wichtigsten rabbinischen Parallelen erläutert," *TSK* 91 (1918) 30-64.

[34]   W. Bauer, "Das Gebot der Feindesliebe und die alten Christen," *ZTK* 27 (1917) 37-54.

[35]   Klassen, *Love of Enemies*. With respect to the origin of the saying, J. Sauer ("Traditionsgeschichtliche Erwägungen zu den synoptischen und paulinischen Aussagen über Feindesliebe und Wiedervergeltungsverzicht," *ZNW* 76 [1985] 1-28) concludes essentially the same thing but does not stress as much the creativity of Jesus and Paul.

[36]   Piper, *"Love Your Enemies."*

[37]   According to Nissen, *Gott und der Nächste*, 316: "A love for the enemy, even for the personal, not religious-moral enemy, consequently does not exist in Judaism; not only is it not present in our preserved sources but is ruled out from the outset and must be ruled out, if not beginning with the starting point the whole structure [*Gesamtgefüge*] of the Jewish ethos and consequently revelation itself be jeopardized [*ins Wanken geraten soll*]."

been challenged recently in a brilliant essay on this topic by Jürgen Sauer.[38] After a careful analysis of the Lukan and Matthean versions he arrives at a "Q" text[39] and compares it with the Pauline materials in detail. He concludes that the tradition on which the Pauline materials on enemy love are based antedates the materials in the Gospels.

Instead of attributing to Jesus the command to love enemies he dates it around the middle fifties but argues that Paul did not have access to it, otherwise he would have used it. It seems to make the most historical sense to give full credit to Jesus himself for having first formed the idea of enemy love into a bold command for his community. The early Christian communities developed their traditions in response to what they remembered Jesus as saying, but they also did a selective recall and no doubt added their own illustrations of what this meant in their context.

Luke and Matthew appear to be drawing from a common source which included at least the words: ἀγαπᾶτε τοὺς ἐχθροὺς ὑμῶν— "love your enemies." Luke repeats the command after giving some illustrations:

> do good to those who hate you
> bless those who curse you
> pray for those who treat you spitefully

These three further imperatives spell out what it means to love enemies but they also spell out more fully the category of an enemy:

Love	Enemy
do good	Those who hate you
bless	Those who curse you
pray for	Those who treat you spitefully

The first of these instructions is rooted in Greek thought and especially the maxim enunciated in many places that the goal of education to maturity (= *paideia*) is to learn to treat your friend right and to take revenge on those who do evil to you. That same idea appears in the Hebrew Bible when Joab is astonished that King David does not follow that pattern but instead: "You love those who hate you and hate those who love you" (2 Sam 19:6). It seems that the King has left behind the notion of vengeance and a society cannot

---

38   Sauer, "Traditionsgeschichtliche Erwägungen," 24.

39   See Appendix B.

survive without it.

The theme of vengeance has received considerable study of late, but there is little evidence that it has been correlated to the love your enemy teaching. Clearly already in Leviticus the love of the neighbor command was to curb vengeance. Likewise in Romans 12 Paul urges that loving deeds towards enemies consume the time between the wrong done to you and God acts to right all wrongs. At the worst, the Psalm writer expects the time to come when, "the righteous will rejoice when they see vengeance done; they will bathe their feet in the blood of the wicked. People will say, 'Surely there is a reward for the righteous'" (Ps 58:10-11). If the righteous will wash their feet in the blood of enemies—Jesus washes the feet of the man perceived by many to be his enemy, Judas.

In a major study on vengeance Laurens Peels seems to minimize the differences between the view of vengeance found in the Hebrew Bible and those in the New Testament and he sees the connection between the love commandment and rejection of vengeance as somewhat illogical; a prohibition of blood vengeance (Lev 19:18a) can hardly be adversely supplemented with a love command (v. 18b). The contrast would have to be: "not blood vengeance but banishment"; not in any event, "not blood vengeance but love." But why cannot vengeance be replaced by love?[40] Professor Vogels concludes that Peels's study is "the best existing study on the vengeance of God, an often shocking and disturbing biblical theme which perhaps for that reason has been avoided in the past or written off as primitive." At any rate it is clearly forbidden in the levitical code: "You shall not seek revenge, or cherish anger towards your kinsfolk; you shall love your neighbor as yourself" (Lev 19:18).

One of the urgent topics deserving research is the theme of vengeance in the Dead Sea Scrolls.[41] For the frequency of that idea

---

[40]   See review of H. G. L. Peels, *The Vengeance of God: The Meaning of the Root NQM and the Function of NQM-Texts in the Context of Divine Revelation in the Old Testament* (OTS 31; Leiden: Brill, 1994), by W. Vogels in *JBL* 115 (1996) 517-18. See also the important book by E. Zenger, *A God of Vengeance? Understanding the Psalms of Divine Wrath* (Louisville: Westminster John Knox, 1996), reviewed by W. Harrelson in *CBQ* 59 (1997) 366-67.

[41]   According to my preliminary survey it occurs in the following places: 1QS 1:10-11; 2:6-9; 5:12; 7:9; 8:7; 9:23; 10:17-21; CD 1:17; 7:9; 8:11; 9:2-5; 19:6-16, 24; 1QH 4:22, 26-27; 7:22-23; 9:8-9; 15:17; 1QM 3:6-7; 4:12; 7:5; 11:13-14; 12:10-15; 14:12; 18:14; 1QpHab 5:3-6; 9:2, 10-13; 12:2-10; 4 QpPs37 1 ii 3-4. See

in the Scrolls may eventually resolve a dilemma about whether the
command to love one's enemies could have been present among
them. There is a fascinating description of the Essenes in Hippolytus
which says that they swore never to take vengeance on anyone and
never to hate their enemies but to pray on their behalf. This conflicts
somewhat with Josephus (*J.W.* 2.8.7 §139). Appendix C shows how
they compare:[42]

The command to love enemies is here used not to curse but to
bring good things and with this statement Jesus declared decisively
that the curse no longer has a place. The Kingdom in which God
rules has no room for curses.

Luke then offers four concrete examples of what the disciple is to
do:

if hit on the cheek	→ offer the other one also
if your coat is taken	→ offer the shirt as well
to everyone who asks	→ give
from one robbing you	→ do not demand it back

In sharp disjunction to this, Luke then introduces the so-called
golden rule which is based on reciprocity. "Treating others as you
would like them to treat you" is, however, to be understood here as
putting yourself in the place of the other.[43] This idea emerges first in
Greek literature in Isocrates but most likely originated in the Greek

---

J. Maier, *Die Texte vom Toten Meer* (2 vols., Munich and Basel: E. Reinhardt,
1960) 2.30, who also argues that "atonement [*Sühneschaffen*] does not take place
through eschatological vengeance but through the uniting or union, *yahad*." He
cites Ps 41:11: "But you O God be gracious to me and lift me up that I may repay
them!" Revenge is mentioned here; H.-J Kraus (*Psalmen* [2 vols., BKAT 15.1-2;
Freiburg: Herder, 1978] 1.314) comments: "Certainly retribution is not to be taken
literally" (cf. Ps 54:7) That the unjust persecutors will be exposed and helped by the
intervention of God, cf. Prov 21:18: "The wicked serves as a ransom for the
righteous, so does a traitor for the upright."

[42]   M. Black, "The Essenes in Hippolytus and Josephus," in W. D. Davies and
D. Daube (eds.), *The Background of the New Testament and its Eschatology:
Studies in Honour of C. H. Dodd* (Cambridge: Cambridge University Press, 1965)
172-75; M. Smith, "The description of the Essenes in Josephus and the Philoso-
phumena," *HUCA* 29 (1958) 273-313. The issue is judiciously assessed by G. M.
Zerbe, *Non-Retaliation in Early Jewish and New Testament Texts: Ethical Themes
in Social Contexts* (JSPSup 13; Sheffield: JSOT Press, 1993) 126-35.

[43]   See W. C. van Unnik, "Die Motivierung der Feindesliebe in Lukas vi 32-
35," *NovT* 8 (1966) 284-300.

theater.[44] It is found in Jewish literature also and both invite the actor to consider the impact of the action if roles are reversed between giver and receiver. It is one of the wisest and most useful rules for human relations, even though it appears to contradict the non-reciprocal teaching on loving the enemy.[45]

Luke follows the example with three queries, each one ending with the same question: "What credit is that to you? If you love only those who love you, do good only to those who do good to you, lend only if you are fully repaid?" What in Matthew becomes the intensified righteousness is here the ποία ὑμῖν χάρις? And the adversative πλήν in v. 35 introduces the standard to which Jesus invites:

> But you must love your enemies and do good and lend without expecting any return. Then you will have a rich reward: you will be children of the Most High, because that one is kind to the ungrateful and wicked. Be compassionate as your Father is compassionate.

What is most important is that for Luke the disciple can become a child of God. The attribute of God which is most important is compassion towards the ungrateful and the wicked. Lacking is any utilitarian motive. This ethical guidance is fully and exclusively rooted in the nature and behavior of God. The only reward which is in sight is a relationship to God.

Can the enemy mentioned here be more closely defined? Some have argued that the illustrations point to personal life and therefore one should not think of international or civic enemies. According to one Jewish source, much newer in written form than the New Testament, an enemy (אויב) is one who has not spoken to the neighbour for three days (cf. *m. Sanh.* 3:5).[46] Horsley has recently concluded that it refers to "village squabbles"; rejecting "foreign enemies" or even outsiders, he sees here a call to "take economic responsibility for one another."[47] Others are persuaded that the term

---

[44]   Klassen, *Love of Enemies*, 14.

[45]   See van Unnik, "Die Motivierung der Feindesliebe"; A. Dihle, *Die goldene Regel: Eine Einführung in die Geschichte der antiken und frühchristlichen Vulgärethik* (Studienhefte zur Altertumswissenschaft 7; Göttingen: Vandenhoeck & Ruprecht, 1962).

[46]   See M. Jastrow, *A Dictionary of the Targumim, the Talmud Babli and Yerushalmi, and the Midrashic Literature* (2 vols., New York: Pardes, 1950) 1.44.

[47]   R. A. Horsley, "Ethics and Exegesis: 'Love Your Enemies' and the Doctrine of Non-Violence," *JAAR* 54 (1989) 3-31, esp. 23. See also idem, *Jesus and the*

ἐχθρός is the standard New Testament term for enemy in its broadest sense and that the occurrence of the plural may indeed stress an inclusive usage.[48] Of course between the time Jesus spoke those words, and the Gospel editors transmitted them the definition of enemy changed; few definitions change as quickly. Nevertheless an increasing number of scholars take this in its broadest sense even as they seek to find the sociological background of the original "Q" source as well as the Matthean and Lukan sources. Out of this broader meaning has come a very intense search on the way in which this commandment can be applied in international and national politics.[49]

For Matthew the "love your enemies" teaching has a bit of an edge against the Jewish tradition, for it is found in the series of antitheses he presents in chap. 5. The first problem which presents itself here is the introduction: "You have heard . . . Love your neighbor, hate your enemy" (5:43). Much time has been spent trying to understand why Matthew added "and hate your enemy." The answer seems to be quite simple. The formula, "be good to (or love) your friends and hate your enemies," was very widespread in the ancient world and occurs in many layers of documentation. Rather than look in vain throughout Jewish sources, including Qumran,[50] for these exact

---

Spiral of Violence (San Francisco: Harper & Row, 1987) 272-73. I have no quarrel with Horsley's attempt to find the social context of this saying. I simply see no reason to restrict it to the immediate social context. The same objections would apply to A. Milavec, "The Social Setting of 'Turning the other Cheek' and 'Loving One's Enemies' in Light of the Didache," *BTB* 25 (1995) 131-43, who sees its context the break-up of families through the attraction of Jesus. It is doubtful that Jesus or Matthew restricted enemies to "members of one's own household," although they were of course included. L. Vaage (*Galilean Upstarts: Jesus' First Followers According to Q* [Valley Forge: Trinity Press International, 1994]) also trivializes these instructions when he depicts them as the same as the Cynic one-up-manship tactics.

48   So W. Schrage, *The Ethics of the New Testament* (Philadelphia: Fortress, 1990) 76: "personal, religious enemies, the enemies of God and of God's people . . . but political and social enemies are also included." Surely few things so clearly indicate the shift in scholarship as the prominent place given to the love your enemies command in Schrage's book.

49   See for example C. F. von Weizsäcker, "Die intelligente Feindesliebe," in idem, *Der bedrohte Friede* (Wien and München: C. Hanser, 1981) 533ff.

50   So James Charlesworth, who follows Yadin and Schubert in arguing that Jesus had Qumran in view. He sees part of Jesus' uniqueness in his rejection of the

words, we should simply treat them as a part of general folk wisdom which Jesus' listeners had heard and were well known to Matthew's audience as well.

The motivation for Matthew is the same as for Luke: becoming a child of God, "only so can you be children of your heavenly Father." Instead of stressing the gentleness and compassion of God Matthew stresses God's impartiality. The sun rises on good and bad alike, the rain is sent on the just and the unjust alike. An insight appearing in Jewish wisdom literature which there drives to cynicism (i.e. so who cares?) is here used to strike forth into a new ethical sphere. Both Luke and Matthew ask: "If you love only those who love you, what credit is that?"

Matthew adds only one further point, the question of greeting not introduced by Luke. Yoḥanan ben Zakkai who escaped from Jerusalem when it was under siege to found the Academy at Yavneh had the reputation of greeting Gentiles and others before they would greet him. In this way there could never be any doubt about his prayerful desire that the one he met should have God's shalom. Along the same lines Matthew invites his readers to exceed the friendliness of the heathen and to greet all whom they meet. It is a striking illustration, too often overlooked, bringing the entire discussion about enemy love into the concreteness of daily life.

Matthew's concluding statement, "Be you therefore mature even as your Father in heaven is mature [τέλειος]" (Matt 5:48), refers to the way in which enemies are treated. Don't play favorites. The term, "perfect" as it is sometimes translated creates difficulties not contained in the original text and suggests an impossible standard; hardly the intention of Jesus for his followers. Rather he provided them with permission and the empowering freedom to live as a child of God who loves even enemies.

Some years ago Hans Windisch published a fascinating study on the correlation of the "peacemaker = child of God" idea.[51] His essay has suffered considerable neglect, but it is far-reaching in its conclusions and forces us to consider the connection between peace-making and love of enemies in the teaching of Jesus. Note for example the beatitude, "Blessed are the peacemakers, for they shall be called children

---

Qumran view, J. H. Charlesworth (ed.), *Jesus and the Dead Sea Scrolls* (ABRL 4; New York, Doubleday, 1992) 23-24.

[51]   H. Windisch, "Friedensbringer—Gottessöhne," *ZNW* 24 (1925) 240-60.

of God" (Matt 5:9). While that beatitude is missing in Luke, this evangelist does place a great deal of emphasis on peace, and indeed in the mission statement in chap. 10 an enigmatic phrase, "child of peace," appears on the lips of Jesus. Both the peacemaker term as well as the designation, "child of peace," show affinity to Judaism and are often dismissed as "Jewish expressions." In fact, it should more accurately be described as "genuine coinage of Jesus."[52] It should be noted that "peacemaker" is most often used by Josephus and in the historical books of the Maccabees for a military general. Jesus, however, relates it to being a child of God and so tied together being a peacemaker and loving one's enemies. When he urged his disciples to be peaceable Hillel urged them to become disciples of Aaron, "loving peace and pursuing it" (*m. ʾAbot* 1:12). Although Judaism affirmed that God was a God of peace and urged Jews to emulate God, so far the only Jew we know who called peacemakers children of God was Jesus. Moreover, the record in Luke 10:4 would seem to indicate that the first followers of Jesus knew each other as "children of peace." There is no reason to doubt that Mark 9:50c is genuine, for it is a hopelessly difficult image; but the mandate is clear: Jesus wants his disciples to be at peace among themselves. It has taken us a while but there is no longer any doubt that Jesus was deeply concerned about peace and that his way of attaining it was clearly that his followers should love their enemies.[53]

Both Matthew and Luke appeal to God's mercy although they use different examples to demonstrate that mercy. In both God's action is to be followed, which becomes in Paul an *imitatio Christi*.

The Gospel of Luke has one parable, the parable of the good Samaritan, which seeks to address the question posed by the lawyer: Who is my neighbor? (Luke 10). What is its point? A recent author listed a series of distinguished interpreters who see the parable as an illustration of how someone viewed traditionally as an enemy can love his enemy, the Jew, and help him in his distress.[54] Thus to be a

---

52   W. Klassen, "A 'Child of Peace' (Luke 10.6) in First Century Context," *NTS* 27 (1981) 484-506. The quotation is from Klassen, "Peace (NT)," *ABD* 5.208.

53   U. Mauser has given us a fine study in *The Gospel of Peace* (Louisville: Westminster John Knox, 1992). It is a thorough study and has not received the attention it deserves. See also the extensive bibliography in W. Swartley and P. Yoder (eds.), *The Meaning of Peace* (Louisville: Westminster John Knox, 1992).

54   W. Monselewski, *Der barmherzige Samariter: Eine auslegungsgeschicht-*

neighbor you love your enemy. The Samaritans were well-liked by Luke, to be sure, for he almost always portrayed them in a favorable light. From Josephus we learn that the Samaritans occasionally terrorized the Jews (*Ant.* 20.6.1-3 §118-136) and little love was lost between these two groups. Yet in the parable, it is the Samaritan who proves neighbor to his "enemy" and shows that categories, like enemies and friends can change to assaulted and the neighbor who assists the one assaulted.

The similarities between this parable and the love your enemies pericopes in Matthew and Luke have often been noted and traced in detail by Monselewski. He sees four elements as determinative: (1) the authority of Jesus; (2) the reference to God's covenant with the people; (3) reward; and (4) the reference to the authority of God and a personal relationship to him. He also believes these motifs may have been at the basis of the parable and with Günther Bornkamm wonders whether the parable may not have been the oldest form of the love your enemies command.[55]

Did Jesus himself love his enemies? Matthew 24 seems to suggest that he did not and other events of his life are often cited. If, however, he saw the injustices around him as being capable of being righted only through the death of those who truly cared for their people, then his teaching and self-sacrifice do harmonize.

CONCLUSION

"It is inconceivable that the primitive Christian community would have made up [these sayings]," the Jesus seminar concluded in their debates about the authenticity of the words, "love your enemies."[56] In addition to this verdict the Seminar also gave a helpful distinction between legally binding commandments and what they refer to as a "case parody which stands on the edge of the possible—just barely." There is then an affirmation that this command of Jesus is an invitation to a real world beyond the world of hatred and anger and war which surrounds us. Jesus struck forth boldly, but he also validated his teaching with his life and death. Moreover the early church believed that God had vindicated Jesus through the

---

liche Untersuchung zu Lukas 10,25-37 (BGBE 5; Tübingen: Mohr [Siebeck], 1967).

[55] Monselewski, *Der barmherzige Samariter*, 166-74.

[56] Funk and Hoover (eds.), *The Five Gospels*, 145.

resurrection and therein they saw their own potential and power to live according to this new path. The ultimate authentication of this word of Jesus then is the one that beckons to be written by the lives of those who follow him.

APPENDIX A

Principal Criteria for Authenticity (Stein and Meier)*

1. Multiple Attestation or Cross-section Approach

3. Multiple Attestation

4. Palestinian Environmental Phenomena

5. Tendencies of the Developing Tradition

2. Discontinuity

9. Environmental Contradiction

10. Contradiction of Authentic Sayings

11. Coherence or Consistency

4. Coherence

1. Embarrassment

5. Rejection and Execution

---

*   The numbering matches the sequence presented in Stein and Meier.

APPENDIX B

Q Text as reconstructed by J. Sauer, "Traditionsgeschichtliche Erwägungen," 14:

λέγω ὑμῖν,

ἀγαπᾶτε τοὺς ἐχθροὺς ὑμῶν,
καλῶς ποιεῖτε τοῖς μισοῦσιν ὑμᾶς,
εὐλογεῖτε τοὺς καταρωμένους ὑμᾶς,
προσεύχεσθε ὑπὲρ τῶν ἐπηρεαζόντων ὑμᾶς.
καὶ ἔσεσθε υἱοὶ τοῦ πατρὸς ὑμῶν
ὅτι τὸν ἥλιον αὐτοῦ ἀνατέλλει ἐπὶ πονηροὺς καὶ ἀγαθοὺς
καὶ βρέχει ἐπὶ δικαίους καὶ ἀδίκους.
εἰ γὰρ ἀγαπᾶτε τοὺς ἀγαπῶντας ὑμᾶς,
τίνα μισθὸν ἔχετε;
οὐχὶ καὶ οἱ τελῶναι τὸ αὐτὸ ποιοῦσιν;
καὶ ἐὰν ἀσπάσησθε τοὺς ἀδελφοὺς ὑμῶν μόνον,
τίνα μισθὸν ἔχετε;
οὐχὶ καὶ οἱ ἐθνικοὶ τὸ αὐτὸ ποιοῦσιν;
γίνεσθε οἰκτίρμονες ὡς ὁ πατὴρ ὑμῶν οἰκτίρμων ἐστίν.

τῷ ῥαπίζοντί σε εἰς τὴν σιαγόνα
στρέψον καὶ τὴν ἄλλην,
καὶ τῷ θέλοντι τὸν χιτῶνά σου λαβεῖν
ἄφες καὶ τὸ ἱμάτιον,
καὶ τῷ ἀγγαρεύοντί σε μίλιον ἕν
ὕπαγε μετ' αὐτοῦ δύο
τῷ αἰτοῦντί σε δός καὶ τὸν ἀπὸ σοῦ δανείσασθαι μὴ ἀποστραφῇς,
καὶ ὡς θέλετε ἵνα ποιῶσιν ὑμῖν οἱ ἄνθρωποι
οὕτως καὶ ὑμεῖς ποιεῖτε αὐτοῖς.

APPENDIX C

Cf. M. Black, "The Account of the Essenes in Hippolytus and Josephus," 172-75.

According to Josephus, the Essenes "swore tremendous oaths": πρὶν δὲ τῆς κοινῆς ἅψασθαι τροφῆς ὅρκους αὐτοῖς ὄμνυσι φρικώδεις, πρῶτον μὲν εὐσεβήσειν τὸ θεῖον, ἔπειτα τὰ πρὸς ἀνθρώπους δίκαια φυλάξειν καὶ μήτε κατὰ γνώμην βλάψειν τινὰ μήτε ἐξ ἐπιτάγματος, μισήσειν δ᾽ ἀεὶ τοὺς ἀδίκους [forever hate the unrighteous] καὶ συναγωνιεῖσθαι τοῖς δικαίοις . . . (Josephus, J.W. 2.8.7 §139). Black leaves the question open whether the Essenes actually taught this.

Hippolytus has them swear: ὅρκοις ὁρικτοῖς ὁρκίζεται πρῶτον μὲν εὐσεβήσειν τὸ θεῖον, ἔπειτα τὰ πρὸς ἀνθρώπους δίκαια φυλάζειν καὶ, κατὰ μηδένα τρόπον ἀδικήσείν τινα [to act unjustly against no one in any way], μηδένα δὲ μήτε ἀδικοῦντα μήτε ἐχθρὸν μισήσειν [nor to avenge or hate an enemy?], προσεύχεσθαι δὲ ὑπὲρ αὐτῶν [but to pray in their behalf], συναγωνίζεσθαι ἀεὶ τοῖς δικαίοις τὸ πίστον πᾶσι παρέζειν, μάλιστα τοῖς κρατοῦσιν. οὐ γὰρ δίχα θεοῦ συμβαίνεν τινι τὸ ἄρχειν . . . (cf. Hippolytus, Refutatio, ed. P. Wendland [Leipzig: Hinrich's, 1916] 9.23).

The issue of Hippolytus' portrayal of the various Jewish parties is analysed by Emmanuelle Main in her 1992 M.A. thesis at Hebrew University: "Esséniens, Pharisiens, Sadducéens chez Hippolyte: la notice de l'Elenchos." While she does not deal specifically with this text, she does treat the morality of the Essenes as described by Josephus and Hippolytus (pp. 58-64) and their position on justice (pp. 79-82).

THE AUTHENTICITY OF THE PARABLE OF THE WARRING KING: A RESPONSE TO THE JESUS SEMINAR

Charles Leland Quarles

Most Christians are at least vaguely familiar with the work of the Jesus Seminar. Newspapers and popular magazines have acclaimed the work of these scholars as a serious challenge to traditional orthodox assessments of the Gospels and the historical Jesus. This group of critics has evaluated the sayings of Jesus in the four New Testament Gospels and the extra-canonical *Gospel of Thomas* ranking them according to the probability of their being authentic statements of Jesus.[1] The Jesus Seminar ranked only eighteen percent of the statements ascribed to Jesus by the Gospel writers as actual or probable statements of Jesus. The Seminar rejected over half of Jesus' statements as having any real connection to Jesus at all.[2] Several scholars have offered trenchant criticism of the work of the Seminar in general. The present study will offer a specific response to the Seminar's treatment of the Parable of the Warring King (Luke 14:31-32).

THE FAVORED CRITERIA OF THE SEMINAR

The Seminar has formulated and adopted twelve rules of written evidence and twenty-four rules of oral evidence to guide them in

---

[1]   The Fellows of the Seminar cast their votes by dropping a colored bead in a box. A red bead indicated that "Jesus undoubtedly said this or something very like it." A pink bead meant, "Jesus probably said something like this." A gray bead meant, "Jesus did not say this, but the ideas contained in it are close to his own." (Gray sometimes indicates lack of consensus on the part of the Seminar.) A black bead meant, "Jesus did not say this; it represents the perspective or content of a later or different tradition." See R. W. Funk and R. W. Hoover (eds.), *The Five Gospels: The Search for the Authentic Words of Jesus* (Sonoma: Polebridge Press; New York: Macmillan, 1993) 36-37. The Jesus Seminar has recently published its assessment of the activities of Jesus, following a similar format; cf. R. W. Funk (ed.), *The Acts of Jesus: What Did Jesus Really Do? The Search for the Authentic Deeds of Jesus* (San Francisco: HarperCollins, 1998).

[2]   Funk and Hoover (eds.), *The Five Gospels*, 5.

assessing the authenticity of Gospel traditions. Most of the rules of oral evidence fall within the standard form-critical categories of. multiple attestation, dissimilarity, and coherence. A brief review of these criteria is necessary.

1. *Multiple attestation*. Critics often assert that a statement of Jesus which is found in independent sources is more likely authentic than a saying unique to a single source or several interdependent texts. The Seminar has adopted three rules of oral evidence which fall under the category of multiple attestation: (1) material attested in two or more independent sources is older than the sources which contain them; (2) material attested in two different contexts probably circulated at an earlier time as an isolated unit independent of its literary context; and (3) identical or similar content attested in multiple forms may stem from older traditions.[3]

The Fellows of the Jesus Seminar did not locate any specific parallels to the Parable of the Warring King. However, they did admit a close thematic connection between this parable and the Parable of the Assassin in *GThom.* §98. The Fellows translated this parable as follows:

> The Father's imperial rule is like a person who wanted to kill someone powerful. While still at home he drew his sword and thrust it into the wall to find out whether his hand would go in. Then he killed the powerful one.[4]

The fellows conceded that "the parable of the assassin is reminiscent of the parables of the tower builder (Luke 14:28-30) and the warring king (Luke 14:31-32), all three of which have to do with estimating the cost of an act or the capability to perform it successfully."[5] Several scholars have argued that this reminiscence constitutes a true parallel.[6] Some of the Fellows evidently agreed. Funk and Hoover

---

3   Funk and Hoover (eds.), *The Five Gospels*, 26.

4   Funk and Hoover (eds.), *The Five Gospels*, 524.

5   Funk and Hoover (eds.), *The Five Gospels*, 524.

6   N. Perrin, *Rediscovering the Teaching of Jesus* (New York: Harper & Row, 1967); C.-H. Hunzinger, "Unbekannte Gleichnisse Jesu aus dem Thomas-Evangelium," in W. Eltester (ed.), *Judentum–Urchristentum–Kirche: Festschrift für Joachim Jeremias* (Berlin: Töpelmann, 1960) 209-17; I. H. Marshall, *The Gospel of Luke* (NIGTC; Grand Rapids: Eerdmans, 1978) 593. J. D. M. Derrett ("Nisi Dominus Aedificaverit Domum: Towers and Wars (Lk XIV 28-32)," *NovT* 19 [1977] 246) acknowledged acceptance of the parallel by Jeremias, Hunzinger, and Perrin, but countered, saying, "To my mind Thomas 98/95 has much more in common with Mk. iii 27, if it is genuine."

confessed that the parallel between the parables was sufficiently close to have "influenced some of the Fellows to vote black on this parable [Parable of the Assassin]."[7] These admissions highlight two faults in the Seminar's application of its methodology. First, in light of their acceptance of the criterion of multiple attestation (particularly rule three mentioned earlier), those scholars who recognized the two parables as literary parallels should have changed their opinion concerning the authenticity of the Lukan parables rather than denying the authenticity of the Parable of the Assassin.[8] Proper application of the criterion of multiple attestation does not lead one to dismiss the authenticity of materials which stand in parallel but rather to affirm the authenticity of materials which stand in parallel. One is given the impression that those scholars who originally voted black with regard to the Parable of the Assassin, under influence of the Lukan parallels, preferred to dismiss both parables for some unstated reason rather than allow each to confirm the other.

This suspicion is also confirmed by the later vote of the Seminar on the Parable of the Assassin, which elevated it from a gray to a pink designation. Two rationales fostered the new confidence in the authenticity of the parable. First and most importantly, the story line of the parable portrayed a reversal. In the words of the Seminar, "the little guy bests the big guy by taking precautions."[9] Appealing to the third rule of "distinctive discourse," which suggested that Jesus' statements elicited surprise and shock through a reversal of expectations, the Seminar concluded that the Parable of the Assassin was likely authentic. However, a closer look at the Parable of the Warring King demonstrates that it depicts a similar reversal. The invading king's intention of destroying the kingdom of the defender is thwarted, or "reversed," through the defending king's reasoned call for terms. The defending king "won" the battle by turning his enemy into an ally. Thus had this rationale been applied consistently, the Parable of the Warring King should perhaps have also qualified for a pink designation.

---

7   Funk and Hoover (eds.), *The Five Gospels*, 524-25. In the initial vote on the parable in 1986, twenty-eight percent of the Fellows voted black. In the final vote four years later, none of the Fellows voted black. See "The Jesus Seminar: Voting Records," *Forum* 6 (1990) 54-55.

8   Some scholars recently have affirmed the probable authenticity of the parable. See R. J. Bauckham, "Gospels (Apocryphal)," *DJG* 287.

9   Funk and Hoover (eds.), *The Five Gospels*, 525.

2. *Dissimilarity*. The Seminar appeals frequently to what has traditionally been called the "criterion of dissimilarity" in its assessment
of Jesus material. E. P. Sanders, who prefers to label the criterion
"the criterion of double dissimilarity," explains: "According to this
criterion, material can be safely attributed to Jesus if it agrees neither
with the early church nor with Judaism contemporary with Jesus."[10]
The rationale behind this criterion is that neither those responsible
for the oral transmission of Gospel traditions nor those who
recorded them were likely to place on Jesus' lips statements which
were contrary to their own thinking. This criterion is described by
the Fellows of the Seminar as the criterion of "false attribution,"
which suggests "words borrowed from the fund of common lore or
the Greek scriptures are often put on the lips of Jesus,"[11] and the
criteria of "distinctive discourse" which insist "Jesus' characteristic
talk was distinctive—it can usually be distinguished from common
lore. Otherwise it is futile to search for the authentic words of Jesus"
and "Jesus' sayings and parables cut against the social and religious
grain."[12]

This criterion provided the grounds for the Seminar to affirm the
authenticity of the Parable of the Assassin. The Seminar affirmed the
authenticity of the parable in *Thomas* because of "the scandalous
nature of the image," that is, the depiction of the inbreaking kingdom
of God as an assassin.[13] The Seminar elaborates:

> The sheer violence and scandal of the image of the assassin suggests that it
> might well have originated with Jesus. It is unlikely that the early Christian
> community would have invented and have attributed such a story to Jesus
> since its imagery is so contrary to the irenic and honorific images, such as
> the good shepherd, they customarily used for him.[14]

Since the description of the incoming kingdom is horrific rather than
honorific, it is probably authentic. One could raise the argument that
the violent image of an invading king is also scandalous and thus
probably authentic. The Seminar anticipated this line of argument:

> In ancient society, it was expected that kings and tyrants would act violently

---

10   E. P. Sanders and M. Davies, *Studying the Synoptic Gospels* (London:
SCM Press; Philadelphia: Trinity Press International, 1989) 316.
11   Funk and Hoover (eds.), *The Five Gospels*, 22.
12   Funk and Hoover (eds.), *The Five Gospels*, 30-31.
13   Funk and Hoover (eds.), *The Five Gospels*, 525.
14   Funk and Hoover (eds.), *The Five Gospels*, 525.

to enforce their will. Ordinary people were expected to refrain from violent behavior, unless, of course, they were brigands or revolutionaries.[15]

However, the Fellows of the Seminar failed to note that the Parable of the Warring King was not merely attributed to Jesus, it portrayed Jesus. While depiction of a king as violent might fit well with the ordinary expectations of ancient society, depiction of Jesus as a violent king borders on the scandalous. At least it does so from the Seminar's perspective, which expects only "irenic" potrayals of Jesus by the early church.

This point requires a brief digression into the meaning and intention of the Parable of the Warring King. Many interpreters regard the parable as a mere restatement of the same basic point contained in the Parable of the Tower-Builder.[16] However, a closer comparison of the two parables suggests that they communicate related but distinct concerns.[17] The Parable of the Tower-Builder shows the foolishness of making hasty commitments. It demonstrates the embarrassment caused by not counting the cost of discipleship. However, the Parable of the Warring King shows the danger of delaying spiritual commitment. It warns of the hazards of not paying the cost of discipleship.

In v. 31 the king who is about to engage in war against another king first sits down and considers whether he is able to defeat his foe. οὐχὶ καθίσας πρῶτον βουλεύσεται (Luke 14:31) is closely parallel to οὐχὶ πρῶτον καθίσας ψηφίζει (Luke 14:28). This suggests that a primary concern of both parables is the need for careful contemplation of the risks and costs involved in discipleship before one commits to Jesus and his message.

After the first half of v. 31, however, the parable moves in a different direction. The reference to ἐρχομένῳ ἐπ' αὐτόν (Luke

---

15   Funk and Hoover (eds.), *The Five Gospels*, 525.

16   Walter Liefeld's comment is typical: "Jesus uses two different circumstances to illustrate his basis point: discipleship requires a conscious advance commitment, made with a realistic estimate of the ultimate personal cost." See Liefeld, "Luke," in F. Gaebelein (ed.), *Matthew, Mark, and Luke* (EBC 8; Grand Rapids: Zondervan, 1984) 979-80.

17   Craig Blomberg saw the second parable of this doublet as climactic, repeating and emphasizing the basic point of the first parable. However, John Sider is probably correct in suggesting that the themes of the parables are complementary rather than identical. See his comparison of the views of Blomberg and A. M. Hunter in Sider, *Interpreting the Parables* (Grand Rapids: Zondervan, 1995) 77-79.

14:31) and the tenor of v. 32 suggest that the main character is on the defensive in this conflict. He must decide how he will respond to his enemy's aggression. A decision is urgent. This urgency is suggested by the words ἔτι αὐτοῦ πόρρω ὄντος (Luke 14:32). The advance of his opponent toward his home front presses him to determine quickly his course of action. If he is going to make a treaty with his enemy, he must do so without delay. The lives of his countrymen, as well as his throne, depend on his prompt response to this crisis. Thus the parable depicts the urgency of making a decision regarding the invading king.

The parable apparently assumes that the king is not able to win the conflict. He is outnumbered two to one. The only sensible response to his situation is to "ask for terms of peace." Hesitation or refusal to make peace with the more powerful king invites the destruction of his kingdom. Thus the parable hints at the serious consequences of hesitating or refusing to make peace with the invading king.

The words ἐρωτᾷ τὰ πρὸς εἰρήνην reflect a Hebrew idiom which originally meant "to surrender unconditionally."[18] Unconditional surrender involved giving the approaching king anything he requested, recognizing that this was the only means by which the other king could spare the lives of himself, his soldiers, and his citizens. The parable served to teach the importance and urgency of unconditional surrender to the invading king as the only means of deliverance.

This interpretation has been supported by the recent research of

---

[18]   J. Jeremias, *The Parables of Jesus* (New York: Scribner's, 1955) 138; H. St. J. Thackeray ("A Study in the Parable of the Two Kings," *JTS* 14 [1913] 389-99) first proposed that the Greek phrase reflects an ancient Hebrew idiom found in 2 Sam 8:10. J. A. Fitzmyer (*The Gospel according to Luke X-XXIV* [AB 24A; Garden City: Doubleday, 1985] 1066) and J. Nolland (*Luke 9:21–18:34* [WBC 35B; Dallas: Word, 1993] 764) have challenged this notion. Appealing to *T. Judah* 9:7, B. Heininger (*Metaphorik, Erzählstruktur und szenisch-dramatische Gestaltung in den Sondergutgleichnissen bei Lukas* [Münster: Aschendorff, 1991] 136) suggested, "Von daher kommt das Friedensangebot hier einer bedingungslosen Unterwerfung gleich." Even if one rejects this phrase as an idiom for "unconditional surrender," the context suggests that the king with the more numerous forces would be able to set forth his own demands in peace negotiations. Jesus laments over Jerusalem, the city which had failed to recognized "the things that make for peace [τὰ πρὸς εἰρήνην]" (Luke 19:42). This language at the very least suggests that the king of the parable under consideration is attempting to reconcile with his approaching opponent.

several major commentators. According to I. H. Marshall, "From this point [v. 32] the parallelism with the previous parable breaks down. The lesson is that one should come to terms with the enemy before it is too late."[19] Leon Morris agrees: "The two parables are similar but they make slightly different points. The builder of the tower is free to build or not as he chooses, but the king is being invaded (the other comes against him). He must do something."[20] Morris cites approvingly A. M. Hunter who wrote: "In the first parable Jesus says, 'Sit down and reckon whether you can afford to follow me.' In the second he says, 'Sit down and reckon whether you can afford to refuse my demands.'"[21] These commentators recognized that Jesus was not only urging his followers to consider carefully the costs of discipleship, but that he was also urging them to consider the cost of refusing to follow him. They recognized that Jesus was calling for a careful but prompt decision. The kingdom was at hand; postponement of decision was not an option.

Although Marshall doubts that the reference to unconditional surrender to an approaching king has any "parabolic significance," he agrees that the parable "emphasizes the ridiculous situation of the man who so far from surrendering plunges his army into complete destruction."[22] While interpreters should respect Marshall's caution about deriving allegorical interpretations of Jesus' parables, the context justifies linking the first king's unconditional surrender to a more powerful king with the unconditional commitment to Jesus, which previously he had demanded.[23] This interpretation is confirmed by the application of the parable made in v. 33. Jesus demands that his followers "give up everything," literally "say goodbye to his possessions," in order to become his disciples. Unconditional surrender involved offering everything to the more powerful king and discipleship involves offering everything one has and is to Jesus, the herald and bringer of the kingdom of God. The Lukan evangelist closely links this conclusion with the Parable of the Warring King by use of the words "in the same way" (οὕτως οὖν). This suggests that

---

19   Marshall, *Luke*, 594.
20   L. Morris, *Luke* (NIC; Grand Rapids: Eerdmans, 1988) 259.
21   Morris, *Luke*, 259.
22   Marshall, *Luke*, 594. Hunter's comment is taken from A. T. Cadoux, *The Parables of Jesus: Their Art and Use* (London: J. Clarke, 1930; New York: Macmillan, 1931) 174.
23   Thackeray, "A Study in the Parable of the Two Kings," 399.

the disciple's surrender of his possessions to Jesus is modeled upon the king's surrender to a more powerful king.[24] Luke frequently uses οὕτως to introduce a parable application (Luke 12:21; 15:7, 10; 17:10; 21:31) and this is its function here.[25] The construction hints that the warring king of the Lukan parable portrays Jesus himself. The message of the parable is that Jesus is like an invading king who threatens destruction to those who do not unconditionally surrender to him.[26]

A close examination of the Parable of the Warring King suggests that it too uses a scandalous image. In the Parable of the Assassin, Jesus merely uses a scandalous image to portray the inbreaking kingdom. But in the Parable of the Warring King, Jesus uses a scandalous image to portray himself. Thus the same criterion which the Seminar uses to establish the authenticity of the Parable of the Assassin ("It is unlikely that the early Christian community would have invented and have attributed such a story to Jesus since its imagery is so contrary to the irenic and honorific images, such as the good shepherd, they customarily used for him") suggests the authenticity of the Parable of the Warring King even more forcefully.

Many scholars have pointed out that the criterion of dissimilarity is of limited help in reconstructing the historical Jesus. Ben Witherington has recently charged:

> If one uses this sort of criterion as an ultimate or final litmus test, one is bound to end up with only the distinctive or unique sayings and a Jesus

---

24   P. G. Jarvis ("Expounding the Parables V: The Tower-builder and the King Going to War (Luke 14:25-33)," *ExpTim* 77 [1965-66] 196-98) identifies the invading king as Satan and has suggested that the parable originally encouraged the disciples by reminding them that their King (God) would never need to surrender to his opponent. I am not suggesting that one should identify these kings as if the parable were an allegory. I am merely suggesting that Jesus is teaching the sensibility of surrender.

25   Pace Nolland, *Luke*, 764.

26   The serious consequences of rejecting Jesus' kingly authority are even more clearly related in Luke 19:27: πλὴν τοὺς ἐχθρούς μου τούτους τοὺς μὴ θελήσαντάς με βασιλεῦσαι ἐπ' αὐτοὺς ἀγάγετε ὧδε καὶ κατασφάξατε αὐτοὺς ἔμπροσθέν μου. Derrett ("Nisi Dominus Aedificaverit Domum," 260) recognized that the parable was a portrayal of Jesus, although he holds Jarvis's view that Jesus was represented by the defending king rather than the invading king. Some of his observations are still pertinent here: "Jews have greatly preferred parables in which kings figure . . . It is known that Luke is interested in Christ as King (Lk. x 24, xix 38, xxiii 2)."

who has nothing in common with either his Jewish heritage or his later Christian followers. Of course the idea of Jesus being totally idiosyncratic, without any analogy, is highly improbable. There has never been such a person in all of human history.[27]

Darrell Bock agrees:

If both sides of the dissimilarity are affirmed, so that Jesus differs from *both* Judaism *and* the early church, then Jesus becomes a decidedly odd figure, totally detached from his cultural heritage and ideologically estranged from the movement he is responsible for founding.[28]

However, the fault of the Seminar lies not only in the over-application of the criterion of dissimilarity but in the inconsistent application of the criterion (a point Bock also emphasizes). This inconsistent application of the methodology which the Seminar has formulated and adopted raises suspicions concerning the validity of their judgments.

3. *Coherence*. The criterion of coherence suggests that a tradition that coheres with or is similar to a tradition otherwise established as authentic can probably be traced back to Jesus. The Seminar affirmed use of this criterion in its rule which states: "The same or similar content attested in two or more different forms has had a life of its own and therefore may stem from old traditions."[29] The Seminar appears to have utilized this criterion in its acceptance of *GThom.* §98: "The image of the assassin may be a distant echo of Matt 11:12, 'Heaven's imperial rule has been breaking in violently, and violent men are attempting to gain it by force,' on which there was a divided vote."[30] Eight percent of the Fellows voted for a red rating.[31] Since both Matt 11:2 and *GThom.* §98 use the imagery of violence to describe the approach of the heavenly imperial rule, those Fellows who affirmed the authenticity of Matt 11:2 were apparently influenced by the coherence of the passage with *GThom.* §98 to accept the authenticity of the Parable of the Assassin.

Again one wonders why the criterion of coherence did not apply

---

[27]   B. Witherington, *The Jesus Quest: The Third Search for the Jew of Nazareth* (Downers Grove: InterVarsity, 1995) 46.

[28]   D. L. Bock, "The Words of Jesus in the Gospels," in M. J. Wilkins and J. P. Moreland (eds.), *Jesus under Fire: Modern Scholarship Reinvents the Historical Jesus* (Grand Rapids: Zondervan, 1995) 73-99, here 91.

[29]   Funk and Hoover (eds.), *The Five Gospels*, 26.

[30]   Funk and Hoover (eds.), *The Five Gospels*, 525.

[31]   "Voting Records," 39.

to Luke 14:31-32. A significant amount of material affirmed as authentic by the Jesus Seminar coheres with the basic message of the. Lukan parable. Mark 10:17-22, which advises people with fortunes to give them away, was ranked in the pink category by the Seminar, with none of the Fellows casting a black vote. This Markan passage is clearly coherent with the unconditional surrender to the warring king, as it portrays abandoning one's possessions to be a disciple of Jesus. Mark 10:23 ("How difficult it is for those who have money to enter God's domain") was given a pink rating by the Seminar. This statement coheres well with the demand of the parable that one must surrender one's possessions in order to become a disciple of Jesus. Mark 10:25 speaks of the difficulty of the wealthy entering the kingdom of God. The Seminar rated the logion pink. No black votes were recorded on the passage. Mark 10:29 was given a gray rating by the Seminar (forty percent of the Fellows voted pink). The logion speaks of Jesus' disciples leaving homes, families, and farms on his account and promises a one hundred-fold reward. Certainly this passage coheres well with the Parable of the Warring King and its demand that one "say goodbye" to his possessions in order to become a disciple of Jesus. Matthew 6:24, which insists that a person must choose between God and money, was given a pink rating by the Seminar. This seems coherent with the application of the Parable of the Warring King and its insistence that one must choose between one's possessions and discipleship. Matt 13:44-46 (graded pink by the Seminar) compares the kingdom of God to a priceless pearl for which a merchant will sell all that he owns and a treasure-laden field for which a person will sell all his possessions. This is similar in theme to Jesus' statement that no one is able to be his disciple without saying goodbye to all that he owns. Luke 14:26 ("If any come to me and do not hate their own father and mother and wife and children and sisters—yes, even their own life—they cannot be my disciples") is graded as likely authentic by the Seminar. This demand coheres with the demand in the Parable of the Warring King to abandon one's possessions for the sake of Christian discipleship. Luke 17:33 ("Whoever tries to hang on to life will forfeit it, but whoever forfeits life will preserve it") was ranked as likely authentic, with forty-five percent of the Seminar judging the logion as definitely authentic. The statement is a close thematic parallel to the Parable of the Warring King, in which the king spares his life by giving his life to the more powerful invading king in an act of unconditional surrender. Thus, if the Fellows of the Seminar had applied the criterion of coherence to the Parable of the Warring King in the same manner in which it was applied to the Parable of the Assassin, the authenticity of the parable should have been confirmed.

OTHER CONSIDERATIONS

1. *The evidence of Palestinian language.* Form critics often use the criterion of Palestinian language and environment to test the authenticity of Jesus material. Critics reason that as oral traditions were transmitted, those who transmitted the tradition adapted it more and more to their own language. Futhermore, since (1) Jesus and his earliest disciples spoke Aramaic, and (2) Greek quickly became the predominant language of the early church, then (3) traces of Aramaic grammar and vocabulary indicate the presence of very old traditions, dating from the earliest stage of the oral period and often deriving from Jesus himself. Although the Fellows of the Seminar did not officially adopt this criterion, they did rightly acknowledge that "Jesus' native tongue was Aramaic."[32] They also concluded that "Jesus undoubtedly employed the term 'Abba' (Aramaic for 'Father') to address God." They did reject the authenticity of the Aramaic words which appeared in Mark 5:41 and 7:34. Though the Aramaic forms normally suggested authenticity, the Gospel writer had used the Aramaic term to make an ordinary command sound like a magical formula to the ear of the Greek-speaker.[33] The Aramaic cry from the cross (Mark 15:34 = Matt 27:46) was rejected since it was an Old Testament quotation such as was imposed on Jesus by the Gospel writers.[34]

Evaluation of the Parable of the Warring King in light of the criterion of Palestinian language suggests the authenticity of the parable and its conclusion. J. Jeremias assigned the parable to pre-Lukan tradition based upon linguistic evidence.[35] Although Jeremias does not specify this linguistic evidence, he likely is referring to suspected Hebrew or Aramaic idioms which lie behind the Greek text. Jeremias believed that the Greek construction ἐρωτᾷ τὰ πρὸς

---

[32] Funk and Hoover (eds.), *The Five Gospels*, 27.

[33] Funk and Hoover (eds.), *The Five Gospels*, 71. Note the concessive "although" in the Seminar's rejection of the Aramaic expression.

[34] Funk and Hoover (eds.), *The Five Gospels*, 126.

[35] Jeremias, *Parables*, 68.

εἰρήνην was a translation of a Hebrew or Aramaic idiom meaning "to greet the opponent, do him homage, surrender unconditionally."[36] This view was popularized by Foerster's article in the *TDNT*, which introduced scholars to the previous work of Thackeray.[37] Thackeray, appealing to the variant in the B text, argued that the Lukan construction was a striking parallel to the Septuagintal rendering of לְשָׁאָל־לֹו לְשָׁלֹום in 2 Sam 8:10. Though the words normally meant merely to salute or greet, in the context of a relationship between two rival kings, the greeting which was typically expressed through bowing the knee in homage constituted an expression of submission and surrender. Thackeray, appealing to evidence in both Assyrian and Egyptian texts, demonstrated that the idiom was shared by other related languages.

In addition to 2 Sam 8:10, this idiomatic use probably occurs in 1 Sam 10:4 and 25:5. Although the authors of Targum Jonathan followed the Hebrew text quite literally here and made no effort to explicate or update the sense of the idiom (presumably because the idiom was functional and current in Aramaic as in Hebrew), modern translators of the Targum have been alert to this idiomatic use.[38] Daniel Harrington and Anthony Saldarini have recognized this idiomatic use and have translated the construction "ask for peace" in these passages. They understand that the construction has another more common sense and so translate it "greet" or "asked about his welfare" in other contexts (e.g. 1 Sam 17:22; Judg 18:15).[39]

The closest parallel to Luke's Greek construction is *T. Judah* 7:7 (αἰτοῦσιν ἡμᾶς τὰ πρὸς εἰρήνην), which is clearly a reference to

---

36   Jeremias, *Parables*, 138.

37   W. Foerster, "εἰρήνη," *TDNT* 2 (1964) 412.

38   The text of the Targum reads "ותשאלון ליה בשמי לשלם," "וישאלון לך לשלם," and "למשאל ליה לשלם," in 1 Sam 10:4; 25:5; and 2 Sam 8:10, respectively. For texts, see A. Sperber (ed.), *The Bible in Aramaic: Based on Old Manuscripts and Printed Texts*, vol. 2: *The Former Prophets according to Targum Jonathan* (Leiden: Brill, 1992).

39   See D. J. Harrington and A. J. Saldarini, *Targum Jonathan of the Former Prophets* (ArBib 10; Wilmington: Glazier, 1987). The recently published graphic concordance of the Dead Sea Scrolls does not list any instances of the combination of שאל and שלם. See J. H. Charlesworth (ed.), *Graphic Concordance to the Dead Sea Scrolls* (Tübingen: Mohr [Siebeck]; Louisville: Westminster/John Knox, 1991). Foerster ("εἰρήνη," 408) notes that the common sense "greet" is expressed using this combination in the Palestinian Talmud.

the peace negotiations of two warring parties. R. H. Charles and other scholars have suggested that this Testament was first written in Hebrew or Aramaic, since Semitic idiom seems to underlie much of the Greek text and since several difficult passages can be explained through an appeal to a Semitic original. The view has received some verification through the discovery of Aramaic fragments of testaments related to the *Testaments of the Twelve Patriarchs*. Although Howard Kee has rejected the opinion that the *Testaments* were first written in Aramaic, since "the absence from the Semitic fragments of some of the fundamental concepts of the Testaments presented here is so complete," he did suggest that the peculiarities of the *Testaments* were best explained "if we assume that it was originally written in Greek, with Hebrew and Aramaic testaments serving loosely as models and perhaps to a very limited extent as sources for details."[40] The fact that Luke's construction appears elsewhere in a document with Semitic influences strengthens the suspicion that an Aramaic construction underlies Luke's awkward expression.

Marshall agrees that a Semitic expression is present here, suggesting that original Hebrew phraseology led to confusion for some early scribes and gave rise to the minor textual variants that appeared in the earliest manuscripts.[41] Slight differences in the expression "ask for terms of peace" in the ancient Greek manuscripts resulted from the difficulty of accomodating Greek syntax to an awkward Hebrew idiom. This hints at the great antiquity of the parable, argues against the notion that the parable was created by a late first-century Greek-speaking church, and strengthens the conviction that the parable was originally spoken by Jesus.

One may object that since the idiom appears in the Septuagint, this is simply another instance of a New Testament writer placing Old Testament expressions on Jesus' lips. That is unlikely, however, in light of an underlying Aramaic word-play which looks beyond the Old Testament expression. After reminding his readers that the Hebrew expression "to surrender unconditionally" in non-royal contexts simply meant "to greet" or "to say 'Hello'," Thackeray pondered:

> Is it not a strange coincidence that immediately after the Hebrew phrase for "to say How do you do?" St Luke employs the κοινή word for "to say

---

40   H. C. Kee, "Testaments of the Twelve Patriarchs," *OTP* 2.776-77.
41   Marshall, *Luke*, 594.

Goodbye" (ἀποτάσσεται)? 'Ασπάζεσθαι would cover both. Was there not perhaps an intentional word-play in St Luke's source?[42]

The word-play "say hello to the coming king" and "say goodbye to your possessions" would be consistent with the form of the communication typical of Jesus. One of the tests for an authentic saying of Jesus involves application of the rule of "distinctive discourse." The Fellows assert that "Jesus' sayings and parables are often characterized by exaggeration, humor, and paradox."[43] This pun satisfies this criterion. The word-play would also serve to make the statement more provocative and memorable to those responsible for the transmission of the oral tradition.[44] Yet the word-play would only be intelligible to those familiar with Hebrew or Aramaic. This suggests that the Semitic idiom reflected in the Parable of the Warring King does not result merely from the evangelist's appeal to the Old Testament but instead marks both the parable and its conclusion as having been crafted by an Aramaic teacher, most likely Jesus himself.

2. *The evidence of the pairable parable*. Jeremias suggested that the parable should be traced to Jesus because it was part of a pair. Jesus frequently employed duplication to emphasize an idea. Pairs of parables that involved a natural contrast "must have been original."[45] Jeremias mentions parables that contrast poor and rich (Matt 13:44-46), wise and foolish (Matt 7:24-27), man and woman (Luke 15:4-10), and great and small (Mark 3:24-27). He includes the Parable of the Tower-Builder and the Warring King in the final category, since building a tower was a small task compared to the greater task of fighting a king who armies doubled the size of one's own forces.[46] The similarities between these two parables and Jesus' teaching form elsewhere strengthen the claim to authenticity for this parable.

3. *The evidence of contemporary events*. The Parable of the Warring King may allude to an actual historical event that could place the origin of the parable in the time of Jesus' ministry. According to his *Antiquities* (18.5.1 §109-115), Josephus reports that the marriage of Herod Antipas to Herodias prompted Aretas, the king of Arabia Petrea and the father of Antipas' former wife, to declare war against

---

42   Thackeray, "A Study in the Parable of the Two Kings," 399.

43   Funk and Hoover (eds.), *The Five Gospels*, 31.

44   Funk and Hoover (eds.), *The Five Gospels*, 27-29.

45   Jeremias, *Parables*, 71.

46   Jeremias, *Parables*, 71.

Antipas. A large number of fugitives from the tetrarchy of Philip joined the army of Aretas. The combined forces greatly out-numbered Antipas' men and destroyed the king's entire army. According to Matt 14:1-12 and Mark 6:14-29, these events occurred during Jesus' ministry. Some interpreters have suggested that the Parable of the Warring King may have deliberately alluded to Antipas' recent disaster.[47] The parallels between the parable and the war between Aretas and Antipas support but do not necessarily confirm this hypothesis.[48] The hypothesis is strengthened when it is remembered that Jesus on other occasions alludes to current events. In Luke 13:1-5 Jesus referred to two contemporary events: Pilate's slaughter of some Galileans and the deadly collapse of the tower of Siloam. Jesus used these episodes to impress upon his hearers the urgent need of repentance. A parable with connections to political events contemporary with Jesus would not likely have developed in the evolution of the tradition in the decades subsequent to Easter. If the relationship between this parable and the experience of Antipas is accepted, it serves to confirm the parable as an authentic utterance of Jesus that has been faithfully preserved by Luke.

PHILOSOPHICAL PREMISES OF THE JESUS SEMINAR

In light of the evidence for the authenticity of the Parable of the Warring King, one is confronted with the question, "Why did the Seminar ignore the evidence supporting the authenticity of this parable but appeal to virtually identical evidence to support the authenticity of an extra-canonical parable?" A careful reading of the Introduction to *The Five Gospels* suggests two reasons for this inconsistency.

1. *Preference for extra-canonical material.* First, the Seminar is driven by a mentality that prefers the novel to the traditional. The Seminar strongly reacts to "the smothering cloud of historic creeds,"

---

[47] C. S. Keener, *The IVP Bible Background Commentary: New Testament* (Downers Grove: IVP, 1993) 231. For older commentators, see A. B. Bruce, "The Synoptic Gospels," in R. Nicoll (ed.), *Expositor's Greek New Testament*, vol. 1 (repr. Grand Rapids: Eerdmans, 1988) 576.

[48] Others have seen a possible allusion in the parable to 2 Sam 8:9-12. This view was argued on both linguistic and contextual grounds by Thackeray, "A Study in the Parable of the Two Kings," 393-95. See also T. W. Manson, *The Sayings of Jesus* (London: SCM Press, 1937) 281.

the "dark ages of theological tyranny," and the "dictatorial tactics of the Southern Baptist Convention and other fundamentalisms."[49] The apparent preference for the *Gospel of Thomas*, as opposed to the New Testament Gospels, is a product of this reactionary mindset. Under the section entitled "The agenda of the Jesus Seminar," the Fellows defined the parameters of their research of the sayings of Jesus with the following rule: "Canonical boundaries are irrelevant in critical assessments of the various sources of information about Jesus."[50] The Fellows further explained that they refuse to "privilege the gospels that came to be regarded as canonical by the church."[51] The inconsistency of the methodology of the Seminar as applied to the *Gospel of Thomas* and New Testament sources leads one to believe that the Fellows have understated the true operating principle of the Seminar. The Seminar has not merely erased canonical boundaries; it prefers material from extra-canonical sources to material in texts recognized as authoritative by the early church.

The Seminar affirms the authenticity of five logia from the *Gospel of Thomas* that, in the assessment of the Seminar, have no canonical parallel—three in the gray category and two in the pink category. The Seminar voted on *GThom.* §97 twice, giving the logion a gray rating both times. When a third vote was taken a pink classification resulted. The Fellows explain:

> The hesitation of the Fellows was occasioned by the unfamiliarity of the parable—it has been known only since the discovery of the Nag Hammadi library in 1945—and the reticence to attribute anything to Jesus not attested by one of the canonical gospels, although, in principle, the Fellows of the Seminar regard canonical boundaries as irrelevant to questions of authenticity. Scholarship, like traditions generally, moves at the speed of a glacier.[52]

The final sentence seems to equate appreciation for the canon with traditionalism, the kind of traditionalism that the Seminar loves to eschew. This suspicion seems confirmed by the Seminar's treatment of *GThom.* §98 examined in the present study. Again, three votes were taken. The first two resulted in a gray classification of the Parable of the Assassin. The third resulted in a pink classification. The editors of *The Five Gospels* applaud the final decision, stating:

---

49   Funk and Hoover (eds.), *The Five Gospels*, 7-8.
50   Funk and Hoover (eds.), *The Five Gospels*, 35.
51   Funk and Hoover (eds.), *The Five Gospels*, 35.
52   Funk and Hoover (eds.), *The Five Gospels*, 524.

"As in the case of Thomas 97, attributing a parable to Jesus not attested in the canonical Gospels and known only for a few years was an act of courage that demanded careful deliberation."[53] The statement is in stark contrast to one made earlier in the Introduction: "Not even the fundamentalists on the far right can produce a credible Jesus out of allegedly inerrant canonical gospels."[54] The inclusion of the adjective "canonical" in this smear gives one the impression that the Seminar associates affirmation of canonical material with (loathed) conservatism, while affirmation of noncanonical material expresses intellectual courage.

In the Introduction, the Fellows describe the *Gospel of Thomas* as a "treasure," a "significant new independent source of data for the study of the historical Jesus" and a "gold mine of comparative material and new information."[55] They assert that the material unique to the *Gospel of Thomas* represents a "tradition quite independent of the other gospels," providing "a 'control group' for the analysis of sayings and parables that appear in the other gospels."[56] They also assert that a "first edition" of the *Gospel of Thomas* was produced in 50–60 CE.[57] These assessments are problematic. Hippolytus, who wrote in the second or early third decade of the third century, was the first to refer to the document. No evidence suggests that the *Gospel of Thomas* originated in the first century.[58] Not only is the *Gospel of Thomas* chronologically distant from the historical Jesus, it is theologically distant from him and his milieu. By the Seminar's own admission, the book clearly contains gnosticizing and ascetic tendencies which were foreign to the historical Jesus.[59] The presence

---

[53]   Funk and Hoover (eds.), *The Five Gospels*, 525.

[54]   Funk and Hoover (eds.), *The Five Gospels*, 5.

[55]   Funk and Hoover (eds.), *The Five Gospels*, 9, 15.

[56]   Funk and Hoover (eds.), *The Five Gospels*, 15.

[57]   Funk and Hoover (eds.), *The Five Gospels*, 128.

[58]   See the discussion in R. J. Bauckham, "Gospels (Apocryphal)," 286-87; B. A. Pearson, "The Gospel according to the Jesus Seminar," *Religion* 25 (1995) 321-22; B. Layton, *The Gnostic Scriptures* (Garden City: Doubleday, 1987) 359-409. The manuscript evidence itself is inconclusive. The oldest of the three Greek fragments (i.e. POxy 1, POxy 654, and POxy 655) may date to 200 CE. Apart from $\mathfrak{P}^{52}$, which dates to 125–150 CE, the oldest mss of the New Testament Gospels date no earlier than 200 CE.

[59]   See *GThom.* §2, §3, §4, §11, §18, §22, §28, §29, §37, §50, §51, §60, §83-85. See especially the notes in Funk and Hoover (eds.), *The Five Gospels*, on logia §18, §19, §29, §50, and §83-84.

of the *Secret Book of James*, the *Dialogue of the Savior*, the *Gospel of Mary*, along with *Thomas*, in the Nag Hammadi collection argues. strongly for the Gnostic origins of the work. These factors should give scholars pause before placing *Thomas* on a par with the canonical Gospels as a source of information for the historical Jesus.[60]

But the sanguine descriptions of the *Gospel of Thomas* stand in sharp contrast with the derogatory comments regarding respect for the canon. Moreover, the Seminar's inequitable treatment of the canonical Gospels compared to extra-canonical Gospels suggests that, far from affirming the equality of *Thomas'* testimony, the Seminar has built a shrine to its supposed superiority. Witherington counters:

> Scholars are right to insist that in principle we must be open to all possible sources of information about the historical Jesus, both canonical and noncanonical . . . But all such sources must be evaluated with critical scrutiny. It is not reasonable to be highly skeptical about the canonical Gospels and highly receptive to the noncanonical Gospels.[61]

2. *Presuppositions and philosophical reductionism.* Perhaps the most troubling aspects of the Seminar's work are what appear to be presuppositions. Although its Fellows will surely deny it, it seems as though the following "rules of evidence" are not conclusions of careful, critical study, but presuppositions through which the evidence is sifted. The Seminar commends three rules:

- Jesus does not as a rule initiate dialogue or debate, nor does he offer to cure people.
- Jesus rarely makes pronouncements or speaks about himself in the first person.
- Jesus makes no claim to be the Anointed, the messiah.[62]

The Fellows insist that Jesus is "like the cowboy hero of the American West exemplified by Gary Cooper."[63] He is a man of few words. He is self-effacing, modest, and unostentatious. He is a man whose

---

60   J. P. Meier, *A Marginal Jew: Rethinking the Historical Jesus.* Volume One: *The Roots of the Problem and the Person* (ABRL 3; New York: Doubleday, 1991) 112-66; J. H. Charlesworth and C. A. Evans, "Jesus in the Agrapha and Apocryphal Gospels," in C. A. Evans and B. Chilton (eds.), *Studying the Historical Jesus: Evaluations of the State of Current Research* (NTTS 19; Leiden: Brill, 1994) 479-533; C. A. Evans, *Jesus and His Contemporaries: Comparative Studies* (AGJU 25; Leiden: Brill, 1995) 26-45.

61   Witherington, *The Jesus Quest:*, 50.

62   Funk and Hoover (eds.), *The Five Gospels*, 32.

63   Funk and Hoover (eds.), *The Five Gospels*, 32.

psychological makeup would have been inconsistent with a messianic self-understanding.[64]

The Jesus Seminar presents itself as the paragon of critical scholarship which makes factual evidence the controlling factor in its judgments. It challenges "non-critical scholars" who "put dogmatic considerations first and insist that the factual evidence confirm theological premises."[65] Yet this is precisely what the Fellows of the Seminar have done. They have produced a psychological profile of the historical Jesus based on their preconceived notions and then have used this profile to test the authenticity of sayings attributed to Jesus. In so doing, the Fellows of the Seminar have imposed their desired conclusions on their criteria. They have insisted that factual evidence confirm their philosophical premises.[66]

Many who have engaged in the quest for the historical Jesus have consciously or unconsciously distorted the Gospel portraits of Jesus to conform Jesus to their own image. The French Catholic modernist Alfred Loisy wrote concerning one scholar engaged in the quest of his time: "The Christ that Harnack sees, looking back through nineteen centuries of Catholic darkness, is only the reflection of a Liberal Protestant face, seen at the bottom of a deep well."[67] Many scholars who have rejected the Gospel portraits of Jesus in whole or in part have constructed a Jesus too much like themselves to make their reconstructions plausible. The Fellows of the Seminar seem to have succumbed to this tendency.

---

[64]   J. R. Edwards ("New Quest, Old Errors," *Touchstone* 9 [1996] 23) has shown that this portrait of the laconic sage has a weak historical foundation. He appeals to the Dead Sea Scrolls and the self-pronouncements of one of the most prominent first-century sages, Rabbi Hillel, to challenge the credibility of the Seminar's assumptions. One might also consider the remarkable claims made by the author of 1QH and 4Q491 (the Teacher of Righteousness?).

[65]   Funk and Hoover (eds.), *The Five Gospels*, 34.

[66]   R. B. Hays ("The Corrected Jesus," *First Things* 43 [1994] 47) is even more scathing in his critique of the Seminar: "Their attempt to present these views as 'the assured results of critical scholarship' is—one must say it—reprehensible deception." D. A. Carson's critique ("Five Gospels, No Christ," *Christianity Today* [25 April 1994] 33) is kinder: "The real irony is that, in some ways, the Jesus Seminar has itself become a parody of what it rejects. In tone and attitude, in its reductionism and self-confident exclusivism, in its self-righteousness and condescending pronouncements, it is more fundamentalistic than the fundamentalism it eschews."

[67]   C. Brown, "Historical Jesus, Quest of," *DJG*, 326-41, here 331.

The Fellows of the Seminar are certainly aware of this danger. They candidly admit:

> In addition to all the safeguards offered by the historical methodologies practiced by all responsible scholars and the protection from idiosyncracies afforded by peer review and open debate, the final test is to ask whether the Jesus we have found is the Jesus we wanted to find. The last temptation is to create Jesus in our own image, to marshal the facts to support preconceived convictions. This fatal pitfall has prompted the Jesus Seminar to adopt as its final general rule of evidence: Beware of finding a Jesus entirely congenial to you.[68]

However, the three criteria that insist that sayings attributed to Jesus which are inconsistent with the Seminar's premise that Jesus was a laconic sage must be rejected preclude a critical reviewer from taking the Seminar's commitment to its final test very seriously. As the Seminar charges the fundamentalist, so may it be said of them: "Their reading of who Jesus was rests on the shifting sands of their own theological constructions."[69] Birger Pearson summarizes the problem with a touch of irony:

> "Seek—you'll find." This is one of the "authentic" sayings of Jesus (Matthew 7:7//Luke 11:9//*Thomas* 92:1, colored pink) in *The Five Gospels*. A group of secularized theologians and secular academics went seeking a secular Jesus, and they found him! They think they found him, but, in fact, they created him.[70]

The dustjacket of *The Five Gospels* contains an advertising blurb that asks "Did Jesus claim to be the Messiah?" and "Did he promise to return and usher in a new age?" The reader is given the impression that these questions are going to be carefully investigated and a new, startling revelation made. But the Seminar does not provide a reasoned and defensible answer to these questions. It presumes a negative response to these questions and then dispenses with sayings attributed to Jesus as necessary to conform him to this preconception.

It is important to note also that the criticisms being directed against the Seminar are coming from scholars of all theological and

---

68   Funk and Hoover (eds.), *The Five Gospels*, 5.

69   Funk and Hoover (eds.), *The Five Gospels*, 5. C. H. Talbert ("Political Correctness Invades Jesus Research," *PRS* 21 [1994] 247) agrees: "One can see that the work of the Jesus Seminar is not a dispassionate intellectual enterprise. It is the pursuit of a specific confessional agenda that owes more to *a priori* assumptions than to reasoned scholarly method."

70   Pearson, "The Gospel according to the Jesus Seminar," 334.

confessional stripes. They are not coming solely from scholars of a more conservative historical or theological inclination.

CONCLUSION

This analysis of the Jesus Seminar's treatment of the Parable of the Warring King suggests that the cowboy Christ of the Seminar is a product of a flawed and inconsistently applied methodology. The Fellows of the Seminar have imposed their view of Jesus on the Gospels rather than deriving their view from the Gospels and other pertinent sources. The criteria utilized by the Seminar were slanted in such a way that they tended to preclude material that might have portrayed a Jesus very different from the one they think they have discovered. Despite the flaws in the Seminar's methodology, if it had been applied in the evaluation of the Parable of the Warring King in a manner consistent with its application elsewhere, the authenticity of this parable would have been affirmed. The Seminar is open to the charge that it manipulates the evidence to fit its agenda. Finally, the Seminar has simply ignored significant evidence that supports the authenticity of the Parable of the Warring King.

THE SAYINGS OF JESUS IN THE LETTER OF JAMES

Wesley Hiram Wachob and Luke Timothy Johnson

The task of this essay is to assess the intertexture of several sayings attributed to "James a servant of God and of the Lord Jesus Christ" (Jas 1:1).[1] Put differently, our interest is the apparent use of Jesus' sayings that appear in the Letter of James. Whether its specific rhetorical category finally be called paraenesis or protrepsis, the Letter of James is certainly a form of wisdom literature that appropriates cross-cultural traditions without explanation, apology, or explicit citation. Determining the precise provenance of any specific expression within James is commensurately difficult, since there are usually too many possibilities. The sayings of Jesus themselves present a similar problem: what parts of the gospel tradition can be said to come from Jesus, and what parts from other sources? Asking about the presence of Jesus sayings in the Letter of James is therefore an invitation to a hazardous and necessarily tentative examination.

James offers some small help in the way it makes use of Leviticus 19. The quotation of Lev 19:18 in Jas 2:8 is the letter's only direct and explicit citation of "scripture" (γραφή). Yet other places in James strongly suggest allusions to Lev 19:11-18: sometimes the wording is close, sometimes not. The important methodological point, however, is this: the clear and explicit citation of one passage legitimates the search for others and makes the detection of each incrementally more plausible. Close analysis shows that James' use of Lev 19:11-18 is considerable: Lev 19:12 = Jas 5:12; Lev 19:13 = Jas 5:4; Lev 19:15 = Jas 2:1, 9; Lev 19:16 = Jas 4:11; Lev 19:17b = Jas 5:20; Lev 19:18c = Jas 2:8.[2] Lev 19:11 and 19:14 are not verbally echoed but the substance of their commands is covered by Jas 2:14-

---

[1]   On the intertexture of texts, see esp. V. K. Robbins, *Exploring the Texture of Texts: A Guide to Socio-Rhetorical Interpretation* (Valley Forge: Trinity Press International, 1996) 40-70.

[2]   L. T. Johnson, "The Use of Leviticus 19 in the Letter of James," *JBL* 101 (1982) 391-401.

16 and 3:13-4:10 respectively.[3] A similar procedure will be followed in this essay: the surest candidate for a saying of Jesus within James will receive the greatest attention, for the simple reason that securing it makes the possibility of the presence of other sayings more likely.

For more than two centuries some scholars have held that James uses a tradition of Jesus' sayings in his letter. They base their conclusion on the perception that a number of the sayings attributed to James have a striking affinity to Jesus logia. Further, as M. Dibelius observed,[4] some of these parallels are similar to Jesus logia in form, style, and convictions. Recently, these scattered opinions have been given the fullest possible airing by D. B. Deppe,[5] who studied the twenty-five most frequently mentioned parallels and concluded that at least eight of them are conscious allusions to Jesus' sayings:

(1) Jas 1:5 = Q^M 7:7 = Q^L 11:9 = *GThom* §92, §94
(2) Jas 4:2c-3 = Q^M 7:7 = Q^L 11:9 = *GThom* §92, §94
(3) Jas 2:5 = Q^M 5:3 = Q^L 6:20b = *GThom* §54
(4) Jas 4:9 = Q^M 5:4 = Q^L 6:21b = *GThom* §69b
(5) Jas 4:10 = Q^M 23:12; Q^L 14:11
(6) Jas 5:2-3a = Q^M 6:20 = Q^L 12:33b = *GThom* §76b
(7) Jas 5:12 = Q^M 5:34-37
(8) Jas 5:1 = Q^L 6:24-25

The present essay focuses on only six sayings: four that Deppe calls "conscious allusions" (Jas 5:12; 1:5 and 4:2c-3; 2:5) and two others that are among the twenty-five sayings he mentions, but not (in his view) "conscious allusions" (Jas 2:8 and 13).

JAMES 5:12 = MATTHEW 5:34-37

Apart from Jesus and James, no one else in the Old or New Testament categorically prohibits oaths. Oaths are, in fact, regarded as an acceptable and important part of life in both Testaments (Gen 22:16; Exod 13:5; 22:10-11; Num 14:16; Deut 6:13; 1 Kgs 7:1; 8:31-

---

[3]   L. T. Johnson, *The Letter of James* (AB 37A; Garden City: Doubleday, 1995) 31.

[4]   M. Dibelius and H. Greeven, *James: A Commentary on the Epistle of James* (11th ed., ed. H. Koester; Hermeneia; Philadelphia: Fortress, 1975) 28.

[5]   D. B. Deppe, *The Sayings of Jesus in the Epistle of James* (Dissertation Amsterdam. Chelsea, MI: Bookcrafters, 1989) 219-20, 222-23. See also W. H. Wachob, "The Relationship Between the Epistle of James and Q" (unpublished paper presented to the Southeastern Regional 1988 SBL Meeting, Macon, GA).

32; Jer 12:16; Matt 23:16-22; Luke 1:73; Acts 2:30; Rom 1:9; 2 Cor
1:23; Gal 1:20; Phil 1:8; Heb 6:13-20; Rev 10:6). There is, to be
sure, criticism within Judaism of frequent and flagrant swearing
(Lev 5:20-24; Num 30:3; Deut 23:22; Ps 23:4; Sir 23:9-11; Philo,
Decalogue 84-95; *m. Nedarim*; *m. Šebu.* 4:1). Such critiques are
found elsewhere in the *Umwelt* (e.g. Epictetus, *Enchr.* 33.5). The
aversion to swearing even led some in the ancient world, like the
Pythagoreans, to prohibit oaths (see Diog. Laert. 8.22; Iambl. *Vit.
Pyth.* 47). Such interdictions, however, are based on different ideas
than those grounding Jesus' and James' prohibitions of oaths.[6] And,
while there was a prohibition of oaths among (one branch of) the
Essenes, the evidence is complicated by the fact that the Dead Sea
sect required an entrance oath (see Josephus, *J.W.* 2.8.6 §135; 2.8.7–
8 §139-43; *Ant.* 15.10.4 §370-372; cf. 1QS 5:8; 1QH 14:17; CD
15:5, 8-12; 16:1-5). The distinctiveness of Jesus and James with
regard to oaths, therefore, is striking.[7] A comparison of James'
prohibition of oaths (Jas 5:12) with the one attributed to Jesus in Matt
5:34-37 shows that they have sixteen Greek words in common:

   . . . μὴ ὀμ[ ] . . . μήτε . . . τ[ ] οὐραν[ ] . . . μήτε . . . τ[ ] γ[ ] . . .
   μήτε . . . [ ] τω δὲ . . . ὑμῶν . . . ναὶ ναὶ . . . οὔ οὔ . . .

James' prohibition ("do not swear") features the present imperative
active, second person plural (μὴ ὀμνύετε), while the Matthean
version has the aorist infinitive active (μὴ ὀμόσαι) with the adverb
ὅλως. In Matt 5:34c and 35a the first two μήτε-phrases ("neither by
the heaven . . . nor by the earth") have ἐν, the dative article and
noun, a Semitic usage;[8] the third μήτε-phrase in Matt 5:35c ("nor by
. . .") has εἰς + an anarthrous noun in the accusative case. In Jas
5:12a the first two μήτε—phrases have the accusative article and
noun, which is ordinary classical usage,[9] and the third μήτε—phrase

---

6   Dibelius and Greeven, *James*, 248 n. 41.

7   Concerning the criteria of authenticity, the prohibition of oaths satisfies the
criterion of dissimilarity. If we may regard Jas 5:12 as a Jamesian performance of a
saying of Jesus, then we have multiple attestation, for Matthew and James are most
probably independent sources for this logion. The prohibition also satisfies the
criterion of embarrassment, since both the Old Testament and New Testament
accept and honor the swearing oaths.

8   See BDF §149, §220; N. Turner, *A Grammar of New Testament Greek*,
vol. 3 (Edinburgh: T. & T. Clark, 1963) 252-53.

9   See H. W. Smyth, *Greek Grammar* (Cambridge: Harvard University Press,
1956) §1596.

also features the accusative case: ἄλλον τινὰ ὅρκον. Both Jas 5:12b
and Matt 5:37a have the imperative third person singular of εἰμί,
("but let be"), though the forms are different (ἤτω and ἔστω,
respectively). And where James has τὸ ναὶ . . . καὶ τὸ οὔ . . . ("your
yes . . . and [your] no . . . "), the compound (articular) subject of the
verb, followed by a compound (anarthrous) predicate, ναὶ . . . οὔ
("yes . . . no"), Matt 5:37a has as its subject λόγος ὑμῶν ("your
word"), and an anarthrous, asyndetic and emphatic ναὶ ναὶ, οὔ οὔ
("yes yes, no, no") as the predicate.[10] The fact that there are
grammatical and syntactical variations in these performances is
anything but surprising, since "recitation of a saying using words
different from the authoritative source" was a common practice in
the culture of the Greco-Roman age, including early Christianity.[11]
Besides, the variations here do not hide what the two texts have in
common. In fact the Jamesian performance is overwhelmingly
regarded as the surest example of James' use of the sayings of
Jesus.[12] For example, H. Koester says, "In Jas 5:12 there can be no
doubt that James is quoting the same injunction that Matthew used in
the third [sic!; should read fourth] antithesis of the Sermon on the

---

[10]   The lack of the article in Matt 5:37a does not prevent the statement from
having the same meaning as that of Jas 5:12. Dibelius and Greeven (*James*, 250-
51), as well as H. Koester (*Ancient Christian Gospels: Their History and
Development* [London: SCM Press; Philadelphia: Trinity Press International, 1990]
73-75), suggest (on the basis of *1 Enoch*) that 5:37a should be understood as
providing a milder and acceptable "oath formula" (as opposed to those in 5:34c-36).
But it is better to understand the second yes and no in 5:37a as emphatic. See W. D.
Davies and D. C. Allison, Jr., *A Critical and Exegetical Commentary on the Gospel
according to Saint Matthew* (ICC; Edinburgh: T. & T. Clark, 1988) 538; H. D.
Betz, *The Sermon on the Mount: A Commentary on the Sermon on the Mount,
including the Sermon on the Plain (Matthew 5:3–7:27 and Luke 6:20-49)*
(Hermeneia. Minneapolis: Fortress, 1995) 271. Moreover, that the emphatic "yes,
yes and no, no" is synonymous with simple "yes and no" is corroborated by Paul's
useage in 2 Cor 1:17-18. See P. Minear, "'Yes and No': The Demand for Honesty
in the Early Church," *NovT* 13 (1971) 1-13.

[11]   See Robbins, *Exploring the Texture of Texts*, 42, and 41-48; and idem, *The
Tapestry of Early Christian Discourse: Rhetoric, Society and Ideology* (London and
New York: Routledge, 1996) 96-143.

[12]   Of the sixty authors listed by Deppe (*The Sayings of Jesus in the Epistle of
James*, 141 n. 500), fifty-nine of them include Jas 5:12. K. A. Credner (*Einleitung
in das Neue Testament* [Halle: Waisenhauses, 1836]), the only exception,
accidentally omitted it, according to Deppe.

Mount. James has preserved an earlier form."[13]

The Matthean performance of Jesus' prohibition of oaths occurs as part of a (so-called[14]) antithesis, which, within the SM, is a rhetorical argument that supports the thesis that Jesus has come "not to abolish the law and the prophets, but to fulfill them" (Matt 5:17).[15] The argument may be outlined as follows:

A testimony of the ancients based on the law:	Do not swear falsely (5:33).
A contrary judgment by Jesus based on the law:	Do not swear at all (5:34b);
Three parallel examples:	by heaven, by earth, by Jerusalem (5:34c, 35a, 35c);
Reason (in three parallel statements):	heaven, earth, Jerusalem belong to God (5:34d, 35b, 35d).
A fourth example:	Do not swear by your head (5:36a);
Reason:	you cannot even make one hair black or white (5:36b).
A judgment by Jesus based on the law:	Let your yes be yes, and your no, no (5:37a);
Reason:	anything more is evil (5:37b).[16]

The antithetical character of Jesus' prohibition of oaths in Matthew

---

13   Koester, *Ancient Christian Gospels*, 74.

14   Although Matt 5:21-48 is usually referred to as "the antitheses," this is, as E. P. Sanders (*The Historical Figure of Jesus* [London: The Penguin Press, 1993] 201) argues, an inaccurate designation. Antithesis in form does not necessarily mean opposition in content. "This section of Matthew has often been cited as showing Jesus' 'opposition' to the law. But heightening the law is not opposing it, though (as we just saw [pp. 210-11]) it implies a kind of criticism. If intensification were against the law, then the main groups of Judaism, the Pharisees and the Essenes, were systematic breakers of the law. But in fact no ancient Jew thought that being super-strict was illegal, nor did the author of Matthew" (p. 212).

15   G. A. Kennedy, *New Testament Interpretation Through Rhetorical Criticism* (Chapel Hill and London: University of North Carolina Press, 1984) 42. Of the six so-called antitheses in the Sermon on the Mount (= SM), the fourth (Matt 5:33-37) begins a second set of three antitheses. See the analyses and discussions in Betz (*Sermon on the Mount*, 259-74), Davies and Allison (*Matthew*, 533-38), and U. Luz (*Matthew 1–7* [Minneapolis: Augsburg, 1989] 310-22).

16   B. L. Mack, *Rhetoric in the New Testament* (Guides to Biblical Scholarship; Minneapolis: Fortress, 1990) 83.

is due to its juxtaposition to an authoritative judgment based on the law "by the men of old" (Matt 5:33). The latter judgment is not a quotation of the law; rather, it appears to be "a Hellenistic-Jewish halakah"[17] or summary based on the law (esp. Lev 19:12; cf. Exod 20:7; Num 30:3-15; Deut 23:21-3). Its probable meaning is, "You have heard that it was said to the men of old: 'All your oaths are to be true.'"[18] To this judgment Jesus authoritatively responds with a different, intensifying judgment, But I say to you, 'do not swear at all, (Matt 5:34a). Jesus' judgment is also based on the law and is not contradictory to it: the person who does not swear obviously would not transgress the law which forbids swearing falsely.[19]

James' instruction occurs at the beginning of a section of the letter that has an undeniably pragmatic and linear relation to earlier advice concerning speech, but does so with specific emphasis on speech acts within the ἐκκλησία (5:14). In James, as in the SM, the judgment about oaths seeks to persuade its addressees to refrain from an action (the swearing of oaths) and to perform an action (speaking frankly, truthfully) in the immediate future.

Jesus' prohibition of oaths is amplified and illustrated by four μήτε—sentences, each of which features a ὅτι-clause as its rationale or basis. The first three sentences (5:34c-35) are parallel and symmetrical; the fourth (5:36) breaks the pattern and flow of the previous three. As illustrations of the tendency to avoid using God's name in swearing, however, they are all examples of the effort to reduce the binding character of oaths, accentuating Jesus' conviction that all oaths are equally serious (cf. Matt 23:16-22).[20]

The formal similarity of the threefold repetition μὴ . . . μήτε . . .

---

17   Betz, *Sermon on the Mount*, 264.

18   Davies and Allison, *Matthew*, 534. It appears that the halakah in 5:33 is closest to Lev 19:12 (but cf. Ps.-Phocylides, *Sent.* 16), where not fulfilling oaths sworn in the name of God is a grievous act of perjury. The amplifications support this by arguing that all oaths used in place of the Holy Name are nevertheless binding (Davies and Allison, *Matthew*, 536; E. P. Sanders, *Jewish Law from Jesus to the Mishnah: Five Studies* [London: SCM Press; Philadelphia: Trinity Press International, 1990] 53).

19   Sanders, *Jewish Law*, 55. He further says, "The position that oaths should not be taken at all implicitly criticizes the law, however, for catering to human weakness" (p. 55; see esp. 51-57).

20   Davies and Allison, *Matthew*, 536; Sanders, *Jewish Law*, 55; and esp. Betz, *Sermon on the Mount*, 266-70.

μήτε . . . μήτε in Jas 5:12a and μὴ . . . μήτε . . . μήτε . . . μήτε . . . μήτε in Matt 5:34-36 is impressive. The formal similarity is only strengthened by the fact that the fourth μήτε clause in Matt 5:36, which is so markedly different from the three in Matt 5:34c-35, is probably a secondary addition. Nor should it be overlooked that the meaning of James' third and climactic μήτε ἄλλον τινα ὅρκον ("nor any other sort of oath") corresponds to the qualification of μὴ ὀμόσαι by ὅλως ("at all") in Matt 5:34.[21]

The similarity of form and content in these two performances is undeniable and raises the question of the relationship of James and Matthew. Most scholars correctly agree that neither James nor Matthew knows the other,[22] so the question of a common source presents itself, along with the issue of which performance, James' or Matthew's, has priority.

Our analysis suggests that Matt 5:36 is most probably a secondary element; furthermore, the three μήτε—clauses in James are the better, smoother performance: in Matt 5:34b the adverb ὅλως makes the subsequent explanations redundant, while James' placement of the limiting phrase, "any other sort of oath," is a rather logical extension and intensification of the prohibition. Matthew's "by Jerusalem" is also probably redactional, though it is uncertain whether the redaction is pre-Matthean (SM) or Matthean.[23] The final clauses in both texts (Matt 5:37b and Jas 5:12b) are most likely redactional statements, as well. In short, although we cannot always argue that the briefer version is the more original, the specific elements of Matthew's longer version support the conclusion that his redactional interests are at work, and that the form of Jas 5:12b may be closer to Jesus' original saying.

With regard to the last point, Justin Martyr's performance of this prohibition is crucial (*1 Apol.* 1.16.5). Like the one in Matthew, it is contextually attributed to Jesus; it reads: "Do not swear at all (μὴ ὀμόσητε ὅλως), but let your yes be yes and your no be no (ἔστω δὲ

---

21   A. H. McNeile, *The Gospel according to St. Matthew* (London: Macmillan, 1915) 67; Johnson, *James*, 328.

22   Pace M. H. Shepherd, "The Epistle of James and the Gospel of Matthew," *JBL* 75 (1956) 40-51.

23   The tension between the categorical prohibition of oaths in the pre-Matthean SM (Matt 5:34-37) and Matt 23:16-22 makes it possible that the understanding of oaths in the SM is not that of the final redactor of Matthew (see Deppe, *Sayings of Jesus*, 137; Betz, *Sermon on the Mount*, 213-14).

ὑμῶν τὸ ναὶ ναὶ καὶ τὸ οὒ οὔ); anything more than this is from evil
(τὸ δὲ περισσὸν τούτων ἐκ τοῦ πονηροῦ). The first and last of these
three clauses are virtually identical to Matt 5:34b and 37b; the only
differences are the form of the verb in the first clause and the ellipsis
of the verb in the last. The second clause, however, is identical to Jas
5:12b, except for the verb ἔστω (which agrees with Matthew). One
may argue that Justin's performance is a harmonization of the
performances of Matthew and James.[24] On the other hand, one can
argue that while Justin clearly depends on Matthew, his agreement
with James in the second clause is due to the fact that the Jamesian
form is broadly and independently known; indeed, it is the Jamesian
form of this clause that is replicated throughout early Christianity,
even in texts that are presumably quoting Matt 5:37a.[25]

Since Luke does not share this material with Matthew, most
scholars do not include the prohibition in Q. This simply shows the
limits of our knowledge of Q: Luke could have chosen not to include
it, if he and Matthew read a shared version; alternatively, Matthew
and Luke could have had different versions of Q, with Q-Matthew
containing the prohibition. H. D. Betz's hypothesis that both the SM
and the SP were pre-synoptic sources suggests that the SM is the
primary source for Jesus' prohibition of oaths. Perhaps the antithesis
before us appeared in both Q-Matthew and in the SM.[26] James, on
the other hand, does not appear to be dependent either upon Q or the
written Gospels.[27] Nevertheless, it is quite possible—perhaps
probable—that James was familiar with a collection of sayings in
which Jesus categorically prohibited oaths. In other words, James
was familiar with a collection of Jesus logia similar to those in the
pre-Matthean SM and/or Q-Matthew.

Our analysis supports the hypothesis that most probably Jas 5:12 is
an independent source for the prohibition of oaths attributed to Jesus
in Matt 5:34-37, and that—in agreement with Koester—the saying in

---

[24]   A. J. Bellinzoni, *The Sayings of Jesus in the Writings of Justin Martyr*
(Leiden: Brill, 1967) 65.

[25]   D. C. Duling, "Against Oaths: Crossan Sayings Parallels 59," *Forum* 6.2
(1990) 99-138, here 133.

[26]   Betz, *Sermon on the Mount*, esp. 42-88. "The conclusion is most likely,"
says Betz, "that Matthew as well as Luke found the SM and the SP, respectively in
their recension of Q (Q^{Matt} and Q^{Luke})" (p. 44).

[27]   W. D. Davies, *The Setting of the Sermon on the Mount* (Cambridge: Cambridge University Press, 1964) 403-404.

James reflects an earlier stage of the tradition than the one in the Matthean SM.[28] The high probability that James in 5:12 recontextualizes without attribution a saying of Jesus also increases the probability that other, less obvious, echoes might have the same source.

JAMES 1:5, 4:2c-3 = Q[M] 7:7, 11 = Q[L] 11:9, 13 = *GTHOM* §92, §94

Jas 1:5 Εἰ δέ τις ὑμῶν λείπεται σοφίας, αἰτείτω παρὰ τοῦ διδόντος θεοῦ πᾶσιν ἁπλῶς καὶ μὴ ὀνειδίζοντος καὶ δοθήσεται αὐτῷ. Jas 4:2-3 οὐκ ἔχετε διὰ τὸ μὴ αἰτεῖσθε ὑμᾶς, αἰτεῖτε καί οὐ λαμβάνετε διότι κακῶς αἰτεῖσθε, ἵνα ἐν ταῖς ἡδοναῖς ὑμῶν δαπανήσατε.

Both Jas 1:5 and 4:2c-3 have a parallel in Matt 7:7, 11 = Luke 11:9, 13. The latter verses are the beginning and ending statements in pericopae (Matt 7:7-11 = Luke 11:9-13) which concern prayer. While some scholars argue for a complex tradition-history behind these synoptic texts,[29] others hold, with better reason, that they defy a history of traditions analysis and conclude that they are unified sections.[30]

In Matthew and Luke, respectively, a three-part exhortation (Matt 7:7 = Luke 11:9) is followed by a three-part rationale (Matt 7:8 = Luke 11:10) which is confirmed by two examples, both of which are arguments from analogy (Matt 7:9-10 = Luke 11:11-12) and warrant the inferred conclusion (Matt 7:11 = Luke 11:13). Moreover, five occurrences of αἰτέω and six formations from δίδωμι—weld the individual parts into unified elaborations.[31]

Shared by Matthew and Luke and almost identical in wording, these elaborations are, according to most scholars, derived from the common source Q.[32] On the other hand, the differences in the wording and order of Matt 7:9-10 (bread/stone and fish/snake) and Luke 11:11-12 (egg/scorpion and snake/fish), are significant and

---

[28]   Koester, *Ancient Christian Gospels*, 74-75.

[29]   J. D. Crossan, *In Fragments: The Aphorisms of Jesus* (San Francisco: Harper & Row, 1983) 95-104.

[30]   Luz, *Matthew 1–7* , 420-25; Davies and Allison, *Matthew*, 677-85. The best and most complete discussion is in Betz, *Sermon on the Mount*, 501-508.

[31]   On "elaboration," see Mack, *Rhetoric in the New Testament*, 31-49, 81-85; and esp. Robbins, *Exploring the Texture of Texts*, 40, 52-59.

[32]   J. S. Kloppenborg, *Q Parallels: Synopsis, Critical Notes and Concordance* (Sonoma: Polebridge, 1988) 86-89.

difficult to explain as either evangelist's redaction. Consequently, a growing number of scholars argue that Matthew and Luke had different recensions of Q and/or other sources.[33] This position is further strengthened by the fact that the pericopae have different contexts and functions in Matthew and Luke. The Lukan pericope fits easily within a large instruction on prayer which begins with the Lord's Prayer (Luke 11:1-13). In contrast, the Matthean pericope, which is part of the SM, seems, at first glance, only loosely connected to its surroundings. Certainly it makes a complete argument for praying confidently, but the function of Matthew's elaboration is less an instruction on prayer than an argument using prayer to emphasize God's generosity. In other words, the primary function of the prayer elaboration in Matt 7:7-11 is to argue that the children of the Father in Heaven should generously give to others (cf. 7:12).[34]

A clue to the secondary emphasis on prayer in Matt 7:7-11 may be reflected in the partial parallels to Matt 7:7 found in the *GThom* §92 and §94 (the latter has a partial parallel in Matt 7:8; and with *GThom* §93; cf. Matt 7:6). These parallels have been overlaid with gnostic emphases and are unrelated to prayer. Likewise, the partial parallels in The Gospel of the Hebrews and in POxy 654 §1 (which is similar to *GThom* §2), while attesting to the widespread popularity of the saying in view, are not necessarily related to prayer and are but faint reminisces of the elaboration in Matt 7:7-11. The history of tradition is opaque.[35]

---

[33]   See I. H. Marshall, *Commentary on Luke* (Grand Rapids: Eerdmans, 1978) 466; Davies and Allison, *Matthew*, 681; G. Strecker, *The Sermon on the Mount* (Abingdon: Nashville, 1988) 11-13; Luz, *Matthew 1–7*, 46-49; and Betz, *Sermon on the Mount*, esp. 42-44.

[34]   See esp. Betz, *Sermon on the Mount*, 423-28, 500-508. The Golden Rule (Matt 7:12), which epitomizes "the law and the prophets," not only supports this assessment of Matt 7:7-11 but, as Betz argues (see esp. *Sermon on the Mount*, 508-19), is (1) also the hermeneutical key for understanding the third section of the SM (Matt 6:19-7:11), and (2) a framing device that, with Matt 5:17- 18, interpreted the Law in terms of fulfilling the love command. In Jas 2:1-13 we are in the same milieu as the SM, for "those who love God" (Jas 2:5) are those who obey the Torah (Jas 2:10 = "the royal law," Jas 2:8) which, summarized in the the the love-command (Jas 2:8; cf. Lev 19:18), coheres with the "faith of Jesus [himself]" (Jas 2:1). See below in the remarks on the parallel between Jas 2:5 and Matt 5:3 = Luke 6:20b.

[35]   Whether the *Gospel of Thomas* depended on Matthew or on presynoptic tradition is uncertain; cf. also John 14:13-14; 15:7; and 16:24 (see Betz, *Sermon on*

In Matt 7:7-11 = Luke 11:9-13 it is only in the final statements (Matt 7:11 = Luke 11:13) that "asking and receiving" ("seeking" and "knocking") are clearly related to prayer. Nonetheless, even if the prayer-connection here is due to secondary interpretation, there is nothing in the history of tradition that violates the integrity of these synoptic sections. In other words, already in the sources used by the evangelists these pericopae were unified wholes. It is certainly conceivable that the original elaboration goes back to Jesus.[36]

Against this background, let us look at Jas 1:5 and 4:2c-3. Both concern prayer and share the pertinent lexical terms: αἰτείτω . . . καὶ δοθήσεται (Jas 1:5) and αἰτεῖτε καί . . . λαμβάνετε (Jas 4:3; cf. Matt 7:8 = Luke 11:10).[37] Additionally, in Jas 1:5 the reference to God as "the God who gives to all liberally and does not upbraid," though clearly different from Matthew's ("our Father, the one in the heavens, [who] will give good things to those who ask him") and Luke's ("the Father, the one from heaven [who] will give the Holy Spirit to those who ask him"), is a linguistic performance that captures the essence of the emphasis on God's generosity in the Jesus logion. Thus, it appears that in Jas 1:5 the author has recited, in his own words, the essence of both the fundamental exhortation (Matt 7:7 = Luke 13:9) and the fundamental conclusion (Matt 7:11 = Luke 13:13) of the saying of Jesus in Matt 7:7-11 = Luke 13:9-13).

Most scholars hold, with good reason, that the Matthean perform-ance, with its reference to "good things," is more original than Luke's reference to the "Holy Spirit." This is extremely significant in light of the connections that James makes between the "wisdom from above" (4:17), which is one of the good and perfect gift(s) which come down from God the Father (1:17, 27; 3:9). Indeed, it is because God the Father is a generous giver of "good things" that one is exhorted in Jas 1:5 to pray with confidence for "wisdom." The pragmatic relations between James' sayings reveal a network of presuppositions that resonate with the saying of Jesus in Matt 7:7-11 = Luke 11:9-13. There is more than enough to suggest that Jas 1:5 is

---

the *Mount*, 426, 503-504; Marshall, *Luke*, 466; Davies and Allison, *Matthew*, 674-75, 678-80, 682.

[36]   Luz, *Matthew 1–7*, 421; also Funk and Hoover (eds.), *The Five Gospels*, 155.

[37]   In Jas 1:5 αἰτέω occurs once; δίδωμι twice. In Jas 4:2c-3 αἰτέω occurs three times; δίδωμι does not occur but its synonym λαμβάνω occurs once. See Philo, *Migr. Abr.* 121.

a Jamesian recitation of a saying attributed to Jesus. Moreover, it appears that Jas 1:5 is closer to the pre-Matthean saying in Matt 7:7, 11.

The lexical terms and the prayer theme in Jas 4:2c-3 recall the language of Jesus in Matt 7:8 = Luke 11:10. On the other hand, some have argued that here James is not using a saying of Jesus. Apart from its lack of attribution to Jesus, the argument against Jas 4:2c-3 is basically this: James, here, is dealing with unanswered prayer (he juxtaposes an unqualified form in 4:2 with a qualified form in 4:3); the format of Jas 4:3 is negative (while the format of Matt 7:8 = Luke 11:10 is positive); and there are grammatical variations in the texts (James has the indicative, rather than imperative, mood, and he shifts voices: middle to active to middle, in 4:2c-3). None of these arguments is persuasive. James here seems to use the active and middle voices interchangeably (see 1 John 5:14-16 and cf. 1 John 3:22); neither the differences in the grammar of Jas 4:2c-3, nor the negative format of Jas 4:3 can disqualify this as a Jamesian recitation of the Jesus logion in Matt 7:8 = Luke 11:10. Moreover, the unity, coherence, and emphasis in Jas 4:2c-3 coheres with the integrity of its grammar, form, and content.

JAMES 2:5 = Q^M 5:3 = Q^L 6:20B = *GTHOM* §54

James 2:5 is one of James' most important parallels to a Jesus logion. It has a strategic function within Jas 2:1-13, which is a well-defined and complete elaboration of the theme introduced in Jas 2:1; namely, that "the faith of our Lord Jesus Christ" is incompatible with acts of partiality.[38] From a rhetorical perspective, it appears that James has adapted a Jesus-beatitude (Matt 5:3 = Luke 6:20b) and partially recited it for his own persuasive purposes.

Besides Jas 2:5, there are four other performances of the saying in question. These are Matt 5:3; Luke 6:20b; *GThom* §54; and Polycarp, *Phil.* 3:2. All five performances share two key terms: "the poor" and "the kingdom." Moreover, all five performances exploit the common terms to produce sentences that feature one common denominator— "God's kingdom is promised to the poor." Apart from this, however,

---

38   W. H. Wachob, *"The Rich in Faith" and "The Poor in Spirit": The Socio-Rhetorical Function of a Saying of Jesus in the Epistle of James* (doctoral dissertation; Atlanta: Emory University, 1993; forthcoming in SNTSMS; Cambridge: Cambridge University Press); Johnson, *James*, 56.

Jas 2:5 is observably different from its four parallels in attribution, form, content, style, and function. For example, the parallels to Jas 2:5 are beatitudes, specifically attributed to Jesus. In addition, they are also enthymemes, rhetorical syllogisms: each consists of a conclusion (a macarism) and a premise (a ὅτι clause), with, as is typical of enthymemes, one premise unstated and tacitly assumed. Because of these differences, and because it emphasizes God's concern for the poor, some scholars separate Jas 2:5 from its context and conclude that it simply states a "principle of the traditional piety of the poor."[39]

There is no doubt that both the OT and Jewish literature reflect the notion that God has a special concern for the poor, and Jas 2:5 clearly evokes "the traditional piety of the poor."[40] On the other hand, as Deppe reminds us, "there are no references in the OT, intertestamental literature, or the Talmud specifically saying that God is giving the kingdom to the poor."[41] This fact alone warrants the conclusion that the most likely source for Jas 2:5 is not the traditional piety of the poor but the teaching of Jesus.

Strong support for this conclusion is found in the following facts. First, the term kingdom appears only here in James, although significantly, βασιλικός occurs immediately in 2:8. Second, this term, which is so distinctive in the language of Jesus, appears in a statement about God that is marked by, subsumed under, and intimately connected to Jesus' own faith (Jas 2:1).[42] Third, previous

---

[39] Koester, *Ancient Christian Gospels*, 74.

[40] H. D. Betz (*Essays on the Sermon on the Mount* [Philadelphia: Fortress, 1985] 34) rightly asserts that Q^M 5:3 also "derives from the Jewish 'piety of the poor.'" See L. T. Johnson, *Sharing Possessions: Mandate and Symbol of Faith* (OBT 9; Philadelphia: Fortress, 1981) 79-116.

[41] Deppe, *Sayings of Jesus*, 90. He further says (*Sayings of Jesus*, 90-91): "The decisive clue for the presence of a saying of Jesus lies in the fact that the word 'kingdom' is not Jamesian vocabulary; Jas 2:5 is the only occurrence of this term in the epistle. Certainly the employment of a term particularly associated with the preaching of Jesus is evidence that James is alluding to the same saying quoted in Matt 5:3 and Luke 6:20. This is confirmed by the fact that even critical exegetes like Dibelius and Laws admit the probablity that Jas is consciously referring to a logion previously spoken by Jesus." He refers to Dibelius and Greeven (*James*, 132) and S. Laws (*The Epistle of James* [HNTC; San Francisco: Harper & Row, 1980] 103-104).

[42] For the suggestion that the reference to Jesus' faith in 2:1 functions as a "global allusion" that evokes the whole of what our author perceives Jesus to have

research has shown that the historical example in Jas 2:5 achieves its rhetorical meaning and function by recalling Jesus' own faith as the measure for the elect community's faith.[43] Fourth, the introduction of historical example in Jas 2:5 ("Has not God promised . . . ?") presupposes that, like Jesus' faith which it recalls, it is already known to James' addressees. In sum, looking at the letter of James as a protreptic wisdom discourse, we find that the first and fundamental supporting proof (Jas 2:5) of the argumentative unit in Jas 2:1-13 is a statement—about God's action with reference to "the poor"—which recalls Jesus' own faith (Jas 2:1) in language that resonates with the texture of a well-known wisdom saying of Jesus in which the poor are promised God's kingdom.[44]

A closer look at the intertextual relations of these five perform-ances only increases the probability that Jas 2:5 is a recitation of a Jesus-beatitude. Recent Q-studies claim that Matt 5:3 = Luke 6:20b belonged to the formative stage in the development of the Synoptic Sayings Source.[45] Supposedly, this stratum of Q was comprised mainly of wisdom sayings, some of which are also found in the *Gospel of Thomas*. Among the latter is *GThom* §54.[46] The source of

---

believed, said, and done, see Wachob (*"The Rich in Faith" and "The Poor in Spirit"*, 263). For the term "global allusion," see R. Alter, *The Pleasures of Reading in an Ideological Age* (New York: Simon & Schuster, 1989) 124.

43   Wachob, *"The Rich in Faith" and "The Poor in Spirit"*, 134-243.

44   Wachob, *"The Rich in Faith" and "The Poor in Spirit"*, 244-329. Because the entire letter presupposes a unity of purpose and action for God and the Lord Jesus Christ (cf. 1:1), this argument presumes a congruence between the faith of the Lord Jesus Christ and God's choice of the poor to inherit the kingdom, and supports the thesis that Jesus' faith and acts of partiality are contrary and incompatible to each other (p. 188).

45   See J. S. Kloppenborg, *The Formation of Q: Trajectories in Ancient Wisdom Collection* (SAC; Philadelphia: Fortress, 1987) 171-73, 174-245. The sayings in this stratum (Q 6:20b-49; 9:57-62 + 10:2-16, 21-24; 11:2-4, 9-13; 12:2-12; 12:22-34; 13:24-30) comprise "clusters or 'speeches'" that are governed by "sapiential themes and devices" and "are directed at the Q community in support of its radical mode of existence." Thus, Kloppenborg classifies Q 6:20b as a "wisdom saying"; on the other hand, Koester (*Ancient Christian Gospels*, 136-38; esp. 149-71) classifies it as a "prophetic saying." The reader notes that such research presup-poses that Q went through several redactional stages; see Kloppenborg (pp. 89-262, 317-28) and Koester (pp. 133-71).

46   Koester (*Ancient Christian Gospels*, 87) finds that forty-six of the seventy-nine sayings shared by the *Gospel of Thomas* and the Synoptic Gospels are Q

this wisdom saying, however, seems not to have been Q itself but most likely a cluster of sayings that also belonged to Q. Both Paul and the author of *1 Clement* (chap. 13) appear to have known this cluster of sayings.[47] This is significant, because Polycarp, *Phil.* 2:3 also suggests an intertextual relation to *1 Clem.* 13:2, (and probably also to the Gospels of Matthew and Luke).[48] If these scholarly hypotheses regarding the development of the Jesus tradition are correct, then the Jesus logion alluded to in Jas 2:5 is an early, widely known and exploited saying of Jesus.

Recent research on the intertexture of Jas 2:5 has shown that there is a difference in the perspectives respectively of Q^L 6:20b, *GThom* §54, and Polycarp, *Phil.* 2:3, and of Q^M 5:3 and Jas 2:5.[49] While all of the latter, except Jas 2:5, are enthymemes, and therefore logical arguments, the reasoning within Q^L 6:20b, *GThom* §54, and Polycarp, *Phil.* 2:3 is different from that in Q^M 5:3. And while all five performances, except (perhaps) *GThom* §54, are dependent upon their respective contexts for their meaning and function, Q^M 5:3 and Jas 2:5 have different rhetorical and theological functions than do Q^L 6:20b, *GThom* §54, and Polycarp, *Phil.* 2:3.[50]

For example, the similar performances of Q^L 6:20b and *GThom* §54 pronounce blessings on people in an ascribed state of socio-economic poverty. In other words, what Koester says of Luke 6:20b, namely, that it "blesses the situation in which those to whom Jesus'

---

sayings (see his list and discussion, pp. 86-95).

[47]   Koester, *Ancient Christian Gospels*, 137.

[48]   Koester, *Ancient Christian Gospels*, 19-20; also idem, *Synoptische Über-lieferung bei den apostolischen Vätern* (TU 65; Berlin: Akademie, 1957) 114-20. Also see W. R. Schoedel, *Polycarp, Martyrdom of Polycarp, Fragments of Papias* (The Apostolic Fathers 5; London: Nelson, 1967) 12.

[49]   According to Wachob, *"The Rich in Faith" and "The Poor in Spirit"*, 326-27 n. 162: "Q^{Matt} 5:3 and Jas 2:5, as the sayings of Jesus and James, respectively, recall the traditional Jewish piety of the poor. Though in different ways, both sayings address 'the Poor of God,' that is, those who in their actions love God by obeying God's law. In neither of the latter are the socially and economically impoverished promised the kingdom on the basis of their situation (as they are in Q^{Luke} 6:20b and *Gos. Thom.* 54). In Q^{Matt} 5:3 and Jas 2:5 the kingdom is the incentive, the reward, of those whose actions conform to the law of God (as it is not in Q^{Luke} 6:20b, *Gos. Thom.* 53, and Pol. Phil. 2:3)."

[50]   For a complete discussion of Polycarp, *Phil.* 2:3, see Wachob, *"The Rich in Faith" and "The Poor in Spirit"*, 317-19.

message comes happen to be,"[51] is also true of *GThom* §54.[52] But this is not the case in Q[M] 5:3 and Jas 2:5—in neither of these sayings are the socially and economically impoverished promised God's kingdom on the basis of their situation. On the contrary, both Q[M] 5:3 and Jas 2:5 argue that the kingdom is the incentive, the reward, of those whose actions conform to the Torah as interpreted by Jesus and summarized in the love command.[53] In their respective contexts, "the poor in spirit" (Q[M] 5:3) and "the rich in faith" (Jas 2:5) designate people (not of an ascribed status but) of an achieved status. Both of these sayings recall the traditional piety of the poor; and each saying, in its own manner, addresses "the Poor of God." James, in particular, plays on the fact that his addressees are for the most part socio-economically impoverished ("the poor before the world"), but Jas 2:5 manipulates their ascribed status from the perspective of the Jewish piety of the poor. In no sense does James suggest that the God's kingdom belongs to the socio-economically poor as a reward for their earthly poverty. The poor are chosen by God, for God, that they might be rich now in obedience to God and therefore receive the promised reward, God's kingdom. In Jas 2:5, "rich in faith" is synonymous with "loving God," and both are functionally equivalent to fulfilling the Torah of God, summarized in the love command.

Deppe[54] reminds us of Spitta's assertion "that if one could somehow show Jas 2:5 to be dependent upon a logion of Jesus, then one could legitimately be convinced that James throughout his epistle alludes to Jesus' sayings."[55] This has been done.[56] It is beyond dispute that in Jas 2:5 the author of James is reciting a saying of Jesus very much like that in Q[M] 5:3, so that "the poor in spirit" of Q[M] 5:3 are "the rich in faith" of Jas 2:5.

JAMES 2:8 AND MATTHEW 22:39; MARK 12:31; LUKE 10:27

James 2:8-11 is a four-part argument based on the written law; the argument is adduced as a judgment, an authoritative witness, that

---

[51]   Koester, *Ancient Christian Gospels*, 156.

[52]   Wachob, *"The Rich in Faith" and "The Poor in Spirit"*, 315-17.

[53]   Betz, *Essays on the Sermon on the Mount*, 34; and Wachob, *"The Rich in Faith" and "The Poor in Spirit"*, 325-29.

[54]   Deppe, *Sayings of Jesus*, 90.

[55]   F. Spitta, "Der Brief des Jakobusbrief," in *Zur Geschichte und Literatur des Urchristentums*, vol. 2 (Göttingen: Vandenhoeck & Ruprecht, 1896) 164.

[56]   Wachob, *"The Rich in Faith" and "The Poor in Spirit"*.

supports the theme introduced in Jas 2:1. In Jas 2:8 the author clearly activates an antecedent text from the LXX, exploiting seven of the twenty-four words in Lev 19:18. Actually, Jas 2:8 is but the third clause in (the four clauses of) Lev 19:18. James marks it with a citation formula as an authoritative text (γραφή), and recites it verbatim. Technically, Jas 2:8 is an "abbreviation" (συστέλλειν) of Lev 19:18; and the Jamesian performance of the love-commandment is properly a rhetorical "recitation" (ἀπαγγελία) of an ancient authority.[57]

Is James aware of the prominence of the love-commandment in the teaching of Jesus?[58] In support of the argument that James is not only citing Lev 19:18 but also alluding to a logion of Jesus is the fact that Jas 2:8 has an unmistakable rhetorical connection to the mention of "Jesus faith" in Jas 2:1; this is a strong indication that—as those who "hold the faith Jesus"—both James and his addressees are aware of Jesus' use of the love-commandment. Moreover, Betz is certainly correct in saying that "early Christianity was historically united on the fact that Jesus taught the fulfillment of the Torah in the love-commandment."[59] The parallels to Jas 2:8 in Matt 22:39; Mark 12:31; and Luke 10:27 bear this out. On the other side, however, the abundance of Jewish and Christian sources that corroborate the use of Lev 19:18 as a summary of the whole law (e.g. Hillel in *b. Šabb.* 31a; R. Aqiba in *Gen. Rab.* 24.7 [on Gen 5:1][60]; and also Matt 5:43; 19:19; Mark 12:31 = Matt 22:39 = Luke 10:27; Rom 13:9; Gal 5:14; *Did.* 1:2; *Barn.* 19:5)[61] makes the argument that James was specifically alluding to logion of Jesus more difficult to sustain.

---

57 Theon, *Progymnasmata* (ed. C. Walz; Rhetores Graeci 1; Stuttgart: Cottae, 1832) 139-42; J. R. Butts, *The Progymnasmata of Theon: A New Text with Translation and Commentary* (doctoral dissertation; Claremont: Claremont Graduate School, 1987) 204-205.

58 On James' use of Leviticus 19, see esp. Johnson, "The Use of Leviticus 19," 391-401; and for a rhetorical analysis of language in Leviticus 19 and the love commandment intertext of Jas 2:8, see Wachob, *"The Rich in Faith" and "The Poor in Spirit"*, 253-60.

59 Betz, *Essays on the Sermon on the Mount*, 37; also Davies, *Setting of the Sermon on the Mount*, 405-13.

60 See H. L. Strack, and P. Billerbeck, *Kommentar zum Neuen Testament aus Talmud und Midrasch* (5 vols., Munich: Beck, 1965) 1.356-58.

61 Cited in H. D. Betz, *Galatians: A Commentary on Paul's Letter to the Churches in Galatia* (Hermeneia; Philadelphia: Fortress, 1979) 276 n. 34.

Nevertheless, it can be asserted that in the context of a wisdom discourse that is addressed to Christian Jews (1:1) and pointedly embraces "the faith of our glorious Lord Jesus Christ," it is hard to imagine that judgments connecting the poor, the promised kingdom, the royal law, and the love-commandment could have been heard without thinking of Jesus' words and deeds.

JAMES 2:13 = Q^M 5:7 = Q^L 6:36

The problem of determining whether this aphorism is reliant on a Jesus logion is even more severe. All commentators agree that the conception expressed in this verse is conventional in Jewish thought and literature from the prophets to the rabbis (Sir 29:1; *T. Zeb.* 5:1; cf. Tob 4:10-11).[62] For example, J. H. Ropes notes that its perform-ance in "Jer. Baba q. viii, 10, 'Every time that thou art merciful, God will be merciful to thee; and if thou art not merciful, God will not show mercy to thee,'" is very close to the performance in Jas 2:13.[63] Betz correctly sums up the evidence: "for all branches of Judaism the exercise of mercy was one of the preeminent religious and social duties. This duty was based on the belief that God is a God of mercy. Early Christian theology continued this tradition in a variety of ways."[64]

The criterion of dissimilarity would also apparently rule out Q^M 5:7 = Q^L 6:36 as a saying of Jesus, given its conventional character both within Judaism and early Christianity (*1 Clem.* 13:1-2). Simi-larly, with respect to Jas 2:13, the well-worn argument and widely accepted view is that James draws on Jewish tradition rather than a Jesus saying. The Jamesian performance certainly reflects thinking similar to the thought emanating from the pre-Matthean SM.[65]

---

62   Cited in Dibelius, *James*, 147-48.

63   J. H. Ropes, *A Critical and Exegetical Commentary on the Epistle of St. James* (ICC; Edinburgh: T. & T. Clark, 1916) 201.

64   Betz, *Sermon on the Mount*, 133, see esp. nn. 313-15.

65   Betz (*Essays on the Sermon of the Mount*) has argued that the SM derives from a Jewish-Christian group in which law and gospel are strongly intertwined (p. 35). "In the SM, Jesus is regarded as the authoritative teacher and interpreter of the Jewish Torah" (p. 91). "According to the SM, Jesus' authority depends upon that of the Torah, though naturally in accordance with his particular interpretation" of it (p. 92). "The Torah taught by Jesus is nothing less than the way revealed by God which corresponds to his kingdom and which leads one into it ([Matt] 7:13-14)" (p. 95). Moreover, as Koester (*Ancient Christian Gospels*, 171) has correctly

Jesus may well have said something like the sayings attributed to him in Q^M 5:7 = Q^L 6:36.[66] Converging lines of evidence (multiple attestation) and the argument from coherence—both of which are more important than the criterion of dissimilarity—based on, for example, the parable of the good Samaritan (Luke 10:30-37) and the command to love one's enemies Q^M 5:44 = Q^L 6:27) certainly support that possibility. The saying coheres with numerous other texts in the tradition which indicate that Jesus' interpretation of the law emphasized justice and mercy. But the road from possibility to probability is a long one, and cannot be traveled for Jas 2:13 with the available evidence.

In this analysis, we have deliberately been minimalist, seeking to avoid sweeping generalizations and grandiose claims, and placing our analysis within the broader scholarly conversation concerning the sayings of Jesus. We argue that there are four passages in James where not simply an echo of Jesus' teaching but a specific use of his words is to be found. The strength of the evidence supporting this claim is shown by contrast with the two passages that we have considered but rejected. We do not deny that Jas 2:8 and 2:13 could have derived from Jesus logia, only that the evidence is insufficent so to assert. The same goes for the other passages in Deppe's extensive list; there is no intrinsic reason why the author of James should not have been so deeply influenced by the teaching of Jesus that his inflections in each of these cases also echoed what had been said by Jesus. But we cannot show it.

The isolation of four passages as performances of Jesus logia, however, is by no means insignificant, especially since, in each case, a further argument can be sustained that the form of the saying in James is closer to the form of tradition commonly hypothesized as Q

---

observed, "the author of this epistle [James] and the redactor of Q who produced the Sermon on the Mount belong to the same Jewish-Christian milieu; both share the decision that the followers of Jesus belong to law-abiding Israel and that fulfillment of the law, though without any emphasis upon circumcision and ritual law, is the appropriate interpretation of the teachings of Jesus."

66   R. W. Funk and R. W. Hoover ([eds.], *The Five Gospels: The Search for the Authentic Words of Jesus* [A Polebridge Press Book; New York: Macmillan, 1993] 296-97) designate Q^M 5:7 = Q^L 6:36 gray. Gray means, "Jesus did not say this, but the ideas in it are close to his own" (p. 36). However, it should be pointed out that often gray means wide disagreement among the members of the Jesus Seminar.

than to the final redaction of Matthew and Luke.[67] On this point, the instinctive assessment of Ropes[68] has been substantiated by all subsequent analysis. The most logical conclusion to draw about the composition of James, given this finding, is that it took place in a setting that was temporally and geographically close to an early stage of the developing tradition. The authors of this essay differ on the judgment concerning authorship. Johnson thinks that the author may very well have been James, the Brother of the Lord;[69] Wachob thinks that an anonymous teacher wrote in the name and ethos of James, the Brother of the Lord, and used the Jesus sayings as a way of strengthening his own instruction.[70] They agree, however, on the following judgment: the use of an early form of the Jesus tradition suggests that the Letter of James was written either before the composition of the Synoptic Gospels, or at the very least before their version of Jesus' teachings became standard.

---

[67] P. J. Hartin, *James and the Q Sayings of Jesus* (JSNTSup 47; Sheffield: JSOT Press, 1991) 140-217, 220-44.

[68] Ropes, *James*, 38-39.

[69] Johnson, *James*, 89-123.

[70] Wachob, *"The Rich in Faith" and "The Poor in Spirit"*.

INDEX OF BIBLICAL LITERATURE

Gen 1:16	91	Num 3	264
Gen 1:27	304	Num 3:42	162 n. 74
Gen 5:2	304	Num 5:6	162 n. 76
Gen 14:14	162 n. 73	Num 6:2	172
Gen 18	279	Num 7:12	162 n. 75
Gen 22:16	432	Num 14:16	432
Gen 33:18	261	Num 26:52-56	92
Gen 49:17	162 n. 75	Num 26:54-56	92
		Num 27:5	172
Exod 5–11	233	Num 30:3-15	436
Exod 8:19	154, 317, 357	Num 30:3	433
Exod 10:3	174 n. 117		
Exod 13:5	432	Deut 5:26	94
Exod 14-15	352	Deut 6:13	432
Exod 15:17	221 n. 49	Deut 14:2	158
Exod 16:17-18	92	Deut 15	165
Exod 20:7	436	Deut 15:3	165, 168
Exod 22:10-11	432	Deut 21:18-21	329
Exod 22:22	171 n. 100, 174	Deut 21:20	329
		Deut 23:21-23	436
Exod 22:24	172	Deut 23:22	433
Exod 23:4-5	66	Deut 24:1-4	304
Exod 23:20	313, 335 n. 7, 355	Deut 30:15	206
		Deut 30:19	206
		Deut 32:39	94
Lev 2:1	175 n. 118	Deut 34:10-12	347
Lev 5:20-24	433		
Lev 13–14	318	Josh 3:10	94
Lev 19:11-18	431	Josh 5:13	279
Lev 19:11	431	Josh 5:14	279
Lev 19:12	431, 436		
Lev 19:13	431	Judg 13:2-20	279
Lev 19:14	431	Judg 18:15	420
Lev 19:15	431		
Lev 19:16	431	Ruth 2:14	160
Lev 19:17	431		
Lev 19:18	397, 431, 447	1 Sam 10:4	420
Lev 25	90	1 Sam 17:22	420
Lev 25:23	167	1 Sam 17:26	94
Lev 25:25-28	167	1 Sam 17:36	94
		1 Sam 17:39	176
Num 1:47	162 n. 74	1 Sam 25:5	420

2 Sam 8:10	420	Ps 84:3	94
2 Sam 19:6	396	Ps 104:29-30	94
		Ps 105:26	305
1 Kgs 3:12	82	Ps 107:29-30	208
1 Kgs 7:1	432		
1 Kgs 8:31-32	432	Prov 1:7	174
1 Kgs 13:1-10	233	Prov 1:10-33	314
1 Kgs 14:15	352	Prov 6:35	174, 175 n.
1 Kgs 17:1	170		119
1 Kgs 17:6	170	Prov 8:1-21	314
1 Kgs 17:8	170	Prov 8:22	218 n. 40
1 Kgs 17:16	170	Prov 8:32-36	331
1 Kgs 18:18	233	Prov 11:13	247
1 Kgs 19:20	267	Prov 15:23	247
1 Kgs 21:20-26	233	Prov 20:19	247
1 Kgs 22:8	233	Prov 23:9	247
1 Kgs 22:17	233	Prov 25:21-22	66
		Prov 30:8	159
2 Kgs 1:10, 12	267	Prov 30:32-33	247
2 Kgs 4:1-7	170		
2 Kgs 19:4	94	Eccl 2:8	158
2 Kgs 19:10	94	Eccl 3:7	247
2 Kgs 22:19	174 n. 117	Eccl 9:12	265
2 Chr 24:20-22	330 n. 42	Isa 2:4	299
		Isa 6:8	345
Job 9:23-24	176	Isa 11:6-9	299 n. 47
Job 13:5	247	Isa 11:6	299
Job 26:11-12	208	Isa 19:2	299 n. 46
Job 34:14-15	94	Isa 26:19	318
		Isa 28:18-20	348
Ps 8	304	Isa 28:23-29	345
Ps 8:3	212 n. 24	Isa 29:18	318, 348, 350
Ps 8:4	281	Isa 32:18	299
Ps 22	245	Isa 35:5-6	12, 318
Ps 22:2	389	Isa 37:4	94
Ps 22:3	245	Isa 40	320, 344
Ps 22:16	245	Isa 40:3	6, 319
Ps 23:4	433	Isa 40:12-13	345
Ps 36:9	94	Isa 40:18	345
Ps 38:14-16	245	Isa 40:21	345
Ps 39:10	245	Isa 40:25	345
Ps 40:8	177 n. 127	Isa 40:27-28	345
Ps 58:10-11	397	Isa 42:1	178 n. 132
Ps 65:8	208	Isa 42:18	318
Ps 66:6	208	Isa 44:28	177 n. 125
Ps 80	307	Isa 48:12	92
Ps 80:14-17	307	Isa 48:14	177 n. 126

Isa 49:7	92	Ezek 36:23	161
Isa 52	90	Ezek 37:24	93,
Isa 52:7-10	90	Ezek 37:26	299
Isa 52:7	90, 91	Ezek 44:10-31	179
Isa 52:9	90	Ezek 44:22-24	179 n. 135
Isa 53:3	307 n. 88		
Isa 53:4	243	Dan 4:10	316 n. 17
Isa 53:6	243	Dan 4:14	316 n. 17
Isa 53:7	241, 242 n. 91, 243, 244, 244 nn.95-97	Dan 4:20	316 n. 17
		Dan 7	95, 273, 274, 277, 281, 282, 284, 285, 286, 307, 308, 309, 310 n. 98, 315
Isa 53:10	243		
Isa 60:17	299 n. 47		
Isa 61	91, 91 n. 22		
Isa 61:1-3	90, 91	Dan 7:1-12	275
Isa 61:1-2	12, 318	Dan 7:12	323
Isa 61:1	90, 91, 318	Dan 7:13-14	274, 278 n. 47, 304, 307
Isa 66:12	299 n. 47		
		Dan 7:13	273, 274
Jer 2:13	94	Dan 7:14	323
Jer 3:1-5	345	Dan 7:15-27	323
Jer 6:14	299	Dan 7:16	276
Jer 7:8-15	140	Dan 7:17-18	276
Jer 7:12-15	221 n. 49	Dan 7:18	316
Jer 7:22-23	70	Dan 7:21	299 n. 46
Jer 8:11	299	Dan 7:27	316
Jer 9:24	177 n. 128	Dan 8:13	316 n. 17
Jer 10:10	94	Dan 9:26	299 n. 46
Jer 12:12	299	Dan 10:16	273, 275
Jer 12:16	433	Dan 10:18	273, 275
Jer 17:13	94	Dan 11:5-45	299 n. 46
Jer 23:36	94	Dan 12:1-3	276
Jer 26:4-6	221 n. 49	Dan 12:1	300
Jer 26:9	221 n. 49	Dan 12:6-13	316
Jer 26:18	297	Dan 18:21	307
Jer 28:9	299	Dan 18:25	307
Jer 30:5	299	Dan 18:27	307
Jer 34:1-7	233		
Jer 37:3-10	233	Hos 2:14-15	351
Jer 37:17	233	Hos 6:6	70, 177 n. 129
Ezek 1	285	Amos 3:3-8	345
Ezek 1:26	285		
Ezek 7:25	299	Obad 1	305
Ezek 13:10	299		
Ezek 13:16	299	Mic 2:6-11	345
Ezek 34:23-24	93	Mic 3:9-12	140
Ezek 34:25	299	Mic 3:12	297 n. 41

Mic 5:5	299 n. 47
Mic 6:15-16	297
Mic 7:6	13, 289, 291, 292, 293, 294, 295, 296, 297, 298, 298 n. 44, 299, 300, 301, 302, 303, 305, 309
Nahu 1:4	208
Nahu 2:1	90
Zech 1:7-11	279
Zech 9:10	299 n. 47
Zech 12:10	93
Zech 13:1-6	93
Zech 13:7-9	93
Zech 14:3	299 n. 46
Mal 1:10	178 n. 130
Mal 2:7-9	178
Mal 2:17	178 n. 131
Mal 3:1	178 n. 132, 313, 319, 335 n. 7, 347, 354, 355
Mal 3:2	179
Mal 3:3	178
Mal 3:4	178 n. 133
Mal 3:5-12	179
Mal 3:5	178
Mal 4:5-6	309 n. 95, 354
Mal 4:5	179, 298, 347
Mal 4:6	298, 298 n. 44, 309
Tob 4:10-11	448
Sir 4:11	331
Sir 5:12	247
Sir 7:26-28	315
Sir 15:7	174 n. 115
Sir 19:5-12	247
Sir 20:1-8	247
Sir 20:1	247 n. 106
Sir 20:5	247
Sir 20:6-7	247
Sir 23:9-11	433
Sir 24:9	218 n. 40
Sir 29:1	448
Sir 33:14	206
Sir 35:12-18	173 n. 112
Sir 35:12-15	175 n. 119
Sir 48:10	180
Matt 1-16	110, 111, 112
Matt 3:1	318
Matt 3:3	319, 320
Matt 3:7-12	11
Matt 3:7-10	380
Matt 3:9	92
Matt 3:16	240 n. 87
Matt 4:1-11	11
Matt 4:10	106
Matt 4:12	349
Matt 4:17	28
Matt 4:18-22	29
Matt 5:1-12	11
Matt 5:1-3	90
Matt 5:3	86, 442, 444
Matt 5:9	402
Matt 5:11	375
Matt 5:13	12, 92, 340
Matt 5:14	83
Matt 5:15	11, 83
Matt 5:16	107
Matt 5:18	12
Matt 5:21	63
Matt 5:23-24	32
Matt 5:23	83
Matt 5:25-26	11, 165
Matt 5:31-32	57
Matt 5:32	12, 109
Matt 5:33-37	62, 63 nn. 50-51; 64 n. 56, 77
Matt 5:33	435, 436
Matt 5:34-37	432, 433
Matt 5:34-36	437
Matt 5:34	433, 435, 436, 437, 438
Matt 5:35	433, 435, 436, 437
Matt 5:36	435, 436, 437

Matt 5:37	434, 435, 437, 438	Matt 7:16-19	83
		Matt 7:20	36
Matt 5:38-48	65, 77	Matt 7:21	11
Matt 5:39-44	150	Matt 7:22-23	12
Matt 5:39-42	11	Matt 7:24-27	11, 422
Matt 5:39	108	Matt 7:27	108
Matt 5:43-48	342	Matt 7:28	11
Matt 5:43	400, 447	Matt 7:29-30	312 n. 4
Matt 5:44-48	11	Matt 8:4	118
Matt 5:44-45	66, 67	Matt 8:5-13	36, 312 n. 3
Matt 5:44	387, 394	Matt 8:5-10	11, 12
Matt 5:45	156	Matt 8:5-6	210
Matt 5:46-47	340	Matt 8:7-13	210
Matt 5:48	401	Matt 8:11-12	12, 90
Matt 6:5	83, 108	Matt 8:11	29, 36
Matt 6:9-13	11	Matt 8:13	11, 12
Matt 6:9b-10	85	Matt 8:19-22	11
Matt 6:11	142	Matt 8:19-20	266
Matt 6:12	142	Matt 8:19	203 n. 3
Matt 6:16	83	Matt 8:20	83, 273 n. 40, 281
Matt 6:19-21	11		
Matt 6:22-23	11, 156	Matt 8:21-22	266
Matt 6:22	84	Matt 8:22	83, 94
Matt 6:24	12, 418	Matt 8:31	210
Matt 6:25-33	11	Matt 8:34	210
Matt 6:25	84	Matt 8:38	372
Matt 6:26	83	Matt 9:2	120
Matt 6:28-30	84	Matt 9:3	211
Matt 6:28	83	Matt 9:5	120, 212
Matt 6:30	83	Matt 9:6	279
Matt 7:1-5	11	Matt 9:8	365, 375
Matt 7:1	110	Matt 9:9	147
Matt 7:3	17	Matt 9:13	90, 178 n. 130
Matt 7:4	17	Matt 9:15	41, 84
Matt 7:5	380,	Matt 9:16-17	84
Matt 7:6	36, 83, 440	Matt 9:23	83
Matt 7:7-11	11, 439, 440, 441	Matt 9:31	250
		Matt 9:32-34	11
Matt 7:7	439, 440, 441, 442	Matt 9:36–11:1	363
		Matt 9:37-38	11
Matt 7:8	440, 441, 442	Matt 9:37	83, 84
Matt 7:9-10	439	Matt 10:1-16	33
Matt 7:11	160, 439, 441, 442	Matt 10:1-2	375
		Matt 10:1	33
Matt 7:12	11, 440	Matt 10:4	36
Matt 7:13-14	11	Matt 10:5	29
Matt 7:13	36	Matt 10:7-16	11
Matt 7:16-20	11	Matt 10:16	83

Matt 10:17-22	372	Matt 11:7-11	11, 335, 336, 350
Matt 10:19-20	11, 240	Matt 11:7-9	344
Matt 10:23	87 n. 12, 273 n. 41	Matt 11:9	354
Matt 10:24-25	11, 203	Matt 11:10	335 n. 7, 350, 354, 355
Matt 10:26-33	11, 371, 372, 374, 376	Matt 11:11	350, 354, 358
Matt 10:26-27	367, 368, 370, 372, 374, 376, 381, 382	Matt 11:12-15	335 n. 7, 355
		Matt 11:12-13	12, 312 n. 4, 315 n. 14, 357
Matt 10:26	370, 373, 376	Matt 11:12	314, 355, 356
Matt 10:27	366, 369, 370, 373, 375	Matt 11:13	355, 356 n. 62
		Matt 11:14	313, 355, 356
Matt 10:28-29	364	Matt 11:15	344, 356
Matt 10:28	94, 262, 365, 371	Matt 11:16-19	11, 334, 335, 346, 359
Matt 10:29-31	263, 364, 370	Matt 11:16-18	336
Matt 10:29-30	84	Matt 11:16	92
Matt 10:29	83, 262	Matt 11:18-19	336
Matt 10:32-33	13, 262, 280, 364, 370, 373	Matt 11:19	273 n. 40, 346, 359
Matt 10:32	274	Matt 11:21-23	11
Matt 10:34-36	11, 13, 289, 294, 297, 309, 375	Matt 11:25-27	11
		Matt 11:25-26	82
		Matt 11:25	360
Matt 10:34	290, 292, 301	Matt 11:27	285
Matt 10:35-36	291	Matt 11:29	82
Matt 10:37-38	12, 387	Matt 12:10	211, 212
Matt 10:39	12, 88, 94	Matt 12:18	240 n. 87
Matt 10:40	11	Matt 12:22-30	11
Matt 11:1	360	Matt 12:25	292
Matt 11:2-19	311, 311 n. 2, 334, 339, 345, 361	Matt 12:28	87 n. 12, 240 n. 87, 357
		Matt 12:32	11, 273 n. 40
Matt 11:2-15	339	Matt 12:33-35	11
Matt 11:2-6	11, 12, 334, 336, 344	Matt 12:33	83
		Matt 12:34	87
Matt 11:2	346, 347, 349, 356, 417	Matt 12:38-42	11
		Matt 12:38	203 n. 3
Matt 11:3-6	346	Matt 12:39	92
Matt 11:3	210, 339	Matt 12:40-42	13
Matt 11:4-6	210, 334	Matt 12:42	82
Matt 11:4	348	Matt 12:43-45	11
Matt 11:5	90, 91, 347	Matt 13:1-9	83
Matt 11:6	339, 344, 347, 350	Matt 13:3-4	83
		Matt 13:6	82
Matt 11:7-15	346	Matt 13:16-17	11
		Matt 13:17	36

Matt 13:24-30	54 n. 25	Matt 19:20	210
Matt 13:31-33	11	Matt 19:21	210
Matt 13:44-46	418, 422	Matt 19:27-28	34
Matt 13:46	176	Matt 19:28	12, 13, 279, 325
Matt 13:52	267		
Matt 14:19	163	Matt 19:30	36
Matt 14:22-23	386	Matt 20:16	12
Matt 15:12	209	Matt 20:21	34
Matt 15:13-14	210	Matt 20:28	36
Matt 15:14	11	Matt 21:13	19, 22
Matt 15:21-28	36	Matt 21:14-17	211
Matt 15:23	210	Matt 21:14-15	17
Matt 15:24	93, 211	Matt 21:15-16	17, 213
Matt 15:31	29	Matt 21:16	211, 213
Matt 16:1-4	212	Matt 21:18-19	386
Matt 16:1	211, 212	Matt 21:20	209
Matt 16:2-3	11, 83	Matt 21:21-22	210
Matt 16:16	34	Matt 21:23-27	342
Matt 16:22	34	Matt 21:23-25	212
Matt 16:23	107	Matt 21:23	212, 213
Matt 16:24	87, 92	Matt 21:28-32	312 n. 4
Matt 16:25	88, 94	Matt 21:31	169
Matt 16:26	273 n. 41	Matt 21:32	314
Matt 16:27	28, 279	Matt 21:34	87 n. 12
Matt 17:6	365, 375	Matt 21:45-46	213
Matt 17:7	365, 375	Matt 22:1-14	84
Matt 17:10-13	309 n. 95	Matt 22:2-10	12
Matt 17:10	179, 209	Matt 22:14	36, 86, 91
Matt 17:11-12	210	Matt 22:15-17	211, 213
Matt 17:16	34	Matt 22:15	211
Matt 17:20	11	Matt 22:16	203 n. 3, 213
Matt 17:24-27	168	Matt 22:18-21	212
Matt 18:1-4	358	Matt 22:18	212, 380
Matt 18:1	209	Matt 22:23-28	211
Matt 18:2-5	210	Matt 22:23	213
Matt 18:7	12	Matt 22:24	203 n. 3
Matt 18:12-14	12	Matt 22:29-32	212
Matt 18:15	12	Matt 22:32	29
Matt 18:21-22	12	Matt 22:34-36	213
Matt 18:23-25	165	Matt 22:35-36	211
Matt 18:30	168	Matt 22:35	213
Matt 18:34	168	Matt 22:36	203 n. 3
Matt 19:3	211	Matt 22:39	446, 447
Matt 19:4-9	212	Matt 22:41-46	95 n. 33
Matt 19:16	203 n. 3	Matt 22:41	213
Matt 19:18-19	210	Matt 22:42-45	213
Matt 19:18	210	Matt 22:46	213
Matt 19:19	447	Matt 23	320

Matt 23:1-31	380	Matt 26:63	204, 224, 232, 242, 250
Matt 23:4	11		
Matt 23:6-7	11	Matt 26:64	95, 104, 224, 224 n. 55, 231, 251, 279, 280
Matt 23:8	203		
Matt 23:11	358		
Matt 23:12	12		
Matt 23:13	11	Matt 26:67-68	204, 222 n. 49
Matt 23:16-22	433, 436	Matt 26:68	232, 251
Matt 23:23	11, 178 n. 130	Matt 27:11	104, 224, 231
Matt 23:25-27	11	Matt 27:12-13	225 n. 57, 232
Matt 23:27-28	178 n. 131	Matt 27:12	225, 242, 252
Matt 23:29-32	11	Matt 27:14	225, 232, 242, 252, 255
Matt 23:30	178 n. 132		
Matt 23:34-36	11	Matt 27:24	225 n. 57
Matt 23:34	178 n. 132	Matt 27:39	245
Matt 23:37-39	12	Matt 27:46	245, 419
Matt 23:39	97	Matt 27:52-53	36
Matt 24:1-2	83	Matt 27:54	365, 375
Matt 24:5	36	Matt 27:55	55
Matt 24:10-11	36	Matt 28:5	365, 375
Matt 24:26-28	12	Matt 28:16-20	38
Matt 24:28	83	Matt 28:19	35
Matt 24:30	28		
Matt 24:32	83	Mark 1-8	10 n. 12
Matt 24:37-41	12, 325	Mark 1:1	9, 151
Matt 24:37-39	92	Mark 1:2-8	7
Matt 24:42-51	325	Mark 1:2-3	319
Matt 24:43-51	11	Mark 1:2	313
Matt 24:44	273 n. 41, 290 n. 4	Mark 1:6	170
		Mark 1:7-8	347
Matt 25:1-13	83	Mark 1:7	322
Matt 25:14-30	165	Mark 1:8	151, 322
Matt 25:14-20	12	Mark 1:9-11	7
Matt 25:31	273 n. 41, 279	Mark 1:10-11	150
Matt 26:18	203	Mark 1:10	151, 240 n. 87
Matt 26:22	210	Mark 1:12-13	7
Matt 26:23-25	210	Mark 1:14	349
Matt 26:25	107, 203 n. 2	Mark 1:15	28, 54 n. 25, 87 n. 12, 90
Matt 26:26	163		
Matt 26:28	36	Mark 1:16-20	7, 29
Matt 26:31	93	Mark 1:24	205
Matt 26:32	93	Mark 1:25	125, 205, 208
Matt 26:39	250	Mark 1:29-34	7
Matt 26:42	250	Mark 1:34	208
Matt 26:49	203 n. 2	Mark 1:38	125
Matt 26:60	36	Mark 1:40-45	7, 156
Matt 26:62	204, 224, 231, 242, 249	Mark 1:44	117, 119, 119 n. 45

Mark 2:1-3:6	381	Mark 4:6	82
Mark 2:1-26	114	Mark 4:8	126
Mark 2:1-12	7	Mark 4:10-12	7
Mark 2:2-5	114	Mark 4:10	204
Mark 2:5	108, 119, 120	Mark 4:11-12	205
Mark 2:7	205	Mark 4:11	126
Mark 2:8-12	206	Mark 4:13-20	7
Mark 2:8-9	114	Mark 4:15	126
Mark 2:9	108, 119, 120, 125	Mark 4:18	127
		Mark 4:19	127
Mark 2:10	273 n. 40, 279	Mark 4:20	127
Mark 2:13-17	7, 207	Mark 4:21-25	382
Mark 2:15	156	Mark 4:21-23	7
Mark 2:16	151, 205	Mark 4:21	127, 382
Mark 2:17	90, 205	Mark 4:22	367, 368, 370, 372, 373, 374, 381, 382, 383
Mark 2:18-22	7		
Mark 2:19	84, 119 n. 45, 125		
		Mark 4:24-25	7
Mark 2:20	41, 375	Mark 4:24	121, 123
Mark 2:21-22	84	Mark 4:26	127
Mark 2:22	110, 125	Mark 4:28	127
Mark 2:23-28	7, 207 n. 10	Mark 4:30-32	7, 176
Mark 2:24	206	Mark 4:30	127
Mark 2:25-26	205	Mark 4:31-32	83
Mark 2:26	119 n. 45	Mark 4:35-41	7
Mark 2:28	273 n. 40	Mark 4:38	203 n. 3
Mark 3:1-6	7, 207 n. 10	Mark 4:39	208
Mark 3:2	206	Mark 4:40	128
Mark 3:3	107	Mark 5:1-20	7
Mark 3:4	125, 126, 178 n. 131, 206	Mark 5:5-13	208
		Mark 5:7	205
Mark 3:5	119 n. 45	Mark 5:9-13	205
Mark 3:6	206, 207 n. 10	Mark 5:9	289 n. 1
Mark 3:7	7	Mark 5:17	205
Mark 3:9-10	208	Mark 5:19	128
Mark 3:12	7, 208	Mark 5:21-43	7
Mark 3:13-19	7	Mark 5:25	169
Mark 3:14-15	33	Mark 5:30	289 n. 1
Mark 3:21	389	Mark 5:41	128, 419
Mark 3:22-27	7, 317	Mark 5:43	156
Mark 3:24-27	422	Mark 6	337
Mark 3:24-25	292	Mark 6:4	7, 128
Mark 3:28-29	7	Mark 6:7-13	7
Mark 3:29	126	Mark 6:7-11	33
Mark 3:31-32	7	Mark 6:7	29
Mark 3:34-35	7	Mark 6:8-9	154 n. 47
Mark 4:1-9	7, 83	Mark 6:11	128
Mark 4:5	126	Mark 6:13	374

Mark 6:14-29	423	Mark 8:20	119 n. 45
Mark 6:14-16	7	Mark 8:23	289 n. 1
Mark 6:14	141, 337	Mark 8:26	129
Mark 6:15	170, 337	Mark 8:27-30	8
Mark 6:16	337	Mark 8:27-29	344
Mark 6:17-29	375	Mark 8:28	170
Mark 6:30-31	114	Mark 8:29	34
Mark 6:30	34, 374	Mark 8:31-38	209
Mark 6:31	128	Mark 8:31	8, 250, 273 n. 40, 330
Mark 6:34-44	156		
Mark 6:35-44	7	Mark 8:32	34
Mark 6:36-37	114	Mark 8:34–9:1	8
Mark 6:38	289 n. 1	Mark 8:34	87, 92, 129, 130
Mark 6:39-41	114		
Mark 6:45-52	386	Mark 8:35	88, 94, 107, 130
Mark 7	70 n. 90, 72 n. 99		
		Mark 8:38	28, 92, 130, 273 n. 41, 279, 280, 281, 284
Mark 7:1-23	70 n. 90, 73 n. 105		
Mark 7:5	205		
Mark 7:6-7	178 n. 130	Mark 9:2-8	8
Mark 7:6	128, 205	Mark 9:4	170
Mark 7:7-9	205	Mark 9:5	203 n. 2
Mark 7:8	128	Mark 9:9	209
Mark 7:9	121, 122, 123, 128	Mark 9:11-13	170, 178 n. 132, 289, 306, 307, 308, 309, 309 n. 96, 310, 310 n. 98
Mark 7:10-12	72 n. 99		
Mark 7:10	205		
Mark 7:11-14	205		
Mark 7:11-12	169	Mark 9:11	204
Mark 7:12	129	Mark 9:12-13	205
Mark 7:13	109	Mark 9:12	130, 289 n. 1, 308
Mark 7:15	70, 70 nn. 89-90; 71, 71 n. 96, 72, 73, 77		
		Mark 9:14-27	8
		Mark 9:16	289 n. 1
Mark 7:17	204	Mark 9:17	203 n. 3
Mark 7:18-23	205	Mark 9:18	34
Mark 7:18	129	Mark 9:19	92, 119 n. 45
Mark 7:19	129	Mark 9:21	130, 289 n. 1
Mark 7:24-30	36	Mark 9:23	130
Mark 7:34	419	Mark 9:25	208
Mark 8-10	10 n. 12	Mark 9:28	204
Mark 8:2	129	Mark 9:29	205
Mark 8:3	129	Mark 9:30-32	8
Mark 8:12	7, 92, 129, 289 n. 1	Mark 9:31	130, 330
		Mark 9:33-37	8
Mark 8:15	7, 129	Mark 9:33	289 n. 1
Mark 8:17	119 n. 45, 129	Mark 9:34	209, 358

Mark 9:36	169	Mark 11-15	10 n. 12
Mark 9:37	130	Mark 11:1-10	8
Mark 9:38-40	8	Mark 11:2	132
Mark 9:38	203 n. 3	Mark 11:3	119 n. 45
Mark 9:40	130, 131	Mark 11:12-14	386
Mark 9:42	8, 131	Mark 11:13	386
Mark 9:43	131	Mark 11:15-19	178 n. 133
Mark 9:47	131	Mark 11:15-18	8
Mark 9:49	131	Mark 11:15-17	181
Mark 9:50	8	Mark 11:16	17
Mark 10:2-9	304	Mark 11:17	19, 22
Mark 10:2	205	Mark 11:21	203 n. 2
Mark 10:3-12	205	Mark 11:23	132
Mark 10:3	289 n. 1	Mark 11:25	150
Mark 10:6	131	Mark 11:27-33	8, 205, 222,
Mark 10:7-8	205		342
Mark 10:10	204	Mark 11:28	205
Mark 10:11-12	8, 205	Mark 12:1-9	222
Mark 10:11	109, 150	Mark 12:1-10, 12	8
Mark 10:12	131	Mark 12:3	132
Mark 10:13-15	8	Mark 12:6	132
Mark 10:17-22	8, 418	Mark 12:7	132
Mark 10:17	203 n. 3, 204	Mark 12:9	344
Mark 10:19	205	Mark 12:13-17	8
Mark 10:20	203 n. 3	Mark 12:14	203 n. 3
Mark 10:21	205	Mark 12:15	119 n. 45, 380
Mark 10:23-31	8	Mark 12:16	344
Mark 10:23	418	Mark 12:18-27	8
Mark 10:25	131, 418	Mark 12:18	205
Mark 10:28	34	Mark 12:19	203 n. 3
Mark 10:29	302, 418	Mark 12:24-27	205
Mark 10:30	131, 156	Mark 12:26	29
Mark 10:32-34	8	Mark 12:29-30	164
Mark 10:33-34	330	Mark 12:29	29, 132
Mark 10:34	132	Mark 12:30	119 n. 45
Mark 10:35	203 n. 3	Mark 12:31	446, 447
Mark 10:37	34	Mark 12:32-34	178 n. 130
Mark 10:38-39	303	Mark 12:32	203 n. 3
Mark 10:40	132	Mark 12:34	207
Mark 10:42-44	8	Mark 12:35-37a	8, 95 n. 33,
Mark 10:42	132		304
Mark 10:43	132	Mark 12:36	132
Mark 10:45	256 n. 139,	Mark 12:38	169
	273 n. 40, 304	Mark 12:39	8
Mark 10:46-52	8	Mark 12:40	169, 181
Mark 10:46	156	Mark 12:41-44	165, 169
Mark 10:48	209	Mark 13	141, 371
Mark 10:51	203 n. 2	Mark 13:1-2	8, 83

Mark 13:1	203 n. 3	Mark 14:59	231
Mark 13:3-13	8	Mark 14:60-61	204, 254 n. 131
Mark 13:3-4	204		
Mark 13:5-37	205	Mark 14:60	221, 231, 240 n. 88, 242
Mark 13:7	132		
Mark 13:9-13	297, 372	Mark 14:61-65	8
Mark 13:9-11	295	Mark 14:61-62	9
Mark 13:11	240	Mark 14:61	221, 222, 232, 243, 250, 251
Mark 13:12	294, 295, 295 n. 29, 296, 298 n. 44, 300, 301	Mark 14:62	95, 151, 222, 222 nn. 50-51; 231, 251, 273 n. 41, 280
Mark 13:13	294, 309		
Mark 13:14-23	8	Mark 14:63-64	223
Mark 13:15	132	Mark 14:65	204, 222 n. 49, 232, 251
Mark 13:22	133		
Mark 13:23	119 n. 45	Mark 14:66-72	8
Mark 13:24-31	8	Mark 15:1-15	8
Mark 13:26	28, 273 n. 41	Mark 15:1	223
Mark 13:28	83	Mark 15:2	104, 223, 231
Mark 13:33, 36	8	Mark 15:3-4	204
Mark 13:35-36	150	Mark 15:3	223, 223 n. 53
Mark 14-16	10 n. 12	Mark 15:4-5	240 n. 88, 252, 254 n. 131
Mark 14:1-12	423		
Mark 14:1-2	8		
Mark 14:1	251	Mark 15:4	223, 232, 243
Mark 14:10-11	8	Mark 15:5	232, 242 n. 91, 243, 252
Mark 14:10	251		
Mark 14:12-25	8	Mark 15:12	223 n. 53
Mark 14:14	203, 289 n. 1	Mark 15:21	8
Mark 14:19	205	Mark 15:22-31	8
Mark 14:20-21	205	Mark 15:29	245
Mark 14:21	119 n. 45, 273 n. 40	Mark 15:33-41	8
Mark 14:24	133	Mark 15:34	133, 245, 389, 419
Mark 14:25	133	Mark 15:39	9
Mark 14:27	93	Mark 15:42-47	8
Mark 14:28	93	Mark 16:1-8	8
Mark 14:30	8	Mark 16:9-20	10
Mark 14:36-38	8	Mark 16:15	9
Mark 14:36	133, 150, 250	Mark 16:17	133
Mark 14:38	119 n. 45	Mark 16:19	9
Mark 14:39	250		
Mark 14:43-49	8	Luke 1:1–11:17	110, 111, 112
Mark 14:45	203 n. 2	Luke 1:1-4	30
Mark 14:53-59	221	Luke 1:17	298 n. 44
Mark 14:54-55	8	Luke 1:68	29
Mark 14:59-60	249	Luke 1:73	433

Luke 2:11	94	Luke 6:23	151
Luke 2:46-47	343	Luke 6:26	109
Luke 3:2-4	151	Luke 6:27-36	11, 65, 77
Luke 3:2-3	318	Luke 6:27-28 + 35	66, 67
Luke 3:4-6	319	Luke 6:27	150, 387, 394
Luke 3:4	320	Luke 6:29	150
Luke 3:7-9	11	Luke 6:33	394
Luke 3:8	92, 164	Luke 6:35	387, 394
Luke 3:16-17	11, 151	Luke 6:37-42	11
Luke 3:18	322	Luke 6:37	109
Luke 3:22	240 n. 87	Luke 6:40	203
Luke 4:1-13	11	Luke 6:42	380
Luke 4:1-2	151	Luke 6:43-45	11
Luke 4:1	240 n. 87	Luke 6:43-44	83
Luke 4:3-4	160	Luke 6:45	87
Luke 4:4	164	Luke 6:46-49	11
Luke 4:7-8	160	Luke 6:49	108
Luke 4:8	106	Luke 7:1-10	11, 12, 36, 312, 312 n. 3
Luke 4:14	240 n. 87		
Luke 4:16-30	343	Luke 7:3	213
Luke 4:17-21	90	Luke 7:6-10	214
Luke 4:18-21	318	Luke 7:11-17	312, 312 n. 3
Luke 4:18-19	178 n. 132, 240 n. 87	Luke 7:11-13	83
		Luke 7:18-35	311, 311 n. 2, 312
Luke 4:18	350		
Luke 4:26	170	Luke 7:18-23	11, 12, 334
Luke 4:38	213	Luke 7:18-20	213, 334
Luke 4:39	214	Luke 7:19	339, 347
Luke 4:42	28	Luke 7:21-23	214
Luke 5:1-11	29	Luke 7:21	334
Luke 5:14	118	Luke 7:22-23	334
Luke 5:20	120	Luke 7:22	90, 91, 348
Luke 5:21	214	Luke 7:23	339
Luke 5:22-26	214	Luke 7:24-35	335
Luke 5:23	120	Luke 7:24-28	11
Luke 5:24	279	Luke 7:27	354
Luke 5:27	335 n. 7	Luke 7:28	354, 358
Luke 5:30-32	214	Luke 7:29-30	314
Luke 5:32	90	Luke 7:31-35	11, 151, 335, 359
Luke 5:34	84		
Luke 5:35	41	Luke 7:34	273 n. 40
Luke 5:36-38	84	Luke 7:35	360
Luke 6:8	107	Luke 7:36	213, 214
Luke 6:20-26	11	Luke 7:40	203 n. 3
Luke 6:20-21	90	Luke 7:41-42	165
Luke 6:20	84, 442, 444, 445	Luke 8:3	141
		Luke 8:4-8	83
Luke 6:22-23	375	Luke 8:6	82

Luke 8:9	213	Luke 11:2	143, 144, 160
Luke 8:10-15	214	Luke 11:3	142
Luke 8:17	367, 368, 370, 372	Luke 11:4	142
		Luke 11:7	83
Luke 8:32	214	Luke 11:9-13	11, 160, 439, 441
Luke 8:37	214		
Luke 8:38	214	Luke 11:9	439
Luke 8:49	203 n. 3	Luke 11:10	441, 442
Luke 9:1-2	33	Luke 11:11-13	156
Luke 9:2-5	33	Luke 11:11-12	439
Luke 9:2	29, 375	Luke 11:13	439, 441
Luke 9:10	34	Luke 11:14-23	151
Luke 9:20	34	Luke 11:14-20, 23	11
Luke 9:23	87, 92	Luke 11:20	87, 154, 176, 357
Luke 9:24	88, 94, 107		
Luke 9:26	28, 279, 372	Luke 11:24-26	11
Luke 9:38	203 n. 3	Luke 11:24	84
Luke 9:40	34	Luke 11:16, 29-32	11, 13
Luke 9:46	358	Luke 11:30	92
Luke 9:51-57	267	Luke 11:31	82
Luke 9:57-62	11	Luke 11:33	11, 83
Luke 9:57-58	266	Luke 11:34-35	11
Luke 9:58	83, 273 n. 40, 281	Luke 11:37	213, 214
		Luke 11:39-41	151
Luke 9:59-60	266	Luke 11:39-52	11, 141
Luke 9:60	83, 94	Luke 11:45	203 n. 3
Luke 10	402	Luke 11:50	92
Luke 10:1-20	35	Luke 11:52	180
Luke 10:2-12	11	Luke 11:53-54	215
Luke 10:2	83, 84	Luke 12:1-12	376
Luke 10:3	83	Luke 12:1-3	374, 376
Luke 10:4-11	151	Luke 12:1	373, 377, 380, 382
Luke 10:9	375		
Luke 10:13-15	11	Luke 12:2-12	11
Luke 10:16	11	Luke 12:2-9	371, 372, 376
Luke 10:21-24	11	Luke 12:2-3	367, 368, 369, 370, 372, 373, 374, 376, 381, 382
Luke 10:21-22	150		
Luke 10:21	82		
Luke 10:22	285		
Luke 10:25	203 n. 3, 214	Luke 12:2	370, 372, 380, 383
Luke 10:26-37	214		
Luke 10:27	446, 447	Luke 12:3	370
Luke 10:29-37	176	Luke 12:4-9	382
Luke 10:30-37	449	Luke 12:4-7	376
Luke 10:32-34	250	Luke 12:4-5	364, 370, 371
Luke 10:36:	344	Luke 12:4	262, 365
Luke 11:1-13	440	Luke 12:5	94
Luke 11:2-4	11, 142, 143		

Luke 12:6-7	84, 262, 263, 272, 364	Luke 14:11	12
		Luke 14:16-24	12, 84
Luke 12:6	83	Luke 14:26-27	12, 386
Luke 12:8-9	13, 263, 272, 273, 274, 280, 364	Luke 14:26	387, 418
		Luke 14:28-30	410
		Luke 14:28	413
Luke 12:8	151, 273 n. 40, 274, 279	Luke 14:31-32	409, 410, 418
		Luke 14:31	413, 414
Luke 12:10	273 n. 40, 376	Luke 14:32	414, 415
Luke 12:11-12	240, 376	Luke 14:33	415
Luke 12:13	203 n. 3	Luke 14:34-35	12
Luke 12:21	416	Luke 14:34	92
Luke 12:22-31	11, 54 n. 25	Luke 15:3-7	93
Luke 12:23	83	Luke 15:4-10	422
Luke 12:26-28	84	Luke 15:4-7	12
Luke 12:27	83	Luke 15:7	416
Luke 12:28	83	Luke 15:10	416
Luke 12:30	156	Luke 15:11-32	156, 176
Luke 12:33-34	11, 172	Luke 15:35b	97
Luke 12:39-46	11	Luke 16:1-8	165
Luke 12:39	150	Luke 16:9-13	97
Luke 12:40	273 n. 41, 290 n. 4	Luke 16:13	12
		Luke 16:14-15	356
Luke 12:41	213	Luke 16:16	12, 312 n. 4, 315, 335 n. 7, 356, 356 n. 62, 357
Luke 12:42-48	214		
Luke 12:49-53	11		
Luke 12:49-50	296		
Luke 12:49	290	Luke 16:17	12, 356
Luke 12:51-53	13, 289, 294, 309, 375	Luke 16:18	12, 109
		Luke 16:19-21	83
Luke 12:51	290, 300, 301	Luke 17:1	12
Luke 12:52-53	291	Luke 17:3-4	12
Luke 12:52	292	Luke 17:6	12
Luke 12:54-56	11	Luke 17:10	416
Luke 12:54	82	Luke 17:20-21	54 n. 25, 215
Luke 12:57-59	11	Luke 17:20	214
Luke 12:58-59	165, 168, 173	Luke 17:21	357
Luke 13:1-5	423	Luke 17:23-24	12
Luke 13:6-9	92	Luke 17:25	92
Luke 13:9	441	Luke 17:26-30	12
Luke 13:18-21	11	Luke 17:26-27	92
Luke 13:18-19	83, 151	Luke 17:31-37	325
Luke 13:20-21	176	Luke 17:33-35	12
Luke 13:23-30	12	Luke 17:33	88, 94, 418
Luke 13:28-29	90	Luke 17:37	12, 83, 213, 214
Luke 13:29	29		
Luke 13:31	141	Luke 18:1	175
Luke 13:34-35	12	Luke 18:2-5	173

Luke 18:4	175	Luke 22:63-71	225
Luke 18:6	174	Luke 22:63-64	222 n. 49
Luke 18:7	175	Luke 22:66	225
Luke 18:8	273 n. 41	Luke 22:67-69	225, 225 n. 58, 231
Luke 18:14	12		
Luke 18:18	203 n. 3, 213	Luke 22:67-68	226
Luke 18:19-22	214	Luke 22:67	9, 225
Luke 19:10	93	Luke 22:69	86, 95, 226, 280
Luke 19:11	290		
Luke 19:12-27	12, 165	Luke 22:70	9, 223 n. 53, 226, 231, 232
Luke 19:39	203 n. 3		
Luke 19:46	19, 22	Luke 23:2	226
Luke 19:47-48	18	Luke 23:3	104, 226, 226 n. 62, 231
Luke 20:1-8	342		
Luke 20:2	214	Luke 23:4	226 n. 62
Luke 20:3-8	215	Luke 23:6-12	227
Luke 20:21	203 n. 3	Luke 23:9	204, 227, 232, 243, 244 n. 95, 248, 253, 254 n. 131
Luke 20:22	214		
Luke 20:23-25	215		
Luke 20:27	214		
Luke 20:28	203 n. 3	Luke 23:28-31	94
Luke 20:34-38	215	Luke 23:34	385
Luke 20:37	29	Luke 23:47	9
Luke 20:39	203 n. 3		
Luke 20:41-44	95 n. 33	John 1:11	19
Luke 21:1-4	169	John 1:32-33	240 n. 87
Luke 21:5	83	John 1:38	203 nn. 2-3
Luke 21:7	203 n. 3, 213	John 1:49	203 n. 2,
Luke 21:8-11	214	John 1:51	280
Luke 21:12-15	240	John 2:15	22
Luke 21:18	372	John 2:17	19
Luke 21:27	28	John 2:18-22	19
Luke 21:29	83	John 3:2	203 nn. 2-3
Luke 21:31	416	John 3:9	217
Luke 21:34	83, 92	John 3:10	217
Luke 22:12	203	John 4:9	217
Luke 22:17-19	150	John 4:31	203 n. 2
Luke 22:24	358	John 4:32-33	215
Luke 22:26	358	John 4:34	216
Luke 22:28-30	12, 13	John 6:16-21	386
Luke 22:30	34	John 6:25	203 nn. 2-3; 216
Luke 22:35-38	94		
Luke 22:35	34	John 6:26	217
Luke 22:37	243, 244 n. 95	John 6:28	217
Luke 22:42	250	John 6:30-31	217
Luke 22:48	273 n. 40	John 6:32-35	217
Luke 22:53	94	John 7:15	217
Luke 22:54	225	John 7:16	217

John 7:37-39	240 n. 87	John 14:27	301
John 8:19	217	John 15:26-27	240
John 8:21-58	217	John 16:16-19	216
John 8:22	21	John 16:20-23	216
John 8:23-24	218	John 16:23	216
John 8:23	218	John 16:33	301
John 8:25	218, 218 n. 40	John 18:12-24	227
John 8:26	218	John 18:19	227
John 8:31-32	218	John 18:20-21	227, 231
John 8:33	218	John 18:23	227, 231
John 8:34-36	218	John 18:28–19:16	227
John 8:37-44	218	John 18:31	227
John 8:45-51	218	John 18:33	227
John 8:57	218	John 18:34-37	223 n. 53
John 8:59	219	John 18:34	227, 231
John 9:2	203 n. 2, 216	John 18:35	227
John 9:3	216	John 18:36-37	254
John 9:16	219	John 18:36	227, 231
John 9:22	219	John 18:37	227, 231
John 9:24	219	John 18:38	227, 344
John 9:28-29	219	John 19:9	204, 227, 232,
John 9:29	219		243, 254
John 9:34	219	John 19:11	227, 231
John 9:39	219	John 20:16	203 nn. 2-3
John 9:40	219	John 20:19	301
John 10:4	93	John 20:21	301
John 10:24	219	John 20:26	301
John 10:25-30	219		
John 10:31	219	Acts 2:2	32
John 10:33	219	Acts 2:30	433
John 10:45	250	Acts 3:12	32
John 11:8	203 n. 2	Acts 3:13	29
John 12:25	88, 94	Acts 3:15	35, 94
John 12:27	250	Acts 4:8-12	239
John 12:34	219, 283	Acts 5:29-32	239
John 12:35-36	220	Acts 5:31	94
John 13:6	216	Acts 5:35	32
John 13:7	216	Acts 7:2-53	239
John 13:8	216	Acts 7:32	29
John 13:24	216	Acts 7:56	280
John 13:25	216	Acts 10:1-8	38
John 13:26	216	Acts 10:9-16	38,
John 13:36	216	Acts 10:36	301
John 13:37	216	Acts 13:16	32
John 13:38	216	Acts 13:23	94
John 14:5	216	Acts 14:27	38
John 14:6-7	217	Acts 15	38
John 14:15-26	240 n. 87	Acts 15:24	38

Acts 16:37-38	239	Eph 2:14-18	301
Acts 18:14-15	239		
Acts 21:40–22:21	239	Phil 1:8	433
Acts 22:25-30	239	Phil 3:5	150
Acts 23:1-6	239		
Acts 24:10-21	239	Col 1:20	301
Acts 25:8-11	239		
Acts 26:1-29	239	1 Thess 2:19	340
		1 Thess 5:2	150
Rom 1:9	433	1 Thess 5:15	65 n. 64
Rom 2:21-23	340		
Rom 5:1	301	2 Thess 3:16	301
Rom 8:11	35		
Rom 8:15-16	150	Titus 2:14	158, 158 n. 61
Rom 8:15	146		
Rom 12	69, 397	Heb 6:13-20	433
Rom 12:9-21	68		
Rom 12:9-12	68	1 Pet 3:9	65 n. 64
Rom 12:14-21	388		
Rom 12:14	65 n. 64, 150	Jas 1:1	431
Rom 12:17-20	65 n. 64	Jas 1:5	432, 439, 441, 442
Rom 12:17-18	69		
Rom 12:17	150	Jas 2:1-13	442, 444
Rom 12:20-21	69	Jas 2:1	431, 442, 443, 444, 447
Rom 13:9	447		
Rom 15	150	Jas 2:5	432, 442, 443, 444, 445, 446
		Jas 2:8-11	446
1 Cor 4:12	65 n. 64	Jas 2:8	431, 432, 443, 446, 447, 449
1 Cor 5-6	141		
1 Cor 7	57	Jas 2:13	432, 448, 449
1 Cor 7:10-11	150	Jas 2:14-16	431
1 Cor 9:14	150	Jas 3:13–4:10	432
1 Cor 10:27	150	Jas 4:2-3	439, 442
1 Cor 11	150	Jas 4:2	432, 441
1 Cor 11:23-25	329	Jas 4:9	432
1 Cor 11:23	150	Jas 4:10	432
1 Cor 15:3	151	Jas 4:11	431
1 Cor 15:7	286	Jas 4:17	441
		Jas 5:1	432
2 Cor 1:23	433	Jas 5:2-3	432
		Jas 5:4	431
Gal 1:12	38	Jas 5:12	431, 432, 433, 434, 437, 438
Gal 1:14	150		
Gal 1:18-20	280	Jas 5:14	436
Gal 1:20	433	Jas 5:20	431
Gal 4:6	146		
Gal 5:14	447	1 John 3:22	442

1 John 5:14-16   442

Rev 1:12-20   278
Rev 1:13   275
Rev 3:10   303
Rev 6:4   300
Rev 10:6   433
Rev 12   36
Rev 14:14   275

Aland, B., 115 n. 37
Aland, K., 115 n. 37
Albright, W. F., 352 n. 51, 354 n. 58
Allen, W. C., 291 n. 15
Allison, D. C. (Jr)., 91 n. 22, 97, 97 n. 1, 146 n. 27, 149 n. 36, 156 n. 54, 210 n. 22, 211 n. 22, 240 n. 86, 290 n. 11, 296 n. 37, 303 n. 69, 304 n. 73, 306 n. 85, 347 nn. 38, 40; 351 n. 49, 352 n. 52, 353 n. 56, 358 n. 70, 370 n. 12, 373, 373 n. 22, 376 n. 28, 381 n. 43, 434 n. 10, 435 n. 15, 436 nn. 18, 20; 439 n. 30, 440 n. 33, 441 n. 35
Alter, R., 444 n. 42
Anderson, F. I., 70 n. 91

Back, S. -O., 54, 54 n. 23
Bahr, G. J., 201, 201 n. 40
Bandstra, A. J., 143 n. 19
Barr, D. L., 27,
Barr, J., 156 n. 54
Barrett, C. K., 216 n. 34, 217 nn. 36-37; 218 n. 42, 219 nn. 43-44
Barton, S. C., 31
Bauckham, R. J., 308 n. 93, 411 n. 8, 425 n. 58
Baum-Bodenbender, R., 254 n. 134
Baumgardt, D., 152 n. 43
Bauer, W., 391 n. 19, 395 n. 34
Beare, F. W., 188 n. 6, 189, 189 n. 7, 190, 190 nn. 9, 11; 196 n. 32
Beasley-Murray, G. R., 302 n. 64
Becker, J., 49 n. 8, 59 n. 40, 65 n. 61, 378 n. 35
Bellinzoni, A. J., 438 n. 24
Bengel, J. A., 252 n. 127
Betz, H. D., 66 n. 64, 145, 145 n. 26, 151 n. 39, 265 n. 18, 434 n. 10, 435 n. 15, 436 nn. 17, 20; 437 n. 23, 438, 438 n. 26, 439 n. 30,

440 nn. 33-34; 443 n. 40, 446 n. 53, 447, 447 nn. 59, 61; 448 nn. 64-65
Betz, O., 222 n. 50, 251 n. 126, 297 n. 40
Bernheim, E., 79, 80 n. 127
Beyer, K., 294 n. 26
Billerbeck, P., 161 n. 72, 176 n. 122, 179 n. 136, 248 n. 114, 447 n. 60
Birnbaum, P., 163 n. 80,
Black, J. S., 75 n. 109
Black, M., 102, 102 n. 19, 273 n. 37, 300 n. 54, 302 n. 61, 306 n. 86, 307 n. 88, 398 n. 42, 407
Blass, F., 101, 101 n. 16
Blau, L., 165, 165 n. 86, 166
Blevins, J. L., 207 n. 11
Blinzer, J., 249 n. 116
Blomberg, C. L., 100 n. 14, 413 n. 17
Bock, D. L., 213 n. 28, 215 n. 30, 225 n. 58, 244 n. 95, 247 n. 106, 248 n. 109, 417, 417 n. 28
Boissard, E., 91, 91 nn. 24-25; 92
Booth, R. P., 70 n. 90, 71 n. 98
Borg, M. J., 49 n. 8, 51 n. 15, 337 n. 13, 338, 338 n. 17, 379 n. 37
Boring, M. E., 49 n. 8, 367, 367 n. 9, 379, 381 n. 42
Bornkamm, G., 337 n. 13
Borsch, F. H., 273 n. 36
Botha, F. J., 145 n. 26
Bowker, J. W., 259 n. 3
Braun, H., 302 n. 63, 391 n. 19
Breech, J., 75, 75 n. 108, 76 n. 110, 389 n. 16
Brocke, M., 193, 193 nn. 22-23, 194 nn. 24-26; 195 n. 30, 196 n. 31
Brooke, G. J., 144 n. 24
Brown, C., 48 n. 3, 427 n. 67
Brown, R. E., 216 n. 34, 217 nn. 35, 37; 218 nn. 40, 42; 220 nn.

45-46; 221 nn. 48-49; 223 nn. 52-54; 224 nn. 55-56; 226 nn. 59, 61; 227 nn. 63-65; 228 n. 66, 239 n. 80, 242 nn. 90-91; 245 n. 100, 248 nn. 112, 114; 249 nn. 117-118; 250 n. 120, 251 n. 123, 252 n. 128, 253 nn. 129, 131; 254 n. 133, 303 n. 65

Bruce, A. B., 423 n. 47

Bruce, F. F., 354 n. 57

Buchanan, G. W., 300 n. 52, 338, 339, 339 nn. 18-19; 347 n. 39, 348, 348 nn. 41-42; 349 n. 47, 351 n. 50, 355 n. 59, 358 n. 68

Buchmann, G., 240 n. 85

Büchner, D. L., 296 nn. 35-36,

Bultmann, R., 48 n. 5, 78, 269, 269 nn. 28-29; 270, 273, 273 n. 38, 281, 299, 306, 306 n. 84, 313, 336, 336 nn. 10-11; 348, 348 nn. 43-44; 350, 350 n. 48, 359, 359 n. 72, 365 n. 5, 370 n. 15, 388, 395

Burney, C. F., 85, 85 n. 5, 86 n. 7, 87 n. 10

Bussmann, C., 6 n. 11

Butts, J. R., 137 n.3, 447 n. 57

Byrskog, S., 203

Cadbury, H. J., 289 n. 2, 290 nn. 8-9

Caird, G. B., 363 n. 1

Calvert, D. G. A., 49 n. 9, 62 n. 46

Cameron, P. S., 356 n. 61

Cameron, R. D., 339, 339 n. 20

Carey, J. W., 334 n. 5

Carroll, J. T., 242 n. 90,

Carson, D. A., 211 n. 22, 218 n. 41, 218 n. 42, 229 n. 68, 241 n. 90, 253 n. 129, 367 n. 9, 370 n. 12, 372 n. 20, 427 n. 66

Casey, P. M., 260 nn. 4-5, 268 n. 19, 272 n. 35, 273, 273 nn. 39, 41; 307 n. 90

Catchpole, D. R., 5 n. 8, 223 n. 53, 273 n. 36, 274 n. 43, 277, 279 n. 55, 335 n. 8, 358 n. 67

Charles, R. H., 421

Charlesworth, J. H., 4 n. 3, 78 n. 121, 79 n. 122, 400 n. 50, 420 n. 39

Chilton, B. D., 4 nn. 3, 5; 13, 16 n. 1, 17 n. 2, 27, 73 n. 105, 78 n. 120, 90 n. 21, 98 n. 5, 99 n. 6, 100 n. 14, 139 n. 7, 149 n. 36, 259 n. 3, 264 nn. 15-16; 268 n. 22, 271 n. 34, 280 n. 57, 284 n. 60; 357, 357 nn. 64-65; 360 n. 76, 426 n. 60

Cheyne, T. K., 75 n. 109

Clarke, K. D., 106 n. 34

Collins, A. Y., 328, 328 n. 37

Collins, J. J., 141 n. 14, 276 n. 45, 316, 316 nn.16-17, 19-20; 318 n. 22

Conzelmann, H., 382 n. 44

Cook, E. M., 85 n. 4

Coote, M. P., 147 n. 32

Coote, R. B., 147 n. 32

Cope, O. L., 296 n. 33

Corley, B., 220 n. 47

Craigie, P. C., 70 n. 91, 245 n. 102

Cranfield, C. E. B., 222 n. 49

Cross, F. L., 106, 106 n. 32

Cross, F. M., 178 n. 134

Crossan, J. D., 4 n. 4, 41, 100, 100 n. 13, 103, n. 22, 204 n. 4, 239 n. 78, 240 n. 84, 241 n. 88, 244 n. 97, 305 n. 78, 439 n. 29

Cullmann, O., 302 n. 63

Cyster, R. F., 155 n. 52

Dahl, N. A., 303 n. 70

Dalman, G., 85, 86, 86 nn. 8-9; 87, 87 nn. 10, 12-13; 93 n. 29, 101, 101 n. 16, 102, 102 n. 18, 103, 104, 104 n. 27, 149, 149 n. 36

Daniel, C., 352 n. 52

Danker, F. W., 190, 190 n. 10, 247 n. 106, 248 n. 109, 355 n. 60

Darr, J. A., 233 nn. 69-70; 234 n. 71

Dauer, A., 227 n. 63

Dautzenberg, G., 63, 63 nn. 52-53; 64, 65 nn. 62-63

Davies, M., 76 n. 112, 412 n. 10

Davies, W. D., 146 n. 27, 149 n. 36, 156 n. 54, 210, 210 n. 22, 211 n. 22, 240 n. 86, 290 n. 11, 304 n. 73, 306 n. 85, 347 nn. 38, 40; 351 n. 49, 352 n. 52, 353 n. 56, 358 n. 70, 370 n. 12, 373, 373 n. 22, 381 n. 43, 388 n. 11, 434 n. 10, 435 n. 15, 436 nn. 18, 20; 438 n. 27, 439 n. 30, 440 n. 33, 441 n. 35, 447 n. 59

Debrunner, 157

Deissmann, A., 157 n. 58

de Jonge, M., 302 n. 63

Delobel, J., 70 n. 89

de Moor, J. C., 149, 149 n. 36, 152 n. 43

Denney, J., 387 n. 5

Deppe, D. B., 432, 432 n. 5, 434 n. 12, 437 n. 23, 443, 443 n. 41, 446, 446 n. 54, 449

Derrett, J. D. M., 173 nn. 112-113; 410 n. 6, 416 n. 26

de Zwaan, J., 102, 102 n. 17

Dibelius, M., 432, 432 n. 4, 433 n. 6, 434 n. 10, 443 n. 41, 448 n. 62

Diebold-Scheuermann, C., 254 n. 134

Dihle, A., 399 n. 45

Dinkler, E., 5 n. 8, 92 n. 28

Doble, P., 279 n. 55

Dodd, C. H., 295 n. 31, 301, 301 n. 55, 392 n. 25

Donahue, J. R., 260 n. 6

Dormeyer, D., 104 n. 28, 203, 239 n. 78

Dodd, C. H., 3 n. 2

Drinkard, J. F., 70 n. 91

Duling, D. C., 27, 137 n. 1, 146 n. 27, 438 n. 25

Dungan, D. L., 49 n. 9

Dunn, J. D. G., 71 n. 96, 207 n. 13, 303, 303 nn. 67-68

Edgar, C., 158 n. 63

Edwards, R. A., 5 n. 8, 327, 327 n. 35, 427 n. 64

Egger, P., 256 n. 138

Eigler, G., 237 n. 76

Eissfeld, O., 178 n. 134, 179 n. 134

Elbogen, I., 152 n. 43

Elliot, J. K., 105 n. 29, 121, 121 n. 51, 368 n. 11

Elliott, J. H., 138 n. 5

Elstester, W., 47 n. 3

Epp, E. J., 105 n. 29, 106 n. 33, 118, 118 n. 41, 119 n. 42

Esler, P. F., 35

Evans, C. A., 3 nn. *, 1; 4 nn. 3, 5; 16 n. 1, 48 n. 3, 49 nn. 8-9; 73 n. 105, 74 n. 106, 75, 75 n. 108, 76 n. 110, 78 n. 120, 97 n. 1, 98, 98 nn. 3, 5; 99 nn. 6-7; 100, 100 nn. 14-15; 101, 104 n. 26, 121 n. 49, 207 n. 13, 222 n. 50, 235 n. 72, 294 n. 28, 426 n. 60

Faierstein, M., 307 n. 92

Falk, H., 269, 269 n. 26

Fee, G. D., 105 n. 29

Fishbane, M., 303 n. 70.

Fitzmyer, J. A., 57 n. 34, 85 n. 4, 104 n. 28, 120 n. 47, 146 n. 28, 149, 149 nn. 36-37; 158 n. 60, 159, 159 n. 66, 174 n. 114, 188 n. 3, 190 n. 10, 191, 191 n. 14, 193, 196 n. 32, 248 n. 110, 259 n. 2, 260 n. 6, 263, 278 n. 47, 292 n. 21, 305 n. 80, 308 n. 92, 318 n. 21, 330 n. 44, 377 n. 30, 385 n. 1, 414 n. 18

Fleddermann, H. T., 122, 122 n. 55, 123, 123 n. 56

Fling, F. M., 48 n. 7

Flint, P., 85 n. 4

Flusser, D., 388, 388 n. 11, 389 nn. 12-14

Foerster, W., 157 n. 58, 420, 420 nn. 37, 39

France, R. T., 48 n. 3, 49 n. 9, 55 n. 27, 224 n. 56, 225 n. 57, 243 n. 94

Frankemölle, H., 66 n. 67

Freedman, D. N., 70 n. 91

Freedman, H., 162, n. 73, 172 nn. 107, 108, 110

Fuchs, E., 99, 99 n. 10, 270, 270 n. 30

Fuellenbach, J., 187 n. 1, 191 n. 13, 197 n. 33, 199 n. 35

Fuller, R. H., 302 n. 63

Funk, R. W., 51 n. 14, 100, 100 n. 11, 103, 103 n. 23, 137 n. 3, 153 n. 45, 187 n. 2, 269 n. 24, 280 n. 58, 385 n. 2, 386 n. 4, 403 n. 56, 409 n. 2, 410, 410 nn. 3-5; 411 nn. 7, 9; 412 nn. 11-14; 413 n. 15, 417 nn. 29-30; 419 nn. 32-34; 422 nn. 43-44; 424 nn. 49-52; 425 nn. 53-57, 59; 426 nn. 61-62; 427 n. 65, 428 nn. 68-69; 441 n. 36, 449 n. 66

Furnish, V. P., 150, 150 n. 38, 387 n. 8

Gager, J., 389, 389 n. 15

Garland, D. E., 363 n. 1

Garnsey, P., 253 n. 129

Geldenhuys, N., 385 n. 1

Giesen, H., 363 n. 1

Ginzberg, E., 170 n. 97

Gnilka, J., 49 n. 8, 63 n. 50, 65 n. 61, 206 n. 8, 208 n. 15, 209 n. 20, 212 n. 24, 224 nn. 55-56; 241 n. 90, 242 n. 91, 245 n. 98, 294 n. 27, 297 n. 38, 369 n. 12, 371 n. 16

Goldschmidt, E. D., 163 n. 79

Gooch, P. W., 204 n. 4, 237 n. 75, 238 n. 77

Goodman, M., 165 n. 84, 167, 167 n. 92

Goodspeed, E. J., 142, 142 n. 15, 143, 143 nn. 16-18

Goppelt, L., 395

Goulder, M., 337, 337 nn. 14-16; 338, 345, 345 n. 36, 359 nn. 72-74

Grams, R., 342, 342 n. 31

Grant, F. C., 47 n. 3

Gray, J. 90, 90 n. 19

Green, J. B., 226 n. 60, 228 n. 67, 242 n. 90, 243 nn. 93-94; 245 n. 103, 257 n. 140, 363 n. 1, 364 n. 2

Green, M., 269 n. 25

Greeven, H., 432 n. 4, 433 n. 6, 434 n. 10, 443 n. 41

Grelot, P., 297, 297 n. 42

Grotius, H., 157

Guelich, R. A., 71 n. 93, 207 n. 9, 368 n. 10, 382 n. 47

Gundry, R. H., 10 n. 12, 187 n. 3, 188 n. 6, 190, 190 n. 10, 191, 191 n. 15, 192, 192 nn. 16-18; 193, 205 n. 5, 206 n. 7, 207 n. 10, 208 nn. 16-17; 209 n. 19, 212 n. 24, 221 n. 49, 222 n. 50, 223 nn. 51; 53; 224 n. 55, 242 n. 91, 245 n. 99, 248 n. 113, 250 n. 119, 251 n. 124, 291 n. 16, 292 n. 19, 375 n. 25

Gunkel, H., 391, 392, 392 nn. 23-24

Haacker, K., 223 n. 53, 253 n. 129

Haas, H., 394

Haenchen, E., 218 n. 39, 242 n. 90

Hagner, D. A., 210 n. 21, 211 nn. 23-24; 212 nn. 24-25; 224 nn. 55-56; 225 n. 57, 241 n. 90, 245 n. 98, 248 n. 113, 250 n. 121, 370 n. 12, 373 n. 21

Hahn, F., 47 n. 3, 227 n. 63, 300 n. 51

Hamilton, V. P., 243 n. 92

Hanson, J. S., 140 n. 8, 164 n. 82

Harding, M., 137 n. 2

Hare, D. R. A., 274 n. 42

Harrington, D., 420, 420 n. 39

Hartin, P. J., 450

Hartman, L., 294, 294 n. 28

Hawkins, J. C., 290, 290 n. 12

Hays, R. B., 427 n. 66

Headlam, A. C., 195, 195 nn. 28-29

Heininger, B., 414 n. 18

Hemer, C., 157

Hengel, M., 10 n. 13, 49 n. 8, 208 n. 13, 295 n. 30

Hennecke, E., 286

Hermisson, H. J., 243 n. 92

Hiers, R. H., 302 n. 64
Hill, D., 224 n. 56, 309 n. 97, 370 n. 12, 371, 371 nn. 17-18; 372, 372 n. 19
Hockett, H. C., 79 n. 126
Holladay, W. L., 297 n. 41
Holmberg, B., 78 n. 120
Holmen, T., 14, 57 n. 34
Holtz, T., 292 n. 18
Honecker, M., 390 n. 18
Honoré, A. T., 6 n. 11
Hooker, M. D., 48 n. 6, 49 n. 9, 50 n. 11, 51 n. 13, 53, 53 nn. 19-20; 54 n. 21, 242 n. 91, 307 n. 91
Hoover, R. W., 137 n. 3, 153 n. 45, 187 n. 2, 269 n. 24, 280 n. 58, 385 n. 2, 403 n. 56, 409 n. 2, 410, 410 nn. 3-5; 411 n. 7, 9; 412 nn. 11-14; 413 n. 15, 417 nn. 29-30; 419 nn. 32-34; 422 nn. 43-44; 424 nn. 49-52; 425 nn. 53-57, 59; 426 nn. 62-63; 427 n. 65, 428 nn. 68-69; 441 n. 36, 449 n. 66
Horgan, M. P., 297 n. 39
Horsley, G. H. R., 31
Horsley, R. A., 41, 138 n. 6, 140 n. 8, 164 n. 82, 309 n. 97, 326, 327, 327 nn. 34, 36; 328, 328 nn. 38-40; 353 n. 56, 399, 399 n. 47
Hort, 142, 142 n. 15
Howard, W. F., 159 n. 64
Hübner, H., 207 n. 12
Huck, A., 106, 106 n. 32
Hun, A., 158 n. 63
Hunter, A. M., 415
Hunzinger, C. H., 410 n. 6
Hurst, L. D., 104, 104 n. 26

Idel, M., 285 n. 61
Ito, A., 64, 64 nn. 56-58; 65, 65 n. 59

Jacobson, A. D., 5 n. 8, 145 n. 26, 147 n. 30, 148 n. 33, 377, 377 n. 32
Jarvis, P. G., 416 n. 24

Jastrow, M., 158 n. 62, 159 n. 68, 160 n. 69, 162 n. 73, 165 n. 87, 174 n. 116, 277 n. 47, 399 n. 46
Jeremias, J., 86 nn. 6-7; 87 nn. 10-12, 88 nn. 14-15; 91 n. 22, 92, 92 n. 27, 93 n. 30, 94 n. 32, 95 n. 34, 99, 99 n. 9, 100, 103, 103 n. 21, 146, 146 n. 28, 147, 147 n. 29, 149, 149 n. 36, 152, 154 n. 48, 156 n. 53, 161, 161 n. 71, 179 n. 136, 180 nn. 137-138; 199 n. 35, 200 n. 39, 243 n. 94, 292, 292 n. 22, 303 nn. 65, 67; 305 n. 80, 329, 359 n. 72, 379 n. 38, 414 n. 18, 419, 419 n. 35, 420 n. 36, 422 nn. 45-46
Johnson, L. T., 431 n. 2, 432 n. 3, 443 n. 40, 450
Joüon, P., 87, 87 n. 12, 90, 90 n. 21, 94 n. 31
Jüngel, E., 99, 99 n. 10

Karrer, M., 203 n. 1
Käsemann, E., 48, 48 n. 5, 49, 50 n. 10, 381 n. 42
Kaser, M., 253 n. 130
Keck, L. E., 270, 270 n. 32
Kee, H. C., 421, 421 n. 40
Keener, C. S., 423 n. 47
Keil, C. F., 309 n. 95
Kelber, W. H., 10 n. 13
Kelley, P. H., 70 n. 91
Kennedy, G., 340 n. 22, 342, 342 nn. 29-30; 435 n. 15
Kertelge, K., 66 n. 67
Kilpatrick, G. D., 105 n. 29
Kingsbury, J. D., 212, 213 n. 26
Kippenberg, H. G., 166, 166 n. 88
Klassen, W., 69 n. 83, 391 nn. 19-20; 395 n. 35, 399 n. 44, 402 n. 52
Klausner, J., 141 n. 11
Kleinknecht, K. T., 245 n. 98
Kloppenborg, J. S., 5 n. 8, 31, 141 n. 12, 145,145 nn. 25-26; 147, 147 nn. 30-31; 148 n. 35, 151, 156 n. 56, 166 n. 90, 299 n. 48, 312, 312 n. 5, 313 nn. 6-8; 314,

314 nn. 10, 12; 315, 315 n. 14, 320 n. 25, 327, 335 n. 8, 348, 364 nn. 3-4; 365 n. 5, 369 n. 12, 370, 370 nn. 14-15; 372 n. 21, 376 n. 28, 377 n. 33, 439 n. 32, 444 n. 45

Koester, H., 5 n. 8, 69 n. 83, 327, 327 n. 36, 394 n. 28, 434, 434 n. 10, 435 n. 13, 438, 439 n. 28, 443 n. 39, 444 nn. 45-46; 445, 445 nn. 47-48; 446 n. 51, 448 n. 65

Kosch, D., 49 n. 8

Kosmala, H., 242 n. 91

Kruse, H, 71 nn. 92, 95-96

Kuhn, H, -W., 66 n. 67, 67, 67 nn. 72, 76-78; 68 n. 82, 69 nn. 85-87; 393 n. 27

Kümmel, W. G., 58 n. 35, 72 n. 100

Kunkel, W., 252 n. 129, 253 n. 130

Lachs, T., 153 nn. 43-44

Lambrecht, J., 70 n. 90, 72 n. 100

Lampe, G. W. H., 290 n. 13

Laufen, R., 364 n. 3, 372 n. 21, 378 n. 34, 379 n. 36, 382 n. 45

Laws, S., 443 n. 41

Layton, B., 425 n. 58

Lehmann, M., 47 n. 3

Lentzen-Deis, F., 47 n. 3

Levine, J. M., 33, 35

Lewis, N., 93 n. 168

Liefeld, W., 413 n. 16

Lietzmann, H., 106, 106 n. 32,

Lightfoot, J., 157, 179 n. 136, 239 n. 79

Lindars, B., 259 n. 3, 263, 263 n. 13

Lindblom, J., 297 n. 42

Linnemann, E., 99, 99 n. 10, 242 n. 90

Lohmeyer, E., 206 n. 8, 241 n. 90

Loisy, A., 427

Lonergan, B. 341, 341 n. 24-26, 343 n. 33, 344 n. 34

Lührmann, D., 364 n. 3, 376 n. 28, 390 n. 17, 391, 391 nn. 19, 21

Luz, U., 63 n. 50, 64, 64 n. 55, 65 nn. 61, 63; 66 n. 68, 67 n. 75,

212 n. 24, 296 n. 34, 297 n. 38, 304, 305 n. 78, 435 n. 15, 439 n. 30, 440 n. 33, 441 n. 36

Mack, B. L., 5 n. 8, 41, 435 n. 16, 439 n. 31

Main, E., 407

Malina, B. J., 14, 25, 25 n. 5, 27, 28, 30, 31, 32, 33, 36, 138 n. 5, 139 n. 7, 156 n. 56

Mann, C. S., 352 n. 51, 354 n. 58

Manson, T. W., 102, 102 n. 18, 104, 104 n. 28, 145, 173 n. 112, 309 n. 97, 334, 334 n. 6, 335, 335 n. 7, 377 n. 32, 423 n. 48

Marcus, J., 71 n. 99, 73 n. 104, 306, 306 n. 83, 307, 307 n. 89, 308 n. 92, 309

Marguerat, D., 246 n. 104

Marshall, I. H., 190, 190 nn. 10, 12; 192, 192 n. 20, 193 n. 21, 213 nn. 27-28; 215 n. 31, 242 n. 90, 367, 367 n. 8, 373 n. 21, 376 nn. 27, 29; 385 n. 1, 410 n. 6, 415, 415 nn. 19, 22; 421, 421 n. 41, 439, 440 n. 33, 441 n. 35

Martens, E. A., 243 n. 92

Martianaie, J., 286 n. 62

Martinez, F. G., 171 n. 105

Mason, S., 349, 349 n. 45

Mauser, U., 402 n. 53

McCasland, S. V., 177 nn. 123-124

McEleney, N. J., 386 n. 3

McKnight, S., 375 n. 26, 380 n. 40

McNeile, A. H., 309 n. 97, 437 n. 21

Mealand, D. L., 47 n. 2, 49 n. 9, 51 n. 13

Meier, C., 79 n. 125

Meier, J. P., 47 n. 1, 48 n. 3, 49 n. 8, 50 n. 13, 58 n. 35, 74 n. 106, 75, 75 nn. 108-109; 76 nn. 110-111; 97 n. 2, 104, 104 n. 25, 119 n. 44, 161 n. 70, 378 n. 35, 405, 426 n. 60

Merkel, H., 49 n. 8, 52 n. 18

Merklein, H., 63 n. 49, 68 n. 82, 77, 78 n. 115

Merz, A., 208 n. 13
Metzger, B. M., 105, 105 n. 30, 106
    n. 34, 107, 119 n. 43, 120, 120 n.
    46, 121, 121 n. 50, 122 n. 53,
    123, 123 n. 57, 144 nn. 21-22
Metzler, N., 199 nn. 36-37
Meyer, B. F., 14, 24, 24 n. 3, 49 n.
    9, 50 n. 12, 51, 51 n. 16, 52, 53,
    53 n. 20, 54, 54 n. 23, 60, 61, 61
    nn. 43-45; 62, 89 n. 18, 90 n. 20,
    91 n. 23, 95 n. 34, 302 n. 63, 333
    n. 3, 378 n. 35, 386 n. 3
Michel, O., 305 n. 81
Milik, J. T., 166 nn. 89-90
Miller, S. S., 147 n. 32
Milligan, G., 251 n. 123
Minear, P., 434 n. 10
Moffatt, 143
Mohr, T. A., 208 n. 14, 239 n. 78,
    240 n. 88, 242 n. 90
Moltmann, J., 199
Monselewski, W., 402 n. 54, 403 n.
    55
Moo, D. J., 242 nn. 90-91
Moran, W. L., 81 n. 1
Moreland, R. L., 33, 35
Morris, L., 415, 415 nn. 20-21
Moule, C. F. D., 275 n. 44, 277,
    277 n. 47, 282, 282 n. 59
Moulton, J. H., 157, 159 n. 64, 251
    n. 123
Mussner, F., 301, 301 n. 58, 305 n.
    78

Neirynck, F., 11 n. 14, 98, 98 n. 4
Nestle, E., 101, 101 n. 16
Netzer, E., 319 n. 23
Neusner, J., 166 n. 89, 167 n. 91,
    170 n. 97
Neyrey, J. H., 42

Nineham, D. E., 303 n. 66
Nissen, 395, 395 n. 37
Nolland, J., 215 n. 29, 226 nn. 60-
    62; 242 n. 90, 253 n. 131, 254 n.
    132, 373 n. 21, 414 n. 18, 416 n.
    25

Oakman, D. E., 138 n. 6, 139 n. 7,
    140 n. 10, 141 n. 11, 153 n. 46,
    155 n. 49, 157 n. 57, 159 n. 67,
    164 nn. 83-84
Odeberg, H., 261, 261 nn. 9, 11;
    262, 263, 265
O'Donnell, M. B., 14
Okoye, J. I., 247 n. 107
Olbrechts-Tyteca, L., 341 n. 27, 343
    n. 32
O'Neill, J. C., 204 n. 4
Osborn, E., 394 n. 29
Otto, R., 302 n. 63, 360, 360 n. 76
Overman, J. A., 321 n. 27

Pannenberg, W., 191, 191 n. 13,
    199, 200 n. 38
Park, E. C., 364 n. 3
Patterson, S. J., 295 n. 32, 305 nn.
    79, 81
Pearson, B, A., 425 n. 58, 428, 428
    n. 70
Pearson, B. W. R., 122 n. 54
Peels, L., 397, 397 n. 40
Peirce, C. S., 24, 24 n. 4, 27
Perelman, C., 341 n. 27, 343 n. 32
Perkins, P., 203 n. 1
Perrin, N., 49 n. 7, 51 n. 15, 54 n.
    24, 71 n. 99, 72 nn. 100, 102; 99,
    99 nn. 8-10; 100, 100 nn. 11-13;
    137 n. 1, 146 n. 27, 154 n. 84,
    302, 302 n. 64, 309 n. 96, 410 n.
    6
Pesch, R., 72 n. 100, 89 n. 17, 205
    n. 6, 207 n. 12, 209 n. 20, 212 n.
    24, 220 n. 48, 222 n. 50, 223 n.
    53, 241 n. 90, 245 n. 98
Petuchowski, J. J., 193, 193 nn. 22-
    23, 194 nn. 24-26; 195 n. 30, 196
    n. 31
Phillips, J. B., 196 n. 32
Piper, J., 65 n. 64, 247 n. 108, 370
    n. 13, 373 n. 21, 375, 375 n. 23,
    376 n. 28, 391, 391 n. 22, 395,
    395 n. 36
Polag, A., 5 n. 8, 323 n. 28, 377 n.
    34
Polkow, D., 48 nn. 3, 6; 53 n. 21

Porter, S. E., 3 nn. *, 1; 4 n. 5, 14, 97 n. 1, 99 nn. 6-7; 100 n. 15, 103 n. 24, 104 n. 28, 106 n. 31, 110 n. 35, 122 n. 54
Porter, W. J., 106 n. 31
Pound, E., 82, 82 n. 2, 84, 88
Preisigke, F., 166 n. 88
Pritchard, J., 171 nn. 101, 103

Radl, W., 6 n. 11, 253 n. 131
Raisanen, H., 70 nn. 89-90; 73 n. 104, 207 n. 12
Randlinger, S., 394 n. 32
Redfield, R., 139 n. 7
Reicke, B., 297 n. 42
Reinbold, W., 220 n. 47, 242 n. 90, 245 n. 98
Reiser, M., 377 n. 31, 379 n. 38, 380 n. 39
Richards, K. H., 48 n. 3
Riches, J., 70 n. 89, 78, 78 nn. 117-118; 386 n. 3
Riesner, R., 49 nn. 8-9, 63 n. 52, 84 n. 3, 170 n. 98, 203 n. 1
Ritschl, A., 199, 199 n. 37
Robbins, V. K., 141 n. 13, 203 n. 1, 431 n. 1, 434 n. 11, 439 n. 31
Robertson, R. G., 154 n. 47
Robinson, J. A. T., 305 n. 77, 327
Robinson, J. M., 5 n. 8, 6, 6 n. 10, 247 n. 108, 270, 270 n. 31, 337 n. 13
Rohrbaugh, R. L., 28
Ropes, J. H., 448, 448 n. 63, 450, 450 n. 68
Ruppert, L., 245 n. 98
Rüsen, J., 79 n. 125

Saldarini, A. J., 420, 420 n. 39
Sand, A., 256 n. 137, 292 n. 19, 369 n. 12
Sanday, W., 195 nn. 28-29
Sanders, E. P., 49 n. 8, 76 n. 112, 304 n. 76, 378 n. 35, 412, 412 n. 10, 435 n. 14, 436 nn. 19-20
Sauer, J., 66 n. 64, 67 n. 75, 68, 68 nn. 79-81, 69, 69 n. 84, 396 n. 38, 406

Schenk, W., 239 n. 78
Schlatter, A., 216 n. 32, 298 n. 45, 301 n. 59, 385 n. 1
Schmidt, K. L., 239 n. 79
Schmiedel, P. W., 75 n. 109
Schnackenburg, R., 216 n. 34, 227 n. 63
Schneider, G., 68 n. 82
Schoedel, W. R., 445 n. 48
Scholem, G., 303 n. 69
Schottroff, L., 66 n. 65, 169 n. 95
Schrage, W., 400 n. 48
Schreiber, J., 204 n. 4, 238 n. 78, 242 n. 90, 248 nn. 111, 114; 250 n. 119, 251 n. 125, 253 n. 131
Schrenk, G., 314, 314 n. 11, 320
Schrenk, W., 177 n. 123
Schulz, S., 5 n. 8, 292 n. 17, 364 n. 3, 365 n. 5, 366 n. 6, 375 n. 24, 382 n. 44
Schürmann, H., 6 n. 11, 244 n. 95
Schweitzer, A., 199, 199 n. 37, 268, 268 n. 22, 302 n. 63
Schweizer, E., 193 n. 21, 303, 303 n. 68, 352 n. 51
Scott, B. B., 137 n. 3
Seccombe, D. P., 243 n. 94
Seeley, D., 331 n. 45
Seesemann, J., 175 n. 120
Sellew, P., 295 n. 32
Shafer, R. J., 79 n. 126
Shepherd, M. H., 437 n. 22
Sherwin-White, A. N., 249 n. 115, 253 n. 129
Shillington, G., 334 n. 4
Sider, J., 413 n. 17
Simon, M., 162, 172 nn. 107, 108, 110
Simonis, W., 52 n. 18
Smith, B. T. D., 163, 180 n. 139
Smith, M. H., 268 nn. 19, 21; 271 n. 34, 304 n. 74, 398 n. 42
Smyth, H. W., 433 n. 9
Soards, M. L., 204 n. 4, 236 n. 73, 242 n. 90, 244 n. 95
Spitta, F., 446, 446 n. 55
Stählin, G., 170 n. 99, 171 nn. 102, 104

Steck, O. H., 330 n. 45
Stegemann, W., 169 n. 95
Stein, R. H., 48 n. 3, 50 n. 11, 54, 54 n. 23, 64 n. 58, 119 n. 44, 386 n. 3, 389 n. 16, 405
Stendahl, K., 173 n. 111, 352 n. 52
Stenstrom, A. B., 340 n. 41
Stone, M. E., 293 n. 25
Strack, H. L., 161, 176 n. 122, 447 n. 60
Strauss, M. L., 243 n. 94
Strecker, G., 63, 65, 65 n. 60, 66 n. 69, 67 nn. 70, 73; 207 n. 12
Streeter, B. H., 334
Strobel, A., 220 n. 47, 245 n. 98, 255 n. 135
Stuart, D., 70 n. 91
Stuhlmacher, P., 207 n. 13, 242 n. 91, 256 n. 139, 304 n. 73,
Suggs, M. J., 247 n. 108
Swartley, W., 387 n. 9

Tabor, J. D., 13 n. 15
Talbert, C. H., 292 n. 23, 428 n. 69
Tan, K. H., 380 n. 40
Tappert, T. G., 188 nn. 5-6; 190 n. 10, 192 n. 19
Taussig, H., 152, 152 n. 42, 153
Taylor, J. E., 352 n. 53, 353 n. 55
Taylor, V., 117, 117 n. 39, 118, 118 n. 40, 206 n. 8, 239 n. 79, 295, 295 n. 31, 303 n. 66, 336 n. 9
Telford, W. R., 16 n. 1, 78 n. 120, 98 n. 5, 270 n. 33, 333 n. 2, 336 n. 12
Thackeray, H. St. J., 414 n. 18, 415 n. 23, 420, 421, 422 n. 42, 423 n. 48
Theissen, G., 48 n. 4, 49 n. 8, 54 n. 22, 73 n. 106, 74 n. 106, 151 n. 40, 208 n. 13, 295 n. 30, 326, 326 n. 32, 352, 352 n. 54
Thompson, J. A., 243 n. 92
Tischendorf, C., 120 n. 48, 142
Tombs, D., 4 n. 5
Torrey, C. C., 101, 102 n. 17,

Tuckett, C. M., 5 n. 8, 72 n. 99, 207 n.11, 278 n. 48, 335 n. 8, 338, 356 n. 63
Tuckman, B. W., 33
Turner, N., 159 n. 68, 433 n. 8

van Bruggen, J., 143 n. 19
VanderKam, J. C., 85 n. 4
Van Segbroeck, F., 6 n. 10
van Unnik, W. C., 398 n. 43, 399 n. 45
Vermes, G., 222 n. 51, 259, 259 n. 1, 260, 260 n. 6, 261, 261 n. 10, 262 n. 12, 263, 269, 269 n. 27, 304 n. 76, 358 n. 69
Via, D. O, 100, 100 n. 12
Vinson, R. B., 340 n. 23
Viviano, B. T., 173 n. 111
Vogels, W., 397
Vögtle, A., 198, 199 n. 35
von Harnack, A., 5 n. 8
von Lips, H., 247 n. 108
von Weizsacker, C. F., 400 n. 49

Wachob, W. H., 432 n. 5, 442 n. 38, 444 nn. 42-44; 445 nn. 49-50; 446 nn. 52-53, 56; 447 n. 58, 450
Waldmann, M., 394, 394 n. 31
Walker, W. O., 47 n. 3, 273 n. 41
Watson, A., 304 n. 75,
Weaver, D. J., 366 n. 7
Webb, R. L., 348 n. 43, 349 n. 46
Weber, M., 139 n. 7
Weeden, T., 9, 10 n. 12
Weiss, J., 199, 199 n. 37, 248 n. 114
Weiss, W., 72 n. 101, 78, 78 n. 119
Wellhausen, J., 101, 101 n. 16
Wenham, D., 4 n. 3
Wenham, J. W., 269 n. 25
Westcott, 142, 142 n. 15, 387 n. 7
Westerhom, S., 71 nn. 94, 96-97
Westermann, C., 345, 345 n. 35
Wettstein, J. J., 157
Weymouth, R. F., 143
Wiener, P. P., 24 n. 4
Wilckens, U., 216 n. 34, 218 n. 38
Wilder, A. N., 92 n. 28